PHILOSOPHICAL
EXPLORATIONS

Peter A. French
University of Minnesota, Morris

GENERAL LEARNING PRESS
250 James Street
Morristown, New Jersey 07960

to Sandra

Manufactured in the United States of America

Published simultaneously in Canada

Library of Congress Catalog Card Number 75–736

ISBN O–382–18219–7

TO THE INSTRUCTOR

INTRODUCTORY students often view philosophy as a series of difficult-to-read opinions, without knowing the problems or questions with which philosophers deal. For such students introductory philosophy becomes a kind of academic archeology. This book is an attempt to alter that misconception of a dynamic subject. It is designed to aid the students in their exploration of certain problems in philosophy.

Each part begins with nonphilosophic selections chosen because of their provocative nature. There follows an inquiry into the philosophic problem that arises out of the introductory readings, with guidelines for examining the ideas of well-respected philosophers on the problem. No attempt has been made to present a historical account of the problems or to structure the readings in a historical pattern. Most of the selections are from contemporary sources. But if the students or the instructor wish to examine the problems within their historical context, the book provides suggestions for such an analysis.

In each of the part inquiries, several questions are posed in order to stimulate a discussion of the problem. Frequently the students are called upon to stop their reading and attempt to find answers to questions, to imagine circumstances, or to construct examples relative to the problem. The intention is to involve the students and the instructor in a probing intellectual activity that will reveal the complexities of the issues under examination. Philosophy cannot just be read. The participants in its activity must constantly reevaluate the issues and themselves. At the discretion of the instructor some of the questions raised in the introductions may be emphasized, others ignored.

The brief headnotes to each philosophical selection serve a number of purposes. Most of them give a concise, though obviously incomplete, statement of that particular philosopher's general position and clues concerning what to look for in the reading. Also included in the headnotes are some questions not raised in the part introductions, questions that might lead to discussion of related issues or to cross-referencing other articles. Wherever possible, philosophical jargon has been avoided. Where it has been necessary to use technical terms, they have been parenthetically defined.

Parts I through III deal with problems related to our social lives, problems of which our newspapers and televisions make us painfully aware. The next parts, IV and V, concern the individual, his or her identity, mind/body dualism, idea of death, and concept of knowledge (the traditional areas of metaphysics and epistemology). We then turn in Parts VI through VIII to issues that arise in areas of three of humanity's most important pursuits: science, religion, and art.

This book is the result of the recognition, by my fellow professors of philosophy and myself, of the need to involve the introductory students of philosophy in a dynamic and relevant way, to make their experience in philosophy an ongoing activity and not a passive memorization of antiquity. This edition is a major revision of the original book, *Exploring Philosophy*. It includes twenty articles not found in the original (many of the original articles have been deleted), and most of the introductory selections have been changed. All of the inquiries to the eight parts are either new or thoroughly revised. The formerly separate parts on personal identity and dualism and survival have been conflated, and the part entitled Social Action and Human Nature has been dropped. Two entirely new parts have been added, one on violence, the other on epistemology.

I must express my gratitude to those members of my profession who have encouraged and criticized my work on this book in its various forms. I am indebted to my colleague Professor Theodore Uehling and many of my students at the University of Minnesota, Morris, for their thoughtful suggestions. I want to thank Mr. P. Knecht of Warner Brothers studios for his aid in obtaining photographs for the book. My gratitude goes to Professor H. H. Price, Professor William Werkmeister, and Professor H. D. Lewis for their generous comments on the text. This book has also benefited from my association with Professors Richard C. Hall, Jere Jones, William O'Neill, James W. Oliver, Haskell Fain, and David E. Cooper. Their suggestions and inspiration, I hope, have found their way through my style.

P. A. F.

TO THE STUDENT

PHILOSOPHY is an activity; it is done, not read or watched. You can have no real appreciation of the philosophic enterprise unless you do it. Unless you are a participant in its explorations and inquiries, all descriptions of philosophy are rather like word games. This book is designed to involve you in the exploration of certain philosophical problems that are relevant to our daily lives.

One of the characteristics of philosophical problems is that almost all of us have answers to them, even if we have not considered the reasons behind our answers. They are problems that occur in living, problems related to "my responsibilities in social situations, my idea of God, my concept of death, my reaction to violence," etc. Philosophy is much more than the study of highly technical and complex questions of metaphysics. Doing philosophy forces you to engage in one of the most difficult of human tasks: trying "to think, really honestly, about your life and other people's lives," as philosopher Ludwig Wittgenstein wrote to Norman Malcolm. He added, Malcolm reports, "And the trouble is that thinking about these things is *not thrilling* but often downright nasty. And when it's nasty then it's most important." Philosophy is a serious endeavor!

What constitutes philosophical problems? They are not the kind of problems that science can solve or even provide much aid in solving. They are embedded in our language, our feelings, our way of life. They are the sort of problems that the adding of new information fails to alter. They lie just below the surface of our activities, deeply involved in most of what we do. The solutions we accept for these problems are of more concern to us than any in mathematics or the sciences. Sometimes we are called upon to die for them.

Philosophical Explorations is an attempt to bring into the open the causes of these problems. Philosophers attempt to clarify the confusions and misunderstandings into which we often fall. They examine the complexities of problems that seem at first to be so simple. They attempt to help us understand the depths of our commitments and theories about our society, ourselves, our religion, our art, our science.

Wittgenstein characterized a philosophical problem as having the form, "I don't know my way about." We get tangled up in our language and our theorizing on the issues of our day and on the way we think about ourselves. Perhaps we even lose sight of the very questions we are trying to answer. *Philosophical Explorations* puts before you many of the alternative viewpoints and perspectives on these issues. It examines the depths of our concerns relieved of the demands of prejudice. The exploration of philosophical problems has a kind of therapeutic effect. Your goal when doing philosophy ought to be a clear view of the problem, how it arises, and how it is seen by others as well as yourself. Only then will you be in a position to make meaningful evaluations and suggestions relative to it. In fact, in the process of clarifying the intricacies of the problem it may cease to be a problem.

Another twentieth-century philosopher, Alfred North Whitehead, reminded us that "the pursuit of philosophy is the one avocation denied to omniscience." Philosophy is something an all-knowing divinity cannot do. No one philosophical position can claim to be any more philosophic than any other position. "No one truth, thoroughly understood in all of the infinitude of its bearings, is more or less philosophical than any other truth." Philosophy is our task, if only because it deals with the uncertainties of being a man. We must live with ourselves.

Each part of this book confronts you first with philosophical problems as they arise in literature or life. The more subtle aspects of the problems are then outlined in the inquiries. Many questions are raised that you should investigate within your own frame of reference. Then you are ready to explore the ways in which some outstanding philosophers have dealt with the problems.

You cannot expect to create a complete and systematic philosophical position that will provide a suitable answer to all the questions raised in this book. As an introductory student you must first become aware of what philosophical problems are and why they are so important in our lives. This book is designed for that purpose.

CONTENTS

Selected Sources

PART III
VIOLENCE AND THE NATURE OF MAN

Selected Sources

PART IV
PERSONS, MINDS, AND SURVIVAL AFTER DEATH

Selected Sources

PART V
KNOWLEDGE, CERTAINTY, AND DOUBT

Selected Sources

PART VI
SCIENTIFIC DISCOVERY

PART VII
FAITH AND RELIGIOUS EXPERIENCE

PART VIII
AESTHETIC JUDGMENT

EPILOGUE
METAPHILOSOPHY

PART I

DUTY AND RESPONSIBILITY

The Watergate Affair

By RICHARD M. NIXON,
President of the United States
Broadcast from Washington, D.C., April 30, 1973

GOOD EVENING. I WANT TO TALK TO YOU TONIGHT FROM MY HEART on a subject of deep concern to every American. In recent months members of my Administration and officials of the Committee for the Re-election of the President—including some of my closest friends and most trusted aides—have been charged with involvement in what has come to be known as the Watergate affair.

They include charges of illegal activity during and preceding the 1972 Presidential election and charges that responsible officials participated in efforts to cover up that illegal activity.

The inevitable result of these charges has been to raise serious questions about the integrity of the White House itself. Tonight I wish to address those questions.

Last June 17 while I was in Florida trying to get a few days' rest after my visit to Moscow, I first learned from news reports of the Watergate break-in. I was appalled at this senseless, illegal action, and I was shocked to learn that employes of the re-election committee were apparently among those guilty. I immediately ordered an investigation by appropriate Government authorities.

On Sept. 15, as you will recall, indictments were brought against seven defendants in the case.

As the investigation went forward, I repeatedly asked those conducting the investigation whether there was any reason to believe that members of my administration were in any way involved. I received repeated assurances that there were not. Because of these continuing reassurances, because I believed the reports I was getting, because I had faith in the persons from whom I was getting them, I discounted the stories in the press that appeared to implicate members of my Administration or other officials of the campaign committee.

Until March of this year, I remained convinced that the denials were true and that the charges of involvement by members of the White House staff were false.

The comments I made during this period, the comments made by my press secretary in my behalf, were based on the information provided to us at the time we made those comments.

However, new information then came to me which persuaded me that there was a real possibility that some of these charges were true and suggesting further that there had been an effort to conceal the facts both from the public—from you—and from me.

As a result, on March 21 I personally assumed the responsibility for coordinating intensive new inquiries into the matter and I personally ordered those conducting the investigations to get all the facts and to report them directly to me right here in this office.

I again ordered that all persons in the Government or at the re-election committee should cooperate fully with the F.B.I., the prosecutors and the grand jury.

I also ordered that anyone who refused to cooperate in telling the truth would be asked to resign from Government service.

And with ground rules adopted that would preserve the basic constitutional separation of powers between the Congress and the Presidency, I directed that members of the White House staff should appear and testify voluntarily under oath before the Senate committee which was investigating Watergate.

I was determined that we should get to the bottom of the matter, and that the truth should be fully brought out no matter who was involved.

At the same time, I was determined not to take precipitive action and to avoid if at all possible any action that would appear to reflect on innocent people.

I wanted to be fair, but I knew that in the final analysis the integrity of this office—public faith in the integrity of this office—would have to take priority over all personal considerations. Today, in one of the most difficult decisions of my Presidency, I accepted the resignations of two of my closest associates in the

White House, Bob Haldeman and John Ehrlichman, two of the finest public servants it has been my privilege to know. I want to stress that in accepting these resignations I mean to leave no implication whatever of personal wrongdoing on their part, and I leave no implication tonight of implication on the part of others who have been charged in this matter. But in matters as sensitive as guarding the integrity of our democratic process, it is essential not only that rigorous legal and ethical standards be observed, but also that the public, you, have total confidence that they are both being observed and enforced by those in authority, and particularly by the President of the United States. They agreed with me that this move was necessary in order to restore that confidence, because Attorney General Kleindienst, though a distinguished public servant, my personal friend for 20 years, with no personal involvement whatever in this matter, has been a close personal and professional associate of some of those who are involved in this case, he and I both felt that it was also necessary to name a new Attorney General.

The counsel to the President, John Dean, has also resigned.

As the new Attorney General, I have today named Elliott Richardson, a man of unimpeachable integrity and rigorously high principle. I have directed him to do everything necessary to insure that the Department of Justice has the confidence and the trust of every law-abiding person in this country. I have given him absolute authority to make all decisions bearing upon the prosecution of the Watergate case and related matters. I have instructed him that if he should consider it appropriate he has the authority to name a special supervising prosecutor for matters arising out of the case.

Whatever may appear to have been the case before, whatever improper activities may yet be discovered in connection with this whole sordid affair, I want the American people, I want you, to know beyond the shadow of a doubt that during my term as President justice will be pursued fairly, fully and impartially, no matter who is involved.

This office is a sacred trust, and I am determined to be worthy of that trust!

Looking back at the history of this case, two questions arise: How could it have happened—who is to blame?

Political commentators have correctly observed that during my 27 years in politics, I've always previously insisted on running my own campaigns for office.

In both domestic and foreign policy, 1972 was a year of crucially important decisions, of intense negotiations, of vital new directions, particularly in working toward the goal which has been my overriding concern throughout my political career—the goal of bringing peace to America, peace to the world.

And that is why I decided as the 1972 campaign approached that the Presidency should come first and politics second. To the maximum extent possible, therefore, I sought to delegate campaign operations to remove the day-to-day campaign decisions from the President's office and from the White House.

I also, as you recall, severely limited the number of my own campaign appearances.

Who then is to blame for what happened in this case?

For specific criminal actions by specific individuals those who committed those actions must of course bear the liability and pay the penalty. For the fact that alleged improper actions took place within the White House or within my campaign organization, the easiest course would be for me to blame those to whom I delegated the responsibility to run the campaign. But that would be a cowardly thing to do.

I will not place the blame on subordinates, on people whose zeal exceeded their judgment and who may have done wrong in a cause they deeply believed to be right. In any organization the man at the top must bear the responsibility.

That responsibility, therefore, belongs here in this office. I accept it.

And I pledge to you tonight from this office that I will do everything in my power to insure that the guilty are brought to justice and that such abuses are purged from our political processes in the years to come long after I have left this office.

Some people, quite properly appalled at the abuses that occurred, will say that Watergate demonstrates the bankruptcy of the American political system. I believe precisely the opposite is true.

Watergate represented a series of illegal acts and bad judgments by a number of individuals. It was the system that has brought the facts to light and that will bring those guilty to justice.

A system that in this case has included a determined grand jury, honest prosecutors, a courageous judge—John Sirica, and a vigorous free press.

It is essential that we place our faith in that system, and especially in the Judicial System.

It is essential that we let the judicial process go forward, respecting those safeguards that are established to protect the innocent as well as to convict the guilty.

It is essential that in reacting to the excesses of others, we not fall into excesses ourselves.

It is also essential that we not be so distracted by events such as this that we neglect the vital work before us, before this nation, before America at a time of critical importance to America and the world.

Since March, when I first learned that the Watergate affair might in fact be far more serious than I had been led to believe, it has claimed far too much of my time and my attention. Whatever may now transpire in the case, whatever the actions of the grand jury, whatever the outcome of any eventual trials, I must now turn my full attention—and I shall do so—once again to the larger duties of this office.

I owe it to this great office that I hold, and I owe it to you, to my country.

I know that, as Attorney General, Elliott Richardson will be both fair and he will be fearless in pursuing this case wherever it leads. I am confident that with him in charge justice will be done.

There is vital work to be done toward our goal of a lasting structure of peace in the world—work that cannot wait, work that I must do.

Tomorrow, for example, Chancellor Brandt of West Germany will visit the White House for talks that are a vital element of the Year of Europe, as 1973 has been called.

We are already preparing for the next Soviet-American summit meeting later this year.

This is also a year in which we are seeking to negotiate a mutual and balanced reduction of armed forces in Europe which will reduce our defense budget and allow us to have funds for other purposes at home so desperately needed.

It is the year when the United States and Soviet negotiators will seek to work out the second and even more important round of our talks on limiting nuclear arms, and of reducing the danger of a nuclear war that would destroy civilization as we know it.

It is a year in which we confront the difficult tasks of maintaining peace in Southeast Asia and in the potentially explosive Middle East.

There's also vital work to be done right here in America to insure prosperity—and that means a good job for everyone who wants to work; to control inflation that I know worries every housewife, everyone who tries to balance the family budget in America. To set in motion new and better ways of insuring progress toward a better life for all Americans.

When I think of this office, of what it means, I think of all the things that I want to accomplish for this nation, of all the things I want to accomplish for you.

On Christmas Eve, during my terrible personal ordeal of the renewed bombing of North Vietnam which, after 12 years of war, finally helped to bring America peace with honor, I sat down just before midnight. I wrote out some of my goals for my second term as President. Let me read them to you.

To make this country be more than ever a land of opportunity —of equal opportunity, full opportunity—for every American; to provide jobs for all who can work and generous help for those who cannot; to establish a climate of decency and civility in which each person respects the feelings and the dignity in the God-given rights of his neighbor; to make this a land in which each person can dare to dream, can live his dreams not in fear but in hope, proud of his community, proud of his country, proud of what America has meant to himself, and to the world.

These are great goals. I believe we can, we must work for them, we can achieve them.

But we cannot achieve these goals unless we dedicate ourselves to another goal. We must maintain the integrity of the White House.

And that integrity must be real, not transparent.

There can be no whitewash at the White House.

We must reform our political process, ridding it not only of the violations of the law but also of the ugly mob violence and other inexcusable campaign tactics that have been too often practiced and too readily accepted in the past including those that may have been a response by one side to the excesses or expected excesses of the other side.

Two wrongs do not make a right.

I've been in public life more than a quarter of a century. Like any other calling, politics has good people and bad people and let me tell you the great majority in politics, in the Congress, in the Federal Government, in the state government are good people.

I know that it can be very easy under the intensive pressures of a campaign for even well-intentioned people to fall into shady tactics, to rationalize this on the grounds that what is at stake is of such importance to the nation that the end justifies the means.

And both of our great parties have been guilty of such tactics.

In recent years, however, the campaign excesses that have occurred on all sides have provided a sobering demonstration of how far this false doctrine can take us.

The lesson is clear. America in its political campaigns must not again fall into the trap of letting the end, however great that end is, justify the means.

I urge the leaders of both political parties, I urge citizens—all of you everywhere—to join in working toward a new set of standards, new rules and procedures to insure that future elections will be as nearly free of such abuses as they possibly can be made. This is my goal. I ask you to join in making it America's goal.

When I was inaugurated for a second term this past January 20, I gave each member of my Cabinet and each member of my senior White House staff a special four-year calendar with each day marked to show the number of days remaining to the Administration.

In the inscription on each calendar I wrote these words:

"The Presidential term which begins today consists of 1,461 days, no more, no less. Each can be a day of strengthening and renewal for America. Each can add depth and dimension to the American experience.

"If we strive together, if we make the most of the challenge and the opportunity that these days offer us, they can stand out as great days for America and great moments in the history of the world."

I looked at my own calendar this morning up at Camp David as I was working on this speech. It showed exactly 1,361 days remaining in my term.

I want these to be the best days in America's history because I love America. I deeply believe that America is the hope of the world, and I know that in the quality and wisdom of the leadership America gives lies the only hope for millions of people all over the world that they can live their lives in peace and freedom.

We must be worthy of that hope in every sense of the word.

Tonight, I ask for your prayers to help me in everything that I do throughout the days of my Presidency to be worthy of their hopes and of yours.

God bless America. And God bless each and every one of you.

INQUIRY

A man said to the universe:
"Sir, I exist!"
"However," replied the universe,
"The fact has not created in me
A sense of obligation."

—STEPHEN CRANE

MUCH transpired in "The Watergate Affair" since the day in April 1973 when President Nixon addressed the American people and for the first time admitted wrongdoing in the White House. Transcripts of his personal conversations with his top aides, in particular those released on August 5, 1974, revealed that Mr. Nixon's protestations of ignorance regarding the attempt to obstruct justice in the Watergate affair were untrue. On the evening of August 8, 1974, Nixon became the first American president to resign from office. In light of those events and regardless of one's political leanings or personal feelings about him, Nixon's speech of April 30, 1973, is a gold mine for moral philosophers. It is couched in both the form and the language of an elaborate excuse, one that at the time it was delivered (although it is now known to have been mendacious) was widely accepted by the general American public. It will prove helpful in launching our examination of the notions of duty and responsibility to consider the function of excuses.

Excuses are speech acts of a particular sort. They differ radically, as J. L. Austin points out, from justifications. When the President tells the American people that because of the pressing nature of foreign and domestic affairs he was unable to run his own campaign for re-election and therefore was ignorant of the illegal behavior of his subordinates, he is not telling us that what he did, or its consequences, was totally good or right and hence justified. He is instead telling us that at least the consequences of his actions were bad, but that he did not voluntarily act in a way designed to bring

about such an outcome. The general form of excuses goes something like, "I did it, but not _____ly." Hence Nixon is saying,
"I failed to police my underlings, but not deliberately." (Remember
that offering an excuse and being excused are not the same thing.
Concentrate on the former.)

Supportable excuses serve in many ways to lessen the burden of
responsibility. As Austin tells us, we learn a great deal of the notion
of responsibility by studying the use of excuses when things go
wrong. Some excuses are mitigatory in that they relieve one of a
portion, though necessarily not all, of the blame for an untoward
act. Others are exculpatory in that their acceptance relieves one
completely of blameworthiness in the case in question. The President says that he is responsible for the acts of his subordinates. He
says that he "will not place the blame on subordinates." But he has
made it clear that he was ignorant, because of his other presidential
duties, of just that for which he is now accepting the responsibility.
Has his excuse, in this form, the force of mitigation, or of exculpa-
tion? If it is meant as an exculpating excuse, then his acceptance
of the responsibility certainly is somewhat vacuous. What kind of
a plea is ignorance?

Aristotle offers a number of pertinent ideas on the excuse of
ignorance. He maintains that involuntary acts usually are not blameworthy. Presumably he means that if someone performs an act that
should not, in the circumstances, have been done, he is responsible
(to blame) for whatever events occur as a result, but he should not
be held responsible (or accountable or blameworthy) if his performance of the act was involuntary. In order to see this point (not
strictly Aristotle's), we must realize that in ordinary usage some
terms like *blame* and *responsible* have many irreducible senses. In
one sense an infant is to blame (the cause of) for breaking a price-
less vase; he toppled it over. But the same child will not be blamed
(held blameworthy) for the broken vase; young children are clumsy
and unsure of their movements.

Aristotle includes in the category of involuntary acts, acts done
out of compulsion and acts done out of ignorance. It is not difficult
to see his point regarding compulsive acts, but acts done out of
ignorance are not in ordinary life usually treated as involuntary.
Aristotle tells us that everything done by reason of ignorance is involuntary. Only when pain and repentance occur is it proper to call
the act involuntary. There are different kinds of ignorance or, better,
different states of being ignorant. Some ignorance is symptomatic
of insanity, for example, ignorance of one's own name. In other

cases sane persons may be properly said to be ignorant of a particular state of affairs, e.g., not knowing the gun was loaded, not knowing the child was going to dart across the street into one's path, etc. The latter cases are legitimately said to be involuntary and, consistent with Aristotle's views, generally are painful and productive of repentative states in the agent, while the former Aristotle would simply describe as not voluntary.

The class of supposedly involuntary acts can be broken down further into those in which the agent was responsible for his ignorance and those in which he was not responsible for it. If a person's state of ignorance is due to drunkenness and he is capable of preventing himself from drinking, then he is said, according to Aristotle, to be responsible for the acts he performs in ignorance. If he is not so responsible for his ignorance, he is blameless. Aristotle also points out that if the person who acted out of ignorance should have known that of which he is ignorant, then he cannot be blameless. "We punish those who are ignorant of anything in the laws that they ought to know and that is not difficult, and so too in the case of anything else that they are thought to be ignorant of through carelessness; we assume that it is in their power not to be ignorant, since they have the power of taking care." Are Aristotle's remarks applicable to President Nixon's position regarding his own ignorance in the Watergate affair?

Excuses reveal much of our concept of responsibility; but how do we determine what our specific responsibilities and duties are? Generally speaking, we all are aware of certain requirements of behavior or certain restraints on behavior that are binding upon us in particular circumstances. In some instances we place ourselves under obligations to behave in specific ways, as when we promise to do something or when we undertake to play a game of chess with a friend. In other cases our duties seem to be thrust upon us by our roles in society.

F. H. Bradley maintains that the concept of duty arises only in conjunction with that of station, that is, social position. People are not isolated entities. We are social animals, which means that we exist and prosper within institutions such as families, communities, societies, and states. Bradley argues then that what a person "has to do depends on what his place is, what his function is, and that all comes from his station in the organism." Bradley's views on the generation of duties, however, entail certain conceptions of social institutions that may not be as obvious as the fact that certain duties arise from the roles we play in various institutions, whether by choice or by birth. Bradley argues that our institutions are organic, natural and, furthermore, that they themselves are moral. This is very difficult for most of us to accept, if only because we tend to look upon our institutions not only as products of individuals but as ultimately reducible to individuals. Generally speaking, for example, we treat statements made about our government as shorthand devices for statements about individual governmental officers. Bradley's position is that "man is a social being; he is real only because he is social," and also that "the assertion that communities have been manufactured . . . is a mere fable." It would seem to follow from Bradley's views that the notion of man as a moral individual divorced from his social role is a myth. The important question from a moral point of view would be, Has X (an individual) fulfilled the tasks requisite of his or her station? Regardless of whatever else people may do, if they have met the requirements in their social roles, they have done their duty and have acted responsibly

Bradley's views on the origins of duty and responsibility are opposed in many ways to those held by Immanuel Kant, who claimed that a formal moral criterion for determining duty and responsibility could be established by reference to the nature of human reason alone. Kant derived his principle of duty by requiring us, as rational beings, to will the maxims of our actions to be universal for all people. In other words, according to Kant, we should only act in ways we would be willing to allow all others to act. He called this principle the "categorical imperative." It commands people to do what is right without external enticements or punishments. According to Kant, we should do right because it is right to do so.

For Kant, morality is always a matter of conscious choice. People cannot be accidentally moral, doing right by chance. The alternatives to the chosen behavior must be actively considered. Inclinations serve as no criterion of right conduct. In fact, Kant tells us that moral goodness is often to be found in acting counter to inclination. Also, according to Kant's thinking, the motive is of prime importance, not the accomplishment. You cannot tell if a person is moral simply by observing his behavior.

What do most people mean when they make judgments of moral worth? Kant is not concerned with distinguishing moral from immoral behavior. There are many different reasons that motivate people to do good deeds, or seeming good deeds. Yet we reserve our highest respect not for people who act from self-centered motives or from natural dispositions to do good, but for people who realize they must do something despite their personal concerns and inhibitions.

Imagine you are interviewing a wealthy businessman who has just given a large sum of money for a park to benefit ghetto children. On the surface the act seems morally commendable. People ought to help those less fortunate whenever possible. You ask the businessman why he did so, and he tells you that it makes him feel very good when he gives to the poor. What is his motive? To make himself feel good. This cannot be a moral motive, Kant argues. If it were, then only those people with certain natural dispositions would be capable of moral actions, and all other people would have to be excused from doing what is morally right. Only if an act is done from a consideration of duty for its own sake can it have moral worth.

There are many difficulties with the Kantian theory of responsibility, not the least of which is his insistence that there can be no justifiable exceptions to moral imperatives. Common experience appears to contradict such absolutism in moral matters. Under certain circumstances we say that a person would be a better person if he did not do what he had promised to do. Occasions also arise in which one is genuinely baffled as to which of two apparently contradictory obligations he ought to fulfill. Suppose a dying man extracts from you a promise to deliver to his nephew the money he has in his possession, a considerable sum. You locate the nephew, but discover him to be a degenerate who has squandered every cent he ever had on self-indulgent living. You are affiliated with a medical foundation that could put the dead man's money to good use in support of its disease research program. Should you keep your promise, or should you tell the nephew that his uncle's last request was that the money be given to the foundation? Kant would adamantly maintain that there can be no duty to lie, even from benevolent motives.

From a consequential point of view one may have reservations about saying that voiding this promise will produce the best results. After all, the foundation may make poor use of the funds, while a newly found fortune might positively affect the character of the nephew and he might mend his ways. Nevertheless, it is a good bet that most of us would rather risk the money on the foundation's future than on the possibility of a metamorphosis in the nephew's life-style. What we would be expressing is an appeal to consequences, to the possibility that the foundation will use the money to produce greater good for more people. The

principle upon which the violation of the promise is thus urged
is utilitarian: persons always have an obligation to choose those
actions that will be productive of the greatest good. The basic
utilitarian belief is that an act is right if its performance results in a
greater amount of happiness or less pain than its nonperformance.
Utilitarianism is in opposition to Kant's moral theory, since it is a
moral theory which maintains that consequences of actions determine their rightness.

There are difficulties with utilitarianism as well. It can be used
to justify actions that go counter to some of our basic moral institutions, as in the example of justified promise-breaking; and it
tends to define moral rules as rules of thumb to be disregarded
if the circumstances so warrant. The relevance of consequences
to the determination of rightness also raises another problem. A
common argument takes this form: "You should not do X, for suppose everyone else did X as well?" The retort usually goes something like this: "But everyone will not do X, so my doing it really
has consequences only for me" or "If everyone does X, my doing
it will certainly make no difference." Moralists, especially those
who espouse some form of utilitarianism, need to determine the
force of the "What if everyone did that?" argument. At least two
different types of things might be meant by someone using the
argument. It might mean that you should not do X because your
so doing will cause others, following your example, to do X. It also
might mean that if your actions were to become universalized,
dire consequences would occur, especially in terms of our basic
institutions. Suppose that the "What if everyone did that?" argument were directed at President Nixon after his Watergate speech
of April 30, 1973? Could it be made effectual from a moral point of
view?

Moralists, such as Kant, Bradley, and the utilitarians, have generally characterized the "good man" as either a doer of good works
or one who has correct motives, consistent with duty, for the
things he attempts to do. But suppose an individual existed who,
despite his successful attempts to abide by moral law no matter
how defined, still in all lacked any real compassion or faith in the
goodness of his fellows. Although he may not actually despise all
other human beings, he has no trust in them either, and he behaves
in such ways as to manifest contempt for their struggles to act
morally despite their frequent misadventures and indiscretions.
Most traditional moralists would label him a "good man," but
would we really consider such a person, who probably minds

everyone's business and delights in the discovery of moral laxity in others, worthy of our praise, a paragon of virtue? Or would we, as Richard Taylor suggests, characterize him with epithets of evil and reward his diligence with the governance of Hell, should that executive office become vacant?

1

J. L. AUSTIN

(1911–1960)

A *Plea* for *Excuses**

Austin and Wittgenstein have been the two most influential philosophers of the English ordinary language school. Austin's approach is far more methodical than Wittgenstein's. In "A Plea for Excuses" he tells us his general views on the enterprise of philosophy. He recommends our examination of what we would say in certain instances, what language is appropriate when certain things occur. Using ordinary language as our guide, we discover the ways to treat problems of responsibility; we study the propensity we have to make certain excuses in certain situations. Austin suggests two major sources for the study of responsibility: the dictionary and the law. Commenting on "A Plea for Excuses" in another paper, "Three Ways of Spilling Ink," Austin writes: "The point of what I had to say there was that there isn't much point to discussing it (responsibility) in general terms. . . . Briefly it is the idea . . . that questions of whether a person was responsible for this or that are prior to questions of freedom . . . to discover whether someone acted freely or not, we must discover whether this, that, or the other plea will pass—for example, duress, or mistake, or accident, or so forth."

* J. L. Austin, "The Presidential Address to the Aristotelian Society, 1956," *Proceedings of the Aristotelian Society*, 1956–1957, Vol. LVII (1957). © 1956 The Aristotelian Society and Mrs. Jean Austin. Reprinted by permission of the Aristotelian Society and Mrs. Jean Austin.

THE subject of this paper, *Excuses,* is one not to be treated, but only to be introduced, within such limits. It is, or might be, the name of a whole branch, even a ramiculated branch, of philosophy, or at least of one fashion of philosophy. I shall try, therefore, first to state *what* the subject is, *why* it is worth studying, and *how* it may be studied, all this at a regrettably lofty level: and then I shall illustrate, in more congenial but desultory detail, some of the methods to be used, together with their limitations, and some of the unexpected results to be expected and lessons to be learned. Much, of course, of the amusement, and of the instruction, comes in drawing the coverts of the microglot, in hounding down the minutiae, and to this I can do no more here than incite you. But I owe it to the subject to say, that it has long afforded me what philosophy is so often thought, and made, barren of—the fun of discovery, the pleasures of cooperation, and the satisfaction of reaching agreement.

What, then, is the subject? I am here using the word "excuses" *for a title*, but it would be unwise to freeze too fast to this one noun and its partner verb: indeed for some time I used to use "extenuation" instead. Still, on the whole "excuses" is probably the most central and embracing term in the field, although this includes others of importance —"plea," "defense," "justification," and so on. When, then, do we "excuse" conduct, our own or somebody else's? When are "excuses" proffered?

In general, the situation is one where someone is *accused* of having done something, or (if that will keep it any cleaner) where someone is *said* to have done something which is bad, wrong, inept, unwelcome, or in some other of the numerous possible ways untoward. Thereupon he, or someone on his behalf, will try to defend his conduct or to get him out of it.

One way of going about this is to admit flatly that he, X, did do that very thing, A, but to argue that it was a good thing, or the right or sensible thing, or a permissible thing to do, either in general or at least in the special circumstances of the occasion. To take this line is to *justify* the action, to give reasons for doing it: not to say, to brazen it out, to glory in it, or the like.

A different way of going about it is to admit that it wasn't a good thing to have done, but to argue that it is not quite fair or correct to say *baldly* "X did A." We may say it isn't fair just to say X did it; perhaps he was under somebody's influence, or was nudged. Or, it isn't fair to say baldly he *did* A; it may have been partly accidental, or an unintentional slip. Or, it isn't fair to say he did simply A—he was really doing something quite different and A was only incidental, or he was looking at the whole thing quite differently. Naturally these arguments can be combined or overlap or run into each other.

In the one defense, briefly, we accept responsibility but deny that it was bad: in the other, we admit that it was bad but don't accept full, or even any, responsibility.

By and large, justifications can be kept distinct from excuses, and I shall not be so anxious to talk about them because they have enjoyed more than their fair share of philosophical attention. But the two certainly can be confused, and can *seem* to go very near to each other, even if they do not perhaps actually do so. You dropped the tea tray: Certainly, but an emotional storm was about to break out: or, Yes, but there was a wasp. In each case the defense, very soundly, insists on a fuller description of the event in its context; but the first is a justification, the second an excuse. Again, if the objection is to the use of such a dyslogistic verb as "murdered," this may be on the ground that the killing was done in battle (justification) or on the ground that it was only accidental if reckless (excuse). It is arguable that we do not use the terms "justification" and "excuse" as carefully as we might; a miscellany of even less-clear terms, such as "extenuation," "palliation," "mitigation," hovers uneasily between partial justification and partial excuse; and when we plead, say, provocation, there is genuine uncertainty or ambiguity as to what we mean—is *he* partly responsible, because he roused a violent impulse or passion in me, so that it wasn't truly or merely me acting "of my own accord" (excuse)? Or is it rather that, he having done me such injury, I was entitled to retaliate (justification)? Such doubts merely make it the more urgent to clear up the usage of these various terms. But that the defenses I have for convenience labeled "justification" and "excuse" are in principle distinct can scarcely be doubted.

This then is the sort of situation we have to consider under "excuses." I will only further point out how very wide a field it covers. We have, of course, to bring in the opposite numbers of excuses—the expressions that *aggravate*, such as "deliberately," "on purpose," and so on, if only for the reason that an excuse often takes the form of a rebuttal of one of these. But we have also to bring in a large number of expressions which at first blush look not so much like excuses as like accusations—"clumsiness," "tactlessness," "thoughtlessness," and the like. Because it has always to be remembered that few excuses get us out of it *completely:* the average excuse, in a poor situation, gets us only out of the fire into the frying-pan—but still, of course, any frying-pan in a fire. If I have broken your dish or your romance, maybe the best defense I can find will be clumsiness.

Why, if this is what "excuses" are, should we trouble to investigate them? It might be thought reason enough that their production has always bulked so large among human activities. But to moral philosophy in particular a study of them will contribute in special ways, both positively towards the development of a cautious, latter-day version of conduct, and negatively towards the correction of older and hastier theories.

In ethics we study, I suppose, the good and the bad, the right and the wrong, and this must be for the most part in some connection with conduct or the doing of actions. Yet before we consider what actions are good or bad, right or wrong, it is proper to consider first what is meant by, and what not, and what is included under, and what not, the expression "doing an action" or "doing something." These are expressions still too little examined on their own account and merits, just as the general notion of "saying something" is still too lightly passed over in logic. There is indeed a vague and comforting idea in the background that, after all, in the last analysis, doing an action must come down to the making of physical movements with parts of the body; but this is about as true as that saying something must, in the last analysis, come down to making movements of the tongue.

The beginning of sense, not to say wisdom, is to realize that "doing an action," as used in philosophy,* is a highly abstract expression—it is a stand-in used in the place of any (or almost any?) verb with a personal subject, in the same sort of way that "thing" is a stand-in for any (or when we remember, almost any) noun substantive, and "quality" a stand-in for the adjective. Nobody, to be sure, relies on such dummies quite implicitly quite indefinitely. Yet notoriously it is possible to arrive at, or to derive the idea for, an oversimplified metaphysics from the obsession with "things" and their "qualities." In a similar way, less commonly recognized even in these semi-sophisticated times, we fall for the myth of the verb. We treat the expression "doing an action" no longer as a stand-in for a verb with a personal subject, as which it has no doubt some uses, and might have more if the range of verbs were not left unspecified, but as a self-explanatory, ground-level description, one which brings adequately into the open the essential features of everything that comes, by simple inspection, under it. We scarcely notice even the most patent exceptions or difficulties (is to think something, or to say something, or to try to do something, to do an action?), any more than we fret, in the *ivresse des grandes profondeurs,* as to whether flames are things or events. So we come easily to think of our behavior over any time, and of a life as a whole, as consisting in doing now action A, next action B, then action C, and so on, just as elsewhere we come to think of the world as consisting of this, that, and the other substance or material thing, each with its properties. All "actions" are, as actions (meaning what?), equal, composing a quarrel with striking a match, winning a war with sneezing: worse still, we assimilate them one and all to the supposedly most obvious and easy cases, such as posting letters or moving fingers, just as we assimilate all "things" to horses or beds.

If we are to continue to use this expression in sober philosophy, we need to ask such questions as: Is to sneeze to do an action? Or is to breathe, or to see, or to checkmate, or each one of countless others? In short, for what range of verbs, as used on what occasions, is "doing an

---

* This use has little to do with the more down-to-earth occurrences of "action" in ordinary speech.

action" a stand-in? What have they in common, and what do those excluded severally lack? Again we need to ask how we decide what is the correct name for "the" action that somebody did—and what, indeed, are the rules for the use of "the" action, "an" action, "one" action, a "part" or "phase" of an action and the like. Further, we need to realize that even the "simplest" named actions are not so simple— certainly are not the mere makings of physical movements, and to ask what more, then, comes in (intentions? conventions?) and what does not (motives?), and what is the detail of the complicated internal machinery we use in "acting"—the receipt of intelligence, the appreciation of the situation, the invocation of principles, the planning, the control of execution and the rest.

In two main ways the study of excuses can throw light on these fundamental matters. First, to examine excuses is to examine cases where there has been some abnormality or failure: and as so often, the abnormal will throw light on the normal, will help us to penetrate the blinding veil of ease and obviousness that hides the mechanisms of the natural successful act. It rapidly becomes plain that the breakdowns signalized by the various excuses are of radically different kinds, affecting different parts or stages of the machinery, which the excuses consequently pick out and sort out for us. Further, it emerges that not *every* slip-up occurs in connection with *everything* that could be called an "action," that not every excuse is apt with every verb—far indeed from it: and this provides us with one means of introducing some classification into the vast miscellany of "actions." If we classify them according to the particular selection of breakdowns to which each is liable, this should assign them their places in some family group or groups of actions, or in some model of the machinery of acting.

In this sort of way, the philosophical study of conduct can get off to a positive fresh start. But by the way, and more negatively, a number of traditional cruces or mistakes in this field can be resolved or removed. First among these comes the problem of Freedom. While it has been the tradition to present this as the "positive" term requiring elucidation, there is little doubt that to say we acted "freely" (in the philosopher's use, which is only faintly related to the everyday use) is to say only that we acted *not* unfreely, in one or another of the many heterogeneous ways of so acting (under duress, or what not). Like "real," "free" is only used to rule out the suggestion of some or all of its recognized antitheses. As "truth" is not a name for a characteristic of assertions, so "freedom" is not a name for a characteristic of actions, but the name of a dimension in which actions are assessed. In examining all the ways in which each action may not be "free," i.e., the cases in which it will not do to say simply "X did A," we may hope to dispose of the problem of Freedom. Aristotle has often been chidden for talking about excuses or pleas and overlooking "the real problem": in my own case, it was when I began to see the injustice of this charge that I first became interested in excuses.

There is much to be said for the view that, philosophical tradition apart, Responsibility would be a better candidate for the role here assigned to Freedom. If ordinary language is to be our guide, it is to evade responsibility, or full responsibility, that we most often make excuses, and I have used the word myself in this way above. But in fact "responsibility" too seems not really apt in all cases: I do not exactly evade responsibility when I plead clumsiness or tactlessness, nor, often, when I plead that I only did it unwillingly or reluctantly, and still less if I plead that I had in the circumstances no choice: here I was constrained and have an excuse (or justification), yet may accept responsibility. It may be, then, that at least two key terms, Freedom and Responsibility, are needed: the relation between them is not clear, and it may be hoped that the investigation of excuses will contribute towards its clarification.*

So much, then, for ways in which the study of excuses may throw light on ethics. But there are also reasons why it is an attractive subject methodologically, at least if we are to proceed from "ordinary language," that is, by examining *what we should say when*, and so why and what we should mean by it. Perhaps this method, at least as *one* philosophical method, scarcely requires justification at present—too evidently, there is gold in them thar hills: more opportune would be a warning about the care and thoroughness needed if it is not to fall into disrepute. I will, however, justify it very briefly.

First, words are our tools, and, as a minimum, we should use clean tools: we should know what we mean and what we do not, and we must forearm ourselves against the traps that language sets us. Secondly, words are not (except in their own little corner) facts or things: we

---

* Another well-flogged horse in these same stakes is Blame. At least two things seem confused together under this term. Sometimes when I blame X for doing A, say for breaking the vase, it is a question simply or mainly of my disapproval of A, breaking the vase, which unquestionably X did: but sometimes it is, rather, a question simply or mainly of how far I think X responsible for A, which unquestionably was bad. Hence if somebody says he blames me for something, I may answer by giving a *justification*, so that he will cease to disapprove of what I did, or else by giving an *excuse*, so that he will cease to hold me, at least entirely and in every way, responsible for doing it.

need therefore to prize them off the world, to hold them apart from and against it, so that we can realize their inadequacies and arbitrariness, and can relook at the world without blinkers. Thirdly, and more hopefully, our common stock of words embodies all the distinctions men have found worth drawing, and the connections they have found worth marking, in the lifetimes of many generations: these surely are likely to be more numerous, more sound, since they have stood up to the long test of the survival of the fittest, and more subtle, at least in all ordinary and reasonably practical matters, than any that you or I are likely to think up in our armchairs of an afternoon—the most favored alternative method.

In view of the prevalence of the slogan "ordinary language," and of such names as "linguistic" or "analytic" philosophy or "the analysis of language," one thing needs specially emphasizing to counter misunderstandings. When we examine what we should say when, what words we should use in what situations, we are looking again not *merely* at words (or "meanings," whatever they may be) but also at the realities we use the words to talk about: we are using a sharpened awareness of words to sharpen our perception of, though not as the final arbiter of, the phenomena. For this reason I think it might be better to use, for this way of doing philosophy, some less misleading name than those given above—for instance, "linguistic phenomenology," only that is rather a mouthful.

Using, then, such a method, it is plainly preferable to investigate a field where ordinary language is rich and subtle, as it is in the pressingly practical matter of Excuses, but certainly is not in the matter, say, of Time. At the same time we should prefer a field which is not too much trodden into bogs or tracks by traditional philosophy, for in that case even "ordinary" language will often have become infected with the jargon of extinct theories, and our own prejudices too, as the upholders or imbibers of theoretical views, will be too readily, and often insensibly, engaged. Here too, Excuses form an admirable topic; we can discuss at least clumsiness, or absence of mind, or inconsiderateness, even spontaneousness, without remembering what Kant thought, and so progress by degrees even to discussing deliberation without for once remembering Aristotle or self-control without Plato. Granted that our subject is, as already claimed for it, neighboring, analogous, or germane in some way to some notorious center of philosophical trouble, then, with these two further requirements satisfied, we should be certain of what we are after: a good site for *field work* in philosophy. Here at last we should be able to unfreeze, to loosen up and get going on agreeing about discoveries, however small, and on agreeing about how to reach agreement.* How much it is to be wished that similar field work will soon be undertaken in, say, aesthetics; if only we could forget for a while about the beautiful and get down instead to the dainty and the dumpy.

There are, I know, or are supposed to be, snags in "linguistic" philosophy, which those not very familiar with it find, sometimes not without glee or relief, daunting. But with snags, as with nettles, the thing to do is to grasp them—and to climb above them. I will mention two in particular, over which the study of excuses may help to encourage us. The first is the snag of Loose (or Divergent or Alternative) Usage; and the second the crux of the Last Word. Do we all say the same, and only the same, things in the same situations? Don't usages differ? And, Why should what we all ordinarily say be the only or the best or final way of putting it? Why should it even be true?

Well, people's usages do vary, and we do talk loosely, and we do say different things apparently indifferently. But first, not nearly as much as one would think. When we come down to cases, it transpires in the very great majority that what we had thought was our wanting to say different things of and in *the same* situation was really not so—we had simply imagined the situation *slightly* differently: which is all too easy to do, because of course no situation (and we are dealing with *imagined* situations) is ever "completely" described. The more we imagine the situation in detail, with a background of story—and it is worth employing the most idiosyncratic or, sometimes, boring means to stimulate and to discipline our wretched imaginations—the less we find we disagree about what we should say. Nevertheless, *sometimes* we do ultimately disagree: sometimes we must allow a usage to be, though appalling, yet actual; sometimes we should genuinely use either or both of two different descriptions. But why should this daunt us? All that is happening is entirely explicable. If our usages disagree, then you use "X" where I use "Y," or more probably (and more intriguingly) your conceptual system is different from mine, though very likely it is at least equally consistent and serviceable: in short, we can find *why* we disagree—you choose to classify in one way, I in another. If the usage is loose, we can understand the temptation that leads to it, and the distinctions that it blurs: if there are "alternative" descriptions, then the situation can be described or can be "structured" in two ways, or perhaps it is one where, for current purposes, the two alternatives come down to the same. A disagreement as to what we should say is not to

* All of which was seen and claimed by Socrates, when he first betook himself to the way of Words.

be shied off, but to be pounced upon: for the explanation of it can hardly fail to be illuminating. If we light on an electron that rotates the wrong way, that is a discovery, a portent to be followed up, not a reason for chucking physics: and by the same token, a genuinely loose or eccentric talker is a rare specimen to be prized.

As practice in learning to handle this bogey, in learning the essential *rubrics*, we could scarcely hope for a more promising exercise than the study of excuses. Here, surely, is just the sort of situation where people will say "almost anything," because they are so flurried, or so anxious to get off. "It was a mistake," "It was an accident"—how readily these can *appear* indifferent, and even be used together. Yet, a story or two, and everybody will not merely agree that they are completely different, but even discover for himself what the difference is and what each means.*

Then, for the Last Word. Certainly ordinary language has no claim to be the last word, if there is such a thing. It embodies, indeed, something better than the metaphysics of the Stone Age, namely, as was said, the inherited experience and acumen of many generations of men. But then, that acumen has been concentrated primarily upon the practical business of life. If a distinction works well for practical purposes in ordinary life (no mean feat, for even ordinary life is full of hard cases), then there is sure to be something in it, it will not mark nothing: yet this is likely enough to be not the best way of arranging things if our interests are more extensive or intellectual than the ordinary. And again, that experience has been derived only from the sources available to ordinary men throughout most of civilized history: it has not been fed from the resources of the microscope and its successors. And it must be added too, that superstition and error and fantasy of all kinds do become incorporated in ordinary language and even sometimes stand up to the survival test (only, when they do, why should we not detect it?). Certainly, then, ordinary language is *not* the last word: in principle it can everywhere be supplemented and improved upon and superseded. Only remember, it *is* the *first* word.†

---

* You have a donkey, so have I, and they graze in the same field. The day comes when I conceive a dislike for mine. I go to shoot it, draw a bead on it, fire: the brute falls in its tracks. I inspect the victim, and find to my horror that it is *your* donkey. I appear on your doorstep with the remains and say—what? "I say, old sport, I'm awfully sorry, etc., I've shot your donkey *by accident*"? Or "*by mistake*"? Then again, I go to shoot my donkey as before, draw a bead on it, fire—but as I do so, the beasts move, and to my horror yours falls. Again the scene on the doorstep—what do I say? "By mistake"? Or "by accident"?

† And forget, for once and for a while, that other curious question "Is it true?" May we?

For this problem too the field of Excuses is a fruitful one. Here is matter both contentious and practically important for everybody, so that ordinary language is on its toes: yet also, on its back it has long had a bigger flea to bite it, in the shape of the Law, and both again have lately attracted the attentions of yet another, and at least a healthily growing, flea, in the shape of psychology. In the law a constant stream of actual cases, more novel and more tortuous than the mere imagination could contrive, are brought up *for decision*—that is, formulas for docketing them must somehow be found. Hence it is necessary first to be careful with, but also to be brutal with, to torture, to fake, and to override, ordinary language: we cannot here evade or forget the whole affair. (In ordinary life we dismiss the puzzles that crop up about time, but we cannot do that indefinitely in physics.) Psychology likewise produces novel cases, but it also produces new methods for bringing phenomena under observation and study: moreover, unlike the law, it has an unbiased interest in the totality of them and is unpressed for decision. Hence its own special and constant need to supplement, to revise and to supersede the classifications of both ordinary life and the law. We have, then, ample material for practice in learning to handle the bogey of the Last Word, however it should be handled.

Suppose, then, that we set out to investigate excuses, what are the methods and resources initially available? Our object is to imagine the varieties of situation in which we make excuses, and to examine the expressions used in making them. If we have a lively imagination, together perhaps with an ample experience of dereliction, we shall go far, only we need system: I do not know how many of you keep a list of the kinds of fool you make of yourselves. It is advisable to use systematic aids, of which there would appear to be three at least. I list them here in order of availability to the layman.

First we may use the dictionary—quite a concise one will do, but the use must be *thorough*. Two methods suggest themselves, both a little tedious, but repaying. One is to read the book through, listing all the words that seem relevant; this does not take as long as many suppose. The other is to start with a widish selection of obviously relevant terms, and to consult the dictionary under each: it will be found that, in the explanations of the various meanings of each, a surprising number of other terms occur, which are germane though of course not often synonymous. We then look up each of *these*, bringing in more for our bag from the "definitions" given in each case; and when we have continued for a little, it will generally be found that the family circle begins to close, until ultimately it is complete and we come only upon repetitions. This method has the advantage of grouping the terms into convenient clusters—but of course a good deal will depend upon the comprehensiveness of our initial selection.

Working the dictionary, it is interesting to find that a high percentage of the terms connected with excuses prove to be *adverbs*, a type of word which has not enjoyed so large a share of the philosophical limelight as the noun, substantive or adjective, and the verb: this is natural because, as was said, the tenor of so many excuses is that I did it but only *in a way*, not just flatly like that—i.e., the verb needs modifying. Besides adverbs, however, there are other words of all kinds, including numerous abstract nouns, "misconception," "accident," "purpose," and the like, and a few verbs too, which often hold key positions for the grouping of excuses into classes at a high level ("couldn't help," "didn't mean to," "didn't realize," or again "intend," and "attempt"). In connection with the nouns another neglected class of words is prominent, namely, prepositions. Not merely does it matter considerably which preposition, often of several, is being used with a given substantive, but further the prepositions deserve study on their own account. For the question suggests itself, Why are the nouns in one group governed by "under," in another by "on," in yet another by "by" or "through" or "from" or "for" or "with," and so on? It will be disappointing if there prove to be no good reasons for such groupings.

Our second sourcebook will naturally be the law. This will provide us with an immense miscellany of untoward cases, and also with a useful list of recognized pleas, together with a good deal of acute analysis of both. No one who tries this resource will long be in doubt, I think, that the common law, and in particular the law of tort, is the richest storehouse; crime and contract contribute some special additions of their own, but tort is altogether more comprehensive and more flexible. But even here, and still more with so old and hardened a branch of the law as crime, much caution is needed with the arguments of counsel and the dicta or decisions of judges: acute though these are, it has always to be remembered that, in legal cases, (1) there is the overriding requirement that a decision be reached, and a relatively black or white decision—guilty or not guilty—for the plaintiff or for the defendant; (2) there is the general requirement that the charge or action and the pleadings be brought under one or another of the heads and procedures that have come in the course of history to be accepted by the courts (These, though fairly numerous, are still few and stereotyped in comparison with the accusations and defenses of daily life. Moreover contentions of many kinds are beneath the law, as too trivial,

or outside it, as too purely moral—for example, inconsiderateness);
(3) there is the general requirement that we argue from and abide by
precedents (The value of this in the law is unquestionable, but it can
certainly lead to distortions of ordinary beliefs and expressions). For
such reasons as these, obviously closely connected and stemming from
the nature and function of the law, practicing lawyers and jurists are
by no means so careful as they might be to give to our ordinary expressions their ordinary meanings and applications. There is special pleading and evasion, stretching and strait-jacketing, besides the invention
of technical terms, or technical senses for common terms. Nevertheless,
it is a perpetual and salutary surprise to discover how much is to be
learned from the law; and it is to be added that if a distinction drawn
is a sound one, even though not yet recognized in law, a lawyer can be
relied upon to take note of it, for it may be dangerous not to—if he
does not, his opponent may.

Finally, the third sourcebook is psychology, with which I include
such studies as anthropology and animal behavior. Here I speak with
even more trepidation than about the Law. But this at least is clear,
that some varieties of behavior, some ways of acting or explanations
of the doing of actions, are here noticed and classified which have not
been observed or named by ordinary men and hallowed by ordinary
language, though perhaps they often might have been so if they had
been of more practical importance. There is real danger in contempt
for the "jargon" of psychology, at least when it sets out to supplement,
and at least sometimes when it sets out to supplant, the language of
ordinary life.

With these sources, and with the aid of the imagination, it will go
hard if we cannot arrive at the meanings of large numbers of expressions and at the understanding and classification of large numbers of
"actions." Then we shall comprehend clearly much that, before, we
only made use of ad hoc. Definition, I would add, explanatory definition, should stand high among our aims: it is not enough to show how
clever we are by showing how obscure everything is. Clarity, too, I
know, has been said to be not enough: but perhaps it will be time to
go into that when we are within measurable distance of achieving
clarity on some matter.

So much for the cackle. It remains to make a few remarks, not, I am
afraid, in any very coherent order, about the types of significant result
to be obtained and the more general lessons to be learned from the
study of Excuses.

1. *No modification without aberration.* When it is stated that X did
A, there is a temptation to suppose that given some, indeed perhaps
any, expression modifying the verb we shall be entitled to insert either
it or its opposite or negation in our statement: that is, we shall be entitled to ask, typically, "Did X do A Mly or not Mly?" (e.g., "Did X
murder Y voluntarily or involuntarily?"), and to answer one or the
other. Or as a minimum it is supposed that if X did A there must be at
least *one* modifying expression that we could, justifiably and informa-
tively, insert with the verb. In the great majority of cases of the use
of the great majority of verbs ("murder" perhaps is not one of the
majority) such suppositions are quite unjustified. The natural economy
of language dictates that for the *standard* case covered by any normal
verb—not, perhaps, a verb of omen such as "murder," but a verb like
"eat" or "kick" or "croquet"—no modifying expression is required or
even permissible. Only if we do the action named in some *special* way
or circumstances, different from those in which such an act is naturally
done (and of course both the normal and the abnormal differ according
to what verb in particular is in question), is a modifying expression
called for, or even in order. I sit in my chair, in the usual way—I am
not in a daze or influenced by threats or the like: here, it will not do to
say either that I sat in it intentionally or that I did not sit in it intentionally,* nor yet that I sat in it automatically or from habit or what
you will. It is bedtime, I am alone, I yawn: but I do not yawn involuntarily (or voluntarily!), nor yet deliberately. To yawn in any such
peculiar way is just not to just yawn.

2. *Limitation of application.* Expressions modifying verbs, typically
adverbs, have limited ranges of application. That is, given any adverb
of excuse, such as "unwittingly" or "spontaneously" or "impulsively,"
it will not be found that it makes good sense to attach it to any and
every verb of "action" in any and every context: indeed, it will often
apply only to a comparatively narrow range of such verbs. Something
in the lad's upturned face appealed to him, he threw a brick at it—
"spontaneously"? The interest then is to discover why some actions
can be excused in a particular way but not others, particularly perhaps
the latter.* This will largely elucidate the meaning of the excuse, and
at the same time will illuminate the characteristics typical of the group
of "actions" it picks out: very often too it will throw light on some
detail of the machinery of "action" in general (see 4), or on our standards of acceptable conduct (see 5). It is specially important in the case

---

* Caveat or hedge: of course we can say "I did *not* sit in it 'intentionally' " as a
way simply of repudiating the suggestion that I sat in it intentionally.

of some of the terms most favored by philosophers or jurists to realize
that at least in ordinary speech (disregarding backseepage of jargon)
they are not used so universally or so dichotomistically. For example,
take "voluntarily" and "involuntarily": we may join the army or make
a gift voluntarily, we may hiccough or make a small gesture involuntarily, and the more we consider further actions which we might naturally be said to do in either of these ways, the more circumscribed and
unlike each other do the two classes become, until we even doubt
whether there is *any* verb with which both adverbs are equally in place.
Perhaps there are some such; but at least sometimes when we may
think we have found one it is an illusion, an apparent exception that
really does prove the rule. I can perhaps "break a cup" voluntarily, *if*
that is done, say, as an act of self-impoverishment: and I can perhaps
break another involuntarily, *if*, say, I make an involuntary movement
which breaks it. Here, plainly, the two acts described each as "breaking
a cup" are really very different, and the one is similar to acts typical of
the "voluntary" class, the other to acts typical of the "involuntary"
class.

3. *The importance of Negations and Opposites.* "Voluntarily" and
"involuntarily," then, are not opposed in the obvious sort of way that
they are made to be in philosophy or jurisprudence. The "opposite,"
or rather "opposites," of "voluntarily" might be "under constraint" of
some sort, duress or obligation or influence;† the opposite of "involuntarily" might be "deliberately" or "on purpose" or the like. Such diver-
gences in opposites indicate that "voluntarily" and "involuntarily," in
spite of their apparent connection, are fish from very different kettles.
In general, it will pay us to take nothing for granted or as obvious
about negations and opposites. It does not pay to assume that a word
must have an opposite, or one opposite, whether it is a "positive" word
like "wilfully" or a "negative" word like "inadvertently." Rather, we
should be asking ourselves such questions as why there is no use for
the adverb "advertently." For above all it will not do to assume that
the "positive" word must be around to wear the trousers; commonly
enough the "negative" (looking) word marks the (positive) abnormality, while the "positive" word, *if* it exists, merely serves to rule out
the suggestion of that abnormality. It is natural enough, in view of what
was said in (1) above, for the "positive" word not to be found at all

---

* For we are sometimes not so good at observing what we *can't* say as what we
can, yet the first is pretty regularly the more revealing.

† But remember, when I sign a check in the normal way, I do *not* do so *either*
"voluntarily" *or* "under constraint."

in some cases. I do an act A_1 (say, crush a snail) *inadvertently* if, in the course of executing by means of movements of my bodily parts some other act A_2 (say, in walking down the public path), I fail to exercise such meticulous supervision over the courses of those movements as would have been needed to ensure that they did not bring about the untoward event (here, the impact on the snail).* By claiming that A_1 was inadvertent we place it, where we imply it belongs, on this special level, in a class of incidental happenings which must occur in the doing of any physical act. To lift the act out of this class, we need and possess the expression "not . . . inadvertently": "advertently," if used for this purpose, would suggest that, if the act was not done inadvertently, then it must have been done noticing what I was doing, which is far from necessarily the case (e.g., if I did it absent-mindedly), or at least that there is *something* in common to the ways of doing all acts not done inadvertently, which is not the case. Again, there is no use for "advertently" at the *same* level as "inadvertently": in passing the butter I do not knock over the cream-jug, though I do (inadvertently) knock over the teacup—yet I do not by-pass the cream-jug *advertently:* for at this level, below supervision in detail, *anything* that we do is, if you like, inadvertent, though we only call it so, and indeed only call it something we have done, if there is something untoward about it.

A further point of interest in studying so-called "negative" terms is the manner of their formation. Why are the words in one group formed with *un-* or *in-*, those in another with *-less* ("aimless," "reckless," "heedless," etc.), and those in another with *mis-* ("mistake," "misconception," "misjudgment," etc.)? Why care*less*ly but *in*attentively? Perhaps care and attention, so often linked, are rather different. Here are remunerative exercises.

4. *The machinery of action.* Not merely do adverbial expressions pick out classes of actions, they also pick out the internal detail of the machinery of doing actions, or the departments into which the business of doing actions is organized. There is for example the stage at which we have actually to *carry out* some action upon which we embark— perhaps we have to make certain bodily movements or to make a

---

* Or analogously: I do an act A_1 (say, divulge my age, or imply you are a liar) *inadvertently* if, in the course of executing by the use of some medium of communication some other act A_2 (say, reminiscing about my war service), I fail to exercise such meticulous supervision over the choice and arrangement of the signs as would have been needed to ensure that. . . . It is interesting to note how such adverbs lead parallel lives, one in connection with physical actions ("doing") and the other in connection with acts of communication ("saying"), or sometimes also in connection with acts of "thinking" ("inadvertently assumed").

speech. In the course of actually *doing* these things (getting weaving) we have to pay (some) attention to what we are doing and to take (some) care to guard against (likely) dangers: we may need to use judgment or tact: we must exercise sufficient control over our bodily parts: and so on. Inattention, carelessness, errors of judgment, tactlessness, clumsiness, all these and others are ills (with attendant excuses) which affect one specific stage in the machinery of action, the *executive* stage, the stage where we *muff* it. But there are many other departments in the business too, each of which is to be traced and mapped through its cluster of appropriate verbs and adverbs. Obviously there are departments of intelligence and planning, of decision and resolve, and so on: but I shall mention one in particular, too often overlooked, where troubles and excuses abound. It happens to us, in military life, to be in receipt of excellent intelligence, to be also in self-conscious possession of excellent principles (the five golden rules for winning victories), and yet to hit upon a plan of action which leads to disaster. One way in which this can happen is through failure at the stage of *appreciation* of the situation, that is at the stage where we are required to cast our excellent intelligence into such a form, under such heads and with such weights attached, that our equally excellent principles can be brought to bear on it properly, in a way to yield the right answer.* So too in real, or rather civilian, life, in moral or practical affairs, we can know the facts and yet look at them mistakenly or perversely, or not fully realize or appreciate something, or even be under a total misconception. Many expressions of excuse indicate failure at this particularly tricky stage: even thoughtlessness, inconsiderateness, lack of imagination, are perhaps less matters of failure in intelligence or planning than might be supposed, and more matters of failure to appreciate the situation. A course of E. M. Forster and we see things differently: yet perhaps we know no more and are no cleverer.

5. *Standards of the unacceptable.* It is characteristic of excuses to be "unacceptable": given, I suppose, almost any excuse, there will be cases of such a kind or of such gravity that "we will not accept" it. It is interesting to detect the standards and codes we thus invoke. The extent of the supervision we exercise over the execution of any act can never be quite unlimited, and usually is expected to fall within fairly definite limits ("due care and attention") in the case of acts of some general kind, though of course we set very different limits in different cases. We

* We know all about how to do quadratics: we know all the needful facts about pipes, cisterns, hours and plumbers: yet we reach the answer "3¾ men." We have failed to cast our facts correctly into mathematical form.

may plead that we trod on the snail inadvertently: but not on a baby —you ought to look where you are putting your great feet. Of course it *was* (*really*), if you like, inadvertence: but that word constitutes a plea, which is not going to be allowed, because of standards. And if you try it on, you will be subscribing to such dreadful standards that your last state will be worse than your first. Or again, we set different standards, and will accept different excuses, in the case of acts which are rule-governed, like spelling, and which we are expected absolutely to get right, from those we set and accept for less stereotyped actions: a wrong spelling may be a slip, but hardly an accident, a winged beater may be an accident, but hardly a slip.

6. *Combination, dissociation, and complication.* A belief in opposites and dichotomies encourages, among other things, a blindness to the combinations and dissociations of adverbs that are possible, even to such obvious facts as that we can act at once on impulse and intentionally, or that we can do an action intentionally yet for all that not deliberately, still less on purpose. We walk along the cliff, and I feel a sudden impulse to push you over, which I promptly do: I acted on impulse, yet I certainly intended to push you over, and may even have devised a little ruse to achieve it: yet even then I did not act deliberately, for I did not (stop to) ask myself whether to do it or not.

It is worth bearing in mind, too, the general rule that we must not expect to find simple labels for complicated cases. If a mistake results in an accident, it will not do to ask whether "it" was an accident or a mistake, or to demand some briefer description of "it." Here the natural economy of language operates: if the words already available for simple cases suffice in combination to describe a complicated case, there will be need for special reasons before a special new word is invented for the complication. Besides, however well-equipped our language, it can never be forearmed against all possible cases that may arise and call for description: fact is richer than diction.

7. *Regina* v. *Finney.* Often the complexity and difficulty of a case is considerable. I will quote the case of *Regina* v. *Finney.**

Shrewsbury Assizes.   1874.   12 Cox 625.
  Prisoner was indicted for the manslaughter of Thomas Watkins.
  The Prisoner was an attendant at a lunatic asylum. Being in charge of a lunatic, who was bathing, he turned on hot water into the bath, and thereby scalded him to death. The facts appeared to be truly set forth in the statement of the prisoner made before the committing magistrate, as follows:

---

* A somewhat distressing favorite in the class that Hart used to conduct with me in the years soon after the war. The italics are mine.

"I had bathed Watkins, and had loosed the bath out. *I intended putting in a clean bath,* and asked Watkins if he would get out. At this time *my attention was drawn* to the next bath by the new attendant, who was asking me a question; and *my attention was taken from the bath* where Watkins was. I put my hand down to turn water on in the bath where Thomas Watkins was. *I did not intend to turn the hot water,* and *I made a mistake in the tap. I did not know what I had done until* I heard Thomas Watkins shout out; and *I did not find my mistake out till* I saw the steam from the water. You cannot get water in this bath when they are drawing water at the other bath; but at other times it shoots out like a water gun when the other baths are not in use. . . ."

(It was proved that the lunatic had such possession of his faculties as would enable him to understand what was said to him, and to get out of the bath.)

A. *Young* (for Prisoner). The death *resulted from accident.* There was no such *culpable negligence* on the part of the prisoner as will support this indictment. A *culpable mistake,* or some degree of *culpable negligence,* causing death, will not support a charge of manslaughter; unless the *negligence* be so gross as to be *reckless.* (*R. v. Noakes.*)

Lush, J. To render a person liable for *neglect of duty* there must be such a degree of culpability as to amount to *gross negligence on his part.* If you accept the prisoner's own statement, you find no such amount of *negligence* as would come within this definition. It is not every little *trip or mistake* that will make a man so liable. It was the duty of the attendant not to let hot water into the bath while the patient was therein. According to the prisoner's own account, *he did not believe that* he was letting the hot water in while the deceased remained there. The lunatic was, we have heard, a man capable of getting out by himself and of understanding what was said to him. He was told to get out. A new attendant who had come on this day, was at an adjoining bath and he *took off the prisoner's attention.* Now, if the prisoner, knowing that the man was in the bath, had turned on the tap, and turned on the hot instead of the cold water, I should have said there was gross negligence; for he ought to have looked to see. But from his own account he had told the deceased to get out, and *thought he had got out.* If you think that indicates gross *carelessness,* then you should find the prisoner guilty of manslaughter. But if you think it *inadvertence* not amounting to culpability—i.e., what is properly termed an *accident*—then the prisoner is not liable.

Verdict, Not guilty.

In this case there are two morals that I will point. (1) Both counsel and judge make very free use of a large number of terms of excuse, using several as though they were, and even stating them to be, indifferent or equivalent when they are not, and presenting as alternatives those that are not. (2) It is constantly difficult to be sure *what* act it is that counsel or judge is suggesting might be qualified by what expression of excuse. The learned judge's concluding direction is a paradigm of these faults.* Finney, by contrast, stands out as an evident master of the Queen's English. He is explicit as to each of his acts and states, mental and physical: he uses different, and the correct, adverbs in connection with each: and he makes no attempt to boil down.

8. *Small distinctions, and big too.* It should go without saying that terms of excuse are not equivalent, and that it matters which we use: we need to distinguish inadvertence not merely from (save the mark) such things as mistake and accident, but from such nearer neighbors as, say, aberration and absence of mind. By imagining cases with vividness and fullness we should be able to decide in which precise terms to describe, say, Miss Plimsoll's action in writing, so carefully, "DAIRY" on her fine new book: we should be able to distinguish between sheer, mere, pure, and simple mistake or inadvertence. Yet unfortunately, at least when in the grip of thought, we fail not merely at these stiffer hurdles. We equate even—I have seen it done—"inadvertently" with "automatically": as though to say I trod on your toe inadvertently means to say I trod on it automatically. Or we collapse succumbing to temptation into losing control of ourselves—a bad patch, this, for telescoping.**

All this is not so much a *lesson* from the study of excuses as the very object of it.

9. *The exact phrase and its place in the sentence.* It is not enough, either, to attend simply to the "key" word: notice must also be taken of

---

* Not but what he probably manages to convey his meaning somehow or other. Judges seem to acquire a knack of conveying meaning, and even carrying conviction, through the use of a pithy Anglo-Saxon which sometimes has literally no meaning at all. Wishing to distinguish the case of shooting at a post in the belief that it was an enemy, as *not* an "attempt," from the case of picking an empty pocket in the belief that money was in it, which *is* an "attempt," the judge explains that in shooting at the post "the man is never on the thing at all."

** Plato, I suppose, and after him Aristotle, fastened this confusion upon us, as bad in its day and way as the later, grotesque, confusion of moral weakness with weakness of will. I am very partial to ice cream, and a bombe is served divided into segments corresponding one to one with the persons at High Table: I am tempted to help myself to two segments and do so, thus succumbing to temptation and even conceivably (but why necessarily?) going against my principles. But do I lose control of myself? Do I raven, do I snatch the morsels from the dish and wolf them down, impervious to the consternation of my colleagues? Not a bit of it. We often succumb to temptation with calm and even with finesse.

† As a matter of fact, most of these examples *can* be understood the other way, especially if we allow ourselves inflections of the voice, or commas, or contexts. a_2 might be a poetic inversion for b_2: b_1, perhaps with commas round the "clumsily," might be used for a_1: and so on. Still, the two senses are clearly enough distinguishable.

the full and exact form of the expression used. In considering mistakes, we have to consider seriatim "by mistake," "owing to a mistake," "mistakenly," "it was a mistake to," "to make a mistake in or over or about," "to be mistaken about," and so on: in considering purpose, we have to consider "on," "with the," "for the," etc., besides "purposeful," "purposeless," and the like. These varying expressions may function quite differently—and usually do, or why should we burden ourselves with more than one of them?

Care must be taken too to observe the precise position of an adverbial expression in the sentence. This should of course indicate what verb it is being used to modify: but more than that, the position can also affect the *sense* of the expression, i.e., the way in which it modifies that verb. Compare, for example:

a_1 He clumsily trod on the snail.
a_2 Clumsily he trod on the snail.
b_1 He trod clumsily on the snail.
b_2 He trod on the snail clumsily.

Here, in a_1 and a_2 we describe his treading on the creature at all as a piece of clumsiness, incidental, we imply, to his performance of some other action: but with b_1 and b_2 to tread on it is, very likely, his aim or policy, what we criticize is his execution of the feat. Many adverbs, though far from all (not, for example, "purposely") are used in these two typically different ways.

10. *The style of performance.* With some adverbs the distinction between the two senses referred to in the last paragraph is carried a stage further. "He ate his soup deliberately" may mean, like "He deliberately ate his soup," that his eating his soup was a deliberate act, one perhaps that he thought would annoy somebody, as it would more commonly if he deliberately ate *my* soup, and which he decided to do: but it will often mean that he went through the performance of eating his soup in a noteworthy manner or *style*—pause after each mouthful, careful choice of point of entry for the spoon, sucking of moustaches, and so on. That is, it will mean that he ate *with* deliberation rather than *after* deliberation. The style of the performance, slow and unhurried, is understandably called "deliberate" because each movement *has the typical look* of a deliberate act: but it is scarcely being said that the making of each motion *is* a deliberate act or that he is "literally" deliberating. This case, then, is more extreme than that of "clumsily," which does in both uses describe literally a manner of performing.

It is worth watching out for this secondary use when scrutinizing any particular adverbial expression: when it definitely does not exist, the reason is worth inquiring into. Sometimes it is very hard to be sure whether it does exist or does not: it does, one would think, with "carelessly," it does not with "inadvertently," but does it or does it not with "absent-mindedly" or "aimlessly"? In some cases a word akin to but distinct from the primary adverb is used for this special role of describing a style of performance: we use "purposefully" in this way, but never "purposely."

11. *What modifies what?* The judge in *Regina* v. *Finney* does not make clear what event is being excused in what way. "If you think that indicates gross carelessness, then. . . . But if you think it inadvertence not amounting to culpability—i.e., what is properly called an accident —then. . . ." Apparently he means that Finney may have *turned on the hot tap* inadvertently:* does he mean also that the tap may have been turned accidentally, or rather that *Watkins may have been scalded* and killed accidentally? And was the carelessness in turning the tap or in thinking Watkins had got out? Many disputes as to what excuse we should properly use arise because we will not trouble to state explicitly *what* is being excused.

To do so is all the more vital because it is in principle always open to us, along various lines, to describe or refer to "what I did" in so many different ways. This is altogether too large a theme to elaborate here. Apart from the more general and obvious problems of the use of "tendentious" descriptive terms, there are many special problems in the particular case of "actions." Should we say, are we saying, that he took her money, or that he robbed her? That he knocked a ball into a hole, or that he sank a putt? That he said "Done," or that he accepted an offer? How far, that is, are motives, intentions, and conventions to be part of the description of actions? And more especially here, what is *an* or *one* or *the* action? For we can generally split up what might be named as one action in several distinct ways, into different *stretches* or *phases* or *stages*. Stages have already been mentioned: we can dismantle the machinery of the act, and describe (and excuse) separately the intelligence, the appreciation, the planning, the decision, the execu-

---

* What Finney says is different: he says he "made a mistake in the tap." This is the basic use of "mistake," where we simply, and not necessarily accountably, take the wrong one. Finney here attempts to account for his mistake, by saying that his attention was distracted. But suppose the order is "Right turn" and I turn left: no doubt the sergeant will insinuate that my attention was distracted, or that I cannot distinguish my right from my left—but it was not and I can; this was a simple, pure mistake. As often happens. Neither I nor the sergeant will suggest that there was any accident, or any inadvertence either. If Finney had turned the hot tap inadvertently, then it would have been knocked, say, in reaching for the cold tap: a different story.

tion, and so forth. Phases are rather different: we can say that he painted a picture or fought a campaign, or else we can say that first he laid on this stroke of paint and then that, first he fought this action and then that. Stretches are different again: a single term descriptive of what he did may be made to cover either a smaller or a larger stretch of events, those excluded by the narrower description being then called "consequences" or "results" or "effects" or the like of his act. So here we can describe Finney's act *either* as turning on the hot tap, which he did by mistake, with the result that Watkins was scalded, *or* as scalding Watkins, which he did *not* do by mistake.

It is very evident that the problems of excuses and those of the different descriptions of actions are throughout bound up with each other.

12. *Trailing clouds of etymology.* It is these considerations that bring us up so forcibly against some of the most difficult words in the whole story of Excuses, such words as "result," "effect," and "consequence," or again as "intention," "purpose," and "motive." I will mention two points of method which are, experience has convinced me, indispensable aids at these levels.

One is that a word never—well, hardly ever—shakes off its etymology and its formation. In spite of all changes in and extensions of and additions to its meanings, and indeed rather pervading and governing these, there will still persist the old idea. In an *accident* something befalls: by *mistake* you take the wrong one: in *error* you stray: when you act *deliberately* you act after weighing it up (*not* after thinking out ways and means). It is worth asking ourselves whether we know the etymology of "result" or of "spontaneously," and worth remembering that "unwillingly" and "involuntarily" come from very different sources.

And the second point is connected with this. Going back into the history of a word, very often into Latin, we come back pretty commonly to pictures or *models* of how things happen or are done. These models may be fairly sophisticated and recent, as is perhaps the case with "motive" or "impulse," but one of the commonest and most primitive types of model is one which is apt to baffle us through its very naturalness and simplicity. We take *some very simple action*, like shoving a stone, usually as done by and viewed by oneself, and use *this*, with the features distinguishable in it, as our model in terms of which to talk about other actions and events: and we continue to do so, scarcely realizing it, even when these other actions are pretty remote and perhaps much more interesting to us in their own right than the acts originally used in constructing the model ever were, and even when the model is really distorting the facts rather than helping us to observe them. In primitive cases we may get to see clearly the differences between, say, "results," "effects," and "consequences," and yet discover that these differences are no longer clear, and the terms them-selves no longer of real service to us, in the more complicated cases where we had been bandying them about most freely. A model must be recognized for what it is. "Causing," I suppose, was a notion taken from a man's own experience of doing simple actions, and by primitive man every event was construed in terms of this model: every event has a cause, that is, every event is an action done by somebody—if not by a man, then by a quasi-man, a spirit. When, later, events which are *not* actions are realized to be such, we still say that they must be "caused," and the word snares us: we are struggling to ascribe to it a new, un-anthropomorphic meaning, yet constantly, in searching for its analysis, we unearth and incorporate the lineaments of the ancient model. As happened even to Hume, and consequently to Kant. Examining such a word historically, we may well find that it has been extended to cases that have by now too tenuous a relation to the model case, that it is a source of confusion and superstition.

There is too another danger in words that invoke models, half-forgotten or not. It must be remembered that there is no necessity whatsoever that the various models used in creating our vocabulary, primitive or recent, should all fit together neatly as parts into one single, total model or scheme of, for instance, the doing of actions. It is pos-sible, and indeed highly likely, that our assortment of models will in-clude some, or many, that are overlapping, conflicting, or more gen-erally simply *disparate.**

13. In spite of the wide and acute observation of the phenomena of action embodied in ordinary speech, modern scientists have been able, it seems to me, to reveal its inadequacy at numerous points, if only because they have had access to more comprehensive data and have studied them with more catholic and dispassionate interest than the ordinary man, or even the lawyer, has had occasion to do. I will con-clude with two examples.

---

* This is by way of a general warning in philosophy. It seems to be too readily assumed that if we can only discover the true meanings of each of a cluster of key terms, usually historic terms, that we use in some particular field (as, for example, "right," "good," and the rest in morals), then it must without question transpire that each will fit into place in some single, interlocking, consistent, conceptual scheme. Not only is there no reason to assume this, but all historical probability is against it, especially in the case of a language derived from such various civiliza-tions as ours. We may cheerfully use, and with weight, terms which are not so much head-on incompatible as simply disparate, which just do not fit in or even on. Just as we cheerfully subscribe to, or have the grace to be torn between, simply disparate ideals—why *must* there be a conceivable amalgam, the Good Life for Man?

Observation of animal behavior shows that regularly, when an animal is embarked on some recognizable pattern of behavior but meets in the course of it with an insuperable obstacle, it will betake itself to energetic, but quite unrelated, activity of some wild kind, such as standing on its head. This phenomenon is called "displacement behavior" and is well identifiable. If now, in the light of this, we look back at ordinary human life, we see that displacement behavior bulks quite large in it: yet we have apparently no word, or at least no clear and simple word, for it. If, when thwarted, we stand on our heads or wiggle our toes, then we are not exactly *just* standing on our heads, don't you know, in the ordinary way, yet is there any convenient adverbial expression we can insert to do the trick? "In desperation"?

Take, again, "compulsive" behavior, however exactly psychologists define it, compulsive washing for example. There are of course hints in ordinary speech that we do things in this way—"just feel I have to," "shouldn't feel comfortable unless I did," and the like: but there is no adverbial expression satisfactorily pre-empted for it, as "compulsively" is. This is understandable enough, since compulsive behavior, like displacement behavior, is not in general going to be of great practical importance.

Here I leave and commend the subject to you.

ARISTOTLE

(384–322 B.C.)

*Blameworthiness**

*Aristotle is one of the most famous philosophers of the Western tradition.
His works span the whole range of philosophic topics, but perhaps his best
known work is* Ethica Nichomachea, *from which this selection is taken. The
title of the book is derived from the belief that it is a record of Aristotle's
lectures prepared by his son Nicomachus. In brief, Aristotle's ethical position
is that the good for man is happiness, which is defined as realization of
man's essential nature, an activity of the soul in accord with reason.
Achieving this involves choosing the mean between the possible extremes
of conduct. The focus of this selection is upon the determination of
blameworthiness. When do we have the right to blame a man for his actions,
and when should we refrain from holding him blameworthy? In offering
an answer to these questions, Aristotle examines in detail the concepts
of involuntariness, compulsion, and such related notions as intention,
ignorance, and inadvertence.*

* Aristotle, *Ethica Nicomachea*, I. Bywater, trans., 1911. From Books II and III.

WE must consider what virtue is. Since things that are found
in the soul are of three kinds—passions, faculties, states of
character, virtue must be one of these. By passions I mean appetite,
anger, fear, confidence, envy, joy, friendly feeling, hatred, longing,
emulation, pity, and in general the feelings that are accompanied by
pleasure or pain; by faculties the things in virtue of which we are
said to be capable of feeling these, e.g. of becoming angry or being
pained or feeling pity; by states of character the things in virtue of
which we stand well or badly with reference to the passions, e.g. with
reference to anger we stand badly if we feel it violently or too weakly,
and well if we feel it moderately; and similarly with reference to the
other passions.

Now neither the virtues nor the vices are *passions*, because we are
not called good or bad on the grounds of our passions, but are so
called on the ground of our virtues and our vices, and because we are
neither praised nor blamed for our passions (for the man who feels
fear or anger is not praised, nor is the man who simply feels anger

blamed, but the man who feels it in a certain way), but for our virtues and our vices we *are* praised or blamed.

Again, we feel anger and fear without choice, but the virtues are modes of choice or involve choice. Further, in respect of the passions we are said to be moved, but in respect of the virtues and the vices we are said not to be moved but to be disposed in a particular way.

For these reasons also they are not *faculties;* for we are neither called good nor bad, nor praised nor blamed, for the simple capacity of feeling the passions; again, we have the faculties by nature, but we are not made good or bad by nature; we have spoken of this before.

If, then, the virtues are neither passions nor faculties, all that remains is that they should be *states of character.*

Thus we have stated what virtue is in respect of its genus.

We must, however, not only describe virtue as a state of character, but also say what sort of state it is. We may remark, then, that every virtue or excellence both brings into good condition the thing of which it is the excellence and makes the work of that thing be done well; e.g. the excellence of the eye makes both the eye and its work good; for it is by the excellence of the eye that we see well. Similarly the excellence of the horse makes a horse both good in itself and good at running and at carrying its rider and at awaiting the attack of the enemy. Therefore, if this is true in every case, the virtue of man also will be the state of character which makes a man good and which makes him do his own work well.

How this is to happen we have stated already, but it will be made plain also by the following consideration of the specific nature of virtue. In everything that is continuous and divisible it is possible to take more, less, or an equal amount, and that either in terms of the thing itself or relatively to us; and the equal is an intermediate between excess and defect. By the intermediate in the object I mean that which is equidistant from each of the extremes, which is one and the same for all men; by the intermediate relatively to us that which is neither too much nor too little—and this is not one, nor the same for all. For instance, if ten is many and two is few, six is the intermediate, taken in terms of the object; for it exceeds and is exceeded by an equal amount; this is intermediate according to arithmetical proportion. But the intermediate relatively to us is not to be taken so; if ten pounds are too much for a particular person to eat and two too little, it does not follow that the trainer will order six pounds; for this also is perhaps too much for the person who is to take it, or too little—too little for Milo, too much for the beginner in athletic exercises. The same is true of running and wrestling. Thus a master of any art avoids excess and defect, but seeks the intermediate and chooses this—the intermediate not in the object but relatively to us.

If it is thus, then, that every art does its work well—by looking to the intermediate and judging its works by this standard (so that we often say of good works of art that it is not possible either to take away or to add anything, implying that excess and defect destroy the goodness of works of art, while the mean preserves it; and good artists, as we say, look to this in their work), and if, further, virtue is more exact and better than any art, as nature also is, then virtue must have the quality of aiming at the intermediate. I mean moral virtue; for it is this that is concerned with passions and actions, and in these there is excess, defect, and the intermediate. For instance, both fear and confidence and appetite and anger and pity and in general pleasure and pain may be felt both too much and too little, and in both cases not well; but to feel them at the right times, with reference to the right objects, towards the right people, with the right motive, and in the right way, is what is both intermediate and best, and this is characteristic of virtue. Similarly with regard to actions also there is excess, defect, and the intermediate. Now virtue is concerned with passions and actions, in which excess is a form of failure, and so is defect, while the intermediate is praised and is a form of success; and being praised and being successful are both characteristics of virtue. Therefore virtue is a kind of mean, since, as we have seen, it aims at what is intermediate.

Again, it is possible to fail in many ways (for evil belongs to the class of the unlimited, as the Pythagoreans conjectured, and good to that of the limited), while to succeed is possible only in one way (for which reason also one is easy and the other difficult—to miss the mark easy, to hit it difficult); for these reasons also, then, excess and defect are characteristic of vice, and the mean of virtue;

For men are good in but one way, but bad in many.

Virtue, then, is a state of character concerned with choice, lying in a mean, i.e. the mean relative to us, this being determined by a rational principle, and by that principle by which the man of practical wisdom would determine it. Now it is a mean between two vices, that which depends on excess and that which depends on defect; and again it is a mean because the vices respectively fall short of or exceed what is right in both passions and actions, while virtue both finds and chooses that which is intermediate. Hence in respect of its substance and the definition which states its essence virtue is a mean, with regard to what is best and right an extreme.

But not every action nor every passion admits of a mean; for some have names that already imply badness, e.g. spite, shamelessness, envy, and in the case of actions adultery, theft, murder; for all of these and suchlike things imply by their names that they are themselves bad, and not the excesses or deficiencies of them. It is not possible, then, ever to be right with regard to them; one must always be wrong. Nor does goodness or badness with regard to such things depend on committing adultery with the right woman, at the right time, and in the right way, but simply to do any of them is to go wrong. It would be equally absurd, then, to expect that in unjust, cowardly, and voluptuous action there should be a mean, an excess, and a deficiency; for at that rate there would be a mean of excess and of deficiency, an excess of excess, and a deficiency of deficiency. But as there is no excess and deficiency of temperance and courage because what is intermediate is in a sense an extreme, so too of the actions we have mentioned there is no mean nor any excess and deficiency, but however they are done they are wrong; for in general there is neither a mean of excess and deficiency, nor excess and deficiency of a mean.

· · ·

That moral virtue is a mean, then, and in what sense it is so, and that it is a mean between two vices, the one involving excess, the other deficiency, and that it is such because its character is to aim at what is intermediate in passions and in actions, has been sufficiently stated. Hence also it is no easy task to be good. For in everything it is no easy task to find the middle, e.g. to find the middle of a circle is not for every one but for him who knows; so, too, any one can get angry— that is easy—or give or spend money; but to do this to the right person, to the right extent, at the right time, with the right motive, and in the right way, *that* is not for every one, nor is it easy; wherefore goodness is both rare and laudable and noble.

Hence he who aims at the intermediate must first depart from what is the more contrary to it, as Calypso advises—

Hold the ship out beyond that surf and spray.

For of the extremes one is more erroneous, one less so; therefore, since to hit the mean is hard in the extreme, we must as a second best, as people say, take the least of the evils; and this will be done best in the way we describe.

But we must consider the things towards which we ourselves also are easily carried away; for some of us tend to one thing, some to another; and this will be recognizable from the pleasure and the pain we feel. We must drag ourselves away to the contrary extreme; for we shall get into the intermediate state by drawing well away from error, as people do in straightening sticks that are bent.

Now in everything the pleasant or pleasure is most to be guarded against; for we do not judge it impartially. We ought, then, to feel towards pleasure as the elders of the people felt towards Helen, and in all circumstances repeat their saying; for if we dismiss pleasure thus we are less likely to go astray. It is by doing this, then, (to sum the matter up) that we shall best be able to hit the mean.

But this is no doubt difficult, and especially in individual cases; for it is not easy to determine both how and with whom and on what provocation and how long one should be angry; for we too sometimes praise those who fall short and call them good-tempered, but sometimes we praise those who get angry and call them manly. The man, however, who deviates little from goodness is not blamed, whether he do so in the direction of the more or of the less, but only the man who deviates more widely; for *he* does not fail to be noticed. But up to that point and to what extent a man must deviate before he becomes blameworthy it is not easy to determine by reasoning, any more than anything else that is perceived by the senses; such things depend on particular facts, and the decision rests with perception. So much, then, is plain, that the intermediate state is in all things to be praised, but that we must incline sometimes towards the excess, sometimes towards the deficiency; for so shall we most easily hit the mean and what is right.

Since virtue is concerned with passions and actions, and on voluntary passions and actions praise and blame are bestowed, on those that are involuntary pardon, and sometimes also pity, to distinguish the voluntary and the involuntary is presumably necessary for those who are studying the nature of virtue, and useful also for legislators with a view to the assigning both of honours and of punishments.

Those things, then, are thought involuntary, which take place under compulsion or owing to ignorance; and that is compulsory of which the moving principle is outside, being a principle in which nothing is contributed by the person who is acting or is feeling the passion, e.g. if he were to be carried somewhere by a wind, or by men who had him in their power.

But with regard to the things that are done from fear of greater evils or for some noble object (e.g. if a tyrant were to order one to do something base, having one's parents and children in his power, and if one did the action they were to be saved, but otherwise would be put to death), it may be debated whether such actions are involuntary or voluntary. Something of the sort happens also with regard to the throwing of goods overboard in a storm; for in the abstract no one throws goods away voluntarily, but on condition of its securing the safety of himself and his crew any sensible man does so. Such actions, then, are mixed, but are more like voluntary actions; for they are worthy of choice at the time when they are done, and the end of an action is relative to the occasion. Both the terms, then, 'voluntary' and 'involuntary,' must be used with reference to the moment of action. Now the man acts voluntarily; for the principle that moves the instrumental parts of the body in such actions is in him, and the things of which the moving principle is in a man himself are in his power to do or not to do. Such actions, therefore, are voluntary, but in the abstract perhaps involuntary; for no one would choose any such act in itself.

For such actions men are sometimes even praised, when they endure something base or painful in return for great and noble objects gained; in the opposite case they are blamed, since to endure the greatest indignities for no noble end or for a trifling end is the mark of an inferior person. On some actions praise indeed is not bestowed, but pardon is, when one does what he ought not under pressure which overstrains human nature and which no one could withstand. But some acts, perhaps, we cannot be forced to do, but ought rather to face death after the most fearful sufferings; for the things that 'forced' Euripides' Alcmaeon to slay his mother seem absurd. It is difficult sometimes to determine what should be chosen at what cost, and what should be endured in return for what gain, and yet more difficult to abide by our decisions; for as a rule what is expected is painful, and what we are forced to do is base, whence praise and blame are bestowed on those who have been compelled or have not.

What sort of acts, then, should be called compulsory? We answer that without qualification actions are so when the cause is in the external circumstances and the agent contributes nothing. But the things that in themselves are involuntary, but now and in return for these gains are worthy of choice, and whose moving principle is in the agent, are in themselves involuntary, but now and in return for these gains voluntary. They are more like voluntary acts; for actions are in the class of particulars, and the particular acts here are voluntary. What sort of things are to be chosen, and in return for what, it is not easy to state; for there are many differences in the particular cases.

But if some one were to say that pleasant and noble objects have a compelling power, forcing us from without, all acts would be for him compulsory; for it is for these objects that all men do everything they do. And those who act under compulsion and unwillingly act with pain, but those who do acts for their pleasantness and nobility do them with pleasure; it is absurd to make external circumstances responsible, and not oneself, as being easily caught by such attractions, and to make oneself responsible for noble acts but the pleasant objects responsible for base acts. The compulsory, then, seems to be that whose moving principle is outside, the person compelled contributing nothing.

Everything that is done by reason of ignorance is *not* voluntary; it is only what produces pain and repentance that is *in*voluntary. For the man who has done something owing to ignorance, and feels not the least vexation at his action, has not acted voluntarily, since he did not know what he was doing, nor yet involuntarily, since he is not pained. Of people, then, who act by reason of ignorance he who repents is thought an involuntary agent, and the man who does not repent may, since he is different, be called a not voluntary agent; for, since he differs from the other, it is better that he should have a name of his own.

Acting by reason of ignorance seems also to be different from acting *in* ignorance; for the man who is drunk or in a rage is thought to act as a result not of ignorance but of one of the causes mentioned, yet not knowingly but in ignorance.

Now every wicked man is ignorant of what he ought to do and what he ought to abstain from, and it is by reason of error of this kind that men become unjust and in general bad; but the term 'involuntary' tends to be used not if a man is ignorant of what is to his advantage— for it is not mistaken purpose that causes involuntary action (it leads rather to wickedness), nor ignorance of the universal (for *that* men are *blamed*), but ignorance of particulars, i.e. of the circumstances of the action and the objects with which it is concerned. For it is on these that both pity and pardon depend, since the person who is ignorant of any of these acts involuntarily.

Perhaps it is just as well, therefore, to determine their nature and number. A man may be ignorant, then, of who he is, what he is doing, what or whom he is acting on, and sometimes also what (e.g. what instrument) he is doing it with, and to what end (e.g. he may think his act will conduce to some one's safety), and how he is doing it (e.g. whether gently or violently). Now of all of these no one could be ignorant unless he were mad, and evidently also he could not be ignorant of the agent; for how could he not know himself? But of what he is doing a man might be ignorant, as for instance people say 'it slipped out of their mouths as they were speaking,' or 'they did not know it was a secret,' as Aeschylus said of the mysteries, or a man might say he 'let it go off when he merely wanted to show its working,' as the man did with the catapult. Again, one might think one's son was an enemy, as Merope did, or that a pointed spear had a button on it, or that a stone was pumice-stone; or one might give a man a draught to save him, and really kill him; or one might want to touch a man, as people do in sparring, and really wound him. The ignorance may relate, then, to any of these things, i.e. of the circumstances of the action, and the man who was ignorant of any of these is thought to have acted involuntarily, and especially if he was ignorant on the most important points; and these are thought to be the circumstances of the action and its end. Further, the doing of an act that is called involuntary in virtue of ignorance of this sort must be painful and involve repentance.

Since that which is done under compulsion or by reason of ignorance is involuntary, the voluntary would seem to be that of which the moving principle is in the agent himself, he being aware of the particular circumstances of the action. Presumably acts done by reason of anger or appetite are not rightly called involuntary. For in the first place, on that showing none of the other animals will act voluntarily, nor will children; and secondly, is it meant that we do not do voluntarily *any* of the acts that are due to appetite or anger, or that we do the noble acts voluntarily and the base acts involuntarily? Is not this absurd, when one and the same thing is the cause? But it would surely be odd to describe as involuntary the things one ought to desire; and we ought both to be angry at certain things and to have an appetite for certain things, e.g. for health and for learning. Also what is involuntary is thought to be painful, but what is in accordance with appetite is thought to be pleasant. Again, what is the difference in respect to involuntariness between errors committed upon calculation and those committed in anger? Both are to be avoided, but the irrational passions are thought not less human than reason is, and therefore also the actions which proceed from anger or appetite are the man's actions. It would be odd, then, to treat them as involuntary.

Both the voluntary and the involuntary having been delimited, we must next discuss choice; for it is thought to be most closely bound up with virtue and to discriminate characters better than actions do.

Choice, then, seems to be voluntary, but not the same thing as the voluntary; the latter extends more widely. For both children and the lower animals share in voluntary action, but not in choice, and acts done on the spur of the moment we describe as voluntary, but not as chosen.

Those who say it is appetite or anger or wish or a kind of opinion do not seem to be right. For choice is not common to irrational creatures as well, but appetite and anger are. Again, the incontinent man acts with appetite, but not with choice; while the continent man on the contrary acts with choice, but not with appetite. Again, appetite relates to the pleasant and the painful, choice neither to the painful nor to the pleasant.

Still less is it anger; for acts due to anger are thought to be less than any others objects of choice.

But neither is it wish, though it seems near to it; for choice cannot relate to impossibles, and if any one said he chose them he would be thought silly; but there may be a wish even for impossibles, e.g. for immortality. And wish may relate to things that could in no way be brought about by one's own efforts, e.g. that a particular actor or athlete should win in a competition; but no one chooses such things, but only the things that he thinks could be brought about by his own efforts. Again, wish relates rather to the end, choice to the means; for instance, we wish to be healthy, but we choose the acts which will make us healthy, and we wish to be happy and say we do, but we cannot well say we choose to be so; for, in general, choice seems to relate to the things that are in our own power.

For this reason, too, it cannot be opinion; for opinion is thought to relate to all kinds of things, no less to eternal things and impossible things than to things in our own power; and it is distinguished by its falsity or truth, not by its badness or goodness, while choice is distinguished rather by these.

Now with opinion in general perhaps no one even says it is identical. But it is not identical even with any kind of opinion; for by choosing what is good or bad we are men of a certain character, which we are not by holding certain opinions. And we choose to get or avoid something good or bad, but we have opinions about what a thing is or whom it is good for or how it is good for him; we can hardly be said to opine to get or avoid anything. And choice is praised for being related to it, opinion for being truly related to its object. And we choose what we best know to be good, but we opine what we do

not quite know; and it is not the same people that are thought to
make the best choices and to have the best opinions, but some are
thought to have fairly good opinions, but by reason of vice to choose
what they should not. If opinion precedes choice or accompanies it,
that makes no difference; for it is not this that we are considering,
but whether it is *identical* with some kind of opinion.

What, then, or what kind of thing is it, since it is none of the things
we have mentioned? It seems to be voluntary, but not all that is
voluntary to be an object of choice. Is it, then, what has been decided
on by previous deliberation? At any rate choice involves a rational
principle and thought. Even the name seems to suggest that it is
what is chosen before other things.

Do we deliberate about everything, and is everything a possible
subject of deliberation, or is deliberation impossible about some
things? We ought presumably to call not what a fool or a madman
would deliberate about, but what a sensible man would deliberate
about, a subject of deliberation. Now about eternal things no one
deliberates, e.g. about the material universe or the incommensurabil-
ity of the diagonal and the side of a square. But no more do we deliberate about the things that involve movement but always happen
in the same way, whether of necessity or by nature or from any other
cause, e.g. the solstices and the risings of the stars; nor about things
that happen now in one way, now in another, e.g. droughts and rains;
nor about chance events, like the finding of treasure. But we do not
deliberate even about all human affairs; for instance, no Spartan deliberates about the best constitution for the Scythians. For none of
these things can be brought about by our own efforts.

We deliberate about things that are in our power and can be done;
and these are in fact what is left. For nature, necessity, and chance
are thought to be causes, and also reason and everything that depends
on man. Now every class of men deliberates about the things that
can be done by their own efforts. And in the case of exact and self-
contained sciences there is no deliberation, e.g. about the letters of
the alphabet (for we have no doubt how they should be written);
but the things that are brought about by our own efforts, but not
always in the same way, are the things about which we deliberate,
e.g. questions of medical treatment or of money-making. And we do
so more in the case of the art of navigation than in that of gymnastics,
inasmuch as it has been less exactly worked out, and again about
other things in the same ratio, and more also in the case of the arts
than in that of the sciences; for we have more doubt about the former.

Deliberation is concerned with things that happen in a certain way for the most part, but in which the event is obscure, and with things in which it is indeterminate. We call in others to aid us in deliberation on important questions, distrusting ourselves as not being equal to deciding.

We deliberate not about ends but about means. For a doctor does not deliberate whether he shall heal, nor an orator whether he shall persuade, nor a statesman whether he shall produce law and order, nor does any one else deliberate about his end. They assume the end and consider how and by what means it is to be attained; and if it seems to be produced by several means they consider by which it is most easily and best produced, while if it is achieved by one only they consider how it will be achieved by this and by what means *this* will be achieved, till they come to the first cause, which in the order of discovery is last. For the person who deliberates seems to investigate and analyse in the way described as though he were analysing a geometrical construction (not all investigation appears to be deliberation—for instance mathematical investigations—but all deliberation is investigation), and what is last in the order of analysis seems to be first in the order of becoming. And if we come on an impossibility, we give up the search, e.g. if we need money and this cannot be got; but if a thing appears possible we try to do it. By 'possible' things I mean things that might be brought about by our own efforts; and these in a sense include things that can be brought about by the efforts of our friends, since the moving principle is in ourselves. The subject of investigation is sometimes the instruments, sometimes the use of them; and similarly in the other cases—sometimes the means, sometimes the mode of using it or the means of bringing it about. It seems, then, as has been said, that man is a moving principle of actions; now deliberation is about the things to be done by the agent himself, and actions are for the sake of things other than themselves. For the end cannot be a subject of deliberation, but only the means; nor indeed can the particular facts be a subject of it, as whether this is bread or has been baked as it should; for these are matters of perception. If we are to be always deliberating, we shall have to go on to infinity.

The same thing is deliberated upon and is chosen, except that the object of choice is already determinate, since it is that which has been decided upon as a result of deliberation that is the object of choice. For every one ceases to inquire how he is to act when he has brought the moving principle back to himself and to the ruling part of himself; for this is what chooses. This is plain also from the ancient constitutions, which Homer represented; for the kings announced their choices to the people. The object of choice being one of the things in our own power which is desired after deliberation, choice will be deliberate desire of things in our own power; for when we have decided as a result of deliberation, we desire in accordance with our deliberation.

We may take it, then, that we have described choice in outline, and stated the nature of its objects and the fact that it is concerned with means.

That *wish* is for the end has already been stated; some think it is for the good, others for the apparent good. Now those who say that the good is the object of wish must admit in consequence that that which the man who does not choose aright wishes for is not an object of wish (for if it is to be so, it must also be good; but it was, if it so happened, bad); while those who say the apparent good is the object of wish must admit that there is no natural object of wish, but only what seems good to each man. Now different things appear good to different people, and, if it so happens, even contrary things.

If these consequences are unpleasing, are we to say that absolutely and in truth the good is the object of wish, but for each person the apparent good; that that which is in truth an object of wish to the good man, while any chance thing may be so to the bad man, as in the case of bodies also the things that are in truth wholesome are wholesome for bodies which are in good condition, while for those that are diseased other things are wholesome—or bitter or sweet or hot or heavy, and so on; since the good man judges each class of things rightly, and in each the truth appears to him? For each state of character has its own ideas of the noble and the pleasant, and perhaps the good man differs from others most by seeing the truth in each class of things, being as it were the norm and measure of them. In most things the error seems to be due to pleasure; for it appears a good when it is not. We therefore choose the pleasant as a good, and avoid pain as an evil.

The end, then, being what we wish for, the means what we deliberate about and choose, actions concerning means must be according to choice and voluntary. Now the exercise of the virtues is concerned with means. Therefore virtue also is in our own power, and so too vice. For where it is in our power to act it is also in our power not to act, and *vice versa;* so that, if to act, where this is noble, is in our power, not to act, which will be base, will also be in our power, and if not to act, where this noble, is in our power, to act, which will be base, will also be in our power. Now if it is in our power to do noble or base acts, and likewise in our power not to do them, and this was what being good or bad meant, then it is in our power to be virtuous or vicious.

The saying that 'no one is voluntarily wicked nor involuntarily happy' seems to be partly false and partly true; for no one is involuntarily happy, but wickedness *is* voluntary. Or else we shall have to dispute what has been said, at any rate, and deny that man is a moving principle or begetter of his actions as of children. But if these facts are evident and we cannot refer actions to moving principles other than those in ourselves, the acts whose moving principles are in us must themselves also be in our power and voluntary.

Witness seems to be borne to this both by individuals in their private capacity and by legislators themselves; for these punish and take vengeance on those who do wicked acts (unless they have acted under compulsion or as a result of ignorance for which they are not themselves responsible), while they honour those who do noble acts, as though they mean to encourage the latter and deter the former. But no one is encouraged to do the things that are neither in our power nor voluntary; it is assumed that there is no gain in being persuaded not to be hot or in pain or hungry or the like, since we shall experience these feelings none the less. Indeed, we punish a man for his very ignorance, if he is thought responsible for the ignorance, as when penalties are doubled in the case of drunkenness; for the moving principle is in the man himself, since he had the power of not getting drunk and his getting drunk was the cause of his ignorance. And we punish those who are ignorant of anything in the laws that they ought to know and that is not difficult, and so too in the case of anything else that they are thought to be ignorant of through carelessness; we assume that it is in their power not to be ignorant, since they have the power of taking care.

But perhaps a man is the kind of man not to take care. Still they are themselves by their slack lives responsible for becoming men of that kind, and men make themselves responsible for being unjust or self-indulgent, in the one case by cheating and in the other by spending their time in drinking bouts and the like; for it is activities exercised on particular objects that make the corresponding character. This is plain from the case of people training for any contest or action; they practise the activity the whole time. Now not to know that it is from the exercise of activities on particular objects that states of character are produced is the mark of a thoroughly senseless person. Again, it is irrational to suppose that a man who acts unjustly does not wish to be unjust or a man who acts self-indulgently to be self-indulgent. But if *without* being ignorant a man does the things which will make him unjust, he will be unjust voluntarily. Yet it does not follow that if he wishes he will cease to be unjust and will be just. For neither does the man who is ill become well on those terms. We may suppose a case in which he is ill voluntarily, through living incontinently and disobeying his doctors. In that case it was *then* open to him not to be ill, but not now, when he has thrown away his chance, just as when you have let a stone go it is too late to recover it; but yet it was in your power to throw it, since the moving principle was in you. So, too, to the unjust and to the self-indulgent man it was open at the beginning not to become men of this kind, and so they are unjust and self-indulgent voluntarily; but now that they have become so it is not possible for them not to be so.

But not only are the vices of the soul voluntary, but those of the body also for some men, whom we accordingly blame; while no one blames those who are ugly by nature, we blame those who are so owing to want of exercise and care. So it is, too, with respect to weakness and infirmity; no one would reproach a man blind from birth or by disease or from a blow, but rather pity him, while every one would blame a man who was blind from drunkenness or some other form of self-indulgence. Of vices of the body, then, those in our own power are blamed, those not in our power are not. And if this be so, in the other cases also the vices that are blamed must be in our own power.

Now some one may say that all men desire the apparent good, but have no control over the appearance, but the end appears to each man in a form answering to his character. We reply that if each man is somehow responsible for his state of mind, he will also be himself somehow responsible for the appearance; but if not, no one is responsible for his own evildoing, but every one does evil acts through ignorance of the end, thinking that by these he will get what is best, and the aiming at the end is not self-chosen but one must be born with an eye, as it were, by which to judge rightly and choose what is truly good, and he is well endowed by nature who is well endowed with this. For it is what is greatest and most noble, and what we cannot get or learn from another, but must have just such as it was when given us at birth, and to be well and nobly endowed with this will be perfect and true excellence of natural endowment. If this is true, then, how will virtue be more voluntary than vice? To both men alike, the good and the bad, the end appears and is fixed by nature or however it may be, and it is by referring everything else to this that men do whatever they do.

Whether, then, it is not by nature that the end appears to each man such as it does appear, but something also depends on him, or the end is natural but because the good man adopts the means voluntarily virtue is voluntary, vice also will be none the less voluntary; for in the case of the bad man there is equally present that which depends on himself in his actions even if not in his end. If, then, as is asserted, the virtues are voluntary (for we are ourselves somehow partly responsible for our states of character, and it is by being persons of a certain kind that we assume the end to be so and so), the vices also will be voluntary; for the same is true of them.

With regard to the virtues in *general* we have stated their genus in outline, viz. that they are means and that they are states of character, and that they tend, and by their own nature, to the doing of the acts by which they are produced, and that they are in our power and voluntary, and act as the right rule prescribes. But actions and states of character are not voluntary in the same way; for we are masters of our actions from the beginning right to the end, if we know the particular facts, but though we control the beginning of our states of character the gradual progress is not obvious, any more than it is in illnesses; because it was in our power, however, to act in this way or not in this way, therefore the states are voluntary.

3   IMMANUEL KANT

(1724–1804)

*The Categorical Imperative**

*Kant's theory of ethics is based on the concept that man is a rational being.
Moral conduct is action performed from respect for duty. Kant tells us that
the only thing which is good without qualification is a good will. By that he
means that the motives by which men act, and not merely the results they
accomplish, are important to questions of duty. It is not enough to appear to
other men to be doing your duty. If actions are not motivated by a sense of
duty, they are not moral. Reason dictates what is necessary, what is one's duty
in particular circumstances of daily life. Kant calls the moral law of duty the
"categorical imperative." Categorical means "universal," and an imperative is a
"command." The categorical imperative is to act only in such a way that you
could will that the maxim of your action become a universal law of nature for
all men. Kant also formulates the law of duty in another way: act always so as
to treat all humanity, yourself and others, always as ends and never as means
only. Compare this to the Golden Rule of Christian ethics. Kant never specifically
tells men what they ought to do. Instead he provides a structure or a plan by
which men can discover for themselves what their moral obligations are.
Kant's analysis of morality, of course, presupposes that men are free to make
moral choices, and he gives no rewards for acting morally. Duty is to be done
for its own sake and for the sake of reason, not in the hope of better crops,
heaven, or social cohesion, or from fear.*

* Immanuel Kant, *Fundamental Principles of the Metaphysics of Morals*,
T. K. Abbott, trans. (New York: Longmans, Green & Co., 1909), Sections 1
and 2.

TRANSITION FROM THE COMMON RATIONAL KNOWLEDGE OF MORALITY TO PHILOSOPHICAL KNOWLEDGE

NOTHING can possibly be conceived in the world, or even out of it,
which can be called good without qualification, except a *good
will*. Intelligence, wit, judgment, and other *talents* of the mind, however
they may be named, or courage, resolution, perseverance, as qualities
of temperament, are undoubtedly good and desirable in many respects;
but these gifts of nature may also become extremely bad and mis-

chievous if the will which is to make use of them, and which, therefore, constitutes what is called *character*, is not good. It is the same with the *gifts of fortune*. Power, riches, honor, even health, and the general well-being and contentment with one's condition which is called *happiness*, inspire pride, and often presumption, if there is not a good will to correct the influence of these on the mind, and with this also to rectify the whole principle of acting, and adapt it to its end. The sight of a being who is not adorned with a single feature of a pure and good will, enjoying unbroken prosperity, can never give pleasure to an impartial rational spectator. Thus a good will appears to constitute the indispensable condition even of being worthy of happiness.

There are even some qualities which are of service to this good will itself, and may facilitate its action, yet which have no intrinsic unconditional value, but always presuppose a good will, and this qualifies the esteem that we justly have for them, and does not permit us to regard them as absolutely good. Moderation in the affections and passions, self-control, and calm deliberation are not only good in many respects, but even seem to constitute part of the intrinsic worth of the person; but they are far from deserving to be called good without qualification, although they have been so unconditionally praised by the ancients. For without the principles of a good will, they may become extremely bad; and the coolness of a villain not only makes him far more dangerous, but also directly makes him more abominable in our eyes than he would have been without it.

A good will is good not because of what it performs or effects, not by its aptness for the attainment of some proposed end, but simply by virtue of the volition—that is, it is good in itself, and considered by itself is to be esteemed much higher than all that can be brought about by it in favor of any inclination, nay, even of the sum-total of all inclinations. Even if it should happen that, owing to special disfavor of fortune, or the niggardly provision of a step-motherly nature, this will should wholly lack power to accomplish its purpose, if with its greatest efforts it should yet achieve nothing, and there should remain only the good will (not, to be sure, a mere wish, but the summoning of all means in our power), then, like a jewel, it would still shine by its own light, as a thing which has its whole value in itself. Its usefulness or fruitlessness can neither add to nor take away anything from this value. It would be, as it were, only the setting to enable us to handle it the more conveniently in common commerce, or to attract to it the attention of those who are not yet connoisseurs, but not to recommend it to true connoisseurs, or to determine its value. . . .

We have then to develop the notion of a will which deserves to be highly esteemed for itself, and is good without a view to anything further, a notion which exists already in the sound natural understanding, requiring rather to be cleared up than to be taught, and which in estimating the value of our actions always takes the first place and constitutes the condition of all the rest. In order to do this, we will take the notion of duty, which includes that of a good will, although implying certain subjective restrictions and hindrances. These, however, far from concealing it or rendering it unrecognizable, rather bring it out by contrast and make it shine forth so much the brighter.

I omit here all actions which are already recognized as inconsistent with duty, although they may be useful for this or that purpose, for with these the question whether they are done *from duty* cannot arise at all, since they even conflict with it. I also set aside those actions which really conform to duty, but to which men have *no* direct *inclination*, performing them because they are impelled thereto by some other inclination. For in this case we can readily distinguish whether the action which agrees with duty is done *from duty* or from a selfish view. It is much harder to make this distinction when the action accords with duty, and the subject has besides a *direct* inclination to it. For example, it is always a matter of duty that a dealer should not over-charge an inexperienced purchaser; and wherever there is much commerce the prudent tradesman does not overcharge, but keeps a fixed price for everyone, so that a child buys of him as well as any other. Men are thus *honestly* served; but this is not enough to make us believe that the tradesman has so acted from duty and from principles of honesty; his own advantage required it; it is out of the question in this case to suppose that he might besides have a direct inclination in favor of the buyers, so that, as it were, from love he should give no advantage to one over another. Accordingly the action was done neither from duty nor from direct inclination, but merely with a selfish view.

On the other hand, it is a duty to maintain one's life; and, in addition, everyone has also a direct inclination to do so. But on this account the often anxious care which most men take for it has no intrinsic worth, and their maxim has no moral import. They preserve their life as *duty requires*, no doubt, but not *because duty requires*. On the other hand, if adversity and hopeless sorrow have completely taken away the relish for life, if the unfortunate one, strong in mind, indignant at his fate rather than desponding or dejected, wishes for death, and yet preserves his life without loving it—not from inclination or fear, but from duty—

then his maxim has a moral worth.

To be beneficent when we can is a duty; and besides this, there are many minds so sympathetically constituted that, without any other motive of vanity or self-interest, they find a pleasure in spreading joy around them, and can take delight in the satisfaction of others so far as it is their own work. But I maintain that in such a case an action of this kind, however proper, however amiable it may be, has nevertheless no true moral worth, but is on a level with other inclinations, for example, the inclination to honor, which, if it is happily directed to that which is in fact of public utility and accordant with duty, and consequently honorable, deserves praise and encouragement, but not esteem. For the maxim lacks the moral import, namely, that such actions be done *from duty*, not from inclination. Put the case that the mind of that philanthropist was clouded by sorrow of his own, extinguishing all sympathy with the lot of others, and that while he still has the power to benefit others in distress, he is not touched by their trouble because he is absorbed with his own; and now suppose that he tears himself out of this dead insensibility and performs the action without any inclination to it, but simply from duty, then first has his action its genuine moral worth. Further still, if nature has put little sympathy in the heart of this or that man, if he, supposed to be an upright man, is by temperament cold and indifferent to the sufferings of others, perhaps because in respect of his own he is provided with the special gift of patience and fortitude, and supposes, or even requires, that others should have the same—and such a man would certainly not be the meanest product of nature—but if nature had not specially framed him for a philanthropist, would he not still find in himself a source from whence to give himself a far higher worth than that of a good-natured temperament could be? Unquestionably. It is just in this that the moral worth of the character is brought out which is incomparably the highest of all, namely, that he is beneficent, not from inclination, but from duty.

To secure one's own happiness is a duty, at least indirectly; for discontent with one's condition, under a pressure of many anxieties and amidst unsatisfied wants, might easily become a great *temptation to transgression of duty*. But here again, without looking to duty, all men have already the strongest and most intimate inclination to happiness, because it is just in this idea that all inclinations are combined in one total. But the precept of happiness is often of such a sort that it greatly interferes with some inclinations, and yet a man cannot form any definite and certain conception of the sum of satisfaction of all of them which is called happiness. It is not then to be wondered at that a single inclination, definite both as to what it promises and as to the time within which it can be gratified, is often able to overcome such a fluctuating idea, and that a gouty patient, for instance, can choose to enjoy what he likes, and to suffer what he may, since, according to his calculation, on this occasion at least, he has [only] not sacrificed the enjoyment of the present moment to a possibly mistaken expectation of a happiness which is supposed to be found in health. But even in this case, if the general desire for happiness did not influence his will, and supposing that in his particular case health was not a necessary element in this calculation, there yet remains in this, as in all other cases, this law—namely, that he should promote his happiness not from inclination but from duty, and by this would his conduct first acquire true moral worth.

It is in this manner, undoubtedly, that we are to understand those passages of Scripture also in which we are commanded to love our neighbor, even our enemy. For love, as an affection, cannot be commanded, but beneficence for duty's sake may, even though we are not impelled to it by any inclination—nay, are even repelled by a natural and unconquerable aversion. This is *practical* love, and not *pathological*—a love which is seated in the will, and not in the propensions of sense—in principles of action and not of tender sympathy; and it is this love alone which can be commanded.

The second* proposition is: That an action done from duty derives its moral worth, *not from the purpose* which is to be attained by it, but from the maxim by which it is determined, and therefore does not depend on the realization of the object of the action, but merely on the *principle of volition* by which the action has taken place, without regard to any object of desire. It is clear from what precedes that the purposes which we may have in view in our actions, or their effects regarded as ends and springs of the will, cannot give to actions any unconditional or moral worth. In what, then, can their worth lie if it is not to consist in the will and in reference to its expected effect? It cannot lie anywhere but in the *principle of the will* without regard to the ends which can be attained by the action. For the will stands between its *a priori* principle, which is formal, and its *a posteriori* spring, which is material, as between two roads, and as it must be determined by something, it follows that it must be determined by the formal principle of volition when an action is done from duty, in which case every material principle has been withdrawn from it.

* The first proposition was that to have moral worth an action must be done from duty. Translator's footnote.

The third proposition, which is a consequence of the two preceding, I would express thus: *Duty is the necessity of acting from respect for the law.* I may have *inclination* for an object as the effect of my proposed action, but I cannot have *respect* for it just for this reason that it is an effect and not an energy of will. Similarly, I cannot have respect for inclination, whether my own or another's; I can at most, if my own, approve it; if another's, sometimes even love it, that is, look on it as favorable to my own interest. It is only what is connected with my will as a principle, by no means as an effect—what does not subserve my inclination, but overpowers it, or at least in case of choice excludes it from its calculation—in other words, simply the law of itself, which can be an object of respect, and hence a command. Now an action done from duty must wholly exclude the influence of inclination, and with it every object of the will, so that nothing remains which can determine the will except objectively the *law*, and subjectively *pure respect* for this practical law, and consequently the maxim that I should follow this law even to the thwarting of all my inclinations.

Thus the moral worth of an action does not lie in the effect expected from it, nor in any principle of action which requires to borrow its motive from this expected effect. For all these effects—agreeableness of one's condition, and even the promotion of the happiness of others—could have been also brought about by other causes, so that for this there would have been no need of the will of a rational being; whereas it is in this alone that the supreme and unconditional good can be found. The pre-eminent good which we call moral can therefore consist in nothing else than *the conception of law* in itself, *which certainly is only possible in a rational being*, in so far as this conception, and not the expected effect, determines the will. This is a good which is already present in the person who acts accordingly, and we have not to wait for it to appear first in the result.

But what sort of law can that be the conception of which must determine the will, even without paying any regard to the effect expected from it, in order that this will may be called good absolutely and without qualification? As I have deprived the will of every impulse which could arise to it from obedience to any law, there remains nothing but the universal conformity of its actions to law in general, which alone is to serve the will as a principle, that is, I am never to act otherwise than so *that I could also will that my maxim should become a universal law.* Here, now, it is the simple conformity to law in general, without assuming any particular law applicable to certain actions, that serves the will as its principle, and must so serve it if duty is not to be a vain delusion and a chimerical notion. The common reason of men in its practical judgments perfectly coincides with this, and always has in view the principle here suggested. Let the question be, for example: May I when in distress make a promise with the intention not to keep it? I readily distinguish here between the two significations which the question may have: whether it is prudent or whether it is right to make a false promise? The former may undoubtedly often be the case. I see clearly indeed that it is not enough to extricate myself from a present difficulty by means of this subterfuge, but it must be well considered whether there may not hereafter spring from this lie much greater inconvenience than that from which I now free myself, and as, with all my supposed *cunning*, the consequences cannot be so easily foreseen but that credit once lost may be much more injurious to me than any mischief which I seek to avoid at present, it should be considered whether it would not be more *prudent* to act herein according to a universal maxim, and to make it a habit to promise nothing except with the intention of keeping it. But it is soon clear to me that such a maxim will still only be based on the fear of consequences. Now it is a wholly different thing to be truthful from duty, and to be so from apprehension of injurious consequences. In the first case, the very notion of the action already implies a law for me; in the second case, I must first look about elsewhere to see what results may be combined with it which would affect myself. For to deviate from the principle of duty is beyond all doubt wicked; but to be unfaithful to my maxim of prudence may often be very advantageous to me, although to abide by it is certainly safer. The shortest way, however, and an unerring one, to discover the answer to this question whether a lying promise is consistent with duty, is to ask myself, Should I be content that my maxim (to extricate myself from difficulty by a false promise) should hold good as a universal law, for myself as well as for others; and should I be able to say to myself, "Every one may make a deceitful promise when he finds himself in a difficulty from which he cannot otherwise extricate himself"? Then I presently become aware that, while I can will the lie, I can by no means will that lying should be a universal law. For with such a law there would be no promises at all, since it would be in vain to allege my intention in regard to my future actions to those who would not believe this allegation, or if they over-hastily did so, would pay me back in my own coin. Hence my maxim, as soon as it should be made a universal law, would necessarily destroy itself.

I do not, therefore, need any far-reaching penetration to discern what I have to do in order that my will may be morally good. Inexperienced in the course of the world, incapable of being prepared for all its contingencies, I only ask myself: Canst thou also will that thy maxim should be a universal law? If not, then it must be rejected, and that not because of a disadvantage accruing from it to myself or even to others, but because it cannot enter as a principle into a possible universal legislation, and reason extorts from me immediate respect for such legislation. I do not indeed as yet *discern* on what this respect is based (this the philosopher may inquire), but at least I understand this—that it is an estimation of the worth which far outweighs all worth of what is recommended by inclination, and that the necessity of acting from *pure* respect for the practical law is what constitutes duty, to which every other motive must give place because it is the condition of a will being good *in itself*, and the worth of such a will is above everything. . . .

TRANSITION FROM POPULAR MORAL PHILOSOPHY TO THE METAPHYSIC OF MORALS

Everything in nature works according to laws. Rational beings alone have the faculty of acting according *to the conception* of laws—that is, according to principles, that is, have a *will*. Since the deduction of actions from principles requires *reason*, the will is nothing but practical reason. If reason infallibly determines the will, then the actions of such a being which are recognized as objectively necessary are subjectively necessary also, that is, the will is a faculty to choose *that only* which reason independent of inclination recognizes as practically necessary, that is, as good. But if reason of itself does not sufficiently determine the will, if the latter is subject also to subjective conditions (particular impulses) which do not always coincide with the objective conditions, in a word, if the will does not *in itself* completely accord with reason (which is actually the case with men), then the actions which objectively are recognized as necessary are subjectively contingent, and the determination of such a will according to objective laws is *obligation*, that is to say, the relation of the objective laws to a will that is not thoroughly good is conceived as the determination of the will of a rational being by principles of reason, but which the will from its nature does not of necessity follow.

The conception of an objective principle, in so far as it is obligatory for a will, is called a command (of reason), and the formula of the command is called an Imperative.

All imperatives are expressed by the word *ought* [or *shall*], and thereby indicate the relation of an objective law of reason to a will which from its subjective constitution is not necessarily determined by it (an obligation). They say that something would be good to do or to forbear, but they say it to a will which does not always do a thing because it is conceived to be good to do it. That is practically *good*, however, which determines the will by means of the conceptions of reason, and consequently not from subjective causes, but objectively, that is, on principles which are valid for every rational being as such. It is distinguished from the *pleasant* as that which influences the will only by means of sensation from merely subjective causes, valid only for the sense of this or that one, and not as a principle of reason which holds for every one.

A perfectly good will would therefore be equally subject to objective laws (viz., laws of good), but could not be conceived as *obliged* thereby to act lawfully, because of itself from its subjective constitution it can only be determined by the conception of good. Therefore no imperatives hold for the Divine will, or in general for a *holy* will; *ought* is here out of place because the volition is already of itself necessarily in unison with the law. Therefore imperatives are only formulae to express the relation of objective laws of all volition to the subjective imperfection of the will of this or that rational being, for example, the human will.

Now all *imperatives* command either *hypothetically* or *categorically*. The former represent the practical necessity of a possible action as means to something else that is willed (or at least which one might possibly will). The categorical imperative would be that which represented an action as necessary of itself without reference to another end, that is, as objectively necessary.

Since every practical law represents a possible action as good, and on this account, for a subject who is practically determinable by reason as necessary, all imperatives are formulae determining an action which is necessary according to the principle of a will good in some respects. If now the action is good only as a means to *something else*, then the imperative is *hypothetical;* if it is conceived as good *in itself* and consequently as being necessarily the principle of a will which of itself conforms to reason, then it is *categorical.*

Thus the imperative declares what action possible by me would be good, and presents the practical rule in relation to a will which does not forthwith perform an action simply because it is good, whether because the subject does not always know that it is good, or because, even if it know this, yet its maxims might be opposed to the objective principles of practical reason.

Accordingly the hypothetical imperative only says that the action is good for some purpose, *possible* or *actual.* In the first case it is a *problematical,* in the second an *assertorial* practical principle. The categorical imperative which declares an action to be objectively necessary in itself without reference to any purpose, that is, without any other end, is valid as an *apodictic* (practical) principle.

Whatever is possible only by the power of some rational being may also be conceived as a possible purpose of some will; and therefore the principles of action as regards the means necessary to attain some possible purpose are in fact infinitely numerous. All sciences have a practical part consisting of problems expressing that some end is possible for us, and of imperatives directing how it may be attained. These may, therefore, be called in general imperatives of *skill.* Here there is no question whether the end is rational and good, but only what one must do in order to attain it. The precepts for the physician to make his patient thoroughly healthy, and for a poisoner to ensure certain death, are of equal value in this respect, that each serves to effect its purpose perfectly. Since in early youth it cannot be known what ends are likely to occur to us in the course of life, parents seek to have their children taught a *great many things,* and provide for their *skill* in the use of means for all sorts of arbitrary ends, of none of which can they determine whether it may not perhaps hereafter be an object to their pupil, but which it is at all events *possible* that he might aim at; and this anxiety is so great that they commonly neglect to form and correct their judgment on the value of the things which may be chosen as ends.

There is *one* end, however, which may be assumed to be actually such to all rational beings (so far as imperatives apply to them, viz., as dependent beings), and, therefore, one purpose which they not merely *may* have, but which we may with certainty assume that they all actually *have* by a natural necessity, and this is *happiness.* The hypothetical imperative which expresses the practical necessity of an action as means to the advancement of happiness is *assertorial.* We are not to present it as necessary for an uncertain and merely possible purpose, but for a purpose which we may presuppose with certainty and *a priori* in every man, because it belongs to his being. Now skill in the choice of means to his own greatest well-being may be called *prudence,* in the narrowest sense. And thus the imperative which refers to the choice of means to one's own happiness, that is, the precept of prudence, is still always *hypothetical;* the action is not commanded absolutely, but only as means to another purpose.

Finally, there is an imperative which commands a certain conduct immediately, without having as its condition any other purpose to be attained by it. This imperative is *categorical*. It concerns not the matter of the action, or its intended result, but its form and the principle of which it is itself a result; and what is essentially good in it consists in the mental disposition, let the consequence be what it may. This imperative may be called that of *morality*. . . .

When I conceive a hypothetical imperative, in general I do not know beforehand what it will contain until I am given the condition. But when I conceive a categorical imperative, I know at once what it contains. For as the imperative contains besides the law only the necessity that the maxims° shall conform to this law, while the law contains no conditions restricting it, there remains nothing but the general statement that the maxim of the action should conform to a universal law, and it is this conformity alone that the imperative properly represents as necessary.

There is therefore but one categorical imperative, namely, this: *Act only on that maxim whereby thou canst at the same time will that it should become a universal law.*

Now if all imperatives of duty can be deduced from this one imperative as from their principle, then, although it should remain undecided whether what is called duty is not merely a vain notion, yet at least we shall be able to show what we understand by it and what this notion means.

Since the universality of the law according to which effects are produced constitutes what is properly called *nature* in the most general sense (as to form)—that is, the existence of things so far as it is determined by general laws—the imperative of duty may be expressed thus: *Act as if the maxim of thy action were to become by thy will a universal law of nature.*

We will now enumerate a few duties, adopting the usual division of them into duties to ourselves and to others, and into perfect and imperfect duties.

1. A man reduced to despair by a series of misfortunes feels wearied of life, but is still so far in possession of his reason that he can ask himself whether it would not be contrary to his duty to himself to take his own life. Now he inquires whether the maxim of his action could become a universal law of nature. His maxim is: From self-love I adopt

---

° A "maxim" is a subjective principle of action, and must be distinguished from the *objective principle,* namely, practical law. The former contains the practical rule set by reason according to the conditions of the subject (often its ignorance or its inclinations), so that it is the principle on which the subject *acts;* but the law is the objective principle valid for every rational being, and is the principle on which it *ought to act*—that is an imperative.

it as a principle to shorten my life when its longer duration is likely to bring more evil than satisfaction. It is asked then simply whether this principle founded on self-love can become a universal law of nature. Now we see at once that a system of nature of which it should be a law to destroy life by means of the very feeling whose special nature it is to impel to the improvement of life would contradict itself, and therefore could not exist as a system of nature; hence that maxim cannot possibly exist as a universal law of nature, and consequently would be wholly inconsistent with the supreme principle of all duty.

2. Another finds himself forced by necessity to borrow money. He knows that he will not be able to repay it, but sees also that nothing will be lent to him unless he promises stoutly to repay it in a definite time. He desires to make this promise, but he has still so much conscience as to ask himself: Is it not unlawful and inconsistent with duty to get out of a difficulty in this way? Suppose, however, that he resolves to do so, then the maxim of his action would be expressed thus: When I think myself in want of money, I will borrow money and promise to repay it, although I know that I never can do so. Now this principle of self-love or of one's own advantage may perhaps be consistent with my whole future welfare; but the question now is, Is it right? I change then the suggestion of self-love into a universal law, and state the question thus: How would it be if my maxim were a universal law? Then I see at once that it could never hold as a universal law of nature, but would necessarily contradict itself. For supposing it to be a universal law that everyone when he thinks himself in a difficulty should be able to promise whatever he pleases, with the purpose of not keeping his promise, the promise itself would become impossible, as well as the end that one might have in view in it, since no one would consider that anything was promised to him, but would ridicule all such statements as vain pretenses.

3. A third finds in himself a talent which with the help of some culture might make him a useful man in many respects. But he finds himself in comfortable circumstances and prefers to indulge in pleasure rather than to take pains in enlarging and improving his happy natural capacities. He asks, however, whether his maxim of neglect of his natural gifts, besides agreeing with his inclination to indulgence, agrees also with what is called duty. He sees then that a system of nature could indeed subsist with such a universal law, although men (like the South Sea islanders) should let their talents rest and resolve to devote their lives merely to idleness, amusement, and propagation of their species—in a word, to enjoyment: but he cannot possibly *will* that this should be a universal law of nature, or be implanted in us as such by a

natural instinct. For, as a rational being, he necessarily wills that his faculties be developed, since they serve him, and have been given him, for all sorts of possible purposes.

4. A fourth, who is in prosperity, while he sees that others have to contend with great wretchedness and that he could help them, thinks: What concern is it of mine? Let everyone be as happy as Heaven pleases, or as he can make himself; I will take nothing from him nor even envy him, only I do not wish to contribute anything to his welfare or to his assistance in distress! Now no doubt, if such a mode of thinking were a universal law, the human race might very well subsist, and doubtless even better than in a state in which everyone talks of sympathy and good-will, or even takes care occasionally to put it into practice, but, on the other side, also cheats when he can, betrays the rights of men, or otherwise violates them. But although it is possible that a universal law of nature might exist in accordance with that maxim, it is impossible to *will* that such a principle should have the universal validity of a law of nature. For a will which resolved this would contradict itself, inasmuch as many cases might occur in which one would have need of the love and sympathy of others, and in which, by such a law of nature, springing from his own will, he would deprive himself of all hope of the aid he desires.

These are a few of the many actual duties, or at least what we regard as such, which obviously fall into two classes on the one principle that we have laid down. We must be *able to will* that a maxim of our action should be a universal law. This is the canon of the moral appreciation of the action generally. Some actions are of such a character that their maxim cannot without contradiction be even *conceived* as a universal law of nature, far from it being possible that we should *will* that it *should* be so. In others, this intrinsic impossibility is not found, but still it is impossible to *will* that their maxim should be raised to the universality of a law of nature, since such a will would contradict itself. It is easily seen that the former violate strict or rigorous (inflexible) duty; the latter only laxer (meritorious) duty. Thus it has been completely shown by these examples how all duties depend as regards the nature of the obligation (not the object of the action) on the same principle.

If now we attend to ourselves on occasion of any transgression of duty, we shall find that we in fact do not will that our maxim should be a universal law, for that is impossible for us; on the contrary, we will that the opposite should remain a universal law, only we assume the liberty of making an *exception* in our own favor or (just for this time only) in favor of our inclination. Consequently, if we considered all cases from one and the same point of view, namely, that of reason, we should find a contradiction in our own will, namely, that a certain principle should be objectively necessary as a universal law, and yet subjectively should not be universal, but admit of exceptions. As, however, we at one moment regard our action from the point of view of a will wholly conformed to reason, and then again look at the same action from the point of view of a will affected by inclination, there is not really any contradiction, but an antagonism of inclination to the precept of reason, whereby the universality of the principle is changed into a mere generality, so that the practical principle of reason shall meet the maxim half way. Now, although this cannot be justified in our own impartial judgment, yet it proves that we do really recognize the validity of the categorical imperative and (with all respect for it) only allow ourselves a few exceptions which we think unimportant and forced from us. . . .

The will is conceived as a faculty of determining oneself to action *in accordance with the conception of certain laws*. And such a faculty can be found only in rational beings. Now that which serves the will as the objective ground of its self-determination is the *end*, and if this is assigned by reason alone, it must hold for all rational beings. On the other hand, that which merely contains the ground of possibility of the action of which the effect is the end, this is called the *means*. The subjective ground of the desire is the *spring*, the objective ground of the volition is the *motive;* hence the distinction between subjective ends which rest on springs, and objective ends which depend on motives valid for every rational being. Practical principles are *formal* when they abstract from all subjective ends; they are *material* when they assume these, and therefore particular, springs of action. The ends which a rational being proposes to himself at pleasure as *effects* of his actions (material ends) are all only relative, for it is only their relation to the particular desires of the subject that gives them their worth, which therefore cannot furnish principles universal and necessary for all rational beings and for every volition, that is to say, practical laws. Hence all these relative ends can give rise only to hypothetical imperatives.

Supposing, however, that there were something *whose existence* has *in itself* an absolute worth, something which, being *an end in itself,* could be a source of definite laws, then in this and this alone would lie the source of a possible categorical imperative, that is, a practical law.

Now I say: man and generally any rational being *exists* as an end in himself, *not merely as a means* to be arbitrarily used by this or that will, but in all his actions, whether they concern himself or other rational beings, must be always regarded at the same time as an end. All objects of the inclinations have only a conditional worth; for if the inclinations and the wants founded on them did not exist, then their object would be without value. But the inclinations themselves, being sources of want, are so far from having an absolute worth for which they should be desired that, on the contrary, it must be the universal wish of every rational being to be wholly free from them. Thus the worth of any object which is *to be acquired* by our action is always conditional. Beings whose existence depends not on our will but on nature's, have nevertheless, if they are not rational beings, only a relative value as means, and are therefore called *things;* rational beings, on the contrary, are called *persons,* because their very nature points them out as ends in themselves, that is, as something which must not be used merely as means, and so far therefore restricts freedom of action (and is an object of respect). These, therefore, are not merely subjective ends whose existence has a worth *for us* as an effect of our action, but *objective ends,* that is, things whose existence is an end in itself—an end, moreover, for which no other can be substituted, which they should subserve *merely* as means, for otherwise nothing whatever would possess *absolute worth;* but if all worth were conditioned and therefore contingent, then there would be no supreme practical principle of reason whatever.

If then there is a supreme practical principle or, in respect of the human will, a categorical imperative, it must be one which, being drawn from the conception of that which is necessarily an end for everyone because it is *an end in itself,* constitutes an *objective* principle of will, and can therefore serve as a universal practical law. The foundation of this principle is: *rational nature exists as an end in itself.* Man necessarily conceives his own existence as being so; so far then this is a *subjective* principle of human actions. But every other rational being regards its existence similarly, just on the same rational principle that holds for me; so that it is at the same time an objective principle from which as a supreme practical law all laws of the will must be capable of being deduced. Accordingly the practical imperative will be as follows: *So act as to treat humanity, whether in thine own person or in that of any other, in every case as an end withal, never as means only.* We will now inquire whether this can be practically carried out.

To abide by the previous examples:

First, under the head of necessary duty to oneself: He who contemplates suicide should ask himself whether his action can be consistent with the idea of humanity *as an end in itself.* If he destroys himself in order to escape from painful circumstances, he uses a person merely as *a mean* to maintain a tolerable condition up to the end of life. But a man is not a thing, that is to say, something which can be used merely as means, but must in all his actions be always considered as an end in himself. I cannot, therefore, dispose in any way of a man in my own person so as to mutilate him, to damage or kill him. (It belongs to ethics proper to define this principle more precisely, so as to avoid all misunderstanding, for example, as to the amputation of the limbs in order to preserve myself; as to exposing my life to danger with a view to preserve it, etc. This question is therefore omitted here.)

Secondly, as regards necessary duties, or those of strict obligation, towards others: He who is thinking of making a lying promise to others will see at once that he would be using another man *merely as a mean,* without the latter containing at the same time the end in himself. For he whom I propose by such a promise to use for my own purposes cannot possibly assent to my mode of acting towards him, and therefore cannot himself contain the end of this action. This violation of the principle of humanity in other men is more obvious if we take in examples of attacks on the freedom and property of others. For then it is clear that he who transgresses the rights of men intends to use the person of others merely as means, without considering that as rational beings they ought always to be esteemed also as ends, that is, as beings who must be capable of containing in themselves the end of the very same action.

Thirdly, as regards contingent (meritorious) duties to oneself: It is not enough that the action does not violate humanity in our own person as an end in itself, it must also *harmonize with it.* Now there are in humanity capacities of greater perfection which belong to the end that nature has in view in regard to humanity in ourselves as the subject; to neglect these might perhaps be consistent with the *maintenance* of humanity as an end in itself, but not with the *advancement* of this end.

Fourthly, as regards meritorious duties towards others: The natural end which all men have is their own happiness. Now humanity might indeed subsist although no one should contribute anything to the happiness of others, provided he did not intentionally withdraw anything from it; but after all, this would only harmonize negatively, not positively, with *humanity as an end in itself,* if everyone does not also endeavor, as far as in him lies, to forward the ends of others. For the ends of any subject which is an end in himself ought as far as possible to be *my* ends also, if that conception is to have its *full* effect with me.

This principle that humanity and generally every rational nature is *an end in itself* (which is the supreme limiting condition of every man's freedom of action), is not borrowed from experience, *first,* because it is universal, applying as it does to all rational beings whatever, and experience is not capable of determining anything about them; *secondly,* because it does not present humanity as an end to men (subjectively), that is, as an object which men do of themselves actually adopt as an end; but as an objective end which must as a law constitute the supreme limiting condition of all our subjective ends, let them be what we will; it must therefore spring from pure reason. In fact the objective principle of all practical legislation lies (according to the first principle) in *the rule* and its form of universality which makes it capable of being a law (say, for example, a law of nature); but the *subjective* principle is in the *end;* now by the second principle, the subject of all ends is each rational being inasmuch as it is an end in itself. Hence follows the third practical principle of the will, which is the ultimate condition of its harmony with the universal practical reason, viz., the idea of *the will of every rational being as a universally legislative will.*

On this principle all maxims are rejected which are inconsistent with the will being itself universal legislator. Thus the will is not subject to the law, but so subject that it must be regarded *as itself giving the law,* and on this ground only subject to the law (of which it can regard itself as the author).

In the previous imperatives, namely, that based on the conception of the conformity of actions to general laws, as in a *physical system of nature,* and that based on the universal *prerogative* of rational beings as *ends* in themselves—these imperatives just because they were conceived as categorical excluded from any share in their authority all admixture of any interest as a spring of action, they were, however, only *assumed* to be categorical, because such an assumption was necessary to explain the conception of duty. But we could not prove independently that there are practical propositions which command categorically, nor can it be proved in this section; one thing, however, could be done, namely, to indicate in the imperative itself, by some determinate expression, that in the case of volition from duty all interest is renounced, which is the specific criterion of categorical as distinguished from hypothetical imperatives. This is done in the present (third) formula of the principle, namely, in the idea of the will of every rational being as a *universally legislating will.*

For although a will *which is subject to laws* may be attached to this law by means of an interest, yet a will which is itself a supreme lawgiver, so far as it is such, cannot possibly depend on any interest, since a will so dependent would itself still need another law restricting the interest of its self-love by the condition that it should be valid as universal law.

Thus the *principle* that every human will is *a will which in all its maxims gives universal laws,*° provided it be otherwise justified, would be very *well adapted* to be the categorical imperative, in this respect, namely, that just because of the idea of universal legislation it is *not based on any interest*, and therefore it alone among all possible imperatives can be *unconditional*. Or still better, converting the proposition, if there is a categorical imperative (that is, a law for the will of every rational being), it can only command that everything be done from maxims of one's will regarded as a will which could at the same time will that it should itself give universal laws, for in that case only the practical principle and the imperative which it obeys are unconditional, since they cannot be based on any interest. . . .

The conception of every rational being as one which must consider itself as giving in all the maxims of its will universal laws, so as to judge itself and its actions from this point of view—this conception leads to another which depends on it and is very fruitful, namely, that of a *kingdom of ends.*

By a "kingdom" I understand the union of different rational beings in a system by common laws. Now since it is by laws that ends are determined as regards their universal validity, hence, if we abstract from the personal differences of rational beings, and likewise from all the content of their private ends, we shall be able to conceive all ends combined in a systematic whole (including both rational beings as ends in themselves, and also the special ends which each may propose to himself), that is to say, we can conceive a kingdom of ends, which on the preceding principles is possible.

For all rational beings come under the *law* that each of them must treat itself and all others *never merely as means*, but in every case *at the same time as ends in themselves*. Hence results a systematic union of rational beings by common objective laws, that is, a kingdom which may be called a kingdom of ends, since what these laws have in view is just the relation of these beings to one another as ends and means. It is certainly only an ideal.

A rational being belongs as a *member* to the kingdom of ends when, although giving universal laws in it, he is also himself subject to these

---

° I may be excused from adducing examples to elucidate this principle, as those which have already been used to elucidate the categorical imperative and its formula would all serve for the like purpose here.

laws. He belongs to it *as sovereign* when, while giving laws, he is not subject to the will of any other.

A rational being must always regard himself as giving laws either as member or as sovereign in a kingdom of ends which is rendered possible by the freedom of will. He cannot, however, maintain the latter position merely by the maxims of his will, but only in case he is a completely independent being without wants and with unrestricted power adequate to his will.

Morality consists then in the reference of all action to the legislation which alone can render a kingdom of ends possible. This legislation must be capable of existing in every rational being, and of emanating from his will, so that the principle of this will is never to act on any maxim which could not without contradiction be also a universal law, and accordingly always so to act *that the will could at the same time regard itself as giving in its maxims universal laws.* If now the maxims of rational beings are not by their own nature coincident with this objective principle, then the necessity of acting on it is called practical necessitation that is, *duty.*

The practical necessity of acting on this principle, that is, duty, does not rest at all on feelings, impulses, or inclinations, but solely on the relation of rational beings to one another, a relation in which the will of a rational being must always be regarded as *legislative,* since otherwise it could not be conceived as *an end in itself.* Reason then refers every maxim of the will, regarding it as legislating universally, to every other will and also to every action towards oneself: and this not on account of any other practical motive or any future advantage, but from the idea of the *dignity* of a rational being, obeying no law but that which he himself also gives.

Whatever has reference to the general inclinations and wants of mankind has a *market value;* whatever, without presupposing a want, corresponds to a certain taste, that is, to a satisfaction in the mere purposeless play of our faculties, has a *fancy value;* but that which constitutes the condition under which alone anything can be an end in itself, this has not merely a relative worth, that is, value, but an intrinsic worth, that is, *dignity.*

4

F. H. BRADLEY

(1846–1924)

My Station and Its Duties*

This famous essay on duty is Bradley's answer to Kant's ethical philosophy. For Bradley, no member of the community can find his function or his duty apart from his involvement with the community. Each man is "but as a 'heart-beat in its system'." There are no individual men for Bradley. Men are what they are because of the community. Each man is simply a particularization of what is common to all men. To know what a man is, is to know his position in society, his relationship to others. Duties arise because of the station a man occupies. Bradley claims that knowledge of right and wrong is based on intuition. A man has feelings of the rightness or wrongness of possible courses of action when he has identified his will with the moral spirit of the community. He begins to feel what is expected of him in his station.

° F. H. Bradley, *Ethical Studies* (Oxford: Oxford Press, 1876), Essay V, with omissions.

WE are not going to enter on a metaphysical question to which we are not equal; we meet the metaphysical assertion of the "individualist" with a mere denial and, turning to facts, we will try to show that they lead us in another direction. To the assertion, then, that selves are "individual" in the sense of exclusive of other selves, we oppose the (equally justified) assertion that this is a mere fancy. We say that, out of theory, no such individual men exist; and we will try to show from fact that, in fact, what we call an individual man is what he is because of and by virtue of community, and that communities are thus not mere names but something real, and can be regarded (if we mean to keep to facts) only as the one in the many.

And to confine the subject and to keep to what is familiar, we will not call to our aid the life of animals, nor early societies, nor the course of history, but we will take men as they are now; we will take ourselves and endeavor to keep wholly to the teaching of experience.

Let us take a man, an Englishman as he is now, and try to point out that apart from what he has in common with others, apart from his sameness with others, he is not an Englishman—nor a man at all; that if you take him as something by himself, he is not what he is. Of course we do not mean to say that he cannot go out of England without disappearing, nor, even if all the rest of the nation perished that he would not survive. What we mean to say is that he is what he is because he is a born and educated social being, and a member of an individual social organism; that if you make abstraction of all this, which is the same in him and in others, what you have left is not an Englishman, nor a man, but some I know not what residuum, which never has existed by itself and does not so exist. If we suppose the world of relations, in which he was born and bred, never to have been, then we suppose the very essence of him not to be; if we take that away, we have taken him away; and hence he now is not an individual, in the sense of owing nothing to the sphere of relations in which he finds himself, but does contain those relations within himself as belonging to his very being; he is what he is, in brief, so far as he is what others also are. . . .

The "individual" man, the man into whose essence his community with others does not enter, who does not include relation to others in his very being, is, we say, a fiction, and in the light of facts we have to examine him. Let us take him in the shape of an English child as soon as he is born, for I suppose we ought not to go further back. Let us take him as soon as he is separated from his mother and occupies a space clear and exclusive of all other human beings. At this time, education and custom will, I imagine, be allowed to have not as yet operated on him or lessened his "individuality." But is he now a mere "individual," in the sense of not implying in his being identity with others? We cannot say that if we hold to the teaching of modern physiology. Physiology would tell us, in one language or another, that even now the child's mind is no passive "tabula rasa"; he has an inner, a yet undeveloped nature, which must largely determine his future individuality. He is born of certain parents who come of certain families, and he has in him the qualities of his parents, and, as breeders would say, of the strains from both sides. Much of it we can see and more we believe to be latent and, given certain (possible or impossible) conditions, ready to come to light. On the descent of mental qualities modern investigation and popular experience, as expressed in uneducated vulgar opinion, altogether, I believe, support one another, and we need not linger here. But if the intellectual and active qualities do descend from ancestors, is it not, I would ask, quite clear that a man may have in him the same that his father and mother had, the same that his brothers and sisters have? And if anyone objects to the word "same," I would put this to him. If, concerning two dogs allied in blood, I were to ask a man, "Is that of the same strain or stock as this?" and were answered,

"No, not the same, but similar," should I not think one of these things, that the man either meant to deceive me, or was a "thinker," or a fool?

But the child is not merely the member of a family; he is born into other spheres, and (passing over the subordinate wholes which nevertheless do in many cases qualify him) he is born a member of the English nation. It is, I believe, a matter of fact that at birth the child of one race is not the same as the child of another; that in the children of the one race there is a certain identity, a developed or undeveloped national type which may be hard to recognize, or which at present may even be unrecognizable, but which nevertheless in some form will appear. If that be the fact, then again we must say that one English child is in some points, though perhaps it does not as yet show itself, the same as another. His being is so far common to him with others; he is not a mere "individual."

We see the child has been born at a certain time of parents of a certain race, and that means also of a certain degree of culture. It is the opinion of those best qualified to speak on the subject that civilization is to some not inconsiderable extent hereditary; that aptitudes are developed, and are latent in the child at birth; and that it is a very different thing, even apart from education, to be born of civilized and of uncivilized ancestors. These "civilized tendencies," if we may use the phrase, are part of the essence of the child. He would only partly (if at all) be himself without them; he owes them to his ancestors, and his ancestors owe them to society. The ancestors were made what they were by the society they lived in. If in answer it be replied, "Yes, but individual ancestors were prior to their society," then that, to say the least of it, is a hazardous and unproved assertion, since man, so far as history can trace him back, is social; and if Mr. Darwin's conjecture as to the development of man from a social animal be received, we must say that man has never been anything but social, and society never was made by individual men. If we suppose then that the results of the social life of the race are present in a latent and potential form in the child, can we deny that they are common property? Can we assert that they are not an element of sameness in all? Can we say that the individual is this individual because he is exclusive, when, if we deduct from him what he includes, he loses characteristics which make him himself, and when again he does include what the others include, and therefore does (how can we escape the consequence?) include in some sense the others do, just as they include him? By himself, then, what are we to call him? I confess I do not know unless we name him a theoretical attempt to isolate what cannot be isolated, and that, I suppose, has, out of our heads, no existence. But what he is really, and not in mere theory, can be described only as the specification or particularization of that which is common, which is the same amid diversity, and without which the "individual" would be so other than he is that we could not call him the same.

Thus the child is at birth; and he is born not into a desert, but into a living world, a whole which has a true individuality of its own, and into a system and order which it is difficult to look at as anything else than an organism, and which, even in England, we are now beginning to call by that name. And I fear that the "individuality" (the particularness) which the child brought into the light with him now stands but a poor chance, and that there is no help for him until he is old enough to become a "philosopher." We have seen that already he has in him inherited habits, or what will of themselves appear as such; but, in addition to this, he is not for one moment left alone, but continually tampered with; and the habituation which is applied from the outside is the more insidious that it answers to this inborn disposition. Who can resist it? Nay, who but a "thinker" could wish to have resisted it? And yet the tender care that receives and guides him is impressing on him habits, habits, alas, not particular to himself, and the "icy chains" of universal custom are hardening themselves round his cradled life. As the poet tells us, he has not yet thought of himself; his earliest notions come mixed to him of things and persons, not distinct from one another, nor divided from the feeling of his own existence. The need that he cannot understand moves him to foolish, but not futile, cries for what only another can give him; and the breast of his mother, and the soft warmth and touches and tones of his nurse, are made one with the feeling of his own pleasure and pain; nor is he yet a moralist to beware of such illusion and to see in them mere means to an end without them in his separate self. For he does not even think of his separate self; he grows with his world, his mind fills and orders itself; and when he can separate himself from that world, and know himself apart from it, then by that time his self, the object of his self-consciousness, is penetrated, infected, characterized by the existence of others. Its content implies in every fiber relations of community. He learns, or already perhaps has learned, to speak, and here he appropriates the common heritage of his race; the tongue that he makes his own is his country's language, it is (or it should be) the same that others speak, and it carries into his mind the ideas and sentiments of the race (over this I need not stay), and stamps them in indelibly. He grows up in an atmosphere of example and general custom, his life widens out from one little world to other and higher worlds, and he apprehends through successive stations the whole in which he lives, and in which he has lived. Is he now to try and develop his "individuality," his self which is not the same as other selves? Where is it? What is it? Where can he find it? The soul within him is saturated, is filled, is qualified by, it has assimilated, has got its substance, has built itself up from, it *is* one and the same life with the universal life, and if he turns against this he turns against himself; if he thrusts it from him, he tears his own vitals; if he attacks it, he sets his weapon against his own heart. He has found his life in the life of the whole, he lives that in himself, "he is a pulse-beat of the whole system, and himself the whole system."

"The child, in his character of the form of the possibility of a moral individual, is something subjective or negative; his growing to manhood is the ceasing to be of this form, and his education is the discipline or the compulsion thereof. The positive side and the essence is that he is suckled at the breast of the universal Ethos, lives in its absolute intuition, as in that of a foreign being first, then comprehends it more and more, and so passes over into the universal mind." The writer proceeds to draw the weighty conclusion that virtue "is not a troubling oneself about a peculiar and isolated morality of one's own, that the striving for a positive morality of one's own is futile, and in its very nature impossible of attainment; that in respect of morality the saying of the wisest men of antiquity is the only one which is true, that to be moral is to live in accordance with the moral tradition of one's country; and in respect of education the one true answer is that which a Pythagorean gave to him who asked what was the best education for his son, If you make him the citizen of a people with good institutions."*

But this is to anticipate. So far, I think, without aid from metaphysics, we have seen that the "individual" apart from the community is an abstraction. It is not anything real and hence not anything that we can realize, however much we may wish to do so. We have seen that I am myself by sharing with others, by including in my essence relations to them, the relations of the social state. If I wish to realize my true being I must therefore realize something beyond my being as a mere this or that, for my true being has in it a life which is not the life of any mere particular, and so must be called a universal life.

What is it then that I am to realize? We have said it in "my station and its duties." To know what a man is (as we have seen) you must not take him in isolation. He is one of a people, he was born in a family, he lives in a certain society, in a certain state. What he has to do depends on what his place is, what his function is, and that all comes from

---

* Hegel, *Philosophische Abhandlungen,* I, 389.

his station in the organism. Are there then such organisms in which he lives, and if so, what is their nature? Here we come to questions which must be answered in full by any complete system of Ethics, but which we cannot enter on. We must content ourselves by pointing out that there are such facts as the family, then in a middle position a man's own profession and society, and, over all, the larger community of the state. Leaving out of sight the question of a society wider than the state, we must say that a man's life with its moral duties is in the main filled up by his station in that system of wholes which the state is, and that this, partly by its laws and institutions.and still more by its spirit, gives him the life which he does live and ought to live. That objective institutions exist is of course an obvious fact; and it is a fact which every day is becoming plainer that these institutions are organic, and further, that they are moral. In short, man is a social being; he is real only because he is social, and can realize himself only because it is as social that he realizes himself. The mere individual is a delusion of theory; and the attempt to realize it in practice is the starvation and mutilation of human nature, with total sterility or the production of monstrosities. . . .

[In] "my station and its duties," I realize myself morally, so that not only what ought to be in the world is, but I am what I ought to be, and find so my contentment and satisfaction. If this were not the case, when we consider that the ordinary moral man is self-contented and happy, we should be forced to accuse him of immorality, and we do not do this; we say he most likely might be better, but we do not say that he is bad, or need consider himself so. Why is this? It is because "my station and its duties" teaches us to identify others and ourselves with the station we fill; to consider that as good, and by virtue of that to consider others and ourselves good too. It teaches us that a man who does his work in the world is good, notwithstanding his faults, if his faults do not prevent him from fulfilling his station. It tells us that the heart is an idle abstraction; we are not to think of it, nor must we look at our insides, but at our work and our life, and say to ourselves, Am I fulfilling my appointed function or not? Fulfill it we can, if we will. What we have to do is not so much better than the world that we cannot do it; the world is there waiting for it; my duties are my rights. On the one hand, I am not likely to be much better than the world asks me to be; on the other hand, if I can take my place in the world I ought not to be discontented. Here we must not be misunderstood; we do not say that the false self, the habits and desires opposed to the good will, are extinguished. Though negated, they never are all of them entirely suppressed, and cannot be. Hence we must not say that any man really does fill his station to the full height of his capacity; nor must we say of any man that he cannot perform his function better than he does, for we all can do so, and should try to do so. We do not wish to deny what are plain moral facts, nor in any way to slur them over.

How then does the contradiction disappear? It disappears by my identifying myself with the good will that I realize in the world, by my refusing to identify myself with the bad will of my private self. So far as I am one with the good will, living as a member in the moral organism, I am to consider myself real and I am not to consider the false self real. That cannot be attributed to me in my character of member in the organism. Even in me the false existence of it has been partly suppressed by that organism; and, so far as the organism is concerned, it is wholly suppressed because contradicted in its results, and allowed no reality. Hence, not existing for the organism, it does not exist for me as a member thereof; and only as a member thereof do I hold myself to be real. And yet this is not justification by faith, for we not only trust, but see, that despite our faults the moral world stands fast, and we in and by it. It is like faith, however, in this, that not merely by thinking ourselves, but by willing ourselves as such, can we look on ourselves as organs in a good whole, and so ourselves good. And further, the knowledge that as members of the system we are real, and not otherwise, encourages us more and more to identify ourselves with that system; to make ourselves better, and so more real, since we see that the good is real, and that nothing else is.

Or, to repeat it, in education my self by habituation has been growing into one with the good self around me, and by my free acceptance of my lot hereafter I consciously make myself one with the good, so that, though bad habits cling to and even arise in me, yet I cannot but be aware of myself as the reality of the good will. That is my essential side; my imperfections are not, and practically they do not matter. The good will in the world realizes itself by and in imperfect instruments, and in spite of them. The work is done, and so long as I will my part of the work and do it (as I do), I feel that, if I perform the function, I *am* the organ, and that my faults, if they do not matter to my station, do not matter to me. My heart I am not to think of, except to tell by my work whether it is in my work, and one with the moral whole; and if that is so, I have the consciousness of absolute reality in the good because of any by myself, and in myself because of and through the good; and with that I am satisfied, and have no right to be dissatisfied.

The individual's consciousness of himself is inseparable from the knowing himself as an organ of the whole; and the residuum falls more and more into the background, so that he thinks of it, if at all, not as himself, but as an idle appendage. For his nature now is not distinct from his "artificial self." He is related to the living moral system not as to a foreign body; his relation to it is "too inward even for faith," since faith implies a certain separation. It is no other-world that he cannot see but must trust to: he feels himself in it, and it in him; in a word, the self-consciousness of himself *is* the self-consciousness of the whole in him, and his will is the will which sees in him its accomplishment by him; it is the free will which knows itself as the free will, and as this beholds its realization and is more than content. . . .

The next point we come to is the question, How do I get to know in particular what is right and wrong? . . .

We know what is right in a particular case by what we may call an immediate judgment, or an intuitive subsumption. These phrases are perhaps not very luminous, and the matter of the "intuitive understanding" in general is doubtless difficult, and the special character or moral judgments not easy to define; and I do not say that I am in a position to explain these subjects at all, nor, I think, could anyone do so, except at considerable length. But the point that I do wish to establish here is, I think, not at all obscure. The reader has first to recognize that moral judgments are not discursive; next, that nevertheless they do start from and rest on a certain basis; and then if he puts the two together, he will see that they involve what he may call the "intuitive understanding," or any other name, so long as he keeps in sight the two elements and holds them together.

On the head that moral judgments are not discursive, no one, I think, will wish me to stay long. If the reader attends to the facts he will not want anything else; and if he does not, I confess I cannot prove my point. In practical morality, no doubt, we *may* reflect on our principles, but I think it is not too much to say that we *never* do so, except where we have come upon a difficulty of particular application. If anyone thinks that a man's *ordinary* judgment, "this is right or wrong," comes from the having a rule *before* the mind and bringing the particular case under it, he may be right, and I cannot try to show that he is wrong. I can only leave it to the reader to judge for himself. We say we "see" and we "feel" in these cases, not we "conclude." . . .

Taking for granted then that our ordinary way of judging in morals is not by reflection and explicit reasoning, we have now to point to the other side of the fact, viz., that these judgments are not mere isolated impressions, but stand in an intimate and vital relation to a certain system, which is their basis. Here again we must ask the reader to pause, if in doubt, and consider the facts for himself. Different men, who have lived in different times and countries, judge a fresh case in morals differently. Why is this? There is probably no "why" before the mind of either when he judges; but *we* perhaps can say, "I know why A said so and B so," because we find some general rule or principle different in each, and in each the basis of the judgment. Different people in the same society may judge points differently, and we sometimes know why. It is because A is struck by one aspect of the case, B by another; and one principle is (not *before*, but) *in* A's mind when he judges, and another in B's. Each has subsumed, but under a different head; the one perhaps justice, the other gratitude. Every man has the morality he has made his own in his mind, and he "sees" or "feels" or "judges" accordingly, though he does not reason explicitly from data to a conclusion. . . .

If a man is to know what is right, he should have imbibed by precept, and still more by example, the spirit of his community, its general and special beliefs as to right and wrong, and, with this whole embodied in his mind should particularize it in any new case, not by a reflective deduction, but by an intuitive subsumption, which does not know that it is a subsumption, by a carrying out of the self into a new case, wherein what is before the mind is the case and not the self to be carried out, and where it is indeed the whole that feels and sees, but all that is seen is seen in the form of *this* case, *this* point, *this* instance. Precept is good, but example is better; for by a series of particulars (as such forgotten) we get the general spirit, we identify ourselves both on the side of will and judgment with the basis, which basis (be it remembered) has not got to be explicit.

What is moral *in any particular given case* is seldom doubtful. Society pronounces beforehand; or, after some one course has been taken, it can say whether it was right or not; though society cannot generalize much, and, if asked to reflect, is helpless and becomes incoherent. But I do not say there are no cases where the morally minded man has to doubt; most certainly such do arise, though not so many as some people think, far fewer than some would be glad to think. A very large number arise from reflection, which wants to act from an explicit principle, and so begins to abstract and divide, and, thus becoming one-sided, makes the relative absolute. Apart from this, however, collisions must take place, and here there is no guide whatever but the intuitive judgment of oneself or others.*

* I may remark on this (after Erdmann, and I suppose Plato) that collisions of duties are avoided mostly by each man keeping to his own immediate duties, and not trying to see from the point of view of other stations than his own.

This intuition must not be confounded with what is sometimes miscalled "conscience." It is not mere individual opinion or caprice. It presupposes the morality of the community as its basis, and is subject to the approval thereof. Here, if anywhere, the idea of universal and impersonal morality is realized. For the final arbiters are the φρόνιμοι, persons with a will to do right, and not full of reflections and theories. If they fail you, you must judge for yourself, but practically they seldom do fail you. Their private peculiarities neutralize each other, and the result is an intuition which does not belong merely to this or that man or collection of men. "Conscience" is the antipodes of this. It wants you to have no law but yourself, and to be better than the world. But this tells you that, if you could be as good as your world, you would be better than most likely you are, and that to wish to be better than the world is to be already on the threshold of immorality.

5   COLIN STRANG

(1922–   )

What If Everyone Did That?*

*In this selection Strang attempts to deal with the common moral argument
that takes the form, "Do you think you ought to do that; have you considered
what it would be like if everyone did it?" Strang constructs a dialogue between
a defaulter (on income tax and military service) and a moralist in order to
examine the validity of the "What if everyone did that?" argument for doing
one's duty. Strang's moralist concludes that an argument for duty can be drawn
by reference to the social situation, the universality of moral behavior, and an idea
of fairness. Basically, his argument is that unless certain things are done at
certain times within society, the consequences will be disastrous, and the burden
of doing these tasks falls equally on particular classes of people within each
society. Every member of one of those classes therefore bears the duty of at least
attempting to do what is called for. By "classes" Strang might refer to young
able-bodied males, or neighbors, or relatives, etc., as the situation demands.*

* From *The Durham University Journal*, Vol. LIII, No. 1 (December, 1960),
pp. 5–10. Used by kind permission of M. E. James, Editor of *The Durham
University Journal*.

I WANT to discuss the force and validity of the familiar type of
ethical argument epitomized in my title. A typical example of it
would be: 'If everyone refrained from voting the result would be
disastrous, therefore *you* ought to vote.' Now since the argument is
addressed to the person concerned simply *qua* member of the class of
people entitled to vote, it could be addressed with equal force to any
member or all members of that class indifferently: so the conclusion
might just as validly be: 'therefore *everyone* ought to vote.'

There is no doubt that this argument has some force. People *are*
sometimes impressed by it. But it is not nearly so obvious that it is a
valid one, i.e. that they *ought* to be impressed by it.

One way of not being impressed by it is to reply: 'Yes, but everyone
won't refrain from voting, so there will be no disaster, so it's all right
for me not to vote.' But this reply is beside the point. The argument
never claimed that this one abstention would lead to disaster, nor did
it claim that universal abstention (which *would* be disastrous) would
occur; indeed it implied, on each point, the very opposite. This brings
out the important fact that the argument does not appeal to the consequences of the action it condemns and so is not of a utilitarian type,

but that it is applicable, if anywhere, just where utilitarian arguments do *not* apply.

The objector, who remains unimpressed, will continue: 'Granted that my first objection is beside the point, I still can't see how you get from your premiss to your conclusion. Your premiss is, roughly: "Everyone's non-voting is to be deplored," and your conclusion is: "Everyone's voting is obligatory." Why should it be irrational to accept the premiss but deny the conclusion? In any case the validity of the argument cannot depend on its form alone. Plenty of arguments of the very same form are plainly invalid. For instance; if everyone switched on their electric fires at 9 a.m. sharp there would be a power breakdown, therefore no one should; furthermore, this argument applies not only to 9 a.m. but to all times, so no one should ever switch on an electric fire. Again, if everyone taught philosophy whole-time we should all starve, so no one should; or if everyone built houses or did anything else whatever (bar farming) whole-time, we should all starve; and if everyone farmed we would be without clothes or shelter and would die of exposure in winter, so no one should farm. It rather looks, on your kind of argument, as if every whole-time activity is forbidden to everyone. Conversely, if no one farmed we would all starve, so everyone should farm; if no one made clothes we would all die of exposure, so everyone ought to make clothes—and so on. So it also looks, on your kind of argument, as if all sorts of part-time activity are obligatory on everybody. You surely do not mean to commit yourself to enjoining self-sufficiency and condemning specialization? What I want to know is why some arguments of this form are valid (as you claim) while others are not (as you must admit).'

In face of this kind of objection the obvious move is to place certain restrictions on the use of arguments of this form, and to show that only those satisfying certain conditions are valid while the rest are not. This is in fact the move adopted in two recent treatments of this problem: one is by A. C. Ewing (*Philosophy*, January 1953), and the other by M. G. Singer (*Mind*, July 1955). These two are independent, since Singer makes no mention of Ewing; and Ewing, incidentally, regards himself as doing pioneer work in the subject, being able to quote only one previous treatment of it (C. D. Broad, *International Journal of Ethics*, 1915–16). But the restrictions these two wish to impose on the argument seem to me *ad hoc;* they fail to explain why the argument is valid in the remaining cases, and it is just this that I aim to discover.

Compare the voting case with this one: 'If everyone here refuses to dig a latrine the camp will be insanitary, therefore everyone ought to dig one.' Surely the conclusion we want is, rather: 'therefore *someone* ought to dig one.' In the voting case, on the other hand, given the premiss 'If everyone refused to vote there would be no government,' the conclusion 'therefore someone ought to vote' clearly will not do; and even the conclusion 'therefore everyone ought to vote' is hardly cogent on the reasonable assumption that a 10% abstention will do no harm. If the argument is to be at all cogent it must make some reference to the percentage vote (say $n\%$) needed, thus: If more than $(100-n)\%$ of the electorate abstained there would be no government'; this allows us to draw an acceptable conclusion, i.e. 'therefore $n\%$ must vote to avert anarchy and one must dig to avert disease. But our argument has gained in cogency and precision (being now of a simple utilitarian kind) only at the expense of being no longer effective, or even seemingly so, against the defaulter. He will reply: 'All right, so $n\%$ ought to vote (someone ought to dig), but why me?' However, there is hope yet for the moralist. To the retort 'Why me?' the argument may not suggest any obvious reply; but the retort itself does suggest the counter-retort 'Why not you?', to which again there is no obvious reply. An impasse is thus reached in which the moralist cannot say why the defaulter should vote or dig, and the defaulter cannot say why he should not. Evidently it was a mistake to amend the original argument, and yet there seemed to be something wrong with it as it stood; and yet, as it stood, it still seemed to be giving an answer, however obscurely, to the baffling question 'Why me?': 'Because if *everyone* did that . . .'

To return to the camp: certainly it is agreed by all members of the party that some digging ought to be done, and it is also agreed that the duty does not lie on anyone outside the party. But just where it lies within the party is hard to say. It does not lie on everyone, nor on anyone in particular. Where then? Whatever the answer to that apparently pressing question may be, we all know what would in fact happen. Someone would volunteer, or a leader would allot duties, or the whole party would cast lots. Or, if the thing to be done were not a once-and-for-all job like digging latrines but a daily routine like washing up, they might take it in turns.

Although various acceptable answers to the question how the duties are to be allotted are readily listed, they leave us quite in the dark as to just *who* ought to dig, wash up, etc. That question hardly seems to arise. In the absence of an argumentative defaulter there is no call to think up reasons why I or you should do this or that or reasons why I or you should not, and we are left with the defaulter's 'Why me?' and the moralist's 'Why not you?' unanswered.

Our enquiry has made little progress, but the fog is beginning to lift from the territory ahead. We are evidently concerned with communities of people and with things that must be done, or not done, if the community is to be saved from damage or destruction; and we want to know whose duty it is to do, or not to do, these things. The complexity of the problem is no longer in doubt. (1) There are some things that need doing once, some that need doing at regular intervals, and some that need doing all the time. (2) Some things need doing by one person, some by a number of people which can be roughly estimated, and some by as many as possible. (3) In practice, who shall do what (though not who *ought* to do what) is determined by economic factors, or by statutory direction (e.g. service with the armed forces in war, paying income tax), or merely by people's inclinations generally, i.e. when enough people are inclined to do the thing anyway.

Somewhere in this territory our quarry has its lair. The following dialogue between defaulter and moralist on the evasion of income tax and military service begins the hunt. Our first steps are taken on already familiar ground:

Defaulter: £ 100 is a drop in the ocean to the exchequer. No one will suffer from their loss of £ 100, but it means a good deal to me.

Moralist: But what if everyone did that and offered the same excuse?

Defaulter: But the vast majority won't, so no one will suffer.

Moralist: Still, would you say it was *in order* for anyone whatever to evade tax and excuse himself on the same grounds as you do?

Defaulter: Certainly.

Moralist: So it would be quite in order for *everyone* to do the same and offer the same excuse?

Defaulter: Yes.

Moralist: Even though disaster would ensue for the exchequer and for everyone?

Defaulter: Yes. The exchequer would no more miss my £ 100 if *everyone* evaded than they would if only I evaded. They wouldn't miss anyone's individual evasion. What they would miss would be the aggregate £ 1,000,000,000 or so, and that isn't my default or yours or anyone's. So even if everyone evades it is still all right for me to evade; and if it's all right for me to evade it's all right for everyone to evade.

Moralist: You seem now to be in the paradoxical position of saying that if everyone evaded it would be disastrous, and yet no one would be to blame.

Defaulter: Paradoxical, perhaps, but instructive. I am not alarmed. Let me recur to one of your previous questions: you asked whether it would be in order for all to evade and give the same excuse. I now want to reply: No, it would not be in order, but only in the sense that it would be disastrous; but it *would* be in order in the sense that each person's grounds for evasion would still be as valid as they would have been if he had been the *only* evader and no disaster had ensued. In other words, none of the defaulters would be to blame for the disaster —and certainly not one of them would blame himself: on the contrary, each one would argue that had he paid he would have been the only one to pay and thus lost his £ 100 without doing himself or anyone else any good. He would have been a mug to pay.

Moralist: But surely there can't be a disaster of this kind for which no one is to blame.

Defaulter: If anyone is to blame it is the person whose job it is to circumvent evasion. If too few people vote, then it should be made illegal not to vote. If too few people volunteer, then you must introduce conscription. If too many people evade taxes, then you must tighten up your system of enforcement. My answer to your 'If everyone did that' is 'Then someone had jolly well better see to it that they don't; it doesn't impress me as a reason why *I* should, however many people do or don't.

Moralist: But surely you are being inconsistent here. Take the case of evading military service.

Defaulter: You mean not volunteering in time of crisis, there being no conscription? I do that too.

Moralist: Good. As I was saying, aren't you being inconsistent? You think *both* that it is all right not to volunteer even if too few other people volunteer (because one soldier more or less could make no difference), *and* think that you ought to be conscripted.

Defaulter: But that is not at all inconsistent. Look: the enemy threatens, a mere handful volunteer, and the writing is on the wall; my volunteering will not affect the outcome, but conscript me with the rest to stay the deluge and I will come without a murmur. In short, no good will come of my volunteering, but a great good will come of a general conscription which gathers me in with the rest. There is no inconsistency. I should add that my volunteering would in fact do positive harm; all who resist and survive are to be executed forthwith. There will be one or two heroes, but I did not think you were requiring me to be heroic.

Moralist: I confirm that I was not, and I concede that your position is not inconsistent, however unedifying. As I see it, the nub of your position is this: Given the premiss 'if everyone did that the result would be disastrous' you cannot conclude 'therefore *you* oughtn't' but only 'therefore someone ought to see to it that they don't.' If you are right, the 'if everyone did' argument, as usually taken, is invalid. But then we are left with the question: Whence does it derive its apparent force?

Defaulter: Whence, indeed?

(*interval*)

Moralist: Suppose when you give your justification for evading ('no one will miss *my* contribution') I reply: But don't you think it *unfair* that other people should bear the burden which you shirk and from the bearing of which by others you derive benefit for yourself?

Defaulter: Well, yes, it is rather unfair. Indeed you make me feel a little ashamed; but I wasn't prepared, and I'm still not, to let your pet argument by without a fight. Just where does fairness come into it?

Moralist: I think I can see. Let me begin by pushing two or three counters from different points on the periphery of the problem with the hope that they will meet at the centre. First, then: if someone is morally obliged (or permitted or forbidden) to do some particular thing, then there is a reason why he is so obliged. Further, if someone is obliged to do something for a particular reason, then anyone else whatever is equally obliged provided the reason applies to him also. The reason why a particular person is obliged to do something will be expressible in general terms, and could be expressed by describing some class to which he belongs. My principle then reads as follows: If someone is obliged to do something *just because* he is a member of a certain class, then any other member of that class will be equally obliged to do that thing. You yourself argued, remember, that any member of the class of people whose contribution would not be missed (here I allude to your reason for evasion) was no less entitled to evade than you.

Defaulter: Agreed.

Moralist: My second counter now comes into play. 'Fairness,' you will agree, is a moral term like 'rightness.' An act is unfair if it results in someone getting a greater or lesser share of something (whether pleasant or unpleasant) than he ought to get—more or less than his fair share, as we say.

Now there are a number of things, burdensome or otherwise, which need to be done if the community is not to suffer. But who precisely is to do them? Why me? Why not me? You will also agree, I hope, to the wide principle that where the thing to be done is burdensome the burden should be fairly distributed?

Defaulter: Certainly. I seldom dispute a truism. But in what does a fair distribution consist?

Moralist: In other words: given two people and a burden, how much of it ought each to bear? I say: *unless there is some reason why one should bear more or less of it than the other, they should both bear the same amount.* This is my Fairness Principle. It concerns both the fair allocation of the burden to some class of community members and the fair distribution of it within that class (and this may mean dividing the class into sub-classes of 'isophoric' members): there must always be a *reason* for treating people differently. For instance, people who are unfit or above or below a certain age are exempted or excluded from military service, and for good reasons; women are exempted or excluded from certain kinds of military service, for what Plato regarded as bad reasons; those with more income pay more tax, while those with more children pay less, and for good reasons—and so on. You will have noticed that the typical complaint about unfair dealing begins with a 'why': 'Why did they charge me more than him?' (unfair distribution), or 'Why should married couples be liable for so much surtax?' (unfair allocation). The maxim governing differential treatment, i.e. which is behind the reasons given for it, seems to be: From each according to his resources, to each according to his need. You might argue that my principle about equal burdens is no more than a special case of this maxim. But that principle is all I need for my argument and all I insist on; I shall not stick my neck out further than necessary.

Defaulter: It is not, thus far, too dangerously exposed, I think.

Moralist: Good. We are now ready to move a little nearer to the core of the problem. But first compare the two principles I have advanced. The first was: if a thing is obligatory etc. for one person, then it is obligatory etc. for anyone in the same class (i.e. the class relevant to the reason given). This is a license to argue from one member of a class to all its members; we will call it the Universalization Principle (U-Principle). The second, which is my Fairness Principle, is: A burden laid on a particular class is to be shared equally by all its members, unless there is reason to the contrary. This, in contrast to the first, is a license to argue from the class itself to each of its members. I take it, by the way, that these two principles are independent, that neither follows from the other.

Defaulter: Granted, granted. I am impatient to know what light all this throws on your 'if everyone did' argument.

Moralist: I am coming to that. You will remember that you used the U-Principle yourself to argue that if it's all right for you to evade it's all right for everyone else. But it was no use to me in pressing my case, and we can now see why: it argues from one to all, and there was

no *one* to argue from. Nor, of course, could I argue from the consequences of your act. 'Why me?' you asked, and I had then no reply. But
I did at least have a retort: 'Why not you?'. Now it seems to me that
it is just my Fairness principle that lies behind the effectiveness of this
retort, for by it you can be shown to have a duty in cases like this
unless you can show that you have not. You would have to show, in
the military service example, that you were not a member of the class
on which the duty of military service is normally (and we will assume,
fairly) regarded as lying. But you cannot show this: you cannot claim
to be under age or over age or blind or lame. All you claim is that you
have a certain property, the property of being one whose contribution
won't be missed, which is shared by every other member of the military
class; and this claim, so far from being a good reason for not volunteering, now stands revealed as no reason at all.

  Defaulter: Still, you didn't dispute my point that the blame for a
disaster following upon wholesale evasion lay upon those whose duty
it was, or in whose power it lay, to prevent such evasion.

  Moralist: You certainly had a point, but I can see now that you
made too much of it. I concede that the authorities failed in their duty,
but then the military class as a whole failed in theirs too. The duty of
both was ultimately the same, to ensure the safety of the state, just as
the duty of wicket-keeper and long-stop is the same, to save byes. To
confine the blame to the authorities is like saying that it's all right to
burn the house down so long as it's insured or that the mere existence
of a police force constitutes a general license to rob banks. As for the
individual defaulter, you wanted to absolve him from all blame—a
claim which seemed at once plausible and paradoxical: plausible because he was not, as you rightly pointed out, to blame for the disaster
(it was not his duty to prevent that, since it was not in his power to do
so); paradoxical because he was surely to blame for *something*, and
we now know what for: failure to bear his share of the burden
allotted to his class.

  Defaulter: Maybe, but it still seems to me that if I volunteer and
others don't I shall be taking on an unfair share of it, and *that* can't be
fair. Then again if I don't volunteer I shall be doing less than my share,
and *that* can't be fair either. Whichever I do, there's something wrong.
And that can't be right.

  Moralist: There are two mistakes here. Whichever you do there's
something wrong, but nothing unfair; the only wrong is people failing
in their duty. Fairness is an attribute of distributions, and whether you
volunteer or not neither you nor anyone else are distributing anything.
Nor, for that matter, are fate or circumstances, for they are not persons.

That is your first mistake. Your second is this: you talk as if the lone volunteer will necessarily do more than his fair share. He may, but he needn't. If he does, that is his own look out: *volenti non fit iniuria.*

Defaulter: It's more dangerous to fight alone than as one among many. How can he ration the danger?

Moralist: He can surrender or run away. Look, he isn't expected to be heroic or to do, or even attempt, ·the impossible. If two are needed to launch and man the lifeboat, the lone volunteer can only stand and wait: *he also* serves. The least a man can do is offer and hold himself ready, though sometimes it is also the most he can do.

Defaulter: Let it be so. But I am still in trouble about one thing: suppose I grant all you say about fairness and the defaulter, I'm still not clear why you choose to make your point against him in just the mysterious way you do, i.e. by fixing him with your glittering eye and beginning 'If everyone did that.'

Moralist: It is a little puzzling, isn't it? But not all that puzzling. After all, the premiss states and implies a good deal: (1) It states that wholesale evasion will have such and such results; (2) it states or implies that the results will be bad; (3) it implies strongly that a duty to prevent them must lie *somewhere;* (4) it implies that the duty does not lie solely on the person addressed (otherwise a quite different kind of argument would apply); (5) it implies, rather weakly, that nevertheless the person addressed has no better excuse for doing nothing about it than anyone else has. The conclusion is then stated that he ought to do something about it. A gap remains, to be sure; but it can't be a very big one, or people wouldn't, as they sometimes do, feel the force of the argument, however obscurely. The 'Why me?' retort brings out implication (4), while the 'Why not you?' counter-retort brings out implication (5); and we didn't really have very far to go from there.

The argument is clearly elliptical and needs filling out with some explicit reference to the Fairness principle. I would formalize it as follows:

> Unless such and such is done, undesirable consequences X will ensue; the burden of preventing X lies upon class Y as a whole;
> each member of class Y has a *prima facie* duty to bear an equal share of the burden by doing Z;
> you are a member of class Y;
> therefore you have a *prima facie* duty to do Z.

I have introduced the notion of a *prima facie* duty at this late stage to cover those cases where only a few members of class Y are required to do Z and it would be silly to put them all to work. In the latrine case only one person needs to dig, and in America only a small proportion of fit persons are required for short-term military service. In such cases it is considered fair to select the requisite number by lot. Until the lot is cast I must hold myself ready; if I am selected my *prima facie* duty becomes an actual duty; if I am spared, it lapses. Why selection by lot should be a fair method I leave you to work out for yourself.

Notice that the argument only holds if the thing to be done is burdensome. Voting isn't really very burdensome; indeed a lot of people seem to enjoy it, and this accounts for the weakness of the argument in this application. If the thing to be done were positively enjoyable one might even have to invoke the Fairness principle against over-indulgence.

Notice, finally, that the argument doesn't apply unless there is a fairly readily isolable class to which a burden can be allotted. This rules out the farming and such like cases. You can't lay it down that the burden of providing food for the nation (if it *is* a burden) lies on the farmers (i.e. the class that provides food for the nation), for that is a tautology, or perhaps it implies the curious proposition that everyone *ought* to be doing the job he *is* doing. Might one say instead that *everyone* has a *prima facie* duty to farm, but that the duty lapses when inclination, ability and economic reward conspire to select a sufficient farming force? Far-fetched, I think. The matter might be pursued, but only at the risk of tedium. Well, are you satisfied?

Defaulter: Up to a point. Your hypothesis obviously calls for a lot more testing yet. But I have carried the burden a good deal further than my fair share of the distance; let others take it from here.

6 DIODORUS CRONUS (RICHARD TAYLOR)

(1919–   )

The Governance of the Kingdom of Darkness*
A Philosopical Fable

Writing under the pseudonym "Diodorus Cronus," Richard Taylor centers his philosophical fable on the notion of evil and reveals much about our conceptions of good and moral worth. As is the case with most fables, the real point of the work is to be found only on careful examination and a reading between the lines. The fable is, on the surface, rather simple. The Devil has been restored to Heaven, and the throne of Hell is vacant. Four candidates are proposed for the office. Their credentials are presented. One is a disease-carrier who has unintentionally killed thousands; another is an executioner who in following orders has led thousands to their deaths. The third is a gangster-type who enjoys the suffering of his many victims, and the fourth is a merely tactless, law-abiding citizen who is not even clear as to why he is in residence in Hell. Taylor does not tell us who wins the throne, but he suggests that it is the last of the candidates who will emerge victorious. Careful consideration should be given to discovering why.

° Diodorus Cronus (Richard Taylor), "The Governance of the Kingdom of Darkness," *Southern Journal of Philosophy,* Summer 1971, pp. 113–118. Used by kind permission of the Editor.

Wherein may be discerned the true essence of moral depravity, or that which really does, like a cesspool, corrupt whatever comes under its influence, as containing within itself all evil and ugliness.

—DIODORUS CRONUS

IT is rare, so rare that no reliable way of coping with it has even yet been evolved, that the office of Prince of Darkness becomes vacant, and the awesome title of Satan must then be bestowed anew upon some candidate chosen from the denizens of Hell.

Lucifer, the first Ruler of Darkness, who was an imperious and exemplary Devil, held sway over the underworld for nearly fourteen thousand years, and it was widely supposed that his tenure of office would be everlasting. There was, therefore, great consternation and amazement in Hell when God, out of his infinite grace, suddenly and without forewarning extended salvation even to Lucifer, restored him to his place in the celestial hierarchy of the angels, and thereby created a vacuum at the summit of the ranks of Hell. Many had come to think that there can be only one supremely wicked being, and that this one's place in the scheme of things was as secure as that of evil itself; but these had to face up to the fact that, this one having departed, there was no longer even one, and a new Prince of Darkness would have to be found.

The first time this emergency was faced the method of popular election was hit upon as the best means of choice. It was thought that this would minimize bias and favoritism, in that the diverse prejudices of the damned would cancel each other out instead, as in fact happened, of augmenting each other. Of course, this was only rationalization, for the true reason for such an inept method of choice was the lack of any really clear criterion of moral depravity. Everyone supposed that this could be supplied by his neighbors.

The democratic method did, in any case, work singularly badly, for the hosts of the damned chose as their Prince one of their number whose wickedness could sometimes be viewed as positively endearing. He had, in his earthly life, been an uncommonly successful jewel thief, having stolen nearly two million dollars worth of gems and baubles from rich ladies without ever spending a day in jail, and before he finally went to Hell he was the most sought after criminal on the face of the globe.

It is needless to say that this fellow cut a very poor figure as Head Devil, and there were some who wondered whether he even belonged in Hell to begin with, in spite of his bad reputation on earth. On more than one occasion he was discovered doing things that bore unmistakable resemblance to virtuous action, and this evoked great uneasiness among his subjects. Thus he was seen tenderly assisting an unregenerate woman who had been nearly overcome by sulphur soon after arriving in Hell. She had borne a bastard child on earth and, dying in childbirth, had of course been banished to Hell. Now the Devil, in rescuing her from the brimstone fumes, claimed that he was only trying to ensure that she would survive to absorb all the pains that were in store for her; but this was not entirely believed. Outwardly, at least, his action had an unmistakable semblance of kindness —and there were other similar instances, which occasioned much misgiving.

This problem was solved, however, in the very manner in which it had been created in the first place; for this second Prince of Darkness was suddenly, like Lucifer, restored to the celestial hierarchy, through the infinite grace of the Almighty, almost before his reign could get started, he having then officially ruled only two hundred and fifty-six years.

To choose the successor to this inept Satan, and to minimize the likelihood of reproducing the embarrassments that his particular style had occasioned, a committee was chosen—or, rather, appointed itself, for there was no semblance of democratic procedure in the manner of its coming into being. This committee, composed of Belial, Beelzebub, and others of the most distinguished of the fallen angels, called itself the Council of Evil, and resolved to find someone who surpassed all others in genuine moral evil, applying this sole criterion with absolute rigor. The choice would be made, they declared, not on the basis of any specious claims, but only the single consideration of total moral depravity.

The field of candidates was eventually narrowed to six, of whom two were eliminated after only cursory consideration. One of these had been a consummate swindler, the other a corrupt politician, and the vices of neither seemed sufficiently distinctive to entitle their possessors to the greatest respect in Hell. Of the four remaining one was finally chosen, and the wisdom of the choice has now been wholly vindicated, for the moral evil of this Prince is so pure and undefiled by any goodness that not only does he still hold sway over Hell, after these four millenia, but his status continuously increases, attesting to the plenitude of his depravity.

The four finalists and their credentials were as follows.

The first candidate: Adama.

There was profound shock and shaking of heads when it was learned that one of the candidates under serious consideration was female, and would accordingly, if chosen, need to be called the Princess of Darkness. Such an appellative seemed wholly inappropriate and even comic, the word "Princess" conjuring in the imagination qualities the very opposite of what could be associated with darkness and evil. Still, it was pointed out that throughout history far more evil had been wrought by women than men, that recognition of this was deserved, and that only arrogance and a jealousy of titles could blind men to the propriety of feminine rule. Such considerations seemed unanswerable, and so in view of what appeared to be the most obvious single qualification, Adama, a female candidate, gained considerable support.

Adama hardly resembled any popular conception of a devil, temptress, or other embodiment of evil. Dowdy in appearance and manner, she conveyed more the impression of a washerwoman. Nevertheless, she had the distinction of having destroyed more people than anyone who had ever walked on the face of the earth, having in her short lifetime caused the deaths of nearly nine-tenths of the inhabitants of two continents. She had, to be sure, never really intended anyone's death, but at the same time she made no effort to avoid spreading sickness and death wherever she went. For Adama, though seemingly in robust health herself, was the carrier of a plague which, once it gained the smallest foothold any place, at once spread like fire over dry weeds, engulfing whole nations. Adama knew this, and thus knew her role in the sorrow and death that spread itself over the land wherever she set foot, but others did not, and it was generally believed that the plagues to which Adama had such remarkable immunity were visited upon men by demons. Adama's knowledge of what she was doing produced in her no desire to limit her movement and thus reduce her threat to the general well-being, however. On the contrary, having all her life cared nothing for others, and having never cared whether any other person lived or died, she went about things exactly as she always had, according to her own convenience, grateful that she was herself spared the effects of the plague she so effectively distributed, but otherwise oblivious to her unusual condition. Thus when she decided to visit a relative she had never seen, she did not hesitate to take the simplest and shortest route to where this person lived, through the most densely populated area of the earth. The result was a staggering decimation of the population, only a few hundred besides Adama being miraculously spared; but she had expected as much, from her previous experience. It was not exactly what she had desired, but at the same time it was no personal loss to herself, as the extra day or two for the more roundabout journey would have been.

Adama finally died, was of course sent to Hell, and there her hopes were quickly kindled by the political developments already described. Murder, she pointed out, was everywhere considered the most flagitious of sins, and her claim to be supremely wicked thus appeared incontestable. Her opponents tried to draw metaphysical distinctions between murdering and causing to die, but these seemed too subtle to alter the overwhelming fact of Adama's monstrous achievement.

The second candidate: Bazel.

Bazel had during his life on earth been an executioner. Of course this was in itself no special distinction, for executioners arrive in Hell with such regularity and in such numbers that it is difficult to find any distinction for them at all. Bazel, however, was able to present himself as a rather special case. He had not merely, like most executioners, hanged men from time to time as a sideline to his proprietorship of a bar or trade as a plumber. Bazel had in the relatively brief span of just eleven years, four months and sixteen days managed to execute a staggering number of men, women and children, most of them inhabitants of recently conquered territories. By his own reckoning he had processed 1,245,308 persons, and he felt certain the figure was accurate within a couple of hundred, plus or minus. This he had done by gassing them in airtight compounds. After only eighteen months of this rather demanding work he had devised ways of increasing his output by nearly thirty percent, without any significant increase in cost of materials, through a cleverly contrived method of packing the specimens into the compounds. Subsequent improvements over the years had enabled him nearly to double his output over the original two hundred or so per day. He had been diligent, too, for while he was obligated by his contract to work only eight hours a day plus a maximum of two hours overtime, at overtime pay, he seldom worked less than twelve in any one day, from devotion to his work, and on a few occasions he kept at it nearly twenty hours at a stretch, clearing away much accumulated backlog. At the conclusion of his tenth year of government service he received a special tribute, which amounted to a modest testimonial dinner and the awarding of a gold watch, inscribed with the record of his service to date. When he was finally dropped, as a result of military reversals abroad and political misfortunes at home, he was tolerably well-to-do, and a rough computation showed that he had averaged about eleven cents for each person dispatched, most of which he had managed to save. He spent his declining years comfortably in a foreign land, protected from his enemies who had never conceded the legitimacy of his vocation, and once granted an interview to a lifelong friend and journalist. In the interview he said, among other things, that he had never harbored any hatred or ill will toward any human being, had never so much as slapped a child or teased a cat, and had always been conscientious in the performance of such tasks as fell to him to perform. He was, as he looked back on things, sometimes astonished at what he had wrought, but he had not thought much of it at the time. He thought it illustrated how, with regular industry day by day, one can in a fair measure of time achieve a genuinely significant total result, and it seemed to him that this lesson was not being sufficiently imparted to the younger generation.

Armed with figures that not even the most decorated bomber pilots could hope to match, Bazel presented himself as candidate for the ruler of Hell. Adama's total figures were, he conceded, far higher, but he argued that her achievements were essentially accidental, resulting from biology rather than true character, whereas his were the product of determination, effort, and devotion to duty.

The third candidate: Calpon.

This candidate was at first unwilling to challenge the candidacy of Bazel, but he eventually convinced himself that he might in fact be the better qualified of the two. Bazel, he decided, was only parading figures to dazzle the Council of Evil and to cover up a considerable deficiency of true baseness. Bazel was, Calpon maintained, entirely motivated by the desires to please his employers and enhance his position in the community, motives which are perfectly commonplace and hardly entitle anyone to any distinction in the area of moral depravity. Bazel was in fact hardly more than a pest control officer, Calpon claimed, and went about his work in about the same way as any other, the single difference being in the species of pest he was hired to eradicate.

Calpon, too, was an executioner, though he had to pursue this calling on his own, in the face of much discouragement and without government support. Calpon belonged to a group of police officers in a small and corrupt country who had taken it upon themselves to do what they could, when off duty, to rid their society of the criminal element, as well as of beggars and similar undesirables. It was, they had found, of little use bringing criminals to justice by traditional means. More often than not they were freed, from lack of evidence against them, and just returned to their criminal pursuits—picking pockets, stealing, smuggling, and so on.

So Calpon and his associates—seven of them altogether—formed themselves into a death squad, and as soon as they heard of anyone being engaged in criminal activity, arranged to eliminate him. They first arrested him, and if no relative or other person inquired of his whereabouts in the next several weeks, and no attorney came forth to ask questions, they removed him from the jail, drove him to some desolate spot, and there disposed of him with knives or guns. Sometimes several were dealt with at once, occasionally as many as five or six. Calpon's role in this operation was somewhat unique, for he had no interest at all in combating crime. He belonged to the group simply because he happened to love the sight of blood, particularly blood flowing from wounds which he had inflicted. It gave him an intense pleasure, akin to but far greater than sexual excitation, he said, to see blood pour forth "like an opening rose." He thus came to be nicknamed "The Rose," and it was always he who was permitted to begin the work, either with gun or knife. He always selected a non-vital spot so he could watch the blood flow unhindered and as long as possible, becoming absorbed at these times in something of a trance. It was quite plainly the most intense joy he could experience. Once, when asked why he held such a hatred for criminals, he protested that he had no hatred for them at all. It was simply that he enjoyed the sight of human suffering, at close range, and that the animal slaughter houses in which he had found such pleasure as a boy had lost their charms for him. He enjoyed drawing blood from criminals, gypsies, beggars and other useless persons only because these happened to be the only people available for this purpose, at least without very great risk. Nor, he declared, did he kill for payment, for he had in fact never been paid for his work with the death squad, doing it all on his own time.

Thus did Calpon lay claim to the office of Prince, not because he had murdered in such staggering numbers as Bazel (he had in fact helped to kill only sixty-three persons) but because, unlike Bazel, he murdered for fun rather than as a means to an honest living.

The fourth candidate: Deprov.

It never occurred to Deprov to compete for the office of Prince, nor did he ever understand why others had wanted to put his name before the Council of Evil. It must, he thought, be some malicious person's idea of a joke. Indeed, Deprov had never understood why he had found himself in Hell in the first place, and always insisted that there had been some ghastly mistake, some confusion of identities.

For Deprov had in fact led a perfectly law-abiding and blameless life, and when he had died, full of years, his record was as clean as when he was born. He had never so much as received a summons for a motor vehicle violation or a delinquent tax payment. He had a dreadful fear and respect for the police and all the forces of law, and felt a deep shame at the mere thought of his integrity being challenged in any way.

Deprov was, to be sure, cruel by nature, but this always expressed itself in acceptable ways within the framework of laws and conventional rules. He had never assaulted anyone in his life. He indulged his ever present cruelty only upon animals, and upon his fellow men only in permissible ways. Thus, when one day he came upon a beautiful young girl sitting in the park, looking disconsolate, he was struck with astonishment to discover that one entire side of her face, the side he had not approached and therefore not at first seen, was horribly discolored and disfigured, apparently from dreadful burns received long ago. Unnoticed, he took several instant pictures of her, from that side, and, with deep satisfaction spread across his face, presented all three to her at once, while she, dumbfounded, stared back at him in blank, unthinking horror. He had, he later said, only taken pictures, and had not tried to make anything seem different from what it really was, thus displaying a respect for truth. On another occasion, seeing the village drunk urinating in the public square, Deprov sought out this man's children and, finding them with numerous playmates in the swings on the playground, loudly announced to them their father's condition, and urged them to fetch their mother before he disgraced them still further. It was, he said, the most effective way of dealing with men of that sort, and children, as well as anyone else, are deserving of truth.

Deprov, along with his reverence for truth, had also a deep respect for law and morality, not only in the sense that he willingly and indeed eagerly guided his own steps within their straight and narrow path, but did whatever he could do to ensure that others did so as well. He regularly strolled about the town evenings, noting the comings and goings of his neighbors, and drawing such inferences as he could concerning their purposes. He was generally rewarded with at least some opportunity to correct large or small transgressions which, had it not been for him, might never have been detected at all. Thus when he found a dog whose owner, the village garbage collector, was well known to him, wandering about the town in violation of ordinance, he carefully amputated all the dog's toes. That dog, he reflected, would never walk again, and its owner would perhaps see that his animals were properly tethered or fenced after this. Again, when he discovered that the local barmaid (in fact a middle-aged divorcee) was spending every night, after work, in the rooming house quarters of the school janitor, who was a black man, he arranged to have the rooms raided by the police and a charge of adultery entered against both of them, and he arranged also for local newspaper coverage of the raid, for it seemed to him that everyone and especially the young would benefit from a dramatic arrest.

Deprov thus acquired a reputation as the sternest defender of law and morality in the county. After one of his more dramatic lessons on the futility of irregular behavior, administered to an ancient, toothless beggar who appeared in the streets one day, he was asked by the local doctor, who had known him for many years, why it was that he seemed to enjoy tormenting the lonely, the sick, and the brokenhearted. Deprov with real astonishment protested that he could never *enjoy* anything of the sort, and that, on the contrary, he had often foregone genuine pleasures and enjoyments in pressing his crusade for truth, law, and morality. A considerable part of his life, he accurately noted, was devoted to this, when he could, easily and without reproof, be spending his time in numberless entertainments and amusements, which he was as capable of enjoying as anyone.

It was thus mystifying to him that he, Deprov, should through some incredible misconception be represented as an *evil* man, when it was well known that he had spent his earthly life combating wickedness; and the more mystifying and astonishing when he viewed, with strenuously suppressed envy, the careers of Adama, Bazel, and Calpon, and their clear qualifications for Satanic governance. Yet certain friends who claimed to know him well thought it worthwhile to present his name along with a dossier of his achievements which, though filled mostly with trivia and the most banal of episodes, turned out to be the bulkiest dossier the Council of Evil had received.

Further Reading On
DUTY AND RESPONSIBILITY

Aristotle. *Ethics* New York: Dutton, 1963.

Barnes, Gerald W. "In Defense of Kant's Doctrine of the Highest Good." *Philosophical Forum,* Summer 1971.

Beran, H. "Ought, Obligation, and Duty." *The Australasian Journal of Philosophy,* December 1972.

Brady, James B. "Status Responsibility." *Philosophy and Phenomenological Research,* March 1973.

Collins, James. *The Existentialists.* Chicago: Henry Regnery Company, 1952.

Compton, John J. "Responsibility and Agency." *The Southern Journal of Philosophy,* Spring–Summer 1973.

Dalrymple, H. B. "Determinism and Moral Responsibility." *Proceedings of the New Mexico–West Texas Philosophical Society,* April 1972.

Duncan, A. R. C. *Practical Reason and Morality.* London: Thomas Nelson and Sons, 1957.

Ewing, A. C. *Ethics.* New York: The Free Press, 1953.

Gupta, R. K. "Kant's Groundwork of Morality." *Studi Internazionali di Filosofia,* Autumn 1971.

Hare, R. M. *The Language of Morals.* Oxford: Clarendon Press, 1953.

Henderson, G. P. "Censure Under Control." *Ratio,* June 1973.

Hunter, J. F. M. "Acting Freely and Being Held Responsible." *Dialogue: Canadian Philosophical Review,* 1972.

Jack, Henry "Note on Doubts About 'Prima Facie' Duties." *Philosophy,* April 1971.

Jack, Henry. "Utilitarianism and Ross's Theory of 'Prima Facie' Duties." *Dialogue: Canadian Philosophical Review,* 1971.

King, James T. "Kierkegaard's Critique of Ethics." *Proceedings of the American Catholic Philosophical Association,* 1972.

Melden, A. I. "The Play of Rights." *The Monist,* October 1972.

Moore, Harold, Robert Neville, and William Sullivan. "The Contours of Responsibility: A New Model." *Man and World,* November 1972.

Murdock, Iris. *The Sovereignty of Good.* New York: Schocken Books, 1971.

Neblett, William R. "W. D. Ross and the Nature of Moral Obligation." *The Journal of Value Inquiry,* September 1973.

Nesbitt, W. and **S. Candlish.** "On Not Being Able to Do Otherwise." *Mind,* July 1973.

Pearl, Leon. "Objective and Subjective Duty." *Mind,* July 1971.

Popov, L. A. "Atheism and Moral Responsibility." *Soviet Studies in Philosophy,* Summer 1973.

Shrag, Francis. "Rights over Children." *The Journal of Value Inquiry,* Summer 1973.

Singer, Marcus G. "The Basis of Rights and Duties." *Philosophical Studies,* Fall 1972.

Stevenson, C. L. *Ethics and Language.* New Haven: Yale University Press, 1944.

Stocker, Michael. "Moral Duties, Institutions, and Natural Facts." *The Monist,* October 1970.

Thomson, J. J. and **Gerald Dworkin.** *Ethics.* New York: Harper & Row, 1968.

Von Wright, Georg Henrik. *Norm and Action.* London: Routledge and Kegan Paul, 1963.

Welding, S. O "On Kant's Concepts of Duty." *Ratio,* December 1971.

Werkmeister, William. *Theories of Ethics.* Lincoln: Johnsen Publishing, 1961.

Wilkerson, T. E. "Duty, Inclination, and Morals." *Philosophical Quarterly,* January 1973.

Woozley, A. D. "Injustice." *American Philosophical Quarterly,* 1973.

Wren, Thomas E. "Rightness and the Formal Level of Action." *Ethics.* July 1973.

PART II

GOVERNMENT, LAW, AND THE PUBLIC MORALS

The Report of the Commission on Obscenity

and Pornography, 1970

MAJORITY REPORT

IN GENERAL OUTLINE, THE COMMISSION RECOMMENDS THAT FEDERAL, state, and local legislation should not seek to interfere with the right of adults who wish to do so to read, obtain, or view explicit sexual materials. On the other hand, we recommend legislative regulations upon the sale of sexual materials to young persons who do not have the consent of their parents, and we also recommend legislation to protect persons from having sexual materials thrust upon them without their consent through the mails or through open public display.

The Commission's specific legislative recommendations and the reasons underlying these recommendations are as follows:

A. Statutes Relating to Adults

The Commission recommends that federal, state, and local legislation prohibiting the sale, exhibition, or distribution of sexual materials to consenting adults should be repealed.

The Commission believes that there is no warrant for continued governmental interference with the full freedom of adults to read, obtain or view whatever such material they wish. Our conclusion is based upon the following considerations:

1. Extensive empirical investigation, both by the Commission and by others, provides no evidence that exposure to or use of explicit sexual materials play a significant role in the causation of social or individual harms such as crime, delinquency, sexual or nonsexual deviancy or severe emotional disturbances. Empirical

investigation supports the opinion of a substantial majority of persons professionally engaged in the treatment of deviancy, delinquency and antisocial behavior, that exposure to sexually explicit materials has no harmful causal role in these areas.

Studies show that a number of factors, such as disorganized family relationships and unfavorable peer influences, are intimately related to harmful sexual behavior or adverse character development. Exposure to sexually explicit materials, however, cannot be counted as among these determinative factors. Despite the existence of widespread legal prohibitions upon the dissemination of such materials, exposure to them appears to be a usual and harmless part of the process of growing up in our society and a frequent and nondamaging occurrence among adults. Indeed, a few Commission studies indicate that a possible distinction between sexual offenders and other people, with regard to experience with explicit sexual materials, is that sex offenders have seen markedly *less* of such materials while maturing.

This is not to say that exposure to explicit sexual materials has no effect upon human behavior. A prominent effect of exposure to sexual materials is that persons tend to talk more about sex as a result of seeing such materials. In addition, many persons become temporarily sexually aroused upon viewing explicit materials and the frequency of their sexual activity may, in consequence, increase for short periods. Such behavior, however, is the type of sexual activity already established as usual activity for the particular individual.

In sum, empirical research designed to clarify the question has found no evidence to date that exposure to explicit sexual materials plays a significant role in the causation of delinquent or criminal behavior among youth or adults.

2. On the positive side, explicit sexual materials are sought as a source of entertainment and information by substantial numbers of American adults. At times, these materials also appear to serve to increase and facilitate constructive communication about sexual matters within marriage. The most frequent purchaser of explicit sexual materials is a college-educated, married male, in his thirties or forties, who is of above average socio-economic status. Even where materials are legally available to them, young adults and older adolescents do not constitute an important portion of the purchases of such materials.

3. Society's attempts to legislate for adults in the area of obscenity have not been successful. Present laws prohibiting the consensual sale or distribution of explicit sexual materials to adults are extremely unsatisfactory in their practical application. The Consti tution permits material to be deemed "obscene" for adults only if, as a whole, it appeals to the "prurient" interest of the average person, is "patently offensive" in light of "community standards," and lacks "redeeming social value." These vague and highly subjective aesthetic, psychological and moral tests do not provide meaningful guidance for law enforcement officials, juries or courts. As a result, law is inconsistently and sometimes erroneously applied and the distinctions made by courts between prohibited and permissible materials often appear indefensible. Errors in the application of the law and uncertainty about its scope also cause interference with the communication of constitutionally protected materials.

4. Public opinion in America does not support the imposition of legal prohibitions upon the right of adults to read or see explicit sexual materials. While a minority of Americans favors such prohibitions, a majority of the American people presently are of the view that adults should be legally able to read or see explicit sexual materials if they wish to do so.

5. The lack of consensus among Americans concerning whether explicit sexual materials should be available to adults in our society, and the significant number of adults who wish to have access to such materials, pose serious problems regarding the enforcement of legal prohibitions upon adults, even aside from the vagueness and subjectivity of present law. Consistent enforcement of even the clearest prohibitions upon consensual adult exposure to explicit sexual materials would require the expenditure of considerable law enforcement resources. In the absence of a persuasive demonstration of damage flowing from consensual exposure to such materials, there seems no justification for thus adding to the overwhelming tasks already placed upon the law enforcement system. Inconsistent enforcement of prohibitions, on the other hand, invites discriminatory action based upon considerations not directly relevant to the policy of the law. The latter alternative also breeds public disrespect for the legal process.

6. The foregoing considerations take on added significance because of the fact that adult obscenity laws deal in the realm of

speech and communication. Americans deeply value the right of
each individual to determine for himself what books he wishes to
read and what pictures or films he wishes to see. Our traditions of
free speech and press also value and protect the right of writers,
publishers, and booksellers to serve the diverse interests of the
public. The spirit and letter of our Constitution tell us that government should not seek to interfere with these rights unless a clear
threat of harm makes that course imperative. Moreover, the possibility of the misuse of general obscenity statutes prohibiting
distributions of books and films to adults constitutes a continuing
threat to the free communication of ideas among Americans—one
of the most important foundations of our liberties.

The concern about the effect of obscenity upon morality is also
expressed as a concern about the impact of sexual materials upon
American values and standards. Such values and standards are
currently in a process of complex change, in both sexual and nonsexual areas. The open availability of increasingly explicit sexual
materials is only one of these changes. The current flux in sexual
values is related to a number of powerful influences, among which
are the ready availability of effective methods of contraception,
changes of the role of women in our society, and the increased
education and mobility of our citizens. The availability of explicit
sexual materials is, the Commission believes, not one of the important influences on sexual morality.

The Commission is of the view that it is exceedingly unwise for
government to attempt to legislate individual moral values and
standards independent of behavior, especially by restrictions upon
consensual communication. This is certainly true in the absence
of a clear public mandate to do so, and our studies have revealed
no such mandate in the area of obscenity.

The Commission recognizes and believes that the existence of
sound moral standards is of vital importance to individuals and to
society. To be effective and meaningful, however, these standards
must be based upon deep personal commitment flowing from
values instilled in the home, in educational and religious training,
and through individual resolutions of personal confrontations with
human experience. Governmental regulation of moral choice can
deprive the individual of the responsibility for personal decision
which is essential to the formation of genuine moral standards.
Such regulation would also tend to establish an official moral or-

thodoxy, contrary to our most fundamental constitutional traditions.

Therefore, the Commission recommends the repeal of existing federal legislation which prohibits or interferes with consensual distribution of "obscene" materials to adults. The Commission also recommends the repeal of existing state and local legislation which may similarly prohibit the consensual sale, exhibition, or the distribution of sexual materials to adults.

B. Statutes Relating to Young Persons

The Commission recommends the adoption by the States of legislation prohibiting the commercial distribution or display for sale of certain sexual materials to young persons.

The Commission's recommendation of juvenile legislation flows from these findings and considerations:

A primary basis for the Commission's recommendation for repeal of adult legislation is the fact that extensive empirical investigations do not indicate any causal relationship between exposure to or use of explicit sexual materials and such social or individual harms such as crime, delinquency, sexual or nonsexual deviancy, or severe emotional disturbances. The absence of empirical evidence supporting such a causal relationship also applies to the exposure of children to erotic materials. However, insufficient research is presently available on the effect of the exposure of children to sexually explicit materials to enable us to reach conclusions with the same degree of confidence as for adult exposure. Strong ethical feelings against experimentally exposing children to sexually explicit materials considerably reduced the possibility of gathering the necessary data and information regarding young persons.

In view of the limited amount of information concerning the effects of sexually explicit materials on children, other considerations have assumed primary importance in the Commission's deliberations. The Commission has been influenced, to a considerable degree, by its finding that a large majority of Americans believe that children should not be exposed to certain sexual materials. In addition, the Commission takes the view that parents should be free to make their own conclusions regarding the suitability of explicit sexual materials for their children and that it is appropriate for legislation to aid parents in controlling the access of their children to such materials during their formative years. The Commission recognizes that legislation cannot possibly isolate children from such materials entirely; it also recognizes that exposure of children to sexual materials may not only do no harm but may, in certain instances, actually facilitate much needed communication between parent and child over sexual matters. The Commission is aware, as well, of the considerable danger of creating an unnatural attraction or an enhanced interest in certain materials by making them "forbidden fruit" for young persons. The Commission believes, however, that these considerations can and should be weighed by individual parents in determining their attitudes toward the exposure of their children to sexual materials, and that legislation should aid, rather than undermine, such parental choice.

Taking account of the above considerations, the model juvenile legislation recommended by the Commission applies only to distributions to children made without parental consent. The recommended legislation applies only to commercial distributions and exhibitions; in the very few instances where noncommercial conduct in this area creates a problem, it can be dealt with under existing legal principles for the protection of young persons, such as prohibitions upon contributing to the delinquency of minors. The model legislation also prohibits displaying certain sexual materials for sale in a manner which permits children to view materials which cannot be sold to them.

. . .

Because of changing standards as to what material, if any, is inappropriate for sale or display to children, the Commission's model statute contains a provision requiring legislative reconsideration of the need for, and scope of, such legislation at six-year intervals.

. . .

The Commission has not fixed upon a precise age limit for inclusion in its recommended juvenile legislation, believing that such a determination is most appropriately made by the States and localities which enact such provisions in light of local standards. All States now fix the age in juvenile obscenity statutes at under 17 or under 18 years. The recommended model statute also excludes married persons, whatever their age, from the category of juveniles protected by the legislation.

. . .

Finally, the Commission considered, but does not affirmatively recommend, the enactment by the federal government of juvenile legislation which would prohibit the sale of certain explicit materials to juveniles through the mails. Such federal legislation would, the Commission believes, be virtually unenforceable since the constitutional requirement of proving the defendant's guilty knowledge means that a prosecution could be successful only if proof were available that the vendor knew that the purchaser was a minor. Except in circumstances which have not been found to be prevalent, as where a sale might be solicited through a mailing list composed of young persons, mail order purchases are made without any knowledge by the vendor of the purchaser's age. Certificates of age by the purchaser would be futile as an enforcement device and to require notarized affidavits to make a purchase through the mails would unduly interfere with purchase by adults. The Commission has found, moreover, that at present juveniles rarely purchase sexually explicit materials through the mail, making federal legislative machinery in this area apparently unnecessary.

Minority Report of Commissioners

Morton A. Hill, S.J.
Winfrey C. Link
concurred in by
Charles H. Keating, Jr.

OUR POSITION

WE STAND IN AGREEMENT WITH THE CONGRESS OF THE UNITED States: the traffic in obscenity and pornography is a matter of national concern.

We believe that pornography has an eroding effect on society, on public morality, on respect for human worth, on attitudes toward family love, on culture.

We believe it is impossible, and totally unnecessary, to attempt to prove or disprove a cause-effect relationship between pornography and criminal behavior.

Sex education, recommended so strongly by the majority, is the panacea for those who advocate license in media. The report suggests sex education, with a plaint for the dearth of instructors and materials. It notes that three schools have used "hard-core pornography" in training potential instructors. The report does not answer the question that comes to mind immediately: Will these instructors not bring the hard-core pornography into the grammar schools? Many other questions are left unanswered: How assure that the instructor's moral or ethical code (or lack of same) will not be communicated to children? Shouldn't parents, not children, be the recipients of sex education courses?

Children cannot grow in love if they are trained with pornography. Pornography is loveless; it degrades the human being, reduces him to the level of animal. And if this Commission majority's recommendations are heeded, there will be a glut of pornography for teachers and children.

In contrast to the Commission report's amazing statement that "public opinion in America does not support the imposition of legal prohibitions upon the consensual distribution" of pornography to adults, we find, as a result of public hearings conducted by two of the undersigned in eight cities throughout the country, that the majority of the American people favor tighter controls. Twenty-six out of twenty-seven witnesses at the hearing in New York City expressed concern and asked for remedial measures. Witnesses were a cross section of the community, ranging from members of the judiciary to members of women's clubs. This pattern was repeated in the cities of New Orleans, Indianapolis, Chicago, Salt Lake City, San Francisco, Washington, D.C., and Buffalo. (And yet, one member of the Commission majority bases his entire position for legalization on the astounding "finding" of the Commission survey that "no more than 35% of our people favor adult controls in the field of obscenity in the absence of some demonstrable social evil related to its presence and use.")

Additionally, law enforcement officers testifying at the Hill-Link hearings were unanimous in declaring that the problem of obscenity and pornography is a serious one. They complained that law enforcement is hampered by the "utterly without redeeming social value" language. The Commission's own survey of prosecuting attorneys indicates that 73% of prosecutors polled said that "social value" is the most serious obstacle to prosecution. The decision not to prosecute is usually a manifestation of this obstacle. This figure and information is strangely missing from the report's "Overview of Findings."

We point also to the results of a Gallup poll, published in the summer of 1969. Eighty-five out of every 100 adults interviewed said they favored stricter state and local laws dealing with pornography sent through the mails, and 76 of every 100 wanted stricter laws on the sort of magazines and newspapers available on newsstands.

We believe government must legislate to regulate pornography, in order to protect the "social interest in order and morality."

SUMMARY AND CONCLUSIONS

1. The Commission on Obscenity and Pornography (majority report) is recommending major changes in laws and social policy in an area of controversy, public concern, and also in an area having health and welfare implications for adults and minors (e.g., remove all controls on pornography for adults and children—except, in the latter case, pictorial materials).

The basis for recommending these changes is that the Commission found no empirical scientific evidence showing a causal relationship between exposure to pornography and any kind of harm to minors or adults.

2. However it should be stated that conclusively proving causal relationships among social science type variables is extremely difficult if not impossible. Among adults whose life histories have included much exposure to pornography it is nearly impossible to disentangle the literally hundreds of causal threads or chains that contributed to their later adjustment or maladjustment. Because of the extreme complexity of the problem and the uniqueness of the human experience it is doubtful that we will ever have absolutely convincing scientific proof that pornography is or isn't harmful. And the issue isn't restricted to, "Does pornography cause or contribute to sex crimes?" The issue has to do with how pornography affects or influences the individual in his total relationship to members of the same as well as opposite sex, children and adults, with all of its ramifications.

The "burden of proof" or demonstration of no harm in a situation such as this, is ordinarily considered to be on the shoulders of he who wishes to introduce change or innovation. It might be noted that in areas where health and welfare are at issue, most government agencies take extremely conservative measures in their efforts to protect the public. In the case of monosodium glutamate which was recently removed from all baby food by government order, the evidence against it, in animal studies, was quite weak. However, because the remote possibility of harm existed, measures were immediately taken to protect children from consuming it.

3. The evidence the Commission presents does not clearly indicate, "no harm." There are also many areas of "neglect" relative to the Commission's studies of pornography's effects (e.g., no

longitudinal studies, no in depth clinical studies, no porno-violence data, no studies in modeling or imitative learning, etc. etc.).

In the Commission's presentation of the scientific evidence there are frequent errors and inaccuracies in their reporting of research results as well as in the basic studies themselves. Frequently conclusions which are not warranted are drawn inappropriately from data. There is a frequent failure to distinguish or discriminate between studies which are badly flawed and weak and those of exceptional merit. But, most serious of all, data from a number of studies which show statistical linkages between high exposure to pornography and promiscuity, deviancy, affiliation with high criminality groups, etc. have gone unreported. This suggests a major bias in the reporting of results which raises a major issue of credibility of the entire report. Regardless of why it occurred, it suggests that at the very least, a panel of independent scientists be called in to reevaluate the Commission research and the conclusions which might be validly drawn from it before any major changes occur in laws and social policy regarding pornography's control.

RECOMMENDATIONS

1. Recommended Test or Definition of Obscenity

A thing is "obscene" if, by contemporary community standards, and considered as a whole, its predominant appeal is to the prurient interest. As a matter of public policy, anything which is obscene by this definition shall be conclusively deemed to be utterly without redeeming social importance. Any slight social value in such obscenity shall be deemed outweighed by the social interest in order and morality.

"Prurient interest" is defined as a shameful or morbid interest in nudity, sex or excretion which goes substantially beyond customary limits of candor in description or representation of such matters. If it appears from the character of the material or the circumstances of its dissemination that the subject matter is designed for, or directed to a specially susceptible audience, the subject matter shall be judged with reference to such audience. When the subject matter is distributed or exhibited to minors who have not attained their 18th birthday, the subject matter shall be judged with reference to an average person in the community of the actual age of the minor to whom such material is distributed or exhibited. In all other cases, the subject matter shall be judged with reference to the average person in the community.

Comment. This formulation is taken from the *Roth* case which is the only case in which the Supreme Court defined obscenity and the *Ginsberg* case, in which the Supreme Court accepts the concept of variable obscenity as it applies to minors. It rejects the suggestion of three of the nine Justices that "utterly without redeeming social value" is a test for obscenity, since the Supreme Court has never adopted this suggestion. In fact, it is this unnecessary "test" that has caused the flood of hard-core pornography in motion pictures, books, magazines and other publications.

A complete review of the lack of constitutional necessity for this so-called "test" is found in Appendix I in our comments under the *Memoirs (Fanny Hill)* case.

The *Roth* Test, it is claimed by some is subjective. Upon examination, however, it is plain that the individual juror is not instructed to apply his subjective concept of what is obscene, but to determine something objective *viz.* "the prurient interest of the average person." This is very similar to what juries are called upon to do in negligence cases where the juror is asked to determine if a person used that degree of care that a "reasonably prudent man" would use. This determination has never been thought to be subjective nor too impractical or difficult to apply. We have confidence in the ability of the Anglo-Saxon jury system to determine obscenity if properly instructed. (See Judge's charge in *Roth* case Appendix I).

Our recommendations are squarely based on the concept that the State has, as the Supreme Court says, a right to enact obscenity legislation based on the "social interest in morality." There is a distinction that should be made between individual morality and the level of general morality which the state needs to protect.

A person's beliefs and practices depend on what he relies on for an authority as to what is right and best. As children grow up, they come under various authorities' influences: parents, relatives, friends, teachers, writers, actors, celebrities, clergymen and a host of others. They are also influenced in various ways by other forces of good and evil.

At every point in life a person has a certain moral character. It is the sum total of what he then believes and practices in the area of right and wrong. This overall moral character is constantly changing under the interplay of the aforementioned influences. Thus if a person accepts higher standards, his moral character improves; if he accepts lower standards, his moral character deteriorates.

Not only does every individual reflect a certain moral character, but so does every group of individuals, a club, a city, a state, or even a nation—*the essence of which is determined by a general consensus of individual standards.* It is, stated another way, the distillation of all the individual moralities or the *level* of morality generally. It is this level, this distillation, this average, this essence, which the state has an interest in protecting. The state protects this level from falling and creates an atmosphere by which it can rise. The obvious morals protected are chastity, modesty, temperance, and self-sacrificing love. The obvious evils being inhibited are lust, excess, adultery, incest, homosexuality, bestiality, masturbation and fornication.

2. Recommended Federal and State Legislation

We recommend: That the United States Codes Sections 1461, 1462, 1463, 1464, 1465 of Title 18, and Section 1305 of Title 19, and Section 4006 of Title 39 be amended to define "obscene" in accordance with our recommended definition of obscenity mentioned above. . . .

We recommend that the Attorney General's Office be required to review for possible prosecution any type of suspected obscenity distributed or about to be distributed, of which he gains knowledge, and which falls into any of the descriptive categories listed below:

1. The Stag Film
2. The Sexploitation Film
3. The Commercial X-rated Film
4. The Commercial Unrated Film
5. Advertisements for X and Unrated Films
6. Underground Sex Publications
7. Underground Newspapers
8. Mimeographed Underground Newspapers

9. Sensational Tabloids
10. Homosexual Magazines
11. Sex-violence Magazines
12. "Spreader" or "Tunnel" Magazines
13. Teenage Sex Magazines
14. Pseudo-Scientific Sex Publications
15. So-called Nudist Magazines
16. Lyrics on Commercially Distributed Rock Records
17. Sex-action Photographs
18. Sex-action Records
19. Sex-action Slides and Tapes
20. Mail Order Advertisements for the Above
21. Paperbacks with themes of: Homosexuality, Sado-masochism, Incest, Bestiality
22. Hardcover Books Devoted to Homosexuality, Sado-masochism, Incest

We advocate the establishment in the office of the Attorney General of each State, a team of one or more skilled attorneys, under the direction of a Deputy Attorney General, to be used to assist in the local prosecutions where intrastate commerce is involved or where federal assistance from the Department of Justice is not readily available.

We advocate the establishment in State Police headquarters of a similar division, working closely with the legal staff just mentioned. The state police have experts in arson, ballistics and other specialties. The formation of a special unit on pornography is long overdue.

We advocate the establishment of a permanent State Commission to examine the laws on obscenity, to make recommendations to the legislature, and recommendations for more effective means of enforcement.

We recommend the establishment of a State Commission to review and classify Motion Pictures and printed materials for minors. . . .

As minimum legislation, we advocate elimination of the phrase "utterly without redeeming social value" in any statute.

Note: The Commission's Majority Report was repudiated by President Richard Nixon, and no action on its recommendations was ever taken in Congress.

INQUIRY

"If the law supposes that," said Mr. Bumble, ...
"the law is an ass, an idiot."

CHARLES DICKENS, *Oliver Twist*

WHAT is a state? What right has a government to legislate and enforce its laws? What controls ought a government exercise over the behavior of its citizenry?

These are complex questions; much rests on the answers one gives to them. Consider the majority and minority reports of the Presidential Commission on Obscenity and Pornography. The question to which the committee addressed itself concerned the extent of the government's province in regulating the materials that citizens can see, read, produce, or distribute. Implicit in that question is the notion that states do have certain rights over their citizens, and difficulties arise in determining exactly what those rights are in particular circumstances. We ought to direct our interest first to that notion.

People do not often raise issue with what we shall call the government's right to govern (Rg for reference). We pay our taxes, we obey traffic laws, we do not rob banks. In effect, our daily behavior is indicative of our tacit assent to Rg. But what does it mean to say the government has a right to anything, let alone to govern? What is a right? In what way do rights, including Rg, arise? On what are they founded? In the case of Rg, a number of possibilities come to mind: (1) divine edict, (2) power as demonstrated through force, (3) consent of the governed, (4) international arrangement.

We need not concern ourselves with (1), for although historically many state sovereignties have been founded on the claim of "divine right," that notion has long since passed out of fashion or has been sufficiently disguised in some other theory as to make its presence all but undetectable.

The view that Rg is founded on overt power demonstrable in terms of coercive force has a good deal of support in historical

examples, but before we investigate (2) it will be wise to clarify what
a right is. In order to do so, let us imagine the following situation:
One man, Jones, is resting on a rock on an island in the middle of
the sea. There is no government of the island, nor even, to Jones's
knowledge, any other resident. To Jones's surprise, Smith appears
from behind a coconut palm and orders Jones off the rock, claiming
that the rock is his and that he is about to sit upon it himself. An
argument arises in which Jones claims the rock and so does Smith.
Such an argument might well center on possession claims, Jones
saying, "This is my rock, get out of here and leave me alone. I saw it
first, I occupied it. You are a usurper!" Smith might well find Jones's
arguments convincing, or at least for the moment he might retreat.
But suppose Jones instead shouts, "I have a right to this rock" or
"Sitting on this rock is my right" or "You have no right to my rock."
Now the situation is different. Jones is claiming not just possession,
but the right of possession. After all, a thief possesses property
although he has no right to it. What then is the difference between
having X and having the right to X (X is usually an action, and the
question should probably be put: What is the difference between
doing X and having the right to do X, e.g., sitting upon the rock?)?
To have the right to do X would seem to entail having been given
leave to do X or permission to do X. On our island, could Jones have
a right to do anything? It would seem best if he were to keep his
arguments to the question of occupation.

The argument for (2), that Rg arises from power, might go something like this: Only those who by whatever means can enforce their
commands by punishing lack of obedience possess the right to
govern. Only those who can exert substantial physical power over
others can with continued success enforce their commands. Hence
only those who can exert physical power over others have the right
to govern. Such an argument might appeal to Jones if Smith were his
physical inferior. Asserting his right to the rock would then come
down to beating Smith over the head. This argument reduces, of
course, to the familiar view that the mightiest have the right to
govern the weaker, and although it has a primitive sound, in slightly
modified fashion it is still often accepted today. Power translates
into financial as well as sheer physical terms; and, of course, in the
case of colonial and military dictatorships, unmasked physical force
purports to support Rg.

There are many important aspects of (2) that should be considered
when weighing its candidacy as the ground of Rg, especially the
question of whether the government that rules by (2) has the right

to govern or only, in fact, governs (Jones has the rock, but not the right to the rock). Rg entails the possession of legitimate authority to command and to be obeyed. If (2) is the ground for Rg, then it follows that the ability to force obedience is equivalent to the right to be obeyed, and that which makes authority legitimate is the power to exercise it.

Imagine that the government of the United States were to fall into the hands of a small junta of military leaders, perhaps the joint chiefs of staff. Undoubtedly they wield immense power and can administer whatever physical force they deem necessary upon the citizenry. They issue a series of edicts demanding various sorts of behavior from the citizens or certain subgroups of citizens. A few of their orders demand that individuals behave in ways that violate their basic moral and/or religious principles. Does the citizenry have the obligation to obey whatever is commanded by the junta? It would appear to be counter to our intuitions for us to maintain that such a body has the right to govern, in spite of its power.

Such problems with (2) have led political philosophers to other grounds for Rg, in particular to various forms of (3). This is the view that Rg is the result of a compact or contractual arrangement between individuals, resulting in the formation of a government and the ordaining of it with certain powers to regulate the behavior of the citizens. By way of illustration, let us return to our island. Smith and Jones decide that the rock issue and any other rights claims could be easily solved if there were some way of establishing permission to possess. Jones argues that if he chisels his name on the rock then he has a right to it, but the clever Mr. Smith points out that artists sign their paintings and the names remain affixed even when they are no longer the artist's property. They decide that they need a way of staking claims and some way of protecting one's claims once properly staked, and Smith convinces Jones that they vest in one of them the power to validate their property claims. Hence they devise an agreement, a contract between them to form a government with regulatory rights, in particular concerning possession of rocks. But is this a solution? In order for Smith and Jones to vest rights in a government, they must have some rights of their own; but what rights have they, and from what source did these rights come? If Jones already has rights, why don't they include the right to sit on the rock? Most contract theorists in political philosophy have argued that men have natural rights. Thomas Jefferson referred to them as inalienable, and among them he identified life, liberty, and the pursuit of happiness. Perhaps property rights are natural rights, and they are the collateral of the social contract. But if Jones already has such rights, would he not be ill-advised to bargain them off to a government that might permit Smith the use and possession of that rock?

Plato argues in the *Republic* that men are naturally social animals and government is a necessity in allowing each man to realize his potential. But such a view does not in itself account for Rg. The international environment suggests that serious consideration be given to some form of the fourth possible ground for Rg. This globe contains just so much land, and, as any political geography map demonstrates, very little land is not partitioned off into political units or states. Every state exercises, in various degrees, control over the lives of those human beings that inhabit it, citizens and noncitizens. If one rejects (1) and (2) and finds difficulties with (3), the possibility still remains that the right to govern is, in part at least, bestowed upon a government not by its citizens but by those other states that occupy the globe. In effect, international agreements in the form of treaties and recognitions bestow Rg upon governments of specific portions of the earth. Haskell Fain argues that the element of international recognition is essential to legitimatize governments. Hence, although inhabitants of a certain section of land may contract to form a "more perfect union," the resultant government lacks the right to govern fully those people living in that area until it has attained international entry into the family of states. Jones and Smith may not know it, but they are residing upon an island in the territorial domain of internationally recognized State Z, and neither has the right to possess the rock despite whatever agreements they ultimately reach, because their government is not a member of the family of internationally recognized states. In Z, by law only those who have registered their rocks with the Bureau of Rocks have the right to possess them.

Perhaps without governments people have no rights. There have been times, usually during international stress, when governments deemed it necessary to suspend all or some of the rights of citizens and noncitizens within their borders. How can such an act be understood?

Assuming for the moment that the question of Rg were settled, another problem arises regarding the rights of the citizen to behave in certain ways. What ought to be the basis for determining the extent of prohibitions that delimit adult behavior? In other words, what controls over private adult behavior ought the state (which possesses the right to govern) exercise? This is really a question about the extent of Rg and could be put in this form: Does the right to govern include the right to regulate the private behavior of adult citizens or adult resident aliens? Many court cases have turned on the philosophical answer to this question.

It has been suggested by some lawyers and philosophers that there is a distinction to be drawn between law and morality, that these are two separate and unrelated concerns. The restraints of morality should not be codified into legal prohibitions on the activities of individuals.

Ask yourself what the real function of laws is. Should laws be designed to mirror moral teachings and to impress the moral views of the majority upon the actions of the members of society as a whole, insuring the continuance of standards the majority thinks good? Or should our laws function entirely outside of moral concern; that is, should they only establish limits on the freedoms of individuals where the lack of a limit would lead to injury of another individual or group? Should law simply keep order? Should law be neutral on moral questions? We may say, when we observe behavior that is offensive to us, "There ought to be a law against that." But consider seriously just which acts found to be offensive ought to be illegal. In large measure that was the task of the Commission on Obscenity and Pornography.

Many people are offended by the sight of nude bodies. Should there be a law against all forms of nudity? Adultery is considered immoral by most Western ethical codes, but should adulterers be made to wear the letter A for the rest of their lives or thrown in jail? What reasons were and are given for laws prohibiting the sale of alcoholic beverages and the use of narcotics? In other words, consider what, if any, so-called moral wrongs ought to be crimes. Murder is certainly both morally wrong and, usually, legally wrong. But some people argue that the same cannot be said of fornication and other private sexual behavior among consenting adults, that law must not impose a particular pattern of moral behavior upon its subjects because we have no objective criterion on morals. Do you find the majority or the minority report of the commission persuasive, and for what reasons?

It may well be that we have created undue criminality. Consider a statement by Sir Herbert Read: "Pornography is a social problem; it is a commodity brought into existence by certain characteristics of a highly developed civilization." Why then are there laws against pornography? The state is surely in the position of limiting personal liberty through law. If it chooses to do so in certain cases, use of narcotics, for example, whom is it protecting from what? In most of the United States, gambling, the use of narcotics, and prostitution are illegal. No one is forced to gamble, use drugs, or contract for the services of a prostitute. Should an act still be illegal when the "victim" consents? The existence of these laws suggests that there is more than the idea of an offended individual involved in the philosophy at the basis of our legal system. Perhaps more philosophical concern should be directed to the notion of the public good.

The Wolfenden Committee in the United Kingdom examined the problems of governmental intervention in the private lives of citizens and concluded that private behavior is no business of the law, a view similar to the majority report of the commission. However, many legal philosophers—most vocally, Lord Devlin—attacked the committee's report on the grounds that laws must be designed to maintain the existence of society and that society, after all, is only a collection of moral attitudes, a view reflected in the minority report. Therefore, Devlin argued, society has not only the right but the obligation to legislate against the deviate moral behavior of individuals, public or private. Such behavior, it is maintained, cannot be allowed to continue or society will crumble from an internal decay of the principles upon which it was founded.

1 PLATO

(427–347 B.C.)

*Crito**

The Crito is set in prison. Socrates is awaiting execution and Crito, one of his students, urges him to escape. Socrates refuses to leave. He explains his reasons to Crito in terms of an imagined conversation between himself and the law. Socrates maintains that loyalty is due the state because it raised and educated him. When punishment is meted out by the exercise of its laws, to seek to escape from such punishment is to do a greater injustice to the state. You would be breaking the implied promise between yourself, your friends and your country. It is better to suffer at the hands of men than to do injury to the state and the law.

* Plato, Crito, 3rd ed., B. Jowett, trans. (Oxford: The Clarendon Press, 1892).

PERSONS OF THE DIALOGUE

SOCRATES   CRITO

SCENE:—The Prison of Socrates

Socrates. Why have you come at this hour, Crito? It must be quite early?

Crito. Yes, certainly.

Socrates. What is the exact time?

Crito. The dawn is breaking.

Socrates. I wonder that the keeper of the prison would let you in.

Crito. He knows me, because I often come, Socrates; moreover, I have done him a kindness.

Socrates. And are you only just arrived?

Crito. No, I came some time ago.

Socrates. Then why did you sit and say nothing, instead of at once awakening me?

Crito. I should not have liked myself, Socrates, to be in such great trouble and unrest as you are—indeed I should not: I have been watching with amazement your peaceful slumbers; and for that reason I did not awake you, because I wished to minimize the pain. I have always thought you to be of a happy disposition; but never did I see anything like the easy, tranquil manner in which you bear this calamity.

Socrates. Why, Crito, when a man has reached my age he ought not to be repining at the approach of death.

Crito. And yet other old men find themselves in similar misfortunes, and age does not prevent them from repining.

Socrates. That is true. But you have not told me why you come at this early hour.

Crito. I come to bring you a message which is sad and painful; not, as I believe, to yourself, but to all of us who are your friends, and saddest of all to me.

Socrates. What? Has the ship come from Delos, on the arrival of which I am to die?

Crito. No, the ship has not actually arrived, but she will probably be here to-day, as persons who have come from Sunium tell me that they left her there; and therefore to-morrow, Socrates, will be the last day of your life.

Socrates. Very well, Crito; if such is the will of God, I am willing; but my belief is that there will be a delay of a day.

Crito. Why do you think so?

Socrates. I will tell you. I am to die on the day after the arrival of the ship.

Crito. Yes; that is what the authorities say.

Socrates. But I do not think that the ship will be here until to-morrow; this I infer from a vision which I had last night, or rather only just now, when you fortunately allowed me to sleep.

Crito. And what was the nature of the vision?

Socrates. There appeared to me the likeness of a woman, fair and comely, clothed in bright raiment, who called to me and said: O Socrates,

'The third day hence to fertile Phthia shalt thou go.'*

Crito. What a singular dream, Socrates!

Socrates. There can be no doubt about the meaning, Crito, I think.

Crito. Yes; the meaning is only too clear. But, oh! my beloved Socrates, let me entreat you once more to take my advice and escape. For if you die I shall not only lose a friend who can never be replaced, but there is another evil: people who do not know you and me will believe that I might have saved you if I had been willing to give money, but that I did not care. Now, can there be a worse disgrace than this— that I should be thought to value money more than the life of a friend?

---

* Homer, *Il* ix. 363.

For the many will not be persuaded that I wanted you to escape, and that you refused.

Socrates. But why, my dear Crito, should we care about the opinion of the many? Good men, and they are the only persons who are worth considering, will think of these things truly as they occurred.

Crito. But you see, Socrates, that the opinion of the many must be regarded, for what is now happening shows that they can do the greatest evil to any one who has lost their good opinion.

Socrates. I only wish it were so, Crito; and that the many could do the greatest evil; for then they would also be able to do the greatest good—and what a fine thing this would be! But in reality they can do neither; for they cannot make a man either wise or foolish; and whatever they do is the result of chance.

Crito. Well, I will not dispute with you; but please to tell me, Socrates, whether you are not acting out of regard to me and your other friends: are you not afraid that if you escape from prison we may get into trouble with the informers for having stolen you away, and lose either the whole or a great part of our property; or that even a worse evil may happen to us? Now, if you fear on our account, be at ease; for in order to save you, we ought surely to run this, or even a greater risk; be persuaded, then, and do as I say.

Socrates. Yes, Crito, that is one fear which you mention, but by no means the only one.

Crito. Fear not—there are persons who are willing to get you out of prison at no great cost; and as for the informers, they are far from being exorbitant in their demands—a little money will satisfy them. I say, therefore, do not hesitate on our account, and do not say, as you did in the court, that you will have a difficulty in knowing what to do with yourself anywhere else. For men will love you in other places to which you may go, and not in Athens only; there are friends of mine in Thessaly, if you like to go to them, who will value and protect you, and no Thessalian will give you any trouble. Nor can I think that you are at all justified, Socrates, in betraying your own life when you might be saved; in acting thus you are playing into the hands of your enemies, who are hurrying on your destruction. And further I should say that you are deserting your own children; for you might bring them up and educate them; instead of which you go away and leave them, and they will have to take their chance; and if they do not meet with the usual fate of orphans, there will be small thanks to you. No man should bring children into the world who is unwilling to persevere to the end in their nurture and education. But you appear to be choosing the easier part, not the better and manlier, which would have been more becoming in one who professes to care for virtue in all his actions, like yourself. And indeed, I am ashamed not only of you, but of us who are your friends, when I reflect that the whole business will be attributed entirely to our want of courage. The trial need never have come on, or might have been managed differently; and this last act, or crowning folly, will seem to have occurred through our negligence and cowardice, who might have saved you, if we had been good for anything; and you might have saved yourself, for there was no difficulty at all. See now, Socrates, how sad and discreditable are the consequences, both to us and you. Make up your mind then, or rather have your mind already made up, for the time of deliberation is over, and there is only one thing to be done, which must be done this very night, and if we delay at all will be no longer practicable or possible; I beseech you therefore, Socrates, be persuaded by me, and do as I say.

Socrates. Dear Crito, your zeal is invaluable, if a right one; but if wrong, the greater the zeal the greater the danger; and therefore we ought to consider whether I shall or shall not do as you say. For I am and always have been one of those natures who must be guided by reason, whatever the reason may be which upon reflection appears to me to be the best; and now that this chance has befallen me, I cannot repudiate my own words: the principles which I have hitherto honoured and revered I still honour, and unless we can at once find other and better principles, I am certain not to agree with you; no, not even if the power of the multitude could inflict many more imprisonments, confiscations, deaths, frightening us like children with hobgoblin terrors. What will be the fairest way of considering the question? Shall I return to your old argument about the opinions of men?—we were saying that some of them are to be regarded, and others not. Now were we right in maintaining this before I was condemned? And has the argument which was once good now proved to be talk for the sake of talking—mere childish nonsense? That is what I want to consider with your help, Crito:—whether, under my present circumstances, the argument appears to be in any way different or not; and is to be allowed by me or disallowed. That argument, which, as I believe, is maintained by many persons of authority, was to the effect, as I was saying, that the opinions of some men are to be regarded, and of other men not to be regarded. Now you, Crito, are not going to die to-morrow—at least, there is no human probability of this—and therefore you are disinterested and not liable to be deceived by the circumstances in which you are placed. Tell me then, whether I am right in saying that some opinions, and the opinions of some men only, are to be valued, and that other opinions, and the opinions of other men, are not to be valued. I ask you whether I was right in maintaining this?

Crito. Certainly.

Socrates. The good are to be regarded, and not the bad?

Crito. Yes.

Socrates. And the opinions of the wise are good, and the opinions of the unwise are evil?

Crito. Certainly.

Socrates. And what was said about another matter? Is the pupil who devotes himself to the practice of gymnastics supposed to attend to the praise and blame and opinion of every man, or of one man only—his physician or trainer, whoever he may be?

Crito. Of one man only.

Socrates. And he ought to fear the censure and welcome the praise of that one only, and not of the many?

Crito. Clearly so.

Socrates. And he ought to act and train, and eat and drink in the way which seems good to his single master who has understanding, rather than according to the opinion of all other men put together?

Crito. True.

Socrates. And if he disobeys and disregards the opinion and approval of the one, and regards the opinion of the many who have no understanding, will he not suffer evil?

Crito. Certainly he will.

Socrates. And what will the evil be, whither tending and what affecting, in the disobedient person?

Crito. Clearly, affecting the body; that is what is destroyed by the evil.

Socrates. Very good; and is not this true, Crito, of other things which we need not separately enumerate? In questions of just and unjust, fair and foul, good and evil, which are the subjects of our present consultation, ought we to follow the opinion of the many and to fear them; or the opinion of the one man who has understanding? ought we not to fear and reverence him more than all the rest of the world: and if we desert him shall we not destroy and injure that principle in us which may be assumed to be improved by justice and deteriorated by injustice;—there is such a principle?

Crito. Certainly there is, Socrates.

Socrates. Take a parallel instance:—if, acting under the advice of those who have no understanding, we destroy that which is improved by health and is deteriorated by disease, would life be worth having?

And that which has been destroyed is—the body?

Crito. Yes.

Socrates. Could we live, having an evil and corrupted body?

Crito. Certainly not.

Socrates. And will life be worth having, if that higher part of man be destroyed, which is improved by justice and depraved by injustice? Do we suppose that principle, whatever it may be in man, which has to do with justice and injustice, to be inferior to the body?

Crito. Certainly not.

Socrates. More honourable than the body?

Crito. Far more.

Socrates. Then, my friend, we must not regard what the many say of us: but what he, the one man who has understanding of just and unjust, will say, and what the truth will say. And therefore you begin in error when you advise that we should regard the opinion of the many about just and unjust, good and evil, honourable and dishonourable.—'Well,' some one will say, 'but the many can kill us.'

Crito. Yes, Socrates; that will clearly be the answer.

Socrates. And it is true: but still I find with surprise that the old argument is unshaken as ever. And I should like to know whether I may say the same of another proposition—that not life, but a good life, is to be chiefly valued?

Crito. Yes, that also remains unshaken.

Socrates. And a good life is equivalent to a just and honourable one —that holds also?

Crito. Yes, it does.

Socrates. From these premises I proceed to argue the question whether I ought or ought not to try and escape without the consent of the Athenians: and if I am clearly right in escaping, then I will make the attempt; but if not, I will abstain. The other considerations which you mention, of money and loss of character and the duty of educating one's children, are, I fear, only the doctrines of the multitude, who would be as ready to restore people to life, if they were able, as they are to put them to death—and with as little reason. But now, since the argument has thus far prevailed, the only question which remains to be considered is, whether we shall do rightly either in escaping or in suffering others to aid in our escape and paying them in money and thanks, or whether in reality we shall not do rightly; and if the latter, then death or any other calamity which may ensue on my remaining here must not be allowed to enter into the calculation.

Crito. I think that you are right, Socrates; how then shall we proceed?

Socrates. Let us consider the matter together, and do you either refute me if you can, and I will be convinced; or else cease, my dear friend, from repeating to me that I ought to escape against the wishes of the Athenians: for I highly value your attempts to persuade me to do so, but I may not be persuaded against my own better judgment. And now please to consider my first position, and try how you can best answer me.

Crito. I will.

Socrates. Are we to say that we are never intentionally to do wrong, or that in one way we ought and in another way we ought not to do wrong, or is doing wrong always evil and dishonourable, as I was just now saying, and as has been already acknowledged by us? Are all our former admissions which were made within a few days to be thrown away? And have we, at our age, been earnestly discoursing with one another all our life long only to discover that we are no better than children? Or, in spite of the opinion of the many, and in spite of consequences whether better or worse, shall we insist on the truth of what was then said, that injustice is always an evil and dishonour to him who acts unjustly? Shall we say so or not?

Crito. Yes.

Socrates. Then we must do no wrong?

Crito. Certainly not.

Socrates. Nor when injured injure in return, as the many imagine; for we must injure no one at all?

Crito. Clearly not.

Socrates. Again, Crito, may we do evil?

Crito. Surely not, Socrates.

Socrates. And what of doing evil in return for evil, which is the morality of the many—is that just or not?

Crito. Not just.

Socrates. For doing evil to another is the same as injuring him?

Crito. Very true.

Socrates. Then we ought not to retaliate or render evil for evil to any one, whatever evil we may have suffered from him. But I would have you consider, Crito, whether you really mean what you are saying. For this opinion has never been held, and never will be held, by any considerable number of persons; and those who are agreed and those who are not agreed upon this point have no common ground, and can only despise one another when they see how widely they differ. Tell me, then, whether you agree with and assent to my first principle, that neither injury nor retaliation nor warding off evil by evil is ever right. And shall that be the premiss of our argument? Or do you decline and dissent from this? For so I have ever thought, and continue to think; but, if you are of another opinion, let me hear what you have to say. If, however, you remain of the same mind as formerly, I will proceed to the next step.

Crito. You may proceed, for I have not changed my mind.

Socrates. Then I will go on to the next point, which may be put in the form of a question:—Ought a man to do what he admits to be right, or ought he to betray the right?

Crito. He ought to do what he thinks right.

Socrates. But if this is true, what is the application? In leaving the prison against the will of the Athenians, do I wrong any? or rather do I not wrong those whom I ought least to wrong? Do I not desert the principles which were acknowledged by us to be just—what do you say?

Crito. I cannot tell, Socrates; for I do not know.

Socrates. Then consider the matter in this way:—Imagine that I am about to play truant (you may call the proceeding by any name which you like), and the laws and the government come and interrogate me: 'Tell us, Socrates,' they say; 'what are you about? are you not going by an act of yours to overturn us—the laws, and the whole state, as far as in you lies? Do you imagine that a state can subsist and not be overthrown, in which the decisions of law have no power, but are set aside and trampled upon by individuals?' What will be our answer, Crito, to these and the like words? Any one, and especially a rhetorician, will have a good deal to say on behalf of the law which requires a sentence to be carried out. He will argue that this law should not be set aside; and shall we reply, 'Yes; but the state has injured us and given an unjust sentence.' Suppose I say that?

Crito. Very good, Socrates.

Socrates. 'And was that our agreement with you?' the law would answer; 'or were you to abide by the sentence of the state?' And if I were to express my astonishment at their words, the law would probably add: 'Answer, Socrates, instead of opening your eyes—you are in the habit of asking and answering questions. Tell us,—What complaint have you to make against us which justifies you in attempting to destroy us and the state? In the first place did we not bring you into existence? Your father married your mother by our aid and begat you. Say whether you have any objection to urge against those of us who regulate marriage?' None, I should reply. 'Or against those of us who after birth regulate the nurture and education of children, in which you also were trained? Were not the laws, which have the charge of education, right in commanding your father to train you in music and gymnastics?' Right, I should reply. 'Well then, since you were brought into the world and nurtured and educated by us, can you deny in the first place that you are our child and slave, as your fathers were before you? And if this is true you are not on equal terms with us, nor can you think that you have a right to do to us what we are doing to you. Would you have any right to strike or revile or do any other evil to your father or your master, if you had one, because you have been struck or reviled by him, or received some other evil at his hands?— you would not say this? And because we think right to destroy you, do you think that you have any right to destroy us in return, and your country as far as in you lies? Will you, O professor of true virtue, pretend that you are justified in this? Has a philosopher like you failed to discover that our country is more to be valued and higher and holier far than mother or father or any ancestor, and more to be regarded in the eyes of the gods and of men of understanding? also to be soothed, and gently and reverently entreated when angry, even more than a father, and either to be persuaded, or if not persuaded, to be obeyed? And when we are punished by her, whether with imprisonment or stripes, the punishment is to be endured in silence; and if she lead us to wounds or death in battle, thither we follow as is right; neither may any one yield or retreat or leave his rank, but whether in battle or in a court of law, or in any other place, he must do what his city and his country order him; or he must change their view of what is just: and if he may do no violence to his father or mother, much less may he do violence to his country.' What answer shall we make to this, Crito? Do the laws speak truly, or do they not?

Crito. I think that they do.

Socrates. Then the laws will say; 'Consider, Socrates, if we are speaking truly that in your present attempt you are going to do us an injury. For, having brought you into the world, and nurtured and educated you, and given you and every other citizen a share in every good which we had to give, we further proclaim to any Athenian by the liberty which we allow him, that if he does not like us when he has become of age and has seen the ways of the city, and made our acquaintance, he may go where he pleases and take his goods with him. None of us laws will forbid him or interfere with him. Any one who does not like us and the city, and who wants to emigrate to a colony or to any other city, may go where he likes, retaining his property. But he who has experience of the manner in which we order justice and administer the state, and still remains, has entered into an implied contract that he will do as we command him. And he who disobeys us is, as we maintain, thrice wrong; first, because in disobeying us he is disobeying his parents; secondly, because we are the authors of his education; thirdly, because he has made an agreement with us that he will duly obey our command; and he neither obeys them nor convinces us that our commands are unjust; and we do not rudely impose them, but give him the alternative of obeying or convincing us;—that is what we offer, and he does neither.

'These are the sort of accusations to which, as we were saying, you, Socrates, will be exposed if you accomplish your intentions; you, above all other Athenians.' Suppose now I ask, why I rather than anybody else? they will justly retort upon me that I above all other men have acknowledged the agreement. 'There is clear proof,' they will say, 'Socrates, that we and the city were not displeasing to you. Of all Athenians you have been the most constant resident in the city, which, as you never leave, you may be supposed to love. For you never went out of the city either to see the games, except once when you went to the Isthmus, or to any other place unless when you were on military service; nor did you travel as other men do. Nor had you any curiosity to know other states or their laws: your affections did not go beyond us and our state; we were your special favourites, and you acquiesced in our government of you; and here in this city you begat your children, which is a proof of your satisfaction. Moreover, you might in the course of the trial, if you had liked, have fixed the penalty at banishment; the state which refuses to let you go now would have let you go then. But you pretended that you preferred death to exile, and that you were not unwilling to die. And now you have forgotten these fine sentiments, and pay no respect to us the laws, of whom you are the destroyer; and are doing what only a miserable slave would do, running away and turning your back upon the compacts and agreements which you made as a citizen. And first of all answer this very question: Are we right in saying that you agreed to be governed according to us in deed, and not in word only? Is that true or not?' How shall we answer, Crito? Must we not assent?

Crito. We cannot help it, Socrates.

Socrates. Then will they not say: 'You, Socrates, are breaking the covenants and agreements which you made with us at your leisure, not in any haste or under any compulsion or deception, but after you have had seventy years to think of them, during which time you were at liberty to leave the city, if we were not to your mind, or if our covenants appeared to you to be unfair. You had your choice, and might have gone either to Lacedaemon or Crete, both which states are often praised by you for their good government, or to some other Hellenic or foreign state. Whereas you, above all other Athenians, seemed to be so fond of the state, or, in other words, of us her laws (and who would care about a state which has no laws?), that you never stirred out of her; the halt, the blind, the maimed were not more stationary in her than you were. And now you run away and forsake your agreements. Not so, Socrates, if you will take our advice; do not make yourself ridiculous by escaping out of the city.

'For just consider, if you transgress and err in this sort of way, what good will you do either to yourself or to your friends? That your friends will be driven into exile and deprived of citizenship, or will lose their property, is tolerably certain; and you yourself, if you fly to one of the neighbouring cities, as, for example, Thebes or Megara, both of which are well governed, will come to them as an enemy, Socrates, and their government will be against you, and all patriotic citizens will cast an evil eye upon you as a subverter of the laws, and you will confirm in the minds of the judges the justice of their own condemnation of you. For he who is a corrupter of the laws is more than likely to be a corrupter of the young and foolish portion of mankind. Will you then flee from well-ordered cities and virtuous men? and is existence worth having on these terms? Or will you go to them without shame, and talk to them, Socrates? And what will you say to them? What you say here about virtue and justice and institutions and laws being the best things among men? Would that be decent of you? Surely not. But if you go away from well-governed states to Crito's friends in Thessaly, where there is great disorder and licence, they will be charmed to hear the tale of your escape from prison, set off with ludicrous particulars of the manner in which you were wrapped in a goatskin or some other disguise, and metamorphosed as the manner is of runaways; but will there be no one to remind you that in your old age you were not ashamed to violate the most sacred laws from a miserable desire of a little more life? Perhaps not, if you keep them in a good temper; but if they are out of temper you will hear many degrading things; you will live, but how?—as the flatterer of all men, and the servant of all men; and doing what?—eating and drinking in Thessaly, having gone abroad in order that you may get a dinner. And where will be your fine sentiments about justice and virtue? Say that you wish to live for the sake of your children—you want to bring them up and educate them—will you take them into Thessaly and deprive them of Athenian citizenship? Is this the benefit which you will confer upon them? Or are you under the impression that they will be better cared for and educated here if you are still alive, although absent from them; for your friends will take care of them? Do you fancy that if you are an inhabitant of Thessaly they will take care of them, and if you are an inhabitant of the other world that they will not take care of them? Nay; but if they who call themselves friends are good for anything, they will—to be sure they will.

'Listen, then, Socrates, to us who have brought you up. Think not of life and children first, and of justice afterwards, but of justice first, that you may be justified before the princes of the world below. For neither will you nor any that belong to you be happier or holier or juster in this life, or happier in another, if you do as Crito bids. Now you depart in innocence, a sufferer and not a doer of evil; a victim, not of the laws but of men. But if you go forth, returning evil for evil, and injury for injury, breaking the covenants and agreements which you have made with us, and wronging those whom you ought least of all to wrong, that is to say, yourself, your friends, your country, and us, we shall be angry with you while you live, and our brethren, the laws in the world below, will receive you as an enemy; for they will know that you have done your best to destroy us. Listen, then, to us and not to Crito.'

This, dear Crito, is the voice which I seem to hear murmuring in my ears, like the sound of the flute in the ears of the mystic; that voice, I say, is humming in my ears, and prevents me from hearing any other. And I know that anything more which you may say will be vain. Yet speak, if you have anything to say.

Crito. I have nothing to say, Socrates.

Socrates. Leave me then, Crito, to fulfil the will of God, and to follow whither he leads.

2   JOHN LOCKE

(1632–1704)

*Second Treatise of Government**

*Locke's political theory has played a major role in the philosophical
foundations of our form of government. For Locke, people in a state of nature
are equally endowed with certain rights, such as life, liberty, and property.
The state of nature, in fact, would be an ideal situation, but some people are
always tempted to intrude upon the rights of others and warfare
results. The majority of people, while attempting to preserve their rights, band
together for protection and place some of their rights in the hands of the
government. Government must be founded on the consent of the
governed. If a government exceeds its established authority and threatens
the personal rights of its citizens, then it must be overthrown. But Locke
does not counsel hasty revolution. Acts of a tyrannical government must
span a number of years to warrant the turmoil of revolt.*

* John Locke, *Two Treatises of Government* (1764), selections from "The
Second Treatise." You might also refer to *Two Treatises of Government*
(London: Thomas Tegg, 1823), Vol. V.

TO understand political power right, and derive it from its original,
we must consider what state all men are naturally in, and that is,
a state of perfect freedom to order their actions and dispose of their
possessions and persons, as they think fit, within the bounds of the
law of nature; without asking leave, or depending upon the will of
any other man.

A state also of equality, wherein all the power and jurisdiction is
reciprocal, no one having more than another; there being nothing more
evident than that creatures of the same species and rank, promiscuously
born to all the same advantages of nature, and the use of the same
faculties, would also be equal one amongst another without subordination or subjection; unless the Lord and Master of them all should, by
any manifest declaration of his will, set one above another, and confer
on him, by an evident and clear appointment, an undoubted right to
dominion and sovereignty.

. . .

Men being, as has been said, by nature all free, equal, and independent, no one can be put out of this estate and subjected to the

political power of another without his own consent. The only way whereby any one divests himself of his natural liberty and puts on the bonds of civil society is by agreeing with other men to join and unite into a community for their comfortable, safe, and peaceable living one amongst another, in a secure enjoyment of their properties and a greater security against any that are not of it. This any number of men may do, because it injures not the freedom of the rest; they are left as they were in the liberty of the state of nature. When any number of men have so consented to make one community or government, they are thereby presently incorporated and make one body politic wherein the majority have a right to act and conclude the rest.

For when any number of men have, by the consent of every individual, made a community, they have thereby made that community one body, with a power to act as one body, which is only by the will and determination of the majority; for that which acts any community being only the consent of the individuals of it, and it being necessary to that which is one body to move one way, it is necessary the body should move that way whither the greater force carries it, which is the consent of the majority; or else it is impossible it should act or continue one body, one community, which the consent of every individual that united into it agreed that it should; and so every one is bound by that consent to be concluded by the majority. And therefore we see that in assemblies impowered to act by positive laws, where no number is set by that positive law which impowers them, the act of the majority passes for the act of the whole and, of course, determines, as having by the law of nature and reason the power of the whole.

And thus every man, by consenting with others to make one body politic under one government, puts himself under an obligation to every one of that society to submit to the determination of the majority and to be concluded by it; or else this original compact, whereby he with others incorporates into one society, would signify nothing, and be no compact, if he be left free and under no other ties than he was in before in the state of nature. For what appearance would there be of any compact? What new engagement if he were no further tied by any decrees of the society than he himself thought fit and did actually consent to? This would be still as great a liberty as he himself had before his compact, or any one else in the state of nature has who may submit himself and consent to any acts of it if he thinks fit.

For if the consent of the majority shall not in reason be received as the act of the whole and conclude every individual, nothing but the consent of every individual can make anything to be the act of the whole; but such a consent is next to impossible ever to be had if we

consider the infirmities of health and avocations of business which in
a number, though much less than that of a commonwealth, will necessarily keep many away from the public assembly. To which, if we
add the variety of opinions and contrariety of interests which unavoid-
ably happen in all collections of men, the coming into society upon
such terms would be only like Cato's coming into the theatre only to
go out again. Such a constitution as this would make the mighty
leviathan of a shorter duration than the feeblest creatures, and not let
it outlast the day it was born in; which cannot be supposed till we can
think that rational creatures should desire and constitute societies only
to be dissolved; for where the majority cannot conclude the rest, there
they cannot act as one body, and consequently will be immediately
dissolved again.

Whosoever, therefore, out of a state of nature unite into a community must be understood to give up all the power necessary to the
ends for which they unite into society to the majority of the community,
unless they expressly agreed in any number greater than the majority.
And this is done by barely agreeing to unite into one political society,
which is all the compact that is, or needs be, between the individuals
that enter into or make up a commonwealth. And thus that which
begins and actually constitutes any political society is nothing but the
consent of any number of freemen capable of a majority to unite and
incorporate into such a society. And this is that, and that only, which
did or could give beginning to any lawful government in the world.

. . .

Every man being, as has been shown, naturally free, and nothing
being able to put him into subjection to any earthly power but only
his own consent, it is to be considered what shall be understood to be
a sufficient declaration of a man's consent to make him subject to the
laws of any government. There is a common distinction of an express
and a tacit consent which will concern our present case. Nobody
doubts but an express consent of any man entering into any society
makes him a perfect member of that society, a subject of that government. The difficulty is, what ought to be looked upon as a tacit consent, and how far it binds—i.e., how far any one shall be looked upon
to have consented and thereby submitted to any government, where
he has made no expressions of it at all. And to this I say that every
man that has any possessions or enjoyment of any part of the dominions
of any government does thereby give his tacit consent and is as far
forth obliged to obedience to the laws of that government, during such
enjoyment, as anyone under it; whether this his possession be of land
to him and his heirs for ever, or a lodging only for a week, or whether

it be barely traveling freely on the highway; and, in effect, it reaches as far as the very being of anyone within the territories of that government.

To understand this the better, it is fit to consider that every man, when he at first incorporates himself into any commonwealth, he, by his uniting himself thereunto, annexes also, and submits to the community, those possessions which he has or shall acquire that do not already belong to any other government; for it would be a direct contradiction for any one to enter into society with others for the securing and regulating of property, and yet to suppose his land, whose property is to be regulated by the laws of the society, should be exempt from the jurisdiction of that government to which he himself, the proprietor of the land, is a subject. By the same act, therefore, whereby any one unites his person, which was before free, to any commonwealth, by the same he unites his possessions which were before free to it also; and they become, both of them, person and possession, subject to the government and dominion of that commonwealth as long as it has a being. Whoever, therefore, from thenceforth by inheritance, purchase, permission, or otherwise, enjoys any part of the land so annexed to, and under the government of that commonwealth, must take it with the condition it is under—that is, of submitting to the government of the commonwealth under whose jurisdiction it is as far forth as any subject of it.

But since the government has a direct jurisdiction only over the land, and reaches the possessor of it—before he has actually incorporated himself in the society—only as he dwells upon and enjoys that, the obligation anyone is under by virtue of such enjoyment, to submit to the government, begins and ends with the enjoyment; so that whenever the owner, who has given nothing but such a tacit consent to the government, will, by donation, sale, or otherwise, quit the said possession, he is at liberty to go and incorporate himself into any other commonwealth, or to agree with others to begin a new one *in vacuis locis,* in any part of the world they can find free and unpossessed. Whereas he that has once, by actual agreement and any express declaration, given his consent to be of any commonwealth is perpetually and indispensably obliged to be and remain unalterably a subject to it, and can never be again in the liberty of the state of nature, unless by any calamity the government he was under comes to be dissolved, or else, by some public act, cuts him off from being any longer a member of it.

But submitting to the laws of any country, living quietly and enjoying privileges and protection under them, makes not a man a member of that society; this is only a local protection and homage due to and from all those who, not being in a state of war, come within the territories belonging to any government, to all parts whereof the force of its laws extends. But this no more makes a man a member of that society, a perpetual subject of that commonwealth, than it would make a man subject to another in whose family he found it convenient to abide for some time, though, while he continued in it, he were obliged to comply with the laws and submit to the government he found there. And thus we see that foreigners, by living all their lives under another government and enjoying the privileges and protection of it, though they are bound, even in conscience, to submit to its administration as far forth as any denizen, yet do not thereby come to be subjects or members of that commonwealth. Nothing can make any man so but his actually entering into it by positive engagement and express promise and compact. That is that which I think concerning the beginning of political societies and that consent which makes any one a member of any commonwealth.

If man in the state of nature be so free, as has been said, if he be absolute lord of his own person and possessions, equal to the greatest, and subject to nobody, why will he part with his freedom, why will he give up his empire and subject himself to the dominion and control of any other power? To which it is obvious to answer that though in the state of nature he has such a right, yet the enjoyment of it is very uncertain and constantly exposed to the invasion of others; for all being kings as much as he, every man his equal, and the greater part no strict observers of equity and justice, the enjoyment of the property he has in this state is very unsafe, very unsecure. This makes him willing to quit a condition which, however free, is full of fears and continual dangers; and it is not without reason that he seeks out and is willing to join in society with others who are already united, or have a mind to unite, for the mutual preservation of their lives, liberties, and estates, which I call by the general name 'property.'

The great and chief end, therefore, of men's uniting into commonwealths and putting themselves under government is the preservation of their property. To which in the state of nature there are many things wanting:

First, there wants an established, settled, known law, received and allowed by common consent to be the standard of right and wrong and the common measure to decide all controversies between them; for though the law of nature be plain and intelligible to all rational creatures, yet men, being biased by their interest as well as ignorant for want of studying it, are not apt to allow of it as a law binding to them in the application of it to their particular cases.

Secondly, in the state of nature there wants a known and indifferent judge with authority to determine all differences according to the established law; for every one in that state being both judge and executioner of the law of nature, men being partial to themselves, passion and revenge is very apt to carry them too far and with too much heat in their own cases, as well as negligence and unconcernedness to make them too remiss in other men's.

Thirdly, in the state of nature there often wants power to back and support the sentence when right, and to give it due execution. They who by any injustice offend will seldom fail, where they are able, by force, to make good their injustice; such resistance many times makes the punishment dangerous and frequently destructive to those who attempt it.

Thus mankind, notwithstanding all the privileges of the state of nature, being but in an ill condition while they remain in it, are quickly driven into society. Hence it comes to pass that we seldom find any number of men live any time together in this state. The inconveniences that they are therein exposed to by the irregular and uncertain exercise of the power every man has of punishing the transgressions of others make them take sanctuary under the established laws of government and therein seek the preservation of their property. It is this makes them so willingly give up every one his single power of punishing, to be exercised by such alone as shall be appointed to it amongst them; and by such rules as the community, or those authorized by them to that purpose, shall agree on. And in this we have the original right of both the legislative and executive power, as well as of the governments and societies themselves.

For in the state of nature, to omit the liberty he has of innocent delights, a man has two powers:

The first is to do whatsoever he thinks fit for the preservation of himself and others within the permission of the law of nature, by which law, common to them all, he and all the rest of mankind are one community, make up one society, distinct from all other creatures. And, were it not for the corruption and viciousness of degenerate men, there would be no need of any other, no necessity that men should separate from this great and natural community and by positive agreements combine into smaller and divided associations.

The other power a man has in the state of nature is the power to punish the crimes committed against the law. Both these he gives up when he joins in a private, if I may so call it, or particular politic society and incorporates into any commonwealth separate from the rest of mankind.

The first power, viz., of doing whatsoever he thought fit for the preservation of himself and the rest of mankind, he gives up to be regulated by laws made by the society, so far forth as the preservation of himself and the rest of that society shall require; which laws of the society in many things confine the liberty he had by the law of nature.

Secondly, the power of punishing he wholly gives up, and engages his natural force—which he might before employ in the execution of the law of nature by his own single authority, as he thought fit—to assist the executive power of the society, as the law thereof shall require; for being now in a new state, wherein he is to enjoy many conveniences from the labor, assistance, and society of others in the same community as well as protection from its whole strength, he is to part also with as much of his natural liberty, in providing for himself, as the good, prosperity, and safety of the society shall require, which is not only necessary, but just, since the other members of the society do the like.

But though men when they enter into society give up the equality, liberty, and executive power they had in the state of nature into the hands of the society, to be so far disposed of by the legislative as the good of the society shall require, yet it being only with an intention in every one the better to preserve himself, his liberty and property—for no rational creature can be supposed to change his condition with an intention to be worse—the power of the society, or legislative constituted by them, can never be supposed to extend farther than the common good, but is obliged to secure every one's property by providing against those three defects above-mentioned that made the state of nature so unsafe and uneasy. And so whoever has the legislative or supreme power of any commonwealth is bound to govern by established standing laws, promulgated and known to the people, and not by extemporary decrees; by indifferent and upright judges who are to decide controversies by those laws; and to employ the force of the community at home only in the execution of such laws, or abroad to prevent or redress foreign injuries, and secure the community from inroads and invasion. And all this to be directed to no other end by the peace, safety, and public good of the people.

. . .

Wherever law ends, tyranny begins if the law be transgressed to another's harm. And whosoever in authority exceeds the power given him by the law, and makes use of the force he has under his command to compass that upon the subject which the law allows not, ceases in that to be a magistrate and, acting without authority, may be opposed as any other man who by force invades the right of another. This is acknowledged in subordinate magistrates. He that has authority to seize my person in the street may be opposed as a thief and a robber if he endeavors to break into my house to execute a writ, notwithstanding that I know he has such a warrant and such a legal authority as will empower him to arrest me abroad. And why this should not hold in the highest as well as in the most inferior magistrate, I would gladly be informed. Exceeding the bounds of authority is no more a right in a great than in a petty officer, no more justifiable in a king than in a constable; but is so much the worse in him in that he has more trust put in him, has already a much greater share than the rest of his brethren, and is supposed, from the advantages of his education, employment, and counselors, to be more knowing in the measures of right and wrong.

May the commands, then, of a prince be opposed? May he be resisted as often as any one shall find himself aggrieved, and but imagine he has not right done him? This will unhinge and overturn all politics, and, instead of government and order, leave nothing but anarchy and confusion.

To this I answer that force is to be opposed to nothing but to unjust and unlawful force; whoever makes any opposition in any other case draws on himself a just condemnation both from God and man.

Revolutions happen not upon every little mismanagement in public affairs. Great mistakes in the ruling part, many wrong and inconvenient laws, and all the slips of human frailty will be born by the people without mutiny or murmur. But if a long train of abuses, prevarications, and artifices, all tending the same way, make the design visible to the people, and they cannot but feel what they lie under and see whither they are going, it is not to be wondered that they should then rouse themselves and endeavor to put the rule into such hands which may secure to them the ends for which government was at first erected, and without which ancient names and specious forms are so far from being better that they are much worse than the state of nature or pure anarchy—the inconveniences being all as great and as near, but the remedy farther off and more difficult.

The doctrine of a power in the people of providing for their safety anew by a new legislative, when their legislators have acted contrary to their trust by invading their property, is the best fence against rebellion, and the probablest means to hinder it; for rebellion being an opposition, not to persons, but authority which is founded only in the constitutions and laws of the government. . . .

Who shall be judge whether the prince or legislative act contrary to their trust? This, perhaps, ill-affected and factious men may spread

amongst the people, when the prince only makes use of his due prerogative. To this I reply: The people shall be judge; for who shall be
judge whether his trustee or deputy acts well and according to the
trust reposed in him but he who deputes him and must, by having
deputed him, have still a power to discard him when he fails in his
trust? If this be reasonable in particular cases of private men, why
should it be otherwise in that of the greatest moment where the welfare
of millions is concerned, and also where the evil, if not prevented, is
greater and the redress very difficult, dear, and dangerous?

But further, this question, Who shall be judge? cannot mean that
there is no judge at all; for where there is no judicature on earth to
decide controversies amongst men, God in heaven is Judge. He alone,
it is true, is Judge of the right. But every man is judge for himself, as
in all other cases, so in this, whether another has put himself into a state
of war with him, and whether he should appeal to the Supreme Judge.

If a controversy arise betwixt a prince and some of the people in a
matter where the law is silent or doubtful, and the thing be of great
consequence, I should think the proper umpire in such a case should
be the body of the people; for in cases where the prince has a trust
reposed in him and is dispensed from the common ordinary rules of
the law, there, if any men find themselves aggrieved and think the
prince acts contrary to or beyond that trust, who so proper to judge as
the body of the people (who, at first, lodged that trust in him) how far
they meant it should extend? But if the prince, or whoever they be in
the administration, decline that way of determination, the appeal then
lies nowhere but to heaven; force between either persons who have no
known superior on earth, or which permits no appeal to a judge on
earth, being properly a state of war wherein the appeal lies only to
heaven; and in that state the injured party must judge for himself
when he will think fit to make use of that appeal and put himself
upon it.

To conclude, the power that every individual gave the society when
he entered into it can never revert to the individuals again as long as
the society lasts, but will always remain in the community, because
without this there can be no community, no commonwealth, which is
contrary to the original agreement; so also when the society has placed
the legislative in any assembly of men, to continue in them and their
successors with direction and authority for providing such successors,
the legislative can never revert to the people while that government
lasts, because having provided a legislative with power to continue
for ever, they have given up their political power to the legislative and
cannot resume it. But if they have set limits to the duration of their

legislative and made this supreme power in any person or assembly only temporary, or else when by the miscarriages of those in authority it is forfeited, upon the forfeiture, or at the determination of the time set, it reverts to the society, and the people have a right to act as supreme and continue the legislative in themselves, or erect a new form, or under the old form place it in new hands, as they think good.

3

HASKELL FAIN

(1926–   )

*The Idea of the State**

*Fain's analysis of the idea of the state is quite different from that of traditional
Western political philosophers. As we have seen with Locke, the usual starting point
when considering the origins of the right to govern a state is the agreement by
citizens to be governed. Fain is not content to accept such a view, because it is
not, he points out, consistent with the international situation. The globe is composed
of a certain amount of land, most of which is under the rule of governments whose
legitimacy is more a matter of international agreement often solidified in the act of
recognition than a matter of citizen consent. Hence, in terms of the external
conditions of being a state, a state must have a central government, territory and
recognition by other states, and not necessarily consent of the governed.*

* Haskell Fain, "The Idea of the State," *Noûs*, 1972, pp 15–20. Used by permission
of the author and the Editor.

IF The State did not exist, man would find it necessary to invent it. No
political arrangement has been so extravagantly worshipped. No
arrangement has served as the scape-goat for so many sins. "The State,"
Hegel proclaimed, "is the Divine Idea as it exists on earth." ([5], p. 39)
"The State—any State, whether monarchy or republic," Bakunin maintained, "is the negation of humanity." ([1], p. 143)

Does The State exist? And if it exists, is it omnipotent and benevolent, as Fichte, Hegel and Bosanquet thought; or is it omnipotent and
malevolent, as Godwin, Bakunin and Kropotkin thought; or is it benevolent but not omnipotent, as Locke and J. S. Mill thought; or is it
just plain omnipotent, as Hobbes and Lyndon Baines Johnson thought?
Or perhaps The State does not really exist after all. Randolph Bourne,
writing just before his death in 1918, presented a feverish double vision
of two Americas, each having its own history: ([2], p. 230)

> The history of America as a country is quite different from that of
> America as a State. In one case it is the drama of the pioneering
> conquest of the land, of the growth of wealth and the ways in which
> it was used, of the enterprise of education, and the carrying out of
> spiritual ideals, of the struggle of economic classes. But as a State, its
> history is that of playing a part in the world, making war, obstructing
> international trade, preventing itself from being split to pieces, punish-

ing those citizens whom society agrees are offensive, and collecting money to pay for all. . . .

In times of peace, the American State lies dormant, the history of America revealing the benign American Nation. During war, however, the American State awakes and crushes the nation: "War is the health of the State." ([2], p. 145) What is Jerry Rubin invoking when he spells "America" with a "k"? Is The State just a bogey man, invoked to spook us when, tired and depressed by our inability to avert national disaster, we are ready to believe that there are terminal malignancies in the American body politic?

The State may not exist, but states certainly do. They are as real as flags, passports, dispiriting post offices, and brown wooden chairs. The term "Amerika"—as well as its less Kafka-esque equivalent "United States"—has a much clearer referent than, say, the expression "the American Nation" and certainly more so than "the Woodstock Nation." The principles of individuation of states are much less controversial, conceptually (but not politically) speaking, than those of societies, cultures, peoples or communities. Unlike nations and peoples, states must of necessity be individuated geographically. Peoples, even nations, can migrate from place to place but *Der Staat* remains more or less fixed in place. Two societies can intermingle without clear boundary markers to set them off, but unsettled geographical borders are always a potential *causus belli* for states. The territorial aspect is one of two central ingredients of statehood: the scope of a state's sovereignty—the domain of a state's laws—is primarily defined by geography and only secondarily by persons. When the conquistadors brought the armies of Spain to South America, that continent was, from the European point of view, stateless. Accordingly, the deciding factor in determining that the laws of Spain applied to the territory was the nationality of its conquerors. Usually, though, the situation is the other way around: the territory determines which laws apply to which persons without regard to their nationality. I shall return to this crucial point later on.

The second main ingredient of statehood is government—but government of a certain kind. The anthropologists M. Fortes and E. E. Evans-Pritchard, in a survey of various African societies, classified the political systems they studied into two main categories: a) societies "with centralized authority, administrative machinery and judicial institutions" ([3], p. 5) and b) societies which lacked them. The former were labelled "primitive states," the latter "stateless" societies. Sharp differences in the distribution of wealth, status and privileges, corresponding to the distribution of power and authority, were observed in all primitive states. Stateless societies, on the other hand, had no great distinctions between the rank, status, or wealth of their members. The Tallensi of the Northern Gold Coast, a stateless society, well recognize political authority and obligation. Political authority among them is usually vested in the oldest male of an agnatic lineage chain. The basic social organization consists of clan-like settlements, each made up of several different lineage groups. Thus, in a clan settlement consisting of two lineage groups, the members of the different lineages will owe primary political allegience to different senior males, neither of whom may reside in the clan settlement itself. To complicate things further, all members of a clan settlement pretend that they really have a common lineage; the rules of exogamy extend to one's clan as well as to one's lineage. As a result, there is a complex network of political loyalties, the members of each clan settlement recognizing at least two political authorities. The chains of political authority do not converge, for Tallensi society is acephalus. "Twenty-five years ago," Fortes writes, ([4], pp. 240–1)

> there was no one who had authority over all the Tallensi; no one who could exact tax, tribute or service from all. They never united for war, or self-protection against a common enemy. They had, in short, no 'tribal' government or 'tribal' citizenship, no centralized State exercising legislative, administrative, juridical, and military functions in the interests of the whole society. Until British rule made them the subjects of a foreign State, obliged to render certain services and to obey certain laws and entitled in return to protection and freedom of movement, it was dangerous for anybody to travel outside his own community, except under the safe-conduct of kinsmen in other clans.

The disadvantages of having no central authority to keep the peace were somewhat compensated for by the fact that wars, when they occasionally broke out between groups of Tallensi clans, lasted for no more than two or three days. It was not simply that the Tallensi had an unnatural distaste for killing in-laws likely to be residing in those clans with whom they went to war; rather, the lack of central authority made it difficult to organize for prolonged war.

The main ingredients of statehood, then, are the concepts of territorial sovereignty and central government. The government of a state exhibits "chains of command" converging at an apex, and the scope of the central government directives is conceived as applying to a piece of well-defined territory. Apparently these two defining features of statehood always appear together. In the one group of societies described by Fortes and Evans-Pritchard, "the administrative unit is a territorial unit; political rights and obligations are territorially de-limited . . . the head of the state is a territorial ruler." "In the other group of societies," however, "there are no territorial units defined by an administrative system . . ." ([3], p. 10)

Once one has laid aside the Idea of the State, is there anything left that is philosophically interesting about the concept of statehood? I have pointed to the notion of territorial dominion as a major ingredient in the concept of statehood, but this is a feature given only passing notice by philosophers. The focus of orthodox political philosophy has been the connection between citizen and government, a relationship which would appear to have no geographical component whatever. When the word "state" occurs in political theory, it is generally used as a stand-in for "government." Ordinary usage partially supports this: we speak of state property and state employees when we mean prop-erty owned by the government and persons employed by the govern-ment. Sometimes philosophers will confuse the relationship between state and resident with that of state and subject. The term "subject" is appropriate when one refers to citizens living under a certain kind of government: A British subject and a French citizen differ in that one of them presently lacks a non-bald monarch. The state-subject re-lationship, as it is usually conceived, is simply the relationship between government and citizen; both relationships are treated as if neither contained a geographical component. Anarchists have at times con-tributed to the confusion of a state with its government by not making clear whether they were calling for the dissolution of the state, or for the abolition of government, or both.

The citizen-resident, in a modern state, has no more political control over affairs of state than does the resident-alien. Democracies, as states, function much the same as states governed by so-called "autocratic" regimes. The foreign policies pursued by a state can create unwar-ranted and often unwanted institutional obligations. The citizen not only endures the hardships imposed by his state's foreign policy but, in the end, is expected to share the blame, the reparations, for his state's misadventures in its dealings with other states. Citizens differ from aliens in that the former are given at least a ceremonial role in the determination of a government's domestic policies. When, however, it comes to foreign policy which involves the dealings of one state with another, the citizen-resident simply has no more role to play than the resident-alien. What is needed in political philosophy is an orientation that puts these facts in proper perspective, that makes room for the concept of the state by fixing upon the relationship residents have to states rather than the relationship citizens have to governments.

Political philosophers have been concerned, almost exclusively, with certain kinds of relationships which citizens supposedly have to their own government and to no other government. They generally assume that certain types of fundamental arrangements between citizens, or between citizens and their government, can generate systems of political rights and obligations. Formerly, philosophers usually thought about such matters in terms of a specific transaction—a contract. In recent times, however, philosophers have been interested more in the arrangements possible between citizens and government which could maintain various systems of rights and obligations. The shift in emphasis from transaction to arrangement reflects a certain realism. The lesson contained in Hume's "Of the Original Contract" has not been wholly forgotten. Yet though philosophers may disagree about the extent to which the rights and obligations of actual societies reflect fundamental arrangements, almost all agree that it is at least *theoretically* possible that *some* arrangement between citizens and governments can generate the following system:

1. Every citizen has a *prima facie* obligation to obey some governmental directives whose scope includes all citizens, whether such directives be in the form of law or executive order.

2. The government has the right to have some of its directives obeyed, where the scope of the directives includes all citizens.

3. The government has the right to punish any citizen, by death if necessary, for violations of any of its legislative enactments.

4. The government has the *prima facie* obligation to protect any and all citizen rights, whether those rights are "residual" or created directly by governmental order.

The above list, of course, is not exhaustive. Nor are (1)–(4) thought to be independent. It is widely believed, for example, that (1) is logically equivalent with (2)—that the obligation to obey is correlative with the right to command. Political philosophers differ in their assessments of the extent to which the system of mutual rights and obligations of citizens and *existing* government can be traced to some fundamental generic relationship or transaction. Anglo-American political philosophers have usually confined themselves to the rights and obligations of citizens living under a democratic form of government and have not bothered about the rights and obligations of, say, German citizens and the German government under the Third *Reich*. The reason for this preoccupation with democratic forms of government is plain. Only a sub-class of political rights and obligations is usually considered to be of philosophical interest: namely, those rights and obligations which can be morally rationalized. Democracy is generally reputed to be the fairest form of government, and it is natural to suppose that it is easier to justify political and legal rights and obligations in a democracy than in other forms of government.

Philosophers, in addition to an interest in possible moral justifications of political and legal rights and obligations, have been concerned with the problem of legitimacy, or authority. The problem is often dramatized as one of distinguishing between the tax collector and the highwayman. One is in either case obliged to part with one's money; however, it is presumed that, in addition to paying the tax collector because of fear of punishment for noncompliance, one is also *obligated* to do so. The general problem of authority, then, is taken to be that of accounting for the legitimacy of government as it is exhibited in the authority of the tax collector. Furthermore, the problem of morally justifying the political obligations of citizens is often taken to be one and the same problem as that of accounting for the legitimacy of government. Many philosophers have feared that, were it to prove impossible to justify a citizen's obligation to obey, the authority of government would prove illusory. However, one philosopher, Robert Paul Wolff, exploits this line of thought in an opposite direction. Taking a position he professes to be anarchist, Wolff argues, *modus tolendo-ly*, that since obedience to law always constitutes a surrender of moral autonomy, and one is morally obligated never to surrender moral autonomy, one is never obligated to obey governmental directives. Furthermore, because governments are legitimate only if citizens are obligated to obey them, the demonstration that citizens are not obligated to obey is tantamount to undermining all claims of legitimacy: ([7], p. 19)

> The dilemmas which we have posed can be succinctly expressed in terms of the concept of a *de jure* state. If all men have a continuing obligation to achieve the highest degree of autonomy possible, then there would appear no state whose subjects have a moral obligation to obey its commands. Hence, the concept of a *de jure* legitimate state would appear to be vacuous and philosophical anarchism would seem to be the only reasonable political belief for an enlightened man.

One may quarrel with Wolff's argument in any number of ways. Wolff's general position, which I do not propose to discuss, would seem to have the disturbing consequence that any promise constitutes, in some way, a surrender of autonomy. Wolff's argument is instructive, nonetheless, for it makes use of a number of widely-held assumptions—assumptions which I intend to challenge. Note, to begin with, that Wolff draws no distinction between the concepts of state and government. Indeed, he defines a state as "a group of persons who have and exercise supreme authority within a given territory" ([7], p. 5), a definition that would seem to make the concept of state identical with that of its government—unless, of course, one follows Rousseau in supposing that the "group of persons who have and exercise supreme authority within a given territory" must be the entire body politic, and not merely its governing subset. But the authority relationship between a state and its subjects may not be the same as the authority relationship between a state and those who inhabit its territory, if only because the class of state subjects is not identical with the class of residents of the territory over which that state exercises sovereignty. What is more, the sovereignty of a modern state over its territory cannot be explained in terms of some transaction or arrangement which the subjects of that state might have had with their government. Statehood primarily involves an arrangement between states, a feature of state sovereignty that is of paramount importance. The authority of a state over its territory is independent of any obligations its subjects may or may not have to obey its directives, as I shall show.

What role, then, does the geographical component play in determining rights and obligations? I stated earlier that almost all philosophers would agree that, *theoretically*, certain arrangements between citizens and their government can generate systems of political rights and obligations. I listed four components of such a system. Consider one of them: the right of the government to punish, by death if necessary, any of its citizens for violation of any of its legislative enactments. Now I have deliberately phrased that right in provocative form in order to call attention to the use of the term "theoretically"; *theoretically*, some arrangements between citizens are supposed to generate that right, at least according to classical theory. Is the objection that an ordinance forbidding spitting on subways ought never to have the death penalty attached to it? But what if citizens were dying of plague and spitting contributed to its spread? The stock arguments against the death penalty do not deny the ultimate *right* of a government to employ it. How can such a governmental right be theoretically generated? Let us suppose that the United States government, wishing to form a more perfect union, submits to its citizens a petition requesting that right; further, that the petition receives universal ratification. Now surely, even if the government did not have the right to punish by death any U.S. citizen prior to ratification of its petition, it seems as if it must have that right after the petition has been universally ratified. It would appear, then, that, theoretically, the citizens of the U.S. *could* grant the U.S. government the right to punish any citizen for any violation of its legislative enactments. At least it *seems* so as long as one focuses on the relationship of citizen to government and neglects to consider that the sovereignty of the U.S. government is limited by geographical boundaries. The citizens of the United States simply cannot grant the U.S. government the right to punish U.S. citizens for violations of U.S. law *wherever* such violations occur. Since no government of any state has a right to punish its citizens for violation of its laws wherever such violations occur—unless, of course, it is given that right by arrangement with *all other states*—it is idle to seek the sole foundation of that right in some special arrangement or transaction a government has *with its citizens*. Conversely, because the government of a state does have the right to punish crime in its own territory, whether committed by any resident, alien or citizen, why seek the foundation of that right in some arrangement of citizenry; or suppose that the right to punish aliens is somehow different from the right to punish citizens? Then, we may ask, what of the *rights* or *authority* of a government of a state over its own territory, as well as the *obligation* to obey on the parts of those who happen to be spatially located in that territory? How are these rights and obligations related? Can they be theoretically founded solely upon special arrangements or transactions of citizenry?

The root of many philosophical justifications of political obligation is contained in the idea that citizens, unless they have special obligations, are free to leave their own state and reside wherever they choose. It is surely unjust for a state to forbid, without any reason, its citizens from leaving its borders. With certain exceptions, however, the government of a given state has no right to have its directives obeyed by those of its subjects who reside in another state. Except during international crisis, citizens of various states are scattered over the globe. Their primary legal obligation is to the state in which they reside, and not to the country of which they are citizens. The geographical element of statehood overrides almost all other considerations.

It is widely thought that the political authority a state exercises over its territory is solely a function of the obligations its subjects have to obey its directives: that the obligation to obey generates the authority to command; even worse, that the authority to command generates the *right* to be obeyed—as if a person could complain about having his *rights* violated when those, over whom he had authority, disobeyed his commands. Not even parental right includes *the right* to obedience, though it carries with it *the obligation* to exact obedience on certain occasions. For those wedded to the correlativity of rights and obligations doctrine, let them seek the correlative of the right to command, not in the obligation to obey, but in the obligation not to usurp. A state's authority over a territory is conceptually quite independent of any obligations its residents may have to obey its directives. The locus of the political authority of the state is not to be found in fundamental arrangements of its subjects, as conceived so often in traditional political philosophy. Rather, it is founded upon arrangements with *other states*.

Imagine, if you will, the Woodstock Nation getting it all together, on rafts gently drifting in the middle of the Sargasso Sea, there with solemn compact to form a new government and live upon kelp and seaweed. Statehood is not for them. Their obligations and loyalties are to each other; the scope of their government's sovereignty includes only The Nation. The Woodstock Nation *could not* become a state, no matter how many oaths of fealty, pacts of blood, observances of fair play among them, unless other existing states agreed to their statehood, to their dominion over wave and brine. The high seas, by consent of all states, are stateless. (Except, of course, for those occasions upon which great powers seize great stretches for testing nuclear weapons.) However, the Woodstock Nation could not expect to transform itself into the *Holzstock Staat* unless the Woodstockers could convince other states that they had a responsible government, one which could at least guarantee the safety of other nationals who might dwell among them. Neither mystical ties with the Sargasso nor observance of fair play is sufficient to generate the required authority over territory. Should the Woodstockers disport themselves in the manner of existing states, without obtaining prior recognition, their actions would be denounced as piracy.

Any obligations the Woodstockers might have to obey the laws of the Woodstock Nation, prior to statehood, are conceptually independent of the authority the Woodstock government would have over the Sargasso should statehood be granted. Suppose the Woodstockers disavowed in advance all obligations to obey the Woodstock government, though they slyly elected all manner of officials to office, and honored their many and complicated rules of establishment. Suppose, further, that other states were insane enough to grant statehood to the Woodstock Nation. The Woodstock Government, surely, would then possess Sargassoian Sovereignty, though the Government's right to command the territory would be rather empty. Practically speaking, empty rights may be no better than none at all, but an empty right is still a right. Whether or not the Woodstockers promise to obey their government, there is no doubt which persons have the right to enact laws, issue orders and so on. The right to command is conceptually distinct from the obligation to obey; the one can certainly exist without the other.

The *right* or authority of a government to command a territory is quite different from any *power* it has to do so, though, presumably, other states would not recognize the territorial sovereignty of any government lacking sufficient power to keep the peace within its own borders. The major share of a state government's power to keep the peace derives, no doubt, from the general readiness of its subjects to comply with its laws. But the source of power, in a modern political state, is distinct from the source of a state's authority over territory. That authority is derived from a state's external arrangements with other states, which is why a state's treaty obligations may override its obligations to its own citizens, as is indicated in Article VI of the Constitution of the U.S. (see a discussion of this point in [6], pp. 127–130) It is a grave mistake to suppose that the internal political obligations of the subjects of a state confer any ultimate right to override a state's external arrangements with other states, which may explain why governments pay so little attention to citizens in decisions about war and peace.

This entire discussion of the authority and obligations of states and residents is itself empty, it may be protested, because political philosophy is not concerned with political authority *per se* but with something called *moral* authority; not with political and legal obligations but with *moral* obligations; not with *de facto* states but with *de jure* states. The point of these distinctions varies but the overall purpose is fairly clear. It is widely felt that unless it proves possible to justify morally institutional obligations, rights, and authority—by showing how they accord with obligations or practices designated by philosophers as "strictly moral"—such "de facto" institutional obligations are somehow less real, or less morally important than those which can be morally rationalized according to some philosopher's pet moral theory. Now I do not believe that one can be morally indifferent to *any* of one's actual obligations—if one has a *military* obligation, for example, to obey one's superior officer, and soldiers do, then that obligation has *some* relative moral weight, however minuscule, in determining whether, say, a soldier should obey an order to shoot unarmed civilians. If you don't fancy that kind of moral equation, then abolish the institution that can give even the commands of near-morons moral weight in matters of life and death.

The most important right that states possess, as far as the future of mankind is concerned, is the right to make war—a right that is usually confused with the obligation to defend resident subjects from other states. A state's sovereignty over territory gives it the right, unless it has specifically renounced it, to go to war for any slights of that sovereignty; not merely for attacks upon its subjects, but for insults to its flag. Should one state plant its flag upon an uninhabitable island belonging to another state, the second state has the right to kill all the inhabitants of the first state, if that is necessary to regain its territory, for the state stands in the same relationship to its territory that a person does to his body: a state's territorial interests are vital. If considerations such as these, and those mentioned before, suggest that there is something rotten in the state of Denmark—to say nothing of Amerika or *Das Dritte Reich*—I shall not dispute that conclusion over much. The State is really not such a good idea

REFERENCES

[1] BAKUNIN, MICHAEL, in *The Anarchists*, Irving L. Horowitz, ed. (New York: Bell, 1964).

[2] DOURNE, RANDOLPH *Untimely Papers* (New York: Huebsch, 1919).

[3] FORTES, M. and EVANS-PRITCHARD, E. E., "Introduction" in *African Political Systems*, M. Fortes and E. E. Evans-Pritchard, ed. (London: Oxford University Press, 1961).

[4] FORTES, M., "The Political System of the Tallensi of the Northern Territories of the Gold Coast," in [3].

[5] HEGEL, G. W. F., *The Philosophy of History* (New York: Dover, 1956).

[6] "Perpetual Peace," in *Kant's Political Writings*, Reiss and Nisbet, eds. (Cambridge: Cambridge University Press, 1970).

[7] WOLFF, ROBERT PAUL, *In Defense of Anarchism* (New York: Harper & Row, 1970).

4   SIR JOHN WOLFENDEN

(1906–   )

Evolution of British Attitudes Toward Homosexuality*

This article presents both a historical and a philosophic account of the discussions of the famous Wolfenden Committee appointed in Great Britain in 1956. The committee was established to consider the laws and practices related to homosexuality and prostitution. The purpose of the committee was to advise the government on what general principles might be applied to establish a consistent policy of law on these two specific types of behavior. The committee's recommendations were that homosexual behavior between consenting males in private should not be the concern of the criminal law, but that solicitation by prostitutes in public places ought to be illegal. The committee concluded that "the function of the criminal law in the area of moral behavior is to safeguard public order and decency and to protect those who for whatever reason are properly regarded as weak." The fact that an act is considered immoral ought not be involved in a decision of its criminality.

* *The American Journal of Psychiatry*, 125 (1968), pp. 792–797.
Copyright © 1968, the American Psychiatric Association. Used by kind permission of the editor and Sir John Wolfenden.

IN order to dispel any exaggerated expectations, I want to make one thing clear from the start. I have no medical or legal qualifications of any kind. Rather more than 12 years ago I became involved, by accident and at the invitation of the then British Secretaries of State for Home Affairs and for Scotland, in the chairmanship of a departmental committee which they set up to inquire into homosexual offenses and offenses in connection with prostitution.

Our precise terms of reference are perhaps worth quoting so that there will be no misunderstanding of what we were and what we were not to examine. We were instructed to consider: a) the law and practice relating to homosexual offenses and the treatment of persons convicted of such offenses by the courts; and b) the law and practice relating to offenses against the criminal law in connection with prostitution and solicitation for immoral purposes; and to report what changes, if any, were in our opinion desirable.

We were not, you will observe, concerned with homosexuality as such or with prostitution as such. This is a point which must be blindingly obvious to a gathering like this present one, but it is a point which we found the greatest difficulty in driving into the heads of the general public in Britain. We were concerned with offenses against the law in these two areas, and, in the case of homosexual offenses, with the treatment of offenders. We were also, for technical reasons which do not concern us here, a departmental committee, not a royal commission.

We were not a committee of experts. Rather, we were a jury listening to the technical evidence of experts, trying to weigh it, and trying to make up our minds on it. We had two distinguished lawyers and two distinguished doctors among our number, but their primary duty was less to behave as experts themselves than to interpret to the rest of us the technical evidence which others gave—and a highly important contribution they made.

At the first meeting I ventured to make three preliminary observations, along the following lines.

We are assembled to try to advise the government on topics which are deeply controversial and to many people extremely distasteful. So let us be clear from the start that whatever we recommend, and I have no idea what that will be, it will almost certainly be passionately opposed by approximately one-half of the population. In short, we can't win. So our business is to listen to the evidence and make up our own minds, never looking over our shoulders to see what is likely to be the outside world's reception of our conclusions, whatever they may turn out to be.

Secondly, I suggest that we should not be content with piecemeal recommendations about particular parts of our field. I hope we may be able to find some valid general principles and then apply them to our special concerns, so that we have a logical position which can be logically defended. Thirdly, although we are technically reporting to the Secretaries of State I hope we may produce a report which will be intelligible to the ordinary intelligent man and woman and may, whatever it turns out to say, be of some general educational value to the country as a whole.

That was our general line of approach, and for three years we worked fairly hard along that line.

It is perhaps worth pointing out that it is nearly 13 years ago that we started, and during that time things have changed quite a bit in many parts of the world. So perhaps a word about the background in Britain at that time is not out of place.

In the three or four years before our appointment there had been a number of rather sensational cases of prosecutions for homosexual offenses. There had been in consequence two quite different kinds of uneasiness expressed. On the one hand there was a widely-voiced fear that what was called "this kind of behavior" was becoming increasingly widespread, especially in certain intellectual and artistic circles, and was damaging the nation's moral fibre. On the other hand, there were increasingly open condemnations, by those who regarded themselves as liberal and progressive, not only of the law as it stood but of the arbitrary and almost capricious way in which it was being applied.

Simultaneously, on the other half of our remit, there was increasing alarm and indignation about the blatant and shameless behavior of prostitutes in public places in London and some of the provincial cities. There was a clamor that "something must be done." But nobody quite knew what. So, in accordance with the best governmental tradition, a departmental committee was set up to investigate.

I will not weary you with a blow-by-blow account of our deliberations or of the reception of our report,* when it was published by the press and the public. But there was one event which I hope you will forgive me for narrating in some detail, because it turned out to be cardinal to our whole thinking. We began, of course, by studying and trying to absorb preliminary memoranda from a wide variety of sources, official and unofficial; after we had done that we thought we were ready to hear oral evidence.

Our first oral witness was the then Lord Chief Justice of England, Lord Goddard. It is rather a disquieting experience for a layman like myself to have in the witness box, as it were, the Lord Chief Justice, open to interrogation and rigorous examination. Fortunately, I had known him personally for many years, so embarrassment was diluted by former acquaintance; but it was still a rather unusual and piquant situation. I explained, as he already knew, that I was not versed in the law. But, still seeking for underlying general principles, I asked him if he could help me, in our consideration of the law on these matters, by telling me what sort of actions he thought ought to be crimes.

After a long and impressive pause he said that that was a question which in that form he could not answer. I asked him if he would put it into a form in which he could answer it, and then answer it. There followed a fascinating hour of conversation on the nature of crime; and although you must not attribute to Lord Goddard anything of what follows it is only right to acknowledge that it was he who knowingly or unknowingly set our feet on the path we trod to the end.

A crime, and here I begin to dogmatize, is any action about which the competent legislative authority says "If you do that we shall pun-

* Report of the Committee on Homosexual Offences and Prostitution, 1957.

ish you." The competent legislative authority may be, in Britain, Parliament in national affairs, or the headmaster of a school, or the relevant committee of a professional organization or a trade union. There is no form of behavior which of its own nature is criminal; an action is only criminal if somebody who is empowered to say so says that it is.

There are, on the other hand, ways of behaving which many people would regard as immoral or sinful. The word "sin" is not very popular nowadays (however prevalent the forms of behavior to which it applies) and the religious and theological presuppositions which underlie it are by no means universally accepted. But even if "sin" is out of fashion (the word, I mean, not the conduct) there still remain many people who would say that such and such an action is "wrong." Or if even that seems too direct and stark a monosyllable, they would agree that such and such an action was "not right."

They may make this judgment for any one of a variety of reasons, depending on their ethical views—that it causes unhappiness, that it is contrary to man's nature, that it is dysgenic, or simply that they don't like it. Whatever their basic moral theory, there are some actions which they call good or right and others which they call bad or wrong or (at the very least) not right. All these adjectives imply moral judgment on some basis or other.

The question for the legislator, the question we could not avoid because we were required to report what changes, if any, in the law we thought ought to be made, was this: What actions, recognized as being wrong or sinful or not right, ought to be made into crimes? There is one circle, so to speak, of actions to which moral adjectives properly belong; they are good or bad, right or wrong. There is another to which adjectives of criminality belong; they are lawful or unlawful, legal or illegal. The question is how far these circles should be made to be identical.

In some societies there is no problem. Under the theocracy of Calvin's Geneva, it was clear that the laws must be such as to punish every action which that theocracy regards as sinful. If a headmaster makes the rules of a school for immature boys he can do so on the basis that if any boy obeys all the rules he will be living the moral life. But I myself happened to have had an experience which cured me of that particular point of view.

Many years ago I too was headmaster of a school. I was in fact in that context what I have earlier called "the competent legislative authority," and I had hauled before me one day, for the appropriate disciplinary action, a boy who had been apprehended in a normal schoolboy crime, copying the answers from the notebook of the boy next to him. Before proceeding with the processes of justice I asked him if he had anything to say. He said "Yes, sir." (He was a very nasty small boy, who is now, I expect, making a lot of money at the bar.) I asked him what. He said "Sir, there is no school rule against it."

You see. If you once begin to legislate in order to ensure that compliance with the law is synonymous with the moral life, you have to legislate for everything; and although that may be excusable in a society of immature persons (though I do not myself believe that it is) it seems to me to be quite inappropriate behavior in those who are legislating for adult mature citizens of a democracy.

Short of that complete identification of the criminal and the immoral, is there any position which makes more sense? We did not, of course, set the criminal and the morally wrong in opposition or antithesis to each other. But we did set them in disjunction from one another; and this is, I believe, a position which is confirmed by experience and common sense.

There are many daily infringements of the law which their perpetrators would not regard as immoral or repugnant to conscience. I do not know how it is with you, but I am prepared to believe that I break one law or another every day without knowing it—and if I do not know I am doing it my moral withers are unwrung. If I were slightly to exceed a speed limit (which I never do, because I do not drive a car) I should not, I suspect, regard myself as morally culpable in any very serious sense.

More important, the converse is true. There are a good many ways of behaving which most people would regard as morally reprehensible but which are not against the laws. Acts of meanness, selfishness, cowardice, cruelty are not criminal offenses except in those rare particular cases where laws have been made about them.

More important for our present concern, there are a good many forms of sexual behavior which most people would regard as deserving moral condemnation but which are not offenses against the criminal law. Adultery, in England at least (there is a fascinating doubt about the law in Scotland), is not a legal offense; nor, for that matter is fornication; nor, for some odd reason, is homosexual behavior between women. Yet all of these, in various degrees, might well be considered by many to be sinful, or wrong, or (at the very least) not right. So I think we were not being outrageous or provocative or mischievous when we suggested that it is legitimate to draw a distinction between what we may perhaps call, in time-saving monosyllables, crime and sin.

Granted that this is so, we go back to the question I asked of Lord Goddard: "What sort of actions ought to be crimes?" Or, to put it another way, at what level and in what instances or on what general principles ought the competent legislative authority to designate as crimes forms of behavior which are held to be sins?

Problems arise at once. I said "held to be sins." So held by whom? Whose pattern of moral judgments is to determine legislation? It is easy enough, as I hinted earlier, if one lives in Calvin's Geneva; and it may be that there were parallels in the early history of New England. But if you were to start with the competent legislative authority in Britain, our two Houses of Parliament, it would be mighty difficult to discover an agreed pattern or (as the lately fashionable word is) consensus of moral judgments that legislation could translate into a code of criminal law. Are we talking about sin as defined by Roman Catholic theology or by austere Puritanism? Are we talking about the current sexual standards of our mid-20th-century permissive society?

That is one problem. The second is this: if you once try to enshrine in the criminal law the accepted standards of any one age, how do you ever change the law if the accepted standards change? It is a commonplace that different standards of sexual behavior are the accepted standards in different places at the same time and in the same place at different times. Which standards at which place at which time should determine if a man is to be sent to prison?

Our own conclusion—and it is time I came out with it instead of continuing to ask these tedious rhetorical questions—was this. We came to the view that the function of the criminal law in this area of behavior is to safeguard public order and decency and to protect those who for whatever reason are properly regarded as the weak and therefore deserving society's protection. We concluded that in this area the private behavior of an adult individual, male or female, is no concern of the criminal law. I stress "an adult individual" because we were as deeply concerned as any other collection of 15 citizens to protect children, the mentally weak, and the officially subordinate. But I suggest that if this guideline is followed a coherent and logical pattern emerges. Let me be more explicit.

It is no concern of the criminal law if two adult consenting males indulge in homosexual behavior in private. It may be a form of behavior of which you and I disapprove; we may be disgusted by it; we may, on all sorts of moral grounds, find it repugnant. But none of those subjective reactions of ours have anything to do with criminality. Every day I come across forms of behavior to which all these descriptions apply; but that fact does not entitle me to demand that those who behave in this way should be sent to prison.

I disapprove of adultery; and so do a good many other people. We do so because we think this sort of behavior is immoral, or wrong, or "not right." But I do not demand that adulterers and adulteresses should be subject to the criminal law. If men and women, or men and men, or women and women, indulge in sexual acts in public, I not only disapprove, I think the law ought to do something about it. And I think this because I think the law's business is to protect me and my wife and children from affronts against decency.

I do not think this because I think such behavior immoral. That seems to me not to be the point. I do not think the law has a right to enter, as it were, anybody's bedroom. Sexual behavior is nobody's business except that of those immediately concerned, unless their behavior offends against public order and decency.

This is the basis in logic for the two halves of our recommendations, that homosexual behavior between consenting males in private should be no concern of the criminal law and that solicitation by prostitutes in public places should render them liable to prosecution. We were not concerned with prostitution or fornication as such; we were concerned with the criminal law and its function as the protector of public order and decency.

It is easy to say that the Street Offences Act, which was introduced on the basis of our recommendations, did no more than sweep prostitutes off the streets and under the carpet—in fact into the striptease joints and cryptobrothels of notorious parts of London. Again, my withers are unwrung. We were not so starry-eyed as to imagine that prostitution can be abolished. Our objective was to make the streets of London tolerable for the ordinary citizen and safe for an attractive girl who is not a prostitute. And if prostitution continues, in London or elsewhere, I am not surprised.

Nor am I moved when I am told that I am a hypocrite or a self-deceiver if I think that because the streets of London are now less thickly populated by nightwalkers or loiterers the standard of sexual morals in London has improved. Quite simply, our objective was not social reform; it was something which was quite different and which was within our terms of reference as a committee. I may have all kinds of private and personal views about prostitution, but I am not so arrogant as to suppose that my personal views about sexual morality should be sanctified by the criminal law.

May I give just one example of the difficulty which quite intelligent people seem to have in making this distinction? After our report was published I was in conversation with an extremely distinguished ecclesiastic in Britain, an old friend of mine. He took me sharply to task for what he called discrimination against the women. "Surely," he said, "you would agree that the man who goes with a prostitute is as guilty as the woman is." "My dear Archbishop," I said—because that is what he was—"Of course the man is as guilty as the woman is of what you and I would both call the sin of fornication. The man is not as guilty as the woman is of what I regard as the offense against public order and decency involved in cluttering up the streets of London and soliciting all the available male passersby."

I have tried to explain what our concerns were and what they were not. I am well aware that these are highly controversial matters, and I have heard much talk—perhaps more than most people—of national decadence, of unnatural behavior, or disgust and scorn. I believe, still, after 13 years, that we were right.

In all the debates in both Houses of Parliament, all the arguments, prejudices, convictions, apprehensions, indignations, sympathies have been marshalled, deployed, and recapitulated time after time. In the end what I regard as unsentimental logic prevailed. Gradually public opinion changed, not dramatically overnight but by what I regard as a dispassionate assessment of the nature of human beings and the nature of the criminal law. In the end, on the initiative of a Conservative peer, the Earl of Arran, in the House of Lords, and with the support of an eloquent advocate, Mr. Leo Abse, in the House of Commons, the law in Britain was changed, almost exactly ten years after the publication of our report.

It is not for me to say whether or not, from the legal or medical point of view, this is a good thing. Still less is it for me to say whether other countries, whose laws are what Britain's used to be, should change them. I never thought it my business, at home, to campaign for a change in the law. My colleagues and I took the responsibility of making certain recommendations for what we thought to be valid and defensible reasons. The legislators eventually accepted those recommendations and wrote them into the law. It is for them and for you to judge what public opinion is in these matters and to decide how far the law should lead public opinion or follow it. I am content to have our stated position judged in terms of rational thinking and human happiness.

5

JOHN STUART MILL

(1806–1873)

Of the Limits to the Authority of Society over the Individual*

In his famous essay On Liberty, Mill discusses some of the same issues that confronted the Wolfenden Committee. He argues that the greatest possible latitude in personal freedom ought to be the aim of society. The government should use as its guideline what Mill calls the "self-protection principle," which maintains that society is justified in interfering with the conduct of individuals only in so far as it may harm others. The individual's own good is not sufficient reason for a law. Any act of what Mill calls private morality (self-regarding acts) is no concern of law. Society may only advise or caution on private matters. Mill argues that in no case ought the moral attitudes of the majority be the grounds for law. Certainly men have always judged others on the basis of their own standards of conduct and feelings, but this has led to religious and racial persecution in civil societies. If law were to use this tendency as a principle of public interference in the conduct of individuals that does not affect the public, then individual human liberty would be a meaningless idea.

* John Stuart Mill, *On Liberty* (London: John W. Parker & Son, 1859), Chap. IV.

WHAT, then, is the rightful limit to the sovereignty of the individual over himself? Where does the authority of society begin? How much of human life should be assigned to individuality, and how much to society?

Each will receive its proper share, if each has that which more particularly concerns it. To individuality should belong the part of life in which it is chiefly the individual that is interested; to society, the part which chiefly interests society.

Though society is not founded on a contract, and though no good purpose is answered by inventing a contract in order to deduce social obligations from it, everyone who receives the protection of society owes a return for the benefit, and the fact of living in society renders it indispensable that each should be bound to observe a certain line of conduct towards the rest. This conduct consists, *first*, in not injuring the interests of one another; or rather certain interests, which, either by express legal provision or by tacit understanding, ought to be considered as rights; and *secondly,* in each person's bearing his share (to be fixed on some equitable principle) of the labors and sacrifices incurred for defending the society or its members from injury and molestation. These conditions society is justified in enforcing, at all costs to those who endeavor to withhold fulfillment. Nor is this all that society may do. The acts of an individual may be hurtful to others, or wanting in due consideration for their welfare, without going to the length of violating any of their constituted rights. The offender may then be justly punished by opinion, though not by law. As soon as any part of a person's conduct affects prejudicially the interests of others, society has jurisdiction over it, and the question whether the general welfare will or will not be promoted by interfering with it, becomes open to discussion. But there is no room for entertaining any such question when a person's conduct affects the interests of no persons besides himself, or need not affect them unless they like (all the persons concerned being of full age, and the ordinary amount of understanding). In all such cases, there should be perfect freedom, legal and social, to do the action and stand the consequences

It would be a great misunderstanding of this doctrine to suppose that it is one of selfish indifference, which pretends that human beings have no business with each other's conduct in life, and that they should not concern themselves about the well-doing or well-being of one another, unless their own interest is involved. Instead of any diminution, there is need of a great increase of disinterested exertion to promote the good of others. But disinterested benevolence can find other instruments to persuade people to their good than whips and scourges, either of the literal or the metaphorical sort. I am the last person to undervalue the self-regarding virtues: they are only second in importance, if even second, to the social. It is equally the business of education to cultivate both. But even education works by conviction and persuasion as well as by compulsion, and it is by the former only that, when the period of education is passed, the self-regarding virtues should be inculcated. Human beings owe to each other help to distinguish the better from the worse, and encouragement to choose the former and avoid the latter. They should be forever stimulating each other to increased exercise of their higher faculties, and increased direction of their feelings and aims towards wise instead of foolish, elevating instead of degrading, objects and contemplations. But neither one person, nor any number of persons, is warranted in saying to another human creature of ripe years, that he shall not do with his life for his own benefit what he chooses to do with it. He is the person most interested in his own well-being: the interest which any other person, except in cases of strong personal attachment, can have in it, is trifling, compared with that which he himself has; the interest which society has in him individually (except as to his conduct to others) is fractional, and altogether indirect; while with respect to his own feelings and circumstances, the most ordinary man or woman has means of knowledge immeasurably surpassing those that can be possessed by anyone else. The interference of society to overrule his judgment and purposes in what only regards himself must be grounded on general presumptions; which may be altogether wrong, and even if right, are as likely as not to be misapplied to individual cases, by persons no better acquainted with the circumstances of such cases than those are who look at them merely from without. In this department, therefore, of human affairs, individuality has its proper field of action. In the conduct of human beings towards one another it is necessary that general rules should for the most part be observed, in order that people may know what they have to expect; but in each person's own concerns his individual spontaneity is entitled to free exercise. Considerations to aid his judgment, exhortations to strengthen his will, may be offered to him, even obtruded on him, by others: but he himself is the final judge. All errors which he is likely to commit against advice and warning are far outweighed by the evil of allowing others to constrain him to what they deem his good.

I do not mean that the feelings with which a person is regarded by others ought not to be in any way affected by his self-regarding qualities or deficiencies. This is neither possible nor desirable. If he is eminent in any of the qualities which conduce to his own good, he is, so far, a proper object of admiration. He is so much the nearer to the ideal perfection of human nature. If he is grossly deficient in those qualities, a sentiment the opposite of admiration will follow. There is a degree of folly, and a degree of what may be called (though the phrase is not unobjectionable) lowness or depravation of taste, which, though it cannot justify doing harm to the person who manifests it, renders him necessarily and properly a subject of distaste, or, in extreme cases, even of contempt: a person could not have the opposite qualities in due strength without entertaining these feelings. Though doing no wrong to anyone, a person may so act as to compel us to judge him, and feel to him, as a fool, or as a being of an inferior order; and since this judgment and feeling are a fact which he would prefer to avoid, it is doing him a service to warn him of it beforehand, as of any other disagreeable consequence to which he exposes himself. It would be well, indeed, if this good office were much more freely rendered than the common notions of politeness at present permit, and if one person could honestly point out to another that he thinks him in fault, without being considered unmannerly or presuming. We have a right, also, in various ways, to act upon our unfavorable opinion of anyone, not to the oppression of his individuality, but in the exercise of ours. We are not bound, for example, to seek his society; we have a right to avoid it (though not to parade the avoidance), for we have a right to choose the society most acceptable to us. We have a right, and it may be our duty, to caution others against him, if we think his example or conversation likely to have a pernicious effect on those with whom he associates.

What I contend for is, that the inconveniences which are strictly inseparable from the unfavorable judgment of others, are the only ones to which a person should ever be subjected for that portion of his conduct and character which concerns his own good, but which does not affect the interest of others in their relations with him. Acts injurious to others require a totally different treatment. Encroachment on their rights; infliction on them of any loss or damage not justified by his own rights; falsehood or duplicity in dealing with them; unfair or ungenerous use of advantages over them; even selfish abstinence from defending them against injury—these are fit objects of moral reprobation, and, in grave cases, of moral retribution and punishment. And not only these acts, but the dispositions which lead to them, are properly immoral, and fit subjects of disapprobation which may rise to abhorrence. Cruelty of disposition; malice and ill-nature; that most anti-social and odious of all passions, envy; dissimulation and insincerity, irascibility on insufficient cause, and resentment disproportioned to the provocation; the love of domineering over others; the desire to engross more than one's share of advantages (the πλεονεξια of the Greeks); the pride which derives gratification from the abasement of others; the egotism which thinks self and its concerns more important than everything else, and decides all doubtful questions in its own favor;—these are moral vices, and constitute a bad and odious moral character: unlike the self-regarding faults previously mentioned, which are not properly immoralities, and to whatever pitch they may be carried, do not constitute wickedness. They may be proofs of any amount of folly, or want of personal dignity and self-respect; but they are only a subject of moral reprobation when they involve a breach of duty to others, for whose sake the individual is bound to have care for himself. What are called duties to ourselves are not socially obligatory, unless circumstances render them at the same time duties to others. The term "duty to oneself," when it means anything more than prudence, means self-respect or self-development, and for none of these is anyone accountable to his fellow-creatures, because for none of them is it for the good of mankind that he be held accountable to them.

The distinction between the loss of consideration which a person may rightly incur by defect of prudence or of personal dignity, and the reprobation which is due to him for an offense against the rights of others, is not a merely nominal distinction. It makes a vast difference both in our feelings and in our conduct towards him whether he displeases us in things in which we think we have a right to control him, or in things in which we know that we have not. If he displeases us, we may express our distaste, and we may stand aloof from a person as well as from a thing that displeases us; but we shall not therefore feel called on to make his life uncomfortable. We shall reflect that he already bears, or will bear, the whole penalty of his error; if he spoils his life by mismanagement, we shall not, for that reason, desire to spoil it still further: instead of wishing to punish him, we shall rather endeavor to alleviate his punishment, by showing him how he may avoid or cure the evils his conduct tends to bring upon him. He may be to us an object of pity, perhaps of dislike, but not of anger or resentment; we shall not treat him like an enemy of society: the worst we shall think ourselves justified in doing is leaving him to himself, if we do not interfere benevolently by showing interest or concern for him. It is far otherwise if he has infringed the rules necessary for the protection of his fellow-creatures, individually or collectively. The evil consequences of his acts do not then fall on himself, but on others; and society, as the protector of all its members, must retaliate on him; must inflict pain on him for the express purpose of punishment, and must take care that it be sufficiently severe. In the one case, he is an offender at our bar, and we are called on not only to sit in judgment on him, but, in one shape or another, to execute our own sentence: in the other case, it is not our part to inflict any suffering on him, except what may incidentally follow from our using the same liberty in the regulation of our own affairs, which we allow to him in his.

The distinction here pointed out between the part of a person's life which concerns only himself, and that which concerns others, many persons will refuse to admit. How (it may be asked) can any part of the conduct of a member of society be a matter of indifference to the other members? No person is an entirely isolated being; it is impossible for a person to do anything seriously or permanently hurtful to himself, without mischief reaching at least to his near connections, and often far beyond them. If he injures his property, he does harm to those who directly or indirectly derived support from it, and usually diminishes, by a greater or less amount, the general resources of the community. If he deteriorates his bodily or mental faculties, he not only brings evil upon all who depended on him for any portion of their happiness, but disqualifies himself for rendering the services which he owes to his fellow-creatures generally; perhaps becomes a burden on their affection or benevolence; and if such conduct were very frequent, hardly an offense that is committed would detract more from the general sum of good. Finally, if by his vices or follies a person does no direct harm to others, he is nevertheless (it may be said) injurious by his example; and ought to be compelled to control himself, for the sake of those whom the sight or knowledge of his conduct might corrupt or mislead.

And even (it will be added) if the consequences of misconduct could be confined to the vicious or thoughtless individual, ought society to abandon to their own guidance those who are manifestly unfit for it? If protection against themselves is confessedly due to children and persons under age, is not society equally bound to afford it to persons of mature years who are equally incapable of self-government? If gambling, or drunkenness, or incontinence, or idleness, or uncleanliness, are as injurious to happiness, and as great a hindrance to improvement, as many or most of the acts prohibited by law, why (it may be asked) should not law, so far as is consistent with practicability and social convenience, endeavor to repress these also? And as a supplement to the unavoidable imperfections of law, ought not opinion at least to organize a powerful police against these vices, and visit rigidly with social penalties those who are known to practice them? There is no question here (it may be said) about restricting individuality, or impeding the trial of new and original experiments in living. The only things it is sought to prevent are things which have been tried and condemned from the beginning of the world until now; things which experience has shown not to be useful or suitable to any person's individuality. There must be some length of time and amount of experience after which a moral or prudential truth may be regarded as established: and it is merely desired to prevent generation after generation from falling over the same precipice which has been fatal to their predecessors.

I fully admit that the mischief which a person does to himself may seriously affect, both through their sympathies and their interests, those nearly connected with him and, in a minor degree, society at large. When, by conduct of this sort, a person is led to violate a distinct and assignable obligation to any other person or persons, the case is taken out of the self-regarding class, and becomes amenable to moral disapprobation in the proper sense of the term. If, for example, a man, through intemperance or extravagance, becomes unable to pay his debts, or, having undertaken the moral responsibility of a family, becomes from the same cause incapable of supporting or educating them, he is deservedly reprobated, and might be justly punished; but it is for the breach of duty to his family or creditors, not for the extravagance. If the resources which ought to have been devoted to them, had been diverted from them for the most prudent investment, the moral culpability would have been the same. George Barnwell murdered his uncle to get money for his mistress, but if he had done it to set himself up in business, he would equally have been hanged. Again, in the frequent case of a man who causes grief to his family by addiction to bad habits, he deserves reproach for his unkindness or ingratitude; but so he may for cultivating habits not in themselves vicious, if they are painful to those with whom he passes his life, or who from personal ties are dependent on him for their comfort. Whoever fails in the consideration generally due to the interests and feelings of others, not being compelled by some more imperative duty, or justified by allowable self-preference, is a subject of moral disapprobation for that failure, but not for the cause of it, nor for the errors, merely personal to himself, which may have remotely led to it. In like manner, when a person disables himself, by conduct purely self-regarding, from the performance of some definite duty incumbent on him to the public, he is guilty of a social offense. No person ought to be punished simply for being drunk; but a soldier or a policeman should be punished for being drunk on duty. Whenever, in short, there is a definite damage, or a definite risk of damage, either to an individual or to the public, the case is taken out of the province of liberty, and placed in that of morality or law.

But with regard to the merely contingent, or, as it may be called, constructive injury which a person causes to society, by conduct which neither violates any specific duty to the public, nor occasions perceptible hurt to any assignable individual except himself, the inconvenience is one which society can afford to bear, for the sake of the greater good of human freedom. If grown persons are to be punished for not taking proper care of themselves, I would rather it were for their own sake, than under pretense of preventing them from impairing their capacity of rendering to society benefits which society does not pretend it has a right to exact. But I cannot consent to argue the point as if society had no means of bringing its weaker members up to its ordinary standard of rational conduct, except waiting till they do something irrational, and then punishing them, legally or morally, for it. Society has had absolute power over them during all the early portion of their existence: it has had the whole period of childhood and nonage in which to try whether it could make them capable of rational conduct in life. The existing generation is master both of the training and the entire circumstances of the generation to come; it cannot indeed make them perfectly wise and good, because it is itself so lamentably deficient in goodness and wisdom; and its best efforts are not always, in individual cases, its most successful ones; but it is perfectly well able to make the rising generation, as a whole, as good as, and a little better than, itself. If society lets any considerable number of its members grow up mere children, incapable of being acted on by rational consideration of distant motives, society has itself to blame for the consequences. Armed not only with all the powers of education, but with the ascendency which the authority of a received opinion always exercises over the minds who are least fitted to judge for themselves; and aided by the *natural* penalties which cannot be prevented from falling on those who incur the distaste or the contempt of those who know them; let not society pretend that it needs, besides all this, the power to issue commands and enforce obedience in the personal concerns of individuals, in which, on all principles of justice and policy, the decision ought to rest with those who are to abide the consequences. Nor is there anything which tends more to discredit and frustrate the better means of influencing conduct than a resort to the worse. If there be among those whom it is attempted to coerce into prudence or temperance any of the material of which vigorous and independent characters are made, they will infallibly rebel against the yoke. No such person will ever feel that others have a right to control him in his concerns, such as they have to prevent him from injuring them in theirs; and it easily comes to be considered a mark of spirit and courage to fly in the face of such usurped authority, and do with ostentation the exact opposite of what it enjoins; as in the fashion of grossness which succeeded, in the time of Charles II, to the fanatical moral intolerance of the Puritans. With respect to what is said of the necessity of protecting society from the bad example set to others by the vicious or the self-indulgent, it is true that bad example may have a pernicious effect, especially the example of doing wrong to others with impunity to the wrong-doer. But we are now speaking of conduct which, while it does no wrong to others, is supposed to do great harm to the agent himself: and I do not see how those who believe this can think otherwise than that the example, on the whole, must be more salutary than hurtful; since, if it displays the misconduct, it displays also the painful or degrading consequences which, if the conduct is justly censured, must be supposed to be in all or most cases attendant on it.

But the strongest of all the arguments against the interference of the public with purely personal conduct is that, when it does interfere, the odds are that it interferes wrongly, and in the wrong place. On questions of social morality, of duty to others, the opinion of the public, that is, of an overruling majority, though often wrong, is likely to be still oftener right; because on such questions they are only required to judge of their own interests; of the manner in which some mode of conduct, if allowed to be practiced, would affect themselves. But the opinion of a similar majority, imposed as a law on the minority, on questions of self-regarding conduct, is quite as likely to be wrong as right; for in these cases public opinion means, at the best, some people's opinion of what is good or bad for other people; while very often it does not even mean that; the public, with the most perfect indifference, passing over the pleasure or convenience of those whose conduct they censure, and considering only their own preference. There are many who consider as an injury to themselves any conduct which they have a distaste for, and resent it as an outrage to their feelings; as a religious bigot, when charged with disregarding the religious feelings of others, has been known to retort that they disregard his feelings, by persisting in their abominable worship or creed. But there is no parity between the feeling of a person for his own opinion, and the feeling of another who is offended at his holding it; no more than between the desire of a thief to take a purse, and the desire of the right owner to keep it. And a person's taste is as much his own peculiar concern as his opinion or his purse. It is easy for anyone to imagine an ideal public which leaves the freedom and choice of individuals in all uncertain matters undisturbed, and only requires them to abstain from modes of conduct which universal experience has condemned. But where has there been seen a public which set any such limit to its censorship? or when does the public trouble itself about universal experience? In its interferences with personal conduct it is seldom thinking of anything but the enormity of acting or feeling differently from itself; and this standard of judgment, thinly disguised, is held up to mankind as the dictate of religion and philosophy, by nine-tenths of all moralists and speculative writers. These teach that things are right because they are right; because we feel them to be so. They tell us to search in our own minds and hearts for laws of conduct binding on ourselves and on all others. What can the poor public do but apply these instructions, and make their own personal feelings of good and evil, if they are tolerably unanimous in them, obligatory on all the world?

6

LORD DEVLIN

(1905–   )

*Law, Democracy and Morality**

Devlin has been a powerful and vocal opponent of the libertarian point of view as expressed by the Wolfenden Committee and John Stuart Mill. In his famous The Enforcement of Morals *lecture, Devlin defended the position that morality must be the basis of criminal law. His reasoning was that a society is nothing more than its basic cohesive moral beliefs. Society not only has the right to punish immorality; it is obligated to do so to preserve itself. Society cannot exist without morals. Devlin asks: What then is the duty of the lawmaker in a democracy? In this selection, Devlin attempts to wrestle with that issue. Criminal law should be properly used when the weight of public opinion on a public moral principle is outraged. The democratic legislator cannot pass laws that are too far removed from the common sense of the society or he does disservice to the democratic system. Yet that does not change the fact, as Devlin finds it, that a society's law must mirror morality, and that the majority's moral principles must be enforced on the erring minority.*

* Lord Devlin, "Law, Democracy, and Morality," *University of Pennsylvania Law Review*, 110:635 (1962), pp. 635–649. Copyright *University of Pennsylvania Law Review*. Used by kind permission of the *University of Pennsylvania Law Review*.

WHEN a state recognizes freedom of worship and of conscience, it sets a problem for jurists which they have not yet entirely succeeded in solving. Now, when the law divides right from wrong, it cannot appeal to any absolute authority outside itself as justifying the division. All the questions which before were settled by divine law as pronounced by the churches are thrown open to debate when the decision is taken to admit freedom of conscience.†

The nineteenth century English philosophers drew what appeared to be the logical conclusion from the change. While the political scientists and constitution-makers of the age were engaged in separating

---

† This decision, and not the separation of church from state, is crucial. In England, the church has never been formally separated from the state, but by the beginning of the nineteenth century an Englishman was effectively set free to worship or not as he chose. It was freedom not to worship at all and to disbelieve in revelation that was important, for it deprived the law of spiritual sustenance. In the eyes of the law the only judgment upon right and wrong which a man could be expected to follow was that of his own conscience, and it did not matter whether he taught himself on matters of morals or was taught by others.

church and state, the philosophers came near to separating law and morality. Austin taught that the only force behind the law was physical force, and Mill declared that the only purpose for which that force could rightfully be used against any member of the community was to prevent harm to others; his own good, physical or moral, was not sufficient warrant.

But this sort of thinking made no impact at all upon the development or administration of the English criminal law. This was doubtless because no practical problems arose. If there had been a deep division in the country on matters of morals—if there had been, for example, a large minority who wished to practice polygamy—the theoretical basis for legislation on morals would have had to have been scrutinized. But the Englishman's hundred religions about which Voltaire made his jibe gave rise to no differences on morals grave enough to affect the criminal law. Parliament added incest and homosexual offenses to the list of crimes without inquiring what harm they did to the community if they were committed in private; it was enough that they were morally wrong. The judges continued to administer the law on the footing that England was a Christian country. Reluctantly they recognized respectful criticism of Christian doctrine as permissible, and the crime of blasphemy virtually disappeared. But Christian morals remained embedded in the law.

It is only recently that there has emerged a moral problem needing a practical solution. There have long been cases in which men have violated various precepts of moral law, but there has been no body of men who asserted that the law ought not to interfere with immoral behavior. But there is now in England, and I daresay in other countries, a body of men who see nothing wrong with the homosexual relationship. There are others, to be found mainly among the educated classes, who, while not themselves practicing homosexuality, are not repelled by it, think it a permissible way of life for those so constituted as to enjoy it, and deplore the misery the law inflicts on the comparatively few victims it detects. In September 1957 the Wolfenden Committee of thirteen distinguished men and women appointed by the Home Secretary recommended with only one dissenter that homosexual behaviour between consenting adults in private should no longer be a criminal offense; and they based their recommendation on the ground that such offenses were within "a realm of private morality and immorality which is, in brief and crude terms, not the law's business."[*] The Home Secretary did not accept this recommendation;

[*] Homosexual Offenses and Prostitution Committee, *Report*, CMD. No. 247, at 24 (1957).

nevertheless, the report, in addition to its sociological value, is an important statement on the relationship between the criminal and the moral law.

Another landmark was made in May of last year by the decision of the House of Lords in *Shaw v. Director of Public Prosecutions.* This case arose indirectly out of another recommendation by the Wolfenden Committee. They were asked to report also upon offenses in connection with prostitution; and as a result the Street Offences Act, 1959, which made it impossible for prostitutes to continue soliciting in the streets, was passed. Mr. Shaw naively considered that since Parliament had not prohibited the trade of prostitution, there could be nothing objectionable or illegal about his supplying for prostitutes some means of advertisement in place of that which Parliament had denied them. So he published a magazine, which he called "The Ladies' Directory," containing the names, addresses, and telephone numbers of prostitutes. If that were all that he had done and if he had been content to remunerate himself simply by the proceeds from the sale of the magazine, he would have committed no specific offense. But the magazine contained additional matter which made it an obscene libel; and by taking payment from the prostitutes themselves the defendant had committed the statutory offense of living "wholly or in part on the earnings of prostitution." The importance of the case comes from the first count in the indictment, which was independent of the two statutory offenses and alleged a conspiracy at common law to corrupt public morals, the particulars being that the defendant and the prostitutes who advertised themselves in his magazine conspired "to induce readers thereof to resort to the said advertisers for the purposes of fornication." The defense argued that there was no such general offense known to the law as a conspiracy to corrupt public morals, but the House of Lords held by a majority of four to one that there was and that the accused was rightly found guilty of it. Viscount Simonds said: "There remains in the courts of law a residual power to enforce the supreme and fundamental purpose of the law, to conserve not only the safety and order but also the moral welfare of the State";* and he approved the assertion of Lord Mansfield two centuries before that the Court of King's Bench was the *custos morum* of the people and had the superintendency of offenses *contra bonos mores.*

With this cardinal enunciation of principle the courts rejected the teaching of John Stuart Mill and proclaimed themselves keepers of the nation's morals. From what source do they draw that power and how do they ascertain the moral standards they enforce?

* Shaw v. Director of Pub. Prosecutions, [1961] 2 Weekly L.R. 897, 917 (H.L.).

The state may claim on two grounds to legislate on matters of morals. The Platonic ideal is that the state exists to promote virtue among its citizens. If that is its function, then whatever power is sovereign in the state—an autocrat, if there be one, or in a democracy the majority —must have the right and duty to declare what standards of morality are to be observed as virtuous and must ascertain them as it thinks best. This is not acceptable to Anglo-American thought. It invests the state with power of determination between good and evil, destroys freedom of conscience, and is the paved road to tyranny. It is against this concept of the state's power that Mill's words are chiefly directed.

The alternative ground is that society may legislate to preserve itself. This is the ground, I think, taken by Lord Simonds when he says that the purpose of the law is to conserve the moral welfare of the state; and all the speeches in the House show, especially when they are laying down the part to be played by the jury, that the work of the courts is to be the guarding of a heritage and not the creation of a system. "The ultimate foundation of a free society is the binding tie of cohesive sentiment."* What makes a society is a community of ideas, not political ideas alone but also ideas about the way its members should behave and govern their lives.

If men and women try to create a society in which there is no fundamental agreement about good and evil they will fail; if having based it on common agreement, the agreement goes, the society will disintegrate. For society is not something that is kept together physically; it is held by the invisible bonds of common thought. If the bonds were too far relaxed the members would drift apart. A common morality is part of the bondage. The bondage is part of the price of society; and mankind, which needs society, must pay its price.

A law that enforces moral standards must like any other law be enacted by the appropriate constitutional organ, the monarch or the legislative majority as the case may be. The essential difference between the two theories is that under the first the lawmaker must determine for himself what is good for his subjects. He may be expected to do so not arbitrarily but to the best of his understanding; but it is his decision, based on his judgment of what is best, from which alone the law derives authority. The democratic system of government goes some way—not all the way, for no representative can be the mirror of the voter's thoughts—to insure that the decision of the lawmaker will be acceptable to the majority, but the majority is not the whole. A written constitution may safeguard to a great extent and for a long time the conscience of a minority, but not entirely and forever; for a

* Minersville School Dist. v. Gobitis, 310 U.S. 586, 596 (1940) (Frankfurter, J.).

written constitution is only a fundamental enactment that is difficult to alter.

But under the second theory the lawmaker is not required to make any judgment about what is good and what is bad. The morals which he enforces are those ideas about right and wrong which are already accepted by the society for which he is legislating and which are necessary to preserve its integrity. He has not to argue with himself about the merits of monogamy and polygamy; he has merely to observe that monogamy is an essential part of the structure of the society to which he belongs. Naturally he will assume that the morals of his society are good and true; if he does not, he should not be playing an active part in government. But he has not to vouch for their goodness and truth. His mandate is to preserve the essentials of his society, not to reconstruct them according to his own ideas.

How does the lawmaker ascertain the moral principles that are accepted by the society to which he belongs? He is concerned only with the fundament that is surely accepted, for legal sanctions are inappropriate for the enforcement of moral standards that are in dispute. He does not therefore need the assistance of moral philosophers, nor does he have to study the arguments upon peripheral questions. He is concerned with what is acceptable to the ordinary man, the man in the jury box, who might also be called the reasonable man or the right-minded man. When I call him the man in the jury box, I do not mean to imply that the ordinary citizen when he enters the jury box is invested with some peculiar quality that enables him to pronounce *ex cathedra* on morals. I still think of him simply as the ordinary reasonable man, but by placing him in the jury box I call attention to three points. First, the verdict of a jury must be unanimous; so a moral principle, if it is to be given the force of law, should be one which twelve men and women drawn at random from the community can be expected not only to approve but to take so seriously that they regard a breach of it as fit for punishment. Second, the man in the jury box does not give a snap judgment but returns his verdict after argument, instruction, and deliberation. Third, the jury box is a place in which the ordinary man's views on morals become directly effective. The lawmaker who makes the mistake of thinking that what he has to preserve is not the health of society but a particular regimen, will find that particular laws wither away. An important part of the machinery for hastening obsolescence is the lay element in the administration of English justice, the man in the jury box and the lay magistrate. The magistrates can act by the imposition of nominal penalties; the juryman acts by acquittal. If he gravely dislikes a law or thinks its application too harsh, he has the power, which from time immemorial he has exercised, to return a verdict of acquittal that is unassailable. . . .

What I want to discuss immediately is the reaction that many philosophers and academic lawyers have to the doctrine I have just outlined. They dislike it very much. It reduces morality, they feel, to the level of a question of fact. What Professor H. L. A. Hart calls rationalist morality, which I take to be morality embodied in the rational judgment of men who have studied moral questions and pondered long on what the answers ought to be, will be blown aside by a gust of popular morality compounded of all the irrational prejudices and emotions of the man-in-the-street. Societies in the past have tolerated witch-hunting and burnt heretics: was that done in the name of morality? There are societies today whose moral standards permit them to discriminate against men because of their color: have we to accept that? Is reason to play no part in the separation of right from wrong?

The most significant thing about questions of this type is that none of the questioners would think them worth asking if the point at issue had nothing in it of the spiritual. It is a commonplace that in our sort of society questions of great moment are settled in accordance with the opinion of the ordinary citizen who acts no more and no less rationally in matters of policy than in matters of morals. Such is the consequence of democracy and universal suffrage. Those who have had the benefit of a higher education and feel themselves better equipped to solve the nation's problems than the average may find it distasteful to submit to herd opinion. History tells them that democracies are far from perfect and have in the past done many foolish and even wicked things. But they do not dispute that in the end the will of the people must prevail, nor do they seek to appeal from it to the throne of reason.

But when it comes to a pure point of morals—for example, is homosexuality immoral and sinful—the first reaction of most of us is different. That reaction illustrates vividly the vacuum that is created when a society no longer acknowledges a supreme spiritual authority. For most of the history of mankind this sort of question has been settled, for men in society as well as for men as individuals, by priests claiming to speak with the voice of God. Today a man's own conscience is for him the final arbiter: but what for society?

This question, it seems to me, has received less study than it ought to have. The lawyers have evaded it by means of the assumption, substantially justifiable in fact though not in theory, that Christian morality remains just as valid for the purposes of the law as it was in the days of a universal church. The philosophers seem to have assumed that because a man's conscience could do for him, if he so chose, all that in the age of faith the priest had done, it could likewise do for society all that the priest had done; it cannot, unless some way be found of making up a collective conscience.

It is said or implied that this can be done by accepting the sovereignty of reason which will direct the conscience of every man to the same conclusion. The humbler way of using the power of reason is to hold, as Aquinas did, that through it it is possible to ascertain the law as God ordered it, the natural law, the law as it ought to be; the prouder is to assert that the reason of man unaided can construct the law as it ought to be. If the latter view is right, then one must ask: As men of reason are all men equal? If they are, if every man has equivalent power of reasoning and strength of mind to subdue the baser faculties of feeling and emotion, there can be no objection to morality being a matter for the popular vote. The objection is sustainable only upon the view that the opinion of the trained and educated mind, reached as its owner believes by an unimpassioned rational process, is as a source of morals superior to the opinion of ordinary men.

To the whole of this thesis, however it be put and whether or not it is valid for the individual mind that is governed by philosophy or faith, the lawmaker in a democratic society must advance insuperable objections, both practical and theoretical. The practical objection is that after centuries of debate men of undoubted reasoning power and honesty of purpose have shown themselves unable to agree on what the moral law should be, differing sometimes upon the answer to the simplest moral problem. To say this is not to deny the value of discussion among moral philosophers or to overlook the possibility that sometime between now and the end of the world universal agreement may be reached, but it is to say that as a guide to the degree of definition required by the lawmaker the method is valueless. Theoretically the method is inadmissable. If what the reason has to discover is the law of God, it is inadmissable because it assumes, as of course Aquinas did, belief in God as a lawgiver. If it is the law of man and if a common opinion on any point is held by the educated elite, what is obtained except to substitute for the voice of God the voice of the Superior Person? A free society is as much offended by the dictates of an intellectual oligarchy as by those of an autocrat.

For myself I have found no satisfactory alternative to the thesis I have proposed. The opposition to it, I cannot help thinking, has not rid itself

of the idea, natural to a philosopher, that a man who is seeking a moral
law ought also to be in pursuit of absolute truth. If he were, they
would think it surprising if he found truth at the bottom of the popular
vote. I do not think it as far from this as some learned people suppose,
and I have known them to search for it in what seem to me to be odder
places. But that is a subject outside the scope of this paper, which is
not concerned with absolute truth. I have said that a sense of right
and wrong is necessary for the life of a community. It is not necessary
that their appreciation of right and wrong, tested in the light of one
set or another of those abstract propositions about which men forever
dispute, should be correct. If it were, only one society at most could
survive. What the lawmaker has to ascertain is not the true belief but
the common belief.

When I talk of the lawmaker I mean a man whose business it is
to make the law whether it takes the form of a legislative enactment
or of a judicial decision, as contrasted with the lawyer whose business
is to interpret and apply the law as it is. Of course the two functions
often overlap; judges especially are thought of as performing both. No
one now is shocked by the idea that the lawyer is concerned simply
with the law as it is and not as he thinks it ought to be. No one need
be shocked by the idea that the lawmaker is concerned with morality
as it is. There are, have been, and will be bad laws, bad morals, and
bad societies. Probably no lawmaker believes that the morality he is
enacting is false, but that does not make it true. Unfortunately bad
societies can live on bad morals just as well as good societies on
good ones.

In a democracy educated men cannot be put into a separate category for the decision of moral questions. But that does not mean that
in a free society they cannot enjoy and exploit the advantage of the
superior mind. The lawmaker's task, even in a democracy, is not the
drab one of counting heads or of synthesizing answers to moral questions set up in a Gallup poll. In theory a sharp line can be drawn between law and morality as they are—positive law and positive morality
—and as they ought to be; but in practice no such line can be drawn,
because positive morality, like every other basis for the law, is subject
to change, and consequently the law has to be developed. A judge is
tethered to the positive law but not tied to it. So long as he does not
break away from the positive law, that is, from the precedents which
are set for him or the clear language of the statute which he is applying, he can determine for himself the distance and direction of his
advance. Naturally he will move towards the law as he thinks it ought
to be. If he has moved in the right direction, along the way his society
would wish to go, there will come a time when the tethering-point is

uprooted and moved nearer to the position he has taken; if he has moved in the wrong direction, he or his successors will be pulled back.

The legislator as an enforcer of morals has far greater latitude than the modern judge. Legislation of that sort is not usually made an election issue but is left to the initiative of those who are returned to power. In deciding whether or not to take the initiative the relevant question nearly always is not what popular morality is but whether it should be enforced by the criminal law. If there is a reasonable doubt on the first point, that doubt of itself answers the whole question in the negative. The legislator must gauge the intensity with which a popular moral conviction is held, because it is only when the obverse is generally thought to be intolerable that the criminal law can safely and properly be used. But if he decides that point in favor of the proposed legislation, there are many other factors, some of principle and some of expediency, to be weighed, and these give the legislator a very wide discretion in determining how far he will go in the direction of the law as he thinks it ought to be. The restraint upon him is that if he moves too far from the common sense of his society, he will forfeit the popular goodwill and risk seeing his work undone by his successor.

This is the method of lawmaking common to both our countries; the popular vote does not itself enact or veto; rather, the initiative is put into the hands of a very few men. Under this method the law reformer has a double opportunity. He may work upon the popular opinion which is the lawmaker's base, or he may influence the lawmaker directly. At each of these stages the educated man is at an advantage in a democratic society.

Let us consider the first stage. True it is that in the final count the word of the educated man goes for no more than that of any other sort of man. But in the making up of the tally he has or should have the advantage of powers of persuasion above the ordinary. I do not mean by that simply powers of reasoning. If he is to be effective he must be ready to persuade and not just to teach, and he must accept that reason is not the plain man's only guide. "The common morality of a society at any time," says Dean Rostow, "is a blend of custom and conviction, of reason and feeling, of experience and prejudice."* If an educated man is armed only with reason, if he is disdainful of custom and ignores strength of feeling, if he thinks of "prejudice" and "intolerance" as words with no connotations that are not disgraceful and is blind to religious conviction, he had better not venture outside

* Dean Rostow, *The Enforcement of Morals,* 1960 Camb. L. J. 197.

his academy, for if he does he will have to deal with forces he cannot understand. Not all learned men are prepared like Bertrand Russell to sit on the pavement outside No. 10 Downing Street. Not all are lucid as well as erudite. Many a man will find satisfaction in teaching others to do what he is not equipped to do himself; but it is naive for such a man to reproach judges and legislators for making what he deems to be irrational law, as if in a democratic society they were the agents only of reason and the controllers of a nation's thought.

The other advantage which the educated man possesses is that he has easier access to the ear of the lawmaker. I do not mean merely by lobbying. When—with such latitude as our democratic and judicial system allows—the lawmaker is determining the pace and direction of his advance from the law that is towards the law that ought to be, he does and should inform himself of the views of wise and experienced men and pay extra attention to them.

These are the ways by which well-informed and articulate men can play a part in the shaping of the law quite disproportionate to their numbers. Under a system in which no single question is submitted to the electorate for direct decision, an ardent minority for or against a particular measure may often count for more than an apathetic majority. Recently in England in the reform of the criminal law a minority has had some remarkable successes. In 1948 flogging was abolished as a judicial punishment; it is doubtful whether that would have been the result of a majority vote, and it is still uncertain whether the gain will be held. Some years later much the same body of opinion was very nearly successful in abolishing capital punishment; I do not believe that in the country as a whole there is a majority against capital punishment. In 1959 the common law on obscenity was altered by statute. Notwithstanding that the tendency of a book is to deprave and corrupt, it is a good defense if its publication is in the interests of some "object of general concern," such as literature or art; and the opinion of experts is made admissable on the merits of the work. Under this latter provision in the recent case of *Lady Chatterley's Lover*, thirty-five witnesses distinguished in the fields of literature and morals were permitted to discuss at large the merits of the book, and thus a specially qualified body of opinion was brought into direct communication with the jury. On the other hand there has so far been a failure to reform the law against homosexuality. The conclusion of the Wolfenden Committee is an indication—I believe a correct one—that a substantial majority of "educated opinion" is in favor of some modification; but I believe also that the Home Secretary was right in his conclusion that public opinion as a whole was too strongly against the proposed amendments to permit legislation.

I have been considering this subject on the assumption that the extent to which the moral law is translated into the law of the land is determined chiefly by the legislature. In England that has appeared to be so at any rate during the last hundred years. The law that is now consolidated in the Sexual Offences Act of 1956 is mainly the creation of statute. Incest, for example, all homosexual offenses, and carnal knowledge of girls under the age of sixteen were never crimes at common law. Parliament in a series of statutes felt its way cautiously towards the curbing of prostitution, approaching the situation obliquely and at several different angles. The second cardinal enunciation of principles in *Shaw's* case, to which I must now return, is that in matters of morals the common law has abandoned none of its rights and duties; and the third relates to the function of the jury.

What exactly is meant by a conspiracy to corrupt public morals? We all know what a conspiracy is in law. Since acts of immorality are rarely committed by one person only, it is not in this branch of the law an element of much importance; indeed, it is uncertain whether it is a necessary ingredient in the crime. What limits, if any, are implicit in the words "public" and "corrupt"? Is it corruption to offer an adult an opportunity of committing, not for the first time, an immoral act? If so, what element of publicity has there to be about it? In the course of a very strong dissenting speech Lord Reid reached the conclusion that the successful argument by the Crown made "unlawful every act which tends to lead a single individual morally astray."[*] Their lordships in the majority refrained—I think, deliberately—from defining their terms. They left the work to the jury. Lord Simonds said: "The uncertainty that necessarily arises from the vagueness of general words can only be resolved by the opinion of twelve chosen men and women."[†] On the question of what was meant by the words in the indictment Lord Tucker said: "It is for the jury to construe and apply these words to the facts proved in evidence and reach their own decision . . . ."[‡] Lord Morris said: "Even if accepted public standards may to some extent vary from generation to generation, current standards are in the keeping of juries, who can be trusted to maintain the corporate good sense of the community and to discern attacks upon values that must be preserved."[**] Lord Hodson said that the function of *custos morum* would ultimately be performed by the jury: "[I]n the field of public morals it will thus be the morality of the man in the jury box that will determine the fate of the accused . . . ."[***]

---

[*] Shaw v. Director of Pub. Prosecutions, [1961] 2 Weekly L.R. 926 (H.L.) (Lord Reid).   [†] *Id.* at 919.   [‡] *Id.* at 937.   [**] *Id.* at 938.   [***] *Id.* at 940.

The opinions in *Shaw*'s case will certainly give rise to much debate. Critics of the majority view complain that it removes from the criminal law on morals the element of reasonable certainty. The relationship between statute and common law surely needs further elucidation. In this respect the immediate impact of the case is sharp. The legislators in Whitehall, inching forward clause by clause towards their moral objectives, topped a rise only to find the flag of their ally, the common law, whom they erroneously believed to be comatose (the Crown cited only three reported cases of conspiracy to corrupt public morals since Lord Mansfield's dictum in 1763), flying over the whole territory, a small part of which they had laboriously occupied.

There is another important aspect of the case, and that is whether, in placing so heavy a burden on the jury, it has brought about a shift of responsibility for decisions in the moral field that affects the democratic process I have endeavoured to describe.

If the only question the jury had to decide was whether or not a moral belief was generally held in the community, the jury would, I think, be an excellent tribunal. It will be objected that the decision would not be that of a jury alone but of a jury assisted by a judge; and in the minds of many reformers, some of whom identify liberalism with relaxation, the views of a judge on what is immoral are suspect. It is true that on this question a judge usually takes the conservative view, but then, so does the British public.

This is, however, as I have now stressed several times, unlikely to be the issue. The argument will not usually be about the immorality of the act but about whether the arm of the law should be used to suppress it. Hitherto the role of the jury has been negative and never formally recognized. The jury resists the enforcement of laws which it thinks to be too harsh. The law has never conceded that it has the right to do that, but it has been accepted that in practice it will exercise its power in that way. The novelty in the dicta in *Shaw*'s case is that they formally confer on the jury a positive function in law enforcement. It cannot be intended that the jury's only duty is to draw the line between public morality and immorality. If, for example, a man and a woman were charged with conspiring to corrupt public morals by openly living in sin, a jury today might be expected to acquit. If homosexuality were to cease to be per se criminal and two men were to be similarly charged with flaunting their relationship in public, a jury today might be expected—I think that this is what Lord Simonds and Lord Tucker would contemplate—to convict. The distinction can be made only on the basis that one sort of immorality ought to be condemned and punished and the other not. That is a matter on which many people besides lawyers are qualified to speak and would desire to be heard before a decision is reached. When a minister submits the issue to Parliament, they can be heard; when a judge submits it to a jury, they cannot. The main burden of Lord Reid's trenchant criticism of the majority opinion is that it allows and requires the jury to perform the function of the legislator.

Of course the courts would never deny the supremacy of Parliament. If Parliament dislikes the fruits of the legal process, it can say so; frequently in the past it has altered the law declared by the courts. But in the legislative process the forces of inertia are considerable; and in matters of morals negative legislation is especially difficult, because relaxation is thought to imply approval. So whoever has the initiative has the advantage. For the moment it appears that the common law has regained the initiative.

Whether it retains it or not, *Shaw's* case settles for the purposes of the law that morality in England means what twelve men and women think it means—in other words, it is to be ascertained as a question of fact. I am not repelled by that phrase, nor do I resent in such a matter submission to the mentality of the common man. Those who believe in God and that He made man in His image will believe also that He gave to each in equal measure the knowledge of good and evil, placing it not in the intellect wherein His grant to some was more bountiful than to others, but in the heart and understanding, building there in each man the temple of the Holy Ghost. Those who do not believe in God must ask themselves what they *mean* when they say that they believe in democracy. Not that all men are born with equal brains— we cannot believe that; but that they have at their command—and that in this they are all born in the same degree—the faculty of telling right from wrong: this is the whole meaning of democracy, for if in this endowment men were not equal, it would be pernicious that in the government of any society they should have equal rights.

To hold that morality is a question of fact is not to deify the *status quo* or to deny the perfectibility of man. The unending search for truth goes on and so does the struggle towards the perfect society. It is our common creed that no society can be perfect unless it is a free society; and a free society is one that is created not as an end in itself but as a means of securing and advancing the bounds of freedom for the individuals who live within it. This is not the creed of all mankind. In this world as it is no man can be free unless he lives within the protection of a free society; if a free man needed society for no other reason, he would need it for this, that if he stood alone his freedom would be in peril. In the free society there are men, fighters for freedom, who strain at the bonds of their society, having a vision of life as they feel it ought to be. They live gloriously, and many of them die gloriously, and in life and death they magnify freedom. What they gain and as they gain it becomes the property of their society and is to be kept: the law is its keeper. So there are others, defenders and not attackers, but also fighters for freedom, for those who defend a free society defend freedom. These others are those who serve the law. They do not look up too often to the heights of what ought to be lest they lose sight of the ground on which they stand and which it is their duty to defend—the law as it is, morality as it is, freedom as it is— none of them perfect but the things that their society has got and must not let go. It is the faith of the English lawyer, as it is of all those other lawyers who took and enriched the law that Englishmen first made, that most of what their societies have got is good. With that faith they serve the law, saying as Cicero said, "*Legum deniquo . . . omnos oorvi sumus ut liberi esse possimus.*" In the end we are all of us slaves to the law, for that is the condition of our freedom.

Further Reading On
GOVERNMENT, LAW, AND THE PUBLIC MORALS

Armour, Leslie. "The Concept of Crime." *Philosophy in Context.* 1973.

Bedau, Hugo (ed.). *Civil Disobedience.* New York: Pegasus, 1969.

Blake, Ralph Mason. "On Natural Rights." *Ethics,* Vol. 36, No. 1, October 1925.

Broad, Charles D. *Five Types of Ethical Theory.* New York: Harcourt, 1954.

Cassier, Ernst. *The Myth of the State.* New Haven: Yale University Press, 1946.

d'Entrenes, A. P. *Natural Law.* London: Hutchinson, 1951.

Ebenstein, William. *Great Political Thinkers.* New York: Holt, Rinehart and Winston, 1951.

Ewing, A. C. *Ethics.* London: English Universities Press, 1953.

Friedman, W. *Legal Theory.* London: Stevens and Sons, 1960.

Gough, J. W. *John Locke's Political Philosophy.* Oxford: Clarendon Press, 1950.

Hart, H. L. A. *Law, Liberty, and Morality.* Stanford: Stanford University Press, 1963.

Hart, H. L. A. *The Concept of Law.* Oxford: Clarendon Press, 1961.

Hill, Thomas English. *Contemporary Ethical Theories.* New York: Macmillan, 1950.

Hobbes, Thomas. *Leviathan.* 1651.

Hook, Sidney (ed.). *Law and Philosophy.* New York: New York University Press, 1964.

Kelsen, Hans. *What Is Justice?* Berkeley: University of California Press, 1960.

Laslett, Peter. *Philosophy, Politics, and Society.* Oxford: Basil Blackwell, 1967.

Margolis, Joseph. "Punishment." *Social Theory and Practice,* Spring 1973.

Mayer, Peter (ed.). *The Pacifist Conscience.* Chicago: Henry Regnery, 1966.

McCloskey, H. J. "Ross and the Concept of Prima Facie Duty." *Australasian Journal of Philosophy,* 1963.

Moore, G. E. *Ethics*. New York: Oxford, 1949.

Nielsen, Kai. "When Are Immoralities Crimes?" *Philosophia* (*Israel*), July 1971.

Olafson, Frederick A. *Society, Law, and Morality*. Englewood Cliffs: Prentice Hall, 1961.

Perelman, Chaim. *The Idea of Justice and the Problem of Argument*. London: Routledge and Kegan Paul, 1963.

Rader, Melvin. *Ethics and Society*. New York: Holt, 1950.

Rousseau, Jean Jacques. *The Social Contract*. 1763.

Sidgwick, Henry. *Methods of Ethics*. London: Macmillan & Co. Ltd., 1922.

Stace, Walter. *The Concept of Morals*. New York: Macmillan, 1937.

Stumpf, Samuel Enoch. *Morality and the Law* Nashville: Vanderbilt University Press, 1966.

Wasserstrom, Richard. "The Relevance of Nuremberg." *Philosophy and Public Affairs*, Fall 1971.

Wasserstrom, Richard (ed.). *War and Morality* Belmont, California: Wadsworth, 1971.

Weinroth, Jay. "A Marxian View of Crime." *Philosophy in Context*, 1973.

PART III

VIOLENCE AND THE NATURE OF MAN

INTRODUCTORY ILLUSTRATION

. . . He was sort of flattened to the wall and his platties were a disgrace, all creased and untidy and covered in cal and mud and filth and stuff. So we got hold of him and cracked him with a few good horrorshow tolchocks, but he still went on singing. . . .

So we cracked into him lovely, grinning all over our litsos, but he still went on singing. Then we tripped him so he laid down flat and heavy and a bucketload of beer-vomit came whooshing out. That was disgusting so we gave him the boot, one go each, and then itwas blood, not song nor vomit, that came out of his filthy-old rot. Then we went on our way.

Anthony Burgess, *A Clockwork Orange* (New York: Ballantine Books, 1962), p. 20 and p. 21.

INTRODUCTORY ILLUSTRATION

. . . so I gave her a malenky fair kick in the litso, and she didn't like that, crying: 'Waaaaah,' and you could viddy her veiny mottled litso going purplewurple where I'd landed the old noga . . . and the old forella started to fist me on the litso, both of us being on the floor, creeching: 'Thrash him, beat him, pull out his finger-nails, the poisonous young beetle' . . . So then I creeched: 'You filthy old smooka,' and upped with the little malenky like silver statue and cracked her a fine fair tolchock on the gulliver and that shut her up real horrorshow and lovely.

Anthony Burgess, *A Clockwork Orange* (New York: Ballantine Books, 1962), pp. 63 and 64.

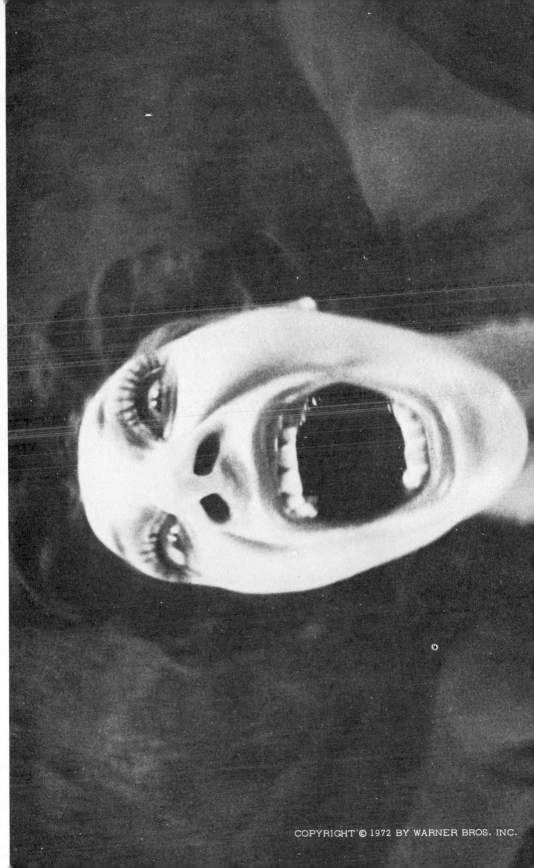

INQUIRY

The whole structure depended on the first premise: that man was decent.

T. H. WHITE, *The Once and Future King*

IT is commonplace to proclaim that we human beings are a violent species. History is replete with violence: our wars, our revolutions, our assassinations and massacres, our destructions of persons and natural environments. Although it may seem that in the 1960's and 1970's human life has taken a peculiarly violent turn, such an appearance is more likely due to the pervasive nature of our mass media daily bringing stories of violence into our homes than to any qualitative change in human behavior.

Most of us claim to be revolted by violence. Some political leaders, M. K. Gandhi and Martin Luther King, Jr., in particular, renounced violence and yet were assassinated. What is this that revolts us? What have some men renounced? What have others, such as Frantz Fanon and members of many radical organizations and urban guerrilla groups, espoused? In short, what is our idea of violence and how does it relate to our idea of human nature?

We could begin by constructing examples that strike us as illustrative of violent acts. There would be no philosophically important point in seeing whether one could narrate the most gruesome, ugly, or heinous crime. A true borderline case, however, one in which uncertainty exists in regard to the appropriateness of labeling the acts in question "violent," reveals much of our concept of violence. Such storytelling might begin with what seems a clear-cut case, such as Alex and his droogs in *A Clockwork Orange* raping and murdering women and kicking old men, and then proceed to more and more subtle manifestations of violence, e.g., psychological violence. But the elusive border between acts of violence and acts that do not do violence will probably still remain vague and uncertain. In fact, many purported nonviolent acts do real personal (if not physical) harm to those against whom they are directed. Is this not what in part motivates civil rights sit-ins, lettuce boycotts, etc.?

The *Oxford English Dictionary* begins its catalogue of definitions of *violence* with "the exercise of physical force so as to inflict injury on, or cause damage to persons or property. . . ." The idea of force, especially physical force, often has been tied to that of violence and would doubtless be a major element in any ordinary man's attempt to characterize a violent act. Utterance of the word "violence" brings forth pictures not unlike those at the beginning of this part of the text. Physical force, however, is not a sufficient condition of violence; it may not even be a necessary condition. Consider, for example, the dentist who must exert considerable force to remove an impacted tooth. He is not performing an act of violence, though we might say that he tugged violently at the tooth. Should he be ill-trained or lack skill in dentistry, however, he may well do violence to his patients. The key, of course, is not "force," but "force that inflicts injury." But what kinds of force and what sort of injury?

J. L. Austin's "trailing clouds of etymology" are helpful. The word *violence* has the same Latin root as the word *violate*. Alex violates the Catlady; he does her violence, he acts violently. What sort of things can be violated? We talk of the violation of persons, rights, property, laws, rules, etc. However, these are not all of the same class. In fact, the violation of rules or laws is not necessarily violent unless those rules primarily concern people, property, animals, or various rights. Hence the violation of a rule of baseball is not generally a violent act unless that violation is, for example, the deliberate beaning of a batter by a pitcher.

Let us examine the notion of violating a person. What does it mean to say that Alex violated the Catlady? The obvious answer is that he infringed upon her rights, in particular her right to her own body and life. In Part II of this book the notion of rights was examined. As we saw, some philosophers hold that each individual has certain natural rights, among which might be found the right to one's own body and life. Hence the acts of rape and murder are violent acts because the rapist and murderer violate a natural right of their victims. The idea of natural rights, however, is problematical, and our attempt to understand the concept of violence would only be postponed by wading again into that topic. (It should not be forgotten, however, that many classical political philosophers believed the right of property is paramount even to that of life.) At any rate, the notion of violence does seem to involve some sense of violation and most probably, in the case of persons, that of rights.

The fact that the idea of force usually accompanies that of violence suggests another important issue in our attempt to understand what violence is. Some philosophers have maintained that force in itself is not violent, even if it is used to bring others to act against their own will. For example, incarcerating criminals is a form of force directed specifically at preventing prisoners from exercising their will, though prisons are not considered to be institutions of violence for this reason by most people. What grounds can then be found for differentiating between violent force and force that is not violent?

Robert Paul Wolff argues that violence should be defined as the *illegitimate* use of force. Thus conscription into the armed forces by a legitimate authority is not violence, while an act of impression into servitude by a slaver is an act of violence. Slavery itself may be an act of violence. Then Wolff argues that from a moral point of view there is no legitimate authority other than each individual himself, that morally no man can relinquish his authority to another authority. Hence there is ultimately no clear-cut way of distinguishing violent from nonviolent acts as made in political contexts, because any sense of "legitimate authority" is, if not destroyed, made irrelevant.

"Violent" is a way of characterizing actions and in a derivative way people and animals, and "violence" would seem to characterize a class of actions. Although the term "violent" is descriptive and "violence" classificatory, they also appear to connote the evaluative sense of bad, evil, or wrong. "Alex acts violently, Alex enjoys violence" and "Violence has become his life-style" all sound negative and disapproving. Perhaps the supposed attachment of violence to evil is due to the persuasive rhetoric of many religious leaders and other champions of nonviolence such as Gandhi. But is violence necessarily evil? Is nonviolence always virtuous? Frantz Fanon, for example, argues that a case cannot be made that violence is never a creative and positive force in human history. In his famous book *The Wretched of the Earth,* he writes:

> ... for the colonized people this violence, because it constitutes their only work, invests their characters with positive and creative qualities. The practice of violence binds them together as a whole, since each individual forms a violent link in the great chain, a part of the great organism of violence. . . .*

* Frantz Fanon, *The Wretched of the Earth* (New York: Grove Press, 1965), p. 93.

One might picture Arab terrorists, linked in violence, defending their acts as creative, as molding the future of Palestine, as positive, in fact, virtuous actions—not despite of but because of their violence, leaving in their wake hundreds of mangled victims. Lt. William Calley used a somewhat similar defense of his behavior during the massacre at My Lai 4.

The argument that violence, at least under certain conditions, is not only defensible but virtuous should not be dismissed lightly. Ecologists and environmentalists tell us that the earth's resources are being exhausted at an ever accelerating pace and that the future holds serious survival problems for the human population. The earth just will not, they claim, support a human population that is growing at the current rate. Let us simplify the situation in order to better grasp the problems. Suppose the time arrives when the earth and human technology will be able to support only 500 million people and at that time 4 billion people are living, if but barely. If the resources available were to be equitably distributed, all would eventually perish of starvation or poisoning from pollution. Reason would seem to dictate the systematic elimination of large numbers of people (genocide) and the institution of practices designed to prevent a future growth of the surviving population (sterilization, abortion, infanticide, killing of the elderly). All acts of this sort are surely violent and would certainly be so in the circumstances envisioned, for few could be expected to submit willingly. But, granted the circumstances, would they not be the right things to do? Would not violence, perhaps even murder for play and genocide for entertainment, become a virtue because it would lengthen the odds that others would die of starvation? Alex and his droogs in such a world might even be heroic.

This scenario may sound terribly concocted, and many will say that it will never happen because people will not allow violence to become virtue. Recently, anthropologist Colin Turnbull, however, has published a study of a people in the northern mountains of Uganda who already live in such a world.* The Ik were once a happy, closely related, socially active society that hunted successfully in the regions of Uganda, Sudan, and Kenya. Political reality in the form of emerging nationalisms in that region, however, served to force the Ik into a restricted area of the Ugandan mountains and isolated them from their most productive hunting grounds. They were forced to farm. The land was poor, the drought came, and the

* Colin Turnbull, *The Mountain People* (New York: Simon and Schuster, 1972).

Ik began en masse to starve to death. The old were the first to die, and the younger Ik, according to Turnbull, made a choice to survive at the cost of their traditions, values, and principles—their very way of life. Today few Iks remain, but they do survive, though reduced in number, because they have adopted various forms of violence toward each other as a way of life. They steal food from the mouths of the old, they turn the young out at the age of three to roam in gangs not unlike Alex's droogs, and when they observe each other suffering or dying they laugh.

> I went to see what the excitement was about. It was . . . Lo'ono. She too had been abandoned, and had tried to make her way down the mountainside. But she was totally blind and had tripped and rolled to the bottom . . . and there she lay on her back, her legs and arms thrashing feebly, while a little crowd standing on the edge above looked down at her and laughed at the spectacle.†

We must keep in mind that the study of violence is the study, generally speaking, of a tactic that violence is a means toward some end and only in certain pathological cases is it an end in itself. Often the question of violence arises only after the ends or goals or needs have been chosen or have manifested themselves. It is often asked, What restraints should be placed on the choice of the means of attaining the goal? But is that really a viable question? Traditional answers from moralists and politicians have been inconclusive and often inconsistent regarding the uses of violence. We have been taught that when the need is to prevent a foreign invasion, all normal restraints against violence are inoperative. What will happen when the goal is mere subsistence-level survival? Troy Organ tells us that "violence may be . . . part of the only possible heaven on earth. Violence may be the religion of the future." The notion of restraint, the view that violence is necessarily evil and destructive, the idea of virtue itself may prove to be only the fruits of affluence and may soon have the hollow sound of echoes in the cornucopia of plenty, depleted and unreplenished.

† Ibid., p. 226.

1 TROY ORGAN

(1912–   )

*The Anatomy of Violence**

Organ analyzes the concept of violence in terms of violent acts. Violent acts are those perpetrated by sentient beings upon other sentient beings without regard for the feelings and wishes of the other. Traditionally nonviolence has been taught as a virtue and violence as a vice, but Organ raises serious questions regarding that view. Nonviolence, he claims, is an offspring of affluence, which in a world of lessening resources may not be the rational way to behave. He dissects the forms in which violence appears, hedonic, frustrated, and committed, in terms of motivation. Hence some violent acts are done because they are enjoyed, some out of sheer frustration (disapproval of the status quo), while still other violent acts are the result of commitment to some ideal or principle. In its third form violence is often an uncontestable proof of conviction, the final affirmation of belief.

* Troy Organ, "The Anatomy of Violence," *The Personalist*, Vol. 51, Fall 1970, pp. 417–433. Used by permission of the Editor.

O NE of man's most persistent self-delusions is that he is the rational animal. The nonrational animals—the lower animals—are red in tooth and claw, but man uses the intellect to solve problems—so he thinks. Yet with the exception of the deer, the dove, the Siamese fighting fish and a few others, the lower animals do no serious physical harm upon other members of their own species. The human animal on the other hand has been involved in internecine warfare during much of his appearance on the earth. Although man supposes that to be rational is to be human, one could more truthfully state that to be violent is to be human.

Violence refers primarily to acts. Thoughts or feelings may be said to be violent only if they lead to violent acts. Violent acts form a subclass of acts done directly or indirectly upon beings capable of sensation and consciousness. To speak of breaking rocks violently or slapping water violently is to speak animistically. Destruction of property may be said to be violent only in the sense that it is an act against the owner of the property. A violent act is always an act in which the actor imposes his will upon another without regard for the will and desire of the one upon whom the act is directed. A dog may be treated violently;

a dogwood tree probably cannot be treated violently; a piece of wood certainly cannot be so treated. Violence may be characterized as an act of a sentient being upon another sentient being without regard for his feelings or wishes. A violent act imposes the will of the actor upon another. The intent may be either good or evil.

Non-violence has been praised almost universally by religious and ethical teachers. Peace, good will, harmlessness, compassion, charity, and love are the chief masks non-violence wears in various human cultures. But man has not heeded his prophets and seers. While giving lip service to the virtue of non-violence, he has not felt secure without a weapon in hand, a weapon that may range from fist axe to hydrogen bomb.

Man's moral evolution from savage to savant is believed to be a passage from passion to reason. Civilization is thought to be the desertion of the old ways of violence and the inauguration of non-violent techniques for promoting orderly change. Hebrew moral law, Greek philosophy, Christian theology, and Roman politics were civilizing influences in the development of Western culture. Correlative developments appeared in Eastern culture. Yet both in East and West the rejection of the ways of violence has been neither widespread nor lasting. In India at the time when Gandhi was pleading for non-violence, Shaheed Suhrarwardy, the Chief Minister of Bengal, wrote, "Bloodshed and disorder are not necessarily evil in themselves, if resorted to for a noble cause." [1] At the same time B. R. Ambedkar, the chairman of the Constitution Committee, offered the admonition, "Non-violence wherever possible; violence wherever necessary." [2] One of the most beautiful apologies for violence couched in the language of the Enlightenment begins with these words: "When in the course of human events, it becomes necessary for one people to dissolve the political bands which have connected them with another, and to assume among the powers of the earth, the separate and equal station to which the Laws of Nature and of Nature's God entitle them, a decent respect to the opinions of mankind requires that they should declare the causes which impel them to the separation." This document, like the words of Suhrarwardy and Ambedkar, recognizes the necessity of the resort to violence: "We must, therefore, acquiesce in the necessity, which denounces our Separation, and hold them (i.e., the British), as we hold the rest of mankind, Enemies in War, in peace, Friends." The rational

---

[1] *The Statesman* (Calcutta), August 5, 1946.
[2] Dhananjay Kerr, *Dr. Ambedkar, Life and Mission.* Bombay: A. V. Kerr, 1954, p. 87.

animal must have reason for his irrationality! He must find some causes which require him to act violently.

Although the United States of America was conceived in violence, the new nation became a haven of freedom, opportunity, and security for millions of oppressed peoples. The Statue of Liberty's invitation

> Give me your tired, your poor,
> Your huddled masses yearning to breathe free,
> The wretched refuse of your teeming shore.
> Send these, the homeless, tempest-tost to me,
> I lift my lamp beside the golden door!

symbolized the hopes and aspirations of those who came to this land. The more energetic Europeans emigrated to America. Hence it is not surprising that it was these people who drove the Indians from their land and who fought one of the most savage civil wars of all time. In the twentieth century America has engaged in two World Wars, a Korean War, a Viet Nam War, and several lesser armed conflicts, yet her self-image is that of a peaceful nation. At the same time her leaders insist that she not allow other nations to surpass her in military might. "Bargaining from a position of strength" is the politicians' cliché. In addition to her stockpile of atomic weapons the United States has stored sufficient nerve gas to kill the human population of the world thirty times over. Other gases kept in reserve include vast quantities of vomit gas, tear gas, and incapacitating gas. Also in the "peace-keeping arsenal" are agents to induce anthrax, tularemia, Q-fever, and psittacosis. Work progresses on techniques for inducing plagues of undulant fever, coccidioidomycosis, botulism, cholera, encephalitis, Rocky Mountain spotted fever, and other diseases. Yet the United States agreed to the 1966 United Nations resolution outlawing the use of chemical-biological weapons. She has given notice on several occasions that she will not be the first to use chemical-biological weapons, but the peoples of the world cannot forget that America is the only nation that has used atomic bombs—nor can they forget the bombs were dropped on Oriental cities.

The violence syndrome is coming to a head in America. How to explain to the ghetto dweller and the college student that total warfare is approved as foreign policy but not as instrument of internal social pressure? That violence is allowable for a nation but not for the people of the nation? That unconditional surrender may be demanded of foreign enemies but non-negotiable demands have no place in American society? That violence is an unfortunate necessity internationally but law and order must be maintained on streets and campuses? That what a nation wants may be secured by violence but what a group within the nation wants must be secured by legal means?

If man must find convincing arguments for violence, so also he must give reasons for those occasions when he acts non-violently. When is non-violence a virtue? When may we justifiably be asked to turn the other cheek, to go the second mile, to share a loaf of bread, and to give cloak and coat? The answer may shock at first, for it may not be what the man of good will expected. In simplest terms it is this: Benevolent acts may be done and benevolent gifts may be given to a member of the secondary group only when doing so does not deprive one of performing the proper acts toward those of the primary group. If giving food and clothing to a stranger takes needed food away from one's child, this act is not virtuous. Non-violence in this respect is like benevolence. Acting non-violently is virtuous only when this way of acting does not conflict with what society considers to be its primary obligations. Who would praise the man who gave away his family's food supply when there was no food available to replace it? Who would call virtuous the man who offered no resistance to a kidnapper stealing his child? Non-violence is a prodigality of affluence. The rich do not need to act violently, and with bread and circuses, dole and social security, they may induce the poor not to seize more than they have. But the good earth is not boundless in resources for life. The time will come when mines are exhausted, when rivers, lakes and oceans can no longer support aquatic life, and when the land can no longer produce enough food for the human population. Will non-violence then be a virtue? Long before living space per man has shrunk to the spatial limitations of the human body we shall have given up the view of non-violence as a virtue. In order to preserve human life on this planet we shall need to declare some violent acts virtuous. Specifically we shall need to limit births. Voluntary limitation has not worked thus far, and we see little hope that it will work in the future. The time will come when sterilization, abortion, infanticide, mercy slaying, and other techniques of limiting the number of human beings on this planet must be imposed without consideration for individual wishes. These acts will be violent, and they will be done without apology, for they will be virtuous.

We who love democracy and cherish the liberal tradition may not wish to contemplate the collapse of our freedom, our egalitarianism, and our individualism, but human survival on this planet and on any planet capable of supporting human life depends upon the control of human population. Society will ultimately be based on forced controls. The best that lovers of democracy can hope is that the inevitable be postponed as long as possible. We are approaching the end of the fruitfulness of the Hebrew-Greek-Christian-Roman tradition in the West, and also, we may add, of the Buddhist-Hindu-Confucian-Taoist tradition in the East. Man's continued existence on this globe will depend either upon ways of behaving far different from any he has been able to muster in social situations other than those in a monastery or convent, or upon what we have chosen to call violence. The former seems highly improbable; the latter unavoidable—unless man chooses genocide. Looking at man's future from the point of view of a secular eschatology gives us little ground for hoping we can escape violence. There is only the remotest possibility that man can discipline his self-destructive propensities in time to stave off ultimate destruction. The programs and sanctions of religion—the Buddhist middle path, the Hindu tolerance, the Hebrew law, and the Christian charity—will be completely inadequate under the ultimate conditions even as they are of limited adequacy under penultimate conditions. The time approaches when the preservation of the human race may depend upon a few in whom wisdom dwells controlling violently the acts of other men. For example, all male children will conceivably be sterilized at birth save for a few breeders who will be the source of sperm to fertilize under laboratory conditions ova selected for development into human replacements. Death will probably be as regulated as birth. Few of us today are prepared to accept such a world, but given man's power to adjust, we can conceive of our descendants welcoming this mode of birth and death as quite normal and proper. We today can at least prepare ourselves for the future state of our race by examining the anatomy of violence.

Violence appears in three forms: the hedonic, the frustrated, and the committed. These may be thought of as motivations of the act. The three are different emphases. Any violent act will be marked more by one than by either of the other two. Seldom, if ever, does one form appear in the total absence of the other two. Let us consider as an example one of the favorite tactics of militant minorities: arson. Churches, libraries, business houses, post offices, buses, railway coaches, apartment houses, shops, and private dwellings have been burned by protesting minorities. But to what end? What appears to the majority as senseless destruction may appear to the minority as essential and meaningful. A specific act of arson may be planned by the minority as a symbol of its dedication to a social ideal: the old must go in order that the new may come. The act may in addition reflect the frustration of the minority caught in what appears to be a hopeless situation and it may also be an effort to experience the hedonic satisfaction of destroying something the minority would like to possess. This plurality of motives may come out in the arsonists' analysis of the act. It is described as an act of commitment in their appearance in a court of law, as an act of frustration in their conversation with a social worker, and as a fun act in the reliving of the event among their peers.

HEDONIC VIOLENCE

In recent years much of the violence in American slums and ghettos has occurred in "the long hot summer." While some have attempted to account for this as the impact of heat and humidity on bodies, the better explanation is that summer is the dull time of the year for dwellers in the innercity. The schools are not in session, the children are on the streets, young people are home from college, and it is a slack time in factories and industries with vacations for men and women who have no place to go but their flats or the streets. It is a time of boredom in which a bit of excitement is a welcome change from the dull monotony of the days. A fist fight, a car accident, or a broken shop window are welcome breaks in a humdrum day. Violence can be fun both for the participant and for the onlooker. Car thieves, bank robbers, kidnappers, and even murderers when brought to trial try to rationalize why they did what they did, when the truth is that there may have been no well thought out motivation. It seemed like fun at the time. But to say "I did it just for kicks" is not the explanation one wants to give in a courtroom, so the hedonic event is couched in fine-sounding words about social justice, protest movements, community frustrations, and economic pressures.

Violence is enjoyable. This is one reason why people attend spectator sports such as cockfights, bullfights, boxing, wrestling, football, hockey, auto races, and rollerskate derbies. These are emotional equivalents for war, the most thrilling "sport" of all the combat sports. General George Patton observed at the close of World War II, "War is hell—and how I love it!"

The component parts of hedonic violence are four. The first is relief of monotony. Any human activity pursued for a long period of time must be broken. The coffee break is based on the sound principle of alternation in human life. Human effort, physical or mental, must be interrupted or there is a noticeable loss of efficiency, creativity, and enjoyment. Examples are numerous: the athlete must occasionally break training lest he overtrain; the Zen master breaks into a long period of meditation with the order "Let us laugh!"; the Epicureans supplanted their simple diet of bread and gruel with a banquet once a month; the Lenten season is often divided by a day in which restrictions are rescinded. Moral holidays, emotional outbursts, laughs over a simple joke, and violent acts have one common denominator: they serve to break the strain, concentration, and dullness of one way of acting, thinking, evaluating.

A second component of hedonic violence is its unpredictability. Probability or statistical predictability is the rule of all human life. The farmer who sows his seed knows that if he does not sow he will not reap, but he also knows that sowing is no guarantee that there will be reaping. Acts of violence are even more unpredictable. War, which is violence in the extreme, has been characterized as a science, but the truth is that it bears a greater resemblance to art. Victory in war is not merely a matter of materiel and strategy; it depends still more on the intangibles of determination, the will to fight, the desire to victory, the conciousness of destiny, and other highly unpredictable psychological features. All violent acts are like that Violent acts are, as we have said, the imposition of the will of one sentient being on the will of another sentient being. The response of persons to violence is not predictable. One person offers resistance at one time, acquiescence at another. This is part of the tantalizing nature of a violent act

A third feature of hedonic violence is the thrill of destruction. The enjoyment of destroying is noticed early in the life of the human infant. The child soon experiences the excitement of knocking down piles of blocks and smashing sand castles. Why such acts are enjoyable is difficult to say. Perhaps the satisfaction is in the feeling of mastery and domination over inanimate objects. The phenomenon appears in adult years in watching a four-alarm fire in an apartment building, a free-standing chimney dropped by a dynamite blast, a demolition ball smash a brick wall, and a bulldozer push over trees. How much of the violence in the streets of Watts and Detroit was the result of the fun of destroying something? Destruction has not been incorporated into the philosophies and religions of the Establishment in the West. We keep the devil out of the godhead. Not so in India. The Trimurti (three forms) of the godhead in Hinduism is Creation (Bramā), Preservation (Viṣṇu), and Destruction (Śiva). This is probably more in accord with the nature of things; it is certainly more in accord with the nature of the human psyche. It is fun to destroy.

The last component of hedonic violence to be mentioned is what may be called the fascination of the terrible. John Bunyan, writes J. B. Pratt, was "extremely suggestible and peculiarly subject to the fascination of the terrible." [3] Bunyan, having read about the unpardon-

[3] *The Religious Consciousness*. New York: The Macmillan Company, 1923, p. 142.

able sin, concluded it consisted of certain words which if spoken would bring eternal damnation. Bunyan became attracted by the heinousness of this sin, and was so fascinated by the thought of saying a word which would produce everlasting punishment that he found himself saying certain blasphemous words over and over again. In *Grace Abounding* Bunyan says, "And in so strong a measure was this temptation upon me that often I have been ready to clap my hand under my chin to hold my mouth from opening, and to that end also I have thought other times to leap with my head downwards into some muckhill hole or other, to keep my mouth from speaking." [4] Bunyan wanted to do the terrible. Plato gives an example of wanting to see the terrible: "Leontius; the son of Aglaion, coming up one day from the Piraeus, under the north wall on the outside, observed some dead bodies lying on the ground at the place of execution. He felt a desire to see them, and also a dread and abhorrence of them; for a time he struggled and covered his eyes, but at length the desire got the better of him and forcing them open, he ran to the dead bodies, saying, "Look, ye wretches, take your fill of the fair sight." [5] Man is fascinated with the unusual, the ugly, the tragic, the grotesque, the hideous, and the evil.

A violent act may be repulsive to the actor and to the observer, but both may find a strange attraction for it. This attraction need not be a perversion. This fascination of the terrible is inherent in the animal that seeks to experience and to know.

Thus far we have had limited success in rooting hedonic violence out of human behavior. Nor is it clear why such an alteration would be desirable if possible. "I found them witless and gave them the use of their wits and made them masters of their minds," boasted the arrogant Prometheus.[6] He gave them something else: the Promethean enthusiasm which expresses itself in the will to live, the will to dominate, and the will to endure, and in the enjoyment of the unusual, the unpredictable, the destructive, and the terrible.

VIOLENCE OF FRUSTRATION

Violence of frustration and violence of commitment are distinguished from hedonic violence in that they are motivated externally rather than

---

[4] Section 104.
[5] *The Republic* 439E. Translation by B. Jowett.
[6] Aeschylus, *Prometheus Bound*, line 442. Translation by David Grene.

internally. They are directed either against or in favor of a specific thing, person, plan, or existing form of behavior. The violence of frustration is negative in the sense that it is primarily aimed at stopping a state of affairs; the violence of commitment is positive in the sense that it is primarily aimed at originating a different state of affairs. An act of frustration, though negative, may be extremely effective in uniting a group of people in a common cause. The Boston Tea Party focused the attention of the American colonists on their common opposition to taxation without representation. Later, after winning a military victory over the British forces, the colonists found great diffculty in attaining the liberty propounded by Patrick Henry and the egalitarianism of Thomas Jefferson. In Germany in July 1944 a group of men united in planning one violent act: the assassination of Adolf Hitler. Some of these men were discouraged Nazi officers who believed Hitler had lost the war, and some were church leaders who opposed National Socialism on the grounds of justice, goodness, and decency, but all had come to the conclusion that Hitler must be killed. The plotters were discovered and executed. Among them was the Protestant theologian Dietrich Bonhoeffer. Preparation for violence growing out of their frustrations had brought them together. We cannot imagine what they would have done next had they succeeded, for their aspirations for Germany and the German people were widely divergent.

Three features of the violence of frustration are to be considered: it springs out of despair, it may serve as a catharsis of emotions, and it is a protest rather than a plan for positive action. This form of violence stands midway between the other two forms with respect to its motivation. If hedonic violence springs from boredom and if violence of commitment springs from hope of improvement, violence of frustration may be said to spring out of such emotions as defeat, impotence, futility, anguish, and distress. It is the act of the person who does not like what he sees, has no power to change it, and does not have all the facts needed to formulate an alternative plan. During the 1930's and 1940's many Americans were asking why the Germans allowed the Nazi system to develop, and why they did not do something to stop it. Now many Americans find themselves in a similar situation. They do not know how the United States got itself involved in an Asian land war, they are much distressed over our involvement in Viet Nam, and they do not know how we can get out of the mess. As individual citizens what can they do? March in peace parades? Write letters to Congressmen? Join peace organizations? Refuse to pay federal income tax? Carry signs "Hell no! I won't go!" Move to Canada? Register as conscientious objectors? Most of the ways open to them are expressions of their frustration and their repudiation of current practices in international and domestic affairs.

The violence of frustration is a climate in which martyrs are made. The individual may engage in acts against the Establishment which in our terminology will have to be called "non-violent violence." He may lie down in front of a bulldozer to prevent the destruction of a low income residence, or parade for civil rights without a permit, or burn his draft card. In such acts he is saying to the Establishment, "Stop doing what you are doing!" Or the individual may express his frustration by an act on his body which calls attention to the depth of his anguish: fasting or self-immolation are examples. In these acts he is saying, "See how much I am opposed to this!" An act of violence of frustration is a ceremonial act. It is not designed to improve or to change the object. It celebrates frustration. How much exhibitionism or masochism is involved in these acts is difficult to determine. But even so, it is a serious mistake to underestimate the importance of an act of violence as symbolic of the utter frustration of the person.

An act of violence of frustration may serve as a catharsis of emotions. A person in a helpless and hopeless situation continues to build up emotional resentment unless there is a means by which the emotion can be expended. A ceremonial act of violence can be the means for such release. A parade in the streets may not solve the problem, but it may diminish the emotional buildup. Wise administrators provide suggestion boxes for their employees. Even though the usable suggestions are very few, the box serves its purpose by providing an employee a way to express his complaints and recommendations. The ceremonial act, however, will lose its therapeutic value if it is known to be only therapeutical, even as prayer ceases to be meaningful for the average person when he realizes that prayer is a monologue rather than a dialogue.

An act of violence of frustration is essentially a protest, a disapproval of the status quo. Protest angers the Establishment. "Don't complain unless you have a better solution to offer," say those in power. But this is to ignore the fact that raising objections may prepare the way for desirable change. The Protestant Reformation was triggered by a list of ninety-five complaints. The violence of frustration is the first expression of dislike of things as they are. Two cautions may be appropriate. One is that there are professional complainers who find fault with everything on principle. They may be ignored. The other is that violence of frustration is a symptom of life and concern. While the act of the protester may irritate the Establishment man, he, unless he be a tyrant, ought to be grateful that people care enough to protest. In modern democratic society it is not the protesters who are social liabilities, rather it is those who do not care. If democracy weakens and dies, its onus is to be placed on the vast indifferent majority.

VIOLENCE OF COMMITMENT

We have defined violence as any act in which the actor imposes his will upon another without regard for the will and the desire of the other being. The act may be motivated by the desire to seek a pleasant relief from boredom, or by frustration, or by commitment. The third form is the most significant. When John Dewey defined the religious quality as "any activity pursued in behalf of an ideal and against obstacles and in spite of threats of personal loss because of conviction of its general enduring value" [7] he was also giving a definition of what we have called the violence of commitment. Likewise T. R. V. Murti's statement on philosophy can be regarded as a characterization of the violence of commitment: "Philosophy, when cultivated seriously and systematically, leads to interminable and total conflict." [8] It is a rare war that is not defended by its supporters as demanding total dedication because of the good which will spring from victory. The Viet Nam War is one of these rare wars! Violence of commitment is action to make that which matters most prevail. Such action has highest priority. "Give me this, or give me death!" is the voice of the violence of commitment.

Violence of commitment is the ultimate proof of the degree to which one holds a belief. It is existential conviction, pragmatic affirmation, overt evidence. If one is fully dedicated to a program of thought and action, one will act to make that program prevail. One will cease from such action only when this action is in conflict with another program which is placed higher in the hierarchy of beliefs and actions. A belief which will be given up intellectually and existentially when shown to be in conflict with another belief we shall call a contingent belief. A belief which trancsends all contingent beliefs, one for which no other belief will cause us to cease our efforts to advance it, we shall call an absolute belief. Absolute beliefs are absolutely valued. Any act which will make an absolute belief triumph is justified. Such a belief is the end which justifies any means. We moderns think that absolutism was

[7] *A Common Faith.* New Haven: Yale University Press, 1934, p. 27.
[8] *The Central Philosophy of Buddhism.* London: George Allen and Unwin, 1960, p. 126.

a medieval notion which we have outgrown, but in truth it is we who are the absolutists. The fanaticism of the Nazis was matched by the fanaticism of the allied forces. Hitler could not ask for greater dedication to the Third Reich than that which Churchill asked of the English. The concept of total war with the bombing of cities, the eliminating of distinction between combatant and non-combatant, and, finally, the dropping of atomic bombs on civilians thrust mankind into the era of violence, the era of total commitment.

The paradox of absolute commitment is that the violence inherent in the commitment itself may be in conflict with violence. We Americans find ourselves in the position of inflicting violence upon people in order that peace, love, good will, brotherhood, and harmony will characterize the affairs of man. We attempt to advance love hatefully, peace aggressively, good will evilly, moderation immoderately, and life murderously!

What is to be done? Two possibilities are open. One is to continue to seek the Good beyond good which is worthy of ultimate commitment, confident that it will be found and that it can be translated into human action. Fundamentally this is the idealistic tradition stemming from Plato in the West and from the Upanisadic tradition as interpreted by Śankara in the East. The other possibility is to desist from seeking the Good beyond good, and to advise men to cease playing God. Leave ultimacy to the gods. If anyone has ultimate truth, ultimate goodness, and ultimate beauty, it is they. Our speculations about the real and the valuable are human constructions subject to human limitations. This is the realistic tradition rooted in the West in Aristotle and in the East in Confucius. This tradition reminds us of the importance of incorporating metaphilosophical insights into each philosophical system and metareligious insights into each religion. If we wish to keep the concept of deity in our system, let us make God the consolation prize we award ourselves when we discover our finitude. The only absolute is that there is no absolute. Let us recognize with the Hindu *tat tvam asi* (The That is you), with the Buddhist *saṃsāra* is *nirvāṇa* (The phenomenal is the Real), and with the Christ "*This* is eternal life."

John R. Platt of the University of Chicago has been quoted as saying, "The world has become too dangerous for anything less than utopias." [9] The saving grace of his statement is the fact that he has put the word "utopia" in the plural. There is no Utopia; there are only utopias, that is, various conceptions of the good life. Man, the creature

---

[9] *The New York Times,* March 27, 1968, Section E, p. 12.

in whom has evolved self-consciousness, now takes on his own evolution. "He makes his own soul throughout all his earthly days," said Teilhard de Chardin.[10] But the optimism of the pluralistic possibilities of man and the world must not cloud from our minds the ugly truth that man now must include genocide among those possibilities. Life is a necessary condition of any good life. And future existence of man on the earth is now problematical.

The early Christians looked hopefully to the end of man. They were awaiting a community. They were waiting for the immanent end of history and the beginning of a new dimension of reality. The medieval Christians may be said to have been an expectant community. They expected that there would be an end of history, but in the meanwhile they were preparing themselves both for the possibility of a full life on earth and a later entrance into heaven. Both the early and the medieval Christians held that somehow their God would save them.[11] Today some Christian theologians are inaugurating a new theology called the theology of hope. They have even coined a new word—mellontology—to displace the term eschatology. This is to suggest the shift from a study of last things to a study of possibilities. They want Christians to look forward eagerly and optimistically rather than apprehensively. But is this whistling in the dark? Perhaps a more realistic view, based on the present overkill weapons of at least two nations, is a secular eschatology which holds that there will be no future unless worldwide controls of the most rigid nature are clamped soon on nations stockpiling doomsday weapons.

Human civilization is in a race with time. Can we control men and nations before we destroy ourselves and our world? The race is not merely between education and catastrophe, for there is a third contestant. This is coercion, enlightened force, violence of commitment, or whatever label may be applied to that situation described by Plato when wisdom and strength are united. Those of us reared in genteel traditions who had hoped that the liberal democratic tradition would through education and the popular ballot lead mankind into Elysian fields may not be happy about the conclusion to which we must come. We should like to believe that through the slow and torturous democratic processes of decision-making a social and political system will evolve in which each citizen of the world community has an oppor-

---

[10] *Le Milieu Divin.* Translation by Bernard Wall. London: Collins, Fontana Books, 1964, p. 61.
[11] Cf. "From the gods who sit in grandeur grace comes somehow violent." Aeschylus, *Agamemnon,* Line 182. Translation by Richard Lattimore.

tunity to express his opinion. We should like to believe that rule will be by consent of the governed, and that persuasion will be by education and argument. We should like to believe that the day will come when each individual's intelligence, rights, and freedom will be respected. But the hopes for such a day are fading. Our world is rapidly moving into that state of urgency when action must be taken which cannot wait for a head count. The slow, wasteful, and cumbersome democratic processes are luxuries tolerable only as long as there is more land, more water, more air, and more space than is necessary for the support of the people now living on the earth. But when there will be scarcely enough land, water, air, and space to preserve the human race, then the democratic ways will be drastically modified by the ways of violence. We foresee the approach of that terrible condition. The depletion of the natural resources of the planet and the multiplication of the human population will bring us to that awful day when we must decide between extinction or preservation of our species. If men cannot be educated to restrain voluntarily their exploitation of natural resources, warfare among nations, and sex relation to births, then a Grand Inquisitor policy must enter our political life, and men must be coerced for their own good.

Those appalled by the revolutionary ideas of Marx and Engels may well prepare themselves for other ideas far more revolutionary. Marx saw though the gunsmoke of the revolution to the classless society and the withering away of the state. But the anatomy of violence offers no such utopia. There is no age of peace in the offing when the lion and the lamb will lie down together. The age of violence is not a threshold to an age of peace. It is the necessary condition of man's survival. Violence may be not only part of the soteriological process but also part of the only possible heaven on earth. Violence may be the religion of the future. The preservation of the rational animal on the face of this planet depends upon the rational uses of violence. An alternative is to follow the ways of human behavior which are turning the earth into a slag heap.

2

M. K. GANDHI

(1869–1948)

Satyagraha

Nationalist and spiritual leader of emerging India, Gandhi espoused a philosophy of passive resistance (Satyagraha: Truth-seeking) that has affected the revolutionary thinking of many black civil rights leaders, most notably Martin Luther King, Jr. Gandhi's is a philosophy of means, not necessarily ends. It is a way of life, not just a tactic. His organization and leadership of resistance movements in India eventually culminated in independence for his country. In 1947 Viscount Mountbatten, former viceroy of the Indian Empire, called Gandhi "the architect of India's freedom through nonviolence." The Satyagraha method is not designed to humble one's opponents, but to lead them to find the truth.

In these selections, Gandhi recounts his thinking on the matter and method of passive resistance, an idea not original with Gandhi. Interestingly, it is a Western theory seen in the works of Thoreau and Tolstoy. On the question of means and ends Gandhi counters the tactical thinking of men like Mao with his theory of soul force, which elevates the resister instead of lowering him to the level of the brute force of his oppressor.

In defining his motives for revealing the Pentagon Papers to the public, Daniel Ellsberg said, "You know what Gandhi's term is for what is otherwise called nonviolent civil disobedience? He called it 'Satyagraha.' That means 'truth force.' The people always focus on the nonviolent aspect of this Gandhian approach, but, in fact, the theme of honesty and openness was at least as strong as the nonviolence. The courts, the press, the Congress—all together have been cooperating in a massive effort at truth telling."

SATYAGRAHA, CIVIL DISOBEDIENCE, PASSIVE RESISTANCE, NON-CO-OPERATION*

Satyagraha is literally holding on to Truth and it means, therefore, Truth-force. Truth is soul or spirit. It is, therefore, known as soul-force. It excludes the use of violence because man is not capable of knowing the absolute truth and, therefore, not competent to punish. The word was coined in South Africa to distinguish the non-violent resistance of the Indians of South Africa from the contemporary "passive resistance" of the suffragettes and others. It is not conceived as a weapon of the weak.

* From *Young India* (1924), 23-3-1921. Used by permission of the Navajivan Trust.

Passive resistance is used in the orthodox English sense and covers the suffragette movement as well as the resistance of the Non-conformists. Passive resistance has been conceived and is regarded as a weapon of the weak. Whilst it avoids violence, being not open to the weak, it does not exclude its use if, in the opinion of a passive resister, the occasion demands it. However, it has always been distinguished from armed resistance and its application was at one time confined to Christian martyrs.

Civil Disobedience is civil breach of unmoral statutory enactments. The expression was, so far as I am aware, coined by Thoreau to signify his own resistance to the laws of a slave State. He has left a masterly treatise on the duty of Civil Disobedience. But Thoreau was not perhaps an out and out champion of non-violence. Probably, also, Thoreau limited his breach of statutory laws to the revenue law, i.e. payment of taxes. Whereas the term Civil Disobedience as practised in 1919 covered a breach of any statutory and unmoral law. It signified the resister's outlawry in a civil, i.e., non-violent manner. He invoked the sanctions of the law and cheerfully suffered imprisonment. It is a branch of Satyagraha.

Non-co-operation predominantly implies withdrawing of co-operation from the State that in the non-co-operator's view has become corrupt and excludes Civil Disobedience of the fierce type described above. By its very nature, non-co-operation is even open to children of understanding and can be safely practised by the masses. Civil Disobedience presupposes the habit of willing obedience to laws without fear of their sanctions. It can, therefore, be practised only as a last resort and by a select few in the first instance at any rate. Non-co-operation, too, like Civil Disobedience is a branch of Satyagraha which includes all non-violent resistance for the vindication of Truth.

MEANS AND ENDS*

Reader: Why should we not obtain our goal, which is good, by any means whatsoever, even by using violence? Shall I think of the means when I have to deal with a thief in the house? My duty is to drive him out anyhow. You seem to admit that we have received nothing, and that we shall receive nothing by petitioning. Why, then, may we not do so by using brute force? And, to retain what we may receive we shall keep up the fear by using the same force to the extent that it may be

---

* From *Indian Home Rule* (1922), Chap. XVI. Used by permission of the Navajivan Trust.

necessary. You will not find fault with a continuance of force to prevent a child from thrusting its foot into fire? Somehow or other we have to gain our end.

Editor: Your reasoning is plausible. It has deluded many. I have used similar arguments before now. But I think I know better now, and I shall endeavour to undeceive you. Let us first take the argument that we are justified in gaining our end by using brute force because the English gained theirs by using similar means. It is perfectly true that they used brute force and that it is possible for us to do likewise, but by using similar means we can get only the same thing that they got. You will admit that we do not want that. Your belief that there is no connection between the means and the end is a great mistake. Through that mistake even men who have been considered religious have committed grievous crimes. Your reasoning is the same as saying that we can get a rose through planting a noxious weed. If I want to cross the ocean, I can do so only by means of a vessel; if I were to use a cart for that purpose, both the cart and I would soon find the bottom. "As is the God, so is the votary," is a maxim worth considering. Its meaning has been distorted and men have gone astray. The means may be likened to a seed, the end to a tree; and there is just the same inviolable connection between the means and the end as there is between the seed and the tree. I am not likely to obtain the result flowing from the worship of God by laying myself prostrate before Satan. If, therefore, any one were to say: "I want to worship God; it does not matter that I do so by means of Satan," it would be set down as ignorant folly. We reap exactly as we sow. If I want to deprive you of your watch, I shall certainly have to fight for it; if I want to buy your watch, I shall have to pay for it; and if I want a gift, I shall have to plead for it; and, according to the means I employ, the watch is stolen property, my own property, or a donation. Thus we see three different results from three different means. Will you still say that means do not matter?

Now we shall take the example given by you of the thief to be driven out. I do not agree with you that the thief may be driven out by any means. If it is my father who has come to steal I shall use one kind of means. If it is an acquaintance I shall use another; and in the case of a perfect stranger I shall use a third. If it is a white man, you will perhaps say you will use means different from those you will adopt with an Indian thief. If it is a weakling, the means will be different from those to be adopted for dealing with an equal in physical strength; and if the thief is armed from top to toe, I shall simply remain quiet. Thus we have a variety of means between the father and the armed man. Again, I fancy that I should pretend to be sleeping whether the thief was my father or that strong armed man. The reason for this is that my father would also be armed and I should succumb to the strength possessed by either and allow my things to be stolen. The strength of my father would make me weep with pity; the strength of the armed man would rouse in me anger and we should become enemies. Such is the curious situation. From these examples we may not be able to agree as to the means to be adopted in each case. I myself seem clearly to see what should be done in all these cases, but the remedy may frighten you. I therefore hesitate to place it before you. For the time being I will leave you to guess it, and if you cannot, it is clear you will have to adopt different means in each case. You will also have seen that any means will not avail to drive away the thief. You will have to adopt means to fit each case. Hence it follows that your duty is not to drive away the thief by any means you like.

Let us proceed a little further. That well-armed man has stolen your property; you have harboured the thought of his act; you are filled with anger; you argue that you want to punish that rogue, not for your own sake, but for the good of your neighbours; you have collected a number of armed men, you want to take his house by assault; he is duly informed of it, he runs away; he too is incensed. He collects his brother robbers, and sends you a defiant message that he will commit robbery in broad daylight. You are strong, you do not fear him, you are prepared to receive him. Meanwhile, the robber pesters your neighbours. They complain before you. You reply that you are doing all for their sake, you do not mind that your own goods have been stolen. Your neighbours reply that the robber never pestered them before, and that he commenced his depredations only after you declared hostilities against him. You are between Scylla and Charybdis. You are full of pity for the poor men. What they say is true. What are you to do? You will be disgraced if you now leave the robber alone. You, therefore, tell the poor men: "Never mind. Come, my wealth is yours, I will give you arms, I will teach you how to use them; you should belabour the rogue; don't you leave him alone." And so the battle grows; the robbers increase in numbers; your neighbours have deliberately put themselves to inconvenience. Thus the result of wanting to take revenge upon the robber is that you have disturbed your own peace; you are in perpetual fear of being robbed and assaulted; your courage has given place to cowardice. If you will patiently examine the argument, you will see that I have not overdrawn the picture. This is one of the means. Now let us examine the other. You set this armed robber down as an ignorant brother; you intend to reason with him at a suitable opportunity; you argue that he is, after all, a fellow man; you do not know what prompted him to steal. You, therefore, decide that, when you can, you will destroy the man's motive for stealing. Whilst you are thus reasoning with yourself, the man comes again to steal. Instead of being angry with him you take pity on him. You think that this stealing habit must be a disease with him. Henceforth, you, therefore, keep your doors and windows open, you change your sleeping-place, and you keep your things in a manner most accessible to him. The robber comes again and is confused as all this is new to him; nevertheless, he takes away your things. But his mind is agitated. He inquires about you in the village, he comes to learn about your broad and loving heart, he repents, he begs your pardon, returns you your things, and leaves off the stealing habit. He becomes your servant, and you will find for him honourable employment. This is the second method. Thus, you see, different means have brought about totally different results. I do not wish to deduce from this that robbers will act in the above manner or that all will have the same pity and love like you, but I only wish to show that fair means alone can produce fair results, and that, at least in the majority of cases, if not indeed in all, the force of love and pity is infinitely greater than the force of arms. There is harm in the exercise of brute force, never in that of pity.

Now we will take the question of petitioning. It is a fact beyond dispute that a petition, without the backing of force, is useless. However, the late Justice Ranade used to say that petitions served a useful purpose because they were a means of educating people. They give the latter an idea of their condition and warn the rulers. From this point of view, they are not altogether useless. A petition of an equal is a sign of courtesy; a petition from a slave is a symbol of his slavery. A petition backed by force is a petition from an equal and, when he transmits his demand in the form of a petition, it testifies to his nobility. Two kinds of force can back petitions. "We shall hurt you if you do not give this," is one kind of force; it is the force of arms, whose evil results we have already examined. The second kind of force can thus be stated: "If you do not concede our demand, we shall be no longer your petitioners. You can govern us only so long as we remain the governed; we shall no longer have any dealings with you." The force implied in this may be described as love-force, soul-force, or, more popularly but less accurately, passive resistance. This force is indestructible. He who uses it perfectly understands his position. We have an ancient proverb which literally means: "One negative cures thirty-six diseases." The force of arms is powerless when matched against the force of love or the soul.

Now we shall take your last illustration, that of the child thrusting its foot into fire. It will not avail you. What do you really do to the child? Supposing that it can exert so much physical force that it renders you powerless and rushes into fire; then you cannot prevent it. There are only two remedies open to you—either you must kill it in order to prevent it from perishing in their flames, or you must give your own life because you do not wish to see it perish before your very eyes. You will not kill it. If your heart is not quite full of pity, it is possible that you will not surrender yourself by preceding the child and going into the fire yourself. You, therefore, helplessly allow it to go to the flames. Thus, at any rate, you are not using physical force. I hope you will not consider that it is still physical force, though of a low order, when you would forcibly prevent the child from rushing towards the fire if you could. That force is of a different order and we have to understand what it is.

Remember that, in thus preventing the child, you are minding entirely its own interest, you are exercising authority for its sole benefit. Your example does not apply to the English. In using brute force against the English you consult entirely your own, that is the national, interest. There is no question here either of pity or of love. If you say that the actions of the English, being evil, represent fire, and that they proceed to their actions through ignorance, and that therefore they occupy the position of a child and that you want to protect such a child, then you will have to overtake every evil action of that kind by whomsoever committed and, as in the case of the evil child, you will have to sacrifice yourself. If you are capable of such immeasurable pity, I wish you well in its exercise.

SATYAGRAHA OR PASSIVE RESISTANCE*

Reader: Is there any historical evidence as to the success of what you have called soul-force or truth-force? No instance seems to have happened of any nation having risen through soul-force. I still think that the evil-doers will not cease doing evil without physical punishment.

Editor: The poet Tulsidas has said: "Of religion, pity, or love, is the root, as egotism of the body. Therefore, we should not abandon pity so long as we are alive." This appears to me to be a scientific truth. I believe in it as much as I believe in two and two being four. The force of love is the same as the force of the soul or truth. We have evidence of its working at every step. The universe would disappear without the existence of that force. But you ask for historical evidence. It is, there-

---

* From *Indian Home Rule,* Chap. XVII. Used by permission of the Navajivan Trust.

fore, necessary to know what history means. The Gujarati equivalent means: "It so happened." If that is the meaning of history, it is possible to give copious evidence. But, if it means the doings of kings and emperors, there can be no evidence of soul-force or passive resistance in such history. You cannot expect silver ore in a tin mine. History, as we know it, is a record of the wars of the world, and so there is a proverb among Englishmen that a nation which has no history, that is, no wars, is a happy nation.

The fact that there are so many men still alive in the world shows that it is based not on the force of arms but on the force of truth or love. Therefore, the greatest and most unimpeachable evidence of the success of this force is to be found in the fact that, in spite of the wars of the world, it still lives on.

Thousands, indeed tens of thousands, depend for their existence on a very active working of this force. Little quarrels of millions of families in their daily lives disappear before the exercise of this force. Hundreds of nations live in peace. History does not and cannot take note of this fact. History is really a record of every interruption of the even working of the force of love or of the soul. Two brothers quarrel; one of them repents and re-awakens the love that was lying dormant in him; the two again begin to live in peace; nobody takes note of this. But if the two brothers, through the intervention of solicitors or some other reason, take up arms or go to law—which is another form of the exhibition of brute force—their doing would be immediately noticed in the press, they would be the talk of their neighbours and would probably go down to history. And what is true of families and communities is true of nations. There is no reason to believe that there is one law for families and another for nations. History, then, is a record of an interruption of the course of nature. Soul-force, being natural, is not noted in history.

Reader: According to what you say, it is plain that instances of this kind of passive resistance are not to be found in history. It is necessary to understand this passive resistance more fully. It will be better, therefore, if you enlarge upon it.

Editor: Passive resistance is a method of securing rights by personal suffering; it is the reverse of resistance by arms. When I refuse to do a thing that is repugnant to my conscience, I use soul-force. For instance, the Government of the day has passed a law which is applicable to me. I do not like it. If by using violence I force the Government to repeal the law, I am employing what may be termed body-force. If I do not obey the law and accept the penalty for its breach, I use soul-force. It involves sacrifice of self.

Everybody admits that sacrifice of self is infinitely superior to sacrifice of others. Moreover, if this kind of force is used in a cause that is unjust, only the person using it suffers. He does not make others suffer for his mistakes. Men have before now done many things which were subsequently found to have been wrong. No man can claim that he is absolutely in the right or that a particular thing is wrong because he thinks so, but it is wrong for him so long as that is his deliberate judgment. It is therefore meet that he should not do that which he knows to be wrong, and suffer the consequence whatever it may be. This is the key to the use of soul-force.

Reader: You would then disregard laws—this is rank disloyalty. We have always been considered a law-abiding nation. You seem to be going even beyond the extremists. They say that we must obey the laws that have been passed, but that if the laws be bad, we must drive out the law-givers even by force.

Editor: Whether I go beyond them or whether I do not is a matter of no consequence to either of us. We simply want to find out what is right and to act accordingly. The real meaning of the statement that we are a law-abiding nation is that we are passive resisters. When we do not like certain laws, we do not break the heads of law-givers but we suffer and do not submit to the laws. That we should obey laws whether good or bad is a newfangled notion. There was no such thing in former days. The people disregarded those laws they did not like and suffered the penalties for their breach. It is contrary to our manhood if we obey laws repugnant to our conscience.

A man who has realized his manhood, who fears only God, will fear no one else. Man-made laws are not necessarily binding on him. Even the Government does not expect any such thing from us. They do not say: "You must do such and such a thing," but they say: "If you do not do it, we will punish you." We are sunk so low that we fancy that it is our duty and our religion to do what the law lays down. If man will only realize that it is unmanly to obey laws that are unjust, no man's tyranny will enslave him. This is the key to self-rule or home-rule.

It is a superstition and ungodly thing to believe that an act of a majority binds a minority. Many examples can be given in which acts of majorities will be found to have been wrong and those of minorities to have been right. All reforms owe their origin to the initiation of minorities in opposition to majorities. If among a band of robbers a knowledge of robbing is obligatory, is a pious man to accept the obligation? So long as the superstition that men should obey unjust laws exists, so long will their slavery exist. And a passive resister alone can remove such a superstition.

To use brute-force, to use gunpowder, is contrary to passive resistance, for it means that we want our opponent to do by force that which we desire but he does not. And, if such a use of force is justifiable, surely he is entitled to do likewise by us. And so we should never come to an agreement. We may simply fancy, like the blind horse moving in a circle round a mill, that we are making progress. Those who believe that they are not bound to obey laws which are repugnant to their conscience have only the remedy of passive resistance open to them. Any other must lead to disaster.

3   ROBERT PAUL WOLFF

(1933–   )

*On Violence**

Wolff defends three basic propositions about violence that he says are unoriginal but true and worth attention because they are often muddled or forgotten in contemporary analyses of violence. The first proposition is that the concept of violence is inherently confused, since it depends for its sense on the notion of legitimate authority, which is itself incoherent. Questions about violent tactics are also confused, Wolff maintains, and the dispute between adherents of violence and of nonviolence is just so much ideological rhetoric. The key to his analysis lies in the first proposition and specifically is dependent upon his view that there cannot be such a thing as legitimate political authority. His position, he claims, is but an extension of a Kantian moral theory. Kant demanded that in order to be moral a person must be autonomous; hence the only legitimate authority over a person is himself, and that would seem to entail that anarchy is the only legitimate state. Wolff's views should be compared not only with others in this part, but also with those in Parts I and II.

* Robert Paul Wolff, "On Violence," *Journal of Philosophy*, Volume LXVI, No. 19 (October 2, 1969), pp. 601–616. Used by permission of the author and the Editors.

EVERYTHING I shall say in this essay has been said before, and much of it seems to me to be obvious as well as unoriginal. I offer two excuses for laying used goods before you. In the first place, I think that what I have to say about violence is true. Now, there are many ways to speak falsehood and only one way to speak truth. It follows, as Kierkegaard pointed out, that the truth is likely to become boring. On a subject as ancient and much discussed as ours today, we may probably assume that a novel—and, hence, interesting—view of violence is likely to be false.

But truth is not my sole excuse, for the subject before us suffers from the same difficulty that Kant discerned in the area of metaphysics. After refuting the various claims that had been made to transcendent rational knowledge of things-in-themselves, Kant remarked that the refutations had no lasting psychological effect on true believers. The human mind, he concluded, possessed a natural disposition to metaphysical speculation, which philosophy must perpetually keep in check. Somewhat analogously, men everywhere are prone to certain beliefs about the legitimacy of political authority, even though their beliefs are as groundless as metaphysical speculations. The most sophisticated of men persist in supposing that some valid distinction can be made between legitimate and illegitimate commands, on the basis of which they can draw a line, for example, between mere violence and the legitimate use of force. This lingering superstition is shared by those dissenters who call police actions or ghetto living conditions "violent"; for they are merely advancing competing legitimacy claims.

I shall set forth and defend *three* propositions about violence:

First: The concept of violence is inherently confused, as is the correlative concept of nonviolence; these and related concepts depend for their meaning in political discussions on the fundamental notion of legitimate authority, which is also inherently incoherent.

Second: It follows that a number of familiar questions are also confusions to which no coherent answers could ever be given, such as: when it is permissible to resort to violence in politics; whether the black movement and the student movement should be nonviolent; and whether anything good in politics is ever accomplished by violence.

Finally: The dispute over violence and nonviolence in contemporary American politics is ideological rhetoric designed either to halt change and justify the existing distribution of power and privilege or to slow change and justify some features of the existing distribution of power and privilege or else to hasten change and justify a total redistribution of power and privilege.

Let us begin with the first proposition, which is essential to my entire discussion.

I

The fundamental concepts of political philosophy are the concepts of power and authority.[1] Power in general is the ability to make and enforce decisions. Political power is the ability to make and enforce decisions about matters of major social importance. Thus the ability to dispose of my private income as I choose is a form of power, whereas the ability to make and enforce a decision about the disposition of

[1] What follows is a summary of analyses I have published elsewhere. The concept of political power is treated in Chapter III of *The Poverty of Liberalism* (Boston: Beacon Press, 1968). The concepts of legitimacy and authority are analyzed in my essay on "Political Philosophy" in Arthur Danto, ed., *The Harper Guide to Philosophy* (New York: Harper & Row, 1970).

some sizable portion of the tax receipts of the federal government is a form of *political* power. (So too is the ability to direct the decisions of a large private corporation; for the exercise of political power is not confined to the sphere of government.) A complete analysis of the concept of political power would involve a classification both of the means employed in the enforcing of decisions and of the scope and variety of questions about which decisions can be made.[2] It would also require an examination of the kinds of opposition against which the decision could be enforced. There is a very considerable difference between the ability a parliamentary majority has to enforce its decisions against the will of the minority and the ability of a rebel military clique to enforce its decisions against the Parliament as a whole.

Authority, by contrast with power, is not an ability but a right. It is the right to command and, correlatively, the right to be obeyed. Claims to authority are made in virtually every area of social life, and, in a remarkably high proportion of cases, the claims are accepted and acquiesced in by those over whom they are made. Parents claim the right to be obeyed by their children; husbands until quite recently claimed the right to be obeyed by their wives; popes claim the right to be obeyed by the laity and clergy; and of course, most notably, virtually all existing governments claim the right to be obeyed by their subjects.

A claim to authority must be sharply differentiated both from a threat or enticement and from a piece of advice. When the state commands, it usually threatens punishment for disobedience, and it may even on occasion offer a reward for compliance, but the command cannot be reduced to the mere threat or reward. What characteristically distinguishes a state from an occupying army or private party is its insistence, either explicit or implicit, on its *right* to be obeyed. By the same token, an authoritative command is not a mere recommendation. Authority says, "Do this!" not, "Let me suggest this for your consideration."

Claims to authority have been defended on a variety of grounds, most prominent among which are the appeal to God, to tradition, to expertise, to the laws of history, and to the consent of those commanded. We tend to forget that John Locke thought it worth while to devote the first of his *Two Treatises on Civil Government* to the claim that Europe's monarchs held their authority by right of primogenitural descent from Adam. It is common today to give lip service to the theory that authority derives from the consent of the governed, but most of

[2] See Robert A. Dahl, "The Concept of Power," *Behavioral Science* (July 1957), for just such a classification.

us habitually accord *some* weight to any authority claim issuing from a group of men who regularly control the behavior of a population in a territory, particularly if the group tricks itself out with flags, uniforms, courts of law, and printed regulations.

Not all claims to authority are justified. Indeed, I shall suggest shortly that few if any are. Nevertheless, men regularly accept the authority claims asserted against them, and so we must distinguish a descriptive from a normative sense of the term. Let us use the term "*de facto* authority" to refer to *the ability to get one's authority claims accepted by those against whom they are asserted.* "*De jure* authority," then, will refer to *the right to command and to be obeyed.* Obviously, the concept of *de jure* authority is primary, and the concept of *de facto* authority is derivative.

Thus understood, *de facto* authority is a form of power, for it is a means by which its possessor can enforce his decisions. Indeed, as Max Weber—from who much of this analysis is taken—has pointed out, *de facto* authority is the *principal* means on which states rely to carry out their decisions. Threats and inducements play an exceedingly important role in the enforcement of political decisions, to be sure, but a state that must depend upon them entirely will very soon suffer a crippling reduction in its effectiveness, which is to say, in its political power. Modern states especially require for the successful prosecution of their programs an extremely high level of coordination of the behavior of large numbers of individuals. The myth of legitimacy is the only efficient means available to the state for achieving that coordination.

Force is the ability to work some change in the world by the expenditure of physical effort. A man may root up a tree, move a stalled car, drive a nail, or restrain another man, *by force.* Force, in and of itself, is morally neutral. Physically speaking, there may be very little difference between the physical effort of a doctor who resets a dislocated shoulder and that of the ruffian who dislocated it. Sometimes, of course, force is used to work some change in the body of another man—to punch him, shoot him, take out his appendix, hold his arms, or cut his hair. But there is in principle no significant distinction between these uses of force and those uses which involve changing some other part of the world about which he cares. A man who slips into a parking place for which I am heading inflicts an injury on me roughly as great as if he had jostled me in a crowd or stepped on my toe. If he destroys a work of art on which I have lavished my most intense creative efforts, he may harm me more than a physical assault would.

Force is a means to power, but it is not of course a guarantee of power. If I wish to elicit hard work from my employees, I can threaten them with the lash or tempt them with bonuses—both of which are employments of force—but if my workers prefer not to comply, my threats and inducements may be fruitless. It is a commonplace both of domestic and of international politics that the mere possession of a monopoly of force is no guarantee of political power. Those who fail to grasp this truth are repeatedly frustrated by the baffling inability of the strong to impose their will upon the weak.

There are, so far as I can see, *three* means or instruments by which power is exercised—three ways, that is to say, in which men enforce or carry out their social decisions. The first is *force*, the ability to re-arrange the world in ways that other men find appealing or distasteful. In modern society, money is of course the principal measure, exchange medium, and symbol of force. The second instrument of power is *de facto* authority—the ability to elicit obedience, as opposed to mere compliance, from others. *De facto* authority frequently accrues to those with a preponderance of force, for men are fatally prone to suppose that he who can compel compliance deserves obedience. But *de facto* authority does not reduce to the possession of a preponderance of force, for men habitually obey commands they know could not effec-tively be enforced. The third instrument of power is social opinion, or what might be called the "symbolic" use of force. When a runner com-petes in a race, he may want the first-prize money or the commercial endorsements that will come to the winner, or he may even just like blue ribbons—but he may also want the acclaim of the fans. Now, that acclaim is expressed by certain uses of force—by clapping of hands and cheering, which are physical acts. But its value to the runner is sym-bolic; he cherishes it as an expression of approval, not merely as a pleasing sound. To say that man is a social creature is not merely to say that he hangs out in groups, nor even to say that he engages in collective and cooperative enterprises for self-interested purposes; it is most importantly to say that he values symbolic interactions with other men and is influenced by them as well as by the ordinary exercise of force and by claims of authority. This point is important for our discussion, for, as we shall see, many persons who shrink from the use of force as an instrument of political power have no compunctions about the use of social opinion or what I have called the "symbolic" use of force. Anyone who has observed a progressive classroom run by a teacher with scruples of this sort will know that a day "in coventry" can be a far crueler punishment for an unruly ten-year old than a sharp rap on the knuckles with a ruler.

We come, finally, to the concept of violence. Strictly speaking, *vio-*

lence is the illegitimate or unauthorized use of force to effect decisions against the will or desire of others. Thus, murder is an act of violence, but capital punishment *by a legitimate state* is not; theft or extortion is violent, but the collection of taxes *by a legitimate state* is not. Clearly, on this interpretation the concept of violence is normative as well as descriptive, for it involves an implicit appeal to the principle of *de jure* legitimate authority. There is an associated sense of the term which is purely descriptive, relying on the descriptive notion of *de facto* authority. Violence in this latter sense is the use of force in ways that are proscribed or unauthorized by those who are generally accepted as the legitimate authorities in the territory. Descriptively speaking, the attack on Hitler's life during the Second World War was an act of violence, but one might perfectly well deny that it was violent in the strict sense, on the grounds that Hitler's regime was illegitimate. On similar grounds, it is frequently said that police behavior toward workers or ghetto dwellers or demonstrators is violent even when it is clearly within the law, for the authority issuing the law is illegitimate.

It is common, but I think wrong-headed, to restrict the term "violence" to uses of force that involve bodily interference or the direct infliction of physical injury. Carrying a dean out of his office is said to be violent, but not seizing his office when he is absent and locking him out. Physically tearing a man's wallet from his pocket is "violent," but swindling him out of the same amount of money is not. There is a natural enough basis for this distinction. Most of us value our lives and physical well-being above other goods that we enjoy, and we tend therefore to view attacks or threats on our person as different in kind from other sorts of harm we might suffer. Nevertheless, the distinction is not sufficiently sharp to be of any analytical use, and, as we shall see later, it usually serves the ideological purpose of ruling out, as immoral or politically illegitimate, the only instrument of power that is available to certain social classes.

In its strict or normative sense, then, the concept of political violence depends upon the concept of *de jure*, or legitimate authority. If there is no such thing as legitimate political authority, then it is impossible to distinguish between legitimate and illegitmate uses of force. Now, of course, under any circumstances, we can distinguish between right and wrong, justified and unjustified, uses of force. Such a distinction belongs to moral philosophy in general, and our choice of the criteria by which we draw the distinction will depend on our theory of value and obligation. But the distinctive political concept of violence can be given a coherent meaning *only* by appeal to a doctrine of legitimate political authority.

On the basis of a lengthy reflection upon the concept of *de jure* legitimate authority, I have come to the conclusion that philosophical anarchism is true. That is to say, I believe that there is not, and there could not be, a state that has a right to command and whose subjects have a binding obligation to obey. I have defended this view in detail elsewhere, and I can only indicate here the grounds of my conviction.[3] Briefly, I think it can be shown that every man has a fundamental duty to be autonomous, in Kant's sense of the term. Each of us must make himself the author of his actions and take responsibility for them by refusing to act save on the basis of reasons he can see for himself to be good. Autonomy, thus understood, is in direct opposition to obedience, which is submission to the will of another, irrespective of reasons. Following Kant's usage, political obedience is heteronymy of the will.

Now, political theory offers us one great argument designed to make the autonomy of the individual compatible with submission to the putative authority of the state. In a democracy, it is claimed, the citizen is both law-giver and law-obeyer. Since he shares in the authorship of the laws, he submits to his own will in obeying them, and hence is autonomous, not heteronymous.

If this argument were valid, it would provide a genuine ground for a distinction between violent and nonviolent political actions. Violence would be a use of force proscribed by the laws of executive authority of a genuinely democratic state. The only possible justification of illegal or extralegal political acts would be a demonstration of the illegitimacy of the state, and this in turn would involve showing that the commands of the state were not expressions of the will of the people.

But the classic defense of democracy is *not* valid. For a variety of reasons, neither majority rule nor any other method of making decisions in the absence of unanimity can be shown to preserve the autonomy of the individual citizens. In a democracy, as in any state, obedience is heteronymy. The autonomous man is of necessity an anarchist. Consequently, there is no valid *political* criterion for the justified use of force. Legality is, by itself, no justification. Now, of course, there are all manner of utilitarian arguments for submitting to the state and its agents, even if the state's claim to legitimacy is unfounded. The laws may command actions that are in fact morally obligatory or whose effects promise to be beneficial. Widespread submission to law may bring about a high level of order, regularity, and predictability in social relationships which is valuable independently of the particular character of the acts commanded. But in and of themselves, the acts of

[3] See "Political Philosophy," in Danto, *op. cit.*

police and the commands of legislatures have no peculiar legitimacy
or sanction. Men everywhere and always impute authority to established governments, and they are always wrong to do so.

II

The foregoing remarks are quite banal, to be sure. Very few serious
students of politics will maintain either the democratic theory of legitimate authority or any alternatives to it. Nevertheless, like post-theo-
logical, demythologized Protestants who persist in raising prayers to a
God they no longer believe in, modern men go on exhibiting a super-
stitious belief in the authority of the state. Consider, for example, a
question now much debated: When is it permissible to resort to violence in politics? If "violence" is taken to mean an *unjustified* use of
force, then the answer to the question is obviously *never*. If the use of
force were permissible, it would not, by definition, be violence, and if
it were violent, it would not, by definition, be permissible. If "violence"
is taken in the strict sense to mean "an illegitimate or unauthorized use
of force," then *every* political act, whether by private parties or by
agents of the state, is violent, for there is no such thing as legitimate
authority. If "violence' is construed in the restricted sense as "bodily
interference or the direct infliction of physical harm," then the obvious
but correct rule is to resort to violence when less harmful or costly
means fail, providing always that the balance of good and evil produced is superior to that promised by any available alternative.

These answers are all trivial, but that is precisely my point. Once the
concept of violence is seen to rest on the unfounded distinction between legitimate and illegitimate political authority, the question of the
appropriateness of violence simply dissolves. It is mere superstition to
describe a policeman's beating of a helpless suspect as "an excessive use
of force" while characterizing an attack by a crowd on the policeman
as "a resort to violence." The implication of such a distinction is that
the policeman, as the duly appointed representative of a legitimate
government, has a right to use physical force, although no right to use
"excessive" force, whereas the crowd of private citizens has no right at
all to use even moderate physical force. But there are no legitimate
governments, hence no special rights attaching to soldiers, policemen,
magistrates, or other law-enforcement agents, hence no coherent distinction between violence and the legitimate use of force.

Consider, as a particular example, the occupation of buildings and
the student strike at Columbia University during April and May of
1968. The consequences of those acts have not yet played themselves

out, but I think certain general conclusions can be drawn. First, the total harm done by the students and their supporters was very small in comparison with the good results that were achieved. A month of class-work was lost, along with many tempers and a good deal of sleep. Someone—it is still not clear who—burned the research notes of a history professor, an act which, I am happy to say, produced a universal revulsion shared even by the SDS. In the following year, a number of classes were momentarily disrupted by SDS activists in an unsuccessful attempt to repeat the triumph of the previous spring.

Against this, what benefits flowed from the protest? A reactionary and thoroughly unresponsive administration was forced to resign; an all-university Senate of students, professors, and administrators was created, the first such body at Columbia. A callous and antisocial policy of university expansion into the surrounding neighborhood was reversed; some at least of the university's ties with the military were loosened or severed; and an entire community of students and professors were forced to confront moral and political issues which till then they had managed to ignore.

Could these benefits have been won at less cost? Considering the small cost of the uprising, the question seems to me a bit finicky; nevertheless, the answer is clearly, No. The history of administrative intransigence and faculty apathy at Columbia makes it quite clear that nothing short of a dramatic act such as the seizure of buildings could have deposed the university administration and produced a university senate. In retrospect, the affair seems to have been a quite prudent and restrained use of force.

Assuming this assessment to be correct, it is tempting to conclude, "In the Columbia case, violence was justified." But this conclusion is *totally wrong,* for it implies that a line can be drawn between legitimate and illegitimate forms of protest, the latter being justified only under special conditions and when all else has failed. We would all agree, I think, that, under a dictatorship, men have the right to defy the state or even to attack its representatives when their interests are denied and their needs ignored—the only rule that binds them is the general caution against doing more harm than they accomplish good. My purpose here is simply to argue that a modern industrial democracy, whatever merits it may have, is in this regard no different from a dictatorship. No special authority attaches to the laws of a representative, majoritarian state; it is only superstition and the myth of legitimacy that invests the judge, the policeman, or the official with an exclusive right to the exercise of certain kinds of force.

In the light of these arguments, it should be obvious that I see no merit in the doctrine of nonviolence, nor do I believe that any special and complex justification is needed for what is usually called "civil disobedience." A commitment to nonviolence can be understood in two different senses, depending on the interpretation given to the concept of violence. If violence is understood in the strict sense as the political use of force in ways proscribed by a legitimate government, then of course the doctrine of nonviolence depends upon the assumption that there *are* or *could be* legitimate governments. Since I believe this assumption to be false, I can attribute no coherent meaning to this first conception of nonviolence.

If violence is understood, on the other hand, as the use of force to interfere with someone in a direct, bodily way or to injure him physically, then the doctrine of nonviolence is merely a subjective queasiness having no moral rationale. When you occupy the seats at a lunch counter for hours on end, thereby depriving the proprietor of the profits he would have made on ordinary sales during that time, you are taking money out of his pocket quite as effectively as if you had robbed his till or smashed his stock. If you persist in the sit-in until he goes into debt, loses his lunch counter, and takes a job as a day laborer, then you have done him a much greater injury than would be accomplished by a mere beating in a dark alley. He may deserve to be ruined, of course, but, if so, then he probably also deserves to be beaten. A penchant for such indirect coercion as a boycott or a sit-in is morally questionable, for it merely leaves the dirty work to the bank that forecloses on the mortgage or the policeman who carries out the eviction. Emotionally, the commitment to nonviolence is frequently a severely repressed expression of extreme hostility akin to the mortifications and self-flagellations of religious fanatics. Enough testimony has come from Black novelists and psychiatrists to make it clear that the philosophy of nonviolence is, for the American Negro, what Nietzsche called a "slave morality"—the principal difference is that, in traditional Christianity, God bears the guilt for inflicting pain on the wicked; in the social gospel, the law acts as the scourge.

The doctrine of civil disobedience is an American peculiarity growing out of the conflict between the authority claims of the state and the directly contradictory claims of individual conscience. In a futile attempt to deny and affirm the authority of the state simultaneously, a number of conscientious dissenters have claimed the right to disobey what they believe to be immoral laws, so long as they are prepared to submit to punishment by the state. A willingness to go to jail for one's beliefs is widely viewed in this country as evidence of moral sincerity, and even as a sort of argument for the position one is defending.

Now, tactically speaking, there is much to be said for legal martyrdom. As tyrannical governments are perpetually discovering, the sight of one's leader nailed to a cross has a marvelously bracing effect on the faithful members of a dissident sect. When the rulers are afflicted by the very principles they are violating, even the *threat* of self-sacrifice may force a government to its knees. But leaving tactics aside, no one has any moral obligation whatsoever to resist an unjust government openly rather than clandestinely. Nor has anyone a duty to invite and then to suffer unjust punishment. The choice is simple: if the law is right, follow it. If the law is wrong, evade it.

I think it is possible to understand why conscientious and morally concerned men should feel a compulsion to seek punishment for acts they genuinely believe to be right. Conscience is the echo of society's voice within us. The men of strongest and most independent conscience are, in a manner of speaking, just those who have most completely internalized this social voice, so that they hear and obey its commands even when no policeman compels their compliance. Ironically, it is these same men who are most likely to set themselves against the government in the name of ideals and principles to which they feel a higher loyalty. When a society violates the very principles it claims to hold, these men of conscience experience a terrible conflict. They are deeply committed to the principles society has taught them, principles they have truly come to believe. But they can be true to their beliefs only by setting themselves against the laws of the very society that has been their teacher and with whose authority they identify themselves. Such a conflict never occurs in men of weak conscience, who merely obey the law, however much it violates the moral precepts they have only imperfectly learned.

The pain of the conflict is too great to be borne; somehow, it must be alleviated. If the commitment to principle is weak, the individual submits, though he feels morally unclean for doing so. If the identification with society is weak, he rejects the society and becomes alienated, perhaps identifying with some other society. But if both conscience and identification are too strong to be broken, the only solution is to expiate the guilt by seeking social punishment for the breach of society's laws. Oddly enough, the expiation, instead of bringing them back into the fold of law-obeyers, makes it psychologically all the easier for them to continue their defiance of the state.

III

The foregoing conclusions seem to reach far beyond what the argument warrants. The classical theory of political authority may indeed be inadequate; it may even be that the concept of legitimate authority is incoherent; but surely *some* genuine distinction can be drawn between a politics of reason, rules, and compromise on the one hand, and the resort to violent conflict on the other! Are the acts of a rioting mob different only in degree from the calm and orderly processes of a duly constituted court of law? Such a view partakes more of novelty than of truth!

Unless I very much misjudge my audience, most readers will respond roughly in this manner. There may be a few still willing to break a lance for sovereignty and legitimate authority, and a few, I hope, who agree immediately with what I have said, but the distinction between violence and nonviolence in politics is too familiar to be so easily discarded. In this third section of my essay, therefore, I shall try to discover what makes the distinction so plausible, even though it is—I insist—unfounded.

The customary distinction between violent and nonviolent modes of social interaction seems to me to rest on *two* genuine distinctions: the first is the *subjective* distinction between the regular or accepted and the irregular or unexpected uses of force; the second is the *objective* distinction between those interests which are central or vital to an individual and those which are secondary or peripheral.

Consider first the subjective distinction between regular and irregular uses of force in social interactions. It seems perfectly appropriate to us that a conflict between two men who desire the same piece of land should be settled in favor of the one who can pull more money out of his pocket. We consider it regular and orderly that the full weight of the police power of the state be placed behind that settlement in order to ensure that nothing upset it. On the other hand, we consider it violent and disorderly to resolve the dispute by a fist fight or a duel. Yet what is the difference between the use of money, which is one kind of force, and the use of fists, which is another? Well, if we do not appeal to the supposed legitimacy of financial transactions or to the putative authority of the law, then the principal difference is that we are accustomed to settling disputes with dollars and we are no longer accustomed to settling them with fists.

Imagine how barbaric, how unjust, how *violent,* it must seem, to someone unfamiliar with the beauties of capitalism, that a man's ability to obtain medical care for his children should depend solely on the contingency that some other man can make a profit from his productive labor! Is the Federal Government's seizure of my resources for the purpose of killing Asian peasants less violent than a bandit's extortion of tribute at gunpoint? Yet we are accustomed to the one and unaccustomed to the other.

The objective distinction between central and peripheral interests also shapes our conception of what is violent in politics. When my peripheral or secondary interests are at stake in a conflict, I quite naturally consider only a moderate use of force to be justified. Anything more, I will probably call "violence." What I tend to forget, of course, is that other parties to the conflict may find their primary interests challenged and, hence, may have a very different view of what is and is not violent. In the universities, for example, most of the student challenges have touched only on the peripheral interests of professors. No matter what is decided about ROTC, curriculum, the disposition of the endowment, or Black studies, the typical philosophy professor's life will be largely unchanged. His tenure, salary, working conditions, status, and family life remain the same. Hence he is likely to take a tolerant view of building seizures and sit-ins. But let a classroom be disrupted, and he cries out that violence has no place on campus. What he means is that force has been used in a way that touches one of his deeper concerns.

The concept of violence serves as a rhetorical device for proscribing those political uses of force which one considers inimical to one's central interests. Since different social groups have different central interests and can draw on different kinds of force, it follows that there are conflicting definitions of violence. Broadly speaking, in the United States today, there are four conceptions of violence corresponding to four distinct socioeconomic classes.

The first view is associated with the established financial and political interests in the country. It identifies the violent with the illegal, and condemns all challenges to the authority of the state and all assaults on the rights of property as beyond the limits of permissible politics. The older segments of the business community adopt this view, along with the military establishment and the local elites of middle America. Robert Taft was once a perfect symbol of this sector of opinion.

The second view is associated with the affluent, educated, technical and professional middle class in America, together with the new, rapidly growing, future-oriented sectors of the economy, such as the communications industry, electronics, etc. They accept, even welcome, dissent, demonstration, ferment, and—within limits—attacks on property in ghetto areas. They look with favor on civil disobedience and feel at ease with extralegal tactics of social change. Their interests are identified with what is new in American society, and they are confident of coming out on top in the competition for wealth and status within an economy built on the principle of reward for profitable performance.

The "liberals," as this group is normally called, can afford to encourage modes of dissent or disruption that do not challenge the economic and social arrangements on which their success is based. They will defend rent strikes, grape boycotts, or lunch-counter sit-ins with the argument that unemployment and starvation are a form of violence also. Since they are themselves in competition with the older elite for power and prestige, they tend to view student rebels and black militants as their allies, up to the point at which their own interests are attacked. But when tactics are used that threaten their positions in universities, in corporations, or in affluent suburbs, then the liberals cry *violence* also, and call for the police. A poignant example of this class is the liberal professor who cheers the student rebels as they seize the Administration building and then recoils in horror at the demand that he share his authority to determine curriculum and decide promotions.

The third view of violence is that held by working-class and lower-middle-class Americans, those most often referred to as the "white backlash." They perceive the principal threat to their interests as coming from the bottom class of ghetto dwellers, welfare clients, and non-unionized laborers who demand more living space, admission to union jobs with union wages, and a larger share of the social product. To this hard-pressed segment of American society, "violence" means street crime, ghetto riots, civil-rights marches into all-white neighborhoods, and antiwar attacks on the patriotic symbols of constituted authority with which backlash America identifies. Studies of the petty bourgeoisie in Weimar Germany suggest, and George Wallace's presidential campaign of 1968 confirms, that the lower middle class, when it finds itself pressed between inflationary prices and demands from the lower class, identifies its principal enemy as the lower class. So we find the classic political alliance of old established wealth with right-wing populist elements, both of which favor a repressive response to attacks on authority and a strong governmental policy toward the "violence" of demands for change.

The fourth view of violence is the revolutionary counterdefinition put forward by the outclass and its sympathizers within the liberal wing of the established order. Two complementary rhetorical devices are employed. First, the connotation of the term "violence" is accepted, but the application of the term is reversed: police are violent, not rioters; employers, not strikers; the American army, not the enemy. In this way, an attack is mounted on the government's claim to possess the right to rule. Secondly, the denotation of the term is held constant and the connotation reversed. Violence is good, not bad; legitimate, not illegitimate. It is, in H. Rap Brown's great rhetorical flourish, "as American as cherry pie." Since the outclass of rebels has scant access to the instruments of power used by established social classes—wealth, law, police power, legislation—it naturally seeks to legitimize the riots, harassments, and street crime which are its only weapons. Equally naturally, the rest of society labels such means "violent" and suppresses them.

In the complex class struggle for wealth and power in America, each of us must decide for himself which group he will identify with. It is not my purpose here to urge one choice rather than another. My sole aim is to argue that the concept of violence has no useful role to play in the deliberations leading to that choice. Whatever other considerations of utility and social justice one appeals to, no weight should be given to the view that *some* uses of force are prima facie ruled out as illegitimate and hence "violent" or that other uses of force are prima facie ruled in as legitimate, or legal. Furthermore, in the advancement of dissenting positions by illegal means, no special moral merit attaches to the avoiding, as it were, of body contact. Physical harm may be among the most serious injuries that can be done to an opponent, but, if so, it differs only in degree and not in kind from the injuries inflicted by so-called "nonviolent" techniques of political action.

IV

The myth of legitimate authority is the secular reincarnation of that religious superstition which has finally ceased to play a significant role in the affairs of men. Like Christianity, the worship of the state has its fundamentalists, its revisionists, its ecumenicists (or world-Federalists), and its theological rationale. The philosophical anarchist is the atheist of politics. I began my discussion with the observation that the belief in legitimacy, like the penchant for transcendent metaphysics, is an ineradicable irrationality of the human experience. However, the slow extinction of religious faith over the past two centuries may encourage us to hope that in time anarchism, like atheism, will become the accepted conviction of enlightened and rational men.

4   JOHN LAWRENCE

(1938–   )

*Violence**

Lawrence's essay is designed to provide a conceptual framework for the study of
questions about violence. He begins by constructing a working definition of
violence as the class of actions that either result in or are intended to result in
serious injury. Then he discusses the moral issues of responsibility for acts of
violence in terms of types of agents and categories of actions. He concludes with
an attempt to formulate the beginnings of a socially responsive morality of violence
which recognizes that violence is not always wrong. What Lawrence has to say
about the paradox that the least dangerous forms of violence are the most
indignantly disavowed, while those forms of violence that threaten all of us are
often vigorously approved, is of particular interest, especially in light of his
distinctions between individual, group, and institutional violence.

* John Lawrence, "Violence." Reprinted from *Social Theory and Practice*, Vol. 1,
Fall 1970, pp. 31–49. Copyright 1970, *Social Theory and Practice*. Used by permission of the author and the Editors.

VIOLENCE is now a fashionable topic. It evokes diverse questions and
conflicting answers. Is violence an outrage or a necessity? An
enemy of freedom and social order or their indispensable foundation?
A rational means or a self-frustrating instrument? Is it the outcome of
perverted learning or a normal, instinctual need? Is violence a pathological or a voluntary form of behavior for which agents bear full responsibility? Can societies prevent its occurrence or must they resign
themselves to an order including it? The need for philosophical clarity
is evident not only in the controversial answers to these typical questions, but also in the manner in which the very questions are stated.
Their formulation suggests that there is a single form of behavior—
always meriting the same moral assessment, the same psychological or
social explanation. Is there anything in human experience carrying the
label "violence" which justifies such a presumption? Or is violence so
multiform that we must forego such generalizations, making instead
numerous distinctions which necessitate varied methodologies, explanatory principles and moral assessments? The essay that follows provides
clarification for the conceptual, empirical and moral issues associated

with violence which currently proliferate without a coherent framework for their interpretation.

I. DEFINING VIOLENCE

The quest for a useful definition of violence must begin by acknowledging the prevailing definitional variety. There are several conflicting or unrelated conceptions of violence in actual usage. Consulting a dictionary,[1] for example, one may find descriptive, non-moral uses designating the sensory qualities of colors and noises: color schemes and musical compositions can thus exhibit violence. A non-moral use is also evident in describing the dynamics of a sudden or intense action as violent: one can violently close a book or violently shake his hand to remove a sticky substance. Turning to moral uses, where "violence" conveys the notion of injury to human well-being, one finds a variety of types of damage and degrees of seriousness in them, ranging from misinterpretation of an author's words to the destruction of life and property. These divergencies of meaning suggest the absence of any morally or socially significant feature or group of features commonly designated in every application of the terms "violence" or "violent."

This general plurality of conflicting meaning is paralleled by conflict in specialized scholarly usage. One scholar, Raziel Abelson, in attempting to provide a definition of violence that indicates its unique axiological status, writes that " 'violence' connotes illegitimate or excessive force" and that "to apply the term 'violence' to some actions and not to others is to condemn the first group and to excuse the second." [2] On the other hand, Graham and Gurr write, " 'Violence' is narrowly defined . . . as behavior designed to inflict physical injury to people or damage to property. Collectively, and individually, we may regard specific acts of violence as good, bad or neutral, depending on who

---

[1] VIOLENCE . . . 1a: exertion of any physical force so as to injure or abuse (as in warfare or in effecting an entrance into a house) . . . 2: injury in the form of revoking, repudiation, distortion, infringement, or irreverence to a thing, notion, or quality fitly valued or observed . . . 3a: intense, turbulent, or furious action, force or feeling, often destructive . . . b: vehement feeling or expression: FERVOR, PASSION, FURY . . . d: clashing, jarring, discordant, or abrupt quality . . . 4: undue alteration of wording or sense (as in editing or interpreting a text)
VIOLENT . . . 1: characterized by extreme force . . . : marked by abnormally sudden physical activity and intensity . . . 2: furious or vehement to the point of being improper, unjust, or illegal . . . 3: extremely or intensely vivid or loud (colors, noise) *Webster's Third New International Dictionary* (Springfield, Mass.: G. & C. Merriam Co., 1966), p. 2554.
[2] "Letters," *New York Review of Books*, Vol. 12, No. 12, 1969, p. 38.

engages in it and against whom." [3] Definitions treating the forms of responsibility peculiar to violent behavior also reflect severe disagreement. Harold Lief defines violence as "an end point on a continuum of aggressive behavior. It is characterized by extreme force . . . as well as by its irrational nature, so that its original goal-orientation may be lost as it becomes an end-in-itself." [4] Another scholar, H. L. Nieburg, defines violence as "direct or indirect action applied to restrain, injure or destroy persons or property." [5] He makes the claim, ruled out by Lief's definition, that "All acts of violence can be put to rational use, whether they are directed against others or against oneself." [6] Such conflicts destroy the hope that a coherent definition will emerge from a scientific and scholarly vocabulary insulated from the divergent general usages of "violence."

Reflecting on ways in which one might state a significant definition, he should recognize that definitions are always relative to particular purposes and should be judged accordingly. If our definitions should not only mirror the objects of social and moral concern in what is labeled "violence" but also assist us in clarifying the issues which grow out of these concerns, then selectivity, rather than comprehensive fidelity, should guide our search. Our concern with war, riots, homicide, the abuse of police powers, etc., as instances of violence expresses our interest in events which are capable of destroying or severely damaging the human being and his possessions. As compared with these life and death concerns, the violence of color schemes, musical compositions or book closings must be judged peripheral and subordinate. A definition of violence that includes such morally irrelevant sensory qualities would trivialize it and destroy the focus demanded by the more pressing issues associated with violence. Secondly, we must avoid loading a definition with controversial presuppositions. Abelson and Lief both depart from this principle: Abelson embodies a condemnation of all violence in his definition while Lief incorporates his belief that all violent acts are irrational. The effect of such definitions is to foreclose discussion of important topics with the mere application of a label: Abelson's definition excludes any justification of violence and Lief's

[3] Hugh Davis Graham and Ted Robert Gurr, *The History of Violence in America* (New York: Bantam Books, 1969), p. xxx.
[4] Harold I. Lief, "Contemporary Forms of Violence," in *Violence and War, with Clinical Studies,* ed. Jules Masserman (New York: Grune and Stratton, 1963), p. 57.
[5] H. L. Nieburg, "The Uses of Violence," *Toward a Theory of War Prevention,* Vol. I, eds. Richard A. Falk and Saul Mendelovitz (New York: World Law Fund, 1966), p. 157n.
[6] Ibid., p. 160.

definition makes it incoherent to talk about the rational qualities in violent behavior. On Abelson's definition it is nonsensical to say, "Violence in self-defense is approvable." Such an exclusion would have little adverse effect on discussion if "violence" were a term like "murder" or "evil," the application of which commits one to a corollary judgment of the wrongness of the acts so designated. An account omitting this judgment would reflect failure to understand the terms.

This argument would be more appealing if the sentiments toward what people label "violence" were in fact as uniformly negative as they are toward what is labeled "murder" or "evil." But many persons wish to distinguish between good and bad violence. This possibility of justifying violence is implicit in neutral uses of "violence" and seems forced upon us by the existence of certain occupational groups: police, soldiers, athletes, bouncers, prison guards, executioners, etc.; all possess a social license to inflict injury upon other persons in special situations. Such acts are generally approved or tolerated. Should they be described as "unviolent" or "not-violent" because they carry an aura of social legitimacy? Should a policeman who legally kills a person murderously assaulting him be described as "unviolent"? Perhaps the policeman's act will fail any test of ultimate moral justification, but the contention that some violence is good or at least excusable must be capable of being considered. To discuss such an important claim we need a definition of violence neutral enough to permit its formulation, even though all such claims may ultimately be refuted. A neutral definition clearly lends itself to a larger number of interesting assertions: it is compatible with every moral claim that can be made about violence—including the claim that every violent act is unjustified.

Similarly with respect to responsibility, since some contend that violence is rational and that persons can bear full responsibility for their acts of violence, a definition should make it possible to formulate this claim, if only for the purpose of demonstrating its falsity, and a neutral definition would permit this. Therefore, a neutral definition emerges with a powerful advantage in facilitating the clear statement of issues for debate.

Thirdly, we must not allow our definition to be distorted by concentrating on what may be misleading features of "paradigm" cases of violence. A mugging or a riot would be clear examples of body violence or property violence. Body violence carries overtones of physical swiftness, intensity and the intent to inflict bodily harm or death upon the victim. Violent damage to property is associated with intentions to make the owner suffer through the injury to his possessions. There are two relevant aspects of these clear-cut instances of violence: there is a process with certain physical characteristics, and there is an injurious condition which is the usual or intended outcome of that process. In thinking about body or property violence, we should ask which is more important—the *type of process* described as violent or the *outcome* that we normally associate with such processes? Or are they equally important and inseparable except for purposes of analysis? Though suddenness, intensity, etc., are prominent in some uses of "violence," such qualities in isolation from the intended outcome do not form the basis for concern about violence. The injurious results of violence rather than the specific physical qualities of the means take dominance. Consider a case of contemplated murder. It could be carried out by a rapid, intense action like shooting or stabbing and would clearly be labeled "violent." But a murder could also be carried out by giving tiny doses of poison over a period of years. The cumulative effect is fatal. Is such a murder not violent because of its "slow motion" features? Slow murders do not require a separate category isolated from the category of "violence." Speed, intensity, etc., should not be, therefore, thought of as necessary traits of violent acts, though they do figure prominently in the most physically dramatic instances of it. What is important morally about a stabbing or a shooting is the harm to the victim and not the fact that it occurred at a certain rate of speed, with a certain degree of intensity. This viewpoint receives some support from actual usage. The dictionary entry reports that violence can mean "the exertion of *any* physical force so as to injure" and also "injury in the form of revoking, repudiation, distortion, infringement or irreverence." These clearly encompass any type of injurious activity, regardless of its particular physical qualities. ("Violence," incidentally, derives from the Latin verb meaning "to injure or plunder.")

If injury and the fact that it is intentionally inflicted are distinctive traits of violence, there is no reason why the concept "violence" should be restricted solely to cases of body injury or property damage. In actual usage, other types of processes have been designated as "violence" in order to indicate the moral kinship of all serious injuries to human well-being. The phrases "latent violence," "hidden violence," "quiet violence," "covert violence," have all been used to convey the idea that a serious injury is being inflicted even though one cannot immediately perceive any act of biologically incapacitating a victim. The addition of qualifying phrases concedes a departure from the paradigm of simple body violence, but there is no concession that these are any less important as forms of human injury. These forms of violence require additional categories.[7] Using "biological violence" to encompass body wounding or death caused by body wounds, we can conceptualize other forms of violence by using the categories "physical" and "psychological." Physical violence (not to be confused with direct body violence) indicates the imposition of physical restraints on the behavior of a victim so as injuriously to reduce his freedom to act, as in certain forms of enslavement and imprisonment. Property damage should also generally fall under "physical violence." "Psychological violence"—has been used to cover destructive assaults upon psychological autonomy and self-esteem.[8] In the instance of a parent who hates his child, a mixture including each type of violence is easily conceivable—the child can be beaten and injured biologically, restricted in his space of action and harassed verbally.

Why accept extensions of the concept so different from the picture of the mugger assailing his victim? Because, if injury is the most important feature of violence, it would be arbitrary to draw the line at biological wounds and exclude gross restraints on the freedom to act and efforts at psychological tyranny. These exclusions seem more arbitrary in view of the interdependence between physical and psychological injury on the one hand and biological well-being on the other. Second, we should ask, what in a given case is most important to the individuals whose well-being is affected? Is biological violence more important than other types? Taking actual behavior as a guide, the absence of physical restraints and the maintenance of psychological autonomy are in many instances given preference over biological well-being. Given the choice between a life of slavery and the loss of a hand, foot, or limb, how many persons would sacrifice a significant portion of their bodies in order to preserve their freedom? Or given the choice between a loss of limb or vision and the permanent loss of personal identity through a brainwashing treatment, how many would choose to retain the identity which they have achieved through a lifetime of personal choices and actions? The extension of the concept of violence to include the physical and psychological elements of well-being is by no means a descent from the more to the less important, but might well be an ascent from the less important toward the more important. Violence should therefore be sufficiently broadly conceived to

---

[7] I follow here some distinctions proposed by Johan Galtung, "On the Meaning of Non-Violence," *Man and International Relations* Vol. II, *Integration*, ed. J. K. Zawodny (San Francisco: Chandler Publishing Co., 1966), pp. 412ff.

[8] *Cf.* Erving Goffman, "On the Characteristics of Total Institutions" and "The Moral Career of the Mental Patient," *Asylums* (Garden City, N.Y.: Doubleday Anchor, 1961).

reflect the variety of important injuries from which individuals suffer and the enormous variety of means through which those injuries can be produced.

A definition which meets all these requirements can be cast in the following form. *"Violence" shall be defined to mean: the entire class of actions which result, or are intended to result, in serious injury to life or its material conditions.*[9] *Serious injury must include the ideas of biological damage, severe physical restraints or property destruction and psychological impairment.* The above concept of "serious injury" is not a straightforward one concerning which social and moral theorists have no disagreements. Just as the specific meaning "deprivation" depends for its specific meaning upon a normative judgment concerning what a person *ought to have,* so the meaning of "injury" depends on a concept of well-being. But for the purpose of discussing violence, it is safe to assume that there are at least some widely agreed upon aspects of well-being and injury. For example, processes leading to biologically premature death are widely regarded as injurious. One should also notice the definition's neutral character. It indicates varied phenomena but contains no partisan moral or theoretical predispositions and therefore leaves open the possibility for a variety of value judgments and explanations. This neutrality prevents no one from condemning or praising violence or from having theories about its functions, control and causation. Such neutrality simply means we must use words other than "violence" to express our convictions about what we so designate.

II. THE AGENTS OF VIOLENCE AND THEIR INTENTIONS

What forms of activity are capable of inflicting injury? Who is responsible for these activities? How much responsibility do they bear for them? Is it possible to control such activities? If so, how? Answers to these questions will require that conceptual extentions take place which resemble that from the paradigmatic body violence to other types of serious injury. Conceptions of responsibility will appear that implicate unsuspected agents and circumstances.

Violence, as described thus far, is characterized by injurious outcomes of processes. It is a general condition (or rather, many con-

---

[9] This definition reflects a crucial philosophical choice; rather than characterizing violence by uniquely distinguishing traits, I have made "violence" synonymous with "doing serious harm."

ditions) which can be produced by a large number of significantly different processes. "Violence" and "disease" can be fruitfully compared. To the single word "disease," there corresponds no specific, uniform condition. To understand what causes disease is to discriminate the multiple circumstances producing specific diseases. Likewise, to understand violence, we must discriminate agencies and types of activity capable of producing injury. We shall further be led to examine the varying circumstances of mind and volition which can enter into its creation.

Forms of Agency

Violent acts can be performed by individuals or by groups, by individuals acting within the framework of institutions, where "institution" means a socially created agency employing collective means such as taxation, conscription, etc. Examples of biological violence by these agencies would be:

    i. Individual violence—homicide, rape, mugging

    ii. Group violence—lynching, attack on draft center, vigilante justice

    iii. Institutional violence—capital execution, war, riot suppression

Intent and Responsibility

Criminal law recognizes differing types of intent and circumstances in the performance of violent acts which enter into their appraisal. Responsibility for violence varies by degree, ranging from cases where the agent is fully accountable morally to cases in which he is not responsible at all except in a causal sense. The following categories afford a sense of the complexity in the morality and control of violence.

a. An act is *deliberately violent* if the agent consciously intends serious damage or injury.

b. An act is *compulsively violent* if the agent's impulses in performing the act are so powerful that his capacity for choice is irrelevant as a determinant of his behavior.

c. An act is *neglectfully violent* even though the agent does not consciously intend injury if such a consequence could have been avoided had he exercised foresight and control.

d. An act is *accidentally violent* if the injurious results could not be foreseen or if the circumstances leading to the injury could not be controlled.

e. An act (or an omission) is *dilemmatically violent* if serious injury is a consequence of any alternative open in that situation (including the option of failing to act). The agent need not be aware of the injurious consequences of each alternative.

Consistent with the theme of production of injury, these categories further extend the model of violence beyond the paradigm of body violence where an agent willfully harms another person. But this extension is consistent with the dominant element in the concept of violence, which is the production of injury. If injury most deeply concerns us, rather than any single form of intention which leads to it, we must consider the diversity of states of mind and circumstance leading to serious injury. To care seriously and consistently about life is to care about every circumstance resulting in harm. Taking the concept of negligent violence, which might be thought farfetched as an instance of violence, we ought to ask several questions. Should the failure to act in a life or death situation be classified as non violent because the individual did not consciously will the injury of the other person, but rather failed to do what would have prevented the injury? Is the failure to respect a person evidenced as much by what we omit to do for them as by the deliberately injurious acts we undertake? Is one being violent if he allows another to be tortured while possessing the power to prevent it? Failing to apply the concept "violence" to such unusual situations would at least make us uncomfortable. Such extensions augment moral awareness. Items whose kinship was concealed by fragmented terminology now fall naturally together.

Examples can establish the descriptive plausibility of these categories. Cases of deliberate violence are common. First degree homicide, lynching and war, exemplify individual, group, and institutional violence, respectively. This type of violence readily gives rise to the desire for punishment and retaliation because its deliberate character removes the conditions excusing the agent from responsibility.

Compulsive violence at the *individual* level includes acts of insane persons. That individuals may be compulsively violent within group settings is suggested by some forms of crowd behavior.[10] At the institutional level, many national leaders suffering from neuroses or psychoses have mobilized national forces for their deranged purposes.[11]

Examples of *neglectful* violence generally masquerade beneath the label "accident." Large numbers of "accidental gun deaths" (so classi-

[10] *Cf.* Elias Canetti, "Panic," *Crowds and Power* (New York: Viking Press, 1966), pp. 26–27.
[11] *Cf.* Jerome D. Frank, "Insanity or Incapacity of National Leaders," in *Sanity and Survival* (New York: Vintage Books, 1968), pp. 58–64.

fied in official statistics) are failures to exercise foresight and control,[12] as when an *individual* hunter with substandard vision shoots a human being. He should have either refrained from an activity which his faulty vision rendered potentially lethal, or worn corrective lenses. But further: a governmental institution could disqualify hunters with poor vision. Its failure to do so may evidence a neglectful indifference to the fate of potential victims, or it may evidence the difficulty or disadvantages of regulations.[13]

Genuinely *accidental* violence is troubling for the hope [14] of preventing serious injuries which men do to one another. In the strict sense of "accident" requiring unforeseeability and uncontrollability, accidental violence could be eliminated only if every injurious consequence of every action were knowable and preventable, which they are not. Accidental violence affects large numbers, particularly where unknown consequences of a broad institutional policy are at work. A controversial example of *institutional, accidental* violence comes from a recent interpretation of the consequences of nuclear testing. A radiation scientist who has studied statistical patterns of infant and fetal mortality describes "an association which appears to be of a direct causal nature" resulting in 375 . . . mortalities during a fifteen year period in the United States.[15] These numbers dwarf the more publicized forms of violence like robbery and rioting which generally provoke discussions of violence.

Dilemmatic violence also troubles the hope that violence may be eliminated with development of an improved human being. These are situations that involve serious injury as the consequence of every alternative. Consider England's *institutional* adoption of a mass radiography policy, described by Lord Adrian:

> Four-and-a-half million examinations were made in 1957. It has been estimated that bone marrow effects of the radiation might possibly have added as many as twenty cases of lukemia in that year; yet the examinations revealed eighteen thousand cases of pulmonary tuberculosis, as well as thousands of other abnormalities. The twenty deaths from leu-

[12] *Cf.* Carl Bakal, *No Right to Bear Arms* (New York: Paperback Library, 1968), passim.
[13] A similar claim of negligence is plausible regarding the 50,000 victims of auto accidents in the United States each year. *Cf.* the statement of Carl Clark in Ralph Nader, *Unsafe at Any Speed* (New York: Grossman Publishers), pp. 344–345.
[14] *Cf.* "Once we perform the revolutionary but simple act of deciding that we can change, the era of violence can close." John Poppy; "Violence: We Can End It," *Look*, Vol. 33, No. 12, 1969, p. 21.
[15] Ernest J. Sternglass, "Infant Mortality and Nuclear Tests," *Bulletin of Atomic Scientist*, Vol. XXV, No. 4, 1969, p. 20.

kemia were only a remote possibility, but, Lord Adrian asks, if they were a certainty would they have been too high a price for the early detection of tuberculosis in eighteen thousand people? [16]

Similar dilemmas confront numerous institutional policy making decisions. An economist has convincingly described highway planning as a process requiring conscious acceptance of death in the policy alternatives.

> The highway planner is sufficiently bound by budget so that a crusade against death on wheels can be no more than a limited war. Within the limits and because of them he is forced to economize, ration, allocate and reckon.[17]

In such cases, one may only attempt to determine and act upon the least violent alternative. Here total elimination is impossible.

The diversity of the categories and examples should dissuade us from adopting single cause theories of violence. And violence is as complex morally as it is causally. There is no single intention peculiar to the occurrence of violence which uniformly justifies the same attribution of intent, responsibility and moral character. The examples also suggest the complexity and pervasiveness of violence as a social phenomenon. No social unit has a monopoly on violence: we find agencies of violence wherever there are agencies capable of affecting human well-being. Dilemmatic and accidental violence seem woven into the fabric of life, not to be eliminated by any vigorous social campaigns. Moral alternatives will seldom polarize as either totally unviolent and good or wholly violent and bad. Different values will be balanced against one another. Often the choice is between the preserving of a freedom and eliminating it because of the types of violence which flourish in its presence: the freedom to own lethal weapons is the same freedom which can easily destroy the lives of others; the freedom of personal mobility which we derive from our cars is a freedom which results in hundreds of thousands of deaths and injuries; the freedom to enjoy private relations with one's children is a freedom which often results in tyrannized personalities or mangled bodies. Would a society necessarily be better if it could permanently eliminate the possibility for a particular type of violence? The answers are not obvious. These reflections are not meant to suggest that violence

[16] Henry K. Beecher, "Medical Research and the Individual," *Life or Death, Ethics and Options* (Seattle: University of Washington Press, 1968), p. 130.
[17] Peter S. Albin, "Economic Values and the Value of Human Life," *Human Values and Economic Policy*, ed. Sidney Hook (New York: New York University Press, 1967), p. 96.

is inevitable or that its control is impossible or undesirable. Even if we concede that some violence is inevitable, and that every attempt to control violence has its costs, the desire to employ the power of human choice to affect the occurrence of violence remains fully rational.

III. MOTIVES FOR VIOLENCE AND THE CONTROL OF VIOLENCE

Control over violence would be ineffectual where compulsion for violence mechanically translates itself into violent behavior. Some hold that aggression, the will to inflict injury is a normal and human instinct. Konrad Lorenz, writes that "intraspecific aggression is, in man, just as much a spontaneous, instinctive drive as in most other higher vertebrates." [18] Such aggression is "phylogenetically programmed" [19] into human behavior. Another popular author, Robert Ardrey, holds that man is "a predator whose natural instinct is to kill with a weapon." [20] Such language—"spontaneous instinctive drive," "phylogenetically programmed aggression" "natural instinct to kill" evokes the image of toxic quanta of destructiveness that we struggle to release in violent behavior.

Various considerations come to mind in appraising such an account. First, what could "instinct" mean in reference to violence, and how much influence upon conduct would one expect it to exert? Suppose that an "instinct" for aggression is like hunger, sexuality, shelter-seeking, etc. Are these latter unaffected by our choice? The sexual instinct does not inevitably lead to and therefore explain the practice of incest. Nor does hunger lead directly to the diet of the vegetarian or the cannibal. Even the most basic needs have highly differentiated, contextually-related satisfactions. So, to call aggression instinctual and "normal" tells us nothing about the situations and modes for its satisfactions, or the frequency with which the instinct is acted upon. In short, the most interesting and humanly significant questions remain to be answered through a detailed knowledge of actual behavior.

In examining the allegedly "instinctual" character of violent behavior, we must ask, "What are the highly differentiated occasions and satisfactions associated with its performance?" Violence exhibits an enormous range of pragmatic appeals, which occur in all of the contexts

[18] "Ritualized Fighting," *The Natural History of Aggression*, eds. J. D. Carthy and F. J. Ebling (London & New York: Academic Press, 1964), p. 49.
[19] An expression used by Lorenz in *On Aggression* (New York: Harcourt Brace Jovanovich, Inc., 1966), p. 253.
[20] *African Genesis* (New York: Atheneum, 1961), p. 316.

of action suggested by the distinctions regarding the forms of agency in violence. Individuals can use violence to secure life necessities, particularly in crises of scarcity or when the normal channels of competition for goods are closed through discriminatory practice. Violence may be used to acquire goods, as when the threat or employment of violence is used in manipulating others to serve one's interests.[21] It may be used to cope with troublesome situations beyond the reach of the agent's verbal skills. It may be used to break bonds of dependency in establishing one's own personal identity. It may be used as a means of retaliating against others who have denigrated one's reputation and threaten the esteem in which one wishes to be held. It can be a response to those who pose physical dangers to one's safety. One may enjoy the sheer excitement of the violent encounter, as in hunting, or the aesthetic delight of destruction.

Groups may use violence to communicate grievances to those who might otherwise ignore them. Violence may provide the hope that it can change existing distributions of power in ways that place the disaffected group on a more equal footing with other social groups and allow the group to become an effective participant in the institutions from which they have been previously excluded. A group psychological benefit of violence, noted in recent riots in America, is the augmented sense of self-esteem and potency. [22] Since institutions generally grant distinct advantages to some groups at the expense of others, there is bound to be some group disaffection with institutional policy. It is therefore natural that institutions should use violence or its threat to preserve existing distributions of power. Institutional violence raises the cost of changing the existing institutions; this can provide for order and stability (though not without the potential for revolutionary violence in the future). The police and army of a nation are also the visible manifestations of willingness to coerce conformity with existing norms and political arrangements. In its international relations, national institutions can attempt to use war in preserving national security, and attempt to preserve or change existing distributions of political power among other nations. These processes are costly, frequently far more than they are meant to be, but war is far from being institutionally obsolete.

The wide range of instrumental motivations to be discovered in violence suggest that it generally presents itself as a means to be considered in comparison with unviolent alternatives. Rather than being

[21] Several of the points in this paragraph are taken from Han Toch, *Violent Men* (Chicago: Aldine Publishing Co., 1969), pp. 133ff.
[22] *Cf.* Hans Toch, *op. cit.*, pp. 201–202.

the unique satisfaction for an instinctual constant, violence functions as a contextually variable option for action. Given the pervasive pragmatic appeal of violence, one should expect to find a variety of social processes whose purpose is the deliberate and effective control of violence. Since violence always involves at least two roles (agent and victim) who have a significantly different interest in the outcome of the violent act, the concept "control" has a pair of divergent meanings. For the agent "control" means attempting to guide the violent process to a successful conclusion; for him, violence functions as means or as a source of desired qualities of experience (or both). The victim experiences violence as an alien force directed against his well-being; here, "control" means attempting to minimize the violent powers bent upon his injury, perhaps by resorting to his own counterviolence against the initiating agent. As with the highly varied occasions and motivations for violence, control of violence is evidenced in every major social process—whether technological, military, educational, legal-political. In some cases these processes are aimed at efficiently structuring and rationalizing the power to injure; in others they are aimed at the construction or protective barriers against it. Technology, for example, is well known for its contributions to the science of killing. But it can also serve to deter violence or minimize some of its effects. Technology may play an important role in preserving peace by allowing nations to monitor conditions which would indicate adherence to weapons and peace treaties.

Education is as potentially double-edged as technology. On the one hand, it may be devoted to the spread of divisive ideologies and the promotion of demonic stereotypes of groups which are designated as enemies. The talents of intellectuals may be employed to rationalize the necessity for wars against enemies who are viewed through distorted perceptual processes.

Contemporary political-military bureaucracies could not function without large numbers highly trained in the arts of verbalizing and making computations. But educational projects could be enrolled in the task of dispelling twisted perceptions which contribute to willingness for violent conflict. They can also teach attitudes of respect for life and provide training in the non-violent resolution of conflict.

Political-legal processes contribute to violence when they make it possible to conscript soldiers, declare wars and to mobilize populations for destructive purposes. Laws can be used to injure permanently the interests of minority groups, as is explicitly done in legalized segregation. But law can also provide substitutes for violence, making it possible to exchange the judicial process for personal combat. Laws have been used to prohibit, punish, and virtually eliminate particular violent practices, as in the instance of lynching in the United States. The reduced violence following the recognition of the labor movement, the granting of women's suffrage, and the repeal of prohibition suggest that a sense of justice on the part of aggrieved groups stems violence.

In giving these examples of violence control, I have provided only enough information to establish that attempts at violence control take place and not that the controls are actually effective. An adherent of an instinctual interpretation of violent behavior might view these descriptions as optimistic projections arising from overly rationalistic interpretations of behavior, interpretations which uncritically take surface appearances at face value. The only way to finally demonstrate the untenability of the belief in the instinctual, compulsive nature of violence resides in the empirical data describing the violent behavior of men and cultures.

Such empirical data as we possess concerning violence and its control confirms the soundness of an approach which emphasizes the role of choice rather than instinct. Individuals and cultures cope with propensities for violence in such variable fashion as to render a concept of "instinct for aggression" useless as an explanation of why particular acts of violence occur.

As an example, homicide rates for different nations vary from one another by factors of more than 100.[23] A table illustrating this is presented here.

TABLE 1. HOMICIDE RATES AMONG SELECTED NATIONS [24]

Nicaragua	29.3
Columbia	21.3
United States	6.0
Japan	1.5
Sweden	0.8
England and Wales	0.7
Spain	0.1

To compare the highest and lowest rates among the nations listed, Nicaragua's rate is 293X as high as that of Spain. If we accept the Ardrey view that "man is a predator whose natural instinct is to kill

---

[23] Cf. H. L. A. Hart, op. cit., pp. 65–71.
[24] These figures come from "Table 24: Death and death rates by cause and sex: latest available year" (1966 in most cases), Demographic Yearbook 1967 (New York: United Nations, 1968), pp. 455–485. The numbers here appear under entry BE50, Homicide and operations of war, and are rates per 100,000 population. Limitations of these statistics are described on p. 38.

with a weapon," it would appear that Nicaraguans would be relatively unfrustrated (and more human?) than the (less human?) citizens of Spain. The instinct to kill, if it does exist at all, is thus shown to be highly malleable and subject to effective restraint.

The data concerning accidental deaths caused by firearms show a similar variation and lend strong support to the contention that what is labeled "accident" may often involve neglect more than chance.

TABLE 2. ACCIDENTAL FIREARMS DEATHS
(1962–1963) [25]

United States	1.20
Sweden	.36
England and Wales	.16
Japan	.09
Netherlands	.03

Here the lowest nation differs from the highest by a factor of 40.

A final table includes some figures (without intermediate rates) for some additional types of violence.

TABLE 3. RATES FOR SELECTED TYPES OF VIOLENCE

1. Suicide   Rates (international)[26]—Ratio of lowest, highest = 296X (Jordan, 0.1: Hungary, 29.6)
2. National Frequencies of Battle Engagement [27]—Ratio of lowest, highest = 24X (Denmark, 2%: France 47%)
3. Deaths and Casualties Due to Civil Disturbances (international) [28]— Ratio of highest, lowest = 1,200X
4. Murder Rates within the U.S.[29]—Ratio of lowest, highest = 23X (Vermont, 0.5: Alabama, 11.5)

---

[25] Figures from Carl Bakal, op. cit., p. 356. Computing the ratio for the lowest and highest rates within the U.S. gives a figure of 24X (Mass.: Alaska, 4.7).
[26] Demographic Yearbook, op. cit., Table 24.
[27] These figures are taken from Quincy Wright's study of 2600 military battles involving European states during the years 1480–1940. A Study of War (Chicago: University of Chicago, Phoenix abridged edition, 1965), pp. 52–53. Lewis Richardson has reached similar conclusions in his The Statistics of Deadly Quarrels (Pittsburgh: Boxwood Press, 1960).
[28] Figures taken from Hugh Davis Graham and Ted Robert Gurr, op. cit., fn. 3, Table 17–3, p. 579. The figures are taken from the portion of the table describing European and Latin American nations. I arbitrarily assigned a value of 0.1 to Sweden in order to establish a ratio.
[29] Taken from "Table 4: Murder Rates by State, 1965," The Death Penalty in America, ed. Hugo A. Bedau (New York: Anchor Books, revised edition, 1967), p. 68.

If we reject determinism in the form which depicts culture and individual behavior as the product of blind interaction between man and physical environment, and which consequently describes autonomous choice as a fiction; we must assume that these variations express individual acts of choice, whether they be the choices of purely personal action or the choice (or toleration) of group action, social custom or institutional policy.

The figures available are mainly relevant to determining success in the control of violence from a victim's point of view and they tell a story of relative success and failure in large population units. In some of the countries mentioned, rates for particular types of violence are so low that no policy or pattern of individual choices could significantly lower them. An obvious case is Denmark, which had no deaths from civil disturbance over a four year period. Iceland had but one homicide in 1966. The Netherlands had only four accidental deaths due to firearms in 1963.[30] The extent to which these forms of violence are minimized would doubtless be regarded as almost entirely satisfactory from the perspective of potential victims. These minimal rates have been achieved without any radical changes in the nature of man,[31] but rather through means which most cultures possess—legislation, the development of social custom and taboo and the other cultural sanctions which influence conduct.

The agent's perspective on success in the control of violence—success mainly meaning the achievement of one's goal in the performance or toleration of violence—is not reflected in the figures. We often hear the clichés that "Violence never settles anything," or "Violence never pays." These sentiments project negative moral valuations into conceptions of fact. There are successful homicides, robberies, rapes, bombings, etc. in which the agent carries out his aim and is never called to task. Some countries have enormously profited from the practice of slavery.[32] Some nations successfully dominate others by military violence or its threat. Some nations have successfully defended their territorial and cultural integrity by the use of violence. Some communities use the threat of violence as a way of maintaining civil order.[33] Violence can pay very well indeed, though it has its own costs like any other policy, and it can settle many things, though it may do so in a

[30] Carl Bakal, op. cit., p. 356.
[31] Cf. Sarvepalli Radakrishnan, "Violence and the Purpose of Education," Alternatives to Violence, ed. Larry Ng (New York: Time-Life Books, 1968), p. 105.
[32] Cf. Ronald Segal, The Race War (New York: Bantam Books, 1967), pp. 19–119.
[33] Cf. Charles Tilley, "Collective Violence in European Perspective," in Graham and Gurr, op. cit., fn. 3, p. 41.

morally odious fashion. We cannot have a full grasp of the human significance of violence until we have struggled with the moral issues which underlie it.

IV. THE MORALITY OF VIOLENCE

What is right or wrong about violence? Is violence always wrong? What is one morally obliged to do about violence? The agent and victim would doubtless offer conflicting answers. The agent will regard his violent act as justified by the moral worthiness of its end. He might regard the injury he inflicts as an unfortunate moral necessity for dealing with some condition which violates the sanctity of life. The justification for capital punishment often holds that if we respect life, then we must destroy life. The victim takes a different view: violence injures or is meant to injure his life, weakening or destroying the powers whose exercise makes life tolerable and valuable. The victim also feels a moral affront: violence expresses an absence of respect for his person. A major social value is negated—the consciousness of a mutually shared and cherished relationship. Those between whom violence occurs exist in hostile, destructive separateness, a positive evil in itself. Nothing could seem more obvious to the victim than that violence is a terrible wrong, the most evil of which humans are capable.

If tragedy be defined as the conflict of good, then tragedy is clearly evident in the violent encounter, provided we grant partial legitimacy to the viewpoints of both agent and victim. The victim of violence is hardly likely to perceive the injury to himself as a moral necessity. The agent's "necessity" is the victim's gratuity. If anything the injury will increase the victim's sense of righteousness about the behavior which provoked the injury. Hence a sense of tragedy is revealed through the inclusion of agent and victim perspectives. The tragedy is not merely that evil *gratuitously* crushes good (victim's perspective) or that good *must* crush good (agent). Both parties feel morally vindicated.

Is violence always wrong? I hope that this question will appear as maddeningly simplistic in light of the distinctions argued for in this essay. Of course, one can say, "Yes, violence is always wrong because the word 'violence' simply means a wrongful use of force. Therefore, we are always obligated to avoid violence." This type of answer settles nothing. The thrust of the moral question about violence concerns the possibility of justifying a willful injury. Saying that "violence" means "unjustified use of force" does not tell us whether such injury is ever justified, but merely forces us to use other words to entertain the possibility.

A second approach to the normative appraisal of violence can be taken via the categories of intention developed in this essay. If by "wrong action" one means the willful performance of an action whose avoidance is morally obligatory, several answers are dictated by the differing kinds of responsibility for violent acts. Among the circumstances of mind, volition, and violent action described, only two—the deliberate and the negligent, are avoidable. Hence they are the only types of violence to which wrongness could be imputed. In the instances of compulsive, accidental and dilemmatic violence, the possibility for deliberate avoidance is excluded; one cannot ascribe the sort of responsibility which depends upon a prior free choice. The consequences of such actions are bad, but the circumstances prevent the imputation of wrongness to the choice or the moral character of the agent. If one accepts these distinctions, then the question about the wrongness of violence becomes, "Is all avoidable violence (deliberate and neglectful) wrong?" Should one adopt the principle that no one ought ever to inflict injury or fail to prevent the suffering of injury in any circumstance? As one analyzes what would be involved in accepting such a principle, the hope of finding a single moral verdict about violence disappears.

If one answers affirmatively that violence is always wrong, the implicit moral principle is that the avoidance of injury to others is a more compelling moral obligation than any other. But why should one accept such an absolute? Does a belief in the sanctity of life require us to accept an absolute obligation to avoid injury? Consider how the sanctity of life and the avoidance of injury principles might be related to one another in a concrete instance. A person is being mugged and believes that he can protect himself only by injuring his assailant. The principle of always avoiding injury to others would prohibit this as wrong. But by avoiding injury to the assailant, would the victim fulfill the requirement to respect life, its conditions of well-being, etc.? The answer is no. In this situation, avoiding injury to others would mean submitting to the injury which another inflicts upon oneself. Adherence to the absolute prohibition against injury to others would amount to a sacrificial ethic rather than a sanctity of life ethic: it would require him to discriminate against the sanctity of his own life in favor of that of his assailant. But if life is sacred, why does not the sacredness of one's own life deserve equal attention to that of others? What is it about being "other" which justifies special consideration? If we study the implications of the absolute proscription in other contexts, one finds additional difficulties. Should one say, in a revolutionary or counter-revolutionary context, that every existing political institution or distribution of power, no matter how fair, should be sacrificed to attackers in order to avoid doing any injury to them? Should one say, in studying the ineffectiveness of African violence against the slave traders, that the Africans are to be commended for the little injury which they inflicted upon those who took them into captivity? Would it have been morally right for Africans to go peacefully into slavery? Would it be wrong for a physician to withhold help in stemming death by epidemic disease in a country which will later see millions starve because of population pressure?

The defender of an absolute prohibition against violence might claim to find a false presumption behind these problematic questions—the presumption that violence is sometimes a unique means to values whose pursuit is morally obligatory. He could say that for every morally obligatory aim, such as physical security, cultural integrity, etc., traditionally pursued by violence, there is an alternative non-violent means for obtaining it; therefore non-violence is always applicable as an effective, and moreover, morally approvable means: violence is never a unique means in a morally obligatory pursuit. Therefore, the assumption that an absolute prohibition against violence is a disguised ethic of sacrifice must be rejected. Belief in the utility of violence rests upon impatience, unimaginativeness or neurosis.

It is difficult to assess accurately the claim that non-violent means could always be efficacious if only they were tried. One might find examples of the success of non-violence in connection with every conceivable human good. And it may well be true that many, if not most, uses of violence are accompanied by delusory beliefs about the efficacy of fear and threat and are less efficacious than some imaginable non-violent alternative. But as for the universal utility of non-violence, one must have doubts. The claim that non-violence has been shown to work on particular occasions for the achievement of a broadly defined goal like physical security is compatible with countless other contexts in which violence, because of the particular circumstances, is a unique means. The truth, perhaps disappointingly pluralistic, is that non-violence is a unique means in some contexts, violence a unique means in others, with a middle range of cases in which either violence or non-violence can be efficacious in the attainment of morally obligatory goals. This seems in fact to be the position of most pacifists and advocates of the ideology of non-violence, who pragmatically proscribe violence in those contests where failure is likely or certain and prescribe

violence where it is a unique means of attaining what is morally required. Gandhi, for example, wrote,

> I do believe that, where there is only a choice between violence and
> cowardice, I would advise violence. Thus, when my eldest son asked
> me what he should have done, had he been present when I was almost
> fatally assassinated in 1908, whether he would have run away and seen
> me killed or whether he should have used physical force which he
> could and wanted to use, I told him that it was his duty to defend me
> even by using violence.[34]

The fact that neither Gandhi nor most pacifists unqualifiedly accept
the principle of non-violence hints at the difficulty of finding it a
tenable moral option.

The proposition that violence is not always wrong constitutes a feeble
beginning at a socially responsive morality of violence since it merely
expresses a commonly held and acted upon belief. Taken by itself, such
a statement could bring little moral comprehension to a humanity
threatened with collective extinction by several violent possibilities.
Provided that one is interested in suggesting desirable transformations
in the moral world, it is surely more relevant (once having examined
the thesis of total non-violence) to talk about the wrongness and
dangers of violence and the attitudes whose perpetuation sustains these
wrongs and dangers.

If, as I have argued, the rightness of violence on particular occasions
is a function of its efficacy in the fulfillment of moral obligation, it
would follow that the wrongness of violence consists in its failure to
meet this condition. Specifically, violence would be wrong in any one
of several circumstances: (i) where it is employed to achieve purposes
not obligatory, as in murder, or (ii) where it is employed to achieve
an end which, while obligatory, does not require violence as a uniquely
efficacious [35] means, as would be true in a case of serious conflict resolved by a beating when verbal or judicial means would have provided
a satisfactory resolution, or (iii) where it is employed to pursue goals
which are obligatory but for which violence is not efficacious as a

---

[34] Quoted in Donald A. Wells, *The War Myth* (New York: Western Publishing
Co., 1968), p. 99.
[35] The requirement that violence can be right only if it is *uniquely efficacious* as a
means to morally obligatory end depends upon the moral principle that one ought
to avoid unnecessary injury. Violence which is merely efficacious as one among
several alternatives, some of which are unviolent in character, violates this principle. It could be said that the element of injury in violence establishes its *prima
facie* wrongness, but that this does not tell us whether violence is *always* unjustified.
To put it another way, violence always has disvalues, but is not for that reason,
automatically the wrong option.

means; for example, assuming that the Czechs were morally obligated to preserve life during their Russian "normalization," it would have been suicidal and hence wrong for them to attempt their defense by military means. Finally, (iv) violence would be wrong where it serves no means function at all, but simply expresses the neglectful indifference of an agent who does not wish to exert himself to preventing a serious injury.

From the perspective of social concern about violence, one should ask, "Do any of these wrong forms of violence pose any significantly greater dangers than others?" If we take "greater" to mean a greater power to harm or destroy life and also take collective extinction of mankind or the destruction of entire nations as meaningful quantitative measures, several conclusions follow. The first category of wrong violence—violence employed toward non-obligatory ends (i)—poses the least danger, though saying so has a paradoxical air. In our quest for dramatic moral simplicities, we are inclined to believe that the greatest dangers emanate from agents who are self-conscious in their knowledge or evil doing, as was the Archangel Michael who said, "Evil, be thou my good." It is true that the greatest amount of public fear and rage is directed at crimes like arson, rape, mugging, and murder ("crime in the streets") which so clearly lack defensible moral purpose. But such behavior clearly does not constitute dangers for the survival of mankind or even of particular nations. The social order is hardly threatened if I kill my brother in a quarrel about money. On the contrary, the greatest dangers from violence are posed by those forms of it directed toward some aim generally regarded as obligatory or justifiable (ii, iii)—an exemplary instance being national defense, which virtually all persons accept in the abstract. National defense consequently commands infinitely greater resources for human destructiveness than the humble brawler who drunkenly stabs his brother with a butcher-knife. And these resources of defense in their turn call forth matching resources of counter-violence from those who are not convinced that they are wholly defensive in character. It is in the institutional domain of violence that we find the powers—nuclear, chemical-biological—that threaten social order and life. The most destructive powers of violence possess social legitimacy because they rest on policies which are alleged to be (and often are) consensually defined. We are confronted with a kind of paradox here: the forms of violence posing the least danger are the most indignantly disapproved while the forms of violence posing the greatest danger are the most vigorously approved. Who can fail to approve defending oneself? The fact that the means employed may not be uniquely requisite or efficacious is obscured by the socially sanctioned character of institutional military violence, a character which demands commitment and loyalty in the absence of proven efficacy or even in spite of proven, self-destructive inefficacy. ("They shall not have died in vain.")

Historically, socially critical magnitudes of violence have resided in institutions rather than in individuals (though individuals can certainly move and use institutions for their own purposes). The novelty in contemporary forms of violence is that a relatively small number of leaders possess the power to destroy all human life; in the past, it would have required the strenuous efforts of almost all men to do so. Furthermore, the impersonality of the modern technological capability has permitted the processes of human destruction to attain their ultimate potential without the need for the hot-blooded passions previously important in human extermination. The industrialization and rationalization of war has made mass life-destruction possible as nothing more than a dutiful and passionless bureaucratic routine. To confront modern violence and to speak in the interests of human life requires one not to admonish people to do what are generally regarded as their solemn duties, but rather to demonstrate that those socially praised and heavily moralized tasks should not be their duties at all. Appealing to men's "better natures" in the age of giant bureaucracies of death is but to appeal to those same selfless sentiments which loyally sustain the machineries of death. The moral restraint of violence in its most awesome magnitudes requires a reordering of moral priorities in modern culture, so that violent means, if they are necessary at all, are genuinely the servants of human interests rather than their greatest enemies.

To descend from the perceptually remote but real possibility of collective extinction to violences of lesser magnitude involves more controversial problems in moral adjudication. Everyone can agree that collective extinction would be wrong; to think at all is almost to affirm the value of human survival. But to see the wrongness of treating violently some particular person or group is more difficult. Moral agents should be very self-conscious about the delusions and preserve twists in reasoning to which the temptations of violence give rise. As stated previously, violence can only be right if it constitutes a uniquely requisite means to the attainment of a morally obligatory goal. Agents should be aware that in the heat of impatience, it is tempting to believe that violence is uniquely requisite, even though many unviolent alternatives exist. Hence in the natural tendency to act decisively there is a predisposition for violence often unjustified by circumstance. Agents should also be aware of the ways in which violence shifts with so much fluidity from effectiveness to ineffectiveness; the process of violent conflict, because of the frustrations to which it gives rise in coping with counter-violence, can lead the individual to believe that the violent conflict is a self-justifying end, to be pursued "honorably" regardless of cost in means. Even though the agent may have undertaken violence under conditions for moral rightness in violence, the violent means can easily become totally disproportionate in their cost in relation to the morally approvable end they were meant to attain.[36] A scrupulous moral agent will doubtless find many occasions on which violence is tempting, but on further reflection demonstrates itself a clear wrong.

This willingness to sort through deliberatively the relevant considerations while struggling with the peculiar difficulties of violence is doubtless latent with the same potential for self-deceit, half-truth, and the other rationalizing vices characteristic of perverted reasoning. But we should not conclude that the effective moral restraint of violence is impossible. At the very least, the information suggests that there is nothing unattainable about a much less violent world than the one in which we now live. Violence will doubtless never be entirely eliminated; it is a permanent human potential with which every generation copes rather than a "problem" which is given a "solution." That we can hope to place greater amounts of violence within effective moral restraints is sufficient motivation for attempting to moralize intelligently about violence and for trying to alter the contours of violence in the world which challenge our moral sensibilities.[37]

[36] *Cf.* Lewis A. Coser, *The Functions of Social Conflict* (Glencoe, Ill.: Free Press, pb., 1964), pp. 48ff, for his analysis of the shift from realistic conflict to non-realistic conflict.

[37] Many persons have contributed valuable criticism during the writing of the article, among them G. Bowles, R. Jewett, J. N. Jordan, J. M. Miller, R. F. Terry, R. Wallace and above all, R. V. Stone.

Further Reading On
VIOLENCE AND THE NATURE OF MAN

Arendt, Hannah. "Violence." *The New York Review of Books,* February 1969.

Byrne, Edmund F. "The Depersonalization of Violence: Reflection on the Future of Personal Responsibility." *The Journal of Value Inquiry,* Fall 1973.

Fanon, Frantz. *The Wretched of the Earth.* New York: Grove Press, 1968.

Flanigan, Patrick. "Wolff on Violence." *Australasian Journal of Philosophy,* December 1972.

Graham, H., and T. Gurr (eds.). *Violence in America.* New York. Bantam Books, 1969.

Honderich, Ted. "Democratic Violence." *Philosophy and Public Affairs,* Winter 1973.

Kasten, Vance. "Violence and the Free Expression of Ideas." *Journal of Social Philosophy,* April 1975.

Kuvacic, Ivan. "Contemporary Forms of Mental Violence." *Praxis,* 1970.

Lawrence, John S. "The Moral Attractiveness of Violence." *Journal of Social Philosophy,* Fall 1970.

Nielsen, Kai. "Remarks on Violence and Paying the Penalty." *Philosophic Exchange,* Spring 1970 .

Prior, Andrew. "Is the Concept of Violence Coherent?" *Philosophical Papers,* October 1972.

Ranley, Ernest W. "Defining Violence." *Thought,* Autumn 1972.

Schaff, Adam. "Marxist Theory on Revolution and Violence." *Journal of the History of Ideas,* April–June 1973.

Shaffer, Jerome (ed.). *Violence.* New York: McKay, 1971.

Smith, Bruce R. "The Politics of Protest: How Effective Is Violence?" *Urban Riots: Violence and Social Change, Proceedings of the Academy of Political Science,* July 1968.

Somerville, John. "Violence, Politics, and Morality." *Philosophy and Phenomenological Research,* December 1971.

Stott, Laurence. "Values and Violence." *Educational Theory,* Fall 1972.

Wade, Francis C. "On Violence." *Journal of Philosophy,* June 1971.

Willers, Jack C. "Violence—An Educational Dilemma." *Philosophy of Education: Proceedings,* 1970.

PART IV

PERSONS, MINDS, AND SURVIVAL AFTER DEATH

I Double
(Bridge term)*

Walt Kelly

HERE IS A DISCUSSION OF PERSONAL SERPENTS AND WHICH IS THE right side of a mirror, head or tails.

* Walt Kelly, *The Pogo Papers* (New York; Simon and Schuster, 1952, 1953), pp. 60–1, 65–7, 69–73. Used by kind permission of Walt Kelly.

PORKY GETS A GRIP ON HIMSELF DESPITE CERTAIN PHYSICAL problems, holds himself at arm's length and hastily puts himself back.

HEREIN THE RAINS COME DOWN IN THE SOGGY ALONE AND WE FIND a firefly in every ointment.

Phoenix Arizona
Jan 2nd 1946
this is my first and only will and is dated the second day in January 1946. I have no heires (have not been married in my life) after all my funeral expenses have been paid and $100, one hundred dollars, to some preacher of the gospital to say farewell at my grave sell all property which is in cash and stocks with E F Hutton Co Phoenix some in safety box, and have this balance money to go in a research or some scientific proof of a soul of the human body which leaves at death I think in time their can be a Photograph of soul leaving the human at death,
James Kidd

dated 2nd
January 1946
[on side margin]: some cash in Valley bank some in Bank America LA Cal

INQUIRY

> *"God knows!" exclaimed he, at his wits' end. "I'm not myself—I'm somebody else—that's me yonder —no—that's somebody else got into my shoes. I was myself last night, but I fell asleep on the mountain, and they've changed my gun, and everything's changed, and I'm changed, and I can't tell what's my name, or who I am!"*
>
> WASHINGTON IRVING, *Rip Van Winkle*

IS having the same body that you had last week a necessary condition of being the same person now that you were then? That is one form of the classic philosophical problem of personal identity. In a broader sense, the problem is related to the kinds of tests we apply when questions arise regarding whether or not someone is the same person as, for example, someone we used to know. In this part, we will first examine some proposals relative to determining criteria for personal identity (self-identity) and some of the problems that arise when these are applied. The *Pogo* cartoon strip serves to illustrate for us some of the issues involved in personal identity.

Porkypine is perplexed by the appearance in the swamp of his double, who has taken over Porkypine's daily activities and even his home. For all Porkypine knows (we, of course, know that it is an imposter), this other self may be a miraculous reconstruction of himself. That is, Porky could imagine that this other Porkypine might well be a real duplicate of himself. How does he convince his friends that he is not his look-alike? "Eventually ever' man gotta face the problem of tryin' to figger if it's worthwhile to prove that he is himself," says Porkypine.

If two persons claim to be the same person, and they look alike, how do we draw distinctions? What criteria are to be applied? As Pogo says, "A man's own friends ought to recognize him." What does "recognize" mean here? The philosophical problem of personal identity is not "What kind of person am I?" but "What particular person am I?" A key to the question may lie in the way we use the word *same*. When we refer to someone as the same person, "same" implies a standard. It refers us to some criterion or rule. The fact that it is important at times in our lives to make claims about ourselves as "the same person who . . ." should give us a clue to the kinds of criteria we deem appropriate to the problem.

If you had purchased a car seven years ago, and in the course of time every part of that car had to be replaced by a new part, would you be inclined to call it the "same car" you bought seven years ago? If not, during which repair did the car cease to be the old car and become the new, different car? Certainly the car is not the original, but is it a seven-year-old car? A used-car dealer would have to refer to it as such. What of a human being? What constitutes his identity and makes him recognizable after seven years?

Whenever questions of identity arise, we would like a clear-cut uncomplicated criterion to solve the problem. In normal circumstances these questions seldom do arise. Only when some extraordinary events interfere with daily life, when it becomes necessary to establish identity, to have an alibi, to recognize someone in a crowd, or to be recognized by someone, do we confront these issues; and, of course, the question of personal identity is also related to certain theories of afterlife, in particular regarding the question of whether sense can be made of the claim that particular men have survived after their physical deaths.

John Locke distinguishes between the identity of men and the identity of persons. The "same man" for Locke refers to bodily continuity. If we were to know (in the sense that we recognize) a certain man in town, even if he should undergo a severe psychological maladjustment—perhaps even to the point of complete mental derangement—we would still call him the same man, assuming his bodily existence is continuous. But, as Locke points out, the personal identity of the man in question would not necessarily be the same. A "person" for Locke is a "thinking, intelligent being that has reason and reflection and can consider itself as itself in different times and places." If those mental capacities were not a vital part of our identities, then we would not differ in terms of distinguishing qualities from beasts or inanimate objects such as trees. Locke concludes that the identity of a person is a question of consciousness, memory, "as far as this consciousness can be extended backwards to any past action or thought, so far reaches the identity of that person." My personal identity, for Locke, might well be summarized as, "I am what I remember." Is it possible for the same man not to be the same person? Consider the implications of the plea of temporary insanity often used by the defense in murder trials.

Eighteenth-century Scottish philosopher Thomas Reid criticized Locke's theory of personal identity when he pointed out that the memory criterion has a tendency to people the world unnecessarily, thereby confusing the issue as to just who someone is. Reid cited the example of a general who remembers his valiant efforts on the battle-field (when a major, let us say) but has forgotten all of his activities as a schoolboy. Yet while he was a major performing the valiant deeds of battle, he clearly remembered his school days. On Locke's account we would have to say that the general is the same person as the valiant major and that the major was the same person as the schoolboy, but that the schoolboy and the general are not the same person.

A great deal of our Western tradition supports the theory that the identity of persons (personality?) is identical with a nonphysical substance, that there is something called "I," a mind or soul, sep-arate from the body, that need not exist within the particular body it now occupies.

David Hume attempts to uncover this thing "I." Hume concludes, however, that a man has no clear, constant idea of "self" as he carries on the various activities of living. You never catch your self when it is not doing something. In other words, your idea of your self is constantly changing. You are happy, sad, relaxed, working on mathematical problems, doing philosophy; but there is no one invariable "I" or "self" that is ascertainable in this bundle of percep-tions. For Hume, if there is no constant impression of "I," there can be no clear idea of "I" apart from the various things "I" does. Identity is the imagined linking of a series of impressions. I am a bundle of the things I do, feel, think, etc. I am not a thing apart from my activities.

Notice, however, that if we accept the Humean analysis of the self, we are left with acts, both mental and physical, but no actors. We have activities, but no agents performing them. Arthur Koestler, in his novel *Darkness at Noon,* has one of the major characters refer to the self, the pronoun "I," as a "grammatical fiction," something the language makes exist. Is the self nothing but a product of the imagination or language? Common sense and our social, legal, and educational systems would lead us to believe that each of us is an Ego, a center or subject of experience. We attribute states of con-sciousness to ourselves and to others, and we act within our social framework as if each of us has a continuing identity. Is all of this a myth? Is it a product of our imagination and not of fact? If we have no perception of the self, why do we find it necessary to manufacture an entity to serve as a kind of ghostly actor in each of our experiences? What would the possessives *mine, yours,* etc., mean if this were the case?

Today's achievements in medical technology, especially in the area of organ transplants, suggest the possibility of a future experiment in which the brains of two individuals are exchanged.[1] A's body receives B's brain, and B's body receives A's brain. Assume that A's body/B's brain dies during the operation, but that B's body/A's brain survives. Let us call our subject BA. BA awakens. Put yourself in his position. You see the familiar body, lifeless, being wheeled out of the room. You have A's brain and his memory traces, but this body does not quite feel right. You are released from the hospital (perhaps told to return weekly to a local philosopher for a progress report). To whose house do you go? Let us stipulate that A and B and their respective families had never met. Undoubtedly you go to A's house; you remember none other. Mrs. A is at the door. What is to be your relationship with wife A and children A? How would you proceed to convince them that you are husband and father despite appearances? Think of the legal problems. Who is the widow? Who collects the life insurance?

Another and non-Western answer to the perplexing questions of self is found in the Brahmanistic traditions of Hinduism. The self (Atman) is identified with neither the bodily self, the self of memory, nor the self of dreams but is instead best described as the pure self-conscious that is universal and identical with reality (Brahman). The contemporary Indian philosopher Radhakrishnan writes of the self: "All our states of consciousness revolve round this central light. Abolish it, they vanish. Without a subject there will be no flux, no order of sensations in space or sequences in time . . . this subject is the universal ground which is in all individuals. It is hidden in all things and pervades all creation."[2] If personal identity is so understood, the distinctions among persons, not to mention things in the world that create the problem of personal identity for us, must be artificial, the product of confusion, the subject/object grammar of our language, or both.

The will of James Kidd generates issues related to those of per-

[1] This example was suggested by Sydney Shoemaker, *Self-Knowledge and Self-Identity* (Ithaca: Cornell University Press, 1963)

[2] S. Radhakrishnan, *Indian Philosophy* (London: George, Allen and Unwin, Ltd., 1923), p. 158.

sonal identity. During the spring and summer of 1967, it was pro-
bated in the Superior Court of the State of Arizona. Among the many
claimants to the estate, which was valued at $200,000, were philoso-
phers, psychologists, neurologists, religious and academic institutions, and certain individuals who said that they had special powers
of communication with the dead or unique theories on "soul-
searching."

The belief that persons do "live" after death is certainly widespread, although it is not often clear what "living after death"
means. If one is dead, then one does not survive. "The dead" and
"the survivors" are exclusive categories. Do any theories of personal identity (Locke's, Hume's, Shoemaker's, etc.) make the notion
of a "disembodied person" intelligible? Persons have points of
view; but what would be the point of view of the disembodied?
Antony Flew tells us that "persons are what we meet." We learn
about being a person and identifying persons through our physical
experiences. We point out persons, we shake hands, pat persons on
the back. On what basis could we identify something disembodied
as a person?

A good deal of Western religious tradition and much of our
literature incorporate the idea that man is a combination of physical
processes and mental processes, outer and inner existence, a distinction we saw in Locke's theory. The physical is public and the
mental is private. Asking children about death shows us, as Maria
H. Nagy demonstrates in her studies on "The Child's View of
Death," [3] how early in life we distinguish between these "parts" of
ourselves. A child of nine years says:

> What is death? Well I think it is a part of a person's life. . . . Only one
> part of it is earthly. As in school, we go on to a different class. To die
> means to begin a new life. Everyone has to die once, the soul lives on.

This type of thinking, called mind/body dualism, is characterized
by the belief that there are two essentially different parts of man.
The two "parts" of man are taken by dualist philosophers to be
irreducible to each other; that is, minds and mental activity can
never be explained totally by reference to the physical, nor can
bodies and physical activities be explained completely by reference
to the mental. The Renaissance philosopher René Descartes, called

[3] Maria H. Nagy, "The Child's View of Death," *Journal of Genetic Psychology*, 73
(1948), pp. 3–27.

by many the father of modern philosophy, gave a concise statement of the "official doctrine" of the dualist:

> Because I know certainly that I exist, and that meanwhile I do not remark that any other thing necessarily pertains to my nature or essence, excepting that I am a thinking thing, I rightly conclude that my essence consists solely in the fact that I am a thinking thing (or a substance whose whole essence or nature is to think). And although possibly (or rather certainly, as I shall say in a moment) I possess a body with which I am very intimately conjoined, yet because, on the one side, I have a clear and distinct idea of myself inasmuch as I am only a thinking and unextended thing, and as, on the other, I possess a distinct idea of body, inasmuch as it is only an extended and unthinking thing, it is certain that this I (that is to say, my soul by which I am what I am), is entirely and absolutely distinct from my body, and can exist without it.[4]

Notice that not only does Descartes think of himself as a combination of two different entities, a mind and a body, but the real Descartes is to be identified with his mind or soul. British philosopher H. D. Lewis put this idea in the phrase, "I have my body, I am my mind."

If mental states are private, some philosophers have argued, then we cannot account for the fact that we explain many of the activities of others by reference to their mental states: "John is depressed." "John is in pain." How could we understand what another person means by "I am in pain" if his pain were a totally private thing? I could not discover whether he means by "pain" what I mean by "pain." As long as our so-called mental or internal states are private, the statement "He is in pain" cannot really be a comment about him, but it is a roundabout statement about what it is like when I use "pain" in reference to myself.

Twentieth-century philosopher Ludwig Wittgenstein offers an interesting analogy to this problem.[5] He tells us to suppose everyone has a box with something in it that is called a "beetle." No one can look into anyone else's box, and each knows what a "beetle" is only by looking at his own "beetle." Might not everyone have something different in his box? Perhaps someone has an empty box. The concept of beetle then could not even be "something in the box." The

---

[4] René Descartes, *Meditations* (1641).
[5] Ludwig Wittgenstein, *Philosophical Investigations*, E. C. M. Anscombe, trans. (New York: Macmillan, 1953), #293.

word "beetle" would have to be used in such a way as not to be the name of anything. "Beetle" is useless; it could mean anything or nothing. If we knew our mental state only by looking within ourselves, then referring to mental states in others would be as meaningless as talking about the "beetles."

In a contemporary autobiography, *Conundrum*,[6] the British journalist Jan Morris describes her own transformation by medical means from a male into a female. Jan (formerly James) Morris maintains that she always had felt herself in spirit to be a woman. It should be noted that Morris was, as a man, neither a homosexual nor a transvestite. Instead she felt herself trapped in a body alien to her deepest and strongest feelings. Hers was apparently a sense of spiritual alienation from her body. "I was 3 or perhaps 4 years old when I realized that I had been born into the wrong body and should really be a girl." The "conundrum" or puzzle of which Morris writes is the apparent contradiction she experienced between mind and body and its resolution at the hands of a surgeon. The identification of the person with the soul or mind, as suggested by Morris's experience, is quite crucial to our problem in understanding the Kidd will. Even if we could show that souls do not die with bodies, unless the individual is, in some essential way, his soul, we could not say that he had survived physical death.

Does the existence of a separate soul or mind explain anything that cannot already be accounted for by reference to physical activities? I come to know of physical things through my senses, in a somewhat indirect way. On the other hand, I know that certain mental processes, such as thinking, intending, willing, deciding, are going on in me regardless of data received from my senses. I have knowledge of this "mental me" in an immediate way, in a direct way. Interactionist dualists would say that we know we have these private sides of ourselves and also that a great deal of our activity is explainable only if we assume that we intend mentally to do something physical. I intend to open the door; therefore I raise my arm, take the knob, and open the door. My opening the door is no accident, nor simply a series of mechanical gestures.

John Passmore attacks the interactionist notion that the mind and the body affect each other. If the mind is purely mental and the body purely physical, they have nothing in common. There are no grounds for transactions between them. Can you imagine a purely physical thing being moved to act by the "force" of reason? If there is no

---

[6] Jan Morris, *Conundrum* (New York: Harcourt Brace Jovanovich, Inc., 1974).

body in mind (minds apparently can be influenced only by thoughts) and if there is no mind in body (bodies are influenced only by physical forces), then minds can never influence bodies and bodies can never influence minds. The separation of the two must be blurred if we are to talk of interactions between them.

Mr. Kidd may have mistakenly applied concepts of physical matters to matters concerning the soul. This is not uncommon. We say, "The man has sold his house" and "The man has sold his soul"; "The airplane leaves the terminal at midnight" and "The soul leaves the body at death." It seems quite natural to talk this way. If it is possible for one to sell his house, why not his soul? If it is possible for someone to take a picture of an airplane as it leaves the terminal, why not a picture of the soul as it leaves the body at death? However, we might remind ourselves that there are many things we can say about houses and airplanes that we cannot say about souls. For example, one might inquire at the ticket counter as to how late a certain plane was in leaving the terminal. But such a question would not be appropriate concerning a certain soul leaving the body at death. Continue the comparison. "Where is your house?" but not "Where is your soul?" "I see my arm," but not "I see my soul."

Mr. Kidd's will demands photographic evidence of survival, but can we even conceive of what is involved in the so-called "survival hypothesis"? During the court hearings on the will, various mediums claimed that their abilities to contact the "dead" constituted the scientific proof Kidd sought or that they at least established a high probability that survival is a fact. Do we have any way of evaluating such "evidence"? Here again the question of personal identity is central. We would want proof that the subject with whom we are communicating through a medium is the same person he is claiming to be. But also we should need some intelligible notion of the so-called other world in which the "dead" person now "lives."

H. H. Price claims that our experience of dreaming is a key to an intelligible account of "Another World." When we dream, he tells us, we enter a world of mental images; we are not stimulated sensually in the normal ways, and the laws of behavior in dreams are not those of physics. Yet so long as the dream lasts, we are not aware that it is a dream (except during so-called lucid dreams). We take the dream to be reality. Price suggests that the "Next World" might be like our dream world. It might be a world of images. The process of "imaging" would replace normal sense perceiving. Instead of receiving stimuli through the senses, we would be stimulated by our mental images, thoughts, emotions, and wishes. Price argues that we would certainly "feel as much alive" in our image world as we do in the present physical world. The word *survival* then would be appropriate to what happened to us.

Where is this "Next World"? Price suggests, based on the model of the dream, that the next world can be thought of as a space not locatable in the physical world. Nonetheless, it would be a place of spatial coordinates for those who image there. As each of us has his own dream worlds, Price allows that there will be many "Next Worlds," and, perhaps by telepathy, intercommunication between these other-worldly heavens and hells would be possible.

If we accept Price's account of the survival hypothesis and "Another World," are we in a better position to meet the requirements of the Kidd will? Can we imagine a photograph of a soul leaving the body at death? Notice that we do not use movement words to describe the process of beginning to dream. We do not say of the sleeper: Now he is halfway to his dream, now three quarters of the way; he has reached his dreamworld. He simply starts to dream. Might not Price argue that one could not photograph the soul leaving the human body at death because its leaving the body and arriving in "Another World" are simultaneous events? There is nowhere to put the camera, nowhere to aim it.

> nobody nowhere
> except yourself
> not even a mirror
> to make you two
> not a soul
> except your own
> maybe
> and even that
> not there
> maybe
> or not yours
> maybe
> because you're what's called
> dead
> you've reached your station
>
> Descend [7]

[7] Lawrence Ferlinghetti, "The Long Street," *A Coney Island of the Mind*. Copyright © 1958 by Lawrence Ferlinghetti. Reprinted by permission of New Directions Publishing Corporation.

1   JOHN LOCKE

(1632–1704)

Same Man . . . Same Person*

Locke's interests lie mainly in practical and social matters. He is most famous for his contributions to government theory, which were influential in the thought of the founders of the American Republic. Locke's epistemological thinking is an attack on the theory that people are born with certain innate ideas that form the core of our human knowledge. Ideas, Locke claims, arise from sensations and reflections on those sensations. In other words, the source of knowledge is experience. Locke's philosophy is often cited as the first major exposition of English empiricism, the theory that knowledge arises not from deducible first principles, but from interactions with our environment. Locke, on the question of identity, draws a distinction between the recognition of material things and that of persons. We know that material things are the same on the basis of sense perception; they look the same. But ourselves? We know our identities through consciousness, intuition and memory.

* John Locke, *Essay Concerning Human Understanding* (1690), with omissions.

THIS also shows wherein the identity of the same *man* consists; viz. in nothing but a participation of the same continued life, by constantly fleeting particles of matter, in succession vitally united to the same organized body. He that shall place the identity of man in anything else, but, like that of other animals, in one fitly organized body, taken in any one instant, and from thence continued, under one organization of life, in several successively fleeting particles of matter united to it, will find it hard to make an embryo, one of years, mad and sober, the *same* man, by any supposition, that will not make it possible for Seth, Ismael, Socrates, Pilate, St. Austin, and Cæsar Borgia, to be the same man. For if the identity of *soul alone* makes the same *man;* and there be nothing in the nature of matter why the same individual spirit may not be united to different bodies, it will be possible that those men, living in distant ages, and of different tempers, may have been the same man: which way of speaking must be from a very strange use of the word man, applied to an idea out of which body and shape are excluded. And that way of speaking would agree yet worse with the notions of those philosophers who allow of transmigration, and are of opinion that the souls of men may, for their miscarriages, be detruded into the bodies of beasts, as fit habitations, with organs suited to the satisfaction of their brutal inclinations. But yet I think nobody, could he be sure that the *soul* of Heliogabalus were in one of his hogs, would yet say that hog were a *man* or *Heliogabalus*.

It is not therefore unity of substance that comprehends all sorts of identity, or will determine it in every case; but to conceive and judge of it aright, we must consider what idea the word it is applied to stands for: it being one thing to be the same *substance*, another the same *man*, and a third the same *person*, if *person, man,* and *substance,* are three names standing for three different ideas;—for such as is the idea belonging to that name, such must be the identity; which, if it had been a little more carefully attended to, would possibly have prevented a great deal of that confusion which often occurs about this matter, with no small seeming difficulties, especially concerning *personal* identity, which therefore we shall in the next place a little consider.

An animal is a living organized body; and consequently the same animal, as we have observed, is the same continued *life* communicated to different particles of matter, as they happen successively to be united to that organized living body. And whatever is talked of other definitions, ingenious observation puts it past doubt, that the idea in our minds, of which the sound man in our mouths is the sign, is nothing else but of an animal of such a certain form. Since I think I may be confident, that, whoever should see a creature of his own shape or make, though it had no more reason all its life than a cat or a parrot, would call him still a *man;* or whoever should hear a cat or a parrot discourse, reason, and philosophize, would call or think it nothing but a *cat* or a *parrot;* and say, the one was a dull irrational man, and the other a very intelligent rational parrot. [A relation we have in an author of great note, is sufficient to countenance the supposition of a rational parrot. His words are:

'I had a mind to know, from Prince Maurice's own mouth, the account of a common, but much credited story, that I had heard so often from many others, of an old parrot he had in Brazil, during his government there, that spoke, and asked, and answered common questions, like a reasonable creature: so that those of his train there generally concluded it to be witchery or possession; and one of his chaplains, who lived long afterwards in Holland, would never from that time endure a parrot, but said they all had a devil in them. I had heard many particulars of this story, and ássevered by people hard to be discredited,

which made me ask Prince Maurice what there was of it. He said, with
his usual plainness and dryness in talk, there was something true, but
a great deal false of what had been reported. I desired to know of him
what there was of the first. He told me short and coldly, that he had
heard of such an old parrot when he had been at Brazil; and though
he believed nothing of it, and it was a good way off, yet he had so
much curiosity as to send for it: that it was a very great and a very old
one; and when it came first into the room where the prince was, with
a great many Dutchmen about him, it said presently, *What a company
of white men are here!* They asked it, what it thought that man was,
pointing to the prince. It answered, *Some General or other.* When they
brought it close to him, he asked it, *D'où venez-vous?* It answered, *De
Marinnan.* The Prince, *À qui estes-vous?* The parrot, *À un Portugais.*
The Prince, *Que fais-tu là?* Parrot, *Je garde les poulles.* The Prince
laughed, and said, *Vous gardez les poulles?* The parrot answered, *Oui-
moi; et je sçai bien faire;* and made the chuck four or five times that
people use to make to chickens when they call them. I set down the
words of this worthy dialogue in French, just as Prince Maurice said
them to me. I asked him in what language the parrot spoke, and he said
in Brazilian. I asked whether he understood Brazilian; he said No, but
he had taken care to have two interpreters by him, the one a Dutchman
that spoke Brazilian, and the other a Brazilian that spoke Dutch; that
he asked them separately and privately, and both of them agreed in
telling him just the same thing that the parrot had said. I could not but
tell this odd story, because it is so much out of the way, and from the
first hand, and what may pass for a good one; for I dare say this
Prince at least believed himself in all he told me, having ever passed
for a very honest and pious man: I leave it to naturalists to reason, and
to other men to believe, as they please upon it; however, it is not,
perhaps, amiss to relieve or enliven a busy scene sometimes with such
digressions whether to the purpose or no.'

I have taken care that the reader should have the story at large in the
author's own words, because he seems to me not to have thought it
incredible; for it cannot be imagined that so able a man as he, who had
sufficiency enough to warrant all the testimonies he gives of himself,
should take so much pains, in a place where it had nothing to do, to
pin so close, not only a man whom he mentions as his friend, but on a
Prince in whom he acknowledges very great honesty and piety, a story
which, if he himself thought incredible, he could not but also think
ridiculous. The Prince, it is plain, who vouches this story, and our
author, who relates it from him, both of them call this talker a parrot:
and I ask any one else who thinks such a story fit to be told, whether,

if this parrot, and all of its kind, had always talked, as we have a prince's word for it this one did,—whether, I say, they would not have passed for a race of *rational animals;* but yet, whether, for all that, they would have been allowed to be men, and not *parrots?*] For I presume it is not the idea of a thinking or rational being alone that makes the *idea of a man* in most people's sense: but of a body, so and so shaped, joined to it; and if that be the idea of a man, the same successive body not shifted all at once, must, as well as the same immaterial spirit, go to the making of the same man.

This being premised, to find wherein personal identity consists, we must consider what *person* stands for;—which, I think, is a thinking intelligent being, that has reason and reflection, and can consider itself as itself, the same thinking thing, in different times and places; which it does only by that consciousness which is inseparable from thinking, and, as it seems to me, essential to it: it being impossible for any one to perceive without *perceiving* that he does perceive. When we see, hear, smell, taste, feel, meditate, or will anything, we know that we do so. Thus it is always as to our present sensations and perceptions: and by this every one is to himself that which he calls *self:*—it not being considered, in this case, whether the same self be continued in the same or divers substances. For, since consciousness always accompanies thinking, and it is that which makes every one to be what he calls self, and thereby distinguishes himself from all other thinking things, in this alone consists personal identity, i.e. the sameness of a rational being: and as far as this consciousness can be extended backwards to any past action or thought, so far reaches the identity of that person; it is the same self now it was then; and it is by the same self with this present one that now reflects on it, that that action was done.

But it is further inquired, whether it be the same identical substance. This few would think they had reason to doubt of, if these perceptions, with their consciousness, always remained present in the mind, whereby the same thinking thing would be always consciously present, and, as would be thought, evidently the same to itself. But that which seems to make the difficulty is this, that this consciousness being interrupted always by forgetfulness, there being no moment of our lives wherein we have the whole train of all our past actions before our eyes in one view, but even the best memories losing the sight of one part whilst they are viewing another; and we sometimes, and that the greatest part of our lives, not reflecting on our past selves, being intent on our present thoughts, and in sound sleep having no thoughts at all, or at least none with that consciousness which remarks our waking thoughts,—I say, in all these cases, our consciousness being interrupted, and we losing the sight of our past selves, doubts are raised whether we are the same thinking thing, i.e. the same *substance* or no. Which, however reasonable or unreasonable, concerns not *personal* identity at all. The question being what makes the same person; and not whether it be the same identical substance, which always thinks in the same person, which, in this case, matters not at all: different substances, by the same consciousness (where they do partake in it) being united into one person, as well as different bodies by the same life are united into one animal, whose identity is preserved in that change of substances by the unity of one continued life. For, it being the same consciousness that makes a man be himself to himself, personal identity depends on that only, whether it be annexed solely to one individual substance, or can be continued in a succession of several substances. For as far as any intelligent being *can* repeat the idea of any past action with the same consciousness it had of it at first, and with the same consciousness it has of any present action; so far it is the same personal self. For it is by the consciousness it has of its present thoughts and actions, that it is *self to itself* now, and so will be the same self, as far as the same consciousness can extend to actions past or to come; and would be by distance of time, or change of substance, no more two persons, than a man be two men by wearing other clothes to-day than he did yesterday, with a long or a short sleep between: the same consciousness uniting those distant actions into the same person, whatever substances contributed to their production.

But though the same immaterial substance or soul does not alone, wherever it be, and in whatsoever state, make the same *man;* yet it is plain, consciousness, as far as ever it can be extended—should it be to ages past—unites existences and actions very remote in time into the same *person,* as well as it does the existences and actions of the immediately preceding moment: so that whatever has the consciousness of present and past actions, is the same person to whom they both belong. Had I the same consciousness that I saw the ark and Noah's flood, as that I saw an overflowing of the Thames last winter, or as that I write now, I could no more doubt that I who write this now, that saw the Thames overflowed last winter, and that viewed the flood at the general deluge, was the same *self,*—place that self in what *substance* you please —than that I who write this am the same *myself* now whilst I write (whether I consist of all the same substance, material or immaterial, or no) that I was yesterday. For as to this point of being the same self, it matters not whether this present self be made up of the same or other substances—I being as much concerned, and as justly accountable for any action that was done a thousand years since, appropriated to me now by this self-consciousness, as I am for what I did the last moment. . . .

This may show us wherein personal identity consists not in the identity of substance, but, as I have said, in the identity of consciousness, wherein if Socrates and the present mayor of Queinborough agree, they are the same person: if the same Socrates waking and sleeping do not partake of the same consciousness, Socrates waking and sleeping is not the same person. And to punish Socrates waking for what sleeping Socrates thought, and waking Socrates was never conscious of, would be no more of right, than to punish one twin for what his brother-twin did, whereof he knew nothing, because their outsides were so like, that they could not be distinguished; for such twins have been seen.

But yet possibly it will still be objected,—Suppose I wholly lose the memory of some parts of my life, beyond a possibility of retrieving them, so that perhaps I shall never be conscious of them again; yet am I not the same person that did those actions, had those thoughts that I once was conscious of, though I have now forgot them? To which I answer, that we must here take notice what the word I is applied to; which, in this case, is the *man* only. And the same man being presumed to be the same person, I is easily here supposed to stand also for the same person. But if it be possible for the same man to have distinct incommunicable consciousness at different times, it is past doubt the same man would at different times make different persons; which, we see, is the sense of mankind in the solemnest declaration of their opinions, human laws not punishing the mad man for the sober man's actions, nor the sober man for what the mad man did,—thereby making them two persons: which is somewhat explained by our way of speaking in English when we say such an one is 'not himself,' or is 'beside himself'; in which phrases it is insinuated, as if those who now, or at least first used them, thought that self was changed; the self-same person was no longer in that man.

But yet it is hard to conceive that Socrates, the same individual man, should be two persons. To help us a little in this, we must consider what is meant by Socrates, or the same individual *man.*

First, it must be either the same individual, immaterial, thinking substance; in short, the same numerical soul, and nothing else.

Secondly, or the same animal, without any regard to an immaterial soul.

Thirdly, or the same immaterial spirit united to the same animal.

Now, take which of these suppositions you please, it is impossible to make personal identity to consist in anything but consciousness; or reach any further than that does.

For, by the first of them, it must be allowed possible that a man born of different women, and in distant times, may be the same man. A way of speaking which, whoever admits, must allow it possible for the same man to be two distinct persons, as any two that have lived in different ages without the knowledge of one another's thoughts.

By the second and third, Socrates, in this life and after it, cannot be the same man any way, but by the same consciousness; and so making human identity to consist in the same thing wherein we place personal identity, there will be no difficulty to allow the same man to be the same person. But then they who place human identity in consciousness only, and not in something else, must consider how they will make the infant Socrates the same man with Socrates after the resurrection. But whatsoever to some men makes a man, and consequently the same individual man, wherein perhaps few are agreed, personal identity can by us be placed in nothing but consciousness, (which is that alone which makes what we call *self*,) without involving us in great absurdities.

But is not a man drunk and sober the same person? why else is he punished for the fact he commits when drunk, though he be never afterwards conscious of it? Just as much the same person as a man that walks, and does other things in his sleep, is the same person, and is answerable for any mischief he shall do in it. Human laws punish both, with a justice suitable to *their* way of knowledge;—because, in these cases, they cannot distinguish certainly what is real, what counterfeit: and so the ignorance in drunkenness or sleep is not admitted as a plea. [For, though punishment be annexed to personality, and personality to consciousness, and the drunkard perhaps be not conscious of what he did, yet human judicatures justly punish him; because the fact is proved against him, but want of consciousness cannot be proved for him.] But in the Great Day, wherein the secrets of all hearts shall be laid open, it may be reasonable to think, no one shall be made to answer for what he knows nothing of; but shall receive his doom, his conscience accusing or excusing him.

Nothing but consciousness can unite remote existences into the same person: the identity of substance will not do it; for whatever substance there is, however framed, without consciousness there is no person: and a carcass may be a person, as well as any sort of substance be so, without consciousness.

Could we suppose two distinct incommunicable consciousnesses acting the same body, the one constantly by day, the other by night; and, on the other side, the same consciousness, acting by intervals, two distinct bodies: I ask, in the first case, whether the day and the night— man would not be two as distinct persons as Socrates and Plato? And whether, in the second case, there would not be one person in two distinct bodies, as much as one man is the same in two distinct clothings? Nor is it at all material to say, that this same, and this distinct consciousness, in the cases above mentioned, is owing to the same and distinct immaterial substances, bringing it with them to those bodies; which, whether true or no, alters not the case: since it is evident the personal identity would equally be determined by the consciousness, whether that consciousness were annexed to some individual immaterial substance or no. For, granting that the thinking substance in man must be necessarily supposed immaterial, it is evident that immaterial thinking thing may sometimes part with its past consciousness, and be restored to it again: as appears in the forgetfulness men often have of their past actions; and the mind many times recovers the memory of a past consciousness, which it had lost for twenty years together. Make these intervals of memory and forgetfulness to take their turns regularly by day and night, and you have two persons with the same immaterial spirit, as much as in the former instance two persons with the same body. So that self is not determined by identity or diversity of substance, which it cannot be sure of, but only by identity of consciousness. . . .

2   DAVID HUME

(1711–1776)

On the Idea of the Self*

Hume is a thorough-going empiricist, skeptical of any arguments that could not be shown to be founded on perceptual knowledge. He reduces all thought to impressions of the senses and to ideas that are derived from those impressions. We have sense impressions of our bodies and the things we do. Our idea of self is the result of a collection of these various impressions. Self is a bundle of perceptions. It is an aggregation of physical and mental states, constantly changing as we are constantly doing different things. Any idea of stability or of a continuing entity called "self" must be a product of imagination, not of inspection. Thus, Hume discredits the idea that there is a constant entity called "I" that has my experiences, and claims that there is no self apart from the activities, mental and physical, that we perform.

* David Hume, *A Treatise of Human Nature* (1739), Section 6, Pt. IV, Bk. I.

THERE are some philosophers who imagine we are every moment intimately conscious of what we call our *self;* that we feel its existence and its continuance in existence; and are certain, beyond the evidence of a demonstration, both of its perfect identity and simplicity. The strongest sensation, the most violent passion, say they, instead of distracting us from this view, only fix it the more intensely, and make us consider their influence on *self* either by their pain or pleasure. To attempt a further proof of this were to weaken its evidence; since no proof can be derived from any fact of which we are so intimately conscious; nor is there anything of which we can be certain if we doubt of this.

Unluckily all these positive assertions are contrary to that very experience which is pleaded for them; nor have we any idea of *self,* after the manner it is here explained. For, from what impression could this idea be derived? This question it is impossible to answer without a manifest contradiction and absurdity; and yet it is a question which must necessarily be answered, if we would have the idea of self pass for clear and intelligible. It must be some one impression that gives rise to every real idea. But self or person is not any one impression, but that to which our several impressions and ideas are supposed to have a reference. If any impression gives rise to the idea of self, that impression must continue invariably the same, through the whole course of our lives; since self is supposed to exist after that manner. But there is no impression constant and invariable. Pain and pleasure, grief and joy, passions and sensations succeed each other, and never all exist at the same time. It cannot therefore be from any of these impressions, or from any other, that the idea of self is derived; and consequently there is no such idea.

But further, what must become of all our particular perceptions upon this hypothesis? All these are different, and distinguishable, and separable from each other, and may be separately considered, and may exist separately, and have no need of anything to support their existence. After what manner therefore do they belong to self, and how are they connected with it? For my part, when I enter most intimately into what I call *myself*, I always stumble on some particular perception or other, of heat or cold, light or shade, love or hatred, pain or pleasure. I never can catch *myself* at any time without a perception, and never can observe anything but the perception. When my perceptions are removed for any time, as by sound sleep, so long am I insensible of *myself*, and may truly be said not to exist. And were all my perceptions removed by death, and could I neither think, nor feel, nor see, nor love, nor hate, after the dissolution of my body, I should be entirely annihilated, nor do I conceive what is further requisite to make me a perfect nonentity. If any one, upon serious and unprejudiced reflection, thinks he has a different notion of *himself*, I must confess I can reason no longer with him. All I can allow him is, that he may be in the right as well as I, and that we are essentially different in this particular. He may, perhaps, perceive something simple and continued, which he calls *himself;* though I am certain there is no such principle in me.

But setting aside some metaphysicians of this kind, I may venture to affirm of the rest of mankind, that they are nothing but a bundle or collection of different perceptions, which succeed each other with an inconceivable rapidity, and are in a perpetual flux and movement. Our eyes cannot turn in their sockets without varying our perceptions. Our thought is still more variable than our sight; and all our other senses and faculties contribute to this change; nor is there any single power of the soul, which remains unalterably the same, perhaps for one moment. The mind is a kind of theater, where several perceptions successively make their appearance; pass, repass, glide away, and mingle in an infinite variety of postures and situations. There is properly no *simplicity* in it at one time, nor *identity* in different, whatever natural propension we may have to imagine that simplicity and identity. The comparison of the theater must not mislead us. They are the successive perceptions only, that constitute the mind; nor have we the most distant notion of the place where these scenes are represented, or of the materials of which it is composed.

What then gives us so great a propension to ascribe an identity to these successive perceptions, and to suppose ourselves possessed of an invariable and uninterrupted existence through the whole course of our lives? In order to answer this question we must distinguish betwixt personal identity, as it regards our thought or imagination, and as it regards our passions or the concern we take in ourselves. The first is our present subject; and to explain it perfectly we must take the matter pretty deep, and account for that identity, which we attribute to plants and animals; there being a great analogy betwixt it and the identity of a self or person.

We have a distinct idea of an object that remains invariable and uninterrupted through a supposed variation of time; and this idea we call that of *identity* or *sameness*. We have also a distinct idea of several different objects existing in succession, and connected together by a close relation; and this to an accurate view affords as perfect a notion of *diversity* as if there was no manner of relation among the objects. But though these two ideas of identity, and a succession of related objects, be in themselves perfectly distinct, and even contrary, yet it is certain that, in our common way of thinking, they are generally confounded with each other. That action of the imagination, by which we consider the uninterrupted and invariable object, and that by which we reflect on the succession of related objects, are almost the same to the feeling, nor is there much more effort of thought required in the latter case than in the former. The relation facilitates the transition of the mind from one object to another, and renders its passage as smooth as if it contemplated one continued object. This resemblance is the cause of the confusion and mistake, and makes us substitute the notion of identity, instead of that of related objects. However at one instant we may consider the related succession as variable or interrupted, we are sure the next to ascribe to it a perfect identity, and regard it as invariable and uninterrupted. Our propensity to this mistake is so great from the resemblance above mentioned, that we fall into it before we are aware; and though we incessantly correct ourselves by reflection, and return to a more accurate method of thinking, yet we cannot long sustain our philosophy, or take off this bias from the imagination. Our last resource is to yield to it, and boldly assert that these different related objects are in effect the same, however interrupted and variable. In order to justify to ourselves this absurdity, we often feign some new and unintelligible principle, that connects the objects together, and prevents their interruption or variation. Thus we feign the continued existence of the perceptions of our senses, to remove the interruption; and run into the notion of a *soul*, and *self*, and *substance*, to disguise the variation. But, we may further observe, that where we do not give rise to such a fiction, our propension to confound identity with relation is so great, that we are apt to imagine something unknown and mysterious, connecting the parts, beside their relation; and this I take to be the case with regard to the identity we ascribe to plants and vegetables. And even when this does not take place, we still feel a propensity to confound these ideas, though we are not able fully to satisfy ourselves in that particular, nor find anything invariable and uninterrupted to justify our notion of identity.

Thus the controversy concerning identity is not merely a dispute of words. For when we attribute identity, in an improper sense, to variable or interrupted objects, our mistake is not confined to the expression, but is commonly attended with a fiction, either of something invariable and uninterrupted, or of something mysterious and inexplicable, or at least with a propensity to such fictions. What will suffice to prove this hypothesis to the satisfaction of every fair inquirer, is to show, from daily experience and observation, that the objects which are variable or interrupted, and yet are supposed to continue the same, are such only as consist of a succession of parts, connected together by resemblance, contiguity, or causation. For as such a succession answers evidently to our notion of diversity, it can only be by mistake we ascribe to it an identity; and as the relation of parts, which leads us into this mistake, is really nothing but a quality, which produces an association of ideas, and an easy transition of the imagination from one to another, it can only be from the resemblance, which this act of the mind bears to that by which we contemplate one continued object, that the error arises. Our chief business, then, must be to prove, that all objects, to which we ascribe identity, without observing their invariableness and uninterruptedness, are such as consist of a succession of related objects.

In order to this, suppose any mass of matter, of which the parts are contiguous and connected, to be placed before us; it is plain we must attribute a perfect identity to this mass, provided all the parts continue uninterruptedly and invariably the same, whatever motion or change of place we may observe either in the whole or in any of the parts. But supposing some very *small* or *inconsiderable* part to be added to the mass, or subtracted from it; though this absolutely destroys the identity of the whole, strictly speaking, yet as we seldom think so accurately, we scruple not to pronounce a mass of matter the same, where we find so trivial an alteration. The passage of the thought from the object before the change to the object after it, is so smooth and easy, that we scarce perceive the transition, and are apt to imagine, that it is nothing but a continued survey of the same object.

There is a very remarkable circumstance that attends this experiment; which is, that though the change of any considerable part in a mass of matter destroys the identity of the whole, yet we must measure the greatness of the part, not absolutely, but by its *proportion* to the whole. The addition or diminution of a mountain would not be sufficient to produce a diversity in a planet; though the change of a very few inches would be able to destroy the identity of some bodies. It will be impossible to account for this, but by reflecting that objects operate upon the mind, and break or interrupt the continuity of its actions, not according to their real greatness, but according to their proportion to each other; and therefore, since this interruption makes an object cease to appear the same, it must be the uninterrupted progress of the thought which constitutes the imperfect identity.

This may be confirmed by another phenomenon. A change in any considerable part of a body destroys its identity; but it is remarkable, that where the change is produced *gradually* and *insensibly*, we are less apt to ascribe to it the same effect. The reason can plainly be no other, than that the mind, in following the successive changes of the body, feels an easy passage from the surveying its condition in one moment, to the viewing of it in another, and in no particular time perceives any interruption in its actions. From which continued perception, it ascribes a continued existence and identity to the object.

But whatever precaution we may use in introducing the changes gradually, and making them proportionable to the whole, it is certain, that where the changes are at last observed to become considerable, we make a scruple of ascribing identity to such different objects. There is, however, another artifice, by which we may induce the imagination to advance a step further; and that is, by producing a reference of the parts to each other, and a combination to some *common end* or purpose. A ship, of which a considerable part has been changed by frequent reparations, is still considered as the same; nor does the difference of the materials hinder us from ascribing an identity to it. The common end, in which the parts conspire, is the same under all their variations, and affords an easy transition of the imagination from one situation of the body to another.

But this is still more remarkable, when we add a *sympathy* of parts to their *common end*, and suppose that they bear to each other the reciprocal relation of cause and effect in all their actions and operations. This is the case with all animals and vegetables; where not only the several parts have a reference to some general purpose, but also a mutual dependence on, and connection with, each other. The effect of so strong a relation is, that though every one must allow, that in a very few years both vegetables and animals endure a *total* change, yet we still attribute identity to them, while their form, size, and substance, are entirely altered. An oak that grows from a small plant to a large tree is still the same oak, though there be not one particle of matter or figure of its parts the same. An infant becomes a man, and is sometimes fat, sometimes lean, without any change in his identity.

We may also consider the two following phenomena, which are remarkable in their kind. The first is, that though we commonly be able to distinguish pretty exactly betwixt numerical and specific identity, yet it sometimes happens that we confound them, and in our thinking and reasoning employ the one for the other. Thus, a man who hears a noise that is frequently interrupted and renewed, says it is still the same noise, though it is evident the sounds have only a specific identity or resemblance, and there is nothing numerically the same but the cause which produced them. In like manner it may be said, without breach of the propriety of language, that such a church, which was formerly of brick, fell to ruin, and that the parish rebuilt the same church of freestone, and according to modern architecture. Here neither the form nor materials are the same, nor is there anything common to the two objects but their relation to the inhabitants of the parish; and yet this alone is sufficient to make us denominate them the same. But we must observe, that in these cases the first object is in a manner annihilated before the second comes into existence; by which means, we are never presented, in any one point of time, with the idea of difference and multiplicity; and for that reason are less scrupulous in calling them the same.

Secondly, we may remark, that though, in a succession of related objects, it be in a manner requisite that the change of parts be not sudden nor entire, in order to preserve the identity, yet where the objects are in their nature changeable and inconstant, we admit of a more sudden transition than would otherwise be consistent with that relation. Thus, as the nature of a river consists in the motion and change of parts, though in less than four-and-twenty hours these be totally altered, this hinders not the river from continuing the same during several ages. What is natural and essential to anything is, in a manner, expected; and what is expected makes less impression, and appears of less moment than what is unusual and extraordinary. A considerable change of the former kind seems really less to the imagination than the most trivial alteration of the latter; and by breaking less the continuity of the thought, has less influence in destroying the identity.

We now proceed to explain the nature of *personal identity*, which has become so great a question in philosophy, especially of late years, in England, where all the abstruser sciences are studied with a peculiar ardor and application. And here it is evident the same method of reasoning must be continued which has so successfully explained the identity of plants, and animals, and ships, and houses, and of all compounded and changeable productions either of art or nature. The identity which we ascribe to the mind of man is only a fictitious one, and of a like kind with that which we ascribe to vegetable and animal bodies. It cannot therefore have a different origin, but must proceed from a like operation of the imagination upon like objects.

But lest this argument should not convince the reader, though in my opinion perfectly decisive, let him weigh the following reasoning, which is still closer and more immediate. It is evident that the identity which we attribute to the human mind, however perfect we may imagine it to be, is not able to run the several different perceptions into one, and make them lose their characters of distinction and difference, which are essential to them. It is still true that every distinct perception which enters into the composition of the mind, is a distinct existence, and is different, and distinguishable, and separable from every other perception, either contemporary or successive. But as, notwithstanding this distinction and separability, we suppose the whole train of perceptions to be united by identity, a question naturally arises concerning this relation of identity, whether it be something that really binds our several perceptions together, or only associates their ideas in the imagination; that is, in other words, whether, in pronouncing concerning the identity of a person, we observe some real bond among his perception, or only feel one among the ideas we form of them. This question we might easily decide, if we would recollect what has been already proved at large, that the understanding never observes any real connection among objects, and that even the union of cause and effect, when strictly examined, resolves itself into a customary association of ideas. For from thence it evidently follows, that identity is nothing really belonging to these different perceptions, and uniting them altogether, but is merely a quality which we attribute to them, because of the union of their ideas in the imagination when we reflect upon them. Now, the only qualities which can give ideas a union in the imagination, are these three relations above mentioned. These are the uniting principles in the ideal world, and without them every distinct object is separable by the mind, and may be separately considered, and appears not to have any more connection with any other object than if disjoined by the greatest difference and remoteness. It is therefore on some of these three relations of resemblance, contiguity, and causation, that identity depends; and as the very essence of these relations consists in their producing an easy transition of ideas, it follows that our notions of personal identity proceed entirely from the smooth and uninterrupted progress of the thought along a train of connected ideas, according to the principles above explained.

The only question, therefore, which remains is, by what relations this uninterrupted progress of our thought is produced, when we consider existence of a mind or thinking person. And here it is evident we must confine ourselves to resemblance and causation, and must drop contiguity, which has little or no influence in the present case.

To begin with *resemblance;* suppose we could see clearly into the breast of another, and observe that succession of perceptions which constitutes his mind or thinking principle, and suppose that he always preserves the memory of a considerable part of past perceptions, it is evident that nothing could more contribute to the bestowing a relation on this succession amidst all its variations. For what is the memory but a faculty, by which we raise up the images of past perceptions? And as an image necessarily resembles its object, must not the frequent placing of these resembling perceptions in the chain of thought, convey the imagination more easily from one link to another, and make the whole seem like the continuance of one object? In this particular, then, the memory not only discovers the identity, but also contributes to its production, by producing the relation of resemblance among the perceptions. The case is the same, whether we consider ourselves or others.

As to *causation;* we may observe that the true idea of the human mind, is to consider it as a system of different perceptions or different existences, which are linked together by the relation of cause and effect, and mutually produce, destroy, influence, and modify each other. Our impressions give rise to their correspondent ideas; and these ideas, in their turn, produce other impressions. One thought chases another, and draws after it a third, by which it is expelled in its turn.

In this respect, I cannot compare the soul more properly to anything than to a republic or commonwealth, in which the several members are united by the reciprocal ties of government and subordination, and give rise to other persons who propagate the same republic in the incessant changes of its parts. And as the same individual republic may not only change its members, but also its laws and constitutions; in like manner the same person may vary his character and disposition, as well as his impressions and ideas, without losing his identity. Whatever changes he endures, his several parts are still connected by the relation of causation. And in this view our identity with regard to the passions serves to corroborate that with regard to the imagination, by the making our distant perceptions influence each other, and by giving us a present concern for our past or future pains or pleasures.

As memory alone acquaints us with the continuance and extent of this succession of perceptions, it is to be considered, upon that account chiefly, as the source of personal identity. Had we no memory, we never should have any notion of causation, nor consequently of that chain of causes and effects, which constitute our self or person. But having once acquired this notion of causation from the memory, we can extend the same chain of causes, and consequently the identity of our persons beyond our memory, and can comprehend times, and circumstances, and actions, which we have entirely forgot, but suppose in general to have existed. For how few of our past actions are there, of which we have any memory? Who can tell me, for instance, what his thoughts and actions on the first of January 1715, the eleventh of March 1719, and the third of August 1733? Or will he affirm, because he has entirely forgot the incidents of these days, that the present self is not the same person with the self of that time; and by that means overturn all the most established notions of personal identity? In this view, therefore, memory does not so much *produce* as *discover* personal identity, by showing us the relation of cause and effect among our different perceptions. It will be incumbent on those who affirm that memory produces entirely our personal identity, to give a reason why we can thus extend our identity beyond our memory.

The whole of this doctrine leads us to a conclusion, which is of great importance in the present affair, viz. that all the nice and subtile questions concerning personal identity can never possibly be decided, and are to be regarded rather as grammatical than as philosophical difficulties. Identity depends on the relations of ideas; and these relations produce identity, by means of that easy transition they occasion. But as the relations, and the easiness of the transition may diminish by insensible degrees, we have no just standard by which we can decide any dispute concerning the time when they acquire or lose a title to the name of identity. All the disputes concerning the identity of connected objects are merely verbal, except so far as the relation of parts gives rise to some fiction or imaginary principle of union, as we have already observed.

3

SYDNEY S. SHOEMAKER

(1931–   )

Personal Identity and Memory*

Shoemaker examines the claims of philosophers, such as Locke, who stress the importance of memory to personal identity. He asks if memory is really a criterion of identity and, if so, is it the sole criterion. Also, what is the relationship between remembering an event and being the same person as the one who participated in the remembered event? The key lies in how we use the word "remember." How do we know if someone is using the phrase "I remember . . . " correctly? Can we distinguish clearly bodily criteria and memory in this case? Shoemaker argues that we do not use any criteria of identity when making claims on the basis of memory. The criteria of personal identity arise in third-person cases, and memory in such cases is only part of the picture. Unless accompanied by bodily criteria, memory statements of others would fail to provide sufficient grounds for identification. In other words, if memory claims are to be significant in establishing identity, there must be some way of checking those claims. We must know what the person making a memory claim means, and to know that is to involve some form of bodily identity. A criterion of "same person" is prior to establishing memory claims.

* *Journal of Philosophy*, Vol. LVI, No. 22 (October 22, 1959), pp. 868–882. Used by permission of the editors and Professor Shoemaker.

PERSONS, unlike other things, make statements about their own pasts, and can be said to know these statements to be true. This fact would be of little importance, as far as the problem of personal identity is concerned, if these statements were always grounded in the ways in which people's statements about the past history of things other than themselves are grounded. But while our statements about our own pasts are sometimes based on diaries, photographs, fingerprints, and the like, normally they are not. Normally they are based on our own memories, and the way in which one's memory provides one with knowledge concerning one's own past is quite unlike the way in which it provides one with knowledge concerning the past history of another person or thing. It is largely for this reason, I believe, that in addition to whatever problems there are about the notion of identity in general there has always been felt to be a special problem about *personal* identity. It is, for example, the way in which one knows one's own past that has led some philosophers to hold that personal identity is the only *real* identity that we have any knowledge of, the identity we ascribe to ships and stones being only, as Thomas Reid expressed it, "something which, for convenience of speech, we call identity."* What I wish to do in this paper is to consider how the concept of memory and the concept of personal identity are related. In particular, I want to consider the view that memory provides a criterion of personal identity, or, as H. P. Grice expressed it some years ago, that "the self is a logical construction and is to be defined in terms of memory."†

1. Clearly the concepts of memory and personal identity are not logically independent. As has often been pointed out, it is a logical truth that, if a person remembers a past event, then he, the very person who remembers, must have been a witness to that event. It is partly this logical truth that has led some philosophers to hold that personal identity can be wholly or partially defined in terms of memory. And this view may seem to be supported by the fact that we sometimes use, as grounds for saying that a person was present when an event occurred, the fact that he apparently remembers the event, i.e., is able to give a correct and detailed account of it and does not appear to have anything accept this view. For it might be held that while there is a logical rela-other than his own memory on the basis of which he could know of it.

But it does not seem, off-hand, that these considerations force us to tionship between the concepts of memory and personal identity, this is because the former is definable or analyzable in terms of the latter, and not *vice versa*. The assertion that a person A remembers an event X can plausibly be analyzed as meaning (1) that A now has knowledge of X, (2) that A's knowledge is not grounded inductively or based on the testimony of other persons, and (3) that A witnessed X when it occurred. To know with certainty that A remembers X, it might be held, we would have to know all three of these conditions were satisfied, and we could know that (3) is satisfied only if we had a criterion of personal identity by which we could judge that A, the person who now has knowledge of X, is identical with one of the persons who witnessed X. Obviously our criterion of identity here could not be the fact that A remembers X, for we know this fact only if we had already established that such an identity holds.

---

* Thomas Reid, *Essays on the Intellectual Powers of Man*, A. D. Woozley, ed. (London: Macmillan, 1941), p. 206.

† H. P. Grice, "Personal Identity," *Mind*, Vol. L (October, 1941), p. 340.

The view just described, I think, must be the view of any philosopher who thinks that the identity of a human body is the sole criterion of personal identity. And this view seems compatible with the fact that sometimes, when we do not have independent grounds for saying that a person witnessed an event, we accept his being able to describe the event as evidence that we was a witness to it. For it might be held that in such cases we are reasoning inductively. We have, it might be said, found out empirically (using bodily identity as our criterion of personal identity) that when someone claims to remember a past event it is generally the case that such an event did occur and that he was a witness to it. On this view it is an inductively established correlation, and not any logical relationship between memory and personal identity, that justifies us in using the memory claims of persons as evidence for identity judgments about them.

2. On the view just described the criteria of personal identity are simply the criteria of bodily identity (i.e., I suppose, spatio-temporal continuity). But it is often argued that bodily identity is not even a necessary condition of personal identity, let alone a sufficient condition, and the same arguments have been alleged to show that memory is a criterion of personal identity. We must now consider some of these arguments.

Considerable attention has been paid, in discussions of personal identity, to so-called "puzzle cases," ostensible cases of what I will call "bodily transfer." It has been argued that if certain imaginable events were to occur we would be obliged to say, or at least would have good grounds for saying, that someone had changed bodies, i.e., had come to have a body that is numerically different from the body that had been his in the past. Locke, it may be recalled, thought it conceivable that the soul of a prince might "enter and inform" the body of a cobbler, "carrying with it the consciousness of the prince's past life," and said that if this happened the cobbler would become "the same person with the prince, accountable only for the prince's actions."* And it is certainly imaginable that a cobbler, living somewhere in the Bronx, might awake some morning and show great surprise at the appearance of his body, that he might claim to find his surroundings, and the persons who claim to know him, totally unfamiliar, that he might exhibit a detailed knowledge of the past life of Prince Philip,

---

* John Locke, *An Essay Concerning Human Understanding*, Vol. I, Fraser, ed. (Oxford: The Clarendon Press, 1894), p. 457.

reporting the Prince's actions as his own, and that he might, in his subsequent behavior, exhibit all of the mannerisms, interests, and personality and character traits that Prince Philip had displayed in the past. Let us imagine this happening immediately after the death of the man now known as Prince Philip.

What we say about such cases is clearly relevant to the question whether memory is a criterion of personal identity. If the above case inclines us to say that bodily transfer is possible, this is largely because the cobbler is imagined to be able to describe in detail, thereby giving evidence of being able to remember, the past life of Prince Philip. That this so much inclines us to admit the possibility of bodily transfer, whether or not we do admit it, seems to be grounds for saying that bodily identity is not our sole criterion of personal identity, and that memory, and perhaps also sameness of personality, has a place among our criteria.

Many philosophers have held that personal identity and bodily identity are logically quite distinct. This view is implied by the Cartesian conception of the mind (or soul) as a substance distinct from the body, and it also seems to be implied by the view of Locke, that it is "same consciousness" that "makes" the same person, and by the views of those philosophers, such as Hume and (at one time) Russell, who have held that the persistence of a person through time consists simply in the occurrence of a series of mental events ("perceptions," "experiences") that are bound together by a non-physical relationship of "co-personality" (perhaps the relation "being the memory of"). In short, it is implied by any view according to which the identity of a person is essentially the identity of a mind, and according to which a mind (whether regarded as a Cartesian "spiritual substance" or a Humeian "bundle" of mental events) is something logically distinct from a human body. To hold such a view is to admit the possibility of bodily transfer, and it is partly the prevalence of such views that accounts for the attention that philosophers have paid to "puzzle cases" such as the one I have described. But it is hardly plausible to suppose that those who have held such views have come to hold them because they have been persuaded by such cases that bodily transfer is possible. For even if it is admitted that such cases would be cases of bodily transfer, it by no means follows that personal identity and bodily identity are logically independent. It does not follow that bodily transfer could become the rule rather than the exception, and it certainly does not follow that a person could exist without having a body at all. Indeed, the view that bodily transfer is possible is quite compatible with a completely behavioristic view concerning the nature of mind and a completely materialistic conception of the nature of a person. After all, in the case I have imagined it is bodily and behavioral facts (the behavior of the cobbler and the past behavior of Prince Philip) that incline one to say that a bodily transfer has occurred.

So while such cases provide some grounds for thinking that memory is among the criteria of personal identity, we must look further if we wish to account for the plausibility of the view that the criteria of personal identity are "mental" or "psychological," one version of which being the view that memory is, to the exclusion of bodily identity, the sole criterion of personal identity. But we need not look much further; all that we have to do, in fact, is to describe such cases in the first person rather than in the third person. For it is when one considers the way in which one knows, or seems to know, one's *own* identity that it becomes plausible to regard personal identity as something logically independent of bodily identity. One does not have to observe, or (it seems) know anything about, the present state of one's body in order to make past tense statements about oneself on the basis of memory. But such statements imply the persistence of a person through time, and it is natural to regard them as expressing knowledge of one's own identity, knowledge that a "present self" (that to which the word "I" refers) is identical with a "past self" (the person who did such and such in the past). One is inclined to suppose that the real criteria of personal identity must be criteria that one uses in making statements about one's own identity. And since it appears that one can make such statements, and know them to be true, without first knowing the facts that would justify an assertion about the identity of one's body, the conclusion would seem to be that bodily identity cannot be a criterion of personal identity. The real criteria of personal identity, it seems, cannot be bodily or behavioral criteria of any sort, but must be criteria that one can know to be satisfied in one's own case without knowing anything about one's body. For similar reasons one is inclined to reject the view that the notion of memory is definable or analyzable in terms of the notion of personal identity. For when one says that one remembers a past event it is surely not the case that one has first established that one is the same as someone who witnessed the event, and then concluded, on the basis of this fact and others, that one remembers the event. That one remembers an event seems, from one's own point of view, a brute, unanalyzable fact. But if there is a logical relationship between the concepts of memory and personal identity, and if the former is not definable or analyzable in terms of the latter, what seems to follow is that the latter is somehow definable in terms of the former, and that memory provides the criterion of personal identity.

3. Whether or not memory is *a* criterion of personal identity, it is not *the* criterion. As I will argue later, it cannot be the sole criterion that we use in making identity statements about other persons. And while it is true that one does not use bodily identity as a criterion of personal identity when one says on the basis of memory that one did something in the past, this is not because one uses something else as a criterion, but is rather because one uses no criterion at all.

Suppose that I make the statement "I broke the front window yesterday." If this statement is based on a criterion of personal identity it must be the case that I know that someone broke the front window yesterday, and that I have found out, by use of my criterion, that that person was myself. And my statement must be based, at least in part, on what I know about that person as he was at the time at which he broke the window. Let us suppose that my own memory is my only source of knowledge concerning the past event in question, for that is the sort of case that we are interested in. Then my statement must be a conclusion from what I remember about the person who broke the window yesterday, and perhaps from other facts as well (facts about my "present self"), and my criterion of identity must be what justifies me in drawing this conclusion from these facts. Presumably, if I had remembered different facts about that person I would have drawn a different conclusion, namely that he was not myself. It should be noted that, if all of this were so, then, strictly speaking, it would be incorrect for me to say "*I remember* that I broke the front window yesterday." For if my statement "I broke the front window yesterday" expresses a conclusion *from* what I remember it is not itself a memory statement, i.e., is not simply a description or report of what I actually remember. We must distinguish statements that are "based" on memory simply in the sense of being memory statements from those that are "based" on memory in the sense of being conclusions drawn from remembered facts.* If one thinks that one cannot make a first person past tense statement except on the basis of a criterion of identity, one must accept the consequence that no such statement can be a memory statement. In the case at hand, if my statement is grounded on a criterion of identity then what I actually remember cannot be that *I* broke the window yesterday, but must be that someone of such and such a description broke the window, the assertion that it was myself being a conclusion from what I remember about the person.

---

*Roughly speaking, a statement is a memory statement if (supposing it to be an honest assertion) it cannot be false unless the speaker has misremembered. A conclusion from what is remembered, on the other hand, can be false without there being a mistaken memory. E.g., I mistakenly identify the man I saw as John when in fact it was his identical twin.

Now it is a logical truth, as I have already said, that if a person remembers a past event then he, that same person, must have been a witness to the event, i.e., must have been present when it occurred and in a position to know of its occurrence. So if I remember someone breaking the front window yesterday it follows that I was present at the time. And since, if I remember this, I am entitled to say "I remember someone breaking the front window yesterday," I am also entitled to say "I was present yesterday when the front window was broken." But this last statement is a first person past tense statement, so let us see whether it can be grounded on any criterion of personal identity. Clearly it cannot be. It is not, as it would have to be if based on a criterion of identity, a conclusion from what I know about someone who existed in the past. What I know about the past, in the case we are considering, is what I remember, but this statement is not a conclusion from *what* I remember at all; it is a conclusion from the fact *that I remember something*, not from any of the facts that I remember.

But if I can know that I was present when an action was done without using a criterion of identity, why can't I know in this way that I did the action? Is it that I must employ a criterion in order to know *which* of the persons present was myself? In that case, presumably, I would not need to employ my criterion if I remembered that only one person was present, for that person would obviously have to be myself. But the trouble is that he would have to be myself *no matter what* I remembered about him. i.e., even if the remembered facts were such that I would have to conclude, in accordance with my criterion, that he was *not* myself. If I had a criterion of identity that I could use in such cases, it seems to me, it would be possible for me to remember someone doing a certain action, discover by the use of my criterion that he was not myself, and then find, by consulting my memory of the event, that he was the only person present when the action was done. And clearly this is not possible.

It is sometimes suggested that one is able to identify a remembered "past self" as one's own self by the fact that one is able to remember the private thoughts, feelings, sensations, etc., of that self. There does seem to be a sense in which my own thoughts and feelings are the only ones that I can remember. Certainly they are the only ones that I can remember *having*. But it is a mistake to conclude from this that memory is used as a first person criterion of personal identity. The sentence "I remember having a headache yesterday" does not differ in meaning from the sentence "I remember my having a headache yesterday." But if what I remember when I remember a past headache is *my having* a headache, or that *I* had a headache, my statement "I had a headache" is a memory statement, not a conclusion from what I remember, and cannot be grounded on any criterion of identity. If, however, what I remember is that someone had a headache, or that a headache occurred, it is clear that the remembered facts provide no grounds for the conclusion that *I* had a headache. Nor can we say, as some have said, that the relation "being the memory of" is the relation of "co-personality" between mental events, and that I know that a past sensation was mine because I have established that one of my present mental states is a memory of it and therefore co-personal with it. For, contrary to what Hume and others seem to have supposed, in the sort of case we are considering it makes no sense to speak of comparing one's present memory with a past sensation and finding that the one is the memory of (on Hume's theory, that it resembles) the other. One could make such a comparison only if one knew of the past sensation on some grounds other than one's memory of it, and our concern here is with cases in which one's memory is one's only source of knowledge concerning the past events in question. In such a case, comparing a past sensation with one's memory of it could only be comparing one's memory with itself—and comparing something with itself (if that means anything) is certainly not a way of discovering whether two events are related in a certain way. One can raise the question whether two events are related in a particular way (in *any* given way) only if one knows of the occurrence of both events. And if one knows of one of the events on the basis of memory, one must, in inquiring whether it is related in some way to the other event, be relying on one's memory of it, and clearly cannot be raising any question as to whether one does remember it (or whether one of one's present mental states is a memory of it). Indeed, if one's knowledge of a past sensation is memory knowledge it is misleading to say that one knows that one remembers a particular past sensation. It makes sense to speak of knowing that one remembers a particular event (knowing of an event that one remembers it) only where it would also make sense to speak of knowing of that event that one does not remember it (as is the case if one's knowledge of an event is based on something other than, or in addition to, one's memory). When I say that I have a headache I am not mentioning some particular headache and reporting, as a fact that I know about it, that it is experienced by me; likewise, when I say that I remember a headache I am not, in most cases, saying of some particular headache that I remember it. Normally I can identify a past sensation only as one that I remember (or, as I should prefer to say, one that I remember having). And when this is so there cannot arise any question concerning the ownership of the sensation, and there is no room for the employment of criteria of ownership or criteria of personal identity.

4. If, as I have argued, one does not use criteria of identity in making statements about one's own past on the basis of memory, the criteria of personal identity must be third person criteria. And if memory were the sole criterion of personal identity it would have to be the sole criterion that we use in making identity statements about persons other than ourselves. It is easily shown, however, that if we did not have some criterion other than memory that we could use in making statements of personal identity we could not use what others remember, or claim to remember, as evidence of any sort (criteriological or otherwise) for identity statements about them.

To begin with, if the word "remember" is to have any meaning it must be possible to establish whether someone is using it correctly. If some of the utterances that persons make are to count as memory claims, and therefore as evidence of what they remember or seem to remember, it must be possible to establish what a person means by the words he utters. But establishing what a person means by a term, or whether he is using it correctly, involves observing his use of it in various circumstances and over a period of time. This, of course, involves being able to know that it was one and the same person who uttered a given word on two different occasions, and to be able to know this one must have a criterion of identity. What could this criterion be if not bodily identity? It could not be any "psychological" criterion (such as memory or sameness of personality), for the use of such criteria (if criteria they are) involves accepting what a person says as indicating what his psychological state is (e.g., that he seems to remember doing a certain thing), and one could not do this if one were trying to establish what he means by, or whether he understands, the expressions he is using. In *some* circumstances, at least, bodily identity must be a criterion of personal identity.

Moreover, memory claims can be mistaken, and there must, accordingly, be such a thing as checking on the truth of a memory claim, i.e., establishing whether a person remembers something without taking his word for it that he does. And this, if he claims to have done a certain thing in the past, would involve establishing whether he, the person who claims this, is the same as someone who did do such an action in the past. In establishing this we could not use memory as our criterion of personal identity, and it is difficult to see what we could use if not bodily identity. And if, in such cases, we could not use bodily identity (or something other than memory) as a criterion of identity, it would not be possible to establish whether someone understands the use of the term "remember," and that term could not so much as have a meaning. It is, I believe, a logical or conceptual truth, not a contingent truth, that memory beliefs, and therefore honest memory claims, are generally true. If someone frequently prefaced past tense statements with the words "I remember that," and these statements generally turned out to be false, this would be grounds for saying that he did not understand the use of these words. We would not think that we had succeeded in teaching a child the use of the word "remember" if he commonly said "I remember doing such and such" when he had not done the thing in question. Again, suppose that we had discovered a new people whose language we did not know, and that someone had proposed a way of translating their language that involved regarding a certain class of statements (or utterances) as memory statements. Clearly, if all or most of those statements turned out to be false if translated as proposed, there could be no reason for accepting that way of translating them as correct, and there would be every reason for rejecting it as mistaken. But if it is a conceptual truth that memory claims are generally true, establishing that someone understands the use of the term "remember" must surely involve establishing whether his memory claims (or what appear to be his memory claims) are true or false. And to be able to do this we must have something other than memory that we can use as a criterion of personal identity.

5. The arguments of the last section may seem to give support to the view that bodily identity is, to the exclusion of memory, the sole criterion of personal identity. But this view seems to me to be mistaken. Bodily identity is certainly *a* criterion of personal identity, and if it were not, I have argued, nothing else could be so much as evidence of personal identity. But I do not think that it can be the sole criterion, and I think that there is an important sense in which memory, though certainly not the sole criterion, is one of the criteria.

Let us consider one consequence of the view that bodily identity is the sole criterion of personal identity. As I said in section 1, if this view were correct it would have to be the case that we are reasoning inductively when we use the fact that someone claims to remember something as grounds for a statement about his past. It would be a contingent fact, one that we have discovered empirically, that most memory claims are true, or that people generally remember what they claim to remember. This would, indeed, be nothing other than the fact that the memory claims that issue from the mouth of a certain body generally correspond to events in the past history of that same body. But I have argued that it is a logical fact, not a contingent fact, that memory claims are generally true. If this is so, inferences of the form

"He claims to remember doing X, so he probably did X" are not simply inductive inferences, for they are warranted by a generalization that is logically rather than empirically true.

Now let us return briefly to the case of the cobbler and the prince. If one is inclined to use the memory claims of the cobbler as grounds that he is (has become) the prince, the inference one is inclined to make is not of the form "He claims to remember doing X, so he probably did do X," but is of a more complex sort. Roughly, it is of the form "He claims to remember doing X, Y, and Z under such and such circumstances and at such and such times and places, and X, Y, and Z were done by someone under precisely those circumstances and at those times and places, so there is reason to believe that he is the person who did those actions." But it seems to me that if inferences of the first sort are not inductive, neither are inferences of the second sort. And I think that to say that inferences of the second sort are legitimate (as they certainly are, at least under certain circumstances), and that they are noninductive, is tantamount to saying that memory is a criterion of personal identity.

It should be noted that if such inferences were merely inductive, and if bodily identity were the sole criterion of personal identity, it would be patently absurd to make such an inference in a case in which the body of the person making a memory claim is known not to be identical with the body of the person who did the action that he claims to remember. The absurdity would be that of asserting something to be true, or probably true, on the basis of indirect evidence, when one has direct and conclusive evidence that it is false. But in the imaginary case I have described, the claim that the cobbler is (has become) the prince does not, I think, strike us as having *this* sort of absurdity. I have not attempted to say whether, if the events I have described were to occur, it would be correct to say that the cobbler had become the prince, and I do not know how this question could be settled. But this in itself seems to me significant. The fact that such cases so much as incline us to admit the possibility of bodily transfer, or leave us in doubt as to what to say, seems to me *prima facie* evidence that memory is a criterion of personal identity. It is not as if our doubts were due to ignorance of empirical facts that, if known, would settle the issue. Doubts of that sort are easily removed, for we need only add further details to the description of the case. But if, knowing all of the relevant facts, we are in doubt as to how we should answer a question of identity, this is surely an indication that the case is such that the question is not unambiguously decidable by our criterion of identity. This, in turn, suggests that there is a conflict of criteria. In the case at hand, our doubts are evidence that one criterion of personal identity, namely bodily identity, is in conflict with another, namely memory.

But now I must try to meet an objection. It might be argued that while the inference "He claims to remember doing X, so he probably did X" is not inductive, we are nevertheless reasoning inductively when we take what a person says as evidence for a statement about his past history. For what justifies us in taking the sounds that a person utters as expressing a memory claim? As was argued earlier, if a question arises as to whether a person understands the use of the word "remember," or is using it to mean what we mean by it, the question can be settled only by establishing, independently of what he says, whether the things that he claims (or apparently claims) to remember are things he actually did, endured, or witnessed in the past. If in a number of cases it turns out that the actions that he apparently claims to remember having done are actions that he actually did, this is evidence that he does understand the use of such words as "remember," and that his apparent memory claims are really memory claims and can generally be relied upon. Must it not be much the same sort of considerations, i.e., our having observed certain correlations between the sounds that people utter and what they have done in the past, that justifies our general reliance on people's memory claims, or rather our acceptance of people's utterances as memory claims? If so, it would seem that our use of people's memory claims as evidence for statements about their own pasts, including identity statements about them, is, in the end, inductively based. Though it is a logical fact that memory claims are generally true, what does this come to except the fact that if there did not exist correlations of the sort mentioned none of the utterances of persons would be memory claims? But the existence of such correlations is a contingent fact, and it is on this contingent fact, it might be argued, that inferences of the sort "He claims to remember doing X, so he probably did X" are ultimately based. As for the case of the cobbler and the prince, it might be argued that if what I said in section 4 is correct then the fact that I have imagined would be evidence, not that the cobbler had become the prince, but rather that his utterances were not memory claims at all, and that he did not understand the use of the term "remember."

To take the last point first, suppose that we were in doubt as to whether the cobbler really understood the words that he was using. Could we not satisfy ourselves that he did by observing his subsequent behavior, and by establishing (using bodily identity as our criterion of personal identity) that when he claims to have done an action that occurred *after* the alleged bodily transfer it is generally the case that he did do that action? When we are trying to establish whether a person understands the words he utters we must, I have argued, use bodily identity as a criterion of identity, but it does not follow from this that there cannot, in exceptional cases, be personal identity in the absence of bodily identity.

As for the rest of the objection, it is certainly true that unless there existed certain correlations between the sounds people utter and events in the past histories of those who utter them it would be impossible to have knowledge of the past that is based on the memory claims of other persons. These correlations are those that must exist if any of the utterances that people make are to be memory claims. But it cannot be the case, I believe, that we regard certain of the utterances of other persons as memory claims *because* we have established, inductively, that such correlations hold. To be sure, from the fact that a person utters the sounds that I would utter if making a certain memory claim it does not necessarily follow that he speaks the language that I speak and means by those sounds what I would mean by them. Under exceptional circumstances I might raise a question as to whether what sounds to me like a memory claim is really one, and such a question could be settled empirically, by observing the behavior of the person who made the claim. But except when we have definite grounds for supposing the contrary, we must, I believe, regard other persons as speaking a language, our own if the words sound familiar, without having any general empirical justification for doing so. Let us consider whether it would be possible for me to question whether there is anyone at all (other than myself) who speaks the language that I speak, and then to discover empirically, by observing correlations between the sounds people utter and their present and past behavior, that those around me do speak the language that I speak and that certain of their utterances are memory claims and can generally be relied upon. In carrying on such an investigation I would, of course, have to rely on my own memory. But one's memory can be mistaken. It is essential to the very notion of memory that there be a distinction between remembering something and merely seeming to remember something. And for there to be such a distinction there must be such a thing as checking up on one's own memory and finding that one does, or does not, remember what one seems to remember. As Wittgenstein pointed out,[*] there are and must be circumstances

* Ludwig Wittgenstein, *Philosophical Investigations* (Oxford: Basil Blackwell, 1953), Pt. I, paras. 56 and 265.

in which we would accept other sorts of evidence concerning the past as more authoritative than our own memories. But an important—I think essential—check on one's own memory is the testimony of other persons. And this sort of check would not be available to me if I could not even regard the utterances of other persons as testimony until I had completed my investigation and established the required set of correlations. Unless there were some persons whose utterances I would be willing to accept as memory claims without having conducted such an investigation I would in effect be admitting no distinction between remembering and merely seeming to remember, and I could therefore make no distinction between finding the correlations and merely seeming to have found them.

It is, I should like to say, part of the concept of a person that persons are capable of making memory statements about their own pasts. Since it is a conceptual truth that memory statements are generally true, it is a conceptual truth that persons are capable of knowing their own pasts in a special way, a way that does not involve the use of criteria of personal identity, and it is a conceptual truth (or a logical fact) that the memory claims that a person makes can be used by others as grounds for statements about the past history of that person. This, I think, is the kernel of truth that is embodied in the view that personal identity can be defined in terms of memory.

4 CHĀNDOGYA UPANISHAD

(c. 700–600 B.C.)

Parable of the Real Self*

This famous parable of the instruction of Indra by the sage Prajāpati contains the basic Hindu view of self. Self is identified first with the body, second with the dream self, and third with the self of dreamless sleep. All these theories of the self are, however, shown to be inadequate. As Indra says, "I see no good in that." Finally, Prajāpati reveals the true nature of the self as pure self-consciousness and ultimately identical with reality itself, with Brahman. Compare Prajāpati's teachings with the views of Hume and Locke.

* [From *Chāndogya Upanishad*, 8.7–12 *passim*]

"THE Self (ātman) who is free from evil, free from old age, free from death, free from grief, free from hunger, free from thirst, whose desire is the Real [*satya*, or truth], whose intention is the Real—he should be sought after, he should be desired to be comprehended. He obtains all worlds and all desires, who, having found out that Self, knows him." Thus, indeed, did the god Prajāpati speak. Verily, the gods and the demons both heard this. They said among themselves: "Aha! Let us seek after that Self—the Self, having sought after whom one obtains all worlds and all desires." Then Indra from among the gods went forth unto Prajāpati, and Virochana from among the demons. Indeed, without communicating with each other, those two came into the presence of Prajāpati with sacrificial fuel in hand [i.e., as students willing to serve their preceptor]. For thirty-two years the two lived under Prajāpati the disciplined life of a student of sacred knowledge (brahmacharya). Then Prajāpati asked them: "Desiring what have you lived the disciplined life of a student of sacred knowledge under me?" They said: "'The Self, who is free from evil, free from old age, free from death, free from grief, free from hunger, free from thirst, whose desire is the Real, whose intention is the Real—he should be sought after, he should be desired to be comprehended. He obtains all worlds and all desires, who, having found out that Self, knows him.' These, people declare to be the venerable master's words. Desiring him [the Self] have we lived the student's life under you." Prajāpati

325

said to them: "That Purusha who is seen in the eye—he is the Self (ātman)," said he. "That is the immortal, the fearless; that is Brahman." "But this one, Sir, who is perceived in water and in a mirror—who is he?" Prajāpati replied: "The same one, indeed, is perceived in all these." "Having looked at yourself in a pan of water, whatever you do not comprehend of the Self, tell that to me," said Prajāpati. They looked at themselves in the pan of water. Prajāpati asked them: "What do you see?" They replied: "We see here, Sir, our own selves in entirety, the very reproduction of our forms, as it were, correct to the hairs and the nails." Then Prajāpati said to them: "Having become well ornamented, well dressed, and refined, look at yourselves in a pan of water." Having become well ornamented, well dressed, and refined, they looked at themselves in a pan of water. Thereupon Prajāpati asked them: "What do you see?" They replied: "Just as we ourselves here are, Sir, well ornamented, well dressed, and refined. . . ." "That is the Self," said he. "That is the immortal, the fearless; that is Brahman." Then they went away with a tranquil heart. Having looked at them, Prajāpati said to himself "They are going away without having realized, without having found out the Self. Whosoever will accept this doctrine as final, be they gods or demons, they shall perish." Then Virochana, verily, with a tranquil heart, went to the demons and declared to them that doctrine, namely: One's self [one's bodily self] [1] alone is to be made happy here; one's self is to be served. Making oneself alone happy here, serving oneself, does one obtain both worlds, this world and the yonder. Therefore, here, even now, they say of one who is not a giver, who has no faith, who does not offer sacrifices, that he is, indeed, a demon; for this is the doctrine of the demons. They adorn the body of the deceased with perfumes, flowers, etc., which they have begged, with dress and with ornaments, for they think they will thereby win the yonder world.

But then Indra, even before reaching the gods, saw this danger: "Just as, indeed, the bodily self becomes well ornamented when this body is well ornamented, well dressed when this body is well dressed, and refined when this body is refined, even so that one becomes blind when this body is blind, lame when this body is lame, and maimed when this body is maimed. The bodily Self, verily, perishes immediately after the perishing of this body. I see no good in this." With sacrificial fuel in hand, he again came back to Prajāpati. [Indra states his objection to Prajāpati, who admits its truth and asks him to live as a student under him for another thirty-two years.] Indra lived a student's life under Prajāpati for another thirty-two years. Then, Prajāpati said

[1] Ātman can refer to one's bodily self as well as the Supreme Self.

to him: "He who moves about happy in a dream—he is the Self," said he. "That is the immortal, the fearless, that is Brahman." Thereupon, with a tranquil heart, Indra went away.

But then, even before reaching the gods, he saw this danger: "Now, even though this body is blind, the Self in the dream-condition does not become blind; even though this body is lame, he does not become lame; indeed, he does not suffer any defect through the defect of this body. He is not slain with the slaying of this body. He does not become lame with the lameness of this body. Nevertheless, they, as it were, kill him; they, as it were, unclothe him. He, as it were, becomes the experiencer of what is not agreeable; he, as it were, even weeps. I see no good in this." [Again Indra returns to Prajāpati with his objection. The latter admits its truth but asks Indra to be his student for another thirty-two years.] Then Prajāpati said to him: "Now, when one is sound asleep, composed, serene, and knows no dream—that is the Self," said he. "That is the immortal, the fearless; that is Brahman." Thereupon, with a tranquil heart, Indra went away.

But then, even before reaching the gods, he saw this danger: "Assuredly, this Self in the deep sleep condition does not, indeed, now know himself in the form: 'I am he'; nor indeed does he know these things here. He, as it were, becomes one who has gone to annihilation. I see no good in this." [Indra once more returns to Prajāpati, who promises to tell him the final truth after another five years of studentship.] Indra lived a student's life under Prajāpati for another five years. The total number of these years thus came to one hundred and one; thus it is that people say that, verily, for one hundred and one years Maghavan [Indra, the Rewarder] lived under Prajāpati the disciplined life of a student of sacred knowledge. Then Prajāpati said to him: "O Maghavan, mortal, indeed, is this body; it is taken over by death. But it is the basis of that deathless, bodiless Self. Verily, the Self, when embodied, is taken over by pleasure and pain. Verily, there is no freedom from pleasure and pain for one who is associated with the body. The wind is bodiless; cloud, lightning, thunder—these are bodiless. Now as these, having risen up from yonder space and having reached the highest light, appear each with its own form, even so this serene Self, having risen up from this body and having reached the highest light, appears with its own form. That Self is the Supreme Person (*uttama purusa*).

5   C. D. BROAD

(1887–1972)

Mind / Body: Two-Sided Interaction*

Broad has written extensively in many areas of philosophy, but he is perhaps best known for his works in the area of philosophical psychology. He is a dualist and in this essay he attempts to defend the theory of interactionism, the idea that the mind and the body act upon each other though they are irreducible entities.
The two major sources of attack on the idea of interaction have been philosophical and scientific. Broad meets the objections of both types by showing how the philosophical arguments against interaction are inconclusive, while the scientific theories are not really incompatible with the dualist position. Compare Broad's arguments with those of Passmore.

* C. D. Broad, *The Mind and Its Place in Nature* (London: 1925), Chap. III, pp. 95–113. Reprinted by permission of Routledge & Kegan Paul Ltd.

THERE is a question which has been argued about for some centuries now under the name of "Interaction"; this is the question whether minds really do act on the organisms which they animate, and whether organisms really do act on the minds which animate them. (I must point out at once that I imply no particular theory of mind or body by the word "to animate". I use it as a perfectly neutral name to express the fact that a certain mind is connected in some peculiarly intimate way with a certain body and under normal conditions with no other body. This is a fact even on a purely behaviouristic theory of mind; on such a view to say that the mind M animates the body B would mean that the body B, in so far as it behaves in certain ways, *is* the mind M. A body which did not act in these ways would be said not to be animated by a mind. And a different Body B', which acted in the same general way as B, would be said to be animated by a different mind M'.)

The problem of Interaction is generally discussed at the level of enlightened common-sense; where it is assumed that we know pretty well what we mean by "mind", by "matter" and by "causation". Obviously no solution which is reached at that level can claim to be ultimate. If what we call "matter" should turn out to be a collection of spirits of low intelligence, as Leibniz thought, the argument that mind and body are so unlike that their interaction is impossible would become irrelevant. Again, if causation be nothing but regular sequence and concomitance, as some philosophers have held, it is ridiculous to regard psychoneural parallelism and interaction as mutually exclusive alternatives. For interaction will mean no more than parallelism, and parallelism will mean no less than interaction. Nevertheless I am going to discuss the arguments here at the common-sense level, because they are so incredibly bad and yet have imposed upon so many learned men.

We start then by assuming a developed mind and a developed organism as two distinct things, and by admitting that the two are now intimately connected in some way or other which I express by saying that "this mind *animates* this organism". We assume that bodies are very much as enlightened common-sense believes them to be; and that, even if we cannot define "causation", we have some means of recognising when it is present and when it is absent. The question then is: "Does a mind ever act on the body which it animates, and does a body ever act on the mind which animates it?" The answer which common-sense would give to both questions is: "Yes, certainly." On the face of it my body acts on my mind whenever a pin is stuck into the former and a painful sensation thereupon arises in the latter. And, on the face of it, my mind acts on my body whenever a desire to move my arm arises in the former and is followed by this movement in the latter. Let us call this common-sense view "Two-sided Interaction". Although it seems so obvious it has been denied by probably a majority of philosophers and a majority of physiologists. So the question is: "Why should so many distinguished men, who have studied the subject, have denied the apparently obvious fact of Two-sided Interaction?"

The arguments against Two-sided Interaction fall into two sets:— Philosophical and Scientific. We will take the philosophical arguments first; for we shall find that the professedly scientific arguments come back in the end to the principles or prejudices which are made explicit in the philosophical arguments.

No one can deny that there is a close correlation between certain bodily events and certain mental events, and conversely. Therefore anyone who denies that there is action of mind on body and of body on mind must presumbaly hold (*a*) that concomitant variation is not an adequate criterion of causal connexion, and (*b*) that the other feature which is essential for causal connexion is absent in the case of body and mind. Now the common philosophical argument is that minds and mental events are so extremely unlike bodies and bodily states that it is inconceivable that the two should be causally connected. It is certainly true that, if minds and mental events are just what they seem to be to introspection and nothing more, and if bodies and bodily events are just what enlightened common-sense thinks them to be and nothing more, the two *are* extremely unlike. And this fact is supposed to show that, however closely correlated certain pairs of events in mind and body respectively may be, they cannot be causally connected.

Evidently the assumption at the back of this argument is that concomitant variation, together with a high enough degree of likeness, is an adequate test for causation; but that no amount of concomitant variation can establish causation in the absence of a high enough degree of likeness. Now I am inclined to admit part of this assumption. I think it is practically certain that causation does not simply *mean* concomitant variation. (And, if it did, *cadit quœstio*.) Hence the existence of the latter is not *ipso facto* a proof of the presence of the former. Again, I think it is almost certain that concomitant variation between A and B is not in fact a sufficient sign of the presence of a *direct* causal relation between the two. (I think it may perhaps be a sufficient sign of *either* a direct causal relation between A and B *or* of several causal relations which indirectly unite A and B through the medium of other terms C, D, etc.) So far I agree with the assumptions of the argument. But I cannot see the least reason to think that the other characteristic, which must be added to concomitant variation before we can be sure that A and B are causally connected, is a high degree of likeness between the two. One would like to know just how unlike two events may be before it becomes impossible to admit the existence of a causal relation between them. No one hesitates to hold that draughts and colds in the head are causally connected, although the two are extremely unlike each other. If the unlikeness of draughts and colds in the head does not prevent one from admitting a causal connexion between the two, why should the unlikeness of volitions and voluntary movements prevent one from holding that they are causally connected? To sum up. I am willing to admit that an adequate criterion of causal connexion needs some other relation between a pair of events beside concomitant variation; but I do not believe for a moment that this other relation is that of qualitative likeness.

This brings us to a rather more refined form of the argument against Interaction. It is said that, whenever we admit the existence of a causal relation between two events, these two events (to put it crudely) must also form parts of a single substantial whole. *E.g.*, all physical events are spatially related and form one great extended whole. And the mental events which would commonly be admitted to be causally connected are always events in a single mind. A mind is a substantial whole of a peculiar kind too. Now it is said that between bodily events and mental events there are no relations such as those which unite physical events in different parts of the same Space or mental events in the history of the same mind. In the absence of such relations, binding mind and body into a single substantial whole, we cannot admit that bodily and mental events can be causally connected with each other, no matter how closely correlated their variations may be.

This is a much better argument than the argument about qualitative likeness and unlikeness. If we accept the premise that causal relations can subsist only between terms which form parts of a single substantial whole must we deny that mental and bodily events can be causally connected? I do not think that we need. (i) It is of course perfectly true that an organism and the mind which animates it do not form a physical whole, and that they do not form a mental whole; and these, no doubt, are the two kinds of substantial whole with which we are most familiar. But it does not follow that a mind and its organism do not form a substantial whole of *some* kind. There, plainly, is the extraordinarily intimate union between the two which I have called "animation" of one by the other. Even if the mind be just what it seems to introspection, and the body be just what it seems to perception aided by the more precise methods of science, this seems to me to be enough to make a mind and its body a substantial whole. Even so extreme a dualist about Mind and Matter as Descartes occasionally suggests that a mind and its body together form a quasi-substance; and, although we may quarrel with the language of the very numerous philosophers who have said that the mind is "the form" of its body, we must admit that such langauge would never have seemed plausible unless a mind and its body together had formed something very much like a single substantial whole.

(ii) We must, moreover, admit the possibility that minds and mental events have properties and relations which do not reveal themselves to introspection, and that bodies and bodily events may have properties and relations which do not reveal themselves to perception or to physical and chemical experiment. In virtue of these properties and relations the two together may well form a single substantial whole of the kind which is alleged to be needed for causal interaction. Thus, if we accept the premise of the argument, we have no right to assert that mind and body *cannot* interact; but only the much more modest proposition that introspection and perception do not suffice to assure us that mind and body are so interrelated that they *can* interact.

(iii) We must further remember that the Two-sided Interactionist is under no obligation to hold that the *complete* conditions of any mental event are bodily or that the complete conditions of any bodily event are mental. He needs only to assert that some mental events include certain bodily events among their necessary conditions, and that some bodily events include certain mental events among their necessary conditions. If I am paralysed my volition may not move my arm; and, if I am hypnotised or intensely interested or frightened, a wound may not produce a painful sensation. Now, if the complete cause and the complete effect in all interaction include both a bodily and a mental factor, the two wholes will be related by the fact that the mental constituents belong to a single mind, that the bodily constituents belong to a single body, and that this mind animates this body. This amount of connexion should surely be enough to allow of causal interaction.

This will be the most appropriate place to deal with the contention that, in voluntary action, and there only, we are immediately acquainted with an instance of causal connexion. If this be true the controversy is of course settled at once in favour of the Interactionist. It is generally supposed that this view was refuted once and for all by Mr. Hume in his *Enquiry concerning Human Understanding* (Sect. VII, Part I). I should not care to assert that the doctrine in question is true; but I do think that it is plausible, and I am quite sure that Mr. Hume's arguments do not refute it. Mr. Hume uses three closely connected arguments. (1) The connexion between a successful volition and the resulting bodily movement is as mysterious and as little self-evident as the connexion between any other event and its effect. (2) We have to learn from experience which of our volitions will be effective and which will not. E.g., we do not know, until we have tried, that we can voluntarily move our arms and cannot voluntarily move our livers. And again, if a man were suddenly paralysed, he would still expect to be able to move his arm voluntarily, and would be surprised when he found it kept still in spite of his volition. (3) We have discovered that the immediate consequence of a volition is a change in our nerves and muscles, which most people know nothing about; and it is not the movement of a limb, which most people believe to be its immediate and necessary consequence.

The second and third arguments are valid only against the contention that we know immediately that a volition to make a certain movement is the *sufficient* condition for the happening of that movement. They are quite irrelevant to the contention that we know immediately that the volition is a *necessary* condition for the happening of just that movement at just that time. No doubt many other conditions are also necessary, *e.g.*, that our nerves and muscles shall be in the right state; and these other necessary conditions can be discovered only by special investigation. Since our volitions to move our limbs are in fact followed in the vast majority of cases by the willed movement, and since the other necessary conditions are not very obvious, it is natural enough that we should think that we know immediately that our volition is the *sufficient* condition of the movement of our limbs. If we think so, we are certainly wrong; and Mr. Hume's arguments prove that we are. But they prove nothing else. It does not follow that we are wrong in thinking that we know, without having to wait for the result, that the volition is a *necessary* condition of the movement.

It remains to consider the first argument. Is the connexion between cause and effect as mysterious and as little self-evident in the case of the voluntary production of bodily movement as in all other cases? If so, we must hold that the first time a baby wills to move its hand it is just as much surprised to find its hand moving as it would be to find its leg moving or its nurse bursting into flames. I do not profess to know anything about the infant mind; but it seems to me that this is a wildly paradoxical consequence, for which there is no evidence or likelihood. But there is no need to leave the matter there. It is perfectly plain that, in the case of volition and voluntary movement, there *is* a connexion between the cause and the effect which is not present in other cases of causation, and which does make it plausible to hold that in this one case the nature of the effect can be foreseen by merely reflecting on the nature of the cause. The peculiarity of a volition as a cause-factor is that it involves as an essential part of it the idea of the effect. To say that a person has a volition to move his arm involves saying that he has an idea of his arm (and not of his leg or his liver) and an idea of the position in which he wants his arm to be. It is simply silly in view of this fact to say that there is no closer connexion between the desire to move my arm and the movement of my arm than there is between this desire and the movement of my leg or my liver. We cannot detect any analogous connexion between cause and effect in causal transactions which we view wholly from outside, such as the movement of a billiard-ball by a cue. It is therefore by no means unreasonable to suggest that, in the one case of our own voluntary movements, we can see without waiting for the result that such and such a volition is a necessary condition of such and such a bodily movement.

It seems to me then that Mr. Hume's arguments on this point are absolutely irrelevant, and that it may very well be true that in volition we positively know that our desire for such and such a bodily movement is a necessary (though not a sufficient) condition of the happening of just that movement at just that time. On the whole then I conclude that the philosophical arguments certainly do not disprove Two-sided Interaction, and that they do not even raise any strong presumption against it. And, while I am not prepared definitely to commit myself to the view that, in voluntary movement, we positively *know* that the mind acts on the body, I do think that this opinion is quite plausible when properly stated and that the arguments which have been brought against it are worthless. I pass therefore to the scientific arguments.

There are, so far as I know, two of these. One is supposed to be based on the physical principle of the Conservation of Energy, and on certain experiments which have been made on human bodies. The other is based on the close analogy which is said to exist between the structures of the physiological mechanism of reflex action and that of vountary action. I will take them in turn.

It will first be needful to state clearly what is asserted by the principle of the Conservation of Energy. It is found that, if we take certain material systems, *e.g.*, a gun, a cartridge, and a bullet, there is a certain magnitude which keeps approximately constant throughout all their changes. This is called "Energy". When the gun has not been fired it and the bullet have no motion, but the explosive in the cartridge has great chemical energy. When it has been fired the bullet is moving very fast and has great energy of movement. The gun, though not moving fast in its recoil, has also great energy of movement because it is very massive. The gases produced by the explosion have some energy of movement and some heat-energy, but much less chemical energy than the unexploded charge had. These various kinds of energy can be measured in common units according to certain conventions. To an innocent mind there seems to be a good deal of "cooking" at this stage, *i.e.*, the conventions seem to be chosen and various kinds and amounts of concealed energy seem to be postulated in order to make the principle come out right at the end. I do not propose to go into this in detail, for two reasons. In the first place, I think that the conventions adopted and the postulates made, though somewhat suggestive of the fraudulent company-promoter, can be justified by their coherence with certain experimental facts, and that they are not simply made *ad hoc*. Secondly, I shall show that the Conservation of Energy is absolutely irrelevant to the question at issue, so that it would be a waste of time to treat it too seriously in the present connexion. Now it is found that the total energy of all kinds in this system, when measured according to these conventions, is approximately the same in amount though very differently distributed after the explosion and before it. If we had confined our attention to a part of this system and *its* energy this would not have been true. The bullet, *e.g.*, had no energy at all before the explosion and a great deal afterwards. A system like the bullet, the gun, and the charge is called a "Conservative System"; the bullet alone, or the gun and the charge, would be called "Non-conservative Systems". A conservative system might therefore be defined as one whose total energy is redistributed, but not altered in amount, by changes that happen within it. Of course a given system might be conservative for some kinds of change and not for others.

So far we have merely defined a "Conservative System", and admitted that there are systems which, for some kinds of change at any rate, answer approximately to our defiinition. We can now state the Principle of the Conservation of Energy in terms of the conceptions just defined. The principle asserts that every material system is either itself conservative, or, if not, is part of a larger material system which is conservative. We may take it that there is good inductive evidence for this proposition.

The next thing to consider is the experiments on the human body. These tend to prove that a living body, with the air that it breathes and the food that it eats, forms a conservative system to a high degree of approximation. We can measure the chemical energy of the food given to a man, and that which enters his body in the form of Oxygen breathed in. We can also, with suitable apparatus, collect, measure and analyse the air breathed out, and thus find its chemical energy. Similarly, we can find the energy given out in bodily movement, in heat, and in exertion. It is alleged that, on the average, whatever the man may do, the energy of his bodily movements is exactly accounted for by the energy given to him in the form of food and of Oxygen. If you take the energy put in food and Oxygen, and subtract the energy given out in waste-products, the balance is almost exactly equal to the energy put out in bodily movements. Such slight differences as are found are as often on one side as on the other, and are therefore probably due to unavoidable experimental errors. I do not propose to criticise the interpretation of these experiments in detail, because, as I shall show soon, they are completely irrelevant to the problem of whether mind and body interact. But there is just one point that I will make before passing on. It is perfectly clear that such experiments can tell us only what happens on the average over a long time. To know whether the balance was accurately kept at every moment we should have to kill the patient at each moment and analyse his body so as to find out the energy present then in the form of stored-up products. Obviously we cannot keep on killing the patient in order to analyse him, and then reviving him in order to go on with the experiment. Thus it would seem that the results of the experiment are perfectly compatible with the presence of quite large excesses or defects in the total bodily energy at certain moments, provided that these average out over longer periods. However, I do not want to press this criticism; I am quite ready to accept for our present purpose the traditional interpretation which has been put on the experiments.

We now understand the physical principle and the experimental facts. The two together are generally supposed to prove that mind and body cannot interact. What precisely is the argument, and is it valid? I imagine that the argument, when fully stated, would run somewhat as follows: "I will to move my arm, and it moves. If the volition has anything to do with causing the movement we might expect energy to flow from my mind to my body. Thus the energy of my body ought to receive a measurable increase, not accounted for by the food that I eat and the Oxygen that I breathe. But no such physically unaccountable increases of bodily energy are found. Again, I tread on a tin-tack, and a painful sensation arises in my mind. If treading on the tack has anything to do with causing the sensation we might expect energy to flow from my body to my mind. Such energy would cease to be measurable. Thus there ought to be a noticeable decrease in my bodily energy, not balanced by increases anywhere in the physical system. But such unbalanced decreases of bodily energy are not found." So it is concluded that the volition has nothing to do with causing my arm to move, and that treading on the tack has nothing to do with causing the painful sensation.

Is this argument valid? In the first place it is important to notice that the conclusion does not follow from the Conservation of Energy and the experimental facts alone. The real premise is a tacitly assumed proposition about causation; viz., that, if a change in A has anything to do with causing a change in B, energy must leave A and flow into B. This is neither asserted nor entailed by the Conservation of Energy. What *it* says is that, *if* energy leaves A, it must appear in something else, say B; so that A and B together form a conservative system. Since the Conservation of Energy is not itself the premise for the argument against Interaction, and since it does not entail that premise, the evidence for the Conservation of Energy is not evidence against Interaction. Is there any independent evidence for the premise? We may admit that it *is* true of many, though not of all, transactions within the physical realm. But there are cases where it is not true even of purely physical transactions; and, even if it were always true in the physical realm, it would not follow that it must also be true of trans-physical causation. Take the case of a weight swinging at the end of a string hung from a fixed point. The total energy of the weight is the same at all positions in its course. It is thus a conservative system. But at every moment the direction and velocity of the weight's motion are different, and the proportion between its kinetic and its potential energy is constantly changing. These changes are caused by the pull of the string, which acts in a different direction at each different moment. The string makes no difference to the total energy of the weight; but it makes all the difference in the world to the particular way in which the energy is distributed between the potential and the kinetic forms. This is evident when we remember that the weight would begin to move in an utterly different course if at any moment the string were cut.

Here, then, we have a clear case even in the physical realm where a system is conservative but is continually acted on by something which affects its movement and the distribution of its total energy. Why should not the mind act on the body in this way? If you say that you can see how a string can affect the movement of a weight, but cannot see how a volition could affect the movement of a material particle, you have deserted the scientific argument and have gone back to one of the philosophical arguments. Your real difficulty is either that volitions are so very unlike movements, or that the volition is in your mind whilst the movement belongs to the physical realm. And we have seen how little weight can be attached to these objections.

The fact is that, even in purely physical systems, the Conservation of Energy does not explain what changes will happen or when they will happen. It merely imposes a very general limiting condition on the changes that are possible. The fact that the system composed of bullet, charge, and gun, in our earlier example, is conservative does not tell us that the gun ever will be fired, or when it will be fired if at all, or what will cause it to go off, or what forms of energy will appear if and when it does go off. The change in this case is determined by pulling the trigger. Likewise the mere fact that the human body and its neighbourhood form a conservative system does not explain any particular bodily movement; it does not explain why I ever move at all, or why I sometimes write, sometimes walk, and sometimes swim. To explain the happening of these particular movements at certain times it seems to be essential to take into account the volitions which happen from time to time in my mind; just as it is essential to take the string into account to explain the particular behaviour of the weight, and to take the trigger into account to explain the going off of the gun at a certain moment. The difference between the gun-system and the body-system is that a little energy does flow into the former when the trigger is pulled, whilst it is alleged that none does so when a volition starts a bodily movement. But there is not even this amount of difference between the body-system and the swinging weight.

Thus the argument from energy has no tendency to disprove Two-sided Interaction. It has gained a spurious authority from the august name of the Conservation of Energy. But this impressive principle proves to have nothing to do with the case. And the real premise of the argument is not self-evident, and is not universally true even in purely intra-physical transactions. In the end this scientific argument has to lean on the old philosophic arguments; and we have seen that these are but bruised reeds. Nevertheless, the facts brought forward by the argument from energy do throw some light on the *nature* of the inter-action between mind and body, assuming this to happen. They do suggest that all the energy of our bodily actions comes out of and goes back into the physical world, and that minds neither add energy to nor abstract it from the latter. What they do, if they do anything, is to determine that at a given moment so much energy shall change from the chemical form to the form of bodily movement; and they determine this, so far as we can see, without altering the total amount of energy in the physical world.

There are purely reflex actions, like sneezing and blinking, in which there is no reason to suppose that the mind plays any essential part. Now we know the nervous structure which is used in such acts as these. A stimulus is given to the outer end of an efferent nerve; some change or other runs up this nerve, crosses a synapse between this and an afferent nerve, travels down the latter to a muscle, causes the muscle to contract, and so produces a bodily movement. There seems no reason to believe that the mind plays any essential part in this process. The process may be irreducibly vital, and not merely physico-chemical; but there seems no need to assume anything more than this. Now it is said that the whole nervous system is simply an immense complica-tion of interconnected nervous arcs. The result is that a change which travels inwards has an immense number of alternative paths by which it may travel outwards. Thus the reaction to a given stimulus is no longer one definite movement, as in the simple reflex. Almost any movement may follow any stimulus according to the path which the afferent disturbance happens to take. This path will depend on the relative resistance of the various synapses at the time. Now a variable response to the same stimulus is characteristic of deliberate as opposed to reflex action.

These are the facts. The argument based on them runs as follows. It is admitted that the mind has nothing to do with the causation of purely reflex actions. But the nervous structure and the nervous processes involved in deliberate action do not differ in kind from those involved in reflex action; they differ only in degree of complexity. The variability which characterizes deliberate action is fully explained by the variety of alternative paths and the variable resistances of the synapses. So it is unreasonable to suppose that the mind has any more to do with causing deliberate actions than it has to do with causing reflex actions.

I think that this argument is invalid. In the first place I am pretty sure that the persons who use it have before their imagination a kind of picture of how mind and body must interact if they interact at all. They find that the facts do not answer to this picture, and so they conclude that there is no interaction. The picture is of the following kind. They think of the mind as sitting somewhere in a hole in the brain, surrounded by telephones. And they think of the efferent disturbance as coming to an end at one of these telephones and there affecting the mind. The mind is then supposed to respond by sending an afferent impulse down another of these telephones. As no such hole, with efferent nerves stopping at its walls and afferent nerves starting from them, can be found, they conclude that the mind can play no part in the transaction. But another alternative is that this picture of how the mind must act if it acts at all is wrong. To put it shortly, the mistake is to confuse a gap in an explanation with a spatio-temporal gap, and to argue from the absence of the latter to the absence of the former.

The Interactionist's contention is simply that there is a gap in any purely physiological explanation of deliberate action; *i.e.*, that all such explanations fail to account completely for the facts because they leave out one necessary condition. It does not follow in the least that there must be a spatio-temporal breach of continuity in the physiological conditions, and that the missing condition must fill this gap in the way in which the movement of a wire fills the spatio-temporal interval between the pulling of a bell-handle and the ringing of a distant bell. To assume this is to make the mind a kind of physical object, and to make its action a kind of mechanical action. Really, the mind and its actions are not literally in Space at all, and the time which is occupied by the mental event is no doubt *also* occupied by some part of the physiological process. Thus I am inclined to think that much of the

force which this argument actually exercises on many people is simply
due to the presupposition about the *modus operandi* of interaction,
and that it is greatly weakened when this presupposition is shown to
be a mere prejudice due to our limited power of envisaging unfamiliar
alternative possibilities.

We can, however, make more detailed objections to the argument
than this. There is a clear introspective difference between the mental
accompaniment of voluntary action and that of reflex action. What
goes on in our minds when we decide with difficulty to get out of a hot
bath on a cold morning is obviously extremely different from what
goes on in our minds when we sniff pepper and sneeze. And the
difference is qualitative; it is not a mere difference of complexity. This
difference has to be explained somehow; and the theory under discussion gives no plausible explanation of it. The ordinary view that, in
the latter case, the mind is not acting on the body at all; whilst, in the
former, it is acting on the body in a specific way, does at least make
the introspective difference between the two intelligible.

Again, whilst it is true that deliberate action differs from reflex
action in its greater variability of response to the same stimulus, this is
certainly not the whole or the most important part of the difference
between them. The really important difference is that, in deliberate
action, the response is varied *appropriately* to meet the special circumstances which are supposed to exist at the time or are expected
to arise later; whilst reflex action is not varied in this way, but is blind
and almost mechanical. The complexity of the nervous system explains
the *possibility* of variation; it does not in the least explain why the
alternative which actually takes place should as a rule be appropriate
and not merely haphazard. And so again it seems as if some factor were
in operation in deliberate action which is not present in reflex action;
and it is reasonable to suppose that this factor is the volition in the
mind.

It seems to me that this second scientific argument has no tendency
to disprove interaction; but that the facts which it brings forward do
tend to suggest the particular form which interaction probably takes
if it happens at all. They suggest that what the mind does to the body
in voluntary action, if it does anything, is to lower the resistance of
certain synapses and to raise that of others. The result is that the nervous current follows such a course as to produce the particular movement which the mind judges to be appropriate at the time. On such
a view the difference between reflex, habitual, and deliberate actions
for the present purpose becomes fairly plain. In pure reflexes the mind
cannot voluntarily affect the resistance of the synapses concerned, and

so the action takes place in spite of it. In habitual action it deliberately refrains from interfering with the resistance of the synapses, and so the action goes on like a complicated reflex. But it *can* affect these resistances if it wishes, though often only with difficulty; and it is ready to do so if it judges this to be expedient. Finally, it may lose the power altogether. This would be what happens when a person becomes a slave to some habit, such as drug-taking.

I conclude that, at the level of enlightened common-sense at which the ordinary discussion of Interaction moves, no good reason has been produced for doubting that the mind acts on the body in volition, and that the body acts on the mind in sensation. The philosophic arguments are quite inconclusive; and the scientific arguments, when properly understood, are quite compatible with Two-sided Interaction. At most they suggest certain conclusions as to the form which interaction probably takes if it happens at all.

6   JOHN PASSMORE

(1914–   )

*The Humpty-Dumpty Argument**

Passmore attacks the whole fabric of dualistic thinking. Passmore claims, perhaps a bit too hastily, that no creative contemporary philosophers are dualists, that philosophers have found unanswerable what Passmore terms the Humpty-Dumpty Argument. This major criticism rests on the problem of interaction between mind and body, which a dualist must assume to explain much of human behavior. Minds and bodies are supposed to work together in most of our activities, but Passmore argues, where are they related so as to affect each other? Body, according to the dualists, is all physical and mind is all mental. There seems to be no common meeting ground. To the dualists, the kinds of things—persuasive argument, reason, emotion—that might affect mind are not physical, and the things that affect bodies—force, weight, etc.—are certainly not mental. Man has been taken apart, and all the king's horses and men cannot seem to put him back together again without erasing the original clear-cut distinctions of the dualism.

* John Passmore, *Philosophical Reasoning* (New York: Basic Books, 1961), pp. 38–40, 53–57. Excerpts from Chapter 3, "The Two-Worlds Argument," of *Philosophical Reasoning* by John Passmore, Basic Books, Inc., Publishers, New York, 1969. Used by permission of the publisher.

THE general tendency of philosophy is towards monism, in one or the other of its two very different varieties. There have, of course, been distinguished dualists—Plato and Descartes, for example—but they have been the exception. Few philosophers have been satisfied with a doctrine which preserves that sort of absolute separation between the mind and the body, the eternal and the temporal, the supernatural and the natural, which is to be found in the orthodox Christian theologies. This is an important fact about philosophers; the rejection of dualism is indeed one of the few points on which almost all the creative philosophers of modern times have agreed. Why this unwonted unanimity?

I have suggested that there are two different sorts of monism; let us call them 'existence-monism' and 'entity-monism.' Entity-monism is the doctrine that 'ultimately' there is only one real entity. What we normally regard as distinct things—whether they be chairs, or musical compositions, or human beings—are, all of them, appearances of this one entity. Some philosophers describe themselves as materialistic monists, others as spiritualistic monists. But obviously this will not do. For if all differences are unreal, the one real entity cannot properly be described as material rather than as spiritual, or as spiritual rather than material. The most that can be said (if even this can be said) is that there is 'the One' or 'the Absolute.' For anybody to say: 'My monism is corporeal in type' is a contradiction in terms—if, that is, his monism is an entity-monism.

Entity-monism has had relatively few, although some distinguished, exponents. The case is quite different with what, for want of a better name, I have called 'existence-monism.' Existence-monism is difficult to define in general terms. But we might put it thus: when we say that something exists, or that things of a certain kind exist, this *exist* or *exists* has an invariant meaning whatever the 'something' or the 'kind' may be, i.e. there are not sorts, or levels, or orders of existence. More accurately, what is asserted by 'X exists' can always be asserted by a proposition which contains an 'is' which has, in this sense, an invariant meaning. Existence-monism, unlike entity-monism, does admit of varieties. Philosophers might say, and have said, that to exist is to be perceived, or to be in process, or to be spatio-temporal, or to be a possible subject for physical investigation, or to be a thing with properties, and so on.

The possible variations are, one might even think, limitless; any predicate might serve. But most of them we should at once rule out. Nobody could now win credence who asserted that to be is to be a quantity of water, however plausible that doctrine might have looked to Thales. This would not be only for empirical reasons. We should not bring it against Thales' view, simply, that scientists had looked at some substance in a laboratory and found that it was not watery. The objection would run deeper: that 'to be' cannot involve the possession of some specific descriptive property (whatever qualms we might suffer if we were asked to define that phrase more exactly). Such a property as wateriness cannot have the sort of priority which Thales' theory would ascribe to it. So it is not only wateriness in particular but any similar predicate which is now being ruled out. Water is the sort of thing to which we *ascribe* existence; and 'water exists here' is not the mere tautology 'the water here is watery'.

Contrast the view that 'to be is to have a place in Space-Time'; this sort of difficulty does not arise, or not so obviously, for Space-Time is not the sort of thing to which existence is ascribed or which is used to distinguish one thing from another. 'Spatio-temporality exists here', if it means anything at all, does assert the mere identity 'this spatio-temporal region is spatio-temporal'. Of course, specific spatio-temporal predicates are used as modes of distinction—something, that is, may be distinguished from its fellows in virtue of its position, or duration, or size, or shape; but the more general property of being 'spatio-temporal' is not ordinarily a distinguishing predicate—although metaphysicians sometimes try to turn it into one by alleging that there is a non-spatio-temporal kind of existence. As for those who say that 'to be is to be an object of thought', they always pay a certain homage to the force of what I am arguing by setting out to show, in Berkeley's manner, that it would be self-contradictory to attempt to use 'object of thought' as if it were a descriptive predicate.

It is not my present object, although by now it might appear to be, to define monism and to distinguish its types. What I want to do, simply, is to consider why most creative philosophers have been attracted by some sort of existence-monism, whether it has taken the form of an explicitly argued phenomenalism, idealism, physicalism, naturalism, or has merely been the implicit assumption, certainly widespread, that the traditional dichotomies of Mind and Body, God and Nature, are obviously untenable.

The convergence on existence-monism arises, I want to suggest, because philosophers have come to accept as unanswerable a particular philosophical argument, which I have called the 'two-worlds argument', but might, more frivolously, have described as the Humpty Dumpty argument. Its basic point is that once we break up any system in a certain kind of way, it becomes quite impossible to put the pieces together again in a single situation: and yet, unless they can be so put together, the whole point of the breaking-up is lost. . . .

Ryle in *The Concept of Mind* puts the two-world argument in a more fundamental way, which links it with our previous discussion. 'The problem,' he writes, 'how a person's mind and body influence one another is notoriously charged with theoretical difficulties. What the mind wills, the legs, arms and the tongue execute; what affects the ear and the eye has something to do with what the mind perceives; grimaces and smiles betray the mind's moods and bodily castigations lead, it is hoped, to moral improvement. But the actual transactions between the episodes of the private history and those of the public history remain mysterious, since by definition they can belong to neither series. They could not be reported among the happenings described in a person's autobiography of his inner life, but nor could they be reported among those described in someone else's biography of that person's overt career. They can be inspected neither by introspection nor by laboratory experiment. They are theoretical shuttlecocks which are forever being bandied from the physiologist back to the psychologist and from the psychologist back to the physiologist.' He continues thus: 'Underlying this partly metaphorical representation of the bifurcation of a person's two lives, there is a seemingly more profound and philosophical assumption. It is assumed that there are two kinds of existence or status. What exists or happens may have the status of physical existence, or it may have the status of mental existence' (pp. 12–13).

Ryle suggests in this passage that *by definition* the transaction between mind and body can belong to neither the mental nor the physical series. If the mental series is defined as containing only such transactions as are mental this is, of course, true. The two-world argument then becomes a very simple one indeed. It consists in saying· 'According to you, everything is either a part of the mental series or a part of the bodily series, and no transaction can belong to the mental series unless it is between members of the mental series, or to the bodily series unless it is between members of the bodily series. But then you have left no room whatever for transactions between the mental and the bodily series.' More commonly, however, the dualist presumes that the mental series can include any transaction in which one ingredient is mental, and the physical series any transaction in which one ingredient is physical; so that mental-physical transactions belong to *both* series. Describing my mental life I can say, 'At this moment I influenced my body' and describing my physical life I can say: 'At this moment I was influenced by my mind.' Then argument is needed to show that there is something about the conditions laid down for series-membership that would rule out this sort of double membership. But Ryle makes two points on which I have been insisting; first, that if we suppose that the mental life is known in one way and the physical in another, it will be impossible to give any account of our knowledge of the transaction between the two lives; and, secondly, that the crucial questions in the end, all the same, are not epistemological but ontological.

Mind and body are supposed to differ not only in properties, as an explosion differs from a lighted match, but in ontological status; the conditions which have to be fulfilled by a mind in order to exist, on the traditional theory, are entirely different from those which have to be fulfilled by a physical object. To assert that a physical body exists is to say that something is going on at a particular time in a particular place, something which is describable in principle by physical laws. To say that a mind exists is to say that at a particular time, but not in a particular place, something is happening which is describable only by spiritual laws, e.g. by teleological as distinct from efficient causality. Then the difficulty can be put thus; it has to be granted that in some sense the mind influences the body and vice versa. But the only force the mind has at its disposal is spiritual force, the power of rational persuasion; and the only thing that can move it is a purpose. On the other side, a body has no force at its disposal except material force and nothing can influence it except mechanical pressure. This means that bodies cannot appeal to minds to act; they can only push; and minds cannot influence bodies by putting purposes before them, because bodies are not susceptible to this sort of influence. So there is no possible way in which one could influence the other. We cannot nominate any particular place—whether it be the pineal gland or the synapse—where mind interacts with body, because mind is no more in that place, nor next to it, than anywhere else. Yet if once we say that mind itself is spatial, subject to physical force, capable of exercising physical force, and so on, the supposed ontological contrast breaks down.

This type of argument is sometimes described as 'the argument against interactionism'. But if interactionism is simply the view that the mental can affect the non-mental—that, for example, if I am worried about something, this can affect my digestion—then it is obviously true. What the two-world argument is concerned to show is that interactionism cannot be true *if there is an ontological gap between the mental and the non-mental;* it is directed against the gap, not against the interaction.

Once again, evasive action may be taken. 'Psycho-physical parallelism' is the best known form of evasion. Notwithstanding appearances, the parallelist argues, there is in fact no interaction between the mental and the non-mental, for such an interaction is ontologically impossible. Mental events and non-mental events belong to two distinct series, even although the series run parallel to one another. But what does 'parallel' mean here? Not that certain events in the one series are *like* events in the other; this has been ruled out in advance. Nor that they occur in the same place, for the same reason. The only possible parallelism is a temporal one; certain events in the mental series occur at the same time as, or prior to, or subsequent to, certain events in the non-mental series. But this relation is not close enough to do justice to the admitted facts. Events in my mind are related temporally to all sorts of events, inside and outside my body; what 'parallelism' fails to explain is the *special* relation between what goes on in my brain and what goes on in my mind.

Even at the level of temporal relationships, parallelism jams into the single notion of 'being parallel' the fact that my mental operations are regularly preceded and regularly followed by such and such physical operations and the fact that they regularly occur at the same time as certain such operations. (Is my nervousness 'parallel' to the changes it produces in my stomach or to the changes in the brain which coincide with it?) But in any case parallelism does not even *look* plausible once the 'parallelism' between mental and non-mental has been spelled out into 'some temporal relationship or other'; for such a relationship holds between any two things we care to mention. Yet to make the relation more intimate—as it very clearly is—at once threatens the ontological gap.

The difficulties in the two-world thesis cannot be solved, either, by setting up a third entity in Descartes' manner—very, very subtle animal spirits. For, no matter how subtle, the problem persists of relating such spirits to mind if they are describable in terms of physical science; and if they are not, the problem of relating them to body. Or, if they exhibit the properties both of the spiritual and the physical, then again all ground has gone for supposing that the mental and the physical must belong to sharply sundered realms of existence.

It will now be apparent why so many philosophers have held some form of existence-monism, rejecting the view that universals and particulars, minds and bodies, God and Nature, belong to different orders of existence. For even to state such a theory, its exponents are obliged to destroy the ontological contrast which the theory is supposed to be setting up; and this becomes even more obvious as soon as they try to use the theory as a matter of explanation, a use which is the *raison d'être* of the theory. From this point on philosophers have said very different things: some that everything is changing and complex; others that nothing is; some that everything is describable in terms of physical laws; others that nothing is; some that existence-monism, properly understood, leads to entity-monism, others that it does not. These various paths I cannot now follow; but if philosophy can really show, by its own peculiar arguments, not by experimental inference or by mathematical deduction (and surely I have used neither of these), that dualism is untenable, it has made a contribution of the first importance, sufficient by itself to dispel the view that philosophy is either no more than personal vision or no more than analysis.

H. H. PRICE

(1899–   )

Survival and the Idea of "Another World"*

Professor Price has been influential in contemporary philosophy in the area of epistemology (theory of knowledge). In this article, he deals with the Survival Hypothesis: the theory that man can survive death. Price is not involved in establishing empirical criteria to decide the issue. He is seeking to understand what is involved in the concept of personal survival of death and whether or not such an idea is intelligible to us. In other words, Price is trying to make sense of the concepts involved; he is trying to find relationships between what we know to be the case and what we believe about survival of death. Price's analysis starts with the common experience of dreams, from which he thinks an analogy to survival can be drawn. Survival would have to take place in some world or other. Price sees the intelligibility of the hypothesis as resting on our ability to give some reasonable account of "Another World." He tries to establish that the dream world provides the model for our thinking about other worlds.

Upon learning of the Kidd will, Professor Price commented that Mr. Kidd might have wanted a photograph of a so-called "extra body" said to exist by those who have claimed "out-of-body experiences." Price wrote: "The idea is, I think that each of us has this 'extra body' all the time and that normally it is coincident with, or interpenetrates, the physical organism. It is also alleged to be quite different from the 'astral body' which is supposed to be the permanent 'vehicle of the soul' in its post-mortem existence. Apparently it is supposed to leave the physical organism at death. But after a while it disintegrates, whereas the 'astral body' continues. So even if it were photographed this would hardly give Mr. Kidd what he wanted: and even the 'astral body' (if there is such a thing) couldn't be identified with the soul. Nor could it be photographed, for it would surely be in another space."

* From *Proceedings of the Society for Psychical Research,* Vol. L, Pt. 182 (January, 1953) pp. 1–25. Reprinted by kind permission of the editor and the author.

THIS year is the seventieth anniversary of the foundation of the Society for Psychical Research. From the very beginning, the problem of survival has been one of the main interests of the Society; and that is my excuse, if any excuse is needed, for discussing some aspects of the problem this evening. I shall not, however, talk about the evi-

dence for survival. In this lecture I am concerned only with the conception of survival; with the *meaning* of the Survival Hypothesis, and not
with its truth or falsity. When we consider the Survival Hypothesis,
whether we believe it or disbelieve it, what is it that we have in mind?
Can we form any idea, even a rough and provisional one, of what a
disembodied human life might be like? Supposing we cannot, it will
follow that what is called the Survival Hypothesis is a mere set of
words and not a hypothesis at all. The evidence adduced in favour of
it might still be evidence for something, and perhaps for something
important, but we should no longer have the right to claim that it is
evidence for survival. There cannot be evidence for something which is
completely unintelligible to us.

Now let us consider the situation in which we find ourselves after
seventy years of psychical research. A very great deal of work has been
done on the problem of survival, and much of the best work by members of our Society. Yet there are the widest differences of opinion about
the results. A number of intelligent persons would maintain that we now
have a very large mass of evidence in favour of survival; that some of it
is of very good quality indeed, and cannot be explained away unless we
suppose that the super-normal cognitive powers of some embodied
human minds are vastly more extensive and more accurate than we can
easily believe them to be; in short, that on the evidence available the
Survival Hypothesis is more probable than not. Some people—and not
all of them are silly or credulous—would even maintain that the Survival Hypothesis is proved, or as near to being so as any empirical
hypothesis can be. On the other hand, there are also many intelligent
persons who entirely reject these conclusions. Some of them, no doubt,
have not taken the trouble to examine the evidence. But others of them
have; they may even have given years of study to it. They would agree
that the evidence is evidence of *something*, and very likely of something important. But, they would say, it cannot be evidence of survival;
there *must* be some alternative explanation of it, however difficult it
may be to find out. Why do they take this line? I think it is because
they find the very conception of survival unintelligible. The very idea
of a "discarnate human personality" seems to them a muddled or absurd
one; indeed not an idea at all, but just a phrase—an emotionally exciting
one, no doubt—to which no clear meaning can be given.

Moreover, we cannot just ignore the people who have not examined
the evidence. Some of our most intelligent and most highly educated
contemporaries are among them. These men are well aware, by this
time, that the evidence does exist, even if their predecessors fifty years

ago were not. If you asked them why they do not trouble to examine it in detail, they would be able to offer reasons for their attitude. And one of their reasons, and not the least weighty in their eyes, is the contention I mentioned just now, that the very idea of survival is a muddled or absurd one. To borrow an example from Whately Carington, we know pretty well what we mean by asking whether Jones has survived a shipwreck. We are asking whether he continues to live after the shipwreck has occurred. Similarly it makes sense to ask whether he survived a railway accident, or the bombing of London. But if we substitute "his own death" for "a shipwreck," and ask whether he has survived it, our question (it will be urged) becomes unintelligible. Indeed, it *looks* self-contradictory, as if we were asking whether Jones is still alive at a time when he is no longer alive—whether Jones is both alive and not alive at the same time. We may try to escape from this logical absurdity by using phrases like "discarnate existence," "alive, but disembodied." But such phrases, it will be said, have no clear meaning. No amount of facts, however well established, can have the slightest tendency to support a meaningless hypothesis, or to answer an unintelligible question. It would therefore be a waste of time to examine such facts in detail. There are other and more important things to do.

If I am right so far, questions about the meaning of the word "survival" or of the phrase "life after death" are not quite so arid and academic as they may appear. Anyone who wants to maintain that there is empirical evidence for survival ought to consider these questions, whether he thinks the evidence strong or weak. Indeed, anyone who thinks there is a *problem* of survival at all should ask himself what his conception of survival is.

Now why should it be thought that the very idea of life after death is unintelligible? Surely it is easy enough to conceive (whether or not it is true) that experiences might occur after Jones's death which are linked with experiences which he had before his death, in such a way that his personal identity is preserved? But, it will be said, the idea of after-death *experiences* is just the difficulty. What kind of experiences could they conceivably be? In a disembodied state, the supply of sensory stimuli is perforce cut off, because the supposed experient has no sense organs and no nervous system. There can therefore be no sense-perception. One has no means of being aware of material objects any longer; and if one has not, it is hard to see how one could have any emotions or wishes either. For all the emotions and wishes we have in this present life are concerned directly or indirectly with material objects, including of course our own organisms and other organisms, especially other human ones. In short, one could only be said to have experiences at all, if one is aware of some sort of a *world*. In this way, the idea of survival is bound up with the idea of "another world" or a "next world." Anyone who maintains that the idea of survival is after all intelligible must also be claiming that we can form some conception, however rough and provisional, of what "the next world" or "the other world" might be like. The skeptics I have in mind would say that we can form no such conception at all; and this, I think, is one of the main reasons why they hold that the conception of survival itself is unintelligible. I wish to suggest, on the contrary, that we *can* form some conception, in outline at any rate, of what a "next world" or "another world" might be like, and consequently of the kind of experiences which disembodied minds, if indeed there are such, might be supposed to have.

The thoughts which I wish to put before you on this subject are not at all original. Something very like them is to be found in the chapter on survival in Whately Carington's book *Telepathy*,° and in the concluding chapter of Professor C. J. Ducasse's book *Nature, Mind and Death*.† Moreover, if I am not mistaken, the Hindu conception of *Kama Loka* (literally, "the world of desire") is essentially the same as the one I wish to discuss; and something very similar is to be found in Mahayana Buddhism. In these two religions, of course, there is not just one "other world" but several different "other worlds," which we are supposed to experience in succession; not merely the next world, but the next but one, and another after that. But I think it will be quite enough for us to consider just the next world, without troubling ourselves about any additional other worlds which there might be. It is a sufficiently difficult task, for us Western people, to convince ourselves that it makes sense to speak of any sort of after-death world at all. Accordingly, with your permission, I shall use the expressions "next world" and "other world" interchangeably. If anyone thinks this is an oversimplification, it will be easy for him to make the necessary corrections.

The next world, I think, might be conceived as a kind of dream-world. When we are asleep, sensory stimuli are cut off, or at any rate are prevented from having their normal effects upon our brain-centres. But we still manage to have experiences. It is true that sense-perception no longer occurs, but something sufficiently like it does. In sleep, our image-producing powers, which are more or less inhibited in waking

° Whately Carington, *Telepathy* (London: Methuen & Co., Ltd., 1945).
† C. J. Ducasse, *Nature, Mind and Death* (La Salle, Ill.: Open Court Publishing Co., 1951).

life by a continuous bombardment of sensory stimuli, are released from this inhibition. And then we are provided with a multitude of objects of awareness, about which we employ our thoughts and towards which we have desires and emotions. These objects which we are aware of behave in a way which seems very queer to us when we wake up. The laws of their behaviour are not the laws of physics. But however queer their behaviour is, it does not at all disconcert us at the time and our personal identity is not broken.

In other words, my suggestion is that the next world, if there is one, might be a world of mental images. Nor need such a world be so "thin and insubstantial" as you might think. Paradoxical as it may sound, there is nothing imaginary about a mental image. It is an actual entity, as real as anything can be. The seeming paradox arises from the ambiguity of the verb "to imagine." It does sometimes mean "to have mental images." But more usually it means "to entertain propositions without believing them"; and very often they are false propositions, and moreover we *dis*believe them in the act of entertaining them. This is what happens, for example, when we read Shakespeare's play *The Tempest*, and that is why we say that Prospero and Ariel are "imaginary characters." Mental images are not in this sense imaginary at all. We do actually experience them, and they are no more imaginary than sensations. To avoid the paradox, though at the cost of some pedantry, it would be well to distinguish between *imagining* and *imaging*, and to have two different adjectives "imaginary" and "imagy." In this terminology, it is imaging, and not imagining, that I wish to talk about; and the next world, as I am trying to conceive of it, is an *imagy* world, but not on that account an imaginary one.

Indeed, to those who experienced it an image-world would be just as "real" as this present world is; perhaps so like it, that they would have considerable difficulty in realizing that they were dead. We are, of course, sometimes told in mediumistic communications that quite a lot of people do find it difficult to realize that they are dead; and this is just what we should expect if the next world is an image-world. Lord Russell and other philosophers have maintained that a material object in this present physical world is nothing more nor less than a complicated system of *appearances*. So far as I can see, there might be a set of visual images related to each other perspectivally, with front views and side views and back views all fitting neatly together in the way that ordinary visual appearances do now. Such a group of images might contain tactual images too. Similarly it might contain auditory images and smell images. Such a family of interrelated images would make a pretty good object. It would be quite a satisfactory substitute for the material objects which we perceive in this present life. And a whole world composed of such families of mental images would make a perfectly good world.

It is possible, however, and indeed likely, that some of those images would be what Francis Galton called *generic* images. An image representing a dog or a tree need not necessarily be an exact replica of some individual dog or tree one has perceived. It might rather be a representation of a *typical* dog or tree. Our memories are more specific on some subjects than on others. How specific they are depends probably on the degree of interest we had in the individual objects or events at the time when we perceived them. An event which moved us deeply is likely to be remembered specifically and in detail; and so is an individual object to which we were much attached (for example, the home of our childhood). But with other objects which interested us less and were less attended to, we retain only a "general impression" of a whole class of objects collectively. Left to our own resources, as we should be in the other world, with nothing but our memories to depend on, we should probably be able to form only generic images of such objects. In this respect, an image-world would not be an exact replica of this one, not even of those parts of this one which we have actually perceived. To some extent it would be, so to speak, a generalized picture, rather than a detailed reproduction.

Let us now put our question in another way, and ask what kind of experience a disembodied human mind might be supposed to have. We can then answer that it might be an experience in which *imaging* replaces sense-perception: "replaces" it, in the sense that imaging would perform much the same function as sense-perception performs now, by providing us with objects about which we could have thoughts, emotions and wishes. There is no reason why we should not be "as much alive," or at any rate *feel* as much alive, in an image-world as we do now in this present material world, which we perceive by means of our sense-organs and nervous systems. And so the use of the word "survival" ("life after death") would be perfectly justifiable.

It will be objected, perhaps, that one cannot be said to be alive unless one has a body. But what is meant here by "alive"? It is surely conceivable (whether or not it is true) that *experiences* should occur which are not causally connected with a physical organism. If they did, should we or should we not say that "life" was occurring. I do not think it matters much whether we answer Yes or No. It is purely a question of definition. If you define "life" in terms of certain very complicated physico-chemical processes, as some people would, then of course life after death is by definition impossible, because there is no longer anything to be alive. In that case, the problem of survival (*life* after bodily death) is misnamed. Instead, it ought to be called the problem of after-death *experiences*. And this is in fact the problem with which all investigators of the subject have been concerned. After all, what people want to know, when they ask whether we survive death, is simply whether experiences occur after death, or what likelihood, if any, there is that they do; and whether such experiences, if they do occur, are linked with each other and with *ante mortem* ones in such a way that personal identity is preserved. It is not physico-chemical processes which interest us, when we ask such questions. But there is another sense of the words "life" and "alive" which may be called the psychological sense; and in this sense "being alive" just *means* "having experiences of certain sorts." In this psychological sense of the word "life," it is perfectly intelligible to ask whether there is life after death, even though life in the physiological sense does *ex hypothesi* come to an end when someone dies. Or, if you like, the question is whether one could *feel* alive after bodily death, even though (by hypothesis) one would not *be* alive at the time. It will be just enough to satisfy most of us if the *feeling* of being alive continues after death. It will not make a halfpennyworth of difference that one will not then *be* alive in the physiological or biochemical sense of the word.

It may be said, however, that "feeling alive" (life in the psychological sense) cannot just be equated with having experiences in general. Feeling alive, surely, consists in having experiences of a special sort, namely *organic sensations*—bodily feelings of various sorts. In our present experience, these bodily feelings are not as a rule separately attended to unless they are unusually intense or unusually painful. They are a kind of undifferentiated mass in the background of consciousness. All the same, it would be said, they constitute our feeling of being alive; and if they were absent (as surely they must be when the body is dead) the feeling of being alive could not be there.

I am not at all sure that this argument is as strong as it looks. I think we should still feel alive—or alive enough—provided we experienced emotions and wishes, even if no organic sensations accompanied these experiences, as they do now. But in case I am wrong here, I would suggest that *images* of organic sensations could perfectly well provide what is needed. We can quite well image to ourselves what it feels like to be in a warm bath, even when we are not actually in one; and a person who has been crippled can image what it felt like to climb a mountain.

Moreover, I would ask whether we do not feel alive when we are dreaming. It seems to me that we obviously do—or at any rate quite alive enough to go on with.

This is not all. In an image-world, a dream-like world such as I am trying to describe, there is no reason at all why there should not be *visual* images resembling the body which one had in this present world. In this present life (for all who are not blind) visual percepts of one's own body form as it were the constant centre of one's perceptual world. It is perfectly possible that visual images of one's own body might perform the same function in the next. They might form the continuing centre or nucleus of one's image world, remaining more or less constant, while other images altered. If this were so, we should have an additional reason for expecting that recently dead people would find it difficult to realize that they were dead, that is, disembodied. To all appearances they *would* have bodies just as they had before, and pretty much the same ones. But, of course, they might discover in time that these image-bodies were subject to rather peculiar causal laws. For example, it might be found that in an image-world our wishes tend *ipso facto* to fulfil themselves in a way they do not now. A wish to go to Oxford might be immediately followed by the occurrence of a vivid and detailed set of Oxford-like images; even though, at the moment before, one's images had resembled Piccadilly Circus or the palace of the Dalai Lama in Tibet. In that case, one would realize that "going somewhere"—transferring one's body from one place to another—was a rather different process from what it had been in the physical world. Reflecting on such experiences, one might come to the conclusion that one's body was not after all the same as the physical body one had before death. One might conclude perhaps that it must be a "spiritual" or "psychical" body, closely resembling the old body in appearance, but possessed of rather different causal properties. It has been said, of course, that phrases like "spiritual body" or "psychical body" are utterly unintelligible, and that no conceivable empirical meaning could be given to such expressions. But I would rather suggest that they might be a way (rather a misleading way perhaps) of referring to a set of body-like images. If our supposed dead empiricist continued his investigations, he might discover that his whole world—not only his own body, but everything else he was aware of—had different causal properties from the physical world, even though everything in it had shape, size, colour, and other qualities which material objects have now. And so eventually, by the exercise of ordinary inductive good sense, he could draw the conclusion that he was in "the next world" or "the other world" and no longer in this one. If, however, he were a very dogmatic philosopher, who distrusted inductive good sense and preferred a priori reasoning, I do not know what condition he would be in. Probably he would never discover that he was dead at all. Being persuaded, on a priori grounds, that life after death was impossible, he might insist on thinking that he must still be in this world, and refuse to pay any attention to the new and strange causal laws which more empirical thinkers would notice.

I think, then, that there is no difficulty in conceiving that the experience of feeling alive could occur in the absence of a physical organism; or, if you prefer to put it so, a disembodied personality could *be* alive in the psychological sense, even though by definition it would not be alive in the physiological or biochemical sense.

Moreover, I do not see why disembodiment need involve the destruction of personal identity. It is, of course, sometimes supposed that personal identity depends on the continuance of a background of organic sensation—the "mass of bodily feeling" mentioned before. (This may be called the somato-centric analysis of personal identity.) We must notice, however, that this background of organic sensation is not literally the same from one period of time to another. The very most that can happen is that the organic sensations which form the background of my experience now should be *exactly similar* to those which were the background of my experience a minute ago. And as a matter of fact, the present ones need not *all* be exactly similar to the previous ones. I might have a twinge of toothache now which I did not have then. I may even have an over-all feeling of lassitude now which I did not have a minute ago, so that the whole mass of bodily feeling, and not merely part of it, is rather different; and this would not interrupt my personal identity at all. The most that is required is only that the majority (not all) of my organic sensations should be closely (not exactly) similar to those I previously had. And even this is only needed if the two occasions are close together in my private time series; the organic sensations I have now might well be very unlike those I used to have when I was one year old. I say "in my private times series." For when I wake up after eight hours of dreamless sleep my personal identity is not broken, though in the physical or public time series there has been a long interval between the last organic sensations I experienced before falling asleep, and the first ones I experience when I wake up. But if similarity, and not literal sameness, is all that is required of this "continuing organic background," it seems to me that the continuity of it could be perfectly well preserved if there were organic *images* after death very like the organic *sensations* which occurred before death.

As a matter of fact, this whole "somato-centric" analysis of personal identity appears to me highly disputable. I should have thought that Locke was much nearer the truth when he said that personal identity depends on memory. But I have tried to show that even if the "somato-centric" theory of personal identity is right, there is no reason why personal identity need be broken by bodily death, provided there are images after death which sufficiently resemble the organic sensations one had before; and this is very like what happens when one falls asleep and begins dreaming.

There is, however, another argument against the conceivability of a disembodied person, to which some present-day linguistic philosophers would attach great weight. It is neatly expressed by Mr. A. G. N. Flew when he says, "people are what you meet."* By "a person" we are supposed to mean a human organism which behaves in certain ways, and especially one which speaks and can be spoken to. And when we say, "this is the same person whom I saw yesterday," we are supposed to mean just that it is the same human organism which I saw yesterday, and also that it behaves in a recognizably similar way.

"People are what you meet." With all respect to Mr. Flew, I would suggest that he does not in this sense "meet" *himself*. He might indeed have had one of those curious out-of-body experiences which are occasionally mentioned in our records, and he might have seen his body from outside (if he has, I heartily congratulate him); but I do not think we should call this "meeting." And surely the important question is, what constitutes my personal identity *for myself*. It certainly does not consist in the fact that other people can "meet" me. It might be that I was for myself the same person as before, even at a time when it was quite impossible for others to meet me. No one can "meet" me when I am dreaming. They can, of course, come and look at my body lying in bed; but this is not "meeting," because no sort of social relations are possible between them and me. Yet, although temporarily "unmeetable," during my dreams I am still, for myself, the same person that I was. And if I went on dreaming *in perpetuum*, and could never be "met"

* *University*, Vol. II, No. 2, 38, in a symposium on "Death" with Professor D. M. Mackinnon. Mr. Flew obviously uses "people" as the plural of "person"; but if we are to be linguistic, I am inclined to think that the nuances of "people" are not quite the same as those of "person." When we used the word "person," in the singular or the plural, the notion of consciousness is more prominently before our minds than it is when we use the word "people."

again, this need not prevent me from continuing to be, for myself, the same person.

As a matter of fact, however, we can quite easily conceive that "meeting" of a kind might still be possible between discarnate experients. And therefore, even if we do make it part of the definition of "a person," that he is capable of being met by others, it will still make sense to speak of "discarnate persons," provided we allow that telepathy is possible between them. It is true that a special sort of telepathy would be needed; the sort which in life produces *telepathic apparitions*. It would not be sufficient that A's thoughts or emotions should be telepathically affected by B's. If such telepathy were sufficiently prolonged and continuous, and especially if it were reciprocal, it would indeed have some of the characteristics of social intercourse; but I do not think we should call it "meeting," at any rate in Mr. Flew's sense of the word. It would be necessary, in addition, that A should be aware of something which could be called "B's body," or should have an experience not too unlike the experience of *seeing* another person in this life. This additional condition would be satisfied if A experienced a telepathic apparition of B. It would be necessary, further, that the telepathic apparition by means of which B "announces himself" (if one may put it so) should be recognizably similar on different occasions. And if it were a case of meeting some person *again* whom one had previously known in this world, the telepathic apparition would have to be recognizably similar to the physical body which that person had when he was still alive.

There is no reason why an image-world should not contain a number of images which are telepathic apparitions, and if it did, one could quite intelligently speak of "meeting other persons" in such a world. All the experiences I have when I meet another person in this present life could still occur, with only this difference, that percepts would be replaced by images. It would also be possible for another person to "meet" me in the same manner, if I, as a telepathic agent could cause him to experience a suitable telepathic apparition, sufficiently resembling the body I used to have when he formerly "met" me in this life.

I now turn to another problem which may have troubled some of you. If there be a next world, *where* is it? Surely it must be somewhere. But there does not seem to be any room for it. We can hardly suppose that it is up in the sky (i.e., outside the earth's atmosphere) or under the surface of the earth, as Homer and Vergil seemed to think. Such suggestions may have contented our ancestors, and the Ptolemaic astronomy may have made them acceptable, for some ages, even to the learned; but they will hardly content us. Surely the next world, if it exists, must be somewhere; and yet, it seems, there is nowhere for it to be.

The answer to this difficulty is easy if we conceive of the next world in the way I have suggested, as a dream-like world of mental images. Mental images, including dream images, are in a space of their own. They do have spatial properties. Visual images, for instance, have extension and shape, and they have spatial relations to one another. But they have no spatial relation to objects in the physical world. If I dream of a tiger, my tiger-image has extension and shape. The dark stripes have spatial relation to the yellow parts, and to each other; the nose has a spatial relation to the tail. Again, the tiger image as a whole may have spatial relations to another image in my dream, for example to an image resembling a palm tree. But suppose we have to ask how far it is from the foot of my bed, whether it is three inches long, or longer or shorter; is it not obvious that these questions are absurd ones? We cannot answer them, not because we lack the necessary information or find it impracticable to make the necessary measurements, but because the questions themselves have no meaning. In the space of the physical world these images are nowhere at all. But in relation to other images of mine, each of them is somewhere. Each of them is extended, and its parts are in spatial relations to one another. There is no a priori reason why all extended entities must be in physical space.

If we now apply these considerations to the next world, as I am conceiving of it, we see that the question "where is it?" simply does not arise. An image-world would have a space of its own. We could not find it anywhere in the space of the physical world, but this would not in the least prevent it from being a spatial world all the same. If you like, it would be its own "where."

I am tempted to illustrate this point by referring to the fairy-tale of Jack and the Beanstalk. I am not of course suggesting that we should take the story seriously. But if we were asked to try to make sense of it, how should we set about it? Obviously the queer world which Jack found was not at the top of the beanstalk in the literal, spatial sense of the words "at the top of." Perhaps he found some very large pole rather like a beanstalk, and climbed up it. But (we shall say) when he got to the top he suffered an abrupt change of consciousness, and began to have a dream or waking vision of a strange country with a giant in it. To choose another and more respectable illustration: In Book VI of Vergil's *Aeneid,* we are told how Aeneas descended into the Cave of Avernus with the Sibyl and walked from there into the other world. If we wished to make the narrative of the illustrious poet intelligible, how should we set about it? We should suppose that Aeneas did go down into the cave, but that once he was there he suffered a change of consciousness, and all the strange experiences which happened afterwards—seeing the River Styx, the Elysian Fields and the rest—were part of a dream or vision which he had. The space he passed through in his journey was an image-space, and the River Styx was not three Roman miles, or any other number of miles, from the cave in which his body was.

It follows that when we speak of "passing" from this world to the next, this passage is not to be thought of as any sort of movement in space. It should rather be thought of as a change of consciousness, analogous to the change which occurs when we "pass" from waking experience to dreaming. It would be a change from the perceptual type of consciousness to another type of consciousness in which perception ceases and imaging replaces it, but unlike the change from waking consciousness to dreaming in being irreversible. I suppose that nearly everyone nowadays who talks of "passing" from this world to the other does think of the transition in this way, as some kind of irreversible change of consciousness, and not as a literal spatial transition in which one goes from one place to another place.

So much for the question "where the next world is," if there be one. I have tried to show that if the next world is conceived of as a world of mental images, the question simply does not arise. I now turn to another difficulty. It may be felt that an image-world is somehow a deception and a sham, not a *real* world at all. I have said that it would be a kind of dream-world. Now when one has a dream in this life, surely the things one is aware of in the dream are not *real* things. No doubt the dreamer really does have various mental images. These images do actually occur. But this is not all that happens. As a result of having these images, the dreamer believes, or takes for granted, that various material objects exist and various physical events occur; and these beliefs are mistaken. For example, he believes that there is a wall in front of him and that by a mere effort of will he succeeds in flying over the top of it. But the wall did not really exist, and he did not really fly over the top of it. He was in a state of delusion. Because of the images which he really did have, there *seemed* to him to be various objects and events which did not really exist at all. Similarly, you may argue, it may *seem* to discarnate minds (if indeed there are such) that there is a world in which they live, and a world not unlike this one. If they have mental images of the appropriate sort, it may even *seem* to them that they have bodies not unlike the ones they had in this life. But surely they will be mistaken. It is all very well to say, with the poet, that "dreams are real while they last"—that dream-objects are only called "unreal" when one wakes up, and normal sense-perceptions begin to occur with which the dream experiences can be contrasted. And it is all very well to conclude from this that if one did *not* wake up, if the change from sense-perception to imaging were irreversible, one would not call one's dream objects unreal, because there would then be nothing with which to contrast them. But would they not still *be* unreal for all that? Surely discarnate minds, according to my account of them, would be in a state of permanent delusion; whereas a dreamer in this life (fortunately for him) is only in a temporary one. And the fact that a delusion goes on for a long time, even forever and ever, does not make it any less delusive. Delusions do not turn themselves into realities just by going on and on. Nor are they turned into realities by the fact that their victim is deprived of the power of detecting their delusiveness.

Now, of course, if it were true that the next life (supposing there is one) is a condition of permanent delusion, we should just have to put up with it. We might not like it: we might think that a state of permanent delusion is a bad state to be in. But our likes and dislikes are irrelevant to the question. I would suggest, however, that this argument about the "delusiveness" or "unreality" of an image-world is based on confusion.

One may doubt whether there is any clear meaning in using the words "real" and "unreal" *tout court*, in this perfectly general and unspecified way. One may properly say, "this is real silver, and that is not," "this is a real pearl and that is not," or again "this is a real pool of water, and that is only a mirage." The point here is that something X is mistakenly believed to be something else Y, because it does resemble Y in some respects. It makes perfectly good sense, then, to say that X is not really Y. This piece of plated brass is not real silver, true enough. It only looks like silver. But for all that, it cannot be called "unreal" in the unqualified sense, in the sense of not existing at all. Even the mirage is something, though it is not the pool of water you took it to be. It is a perfectly good set of visual appearances, though it is not related to other appearances in the way you thought it was; for example, it does not have the relations to tactual appearances, or to visual appearances from other places, which you expected it to have. You may properly say that the mirage is not a real pool of water, or even that it is not a real physical object, and that anyone who thinks it is must be in a state of delusion. But there is no clear meaning in saying that it is just "unreal" *tout court*, without any further specification or explanation. In short, when the word "unreal" is applied to something, one means that it is different from something else, with which it might be mistakenly identified; what that something else is may not be explicitly stated, but it can be gathered from the context.

What, then, could people mean by saying that a next world such as I have described would be "unreal"? If they are saying anything intelligible, they must mean that it is different from something else, something else which it does resemble in some respects, and might therefore be confused with. And what is that something else? It is the present physical world in which we now live. An image-world, then, is only "unreal" in the sense that it is not really physical, though it might be mistakenly thought to be physical by some of those who experience it. But this only amounts to saying that the world I am describing would be an *other* world, other than this present physical world, which is just what it ought to be; other than this present physical world, and yet sufficiently like it to be possibly confused with it, because images do resemble percepts. And what would this otherness consist in? First, in the fact that it is in a *space* which is other than physical space; secondly, and still more important, in the fact that the *causal laws* of an image-world would be different from the laws of physics. And this is also our ground for saying that the events we experience in dreams are "unreal," that is, not really physical, though mistakenly believed by the dreamer to be so. They do in some ways closely resemble physical events, and that is why the mistake is possible. But the causal laws of their occurrence are quite different, as we recognize when we wake up; and just occasionally we recognize it even while we are still asleep.

Now let us consider the argument that the inhabitants of the other world, as I have described it, would be in a state of delusion. I admit that some of them might be. That would be the condition of the people described in the mediumistic communications already referred to—the people who "do not realize that they are dead." Because their images are so like the normal percepts they were accustomed to in this life, they believe mistakenly that they are still living in the physical world. But, as I have already tried to explain, their state of delusion need not be permanent and irremediable. By attending to the relations between one image and another, and applying the ordinary inductive methods by which we ourselves have discovered the causal laws of this present world in which *we* live, they too could discover in time what the causal laws of *their* world are. These laws, we may suppose, would be more like the laws of Freudian psychology than the laws of physics. And once the discovery was made, they would be cured of their delusion. They would find out, perhaps with surprise, that the world they were experiencing was *other* than the physical world which they experienced before, even though like it in some respects.

Let us now try to explore the conception of a world of mental images a little more fully. Would it not be a "*subjective*" world? And surely there would be many *different* next worlds, not just one; and each of them would be private. Indeed, would there not be as many next worlds as there are discarnate minds, and each of them wholly private to the mind which experiences it? In short, it may seem that each of us, when dead, would have his own dream-world, and there would be no common or public next world at all.

"Subjective," perhaps, is a rather slippery word. Certainly, an image-world would have to be subjective in the sense of being mind-dependent, dependent for its existence upon mental processes of one sort or another; images, after all, are mental entities. But I do not think that such a world need be completely private, if telepathy occurs in the next life. I have already mentioned the part which telepathic apparitions might play in it in connection with Mr. Flew's contention that "people are what you meet." But there is more to be said. It is reasonable to suppose that in a disembodied state telepathy would occur more frequently than it does now. It seems likely that in this present life our telepathic powers are constantly being inhibited by our need to adjust ourselves to our physical environment. It even seems likely that many telepathic "impressions" which we receive at the unconscious level are shut out from consciousness by a kind of biologically motivated censorship. Once the pressure of biological needs is removed, we might expect that telepathy would occur continually, and manifest itself in consciousness by modifying and adding to the images which one experiences. (Even in this life, after all, some dreams are telepathic.)

If this is right, an image-world such as I am describing would not be the product of one single mind only, nor would it be purely private. It would be the joint product of a group of telepathically interacting minds and public to all of them. Nevertheless, one would not expect it to have unrestricted publicity. It is likely that there would still be *many* next worlds, a different one for each group of like-minded personalities. I admit I am not quite sure what might be meant by "like-minded" and "unlike-minded" in this connection. Perhaps we could say that two personalities are like-minded if their memories or their characters are sufficiently similar. It might be that Nero and Marcus Aurelius do not have a world in common, but Socrates and Marcus Aurelius do.

So far, we have a picture of many "semi-public" next worlds, if one may put it so; each of them composed of mental images, and yet not wholly private for all that, but public to a limited group of telepathically interacting minds. Or, if you like, after death everyone does have his own dream, but there is still some overlap between one person's dream and another's, because of telepathy.

8

ANTONY FLEW

(1923–)

Can a Man Witness His Own Funeral?*

Flew, though perhaps better known as the editor of Logic and Language *and the author of various works on the British empiricists as well as religious and epistemological problems, has been actively involved in the issues arising out of parapsychological research. He and H. H. Price carried on a series of debates on Price's "Survival and the Idea of 'Another World' " and on issues related to the question of survival. This selection, though not directed specifically at Price, is an attack on the position of Price and of any dualist that seriously maintains the possibility and/or intelligibility of survival of death. When Flew asks whether a man can witness his own funeral, he refers to the situation in which a person would be watching the funeral of his own body from some other point of view. The key words are "survivor," "dead," "person," and "body." Flew argues that it would take a radical change in the meanings of these words for us to make sense of the idea of witnessing one's own funeral. The dualist conception of man is inconsistent with the ways we generally use language. What is needed, Flew maintains, is a clearer idea of a person. He tells us that persons are what we meet. What would it be like to meet a disembodied person?*

* From *Hibbert Journal* (1956), pp. 242–250. Used by permission of the Hibbert Trust.

"Whether we are to live in a future state, as it is the most important question which can possibly be asked, so it is the most intelligible one which can be expressed in language" (Bishop Butler in the dissertation *Of Personal Identity*).

I

The purposes of this paper are, *first*, to try to begin to raise what Butler called "strange perplexities"* about the meaningfulness of this question and, *second*, to attempt to dispose of the counter-thesis, maintained by Schlick, that it must be significant because the possibility being discussed is not merely conceivable but also imaginable. These are very strictly limited objectives. We shall not, and shall not pretend

* *Op. cit.*

to, do more than attack these two of the vast complex of problems, both
logical and empirical, compendiously described as the questions of
Survival and Immortality.

II

Now suppose someone offers the gambit "We all of us survive death"
or "We all of us live forever." Might we not reply "Whatever in the
world do you mean? For, in the ordinary senses of the words you use,
the former sentence is self-contradictory and the latter denies one of
the most securely established of all empirical generalisations; for it is
the contrary of that traditional darling of the logicians 'All men are
mortal'." As the objections to the two sentences are different, let us deal
with each of them separately.

"We all of us survive death" is self-contradictory because we use the
words "death" and "survival" and their derivatives in such a way that
the classification of the crew of a torpedoed ship into "Dead" and
"Survivors" is both exclusive and exhaustive. Every member of the
crew must (logical "must") have either died or survived: and no member of the crew could (logical "could") have both died and survived.
It is easy to overlook that "We all of us survive death" is self-contradictory because we all habitually and wisely give all utterances the benefit
of the doubt. Generously assuming that other people usually have something intelligible to express even when they speak or write in unusual
or incorrect ways, we attempt to attach sense even to expressions which
are strictly self-contradictory. This tendency is frequently exploited by
advertisers. Posters advertising the film *Bachelor Husband* catch the
eye precisely because the expression "bachelor husband" is self-contradictory, and therefore paradoxical. We tend to puzzle over the title,
to ponder—doubtless to the advertiser's eventual profit—over the non-
linguistic improprieties suggested by this linguistically improper expression. If we see the headline "We survived death!" we do not just
exclaim (in the tone of voice of rigid logical schoolmasters) "Nonsense:
you either survive or you die!", but, curiosity aroused, we read on to
learn how the death was only 'death' (in inverted commas), that the
people in question had only pretended, been reported, appeared, to
die; but had not of course in fact died. Sometimes, for instance, people
show all the usual 'symptoms' of death, all the usually reliable signs
that they will not walk, or talk, or joke again, but then, surprisingly,
recover and do walk and talk and joke once more. This happened quite
often in World War II: Russian doctors in particular reported many
cases of patients who showed the usual indications of death—the heart
not beating and so forth—but were brought back to life by shock
treatments, blood transfusions, and suchlike. These patients thus sur-

vived 'death' (in inverted commas). The doctors then adapted their language—or at least the language of *Soviet War News* (London) was adapted—to meet the new situation: "We cannot survive death" was retained as the expression of a necessary truth; and the expression "clinical death" was introduced as a more precise and less awkward substitute for "death" (in inverted commas) to refer to the condition of the patients who showed all the usual 'symptoms' but who nevertheless might or might not survive to tell the tale. "We survive death" thus was, and remains, self-contradictory. The paradox use of "survives death" in advertising and headlines, and the inverted-comma use of 'death' in which people can be said to return from the "dead" (in inverted commas), do not in the least weigh against this contention. They positively reinforce it: it is precisely because "He survived death" is self-contradictory that it is a good headline; it is precisely because "to survive death" is self-contradictory that the doctors put the word "death" between warning inverted commas when first they had to report that a patient survived 'death,' and later introduced the new expression "clinical death" to replace the makeshift 'death' (in inverted commas) when similar cases occurred repeatedly.

"We all of us live forever" is, on the other hand, not self-contradictory but just as a matter of fact false, being as it is the flat contrary of the massively confirmed generalisation "All men are mortal." (Though if you choose to use the latter expression to express not a factual generalisation but an artificial truth of logic, making it true by definition that all *men* are mortal, thus incurring the probably unwelcome consequence that on this definition neither the prophet Elijah nor—on the Roman view—the Virgin Mary can count as human beings; then, of course, "we all of us [men] live forever" will on your definition become self-contradictory, and not merely false as a matter of manifest empirical fact.) But, like "We all of us survive death," "We all of us live forever" has what we might call 'headline value.' Both are 'shockers' and thus catch the eye and arouse curiosity. They make us wonder what the writer is up to, what is the story which he is going to tell under these arresting headlines. For surely he cannot really be intending to say something so obviously nonsensical or so notoriously false as what at first glance he seems to be saying.

Now many stories have been and still more could be told under these headlines. People have claimed that "We all of us live for ever, *because* the evil (and sometimes even the good) that men do lives after them." People have argued that "We survive death, *because* our descendants will live on after we are dead." And in the variety and irrelevance of their supporting reasons they have revealed the variety and irrelevance of the theses which they have been concerned to maintain when they used these and similar paradoxical expressions. The only use with which we are concerned here—and certainly the only use which would justify Butler's claim that here was "the most important question which can possibly be asked"—is that in which they are intended to support or express what Wisdom has called "the logically unique expectation,"* the expectation that we shall see and feel, or at any rate and more non-committally, that we shall 'have experiences' after we are dead. Therefore we shall take it that the person who has said "We all of us survive death" or "We all of us live forever" was making a move intended to justify such expectations.

And against this move the simple-minded counter-move is to attempt a sort of philosophical fools' mate. Clearly this expectation cannot (logical "cannot") be well grounded unless we are going to exist after our deaths. But we have been insisting that it is not merely false but actually self-contradictory to say that we survive death. So we cannot (logical "cannot") exist after our deaths. Therefore these logically unique expectations cannot be well founded. Indeed the suggestion on which they are based, the assumption which they presuppose (*viz.* that "We survive death") is self-contradictory and therefore senseless.

III

Well, of course there are several possible defences against this sort of attack; and the possible variations on these defences are innumerable. The traditional one depends on the distinction between body and mind, or body and soul (what Professor Ryle, unaccountably ignoring Plato, insists on calling the *Cartesian* Myth; a notion which—far from being a philosopher's fancy—is incapsulated in the idiom of innumerable languages and is a widespread, though not universal, element in folklore and religion). The first stage is to maintain that people consist of two elements, one, the body, visible, tangible and corporeal, the other, the mind or soul, invisible, intangible and incorporeal. The second stage is to maintain that we are our souls or minds. This stage is indispensable: unless we are our souls the survival of our souls will not be our survival; and the news that our souls were to be preserved after we died would be of no more importance or concern to us than the news that any other parts of us—our appendices, say—were to be preserved. Granted these two presuppositions (and "presuppositions" is surely the *mot juste*: for they are rarely either distinguished from one another or argued for) it

---

* In 'Gods' *PAS* 44/5, reprinted in *Logic and Language* I, A. G. N. Flew, ed. (Blackwell, 1951).

is then significant and even plausible to say that we (our incorporeal souls, that is) survive death (which is "the mere death of the body"). The desire to allow doctrines of personal immortality to be significant and plausible is one of the main drives behind dualist conceptions, and one perhaps insufficiently stressed by Professor Ryle in *The Concept of Mind*. But this is a vast and another subject; here we propose to concentrate exclusively on one more modern defence, that which claims that "I shall survive my death" cannot be self-contradictory and therefore senseless, because it refers to a possibility which is not merely conceivable but imaginable.

This argument was used by Moritz Schlick* "I take it for granted that . . . we are concerned with the question of survival after 'death'."— [His inverted commas. These surely tacitly concede the claim that "to survive death" is a self-contradictory expression: compare the similar tacit admission made in the tombstone insistence "Not dead but sleeping". A.F.] I think we may agree with Professor Lewis when he says about this hypothesis: "Our understanding of what would verify it has no lack of clarity. In fact I can easily imagine, e.g. witnessing the funeral of my own body and continuing to exist without a body, for nothing is easier than to describe a world which differs from our ordinary world only in the complete absence of all data which I would call parts of my own body. We must conclude that immortality, in the sense defined, should not be regarded as a metaphysical 'problem', but is an empirical hypothesis, because it possesses logical verifiability. It could be verified by following the prescription 'Wait until you die!'." A briefer and more puckish version of the same argument can be found in John Wisdom's unending saga *Other Minds*. "I know indeed what it would be like to witness my own funeral—the men in tall silk hats, the flowers, and the face beneath the glass-topped coffin"* and it is also deployed by Dr. Casimir Lewy in his 'Is the Notion of Disembodied Existence Self-contradictory?'

So far as I know this argument has never been challenged: presumably partly because we can most of us imagine (image) a scene such as Wisdom describes; and partly because no one wants to arrogate to himself the right to decide what Wisdom or Schlick or anyone other than he himself can or cannot imagine (image). But the argument can and should be challenged: and it can be done without arbitrarily pre-

* *Philosophical Review* (July, 1936), p. 356. Reprinted in Feigl and Sellars' *Readings in Philosophical Analysis*, pp. 159–60.

* *Mind* (1942), p. 2 and *Other Minds* (Blackwell, 1952), p. 36.

scribing any limit to Wisdom's obviously very considerable imaginative powers. For there is all the difference in the world between: imagining what it would be like to witness my own funeral (which requires only a minor effort); and imagining what it would be like to witness me witnessing *my own* funeral (which is logically impossible. Or at least, less dogmatically, is very far from being a logically straightforward matter). If it really is I who witness it then it is not my funeral but only 'my funeral' (in inverted commas): and if it really is my funeral then I cannot be a witness, for I shall be dead and in the coffin.

Of course I can imagine many situations which might be described as my watching 'my own funeral' (in inverted commas): I can remember Harry Lime in the film *The Third Man* watching 'his own funeral,' and of course I can imagine being in the same situation as Harry Lime; but it was not really Harry Lime's own funeral, and what I can imagine would not really be mine. Again I can imagine my own funeral—I shall not try to better Wisdom's whimsical description of such a scene—but now what I am imagining is not *my* witnessing *my own* funeral but merely my own funeral. (Parenthetically, it should be pointed out that Wisdom is far too good a writer to have committed himself to the former—and improper—description of his imaginings (imagings). What he wrote was "I know indeed what it would be like to witness my own funeral." Unfortunately, this will not, under examination, support his thesis: which requires that he should be able to imagine his surviving his own death and his witnessing his own funeral: which seems to be impossible, since the latter supposition, like the former, is apparently self-contradictory).

But surely this is merely slick? Surely I can perfectly well imagine my own funeral, really my own funeral with my body in the coffin and not a substitute corpse or a weight of bricks; with me there watching it all, but invisible, intangible, a disembodied spirit? Well, yes, this seems all right: until someone asks the awkward question "Just how does all this differ from your imagining your own funeral without your being there at all (except as the corpse in the coffin)?"

Certainly Schlick could imagine, as he claimed, "the funeral of his own body": though it is perhaps a pity that he should describe what he imagined in this way and not, more naturally, as "his own funeral." But then he goes on to talk of imagining his "continuing to exist without a body": which he tries to justify by claiming that "nothing is easier than to describe a world which differs from our ordinary world only in the complete absence of all data which I would call parts of my own body." But the fact that we can all of us describe, or even imagine, a world which would differ from our ordinary world only in the complete absence of all data describable as parts of our respective bodies has not, by itself, the slightest tendency to show that anyone could imagine or describe a world in which, after his funeral, he continued to exist without a body. By itself it merely shows that we can each imagine what the world would be like if he were obliterated from it entirely, and no trace of his corpse remained. Schlick has misdescribed what he could imagine. Misled by the fact that a man can easily imagine what his funeral will be like, and hence what it would be like to watch it, it is tempting to insist that he can imagine what it would be like *for him* to watch *his own* funeral. Schlick is thus able to "conclude that immortality, in the sense defined . . . is an empirical hypothesis. . . . It could be verified by following the prescription 'Wait until you die!'." But he has not defined a sense of "immortality" at all: apparently he has merely misdescribed some rather humdrum exercises of his imagination in an extremely exciting and misleading way. He has failed to say anything to prevent his opponent from objecting to his conclusion: "But, on the contrary, nothing whatever could be verified (by me) by (my) following the prescription 'Wait until you die!': (for me my) death is so final that it is logically impossible (for me) to survive it to verify any hypotheses at all."

IV

We have now fulfilled the two strictly limited purposes of this paper. But perhaps it is worth while to add comments on three other possible objections to the attempted philosophical fools' mate; emphasising that nothing we have said or shall say must be interpreted to mean that we ourselves consider it to be decisive. *First* it may be said that this is all too cut and dried, the logic of our ordinary language is not as sharp, clear, and uncomplicated as has been made out. This is true and important. To take only one example: any adequate treatment of the logic of survival and immortality (the enquiry initiated by Plato's *Phaedo*) would demand the use of the distinction between death and dissolution; just as any full discussion of the logic of metempsychosis and pre-existence (the enquiry initiated by Plato's *Meno*) would have to take account of the parallel distinction between birth and conception. But for our first purpose, the raising of "strange perplexities," soft shading and rich detail is confusing, while for the second, dealing with one counter-move crudely made, it is unnecessary.

Second, it may be suggested that, although Schlick and Wisdom as a matter of fact only succeeded in imagining their own funerals and the world going on without them (and then misdescribed and/or mistook the significance of what they did imagine), it would nevertheless be quite possible to imagine all sorts of bizarre phenomena which we should feel inclined to describe as "the activities of disembodied people" or even as "evidence of survival." This again is true and important. Anyone who has read at all widely in the literature of psychical research must often have felt inclined to apply such expressions to phenomena, or putative phenomena, recorded in this literature. But it is all too easy to misinterpret what we shall be doing if we do allow ourselves to describe such *outré* phenomena in these paradoxical ways. In fact we shall be attaching sense to an expression—"disembodied person"—for which previously no sense had been provided: either directly as an idiomatic expression; or indirectly through the uses given to its constituent words. We are thereby introducing a new sense of the word "person." Yet it may appear to us and to others as if we have discovered a new sort of person, or a new state in which a person can be. Whereas a disembodied person is no more a special sort of person than is an imaginary person: and (except in the Services—which have their peculiar sense of the word "disembodied") disembodiment is no more a possible state of a person than is non-existence.

Now it is perfectly possible to specify a sense for the expression "disembodied person": just as it is possible to attach sense to any expression, even one which on present usage would be self-contradictory. The difficulty is to attach a sense to it so that some expression incorporating it will, if true, provide a ground for the logically unique expectation. In their present use person words have logical liaisons of the very greatest importance: personal identity is the necessary condition of both accountability and expectation; which is only to say that it is unjust to reward or punish someone for something unless (as a minimum condition) he is the same person who did the deed; and also that it is absurd to expect experiences for Flew in 1984 unless (as a minimum condition) there is going to be a person in existence in 1984 who will be the same person as I. The difficulty, not necessarily insuperable, is to change the use of person words so radically that it becomes significant to talk of people surviving dissolution, without changing it to such an extent that these vital logical liaisons are lost.

The *third* obvious criticism returns us to the traditional foundation for what we might call a "logic of immortality." The objection might be made that it has been assumed throughout that people are merely bodies, that people are bodies and nothing more. Even though we have excluded discussion of the traditional dualisms from this paper, this criticism has to be met. It is met by pointing out that no one has either argued or assumed anything of the sort. What has been done is merely to take for granted the ordinary meaning and use of person words, and to use them—we hope—in the conventional and proper way: a very different matter. People are what you meet. Person words refer to men and women like you and me and the other fellow. They are taught by pointing at people: indeed how else could they or should they be taught? They do not refer to anything invisible and elusive, to any mysterious incorporeal substances. Even children can be taught them, can and do know what is meant by "Father," "I," "man," "person," or "butcher." But that is not to say that they refer merely or at all to bodies. "Person" is no synonym for "body": though "body" is used peculiarly in the Services as a slightly pejorative substitute for "person," the degrading point of the substitution would be lost if the words were really synonymous; there is a difference, a difference of life and death, between "We brought a person down from the foot of the Z'mutt ridge" and "We brought a body down from the foot of the Z'mutt ridge." Person words do not mean either bodies or souls nor yet any combination of the two: "I" is no synonym for "my body" nor yet for "my mind" or "my soul" nor yet for any combination of these (as anyone who tries a few substitutions must soon discover). If we are indeed compound of two such disparate elements, that is a contingent fact about people and not part of what is meant by "person" and other person words. To suggest that it has been assumed that people are merely bodies is surely to reveal that you yourself assume that everyone must be a dualist—or at least a dualist with one component missing—a sort of one-legged dualist. And this is a mistake. But though this third criticism is mistaken, it does go straight to the heart of the matter. For the whole position does depend on the fact that people are what you meet: we do not just meet the sinewy containers in which other people are kept; they do not just encounter the fleshy houses which we ourselves inhabit. The whole position depends on the obvious, crucial, but constantly neglected fact that person words mean what they do mean. This paper has consisted in insistent and obstinate underlining of this fact; and in pointing out two implications of it, important but limited in scope: that Butler was wrong to deny that there were logical difficulties about the notion of a future life; and that Schlick's short way with these difficulties will not do. Perhaps attention to it can transform discussion of the problems of Survival and Immortality in a way very similar to that in which Moore's insistence that we do know that some material things exist has transformed discussions of Idealism and of the problems of Epistemology. As Berkeley, with his usual insight, remarked, "the grand mistake is that we know not what we mean by 'we', 'selves' or 'mind', etc."

Further Reading On
PERSONS, MINDS, AND SURVIVAL AFTER DEATH

Ayers, A. J. *The Concept of a Person.* London: Macmillan, 1963.

Bain, Alexander. *Mind and Body.* London: Henry King, 1873.

Broad, C. D. *The Mind and Its Place in Nature.* London: Routledge & Kegan Paul, 1925.

Brody, Baruch. "Locke on the Identity of Persons." *American Philosophical Quarterly,* October 1972.

Buford, T. O. (ed.). *Essays on Other Minds.* Urbana: University of Illinois Press, 1970.

Butler, Clarke W. "The Mind-Body Problem: A Nonmaterialistic Identity Thesis." *Idealistic Studies,* September 1972.

Campbell, C. A. *On Selfhood and Godhood.* London: Allen & Unwin, 1957.

Campbell, K. *Body and Mind.* Garden City: Doubleday, 1970.

Carney, James D. "The Compatability of the Identity Theory with Dualism." *Mind,* January 1971.

Chappell, V. C. (ed.). *The Philosophy of David Hume.* New York: Modern Library, 1963.

Chatterjee, S.C., and D. M. Dalta. *An Introduction to Indian Philosophy.* Calcutta: Calcutta University Press, 1955.

Crosson, F. J., and K. M. Sayre (eds.). *Philosophy and Cybernetics.* Notre Dame: Notre Dame University Press, 1967.

Ducasse, C. J. *Nature, Mind, and Death.* LaSalle, Illinois: Open Court, 1951.

Ducasse, C. J. *The Belief in Life After Death.* Springfield: Charles C. Thomas, 1961.

Epstein, Fanny L. "The Metaphysics of Mind-Body Identity Theories." *American Philosophical Quarterly,* April 1973.

Flew, Antony. *Body, Mind, and Death.* New York: Macmillan, 1964.

Frondizi, Risieri. *The Nature of the Self.* New Haven, Connecticut: Yale University Press, 1953.

Gert, Bernard. "Personal Identity and the Body." *Dialogue: Canadian Philosophical Review,* 1971.

Gustafson, Donald (ed.). *Essays in Philosophical Psychology.* Garden City: Doubleday, 1964.

Hiriyana, M. *Outlines of Indian Philosophy*. London: Allen & Unwin, 1964.

James, William. *Principles of Psychology*. New York: Longmans, Green, 1890.

Laird, J. *The Problems of Self*. London: Macmillan, 1917.

Laslett, P. (ed.). *The Physical Basis of Mind*. Oxford: Blackwell, 1951.

Locke, D. *Myself and Others: A Study in Our Knowledge of Minds*. Oxford: Oxford University Press, 1968.

Lovejoy, A. O. *The Revolt Against Dualism*. Lasalle: Open Court, 1955.

MacMurray, John. *The Self as Agent*. London: Faber and Faber, 1953.

Mead, George H. *Mind, Self, and Society*. Chicago: University of Chicago Press, 1934.

Morick, H. (ed.). *Wittgenstein and the Problem of Other Minds*. New York: McGraw Hill, 1967.

Murphy, Gardner. *Challenge of Psychical Research*. New York: Harper & Brothers, 1961.

Nelson, John O. "Criteria and Personal Identity." *Ratio*, June 1973.

Olding, A. "Flew on Souls." *Sophia*, October 1970.

Ousley, J. Douglas. "The Possibility of Life After Death." *Religious Studies*, June 1973.

Penelhem, T. "Hume on Personal Identity." *The Philosophical Review*, October 1955.

Perry, John. "Can the Self Divide?" *Journal of Philosophy*, September 1972.

Pratt, J. B. *Matter and Spirit*. New York: Macmillan, 1926.

Purtill, Richard L. "Disembodied Survival." *Sophia*, July 1973.

Quinton, Anthony M. "The Soul." *Journal of Philosophy*, July 1962.

Radhakrishnan, S. *Indian Philosophy*. London: Allen & Unwin, 1964.

Radhakrishnan, S., and P. T. Raju (eds.). *The Concept of a Man: A Study in Comparative Philosophy*. Allen & Unwin, 1969.

Rorty, Amelie Oksenberg. "Persons, Policies, and Bodies." *International Philosophical Quarterly*, March 1973.

Rorty, Amelie Oksenberg. "The Transformations for Persons." *Philosophy*, July 1973.

Ryle Gilbert. *The Concept of Mind*. London: Hutchinson, 1949.

Shoemaker, Sydney. *Self-Knowledge and Self-Identity*. Ithaca: Cornell University Press, 1963.

Smythies, J. R. (ed.). *Brain and Mind.* London: Routledge & Kegan Paul, 1965.

Stout, G. F. *Mind and Matter.* Cambridge: Cambridge University Press, 1931.

Strawson, P. F. *Individuals.* London: Methuen, 1959.

Vessey, G. N. A. *The Embodied Mind.* London: Allen & Unwin, 1965.

Wisdom, John. *Problems of Mind and Matter.* Cambridge: Cambridge University Press, 1934.

Wittgenstein, Ludwig. *The Blue and Brown Books.* Oxford: Blackwell, 1958.

PART V

KNOWLEDGE, CERTAINTY, AND DOUBT

Walter F. Prince's Dream of the Decapitated Woman

THE DREAM

Date of Dream, Nov. 27, 1917.

On the night following Nov. 27, I dreamed that I had in my hands a small paper with an order printed in red ink, for the execution of the bearer, a woman. I did not seem to have any distinct notion of the reason for her condemnation, but it seemed that I inferred that it was for a political offense, and some thought of the French Revolution seems faintly connected with it; though it may be that I was only reminded of the execution of such as Madame Roland. The woman appeared to have voluntarily brought the order, and she expressed herself as willing to die, if I would only hold her hand.

I remember her looks quite well; she was slender of the willowy type, had blonde hair, small girlish features, and was rather pretty. She sat down to die without any appearance of reluctance, seeming fully calm and resigned. It was not clear where we were, but she seemed to me to be in a chair. I should have thought her about 35.

Then the light went out and it was dark. I could not tell how she was put to death, but soon I felt her hand grip mine (my hand), *and knew that the deed was being done. Then I felt one* hand (of mine) *on the hair of the head, which was loose and severed from the body, and felt the moisture of blood. Then the fingers of my other* hand *were caught in her teeth, and the mouth opened and shut several times as the teeth refastened on my* hand, *and I was filled with the horror of the thought of a severed but living head. Here the dream faded out.*

WALTER F. PRINCE.
New York, Nov. 30, 1917.

THE EVENT

New York Evening Telegram, Nov. 29, 1917

HEAD SEVERED BY TRAIN AS WOMAN ENDS HER LIFE

Deliberately placing her head in front of the wheels of a train that had stopped at the Long Island Rail Road Station at Hollis, L.I., so that the wheels would pass over her when it started, a woman identified by letters in her handbag as Mrs. Sarah A. Hand, thirty years old, of No. —— West —— St., ended her life early to-day. In the handbag, beside the letters, was found a letter rambling in its contents, that predicted the existence of life in her body after death and that her head would still continue to live after it had been severed from her body.

The husband of the woman, —— Hand, was notified at the —— Street address, and he went to Hollis in a taxicab. He said his wife had been missing from home since November 27. Since the death of her little girl several months ago, he asserted, Mrs. Hand had acted strangely.

Long Island Farmer, Nov. 30, 1917

DEMONSTRATED A THEORY

WOMAN WHO BELIEVED HER HEAD AND HER BODY COULD RETAIN

LIFE IF SEPARATED CAUSED BEHEADMENT BY CAR WHEEL

WAS INSANE SEVERAL YEARS

Mrs. Sarah A. Hand, 30, of Manhattan, had a theory that her body and her head could live independently of each other. Her friends said she was crazy; but she had the courage of her convictions. So, late Wednesday night, she went to Hollis and, to prove her contention, lay down on the Long Island Rail Road tracks and permitted a train to run over her neck, cutting off her head as cleanly as though the job had been done with an axe. The finding of her head and body, and of a letter beside it, revealed the theory and its execution. The letter read as follows:

"Please stop all trains immediately. My head is on the track and will be run over by those steam engines and will prevent me from proving my condition. You see, my body is alive without my head, and my head is alive without my body. It is suffering where

*it is, and if smashed in small bits will suffer just the same. So
please, I beg, stop all trains so my head will be saved from this
terrible torture. My head is alive and can see and talk, and I
must get it to prove my case to the law. No one believed me when
I said I would never die and when my head was chopped off I
would still be alive. Everyone laughed and said I was crazy, so
now I have proved this terrible life to all. Please call my husband
up at Audubon ———, or Academy ———, N.Y.*

*"Please have all trains stopped to save my head from being cut
in fragments. I need it to talk to prove my condition and have
the doctor arrested for this terrible life he put me in."*

*This missive was not signed. It was in a plain envelope, ad-
dressed "To whom it may concern."*

*Mrs. Hand's body and head were seen by the crew of an east-
bound train that left Hollis at 11:15 o'clock Wednesday night.
She had placed her neck across the outside westbound rail, close
to the station. The station has an elevated concrete platform. It
is believed Mrs. Hand crouched for some time under this platform, out of sight of anyone, waiting for a train to stop at Hollis.*

*When one did, it was evident by the position of her body that
she crawled out from her shelter and put her head under the
wheels. She lay on her stomach, gripping the ties with her hands,
to prevent the wheel pushing her along the rail. As a result, the
wheel cut her head off without inflicting any other mark or injury
except a deep scratch on her face.*

*Her husband was notified and hurried to Jamaica. He told the
authorities that his wife had been deranged for several years. On
an occasion she became much interested in a murder trial in
progress in Georgia, where the family then lived. The trial preyed
on her mind, and, when her son was born, she conceived the idea
that he would be a murderer. The mother's mental condition grew
steadily worse. Hoping a change of scene would be beneficial,
her husband came to New York.*

*Recently, he said, his wife had been in a sanatorium. She
begged to be taken home for Thanksgiving, so he took her out of
the sanatorium last Saturday, sending for his mother to watch
over her. On Tuesday she seemed perfectly normal, and went to
visit a sister in Manhattan. She never reached her sister's. Following her disappearance her husband spent all his time search-*

ing morgues and hospitals. He also sent out a general police alarm. He said he did not know why she had traveled to Hollis, as she knew no one there.

Near the body was a butcher's knife and cleaver, bright and new. It is thought Mrs. Hand intended at first to demonstrate her theory with them, but finally decided that a railroad train would sever her head more effectually. She had written two other letters besides the one found, but afterwards tore them into pieces so small they could not be put together. These pieces lay beside the butcher's tools under the railroad platform. There was also a pocketbook containing $1.50 and some small personal belongings.

COINCIDENCES BETWEEN THE DREAM AND THE EVENT.

The Dream.	*The Event.*
1. (a) A woman,	1. (a) A woman,
(b) apparently about 35 years old.	(b) about 31 years old,
(c) slender,	(c) slender,
(d) with very light hair;	(d) with "golden-brown" hair Semi-coincidental particular),
(e) was rather pretty.	(e) said to be pretty. (Portrait, however, not recognized by me.)
2. (a) Carried the order of execution, and was "willing to die,"	2. (a) Her death was voluntary and willed by herself,
(b) and she went to the place of "execution."	(b) and she went to the place of suicide.
3. (a) The "execution" was bloody (not electrocution, strangling, *et al.*),	3. (a) Her death was bloody,
(b) by decapitation.	(b) by decapitation,
(c) and the head seemed to be entire afterwards.	(c) and, as the woman hoped it would be, the head was not "smashed."

4. The "execution" took place in darkness.

4. The head was cut off at about 11:15 in the night.

5. The word "hand," or the idea of a hand, kept appearing. The woman asked me to hold her hand, then her hand gripped my hand, then my hand felt her hair, then her teeth fastened on my hand.

5. The woman's name was Sarah A. Hand.

6. (a) After decapitation, the head acted as though, and impressed me very disagreeably that it was, still alive.

6. (a) She left a paper declaring that her head would live apart from her body, and asserting that she had previously maintained that "when my head was chopped off I would still be alive."

(b) The acts which manifested life were in connection with the mouth (gripping my hand).

(b) The act, which the note found with the body stated that the still living head would perform, was also one connected with the mouth (talking).

7. The dream took place in a house on Franklin Place, near Bowne Avenue, Flushing, L.I.

7. The event occurred near the railroad station in Hollis, L.I., about six miles from Flushing.

8. The dream was during the night of Nov. 27–28, 1917.

8. The event took place less than twenty-four hours afterward, at about 11:15 P.M., on Nov. 28, 1917.

INQUIRY

PRINCE'S strange dream of the decapitated woman and its startling similarity to an event that occurred about 24 hours later suggest that he possessed some knowledge about the future. In the parlance of parapsychology, his dream was precognitive; that is, he purportedly learned of certain aspects of an event before it did in fact occur. There are many difficulties with the notion of precognition, not the least of which is that the standard view of time cannot accommodate it.* But our specific concern here is with knowledge claims: what, if anything, could Prince legitimately claim to have known regarding the suicide of Mrs. Sarah Hand on the basis of his dream?

Suppose that upon learning of Mrs. Hand's grotesque death Prince had said, "I knew that was going to happen" or, more generally, "I knew that something like that was about to happen." How should we understand his utterance? Under normal circumstances, what does Prince claim when he claims to know something? What is it to say that someone knows anything at all?

There seem to be at least two different senses of knowing. One sense is illustrated by the sentence, "Henry Aaron knows how to hit a baseball" (S¹), the other by the sentence, "W. F. Prince knows that a pretty blonde woman about age 35 will voluntarily meet death by decapitation" (S²). S¹ is a report on the talents of Henry Aaron. To know *how* to do something is to possess a skill, what some have called "practical knowledge." S², on the other hand, reports that Prince believes or is of the opinion that a certain proposition is true. It has nothing to do with the mastery of a technique or a skill. It is with this S² sense of knowing that we are to be primarily concerned, although we should not lose sight of the fact that a complete divorce of these two senses of knowledge cannot usually be exacted. What

---

* See my *Philosophers in Wonderland: Philosophy and Psychical Research* (St. Paul: Llewellyn Publications, 1975), Symposium III, "Time and Precognition."

one knows how to do is usually intimately related to certain propositions that one knows to be the case, and "I know that X" may often be properly analyzed as "I know how to do X." Saying that Johnny knows that Caesar was assassinated by members of the Roman Senate is saying at least that when he is tested or asked the question "Who assassinated Caesar?" Johnny will know *how* to answer correctly.

If Johnny does know that X (Caesar was assassinated by members of the Roman Senate), then X must be true. How could Johnny know X if X is false? If he were to say that he knows that Caesar was assassinated by a frustrated office-seeker from Gaul, a natural response would be to inform him that he cannot know that. He may *think* he knows it, he may feel certain of it, but if it can be shown to be false, then he does not know it.

In the *Theaetetus* Plato, through Socrates' examination of the theory that knowledge is perception, argues that knowledge cannot be relative to the knower. In effect, Plato argues that the theory that knowledge is perception endorses the view that what seems to be true to someone is true for that person. Hence, if it seems or appears to Johnny to be true that there is a diamond on the rug, then it is true that there is a diamond on the rug. This is but an extension of the old Sophist doctrine that "man is the measure of all things" or that *true* means "true for me." The world of our sense experience is constantly changing. For example, think of what happens when you spot an object (Y) at some way off (D^1), and it seems to you to be a barn. As you approach it (D^2), it appears to be too small to be a barn and seems to be a house. Then, as you finally arrive at it (D^3), you discover it to be a mound of dirt and old branches from a fallen tree. If knowledge is perception, then at D^1 "Object Y is a barn" seems to be true, at D^2 "Object Y is a house" seems to be true, and at D^3 "Object Y is a mound of dirt and branches" seems to be true. Object Y has not, however, changed, as has your observational position, and it would seem correct to say "Object Y is a mound of dirt and branches" at D^1, D^2, and D^3, in spite of what appeared to you to have been the case. Had you stopped at D^2 and decided not to examine object Y further, you might say that you know Y is a house, but anyone knowing the facts most likely would argue that you only think you know that. Its not being the case is a sufficient reason for showing a knowledge claim to be incorrect. Knowing, then, cannot merely be identified with perceiving, though that does not mean there can be no perceptual knowledge.

A further reason for reluctance to accept the relativistic view that knowledge is perception is to be found in the way we use and respond to knowledge claims. J. L. Austin, in a famous paper entitled "Other Minds," * points out that a sentence such as "I know that X is a house but I may be wrong" is always inappropriate as long as "I may be wrong" is understood to be more than a general rider to the effect that human beings are not infallible. It is always possible for one to be wrong, but the clause "I may be wrong" is in order only when one has some concrete reasons to suppose he may be mistaken in the case at issue, and if one has such reasons, he has no business claiming to know. "I know Y is a house" serves to give other people my authority for saying they know it too. I ought to utter it only when I have "covered myself" regarding mistakes. Of course the relativist might maintain that "I know Y is a house" really translates only to "It seems to me to be a house," and because I cannot reasonably be said to make mistakes about what seems to me, then I am warranted in saying, "I know. . . ." This argument, however, misses the point and, even worse, completely destroys the notions of making a mistake and getting something correct. It is not that I cannot be mistaken about what seems to me, and hence I am always correct about it; being correct where there can be no possibility of error is vacuous. Hence it would make little sense to say I am correct. Being mistaken amounts to having not been in a position to transmit authority, having not been in a position to know, despite what seemed to one to have been the case.

Let us return to Johnny's claim to know that Caesar was assassinated by members of the Roman Senate. Could Johnny be said to know that if he did not really believe it and believed instead that Caesar was actually assassinated by a disappointed office-seeker from Gaul? Certainly we would tend to doubt that Johnny really knew who assassinated Caesar. Perhaps knowledge is justified true belief, a view also examined by Plato in the *Theaetetus*.

What is meant by "justified true belief"? Those beliefs one entertains about most matters, for example, obviously may be either true or false. To say a belief is true is to say that it has been or will be proved to be the case, has been or will be verified by experience. My belief that I hear a meadowlark singing in the fields behind my home is true if indeed such a bird is to be found singing in those fields. If no such bird or no traces of such a bird can be located in those fields, or if no one who knows bird calls can verify that the sounds are characteristic of a meadowlark, then the likelihood that

* *Proceedings of the Aristotelian Society*, Suppl. Vol. XX, 1946.

my belief was not a true one increases perhaps to the point where
other people would say that I falsely believed the bird I heard singing was a meadowlark.

Suppose I were to tell you as we walk through the fields that I
believe the bird we just heard was a meadowlark. You ask me how
I came to believe that, and I reply that I have no good reasons for
believing it. I really know nothing of birds, especially meadowlarks,
but it seemed to be the thing to say. It turns out, however, that you
are a dedicated bird watcher and that the bird we just heard was
indeed a meadowlark; hence my belief was true, but my believing
it certainly was not based on evidence and thereby was not justified. Would we say that I knew that the bird was a meadowlark?
Would we not say that I was lucky or that I guessed correctly? And
would it not be more comfortable to describe Prince as having correctly believed, even guessed, a woman (possibly even one named
Hand) would voluntarily submit to a bloody death, rather than to
say that his dream experiences count as evidence and that he was
justified in so believing and therefore that he knew?

We need to clarify the notions of evidence and justification. If
we say that Prince's dream does not count as good evidence for
justifying or grounding a belief, what does count? Under what conditions might we begin to count such dreams as evidence? If I had
answered when asked how I knew that the singing was that of a
meadowlark, that I had studied the songs of field birds, that the
meadowlark is a particular favorite of mine, and that I had just seen
one flying near the spot from which the song seemed to come, then,
chances are, my claim would be accepted. The evidence, even the
gathering of evidence, however, is not isolated. In order to have
evidence to support my claim to know that the bird (assuming it
was a bird and not a person practicing bird calls) we just heard
was a meadowlark, I must know certain other propositions to be
true, e.g., meadowlarks nest in fields, the song of a meadowlark is
a loud and flutelike whistle, and meadowlarks frequent this part
of Minnesota. How is this knowledge established? By evidence? It
would appear that either the definition is circular: to have knowledge is to have evidence which is to have knowledge, etc., or it
must be but a step in an infinite regress series.

In a recently published collection of his last notes,* Ludwig Wittgenstein offers the following characterizations that should help

* *On Certainty*

us better understand the relationship between evidence and knowledge.

> 102. . . . My convictions do form a system, a structure . . . .
>
> 105. All testing, all confirmation and disconfirmation of a hypothesis takes place already within a system. And this system is not a more or less arbitrary and doubtful point of departure for all our arguments: no, it belongs to the essence of what we call an argument. The system is not so much the point of departure, as the element in which argu-ments have their life . . . .
>
> 150. . . . Must I not begin to trust somewhere? That is to say: some-where I must begin with not doubting; and that is not, so to speak, hasty but excusable; it is part of judging . . . .
>
> 253. At the foundation of well-founded belief lies belief that is not founded.

Wittgenstein is arguing that judging, testing, inquiring, arguing are activities that human beings perform within a system of propo-sitions (or world view or form-of-life), some of which must remain untestable, unarguable, or outside the path of inquiry if those ac-tivities are to proceed at all. Some propositions are given or under-stood. They are the bedrock of our knowledge or, to use another metaphor of which Wittgenstein was fond, they are the foundations of our house of inquiry. In one sense we can say that we are certain of those propositions if only because we never bring them to test.

> 343. But it isn't that the situation is like this: We just *can't* investigate everything, and for that reason we are forced to rest content with assumption. If I want the door to turn, the hinges must stay put.

Imagine that our known propositions are a raft on which we float in the middle of the sea. We can examine each plank by dis-connecting it from the raft and holding it up to inspection, but we must always remain on some plank that cannot be under scrutiny while we examine the others or we will drown.

An answer such as Wittgenstein has suggested to the problem of grounding or justifying knowledge claims traditionally has not been very popular. Skeptics, who argue that the ultimate lack of a ground for knowledge claims entails that we really can have no knowledge at all, have been countered by others who seek to prove that we do have some knowledge of which we can be certain, that we cannot doubt. The most famous philosopher to pursue the task of revealing that which is absolutely certain was René Descartes. Descartes's method was to systematically doubt everything until he arrived at a proposition he could not doubt. Descartes decided that all he learned from his senses, including the existence of his own body, was dubitable because on occasion he had been deceived by his senses and while dreaming he had thought himself to be having experiences not unlike those he had while awake; hence he might on any occasion only be dreaming; and, finally, he might even be deceived in his perceptual experiences by some malevolent demon. But Descartes could not doubt that he was doubting while he was doing so, or to put it in a positive way, he could be certain that while he was thinking he was thinking and hence he was existing.

> After having reflected well and carefully examined all things, we must come to the definite conclusion that this proposition: "I am, I exist," is necessarily true each time that I pronounce it, or that I mentally conceive it.

For Descartes it was at least certain that "I think, therefore I exist" (Cogito, ergo sum).

A number of interesting problems arise with Descartes's account of certain knowledge, two of which are of particular concern here: (1) When one is certain of something, does one necessarily know it, and vice versa? and (2) Are dreams a part of one's continuous mental life such that there really are no clearly discernible marks for distinguishing waking states from dreaming? If the latter question is answered affirmatively, as Descarte's views might suggest, then knowledge based on sense perception would be dubitable. But, as Malcolm demonstrates, the question, How can I know whether I am awake or sound asleep? is based on a series of misconceptions, in particular a misconception of the nature of dreaming.

What is our criterion for telling whether or not Prince has had a dream? Malcolm would argue that it is upon awakening that Prince tells his dream. Malcolm maintains that a clear understanding of the notions of sound sleep and dreaming reveals that a skeptical question cannot be raised while dreaming because anyone raising a skeptical question cannot be dreaming. Hence the "dream argument" does not cast real doubts about perceptual knowledge.

Descartes implies that if one is certain of something, he knows it, and if one knows something, he must be certain of it. But is this really the case? Might not someone know something about which he could not claim to be certain? Suppose we are again in the field and we hear a bird song. You quiz me on the type of bird, and I rather timidly respond, "It's a meadowlark." I do not feel certain, but I am correct, and you congratulate me: "You see, you do know some bird calls even if you are not certain." Colin Radford claims that "neither being sure that P nor having the right to be sure that P, can be necessary conditions of knowing that P." "Certainly," Wittgenstein writes, "is *as it were* a tone of voice in which one declares how things are, but one does not infer from the tone of voice that one is justified." (#30 *On Certainty*)

Is it not the case that the view that one may know things about which one would not necessarily claim certainty or sureness leaves the door ajar to the possibility that Prince, from his dream, may have known something of the forthcoming death of Mrs. Sarah Hand, even though he would not have claimed to be certain, to believe, to have the right to believe, or even to believe that he knew what Mrs. Hand was soon to do? Yet if we allow that Prince knew something about Mrs. Hand's suicide before it was committed, would we not be erasing a distinction that most of us normally draw between "He knew that X" and "He guessed that X," a distinction usually drawn even when the guess was based on good evidence, let alone a nightmare?

1

PLATO

(427–347 B.C.)

What Knowledge Is Not *

Plato was a student of Socrates and was greatly influenced by his teacher's inquiries
and theories regarding virtually all the problems associated with philosophy. Most
of Plato's philosophy is written in the form of dialogues, generally led by Socrates.
In the Theaetetus Plato constructs a discussion between Socrates and Theaetetus, a
youth. Socrates asks Theaetetus for a definition of knowledge and receives the
answer that knowledge is perception, a theory Socrates identifies with the
Protagorean view that "man is the measure of all things." This theory is closely
examined and found wanting, and Theaetetus offers yet another theory of
knowledge: knowledge is true belief. Socrates demonstrates faults with that theory,
and Theaetetus amends it; knowledge is true belief supported by an "account" or
reasons. Socrates shows that position to be circular, and the dialogue ends.
Although there seems to be no resolution to the problem in the dialogue, the bases
for the rejection of the various theories lay the groundwork for Plato's only theory
of knowledge and his conception of the immutable and eternal Forms.

* *Theaetetus*, trans. by B. Jowett (with omissions).

Soc. Then now, Theaetetus, you answered that knowledge is perception?

Theaet. I did.

Soc. And if any one were to ask you: With what does a man see
black and white colours? and with what does he hear high and low
sounds?—you would say, if I am not mistaken, "With the eyes and
with the ears."

Theaet. I should.

Soc. The free use of words and phrases, rather than minute precision,
is generally characteristic of a liberal education, and the opposite is
pedantic; but sometimes precision is necessary, and I believe that the
answer which you have just given is open to the charge of incorrect-
ness; for which is more correct, to say that we see or hear with the eyes
and with the ears, or through the eyes and through the ears.

Theaet. I should say "through," Socrates, rather than "with."

Soc. Yes, my boy, for no one can suppose that in each of us, as in a sort of Trojan horse, there are perched a number of unconnected senses, which do not all meet in some one nature, the mind, or whatever we please to call it, of which they are the instruments, and with which through them we perceive objects of sense.

Theaet. I agree with you in that opinion.

Soc. The reason why I am thus precise is, because I want to know whether, when we perceive black and white through the eyes, and again, other qualities through other organs, we do not perceive them with one and the same part of ourselves, and, if you were asked, you might refer all such perceptions to the body. Perhaps, however, I had better allow you to answer for yourself and not interfere. Tell me, then, are not the organs through which you perceive warm and hard and light and sweet, organs of the body?

Theaet. Of the body, certainly.

[185] *Soc.* And you would admit that what you perceive through one faculty you cannot perceive through another; the objects of hearing, for example, cannot be perceived through sight, or the objects of sight through hearing?

Theaet. Of course not.

Soc. If you have any thought about both of them, this common perception cannot come to you, either through the one or the other organ?

Theaet. It cannot.

Soc. How about sounds and colours: in the first place you would admit that they both exist?

Theaet. Yes.

Soc. And that either of them is different from the other, and the same with itself?

Theaet. Certainly.

Soc. And that both are two and each of them one?

Theaet. Yes.

Soc. You can further observe whether they are like or unlike one another?

Theaet. I dare say.

Soc. But through what do you perceive all this about them? For neither through hearing nor yet through seeing can you apprehend that which they have in common. Let me give you an illustration of the point at issue:—If there were any meaning in asking whether sounds and colours are saline or not, you would be able to tell me what faculty would consider the question. It would not be sight or hearing, but some other.

Theaet. Certainly; the faculty of taste.

Soc. Very good; and now tell me what is the power which discerns, not only in sensible objects, but in all things, universal notions, such as those which are called being and not-being, and those others about which we were just asking—what organs will you assign for the perception of these notions?

Theaet. You are thinking of being and not-being, likeness and unlikeness, sameness and difference, and also of unity and other numbers which are applied to objects of sense; and you mean to ask, through what bodily organ the soul perceives odd and even numbers and other arithmetical conceptions.

Soc. You follow me excellently, Theaetetus; that is precisely what I am asking.

Theaet. Indeed, Socrates, I cannot answer; my only notion is, that these, unlike objects of sense, have no separate organ, but that the mind, by a power of her own, contemplates the universals in all things.

Soc. You are a beauty, Theaetetus, and not ugly, as Theodorus was saying; for he who utters the beautiful is himself beautiful and good. And besides being beautiful, you have done me a kindness in releasing me from a very long discussion, if you are clear that the soul views some things by herself and others through the bodily organs. For that was my own opinion, and I wanted you to agree with me.

Theaet. I am quite clear.

[*186*] *Soc.* And to which class would you refer being or essence; for this, of all our notions, is the most universal?

Theaet. I should say, to that class which the soul aspires to know of herself.

Soc. And would you say this also of like and unlike, same and other?

Theaet. Yes.

Soc. And would you say the same of the noble and base, and of good and evil?

Theaet. These I conceive to be notions which are essentially relative, and which the soul also perceives by comparing in herself things past and present with the future.

Soc. And does she not perceive the hardness of that which is hard by the touch, and the softness of that which is soft equally by the touch?

Theaet. Yes.

Soc. But their essence and what they are, and their opposition to one another, and the essential nature of this opposition, the soul herself endeavours to decide for us by the review and comparison of them?

Theaet. Certainly.

Soc. The simple sensations which reach the soul through the body are given at birth to men and animals by nature, but their reflections on the being and use of them are slowly and hardly gained, if they are ever gained, by education and long experience.

Theaet. Assuredly.

Soc. And can a man attain truth who fails of attaining being?

Theaet. Impossible.

Soc. And can he who misses the truth of anything, have a knowledge of that thing?

Theaet. He cannot.

Soc. Then knowledge does not consist in impressions of sense, but in reasoning about them; in that only, and not in the mere impression, truth and being can be attained?

Theaet. Clearly.

Soc. And would you call the two processes by the same name, when there is so great a difference between them?

Theaet. That would certainly not be right.

Soc. And what name would you give to seeing, hearing, smelling, being cold and being hot?

Theaet. I should call all of them perceiving—what other name could be given to them?

Soc. Perception would be the collective name of them?

Theaet. Certainly.

Soc. Which, as we say, has no part in the attainment of truth any more than of being?

Theaet. Certainly not.

Soc. And therefore not in science or knowledge?

Theaet. No.

Soc. Then perception, Theaetetus, can never be the same as knowledge or science?

Theaet. Clearly not, Socrates; and knowledge has now been most distinctly proved to be different from perception.

[187] *Soc.* But the original aim of our discussion was to find out rather what knowledge is than what it is not; at the same time we have made some progress, for we no longer seek for knowledge in perception at all, but in that other process, however called, in which the mind is alone and engaged with being.

Theaet. You mean, Socrates, if I am not mistaken, what is called thinking or opining.

Soc. You conceive truly. And now, my friend, please to begin again at this point; and having wiped out of your memory all that has preceded, see if you have arrived at any clearer view, and once more say what is knowledge.

Theaet. I cannot say, Socrates, that all opinion is knowledge, because there may be a false opinion; but I will venture to assert, that knowledge is true opinion: let this then be my reply; and if this is hereafter disproved, I must try to find another.

Soc. That is the way in which you ought to answer, Theaetetus, and not in your former hesitating strain, for if we are bold we shall gain one of two advantages; either we shall find what we seek, or we shall be less likely to think that we know what we do not know—in either case we shall be richly rewarded. And now, what are you saying?— Are there two sorts of opinion, one true and the other false; and do you define knowledge to be the true?

Theaet. Yes, according to my present view.

Soc. Is it still worth our while to resume the discussion touching opinion?

Theaet. To what are you alluding?

Soc. There is a point which often troubles me, and is a great perplexity to me, both in regard to myself and others. I cannot make out the nature or origin of the mental experience to which I refer.

Theaet. Pray what is it?

Soc. How there can be false opinion—that difficulty still troubles the eye of my mind; and I am uncertain whether I shall leave the question, or begin over again in a new way.

Theaet. Begin again, Socrates,—at least if you think that there is the slightest necessity for doing so. Were not you and Theodorus just now remarking very truly, that in discussions of this kind we may take our own time?

Soc. You are quite right, and perhaps there will be no harm in retracing our steps and beginning again. Better a little which is well done, than a great deal imperfectly.

Theaet. Certainly.

Soc. Well, and what is the difficulty? Do we not speak of false opinion, and say that one man holds a false and another a true opinion, as though there were some natural distinction between them?

Theaet. We certainly say so.

[188] *Soc.* All things and everything are either known or not known. I leave out of view the intermediate conceptions of learning and forgetting, because they have nothing to do with our present question.

Theaet. There can be no doubt, Socrates, if you exclude these, that there is no other alternative but knowing or not knowing a thing.

Soc. That point being now determined, must we not say that he who has an opinion, must have an opinion about something which he knows or does not know?

Theaet. He must.

Soc. He who knows, cannot but know; and he who does not know, cannot know?

Theaet. Of course.

Soc. What shall we say then? When a man has a false opinion does he think that which he knows to be some other thing which he knows, and knowing both, is he at the same time ignorant of both?

Theaet. That, Socrates, is impossible.

Soc. But perhaps he thinks of something which he does not know as some other thing which he does not know; for example, he knows neither Theaetetus nor Socrates, and yet he fancies that Theaetetus is Socrates, or Socrates Theaetetus?

Theaet. How can he?

Soc. But surely he cannot suppose what he knows to be what he does not know, or what he does not know to be what he knows?

Theaet. That would be monstrous.

Soc. Where, then, is false opinion? For if all things are either known or unknown, there can be no opinion which is not comprehended under this alternative, and so false opinion is excluded.

Theaet. Most true.

Soc. Suppose that we remove the question out of the sphere of knowing or not knowing, into that of being and not-being.

Theaet. What do you mean?

Soc. May we not suspect the simple truth to be that he who thinks about anything, that which is not, will necessarily think what is false, whatever in other respects may be the state of his mind?

Theaet. That, again, is not unlikely, Socrates.

Soc. Then suppose some one to say to us, Theaetetus:—Is it possible for any man to think that which is not, either as a self-existent substance or as a predicate of something else? And suppose that we answer, "Yes, he can, when he thinks what is not true."—That will be our answer?

Theaet. Yes.

Soc. But is there any parallel to this?

Theaet. What do you mean?

Soc. Can a man see something and yet see nothing?

Theaet. Impossible.

Soc. But if he sees any one thing, he sees something that exists. Do you suppose that what is one is ever to be found among nonexisting things?

Theaet. I do not.

Soc. He then who sees some one thing, sees something which is?

Theaet. Clearly.

[189] Soc. And he who hears anything, hears some one thing, and hears that which is?

Theaet. Yes.

Soc. And he who touches anything, touches something which is one and therefore is?

Theaet. That again is true.

Soc. And does not he who thinks, think some one thing?

Theaet. Certainly.

Soc. And does not he who thinks some one thing, think something which is?

Theaet. I agree.

Soc. Then he who thinks of that which is not, thinks of nothing?

Theaet. Clearly.

Soc. And he who thinks of nothing, does not think at all?

Theaet. Obviously.

Soc. Then no one can think that which is not, either as a self-existent substance or as a predicate of something else?

Theaet. Clearly not.

Soc. Then to think falsely is different from thinking that which is not?

Theaet. It would seem so.

Soc. Then false opinion has no existence in us, either in the sphere of being or of knowledge?

Theaet. Certainly not.

. . .

Soc. Then when any one thinks of one thing as another, he is saying to himself that one thing is another?

Theaet. Yes.

Soc. But do you ever remember saying to yourself that the noble is certainly base, or the unjust just; or, best of all—have you ever attempted to convince yourself that one thing is another? Nay, not even in sleep, did you ever venture to say to yourself that odd is even, or anything of the kind?

Theaet. Never.

Soc. And do you suppose that any other man, either in his senses or out of them, ever seriously tried to persuade himself that an ox is a horse, or that two are one?

Theaet. Certainly not.

Soc. But if thinking is talking to oneself, no one speaking and thinking of two objects, and apprehending them both in his soul, will say and think that the one is the other of them, and I must add, that even you, lover of dispute as you are, had better let the word "other" alone [i.e., not insist that "one" and "other" are the same].[1] I mean to say, that no one thinks the noble to be base, or anything of the kind.

Theaet. I will give up the word "other," Socrates; and I agree to what you say.

Soc. If a man has both of them in his thoughts, he cannot think that the one of them is the other?

Theaet. True.

Soc. Neither, if he has one of them only in his mind and not the other, can he think that one is the other?

Theaet. True; for we should have to suppose that he apprehends that which is not in his thoughts at all.

Soc. Then no one who has either both or only one of the two objects in his mind can think that the one is the other. And therefore, he who maintains that false opinion is heterodoxy is talking nonsense; for neither in this, any more than in the previous way, can false opinion exist in us.

Theaet. No.

Soc. But if, Theaetetus, this is not admitted, we shall be driven into many absurdities.

Theaet. What are they?

Soc. I will not tell you until I have endeavoured to consider the matter from every point of view. [*191*] For I should be ashamed of us if we were driven in our perplexity to admit the absurd consequences of which I speak. But if we find the solution, and get away from them, we may regard them only as the difficulties of others, and the ridicule will not attach to us. On the other hand, if we utterly fail, I suppose that we must be humble, and allow the argument to trample us under foot, as the sea-sick passenger is trampled upon by the sailor, and to do anything to us. Listen, then, while I tell you how I hope to find a way out of our difficulty.

Theaet. Let me hear.

Soc. I think that we were wrong in denying that a man could think what he knew to be what he did not know; and that there is a way in which such a deception is possible.

Theaet. You mean to say, as I suspected at the time, that I may know Socrates, and at a distance see some one who is unknown to me, and whom I mistake for him—then the deception will occur?

Soc. But has not that position been relinquished by us, because in-

---

[1] Both words in Greek are called ἕτερον: cf. *Parmenides, 147; Euthydemus, 301.*

volving the absurdity that we should know and not know the things which we know?

Theaet. True.

Soc. Let us make the assertion in another form, which may or may not have a favourable issue; but as we are in a great strait, every argument should be turned over and tested. Tell me, then, whether I am right in saying that you may learn a thing which at one time you did not know?

Theaet. Certainly you may.

Soc. And another and another?

Theaet. Yes.

Soc. I would have you imagine, then, that there exists in the mind of man a block of wax, which is of different sizes in different men; harder, moister, and having more or less of purity in one than another, and in some of an intermediate quality.

Theaet. I see.

Soc. Let us say that this tablet is a gift of Memory, the mother of the Muses; and that when we wish to remember anything which we have seen, or heard, or thought in our own minds, we hold the wax to the perceptions and thoughts, and in that material receive the impression of them as from the seal of a ring; and that we remember and know what is imprinted as long as the image lasts; but when the image is effaced, or cannot be taken, then we forget and do not know.

Theaet. Very good.

Soc. Now, when a person has this knowledge, and is considering something which he sees or hears, may not false opinion arise in the following manner?

Theaet. In what manner?

Soc. When he thinks what he knows, sometimes to be what he knows, and sometimes to be what he does not know. We were wrong before in denying the possibility of this. . . .

The only cases, if any, which remain, are the following.

Theaet. What are they? If you tell me, I may perhaps understand you better; but at present I am unable to follow you.

Soc. A person may think that some things which he knows, or which he perceives and does not know, are some other things which he knows and perceives; or that some things which he knows and perceives, are other things which he knows and perceives.

Theaet. I understand you less than ever now.

Soc. Hear me once more, then:—I, knowing Theodorus, and remembering in my own mind what sort of person he is, and also what sort of person Theaetetus is, at one time see them, and at another time do not see them, and sometimes I touch them, and at another time not, or at one time I may hear them or perceive them in some other way, and at another time not perceive them, but still I remember them, and know them in my own mind.

Theaet. Very true.

Soc. Then, first of all, I want you to understand that a man may or may not perceive sensibly that which he knows.

Theaet. True.

Soc. And that which he does not know will sometimes not be perceived by him and sometimes will be perceived and only perceived?

Theaet. That is also true.

[*193*] *Soc.* See whether you can follow me better now: Socrates can recognize Theodorus and Theaetetus, but he sees neither of them, nor does he perceive them in any other way; he cannot then by any possibility imagine in his own mind that Theaetetus is Theodorus. Am I not right?

Theaet. You are quite right.

Soc. Then that was the first case of which I spoke.

Theaet. Yes.

Soc. The second case was, that I, knowing one of you and not knowing the other, and perceiving neither, can never think him whom I know to be him whom I do not know.

Theaet. True.

Soc. In the third case, not knowing and not perceiving either of you, I cannot think that one of you whom I do not know is the other whom I do not know. I need not again go over the catalogue of excluded cases, in which I cannot form a false opinion about you and Theodorus, either when I know both or when I am in ignorance of both, or when I know one and not the other. And the same of perceiving: do you understand me?

Theaet. I do.

Soc. The only possibility of erroneous opinion is, when knowing you and Theodorus, and having on the waxen block the impression of both of you given as by a seal, but seeing you imperfectly and at a distance, I try to assign the right impression of memory to the right visual impression, and to fit this into its own print: if I succeed, recognition will take place; but if I fail and transpose them, putting the foot into the wrong shoe—that is to say, putting the vision of either of you on to the wrong impression, or if my mind, like the sight in a mirror, which is transferred from right to left, err by reason of some similar affection, then "heterodoxy" and false opinion ensues.

Theaet. Yes, Socrates, you have described the nature of opinion with wonderful exactness.

Soc. Or again, when I know both of you, and perceive as well as know one of you, but not the other, and my knowledge of him does not accord with perception.

. . .

Soc. Then now we may admit the existence of false opinion in us?
Theaet. Certainly.
Soc. And of true opinion also?
Theaet. Yes.
Soc. We have at length satisfactorily proven that beyond a doubt there are these two sorts of opinion?
Theaet. Undoubtedly.

. . .

Soc. Then do we not come back to the old difficulty? For he who makes such a mistake does think one thing which he knows to be another thing which he knows; but this, as we said, was impossible, and afforded an irresistible proof of the non-existence of false opinion, because otherwise the same person would inevitably know and not know the same thing at the same time.

Theaet. Most true.

Soc. Then false opinion cannot be explained as a confusion of thought and sense, for in that case we could not have been mistaken about pure conceptions of thought; and thus we are obliged to say, either that false opinion does not exist, or that a man may not know that which he knows;—which alternative do you prefer?

Theaet. It is hard to determine, Socrates.

. . .

Soc. We are wrong in seeking for false opinion until we know what knowledge is; that must be first ascertained; then, the nature of false opinion?

Theaet. I cannot but agree with you, Socrates, so far as we have yet gone.

Soc. Then, once more, what shall we say that knowledge is?—for we are not going to lose heart as yet.

Theaet. Certainly, I shall not lose heart, if you do not.

Soc. What definition will be most consistent with our former views?

Theaet. I cannot think of any but our old one, Socrates.

Soc. What was it?

Theaet. Knowledge was said by us to be true opinion; and true opinion is surely unerring, and the results which follow from it are all noble and good.

Soc. He who led the way into the river, Theaetetus, said "The experiment will show"; [201] and perhaps if we go forward in the search, we may stumble upon the thing which we are looking for; but if we stay where we are, nothing will come to light.

Theaet. Very true; let us go forward and try.

Soc. The trail soon comes to an end, for a whole profession is against us.

Theaet. How is that, and what profession do you mean?

Soc. The profession of the great wise ones who are called orators and lawyers; for these persuade men by their art and make them think whatever they like, but they do not teach them. Do you imagine that there are any teachers in the world so clever as to be able to convince others of the truth about acts of robbery or violence, of which they were not eye-witnesses, while a little water is flowing in the clepsydra?

Theaet. Certainly not, they can only persuade them.

Soc. And would you not say that persuading them is making them have an opinion?

Theaet. To be sure.

Soc. When, therefore, judges are justly persuaded about matters which you can know only by seeing them, and not in any other way, and when thus judging of them from report they attain a true opinion about them, they judge without knowledge and yet are rightly persuaded, if they have judged well.

Theaet. Certainly.

Soc. And yet, O my friend, if true opinion in law courts and knowledge are the same, the perfect judge could not have judged rightly without knowledge; and therefore I must infer that they are not the same.

Theaet. That is a distinction, Socrates, which I have heard made by some one else, but I had forgotten it. He said that true opinion, combined with reason, was knowledge, but that the opinion which had no reason was out of the sphere of knowledge; and that things of which there is no rational account are not knowable—such was the singular expression which he used—and that things which have a reason or explanation are knowable.

Soc. Excellent; but then, how did he distinguish between things which are and are not "knowable"? I wish that you would repeat to me what he said, and then I shall know whether you and I have heard the same tale.

Theaet. I do not know whether I can recall it; but if another person would tell me, I think that I could follow him.

Soc. Let me give you, then, a dream in return for a dream:— Methought that I too had a dream, and I heard in my dream that the primeval letters or elements out of which you and I and all other things are compounded, have no reason or explanation; you can only name them, [202] but no predicate can be either affirmed or denied of them, for in the one case existence, in the other non-existence is already implied, neither of which must be added, if you mean to speak of this or that thing by itself alone. It should not be called itself, or that, or each, or alone, or this, or the like; for these go about everywhere and are applied to all things, but are distinct from them; whereas, if the first elements could be described, and had a definition of their own, they would be spoken of apart from all else. But none of these primeval elements can be defined; they can only be named, for they have nothing but a name, and the things which are compounded of them, as they are complex, are expressed by a combination of names, for the combination of names is the essence of a definition. Thus, then, the elements or letters are only objects of perception, and cannot be defined or known; but the syllables or combinations of them are known and expressed, and are apprehended by true opinion. When, therefore, any one forms the true opinion of anything without rational explanation, you may say that his mind is truly exercised, but has no knowledge; for he who cannot give and receive a reason for a thing, has no knowledge of that thing; but when he adds rational explanation, then, he is perfected in knowledge and may be all that I have been denying of him.

You allow and maintain that true opinion, combined with definition or rational explanation, is knowledge?

Theaet. Exactly.

Soc. Then may we assume, Theaetetus, that to-day, and in this casual manner, we have found a truth which in former times many wise men have grown old and have not found?

Theaet. At any rate, Socrates, I am satisfied with the present statement.

Soc. Which is probably correct—for how can there be knowledge apart from definition and true opinion? And yet there is one point in what has been said which does not quite satisfy me.

Theaet. What was it?

Soc. What might seem to be the most ingenious notion of all:—That the elements or letters are unknown, but the combination or syllables known.

Theaet. And was that wrong?

. . .

Soc. Let us take them and put them to the test, or rather, test ourselves:—What was the way in which we learned letters? and, first of all, are we right in saying that syllables have a definition, but that letters have no definition?

Theaet. I think so.

Soc. I think so too; for, suppose that some one asks you to spell the first syllable of my name:—Theaetetus, he says, what is SO?

Theaet. I should reply S and O.

Soc. That is the definition which you would give of the syllable?

Theaet. I should.

Soc. I wish that you would give me a similar definition of the S.

Theaet. But how can any one, Socrates, tell the elements of an element? I can only reply, that S is a consonant, a mere noise, as of the tongue hissing; B, and most other letters, again, are neither vowel-sounds nor noises. Thus letters may be most truly said to be undefined; for even the most distinct of them, which are the seven vowels, have a sound only, but no definition at all.

Soc. Then, I suppose, my friend, that we have been so far right in our idea about knowledge?

Theaet. Yes; I think that we have.

Soc. Well, but have we been right in maintaining that the syllables can be known, but not the letters?

. . .

Soc. If, then, a syllable is a whole, and has many parts or letters, the letters as well as the syllable must be intelligible and expressible, since all the parts are acknowledged to be the same as the whole?

Theaet. True.

Soc. But if it be one and indivisible, then the syllables and the letters are alike undefined and unknown, and for the same reason?

Theaet. I cannot deny that.

Soc. We cannot, therefore, agree in the opinion of him who says that the syllable can be known and expressed, [206] but not the letters.

Theaet. Certainly not; if we may trust the argument.

Soc. Well, but will you not be equally inclined to disagree with him, when you remember your own experience in learning to read?

Theaet. What experience?

Soc. Why, that in learning you were kept trying to distinguish the separate letters both by the eye and by the ear, in order that, when you heard them spoken or saw them written, you might not be confused by their position.

Theaet. Very true.

Soc. And is the education of the harp-player complete unless he can tell what string answers to a particular note; the notes, as every one would allow, are the elements or letters of music?

Theaet. Exactly.

Soc. Then, if we argue from the letters and syllables which we know to other simples and compounds, we shall say that the letters or simple elements as a class are much more certainly known than the syllables, and much more indispensable to a perfect knowledge of any subject; and if some one says that the syllable is known and the letter unknown, we shall consider that either intentionally or unintentionally he is talking nonsense?

Theaet. Exactly.

Soc. And there might be given other proofs of this belief, if I am not mistaken. But do not let us in looking for them lose sight of the question before us, which is the meaning of the statement, that right opinion with rational definition or explanation is the most perfect form of knowledge.

Theaet. We must not.

Soc. Well, and what is the meaning of the term "explanation"? I think that we have a choice of three meanings.

Theaet. What are they?

Soc. In the first place, the meaning may be, manifesting one's thought by the voice with verbs and nouns, imaging an opinion in the stream which flows from the lips, as in a mirror or water. Does not explanation appear to be of this nature?

Theaet. Certainly; he who so manifests his thought, is said to explain himself.

Soc. And every one who is not born deaf or dumb is able sooner or later to manifest what he thinks of anything; and if so, all those who have a right opinion about anything will also have right explanation; nor will right opinion be anywhere found to exist apart from knowledge.

Theaet. True.

Soc. Let us not, therefore, hastily charge him who gave this account of knowledge with uttering an unmeaning word; for perhaps he only intended to say, that when a person was asked what was the nature of anything, [207] he should be able to answer his questioner by giving the elements of the thing.

Theaet. As for example, Socrates . . . ?

Soc. As, for example, when Hesiod says that a waggon is made up of a hundred planks. Now, neither you nor I could describe all of them individually; but if any one asked what is a waggon, we should be content to answer, that a waggon consists of wheels, axle, body, rims, yoke.

Theaet. Certainly.

Soc. And our opponent will probably laugh at us, just as he would if we professed to be grammarians and to give a grammatical account of the name of Theaetetus, and yet could only tell the syllables and not the letters of your name—that would be true opinion, and not knowledge; for knowledge, as has been already remarked, is not attained until, combined with true opinion, there is an enumeration of the elements out of which anything is composed.

Theaet. Yes.

Soc. In the same general way, we might also have true opinion about a waggon; but he who can describe its essence by an enumeration of the hundred planks, adds rational explanation to true opinion, and instead of opinion has art and knowledge of the nature of a waggon, in that he attains to the whole through the elements.

Theaet. And do you not agree in that view, Socrates?

Soc. If you do, my friend; but I want to know first, whether you admit the resolution of all things into their elements to be a rational explanation of them, and the consideration of them in syllables or larger combinations of them to be irrational—is this your view?

Theaet. Precisely.

Soc. Well, and do you conceive that a man has knowledge of any element who at one time affirms and at another time denies that element of something, or thinks that the same thing is composed of different elements at different times?

Theaet. Assuredly not.

Soc. And do you not remember that in your case and in that of others this often occurred in the process of learning to read?

Theaet. You mean that I mistook the letters and misspelt the syllables?

Soc. Yes.

Theaet. To be sure; I perfectly remember, and I am very far from supposing that they who are in this condition have knowledge.

Soc. When a person at the time of learning writes the name of Theaetetus, [208] and thinks that he ought to write and does write *Th* and *e;* but, again, meaning to write the name of Theodorus, thinks that he ought to write and does write *T* and *e*—can we suppose that he knows the first syllables of your two names?

Theaet. We have already admitted that such a one has not yet attained knowledge.

Soc. And in like manner he may enumerate without knowing them the second and third and fourth syllables of your name?

Theaet. He may.

Soc. And in that case, when he knows the order of the letters and can write them out correctly, he has right opinion?

Theaet. Clearly.

Soc. But although we admit that he has right opinion, he will still be without knowledge?

Theaet. Yes.

Soc. And yet he will have explanations, as well as right opinion, for he knew the order of the letters when he wrote; and this we admit to be explanation.

Theaet. True.

Soc. Then, my friend, there is such a thing as right opinion united with definition or explanation, which does not as yet attain to the exactness of knowledge.

Theaet. It would seem so.

Soc. And what we fancied to be a perfect definition of knowledge is a dream only. But perhaps we had better not say so as yet, for were there not three explanations of knowledge, one of which must, as we said, be adopted by him who maintains knowledge to be true opinion combined with rational explanation? And very likely there may be found some one who will not prefer this but the third.

Theaet. You are quite right; there is still one remaining. The first was the image or expression of the mind in speech; the second, which has just been mentioned, is a way of reaching the whole by an enumeration of the elements. But what is the third definition?

Soc. There is, further, the popular notion of telling the mark or sign of difference which distinguishes the thing in question from all others.

Theaet. Can you give me any example of such a definition?

Soc. As, for example, in the case of the sun, I think that you would be contented with the statement that the sun is the brightest of the heavenly bodies which revolve about the earth.

Theaet. Certainly.

Soc. Understand why:—the reason is, as I was just now saying, that if you get at the difference and distinguishing characteristic of each thing, then, as many persons affirm, you will get at the definition or explanation of it; but while you lay hold only of the common and not of the characteristic notion, you will only have the definition of those things to which this common quality belongs.

Theaet. I understand you, and your account of definition is in my judgment correct.

Soc. But he, who having right opinion about anything, can find out the difference which distinguishes it from other things will know that of which before he had only an opinion.

Theaet. Yes; that is what we are maintaining.

Soc. Nevertheless, Theaetetus, on a nearer view, I find myself quite disappointed; the picture, which at a distance was not so bad, has now become altogether unintelligible.

Theaet. What do you mean?

[209] *Soc.* I will endeavour to explain: I will suppose myself to have true opinion of you, and if to this I add your definition, then I have knowledge, but if not, opinion only.

Theaet. Yes.

Soc. The definition was assumed to be the interpretation of your difference.

Theaet. True.

Soc. But when I had only opinion, I had no conception of your distinguishing characteristics.

Theaet. I suppose not.

Soc. Then I must have conceived of some general or common nature which no more belonged to you than to another.

Theaet. True.

Soc. Tell me, now—How in that case could I have formed a judgment of you any more than of any one else? Suppose that I imagine Theaetetus to be a man who has nose, eyes, and mouth, and every other member complete; how would that enable me to distinguish Theaetetus from Theodorus, or from some outer barbarian?

Theaet. How could it?

Soc. Or if I had further conceived of you, not only as having nose and eyes, but as having a snub nose and prominent eyes, should I have any more notion of you than of myself and others who resemble me?

Theaet. Certainly not.

Soc. Surely I can have no conception of Theaetetus until your snub-nosedness has left an impression on my mind different from the snub-nosedness of all others whom I have ever seen, and until your other peculiarities have a like distinctness; and so when I meet you tomorrow the right opinion will be re-called?

Theaet. Most true.

Soc. Then right opinion implies the perception of differences?

Theaet. Clearly.

Soc. What, then, shall we say of adding reason or explanation to right opinion? If the meaning is, that we should form an opinion of the way in which something differs from another thing, the proposal is ridiculous.

Theaet. How so?

Soc. We are supposed to acquire a right opinion of the differences which distinguish one thing from another when we have already a right opinion of them, and so we go round and round:—the revolution of the scytal, or pestle, or any other rotatory machine, in the same circles, is as nothing compared with such a requirement; and we may be truly described as the blind directing the blind; for to add those things which we already have, in order that we may learn what we already think, is like a soul utterly benighted.

Theaet. Tell me; what were you going to say just now, when you asked the question?

Soc. If, my boy, the argument, in speaking of adding the definition, had used the word to "know," and not merely "have an opinion" of the difference, this which is the most promising of all the definitions of knowledge would have come to a pretty end, for to know is surely to acquire knowledge.

[210] *Theaet.* True.

Soc. And so, when the question is asked, What is knowledge? this fair argument will answer "Right opinion with knowledge,"—knowledge, that is, of difference, for this, as the said argument maintains, is adding the definition.

Theaet. That seems to be true.

Soc. But how utterly foolish, when we are asking what is knowledge, that the reply should only be, right opinion with knowledge of difference or of anything! And so, Theaetetus, knowledge is neither sensation nor true opinion, nor yet definition and explanation accompanying and added to true opinion?

2

BERTRAND RUSSELL

(1872–1970)

Knowledge, Error, and Probable Opinion *

Bertrand Russell is justly famous as one of the great philosophers of this century. Although he began his career as an idealist, he soon found his way to the position of logical atomism, an analytic method of using the techniques of logic to clarify and solve the basic philosophic problems. In this essay, from his book Problems of Philosophy, *he analyzes the concept of knowledge. He, like Plato, investigates the position that knowledge is true belief, but he rejects that view on the grounds that holding it is not in accordance with common linguistic usage. He draws a distinction between what he calls intuitive knowledge and derivative knowledge and centers his attention on the former. What does it mean to say that something is self-evident? Russell identifies two kinds of self-evidence. He then defines knowledge as what we firmly believe if it is true and provided that it is either intuitive or inferred from intuitive knowledge. On such a view, most of what we treat as knowledge shades into what Russell calls probable opinion, identified as what we firmly believe, if it is neither knowledge nor error, and also what we believe hesitatingly because it is not self-evident.*

* Bertrand Russell, *Problems of Philosophy* (London: Home University Library, 1912), Chapter XIII.

THE question as to what we mean by truth and falsehood is of much less interest than the question as to how we can know what is true and what is false. There can be no doubt that *some* of our beliefs are erroneous; thus we are led to inquire what certainty we can ever have that such and such a belief is not erroneous. In other words, can we ever *know* anything at all, or do we merely sometimes by good luck believe what is true? Before we can attack this question, we must, however, first decide what we mean by 'knowing,' and this question is not so easy as might be supposed.

At first sight we might imagine that knowledge could be defined as 'true belief.' When what we believe is true, it might be supposed that we had achieved a knowledge of what we believe. But this would not accord with the way in which the word is commonly used. To take a very trivial instance: If a man believes that the late Prime Minister's last name began with a B, he believes what is true, since the late Prime Minister was Sir Henry Campbell Bannerman. But if he believes that Mr. Balfour was the late Prime Minister, he will still believe that the late Prime Minister's last name began with a B, yet this belief, though true, would not be thought to constitute knowledge. If a newspaper, by an intelligent anticipation, announces the result of a battle before any telegram giving the result has been received, it may by good fortune announce what afterwards turns out to be the right result, and it may produce belief in some of its less experienced readers. But in spite of the truth of their belief, they cannot be said to have knowledge. Thus it is clear that a true belief is not knowledge when it is deduced from a false belief.

In like manner, a true belief cannot be called knowledge when it is deduced by a fallacious process of reasoning, even if the premises from which it is deduced are true. If I know that all Greeks are men and that Socrates was a man, and I infer that Socrates was a Greek, I cannot be said to *know* that Socrates was a Greek, because, although my premisses and my conclusion are true, the conclusion does not follow from the premisses.

But are we to say that nothing is knowledge except what is validly deduced from true premisses? Obviously we cannot say this. Such a definition is at once too wide and too narrow. In the first place, it is too wide, because it is not enough that our premisses should be *true*, they must also be *known*. The man who believes that Mr. Balfour was the late Prime Minister may proceed to draw valid deductions from the true premiss that the late Prime Minister's name began with a B, but he cannot be said to *know* the conclusions reached by these deductions. Thus we shall have to amend our definition by saying that knowledge is what is validly deduced from *known* premisses. This, however, is a circular definition: it assumes that we already know what is meant by 'known premisses.' It can, therefore, at best define one sort of knowledge, the sort we call derivative, as opposed to intuitive knowledge. We may say: '*Derivative* knowledge is what is validly deduced from premisses known intuitively.' In this statement there is no formal defect, but it leaves the definition of *intuitive* knowledge still to seek.

Leaving on one side, for the moment, the question of intuitive knowledge, let us consider the above suggested definition of derivative knowledge. The chief objection to it is that it unduly limits knowledge. It constantly happens that people entertain a true belief, which has grown up in them because of some piece of intuitive knowledge from which it is capable of being validly inferred, but from which it has not, as a matter of fact, been inferred by any logical process.

Take, for example, the beliefs produced by reading. If the newspapers announce the death of the King, we are fairly well justified in believing that the King is dead, since this is the sort of announcement which would not be made if it were false. And we are quite amply justified in believing that the newspaper asserts that the King is dead. But here the intuitive knowledge upon which our belief is based is knowledge of the existence of sense-data derived from looking at the print which gives the news. This knowledge scarcely rises into consciousness, except in a person who cannot read easily. A child may be aware of the shapes of the letters, and pass gradually and painfully to a realization of their meaning. But anybody accustomed to reading passes at once to what the letters mean, and is not aware, except on reflection, that he has derived this knowledge from the sense-data called seeing the printed letters. Thus although a valid inference from the letters to their meaning is possible, and *could* be performed by the reader, it is not in fact performed, since he does not in fact perform any operation which can be called logical inference. Yet it would be absurd to say that the reader does not *know* that the newspaper announces the King's death.

We must, therefore, admit as derivative knowledge whatever is the result of intuitive knowledge even if by mere association, provided there *is* a valid logical connexion, and the person in question could become aware of this connexion by reflection. There are in fact many ways, besides logical inference, by which we pass from one belief to another: the passage from the print to its meaning illustrates these ways. These ways may be called 'psychological inference.' We shall, then, admit such psychological inference as a means of obtaining derivative knowledge, provided there is a discoverable logical inference which runs parallel to the psychological inference. This renders our definition of derivative knowledge less precise than we could wish, since the word 'discoverable' is vague: it does not tell us how much reflection may be needed in order to make the discovery. But in fact 'knowledge' is not a precise conception: it merges into 'probable opinion,' as we shall see more fully in the course of the present chapter. A very precise definition, therefore, should not be sought, since any such definition must be more or less misleading.

The chief difficulty in regard to knowledge, however, does not arise over derivative knowledge, but over intuitive knowledge. So long as we are dealing with derivative knowledge, we have the test of intuitive knowledge to fall back upon. But in regard to intuitive beliefs, it is by no means easy to discover any criterion by which to distinguish some as true and others as erroneous. In this question it is scarcely possible to reach any very precise result: all our knowledge of truths is infected with *some* degree of doubt, and a theory which ignored this fact would be plainly wrong. Something may be done, however, to mitigate the difficulties of the question.

Our theory of truth, to begin with, supplies the possibility of distinguishing certain truths as *self-evident* in a sense which ensures infallibility. When a belief is true, we said, there is a corresponding fact, in which the several objects of the belief form a single complex. The belief is said to constitute *knowledge* of this fact, provided it fulfills those further somewhat vague conditions which we have been considering. But in regard to any fact, besides the knowledge constituted by belief, we may also have the kind of knowledge constituted by *perception* (taking this word in its widest possible sense). For example, if you know the hour of the sunset, you can at that hour know the fact that the sun is setting: this is knowledge of the fact by way of knowledge of *truths;* but you can also, if the weather is fine, look to the west and actually see the setting sun: you then know the same fact by the way of knowledge of *things.*

Thus in regard to any complex fact, there are, theoretically, two ways in which it may be known: (1) by means of a judgement, in which its several parts are judged to be related as they are in fact related; (2) by means of *acquaintance* with the complex fact itself, which may (in a large sense) be called perception, though it is by no means confined to objects of the senses. Now it will be observed that the second way of knowing a complex fact, the way of acquaintance, is only possible when there really is such a fact, while the first way, like all judgement, is liable to error. The second way gives us the complex whole, and is therefore only possible when its parts do actually have that relation which makes them combine to form such a complex. The first way, on the contrary, gives us the parts and the relation severally, and demands only the reality of the parts and the relation: the relation may not relate those parts in that way, and yet the judgement may occur.

We suggested that there might be two kinds of self-evidence, one giving an absolute guarantee of truth, the other only a partial guarantee. These two kinds can now be distinguished.

We may say that a truth is self-evident, in the first and most absolute sense, when we have acquaintance with the fact which corresponds to the truth. When Othello believes that Desdemona loves Cassio, the corresponding fact, if his belief were true, would be 'Desdemona's love for Cassio.' This would be a fact with which no one could have acquaintance except Desdemona; hence in the sense of self-evidence that we are considering, the truth that Desdemona loves Cassio (if it were a truth) could only be self-evident to Desdemona.

All mental facts, and all facts concerning sense-data, have this same privacy: there is only one person to whom they can be self-evident in our present sense, since there is only one person who can be acquainted with the mental things or the sense-data concerned. Thus no fact about any particular existing thing can be self-evident to more than one person. On the other hand, facts about universals do not have this privacy. Many minds may be acquainted with the same universals; hence a relation between universals may be known by acquaintance to many different people. In all cases where we know by acquaintance a complex fact consisting of certain terms in a certain relation, we say that the truth that these terms are so related has the first or absolute kind of self-evidence, and in these cases the judgement that the terms are so related *must* be true. Thus this sort of self-evidence is an absolute guarantee of truth.

But although this sort of self-evidence is an absolute guarantee of truth, it does not enable us to be *absolutely* certain, in the case of any given judgement, that the judgement in question is true. Suppose we first perceive the sun shining, which is a complex fact, and thence proceed to make the judgement 'the sun is shining.' In passing from the perception to the judgement, it is necessary to analyse the given complex fact: we have to separate out 'the sun' and 'shining' as constituents of the fact. In this process it is possible to commit an error; hence even where a *fact* has the first or absolute kind of self-evidence, a judgement believed to correspond to the fact is not absolutely infallible, because it may not really correspond to the fact. But if it does correspond (in the sense explained in the preceding chapter), then it *must* be true.

The second sort of self-evidence will be that which belongs to judgements in the first instance, and is not derived from direct perception of a fact as a single complex whole. This second kind of self-evidence will have degrees, from the very highest degree down to a bare inclination in favour of the belief. Take, for example, the case of a horse trotting away from us along a hard road. At first our certainty that we hear the hoofs is complete; gradually, if we listen intently, there comes a moment when we think perhaps it was imagination or the blind upstairs or our own heartbeats; at last we become doubtful whether there was any noise at all; then we *think* we no longer hear anything, and at last we *know* we no longer hear anything. In this process, there is a continual gradation of self-evidence, from the highest degree to the least, not in the sense-data themselves, but in the judgements based on them.

Or again: Suppose we are comparing two shades of colour, one blue and one green. We can be quite sure they are different shades of colour; but if the green colour is gradually altered to be more and more like the blue, becoming first a blue-green, then a greeny-blue, then blue, there will come a moment when we are doubtful whether we can see any difference, and then a moment when we know that we cannot see any difference. The same thing happens in tuning a musical instrument, or in any other case where there is a continuous gradation. Thus self-evidence of this sort is a matter of degree; and it seems plain that the higher degrees are more to be trusted than the lower degrees.

In derivative knowledge our ultimate premisses must have some degree of self-evidence, and so must their connexion with the conclusions deduced from them. Take for example a piece of reasoning in geometry. It is not enough that the axioms from which we start should be self-evident: it is necessary also that, at each step in the reasoning, the connexion of premiss and conclusion should be self-evident. In difficult reasoning, this connexion has often only a very small degree of self-evidence; hence errors of reasoning are not improbable where the difficulty is great.

From what has been said it is evident that, both as regards intuitive knowledge and as regards derivative knowledge, if we assume that intuitive knowledge is trustworthy in proportion to the degree of its self-evidence, there will be a gradation in trustworthiness, from the existence of noteworthy sense-data and the simpler truths of logic and arithmetic, which may be taken as quite certain, down to judgements which seem only just more probable than their opposites. What we firmly believe, if it is true, is called *knowledge,* provided it is either intuitive or inferred (logically or psychologically) from intuitive knowledge from which it follows logically. What we firmly believe, if it is not true, is called *error.* What we firmly believe, if it is neither knowledge nor error, and also what we believe hesitatingly, because it is, or is derived from, something which has not the highest degree of self-evidence, may be called *probable opinion.* Thus the greater part of what would commonly pass as knowledge is more or less probable opinion.

In regard to probable opinion, we can derive great assistance from *coherence,* which we rejected as the *definition* of truth, but may often use as a *criterion.* A body of individually probable opinions, if they are mutually coherent, become more probable than any one of them would be individually. It is in this way that many scientific hypotheses acquire their probability. They fit into a coherent system of probable opinions, and thus become more probable than they would be in isolation. The same thing applies to general philosophical hypotheses.

Often in a single case such hypotheses may seem highly doubtful, while yet, when we consider the order and coherence which they introduce into a mass of probable opinion, they become pretty nearly certain. This applies, in particular, to such matters as the distinction between dreams and waking life. If our dreams, night after night, were as coherent one with another as our days, we should hardly know whether to believe the dreams or the waking life. As it is, the test of coherence condemns the dreams and confirms the waking life. But this test, though it increases probability where it is successful, never gives absolute certainty, unless there is certainty already at some point in the coherent system. Thus the mere organization of probable opinion will never, by itself, transform it into indubitable knowledge.

3 EDMUND GETTIER

(1927–   )

Is Justified True Belief Knowledge? *

Although Gettier's paper is rather short, it has had a great impact in contemporary epistemology. It is an attempt to show the inadequacy of the view that someone knows something entails that what he knows is true, that he believes it, and that he is justified in (has good reasons for) believing it. Those conditions, Gettier believes, are not sufficient for the truth of the statement that someone knows something. Gettier presents us with two examples to demonstrate that in some cases one may satisfy all the supposed relevant conditions and yet not know the proposition that the traditional theorist would argue that he must know.

* Edmund Gettier, "Is Justified True Belief Knowledge?" *Analysis,* Vol. 23, 1963. Reprinted by permission of Basil Blackwell & Mott Ltd, Oxford.

VARIOUS attempts have been made in recent years to state necessary and sufficient conditions for someone's knowing a given proposition. The attempts have often been such that they can be stated in a form similar to the following: [1]

   (a) S knows that P   *IFF*   (i) P is true,
                                       (ii) S believes that P, and
                                       (iii) S is justified in believing
                                             that P.

For example, Chisholm has held that the following gives the necessary and sufficient conditions for knowledge: [2]

   (b) S knows that P   *IFF*   (i) S accepts P,
                                        (ii) S has adequate evidence
                                           for P, and
                                        (iii) P is true.

Ayer has stated the necessary and sufficient conditions for knowledge as follows: [3]

---

[1] Plato seems to be considering some such definition at *Theaetetus* 201, and perhaps accepting one at *Meno* 98.
[2] Roderick M. Chisholm, *Perceiving: A Philosophical Study,* Cornell University Press (Ithaca, New York, 1957), p. 16.
[3] A. J. Ayer, *The Problem of Knowledge,* Macmillan (London, 1956), p. 34.

(c) S knows that P   *IFF*   (i) is true,
                                     (ii) S is sure that P is true, and
                                     (iii) S has the right to be sure
                                            that P is true.

I shall argue that (a) is false in that the conditions stated therein do not constitute a *sufficient* condition for the truth of the proposition that S knows that P. The same argument will show that (b) and (c) fail if 'has adequate evidence for' or 'has the right to be sure that' is substituted for 'is justified in believing that' throughout.

I shall begin by noting two points. First, in that sense of 'justified' in which S's being justified in believing P is a necessary condition of S's knowing that P, it is possible for a person to be justified in believing a proposition that is in fact false. Secondly, for any proposition P, if S is justified in believing P, and P entails Q, and S deduces Q from P and accepts Q as a result of this deduction, then S is justified in believing Q. Keeping these two points in mind, I shall now present two cases in which the conditions stated in (a) are true for some proposition, though it is at the same time false that the person in question knows that proposition.

CASE I

Suppose that Smith and Jones have applied for a certain job. And suppose that Smith has strong evidence for the following conjunctive proposition:

(d) Jones is the man who will get the job, and Jones has ten coins in his pocket.

Smith's evidence for (d) might be that the president of the company assured him that Jones would in the end be selected, and that he, Smith, had counted the coins in Jones's pocket ten minutes ago. Proposition (d) entails:

(e) The man who will get the job has ten coins in his pocket. Let us suppose that Smith sees the entailment from (d) to (e), and accepts (e) on the grounds of (d), for which he has strong evidence. In this case, Smith is clearly justified in believing that (e) is true.

But imagine, further, that unknown to Smith, he himself, not Jones, will get the job. And, also, unknown to Smith, he himself has ten coins in his pocket. Proposition (e) is then true, though proposition (d), from which Smith inferred (e), is false. In our example, then, all of the following are true: (*i*) (e) is true, (*ii*) Smith believes that (e) is true, and (*iii*) Smith is justified in believing that (e) is true. But it is equally clear that Smith does not *know* that (e) is true; for (e) is true in virtue of the number of coins in Smith's pocket, while Smith does not know how many coins are in Smith's pocket, and bases his belief in (e) on a count of the coins in Jones's pocket, whom he falsely believes to be the man who will get the job.

CASE II

Let us suppose that Smith has strong evidence for the following proposition:

(f) Jones owns a Ford.

Smith's evidence might be that Jones has at all times in the past within Smith's memory owned a car, and always a Ford, and that Jones has just offered Smith a ride while driving a Ford. Let us imagine, now, that Smith has another friend, Brown, of whose whereabouts he is totally ignorant. Smith selects three place-names quite at random, and constructs the following three propositions:

(g) Either Jones owns a Ford, or Brown is in Boston;
(h) Either Jones owns a Ford, or Brown is in Barcelona;
(i) Either Jones owns a Ford, or Brown is in Brest-Litovsk.

Each of these propositions is entailed by (f). Imagine that Smith realizes the entailment of each of these propositions he had constructed by (f), and proceeds to accept (g), (h), and (i) on the basis of (f). Smith has correctly inferred (g), (h), and (i) from a proposition for which he has strong evidence. Smith is therefore, completely justified in believing each of these three propositions. Smith, of course, has no idea where Brown is.

But imagine now that two further conditions hold. First, Jones does *not* own a Ford, but is at present driving a rented car. And secondly, by the sheerest coincidence, and entirely unknown to Smith, the place mentioned in proposition (h) happens really to be the place where Brown is. If these two conditions hold then Smith does *not* know that (h) is true, even though (*i*) (h) *is* true, (*ii*) Smith does believe that (h) is true, and (*iii*) Smith is justified in believing that (h) is true.

These two examples show that definition (a) does not state a *sufficient* condition for someone's knowing a given proposition. The same cases, with appropriate changes, will suffice to show that neither definition (b) nor definition (c) do so either.

4

COLIN RADFORD

(1935–   )

Knowledge—By Examples *

Radford attacks the traditional views of what it means to say someone knows something in a way similar to Gettier, but Radford is concerned to show the lack of correlation between knowing something and being sure or certain of it. The point of his main example is the demonstration that a person may know that something is the case, even if he is neither sure that it is and is almost certain that it is not the case, nor justified in being sure that it is the case, nor has the right to be certain that it is the case. If Radford is correct, then believing, being sure, being confident, being certain of something, etc., are not necessary conditions of knowing. But what is a necessary condition of knowing?

* Colin Radford, "Knowledge—By Examples," *Analysis*, Vol. 27, 1966, 1–11. Reprinted by permission of Basil Blackwell & Mott Ltd., Oxford.

EXAMPLE 1

Man: Look, I *know* I locked the car. Still—I'll go back and make absolutely sure.

Wife (irritated): Aren't you sure?

Man: Well—*yes,* I *am* sure. I'd bet money on it. Still, I could be mistaken. It's possible, isn't it darling? And this is a tough neighborhood.

Wife (surprised): Oh!

Man: Yes. And since it would be disastrous if I hadn't locked it, I might as well go and check. I won't be long.

We may safely assume that, providing he has locked his car, the man knows that he has done so, viz., that P. Even so, it is not absolutely clear whether he is sure that he has or has not. (We should need to know more about him and his relationship with his wife to say.)

So what this example suggests is that a man could know that P and yet not be sure that P.[1]

---

[1] It also suggests that checking up on something does not invariably require or imply doubt on the part of the checker with regard to what he checks up on, nor does it imply or require this to make his action rational. Security procedures at banks, routine daily inspections on aircraft, etc., show that this is so.

The next example is less equivocal.

EXAMPLE 2

Mr. Rea (the new librarian): What did we do with our copies of W. J. Locke's novels, Miss Tercy?

Miss Tercy: Oh!—I'm not absolutely sure. I *think* we may have sold them for pulp.

Mr. Rea: But you're not sure?

Miss Tercy: Well, no, not really, Mr. Rea. I *think* we did. It was several years ago—well, I think it was. Shall I just go and ... (*She leaves.*)

Mr. Rea: ?

Mr. Gee: Oh, that's what'll have happened. She's got a memory like an elephant.

Mr. Rea: Well, why is she so ... so ... ?

Mr. Gee: Anxious? Uncertain? I don't know. Perhaps it's her age —she isn't sure about anything. But she knows everything about this library. What did she say—they may have been pulped? Well, you may be certain that's what'll have happened to them.

This conversation piece shows that a person may be judged both to know something to be the case, viz., that P, and yet not be sure that P. For although Miss Tercy's lack of certainty is, perhaps, neurotic and treated as such, it is also treated as real. She really isn't sure. It isn't that she is simply prone to hedge.

The next example is more ambitious.

EXAMPLE 3

Tom: Right. You won the noughts-and-crosses. Now we'll have a quiz: English history.

Jean: Oh! No! I don't *know* any English history.

Tom: Don't be silly, everyone does. You must have done some at school?

Jean: They don't teach English history at French-Canadian schools.

Tom: Really? Well, this will be educational for you. And it's time I won something. Ready?

Jean: O.K. I'll just guess. Then I'll ask you some questions on French-Canadian history!

Tom: Yes. Well: sixpence on the first question, shilling on the second, one and six on the third and so on up to five bob?

Jean: Why not?

Tom: Right. First question, for sixpence: when did William the Conquerer land in England?

Jean (hesitantly): Ten sixty-six.

Tom: There you are!

Jean: Well, well! Ten sixty-six and all that?

Tom: Yes! Yes—for ´a shilling: whom did he defeat and kill when he landed?

Jean: Oh! Oh. (*Pause.*) Oh—I don't know.

Tom: It's easy. Kids' stuff.

Jean: I told you.

Tom: Harold! Whom had Harold himself defeated just before the Battle of Hastings?

Jean: I'm glad this isn't for real money. (*Pause.*) Frederick?

Tom: Frederick? No. Harald Hadraga. That's—ah?—two bob. For another two bob—um?—um? Well—moving on a bit then: when did Henry the Eighth die?

Jean (pause): He had six wives?

Tom: Yes.

Jean: Oh, I don't know. (*Pause.*) Fifteen seventy-seven?

Tom: Bad luck! Fifteen *forty*-seven. What about Elizabeth?

Jean: Oh! Ah . . . Elizabeth. Elizabeth. Tsst! Ooh . . . Mmm . . . Sixteen-oh-three?

Tom: Yes! Now tell me you haven't done any history!

Jean: No, really.

Tom (sarcastically): That was just a guess, was it?

Jean: Well, I don't know. Perhaps I picked that up on a Shakespeare course or somewhere. We didn't do all these kings and queens. Anyway—you owe me . . . ?

Tom: You owe *me*—four bob take away two and six—one and six. For *three* bob, when did James the First die?

Jean: James the First?

Tom: James Stuart, the Sixth of Scotland and the First of England. The first Stuart. He came after Elizabeth.

Jean: Oh . . . Ah . . . James the First. So he's sixteen-oh-three to . . . to . . . sixteen-oh-three. Sixteen twenty-five?

Tom: Yes! Look here, you must have done these people!

Jean: Well, I certainly don't remember. As far as I can tell I'm just guessing. And don't think you're going to get me to double up or anything like that!

Tom: I wouldn't dream of it; I owe you one-and-six. Well—this is giving you a chance: Charles the First?

Jean: When did he get on and off his English throne?

Tom: Yep. He's the next. This is for three-and-six.

Jean: Ah . . . the *next?* Charles the First? So that's sixteen . . . What was it, sixteen twenty-five? to . . . (*Pause.*) Sixteen-oh-three, sixteen twenty-five—sixteen forty-nine?

Tom: Well, I—

Jean: Is that right?

Tom: You wouldn't like to double your stake on that?

Jean: *Oh* no! Is it right, though?

Tom: Yes. No more clues. Um. (*Thinks.*) Oh! Easy: Victoria. When did she ascend the throne?

Jean: Ah . . . Victoria? Victoria. Victoria. About eighteen twenty?

Tom: What date?

Jean: Eighteen twenty.

Tom: Hmm. When did she die?

Jean: Ah! Ah . . . the Victorian Age. Um . . . Eighteen ninety-eight?

Tom: No. She's eighteen thirty-seven to nineteen-oh-one. You're slipping. All right then. Last question. For five shillings· Edward the Seventh came to the throne in nineteen-oh-one. When did he die?

Jean (*thinking*): Nineteen-nineteen?

Tom: No. Nineteen-ten. That's the last three wrong. Let's see, that's four bob, four and six, five bob, take away five bob—nine and six.

Jean: Well, there you are. Now do you believe me?

Tom: Well, no. You don't know much, that's true. But besides ten sixty-six, you got all the questions right about the Tudor and Stuart kings—apart from Henry the Eighth.

Jean (*reflectively*): Yes.

Tom: And even there you got a kind of near mnemonic miss. You know you must have done them at some time. You couldn't just have been guessing, Jean, could you?

Jean: No, I don't suppose . . . . Yes, you know—come to think of it— I think I remember I *did* once have to learn some dates. . . .

Tom: Ah, yes!

Jean: Some kings and queens. Perhaps it *was* these. As a punishment I think it was. But I'd quite forgotten about it, really.

Tom: Oh . . .

Jean: Yes, I think it *was* these—but *really*—

Tom: No, no, no—I believe you. Freudian forgetting, I expect.

Like the others this is not of course a real-life example, and this time we should consider whether it is a possible one, i.e., whether it is a conversation that could take place, and, if it could and did, whether its participants would be right in concluding, as they do, that the Jean-figure did know some English history.

Clearly such a conversation might take place, and I shall temporarily assume that the participants' conclusion would be correct if it did. I shall also assume for the sake of simplicity that Jean was sincere in everything he said and that the questions about the Tudor and Stuart monarchs that he got right he would have got right without any prompting, cues, or clues at all. For if we allow this as a possibility, then we should have to say about our hypothetical example that prior to the quiz, or at very least during the quiz but before hearing Tom's comments on each correct answer, Jean *did* know some English history, viz., that William landed in 1066, Elizabeth died in 1603, etc. In particular, he knew, e.g., the date of James I's death, viz., 1625; that is to say, he knew that James I died in 1625, that P.

And yet of course, although in this situation Jean knew that P, he was not certain, or sure, or confident that P. Indeed he was fairly certain that his answer to the question was wrong, i.e., that not-P, since he believed it to be a pure guess in a situation where only one of many such guesses could be correct.

Moreover, though he was not sure that P, Jean would not have had any grounds for being sure—or, at least, as he was not aware of them, i.e., of having learned that P, etc.—he would not have been justified in being sure, etc., that his answer was right, viz., that P, had he been sure. For although he had at some stage learned that P, he had quite forgotten that he had done so, and was, indeed, quite sure that he had not. (Of course, when we *are* quite sure about such matters, but cannot remember learning about them, we characteristically infer that, since we are sure, we *must* have learned though we have forgotten doing so. But if Jean were both sure, e.g., that James I had died in 1625, and yet sure that he had never learned or heard of or read the date, he would have no right, no good or adequate reason or justification for being sure that it was 1625 or whatever—unless, for whatever reason, his 'intuitions' about such matters invariably turned out to be right, and he knew this.)

So if Example 3 is a possible one it shows that neither being sure that P nor having the right to be sure that P, can be necessary conditions of knowing that P.[2] Indeed, it shows that a man may know that

---

[2] That is not to say that one is not characteristically or paradigmatically sure of what one knows. But if being sure is a necessary condition, one cannot know unless one is sure. But cf. Cohen's remark, 'Claims to Knowledge,' *Arist. Soc. Supp. Vol.* XXXVI (1962), '... if ... confidence that p is *never* a necessary condition of knowledge that p ...' (p. 46, my italics).

P even though he is *neither* sure that P, and is indeed fairly sure that not-P, *nor* justified in being sure, etc., that P!

This perhaps is surprising. Certainly it contradicts most of what philosophers have had to say about knowledge. Moreover it raises further problems. So, before concluding by discussing a couple of these problems, I want to consider whether and, if so, why, the conclusion that Jean did know some English history is correct.

Since the example is a fabricated one we may properly assume that the participants are right as to the facts, i.e., that they are right in thinking that, e.g., James died in 1625, that Jean had learned this at some time, etc. Given this, then, if the conclusion that Jean knew is one that English speakers who shared this information would generally tend to come to, Jean did indeed know and this conclusion is correct. For, ultimately, whether he 'knows' is a question of what 'know' means, which in turn is very much a matter of when, in what situations, English speakers say or would say that someone knows or does not know. Tom's conclusion, which Jean himself finally accepts, viz., that Jean did know some English history, did know, e.g., the date of James' death, is one, I think, that similarly placed English speakers would make, and is therefore correct.

However, whether we say Jean does or does not know is not simply a matter of appealing to one's intuition and then checking this against the result of some Naessian survey. We can provide reasons for our judgment that he knows—and weigh considerations which seem to tell against it—and this is what Tom and Jean do. After some discussion they agree:

i. That Jean's answers show that he has—he *must* have—*learned* some English history, viz., that which constitutes or, more probably, includes the answers to those questions he got right, which seems to be, almost exclusively, the dates of the Tudor and Stuart monarchs. I.e., at some stage he must have learned that James I died in 1625, etc. He did not get these answers right by sheer fluke or chance (or—a possibility they did not even bother to rule out—as a result of some mysterious intuition).

ii. They also show that he has *not forgotten* all the history, all the dates, that he must have learned—even though he *has* forgotten that he has learned them (it). For he produces various correct dates when asked, and does so in such a way and sufficiently often to preclude the possibility that he might simply be guessing and not remembering—even though he is inclined to think that he *is* guessing.

iii. So he *remembers* some history, and hence he knows some history, including, e.g., that P.

Of course, Jean's knowledge of English history is a poor thing, sparse, uncertain, unwitting, and therefore unimpressive and of little use. But that is not to say that, at the time of the quiz, it is wholly gone, totally forgotten, i.e., that it does not exist.

Although the quiz reveals that Jean does know some English history, he does not know that he knows any until after Tom has told him that certain of his answers are correct.[3] E.g., when asked, Jean knew the date of James I's death, viz., that P, but he did not know that he knew this. For he did not think that he knew the date of James's death and was indeed quite sure that he did not and that he would therefore have to make a guess at it. Moreover, had he been sure that he knew the date, and yet still sure, as he was, that he had never learned it (and sure that if he *had* ever seen or heard or read it, it had left no 'impression,' and had not 'registered,' etc.), he would certainly have had no right to be sure that he knew the date. But this last point is a complication. Jean was not sure that he knew the date of James's death for he was sure that he did not know it, and, having forgotten that he had learned it, and indeed being quite sure that he had never learned it, he did not have the right to be sure that he knew this date.

But although this conclusion is correct, the account above of why Jean did not know that he knew, e.g., that P, is incomplete and in such a way as to seem paradoxical. For it appears to reintroduce at the second level (knowing that one knows that P) precisely those conditions for knowing which, I have argued, are not necessary conditions for knowing at the first level (knowing that P) or at any level at all.

In fact, of course, no paradox is involved here. For to say that being sure and having the right to be sure are not necessary conditions of knowing that ... is not to say that it is possible to know that ϕ without satisfying these conditions for any value of 'ϕ,' but only that one can know that ϕ without satisfying these conditions for at least one value of 'ϕ.' (Cf. footnote 1.)

Even so, the account of why Jean does not know that he knows any English history, including, e.g., that P, is incomplete, and we can remove the air of paradox by seeing both why we want to say that Jean knows at the first level—even though he is not sure and does not have the right to be sure (that P) and that these considerations do not exist or operate at the second level in this particular case.

[3] Hence a gap can appear between knowing that P and knowing that one knows that P. That it does sometimes appear is suggested by remarks made when the gap closes, *cf.* 'I didn't know I knew that—you know, that the molecular weight of oxygen was sixteen. But that it can has been denied e.g. by Richard Taylor, 'Knowing what one knows,' *Analysis*, 16.2 (December 1955, p. 65), and queried e.g., by Michael Clark (*Analysis*, December 1963, p. 48).

We conclude that Jean knows some English history, e.g., the dates of some of the Tudor and Stuart monarchs, because his answers, though different, are *right* sufficiently often and in such a way as to persuade us that he has learned these dates and not simply guessed them, i.e., they persuade us that he has learned some history and has remembered some. And, since he remembers some, he knows some, even though he is not sure, etc. In contrast, had the questions in the quiz been framed slightly differently, 'Do you *know* when...?' (or 'Are you going to have a guess?'), Jean would have consistently and no doubt wearily replied 'No, I don't know. I'll guess. Was it...?' *even when he did know the date.*

Of course Jean would talk in this way precisely because he is sure that he has never come into contact with any English history and is, therefore, quite sure that he does not know any. But this does not mean that a man could not know that he knew that... unless he was sure that he knew and he had the right to be sure. For let us consider a slightly different case in which a man is not sure that he knows any English history and does not have the right to be sure that he knows any as it is years since he did any history. Despite this, he says at the beginning of a history quiz, quite modestly but firmly, that he *does* know a little history. He is then asked ten questions, and on the four occasions that he does know the date he says, sometimes after a little hesitation, that he does know it and gives the correct date, and when he does not know he says that he does not. I think we should have to say of such a man that he did know a little history, and that he knew that he knew a little history. (We could hardly say of him that he *didn't* know that he knew any history.)

So it is perhaps not merely Jean's not being sure, or his not having the right to be sure, or even his not believing that he has the right to be sure, that he knows the answers to any of the questions that Tom asks him, that debars him from knowing that he knows any English history, or knowing that he knows, e.g., that P. It is rather that (being quite sure he does *not* know any) he says at the beginning of the quiz that he does not, and would say that he did not know the answer to any particular question in the quiz even when he did. It is because he gets or would get the answers to the 'Do you know...?' questions wrong (and certain of the dates right) that we say that he is not *aware,* does not realize, i.e., he does not know, that he knows any history. [4]

---

[4] But could a man know that he knew some history if he were not merely unsure that he did, but pretty sure that he did not? Apparently not. But why not?

Secondly: although at the time of the quiz Jean knew some English history, viz., a few dates, before he realised—before he knew—that he knew some, he had no *right* to say that he knew. It would, in some way, have been improper for him to say, e.g., that he knew that James died in 1625, prior to his learning that this was indeed the case, i.e., that he knew. That is not to say that different circumstances could not excuse, justify, or even make praiseworthy Jean's saying this, but only that, whatever the circumstances, a *prima facie* objection remains, i.e., to claiming that one knows that P when one is not sure that P or does not believe that one knows that P.

Cohen (see footnote, p. 424), who distinguishes statements as acts, statements as the contents of a subclass of such acts, and propositions (I am unable to make the latter distinction), argues that a man's lack of confidence that P does not *eo ipso* render his act of 'making the statement' that he knows that P unjustifiable, i.e., *morally* unjustifiable (p. 39), which of course is correct. And for him the only other question of justifiability that can arise is whether the proposition that is 'uttered' when the statement is made is true or not. But although special circumstances could, e.g., make Jean's claiming that he knew that P morally justifiable, that is not to say that the *prima facie* objection would not remain to his doing so or that it would not have to be met and overcome if his action were to be morally justified. It is this *prima facie* impropriety, which Cohen misses or dismisses and which remains even when what Jean says happens to be true, that I want to explain.

Those who claim that being sure and having the right to be sure are necessary conditions of knowledge can give a clear explanation though, as I have argued, an incorrect one. They can say that had Jean claimed that he knew that P, what he said would have been improper in that it would have been false. But, on my thesis, had he said this, it would have been true; Jean did know the date of James's death, and yet it would nonetheless have been improper for him to say this. Why?

The answer is of course simply that, although Jean did know that P, he neither knew that he knew that P nor did he believe that he knew. In exactly the same way, Jean would have had no right *prima facie* to state, assert, claim—or, for that matter, agree, admit, concede, etc.—that P either, since although he did know that P he did not know that he knew that P nor did he believe that he knew that P (for he was neither sure that P, nor did he have the right, or believe that he had the right to be sure that P).

This account presupposes that it is *prima facie* improper for a man to state, etc., that he knows that P, or that P, or whatever, unless he believes that he does know that what he says is true, and his belief that he knows this is confident, sure, certain, etc., and, he believes, well-grounded or reasonable, etc. This may be true, but how so?

i. If a man states, etc., that P, or that he knows that P, or whatever, i.e., states or concedes, etc., whatever he does state or concede (without qualification, 'as if it were a fact'), his doing this implies in some way that he believes that what he says is true, that he is confident that this is so, and that he believes that he has the right to be confident that this is so. (For if he is not sure, etc., he should qualify what he says.) I.e., it implies that he at least *believes* that he knows that what he says is true. But Jean did not believe that he knew that P, and so his stating, etc., that P would have implied something false, and hence would have been *prima facie* improper in this sense.[5]

ii. If a man does not believe that he knows that P, this may be because he is not sure that P, or not sure that he has the right to be sure that P, or sure that he does not know that P, or sure that he knows that not-P, etc. So if a man does not believe that he knows that P, then, *ceteris paribus*, it is not likely that he *does* know that P and entirely problematic (for most values of 'P') that P. So if he says that he knows that P, what he says is likely to be false either because it is not the case that P or because he does not know that P. Hence, what he says is improper in this sense. Moreover, and as we have already seen, if a man states, etc., that he knows that P, or P, or whatever, his doing this implies that he at least believes that he knows that what he says is true. So not only does he say something that may very well be false, his doing this implies that he at least thinks he knows that what he says is true, and this is certainly false. But not only is what is implied by his stating that he knows that P, or P, or whatever, false, it is something which, more than anything else he could imply by what he does, would tend to suggest to others that what he says is true. (Compare what he does, which is to *state*, etc., that he knows that P, with someone's *guessing* that he, the guesser, knows that P. His doing this, viz., guessing that he knows that P, does not imply that he, the guesser, knows or thinks he knows that what he guesses is true. *Au contraire*. So his guessing would not tend to persuade or suggest to a listener who knew what the guesser was doing, viz., guessing, that the guesser did know that he knew that P. It would suggest instead that the guesser was not at

---

[5] Of course, what is implied in this kind of way is not always believed by a hearer, nor is it always morally wrong to mislead or to intend to mislead him. But it is *prima facie* wrong.

all sure that he knew that P.) Thus a man's stating, etc., that he knows
that P when he does not believe that he knows this has implications
that are themselves false and which suggest to the naïve hearer that
he may accept as true what may very well be false, viz., that the
speaker knows that P. Such behaviour is intentionally misleading, and,
of course, remains so even if, like Jean, the speaker does know that P.

I think this does explain how Jean's stating, etc., that he knew that
P, when he did not believe this, would have been *prima facie* improper
even though he did know that P. The explanation, which has the
advantage of allowing that Jean could know without believing that
he knew, also has the advantage of offering an account, and precisely
the same account, of the precisely similar impropriety of a man's stating, etc., that P when he does not believe that he knows this. Now as
in this case the man does not state or claim or assert, etc., that he
knows that P, the rival explanation has no application here and so
cannot possibly explain the impropriety.

'But,' it may now be asked, 'even if it is true that a man's stating,
etc., that P somehow implies that he is confident that he knows, and,
he believes, properly confident that he knows that P, how does it
do this?'

This is not perhaps a question that I ought to try to answer within
the confines of this paper, but since it is interesting and difficult, and
a problem that the paper leaves me with, I shall very briefly try to
say something about it.

It is tempting to say that there is a convention, a linguistic convention, in English and perhaps in other languages too, that one does not
state, etc., that P unless one is confident and, one feels, properly confident that one knows that P. So anyone who breaks this convention
says something or, perhaps, does something, that is misleading, and
if he breaks it deliberately, then he is being deliberately misleading.

But this sketch of an account, though attractive, is not just inadequate but, I suspect, fundamentally incorrect. For it entails that there
could be a language with a convention which allowed one to state, etc.,
that P, even though one did not believe that one knew that P, i.e., a
language in which someone's stating that P did not imply that the
speaker at least thought he knew that what he said was true, and
hence a language in which, if someone did state that P without believing that he knew that P, his doing so would not be regarded as misleading or *prima facie* improper.

The difficulty here is that if there were such a language, we could
not understand its users' 'stating,' 'asserting,' 'claiming,' 'conceding,'
etc., that P, i.e., their saying that P without qualification and as if it

were a fact, as *that*. We should rather understand it, if we could understand it at all, as their analogue of our saying 'I don't know whether
P or not,' but this of course is not a way of saying that P.

The reason for this is that stating, etc., that P, i.e., saying that something is the case, is essentially something that we do to inform. But we
cannot hope or try or intend to inform unless we at least believe that
we are ourselves informed, i.e., have knowledge. Thus we cannot construe something that a person does as his stating, asserting, etc., i.e., as
his saying that something or other is the case, without thinking that
either he at least believes he knows what he is talking about and so
knows that P, if that is what he says, or he is misleading us and, therefore, his saying that P is at least *prima facie* improper.

To briefly summarise my negative conclusions: neither believing that
P nor, *a fortiori*, being confident, sure, quite sure, or certain that P is
a necessary condition of knowing that P. Nor is it a necessary condition
of knowing that P that one should have the right to be, or be justified
in being, or have adequate grounds for being sure that P. Nor is it a
necessary condition that one should *believe* that one has the right to
be, etc., sure that P. It is, perhaps, rather that being sure that P, and
believing that one has the right to be sure that P, are necessary conditions of *believing* that one knows, and hence of having the *prima
facie* right to say that one knows that P.

5   RENÉ DESCARTES

(1596–1650)

Doubt and Certainty *

René Descartes is usually identified as the father of modern philosophy, not only because of the topics of his major works but also because of the methodology that he incorporated in pursuit of his philosophical goals. This selection is taken from his First and Second meditations. Descartes's chief concern was to answer the question, What can we know for certain? The First Meditation is a description of Descartes's struggle to avoid thinking of his world in terms of the language of the senses. His method usually is described as systematic doubt. Descartes asks himself if he can without contradiction doubt all the beliefs he has formerly held. He begins by doubting anything that he has learned or that is dependent upon his senses and then proceeds to doubt even "knowledge" garnered from mathematics

Everything could be an illusion, even the most abstract of mathematical proofs. The path of systematic doubt seems endless, and the foundations of knowledge appear to crumble, but Descartes then "discovers" a certitude that even while doubting he cannot doubt that he is doubting. "I am, I exist" is necessarily true each time it is uttered by oneself. That is indubitable and hence certain knowledge. Compare Descartes's account with Russell's views on intuitive knowledge and derivative knowledge and with Malcolm's criticism of Descartes's grounds for skepticism of the senses.

* From *Meditations on First Philosophy* (1641). Translated by E. S. Haldane and G. R. T. Ross (London: Cambridge University Press, 1912).

MEDITATION I

*Of the Things Which May
Be Brought Within the Sphere
of the Doubtful*

It is now some years since I detected how many were the false beliefs that I had from my earliest youth admitted as true, and how doubtful was everything I had since constructed on this basis; and from that time I was convinced that I must once for all seriously undertake to rid myself of all the opinions which I had formerly accepted, and commence to build anew from the foundation, if I wanted to establish any firm and permanent structure in the sciences. But as this enterprise appeared to be a very great one, I waited until I had

attained an age so mature that I could not hope that at any later date
I should be better fitted to execute my design. This reason caused me
to delay so long that I should feel that I was doing wrong were I to
occupy in deliberation the time that yet remains to me for action.
Today, then, since very opportunely for the plan I have in view I
have delivered my mind from every care [and am happily agitated by
no passions] and since I have procured for myself an assured leisure
in a peaceable retirement, I shall at last seriously and freely address
myself to the general upheaval of all my former opinions.

Now for this object it is not necessary that I should show that all of
these are false—I shall perhaps never arrive at this end. But inasmuch
as reason already persuades me that I ought no less carefully to withhold my assent from matters which are not entirely certain and indubitable than from those which appear to me manifestly to be false, if I
am able to find in each one some reason to doubt, this will suffice to
justify my rejecting the whole. And for that end it will not be requisite
that I should examine each in particular, which would be an endless
undertaking; for owing to the fact that the destruction of the foundations of necessity brings with it the downfall of the rest of the edifice,
I shall only in the first place attack those principles upon which all
my former opinions rested.

All that up to the present time I have accepted as most true and
certain I have learned either from the senses or through the senses;
but it is sometimes proved to me that these senses are deceptive, and
it is wiser not to trust entirely to any thing by which we have once
been deceived.

But it may be that, although the senses sometimes deceive us concerning things which are hardly perceptible, or very far away, there
are yet many others to be met with as to which we cannot reasonably
have any doubt, although we recognize them by their means. For
example, there is the fact that I am here, seated by the fire, attired
in a dressing gown, having this paper in my hands, and other similar
matters. And how could I deny that these hands and this body are
mine, were it not perhaps that I compare myself to certain persons,
devoid of sense, whose cerebella are so troubled and clouded by the
violent vapors of black bile, that they constantly assure us that they
think they are kings when they are really quite poor, or that they are
clothed in purple when they are really without covering, or who
imagine that they have an earthenware head or are nothing but pump-
kins or are made of glass. But they are mad, and I should not be any
the less insane were I to follow examples so extravagant.

At the same time I must remember that I am a man, and that consequently I am in the habit of sleeping, and in my dreams representing to myself the same things or sometimes even less probable things, than do those who are insane in their waking moments. How often has it happened to me that in the night I dreamt that I found myself in this particular place, that I was dressed and seated near the fire, whilst in reality I was lying undressed in bed! At this moment it does indeed seem to me that it is with eyes awake that I am looking at this paper; that this head which I move is not asleep, that it is deliberately and of set purpose that I extend my hand and perceive it; what happens in sleep does not appear so clear nor so distinct as does all this. But in thinking over this I remind myself that on many occasions I have in sleep been deceived by similar illusions, and in dwelling carefully on this reflection I see so manifestly that there are no certain indications by which we may clearly distinguish wakefulness from sleep that I am lost in astonishment. And my astonishment is such that it is almost capable of persuading me that I now dream.

Now let us assume that we are asleep and that all these particulars, e.g., that we open our eyes, shake our head, extend our hands, and so on, are but false delusions; and let us reflect that possibly neither our hands nor our whole body are such as they appear to us to be. At the same time we must at least confess that the things which are represented to us in sleep are like painted representations which can only have been formed as the counterparts of something real and true, and that in this way those general things at least, i.e., eyes, a head, hands, and a whole body, are not imaginary things, but things really existent. For, as a matter of fact, painters, even when they study with the greatest skill to represent sirens and satyrs by forms the most strange and extraordinary, cannot give them natures which are entirely new, but merely make a certain medley of the members of different animals; or if their imagination is extravagant enough to invent something so novel that nothing similar has ever before been seen, and that their work represents a thing purely fictitious and absolutely false, it is certain all the same that the colors of which this is composed are necessarily real. And for the same reason, although these general things, to wit, [a body], eyes, a head, and such like, may be imaginary, we are bound at the same time to confess that there are at least some other objects yet more simple and more universal, which are real and true; and of these just in the same way as with certain real colors, all these images of things which dwell in our thoughts, whether true and real or false and fantastic, are formed.

To such a class of things pertains corporeal nature in general, and its extension, the figure of extended things, their quantity or magnitude

and number, as also the place in which they are, the time which measures their duration, and so on.

That is possibly why our reasoning is not unjust when we conclude
from this that Physics, Astronomy, Medicine, and all other sciences
which have as their end the consideration of composite things, are
very dubious and uncertain; but that Arithmetic, Geometry, and other
sciences of that kind which only treat of things that are very simple
and very general, without taking great trouble to ascertain whether
they are actually existent or not, contain some measure of certainty
and an element of the indubitable. For whether I am awake or asleep,
two and three together always form five, and the square can never
have more than four sides, and it does not seem possible that truths
so clear and apparent can be suspected of any falsity [or uncertainty].

Nevertheless, I have long had fixed in my mind the belief that an
all-powerful God existed by whom I have been created such as I am.
But how do I know that He has not brought it to pass that there is no
earth, no heaven, no extended body, no magnitude, no place, and that
nevertheless [I possess the perceptions of all these things and that]
they seem to me to exist just exactly as I now see them? And besides,
as I sometimes imagine that others deceive themselves in the things
which they think they know best, how do I know that I am not deceived every time that I add two and three, or count the sides of a
square, or judge of things yet simpler, if anything simpler can be
imagined? But possibly God has not desired that I should be thus
deceived, for He is said to be supremely good. If, however, it is contrary to His goodness to have made me such that I constantly deceive
myself, it would also appear to be contrary to His goodness to permit
me to be sometimes deceived, and nevertheless I cannot doubt that
He does permit this.

There may, indeed, be those who would prefer to deny the existence
of a God so powerful, rather than believe that all other things are
uncertain. But let us not oppose them for the present, and grant that
all that is said of a God is a fable; nevertheless, in whatever way they
suppose that I have arrived at the state of being that I have reached—
whether they attribute it to fate or to accident, or make out that it is by
a continual succession of antecedents, or by some other method—since
to err and deceive oneself is a defect, it is clear that the greater will
be the probability of my being so imperfect as to deceive myself ever,
as is the Author to whom they assign my origin the less powerful. To
these reasons I have certainly nothing to reply, but at the end I feel
constrained to confess that there is nothing in all that I formerly believed to be true, of which I cannot in some measure doubt, and that

not merely through want of thought or through levity, but for reasons which are very powerful and maturely considered; so that henceforth I ought not the less carefully to refrain from giving credence to these opinions than to that which is manifestly false, if I desire to arrive at any certainty [in the sciences].

But it is not sufficient to have made these remarks; we must also be careful to keep them in mind. For these ancient and commonly held opinions still revert frequently to my mind, long and familiar custom having given them the right to occupy my mind against my inclination and rendered them almost masters of my belief; nor will I ever lose the habit of deferring to them or of placing my confidence in them, so long as I consider them as they really are, i.e., opinions in some measure doubtful, as I have just shown, and at the same time highly probable, so that there is much more reason to believe than to deny them. That is why I consider that I shall not be acting amiss, if, taking of set purpose a contrary belief, I allow myself to be deceived, and for a certain time pretend that all these opinions are entirely false and imaginary, until at last, having thus balanced my former prejudices with my latter [so that they cannot divert my opinions more to one side than to the other], my judgment will no longer be dominated by bad usage or turned away from the right knowledge of the truth. For I am assured that there can be neither peril nor error in this course, and that I cannot at present yield too much to distrust, since I am not considering the question of action, but only of knowledge.

I shall then suppose, not that God, who is supremely good and the fountain of truth, but some evil genius not less powerful than deceitful, has employed his whole energies in deceiving me; I shall consider that the heavens, the earth, colors, figures, sound, and all other external things are nought but the illusions and dreams of which this genius has availed himself in order to lay traps for my credulity; I shall consider myself as having no hands, no eyes, no flesh, no blood, nor any senses, yet falsely believing myself to possess all these things; I shall remain obstinately attached to this idea, and if by this means it is not in my power to arrive at the knowledge of any truth, I may at least do what is in my power [i.e., suspend my judgment], and with firm purpose avoid giving credence to any false thing, or being imposed upon by this arch deceiver, however powerful and deceptive he may be. But this task is a laborious one, and insensibly a certain lassitude leads me into the course of my ordinary life. And just as a captive who in sleep enjoys imaginary liberty, when he begins to suspect that his liberty is but a dream, fears to awaken, and conspires with these agreeable illusions that the deception may be prolonged, so insensibly of my own accord I fall back into my former opinions, and I dread awakening from this slumber, lest the laborious wakefulness which would follow the tranquillity of this repose should have to be spent, not in daylight, but in the excessive darkness of the difficulties which have just been discussed.

MEDITATION II

Of the Nature of the Human
Mind; and That It Is More Easily
Known Than the Body

The Meditation of yesterday filled my mind with so many doubts that it is no longer in my power to forget them. And yet I do not see in what manner I can resolve them, and, just as if I had all of a sudden fallen into very deep water, I am so disconcerted that I can neither make certain of setting my feet on the bottom, nor can I swim and so support myself on the surface. I shall, nevertheless, make an effort and follow anew the same path as that on which I yesterday entered, i.e., I shall proceed by setting aside all that in which the least doubt could be supposed to exist, just as if I had discovered that it was absolutely false; and I shall ever follow in this road until I have met with something which is certain, or at least, if I can do nothing else, until I have learned for certain that there is nothing in the world that is certain. Archimedes, in order that he might draw the terrestrial globe out of its place, and transport it elsewhere, demanded only that one point should be fixed and immovable; in the same way, I shall have the right to conceive high hopes if I am happy enough to discover one thing only which is certain and indubitable.

I suppose, then, that all the things that I see are false; I persuade myself that nothing has ever existed of all that my fallacious memory represents to me. I consider that I possess no senses; I imagine that body, figure, extension, movement, and place are but the fictions of my mind. What, then, can be esteemed as true? Perhaps nothing at all, unless that there is nothing in the world that is certain.

But how can I know there is not something different from those things that I have just considered, of which one cannot have the slightest doubt? Is there not some God, or some other being by whatever name we call it, who puts these reflections into my mind? That is not necessary, for is it not possible that I am capable of producing them myself? I myself, am I not at least something? But I have already denied that I had senses and body. Yet I hesitate, for what follows from that? Am I so dependent on body and senses that I cannot exist without these? But I was persuaded that there was nothing in all the world, that there was no heaven, no earth, that there were no minds, nor any bodies: was I not then likewise persuaded that I did not exist? Not at all; of a surety I myself did exist since I persuaded myself of something [or merely because I thought of something]. But there is some deceiver or other, very powerful and very cunning, who ever employs his ingenuity in deceiving me. Then, without doubt, I exist also if he deceives me, and let him deceive me as much as he will, he can never cause me to be nothing so long as I think that I am something. So that, after having reflected well and carefully examined all things, we must come to the definite conclusion that this proposition: I am, I exist, is necessarily true each time that I pronounce it, or that I mentally conceive it.

6   NORMAN MALCOLM

(1911–   )

Dreaming and Skepticism *

Malcolm's concern in this essay is to examine Descartes's claim that because we can be deceived in our dreams into believing something that is not happening is happening and because we cannot clearly distinguish our dreaming from our waking states, we must always be skeptical of that which we supposedly learn from our senses. Malcolm's argument, based on his analysis of the notions of sleeping and dreaming, is that Descartes is confused. A major element in that confusion is Descartes's belief that one's dreams are a part of one's continuous mental life, that the thoughts and feelings one has in dreams are just like all of one's thoughts and feelings. Malcolm's philosophy is very much influenced by that of his teacher, Ludwig Wittgenstein, and this essay is a particularly good example of an important way to do philosophy in an analytic fashion.

* From *The Philosophical Review*, LXV (1956), 14 37. Reprinted by permission of the author and *The Philosophical Review*.

I N the *First Meditation,* Descartes represents himself as at first having the thought that surely it is *certain* that he is seated by the fire, and then as rejecting this thought in the following remark: "I cannot, however, but remind myself that on many occasions I have in sleep been deceived by similar illusions; and on more careful study of them I see that there are no certain marks distinguishing waking from sleep. ..." [1] I believe that it is worth while reflecting on his assertion that he has often been *deceived* when asleep. In his reply to the objections against the *Meditations* raised by Hobbes, he repeats this assertion in the form of a rhetorical question: "For who denies that in his sleep a man may be deceived?" [2]

Descartes is clearly implying that while a man is asleep a certain thought may occur to him or he may come to believe something or to

[1] Norman Kemp Smith, *Descartes' Philosophical Writings* (London, 1952), p. 198. hereafter cited as *DPW*.
[2] E. Haldane and G. Ross, *The Philosophical Works of Descartes* (Cambridge, 1934), II, 78; hereafter cited as *H &R*.

affirm something. And there is no doubt that he held this to be so. [3]
In the *Fifth Meditation* he says that "once I have recognized that there
is a God, and that all things depend on Him, and that He is not a deceiver, and from this, in turn, have inferred that all things which I
clearly and distinctly apprehend are of necessity true," then no grounds
remain for doubting any of the things that he remembers as having
been previously demonstrated—for example, the truths of geometry.
He continues:

> Will it be said that perhaps I am dreaming (an objection I myself
> raised a little while ago), that is, that all the thoughts I am now enter-
> taining are no more true than those which come to me in dreams?
> Even so, what difference would that make? For even should I be
> asleep and dreaming, whatever is present to my understanding in an
> evident manner is indisputably true [*DPW*, 247].

Descartes thinks that a man might have thoughts and make judgments while sleeping, and if those thoughts are "clear and distinct"
they are true, despite the fact that he is sleeping. This doctrine is
plainly set forth in his reply to the Jesuit, Bourdin: ". . . everything
which anyone clearly and distinctly perceives is true, although that
person in the meantime may doubt whether he is dreaming or awake,
nay, if you want it so, even though he is really dreaming or is deliri-
ous" (*H & R*, II, 267). In Part IV of the *Discourse*, Descartes remarks that "whether awake or asleep, we ought never to allow ourselves to be persuaded save on the evidence of our reason" (*DPW*,
146). Here he implies that a man can reason, can be persuaded, and
can resist persuasion—though all the while he is asleep!
    His view is that when we sleep the same *kinds* of mental states and
mental occurrences are present in us as when awake; the difference
is that, as a general rule, our minds don't work as well when we are
asleep.[4] But they work. Indeed, they *must* do so; for the "essence" or

---

[3] Other philosophers have held it too. Aristotle, in a short paper on dreams, says:
"It is . . . a fact that the soul makes . . . assertions in sleep" (*De Somnis*, in *The
Basic Works of Aristotle*, ed. by R. McKeon, [New York, 1941] p. 618). Kant, in *An
Inquiry into the Distinctness of the Principles of Natural Theology and Morals*,
says: "In deepest sleep perhaps the greatest perfection of the mind might be exercised in rational thought. For we have no reason for asserting the opposite except
that we do not remember the idea when awake. This reason, however, proves
nothing" (Immanuel Kant, *Critique of Practical Reason and Other Writings in
Moral Philosophy*, ed. by L. W. Beck [Chicago, 1949], p. 275).
[4] As Gilson puts Descartes' view: "Sleep does not constitute in itself a state of
error, but simply, because of physiological conditions, a state less favorable than
waking to the free exercise of thought" (E. Gilson, *René Descartes: Discours de la
Méthode:* Texte et commentaire [Paris, 1930], p. 366).

"principal attribute" of mental substance is consciousness, and so long as a mind exists there must exist "modes" of that essence, i.e., states of consciousness, mental occurrences, mental acts. As Descartes says in a letter:

> I had good reason to assert that the human soul is always conscious in any circumstances—even in a mother's womb. For what more certain or more evident reason could be required than my proof that the soul's nature or essence consists in its being conscious, just as the essence of a body consists in its being extended? A thing can never be deprived of its own essence.[5]

Descartes conceives of a dream as being a part of this continuous mental life. The thoughts of a dream are real thoughts. The feelings in a dream are real feelings. Descartes holds that to be frightened in a dream is to be frightened in the *same* sense as that in which I should be frightened now if half of the ceiling were suddenly to fall. He holds that the proposition "In my dream last night I was frightened" *entails* the proposition "Last night I was frightened." He holds that if in my dream I thought someone was at the door, then I had this thought, while asleep, in the very same sense as that in which I should have it now were I to hear the doorbell. It is only because Descartes conceives of a dream as composed of thoughts and sensations, in the same sense that a period of waking life is, that he is able, in the *First Meditation*, to derive a ground for doubting his senses from the fact that sometimes he dreams. According to his conception, the identical thoughts and sensations that you had when you were wide awake could have occurred to you when you were asleep. The *content* of a dream and of a waking episode could be the same. From this it follows "that there are no certain marks distinguishing waking from sleep." I will try to show that this conception is mistaken.

I

To begin with, I should like to call attention to the familiar distinction between being *sound* asleep and being *half* asleep. It is noteworthy that in American colloquial speech the phrase "dead to the world" is a synonym of the phrase "sound asleep" and not, of course, a synonym of the phrase "half asleep." If a man is half asleep he is also

---

[5] C. Adam and P. Tannery, *Oeuvres de Descartes* (Paris, 1899), III, 423; translation by E. Anscombe and P. Geach, *Descartes: Philosophical Writings* (Edinburgh, 1954), p. 266.

partly awake but not "clear" awake. Many different degrees of being asleep fall under the heading "half asleep." The criteria we commonly use for determining whether another person is or was sound asleep are different from the criteria we use for determining whether he is or was half asleep. It would seem that the former criteria are of two sorts: (1) a "present-tense" criterion, and (2) a "past-tense" criterion. We use the "present-tense" criterion to determine whether someone *is* (not was) sound asleep. It consists of things of this kind: that his eyes are closed, his body inert, his breathing rhythmical, and (more important) that he is unresponsive to questions, commands, and stimuli of moderate intensity. (Example: The sleeper does not react in any way when the carpenter begins hammering in the next room. In contrast, he might have rolled over and muttered a sleepy protest against the noise.) The "past-tense" criterion is used to determine whether a person *was* (not is) sound asleep, and it can be satisfied only when he is awake. It applies when the present-tense criterion has not been fulfilled in such a way that all question is removed as to whether the person is or is not sound asleep. We wait until he is awake and then find out whether he has any knowledge of what transpired in his vicinity while he was asleep: if he has none it is confirmed that he was sound asleep. (Example: He is surprised to learn that there was hammering close by while he slept: he has no recollection of any noise.) These two sorts of criterion can combine or conflict in many ways. It is possible that there should be cases in which there is no correct answer to the question "Was he sound asleep?"

The criteria of someone's being half asleep would seem to fall into the same two categories. The main difference between the present-tense criteria for being sound asleep and for being half asleep is that if someone is merely half asleep he will be in some degree responsive to questions, commands, and disturbances, although only sluggishly or groggily so. The main difference in the past-tense criteria for these two conditions is that if someone was only half asleep then he will be able to produce, when fully awake, some account of what took place in his immediate vicinity while he was half asleep, an account that will, however, be hazy and incomplete.[6] (A refinement of this last difference, pertaining to dreaming, is mentioned in footnote 9.)

[6] The psychoanalyst Lawrence Kubie remarks that "sleep is a psychologically active state, and we are never completely asleep, nor completely awake" (E. Hilgard, L. Kubie, and E. Pumpian-Mindlin, *Psychoanalysis as Science* [Stanford, 1952], p. 95). One wonders whether Kubie is so using the words that no one *could* be "completely awake" or "completely asleep."

II

In the next place, I wish to compare the following two sentences:
1. "I am sound asleep."
2. "I was sound asleep."

Although (1) and (2) differ grammatically only in tense, (1) is seen, straight off, to be a queer sentence, but (2) is not. Wherein lies the oddity of (1)?

Let us say that when a person utters or writes a sentence he can *use* the sentence to claim or affirm or assert something. It will depend on circumstances whether one has used a sentence to claim something, or whether one has merely uttered the sentence in order to call attention to the sentence itself, as I might utter (1) merely to call attention to it. (Also, of course, a sentence may be used to give a command or to put a question, and so on.) Now it is obvious that sentence (2), "I was sound asleep," can be and is used to claim or affirm or assert something. I shall express this by saying that it can be "used as an assertion."

The question now is whether (1) can be used as an assertion. It is not hard to see that there would be an absurdity in attempting to so use it. Suppose that I am in bed and that you come and shake me and ask "Are you asleep?" and that I reply "I am sound asleep." It would be amusing if you took me as claiming that I am sound asleep and then concluded from this that I am sound asleep. ("He says that he is sound asleep, and he ought to know.") The absurdity that would lie in the use of the sentence "I am sound asleep" as an assertion consists in this: if a person *claims* that he is sound asleep then he is *not* sound asleep. Notice that "claims" is a stronger verb here than "says." There is *a* sense of "says" in which a person says whatever words come out of his mouth. In this sense a man who is sound asleep can say things: he may talk in his sleep. He could say, in this sense, "I am sound asleep"; but this would not prove that he is not sound asleep. He is not claiming that he is sound asleep.

The absurdity that I am trying to describe does not lie in my uttering the words "I am sound asleep" but in my claiming or affirming or asserting that I am sound asleep. Whether I make the claim by using spoken or written words or by any other audible or visible signs is, therefore, irrelevant. If I use no physical signs but merely affirm in my mind that I am sound asleep (as I might affirm in my mind that my companion is a bore), it follows that I am not sound asleep.

The matter can be put by saying that the *assertion* "I am sound asleep" would be, in a certain sense, self-contradictory. The sentence

"I am sound asleep" does not express a self-contradiction in the way in which the sentence "A is taller than B and B is taller than A," expresses a self-contradiction. If the latter sentence were written down in front of you, you could straight off deduce a proposition of the form "*p* and not-*p*." You cannot do this with "I am sound asleep." But as soon as you bring in the notion of a person's *asserting* or *claiming* that he is sound asleep then you get a kind of self-contradiction. It would be an assertion of such a nature that *making* the assertion would contradict the *truth* of the assertion. The proposition "I am sound asleep" (if it can be called a "proposition") does not entail the proposition "I am not sound asleep." But if I am asserting that I am sound asleep then I am not sound asleep. If I am asserting that I am sound asleep someone else is entitled to say of me "He claims that he is sound asleep." And this latter proposition, "He claims that he is sound asleep" (if it can be called a "proposition"), entails the proposition "He is not sound asleep." Thus the first-person assertion "I am sound asleep" and the related third-person proposition "He claims that he is sound asleep" may each, with propriety I think, be called "self-contradictory," although in somewhat different senses. In neither case, of course, is it that "strict" kind of self-contradiction that is illustrated by my "taller" sentence: for the latter expresses something from which there follows a proposition of the form "*p* and not-*p*"; whereas neither from "I am sound asleep" nor from "He claims that he is sound asleep" does there follow any proposition of that form. The kind of self-contradiction is this: if someone claims that he is sound asleep then it follows that he is not what he claims. It is an assertion that would necessarily be false each time it was made.

Not only is there a kind of self-contradiction in claiming or affirming that one is sound asleep; there is the same kind of self-contradiction in wondering or conjecturing whether one is sound asleep, or in being in doubt about it. The proposition "He wonders whether he is sound asleep" is absurd in the same way that the proposition "He claims that he is sound asleep" is absurd. From either of them equally there follows the proposition "He is not sound asleep." So not merely is the *assertion* "I am sound asleep" self-contradictory: the *question* "Am I sound asleep?" is self-contradictory in the same sense. And if the *thought* should occur to you that you are sound asleep it would be a self-contradictory thought. And if you should be under the *impression* that you are sound asleep it would be a self-contradictory impression: for the proposition "He is under the impression (it seems to him) that he is sound asleep" entails the proposition "He is not sound asleep."

Finally, it should be mentioned that the proposition "He knows (he realizes, he is aware) that he is sound asleep" is a self-contradictory proposition in the "strict" sense. Therefore, a person who is sound asleep cannot know, realize, or be aware that he is.[7]

Of course, a person can *dream* that he is sound asleep and can *dream* that he *knows* that he is sound asleep. It can be said of a person who dreamt either of these things that "he knew in his dream" that he was sound asleep. What my argument proves is that knowing-in-your-dream that you are sound asleep is not knowing that you are sound asleep.

III

So far I have called attention to the fact that if a person affirms, doubts, thinks, or questions that he is sound asleep then he is not sound asleep—and also to the fact that a person who is sound asleep cannot know that he is. But now it is important to see that if a person affirms, doubts, thinks, or questions *anything whatever* (and not merely that he is sound asleep) then he is not sound asleep. No doubt all of those verbs have "dispositional" senses: for example, you can truly say of a man who is in fact sound asleep that he affirms that war will break out within the year. But it is not that sense of those verbs to which I am referring. If we take "He affirms that there will be a war" in the sense in which it means "At this very moment he is affirming that there will be a war," then it entails "He is not sound asleep." In this "nondispositional" sense of those verbs, "He is affirming (doubting, thinking, questioning) that *p*" entails "He is not sound asleep," *regardless* of what proposition is substituted for "*p*." Surely it is obvious that if "He is claiming that he is sound asleep" entails "He is not sound asleep," then also "He is claiming that someone is at the door" entails "He is not sound asleep." And likewise, if the thought has struck him that there might be someone at the door, or if he wonders whether there is, or if he doubts that there is, or if it seems to him that there is, or if he is afraid that there is—then he is not sound asleep. To state the principle for which I am arguing in its most general form: if a person is in *any* state of consciousness it logically follows that he is not sound asleep. The proposition with which I started my argument—namely, the propo-

---

[7] A proposition of the form "He knows that *p*" differs from a proposition of the form "He claims (thinks, conjectures, doubts) that *p*," in the respect that the former entails "*p*," the latter not. Therefore, "He knows that he is sound asleep" is self-contradictory in the "strict" sense: for, like propositions of the latter form, it entails "He is *not* sound asleep"; and, unlike those of the latter form, it entails "He *is* sound asleep."

sition that "He claims that he is sound asleep" entails "He is not sound asleep"—is a special case of this general principle, which may be expressed in Cartesian terms as follows: *Cogito ergo non dormio.*

When Descartes declared, in the course of his *Reply* to Gassendi's objections to the *Meditations*, that "when we sleep we perceive that we are dreaming" (*H & R*, II, 212), he was mistaken if he meant that when we are *sound* asleep we perceive that we are dreaming.[8]

The fact is that if someone is in bed with his eyes closed, whatever serves as a criterion for saying that just now he is thinking that so-and-so is the case, or is wondering or doubting whether it is, or perceives that it is—also serves as a criterion for saying that he is not sound asleep.

And if one cannot have thoughts while sound asleep, one cannot be *deceived* while sound asleep.

IV

There will be a temptation to conclude that, if all the foregoing is true, then clearly a person cannot *dream* when sound asleep. But this would be a mistake. Our normal criterion for someone's having had a dream is that, upon awaking, he relates ("tells") a dream. Suppose that the present-tense and past-tense criteria of sound sleep were satisfied in the case of a certain person—i.e., his body was inert, his breathing was heavy and rhythmical (perhaps he even snored); he did not react to moderately loud noises or to occurrences in his immediate vicinity that would have provoked his lively interest had he known about them: furthermore, when he woke up he had no suspicion that those noises and incidents had occurred. Also suppose that on awaking he related a dream. It would have been established both that he slept soundly and that he dreamt.[9]

---

[8] Note the following consequence drawn by Freud from his theory of dreams: "Throughout the whole of our sleep we are just as certain that we are dreaming as we are certain that we are sleeping" (*The Interpretation of Dreams*, in *The Basic Writings of Sigmund Freud*, ed. by A. A. Brill [New York, 1938], p. 513).

[9] The proposition "I was sound asleep" has, on my view, the nature of an inference. I *conclude* that I was sound asleep from things that I notice or learn after or as I wake up. For example, I find out that while I slept for the past hour a heavy tractor was making an uproar a hundred feet away, yet I have no recollection of hearing any noise. I infer that I was very soundly asleep.

I must mention here a complicating subtlety. Suppose, in the above example, I *dreamt* that I heard a roaring and clanking (like that of a nearby tractor) and dreamt that this noise was made by a dinosaur. I believe we should be inclined to say that I *heard* the tractor *in my sleep*, although I had no suspicion, upon awak-

V

I will anticipate, at this point, a very general sort of objection to the manner in which I argue. It will be said that I am assuming throughout that there are *criteria* for determining whether a person other than myself is or was thinking, or frightened, or awake, or asleep; i.e., I am assuming that I have criteria for the existence of particular sorts of mental occurrences and states of consciousness in other persons, those criteria being of such a nature that if they are fully satisfied the existence of those occurrences and states is established beyond question—whereas, the objection runs, there are no such criteria and could be none: at best I only have *evidence*, which makes the existence of those mental states and occurrences in others more or less probable. It is true that I make this "assumption." I believe that to deny it leads one to the view that each person *teaches himself* what fright, doubt, thinking, and all other mental phenomena are, by noting his own fright, doubt, etc.: each person "knows from his own case" what these things are. And this view leads to the untenable notion of a language that "I alone *can* understand." I will not attempt here to show either that the denial of the above "assumption" has this consequence or that it is untenable. I believe that both of these things have been established by Wittgenstein in his *Philosophical Investigations*. A rough guide to some of his thoughts on this topic may be found in my review of that book (*Philosophical Review*, October, 1954).

---

ening, that there had been such goings-on, until I was told. I think we should also be inclined to say that my sleep was not completely sound, that I was not utterly "dead to the world." I think that in general a certain degree of similarity between the events of a dream and the events occurring within normal perceptual range of the sleeper counts in favor of saying both that the sleeper faintly perceived the latter events and that his sleep was not an absolutely deep sleep. This would be so even if the sleeper had no idea, after awaking, that the events in question had occurred. I doubt that there is any way of specifying what the degree of similarity must be. I will comment briefly on two examples adduced by T. M. Yost, Jr., and Donald Kalish in their paper "Miss Macdonald on Sleeping and Waking" (*Philosophical Quarterly*, April, 1955). One is of an asthmatic who dreams that he is suffocating and finds on awaking that he is suffocating. The right thing to say here, I think, is that his dream was partly a perception of the reality, and also that it was not a dream of perfectly sound sleep. The other example is that of a person in California who dreams that the Washington Monument is being painted blue. A dream with such a content would not count against the dreamer's having been sound asleep, even if the Monument were being painted blue at the time he slept. What would indicate that a dreamer's sleep was not a very deep one would not be that his dream was veridical, but that the content of the dream suggests that he was to some extent perceptive of things that he would probably have perceived clearly, located as he was, had he been awake.

VI

Let us consider again Descartes' famous remark: "I cannot, however, but remind myself that on many occasions I have in sleep been deceived by similar illusions; and on more careful study of them I see that there are no certain marks distinguishing waking from sleep." Of course, if by "sleep" he means sound sleep, then it is false that in sleep he could ever have been deceived by any illusions whatever. But I want to pay particular attention to the idea that there are no certain marks distinguishing waking from sleep, an idea that has been commonly entertained and accepted by philosophers. Socrates put to Theaetetus the question:

> What evidence could be appealed to, supposing we were asked at this very moment whether we are asleep or awake—dreaming all that passes through our minds or talking to one another in the waking state?

To which Theaetetus replied

> Indeed, Socrates, I do not see by what evidence it is to be proved; for the two conditions correspond in every circumstance like exact counterparts. The conversation we have just had might equally well be one that we merely think we are carrying on in our sleep; and when it comes to thinking in a dream that we are telling other dreams, the two states are extraordinarily alike.[10]

Bertrand Russell says the following:

> I dreamed last night that I was in Germany, in a house which looked out on a ruined church; in my dream I supposed at first that the church had been bombed during the recent war, but was subsequently informed that its destruction dated from the wars of religion in the sixteenth century. All this, so long as I remained asleep, had all the convincingness of waking life. I did really have the dream, and did really have an experience intrinsically indistinguishable from that of seeing a ruined church when awake. It follows that the experience which I call "seeing a church" is not conclusive evidence that there is a church, since it may occur when there is no such external object as I suppose in my dream. It may be said that, though when dreaming I may *think* that I am awake, when I wake up I *know* that I am awake. But I do not see how we are to have any such certainty.... I do not believe that I am now dreaming, but I cannot prove that I am not. I am, however, quite certain that I am having certain experiences, whether they be those of a dream or those of waking life.[11]

---

[10] F. M. Cornford, *Plato's Theory of Knowledge* (London, 1935), p. 53.
[11] B. A. W. Russell, *Human Knowledge* (New York, 1948), pp. 171–172.

This manner of comparing dreaming and waking inevitably results in the skeptical question: "How can I tell whether at this moment I am awake or asleep?" and in the skeptical conclusion: "I *cannot* tell." The conception that underlies the comparison is the following: "Take any sequence of sensations, thoughts, and feelings. That same sequence could occur either when you were awake or when you were asleep and dreaming. The two conditions, being awake and being asleep, can have the same *content* of experience. Therefore, you cannot tell from the sensations, thoughts, and feelings themselves, at the time you are having them, whether you are awake or asleep."

If, however, we state the problem in terms of *sound* sleep, and bear in mind my preceding argument, then we see at least one respect in which this conception is mistaken. When a person is sound asleep he cannot have any sensations, thoughts, and feelings at all; sound sleep cannot, in *this* sense, have any "content of experience." This is so regardless of whether or not the sleeper dreams. Therefore it is not true, but senseless, to say that sound sleep and waking are "indistinguishable" from one another, or that they are "exact counterparts." For the meaning of this philosophical remark is that identically the same sensations, impressions, and thoughts could occur to one in either condition. But one might as well assert that a house and the mental image of a house could have the same weight; it is as meaningless to attribute sensations, impressions, thoughts, or feelings to sound sleep as to attribute weight to a mental image.

It is undoubtedly an ordinary use of language to call a dream an "experience": one may say of an unpleasant dream "I hope that I won't have that experience again." In this sense a man can have experiences when sound asleep. But this use of the word "experience" should not mislead us. In his dream a man may see, hear, think, feel emotion. To say that "in his dream" he thought his bed was on fire and was frightened, is equivalent to saying that he dreamt that he thought his bed was on fire and dreamt that he was frightened. The fallacy I am warning against is to conclude "He was frightened" from "He dreamt that he was frightened," and "He thought his bed was on fire" from "He dreamt that he thought his bed was on fire." The experience of thinking your bed is on fire and (if you are sound asleep) of thinking in your dream that your bed is on fire are "experiences" in different senses of the word.

VII

In the notion of the dream of sound sleep there is no foothold for philosophical skepticism. It is an error to say that a person *cannot tell*

whether he is awake or sound asleep and dreaming. For this implies
(a) that he might *think* he was awake and yet be sound asleep—which
is impossible. And it implies (b) that he might think he was sound
asleep and yet be awake. Now (b), unlike (a), is not impossible: but
the thought that the man has—namely, that he is sound asleep—is self-
contradictory (in the special sense that I explained), and a little reflection could teach him that it is. Whether or not a particular person
would see this point of logic, in any case no general ground for skepticism is provided.

But it is also an error to say that a man *can* tell whether or not he
is sound asleep. For this would imply that he had some criterion or test
at hand for determining the matter, and there is an absurdity in this
idea—for he could not even *use* a criterion unless he were *not* sound
asleep, and so nothing could turn on the "outcome" of using it. Therefore, it is wrong to say *either* that you can tell or cannot tell (in the
sense of *determine*) that you are sound asleep and dreaming, or that
you are awake.

There is a temptation to object to the preceding argument in the
following way: "even if I cannot have thoughts and sensations during
sound sleep, yet when I dream during sound sleep it seems to me that
I am having thoughts and sensations, and so there remains the problem
of determining, at any given time, whether I am having thoughts and
sensations or merely seeming to have them." [12] The pretty obvious
answer to this is that to a person who is sound asleep, "dead to the
world," things cannot even *seem*. He cannot hear the telephone ring
nor can it seem to him that it rings. Suppose that A is apparently sound
asleep, but that B makes the following report to C: "It seems to A that
he hears the telephone ringing." C's natural reply would be: "Why, I
thought that he was sound asleep!" Whatever movements, gestures, or
utterances of A's indicate that it seems to him that the telephone is
ringing, also indicate, to an equal degree, that he is not sound asleep.

Another objection to my argument is the following: "Granted that
while a person is sound asleep he gives no indication of having any
thoughts or of being conscious of anything, nevertheless upon awaking,
he might testify that such and such a thought had occurred to him
while he slept. Likewise, nothing in the demeanor of the man who is
quietly smoking his pipe reveals that the thought of resigning his government post has just occurred to him; but afterwards he may declare

---

[12] Socrates in the *Republic* asks: "Does not dreaming, whether one is awake or
asleep, consist in mistaking a semblance for the reality it resembles?" (F. M. Cornford, *The Republic of Plato* [New York, 1945], p. 183).

that it did first occur to him then. You would accept his testimony. Now, why shouldn't you accept it in the other case too? Since the cases are similar it is merely dogmatic and unreasonable to reject his testimony there while accepting it here."

It is true enough that a man's declaration that a certain thought passed through his mind on a particular occasion in the very recent past is used by others as a criterion of that thought's having passed through his mind on that past occasion, even though his behavior at the time gave no indication of it. Similarly, someone who is calmly discussing something with you and giving no indication of physical discomfort, may later declare that he felt slightly ill just then; and you will probably use his declaration as a criterion of his having felt slightly ill just then, even though he gave no sign of it. But note that we have said that he did not, in fact, give any sign of it. He *could* have done so. Whereas it is false that a man who is sound asleep could, while he is sound asleep, give any signs or indications that a certain thought was occurring to him or that he was experiencing some sensation. For any sign of this would also be a sign that he was at least partly awake.[13]

If a man were to get up from an apparently sound sleep and declare that while he was lying there a certain thought had occurred to him we might conclude that he was about to tell us something that he had dreamt, or we might conclude that, despite appearances, he had not been sound asleep; or we might conclude that he had awakened *with* that thought. Famous men testify to having solved difficult problems in their sleep. This can seem a paradox until we understand what it means: namely, that they went to sleep without a solution and woke up with one. But if a man, who knew English as well as anyone, declared that a certain thought had occurred to him while he was *sound* asleep, and insisted that he did not mean that he dreamt it or that he woke up with it, but that it had occurred to him in the same literal sense in which thoughts sometimes occur to him when he is drinking his coffee or weeding the garden—then I believe that in ordinary life we should not be able to make head or tail of his declaration.

---

[13] [Footnote added 1966] I was assuming here the following principle: If there is a certain state, S, such that it is *logically* impossible for a person in state S to give any *signs* of thinking or having experiences, then it is logically impossible for a person to think or to have experiences while in state S. Unfortunately this principle is not true. One can define a state (e.g. *total* paralysis) such that by definition a person in that state could not give any *signs* of thinking or experiencing: yet it would not follow that a person in that state could not think or have experiences. This problem is treated with greater sophistication in my monograph *Dreaming* (New York: Humanities Press, 1959). My argument there does not assume the foregoing false principle.

VIII

It will appear to some that there is a contradiction in maintaining, as I have, that it is true that someone who is sound asleep can in a dream think it is raining and in a dream seem to hear thunder, and yet that it is not true that he thinks it is raining or seems to hear thunder. One wants to argue: "In your dream you thought such-and-such. Dreams take place during sleep. Therefore, in your sleep you must have thought such-and-such." I have no objection to the conclusion if it merely means that I dreamt that I thought such-and-such: for this repeats the first premise and nothing is proved. It is only when the "argument" is taken, not as platitudinous and redundant, but as proving something, that I wish to attack it: when, that is, it is understood as proving that during a period of sound sleep I could have thoughts, sensations, impressions, and feelings in the *same* sense as that in which I have them during a half-hour of waking reverie.

Consider the second premise: "Dreams take place during sleep." Looked at in one way it is a tautology; looked at in another way it is a dubious proposition. It is a tautology in the sense that the inference from "He had a dream last night" to "He got at least some sleep last night" is valid. It is a dubious proposition when a dream is conceived of as an occurrence during sleep in the sense in which breathing is, or as an occurrence during the night in the sense in which a fright or a toothache can be. What is dubious about it? Well, let us take note of the fact that we have no way of determining *when* a dream occurred or *how long* it lasted. Of course it occurred "while he slept": but *when* while he slept? Some psychologists have conjectured that dreams occur, not during sleep, but during the period of *awaking* from sleep. Our feeling that it is impossible to decide whether this is so or not shows that we have no *criterion* for deciding it—shows that there is no sense in the question "When, while he slept, did he dream?" as there is in the questions "When, last night, did his headache begin?" or "When did his fright occur?" There is a similar lack of any criterion with respect to the duration of dreams: when should you say of a sleeping person, "Now he has begun to dream," "Now he has stopped dreaming?" We know what it means to find out whether someone has had a dream: he tells us a dream on awaking, or tells us he had one. (This concept of verification does not apply, of course, to small children or dogs. Just how much sense is there in the familiar half serious "conjecture" that the dog whose feet are twitching is dreaming of rabbits? And where this concept does apply—namely, to people who can tell dreams—there is much indefiniteness; e.g., a man says, on awaking, "I don't know whether I had a dream or not: perhaps I did." Does it make any sense to insist that either he had a dream or he didn't have one, *regardless* of whether he knows anything about it?) In the way that we find out whether someone had a dream, we sometimes also find out that it was a long dream: i.e., he *says* it was a long dream. But what is the duration of a "long" or "short" dream in "objective" time?

We can imagine the discovery of a uniform correlation between the occurrence of a specific physiological process during sleep and the subsequent reporting of a dream.[14] This correlation might be so impressive that scientists would be tempted to adopt the occurrence of the physiological process as their criterion for the occurrence of a dream. Let us imagine that it even became the criterion in ordinary life. There would then be such a thing as *proving* that a man had dreamt, although on awaking he honestly reported that he had not; and the duration (three minutes, say) of the physiological process, and its time of occurrence, could be made the criterion of the duration and time of occurrence of the dream. It would even have sense to say of someone "He is halfway through his dream!" All of this would amount to the adoption of an extremely different use of the word "dreaming." Its meaning would have to be *taught* differently; and all sorts of remarks would make sense that at present do not.

As things are, the notions of duration and time of occurrence have no application in ordinary discourse to dreams. In *this* sense, a dream is *not* an "occurrence" and, therefore, not an occurrence during sleep. The proposition "Dreams occur during sleep" can now be seen to be a curious one. It is important to ask *why* we say such a thing. The answer, I believe, is not hard to find. When someone "tells" a dream he talks in the *past* tense: after sleeping he relates how he *did* this and *saw* that (none of which is true). It is this peculiar phenomenon of speaking in the past tense after sleep, the phenomenon called "telling a dream," that provides the sense of the proposition that dreams occur during sleep.

One would like to object here that a person who is telling a dream speaks in the past tense *because* he is reporting something that took

14 There is some evidence in favor of there being a positive correlation between the occurrence of strong electrical currents in the bodies of sleeping persons and their subsequently reporting that they dreamt. The experiment in which this evidence was obtained is summarized in *Recent Experiments in Psychology*, by Crafts, Schneirla, Robinson, and Gilbert (New York, 1938), pp. 377–384. I quote: "In 33 cases, series of intense action currents . . . were recorded during sleep. After the action currents had been in progress a short time, but before they had disappeared, the subjects were awakened. In 30 of the 33 cases, subjects reported that they had just been dreaming" (p. 380).

place in the past while he slept, namely, his dream. The objection rests on the idea that his report corresponds to his dream in the same way that my report of yesterday's events corresponds to them. This is wrong. It is senseless to suppose that his dream differed from his report of it unless this means that he might change, add to, or contradict his report. No one knows what it would mean to "verify" his report. Others use his report as their criterion of what his dream was. In contrast, no one uses my report of the events of yesterday's robbery as his *criterion* of what actually happened: there are familiar ways of confirming or disconfirming my report, independently of my inclination or disinclination to amend or contradict it. If you take seriously the idea that the two reports correspond with reality, or fail to, in the *same* way, then you are confronted with the disturbing "possibility" that there are no dreams at all! I am guided here by Wittgenstein's remarks:

> People who on waking tell us certain incidents (that they have been in such-and-such places, etc.). Then we teach them the expression "I dreamt," which precedes the narrative. Afterwards I sometimes ask them "did you dream anything last night?" and am answered yes or no, sometimes with an account of a dream, sometimes not. That is the language-game. . . .

> Now must I make some assumption about whether people are deceived by their memories or not; whether they really had these images while they slept, or whether it merely seems so to them on waking? And what meaning has this question?—And what interest? Do we ever ask ourselves this when someone is telling us his dream? And if not—is it because we are sure his memory won't have deceived him? (And suppose it were a man with a quite specially bad memory?—) [15]

Perhaps when people give accounts of their dreams these accounts correspond to nothing at all! Perhaps it only *seems* to them on awaking that they dreamt!

I hope that I will not be misunderstood. I am not claiming that there are no dreams or that they do not occur in sleep—nor that these are genuine possibilities: of course they are not! If someone talks in a certain way after sleep then we say "He dreamt such-and-such while he slept." That is how the words are used! What I am trying to show is that *if* one thinks that a man's account of his dream is related to his dream just as my account of yesterday's happenings is related to them, one is in a hopeless difficulty: for then it *would* appear that our osten-

[15] *Philosophical Investigations* (New York, 1953), p. 184.

sible remembering that we dreamt such-and-such could be mistaken, not just once but all the time. If the report of the dream is "externally" related to the dream, then it may be that we are always only under the *illusion* of having had a dream, an illusion that comes to us as we awake. Trying to look at the matter in this way, we see that the notion that dreams really take place during sleep would become senseless: we should have no idea as to what would go to prove that they do.

We get out of this impasse only by realizing that there is nothing to be proved. If after sleep a person relates that he thought and did and experienced such-and-such (all of this being false), and if he is not lying, pretending, or inventing, then we say "he dreamt it." "That is the language-game!" That he really had a dream and that he is under the impression that he had a dream: these are the same thing.

There is a sharp break between the concept of "remembering a dream" and the concept of remembering what happened downtown yesterday. If a man confidently relates that he witnessed such-and-such happen in the street the day before, it can turn out that it didn't happen that way at all; it merely seems to him that he remembers such-and-such. When he gives an account of his dream there is no sense in supposing that it merely seems to him that he dreamt such-and-such. In the case of remembering a dream there is no contrast between correctly remembering and seeming to oneself to remember—here they are identical! (It can even appear surprising that we should speak of "remembering" a dream.)

IX

I have put forward an argument intended to prove that a person who is sound asleep cannot have any thoughts or impressions or sensations. Many persons will not be convinced by this argument, which is perfectly sound, one reason being that they tend to misapprehend the concept of the dream. They think: You can dream in sound sleep (which is true enough); in your dream you can have various thoughts, impressions, sensations (also true); therefore, while you are sound asleep you can have thoughts, etc. (which is false, unless it is the redundant conclusion that *in the dream* you have in sound sleep there can be thoughts, etc.).

The inclination to draw the false conclusion comes from the mistake of thinking that someone's report that in his dream he was, say, afraid of snakes, is a report that he was afraid of snakes *in the sense* in which his report that he was afraid of snakes when he was in the woods an hour ago is a report that he was afraid of snakes. But if his demeanor and behavior when he was in the woods expressed fearlessness of snakes, this would be in conflict with this report and would make its truth at least doubtful. Similarly, if in the woods he did show fear of snakes this would fit in with and confirm his report.

The logic of the matter is entirely different in the case of the report of a dream. If when he was in bed he had, by utterances and behavior, expressed a fear of snakes, this would have no tendency to confirm his report that he dreamt that he was afraid of snakes. Quite the opposite! It would tend to establish that he had *really* felt fear of snakes and not dreamt it at all! It would also tend to establish, in the same degree, that he had not been asleep, or at least not sound asleep, not "dead to the world." It is a logical impossibility that he should, when sound asleep, express fear or fearlessness or any other state of consciousness.

If a man declares that he was in a certain state of consciousness, what would count against his assertion would be evidence that he was, at the time referred to, either in an opposite state of consciousness or else not in any state of consciousness. Evidence that he was sound asleep would be evidence for the latter. His assertion that he dreamt last night that he was afraid of snakes (an assertion that could be true even though he slept soundly) does *not*, therefore, imply the proposition that in the night he was afraid of snakes, *in the sense* of this proposition in which it would be confirmed by his having manifested a fear of snakes in the night. And that is the normal sense of the proposition! When we say "He was afraid of snakes last night" we usually mean something that would be confirmed by the fact that during the night he expressed, by some demeanor or behavior of his, a fear of snakes. When we say "He dreamt last night that he was afraid of snakes" we do not mean anything of the sort. The latter proposition, therefore, does not imply the former one. In general, and contrary to Descartes, the proposition that a certain person had in his dream last night various thoughts, sensations, impressions, or feelings does not imply the proposition that last night he had those thoughts, sensations, impressions, or feelings, in the normal sense of the latter proposition.

X

So far I have discussed the notion of dreaming only in relation to sound sleep. The concept of dreaming when partly awake is different. A person who is partly awake can have thoughts (however groggy and confused) and so can be deceived. But he does not *have* to be deceived.

He is not "trapped in a dream." If it seems to him that he is sailing in the air high over green meadows he can decide to investigate—for example, to open his eyes and see where he is. The person who is sound asleep, in contrast, cannot *decide* to do anything; he can only dream that he decides; and, unlike the man who is half asleep, he cannot *find out* anything but can only dream that he does.[16] He who is sound asleep cannot realize that he sleeps; but neither can he mistakenly think

[16] A. Baillet, in his *Vie de Descartes* (Paris, 1691), Bk. II, ch. i. pp. 81–86, gives an account of the famous three dreams that apparently had an important influence on Descartes' life. In the third dream a man and a book appeared before him and then suddenly disappeared. I quote: "What especially calls for remark is that in doubt whether what he had just seen was dream or actual vision, not merely did he decide in his sleep that it was a dream, but proceeded to interpret the dream prior to his awaking" (translated by Norman Kemp Smith, *New Studies in the Philosophy of Descartes* [London, 1952], p. 36). If my argument is correct either Descartes was not sound asleep or else he *dreamt* that he decided and interpreted.

Miss Margaret Macdonald, in her paper "Sleeping and Waking" (*Mind*, April, 1953), observes that "it makes no sense to assert that one could employ any confirming technique in a dream. For one would but dream such employment" (p. 205); that a person who is asleep cannot choose to do anything, e.g., to stop dreaming, for "once asleep, a dreamer can only dream that he makes such a choice" (p. 214); that if I saw the Hebrides in a dream it does not follow either that I saw them or seemed to see them or thought I saw them (p. 210); and that dreaming is neither a form of perception nor of illusion (*passim*). Assuming that she refers to dreaming in sound sleep, I am in agreement with these contentions although her method of argument does not resemble mine. Unfortunately Macdonald seems to have made a blunder. After noting important distinctions between the concepts of sleeping and waking, she adds, "I suggest that these differences destroy the need for Descartes' lament that 'there exist no certain marks by which the state of waking may be distinguished from sleep.' For if what is said of one state is nonsensical when applied to the other, then this provides at least one certain mark by which to distinguish between them" (p. 215). From the fact that there are differences between the concepts of the two states it does not follow that I can tell whether I am in the one state or the other. I have argued (Sec. VII *supra*) that the notion of a person's determining whether he himself is awake or sound asleep is senseless. Macdonald is attacked on the above point by M. J. Baker ("Sleeping and Waking," *Mind*, October, 1954).

Yost and Kalish (*op. cit.*) give an elaborate analysis of Macdonald's paper. Some of their critical remarks are in disagreement with what I have contended: e.g., "To say that one dreams is to say that one sees, hears, touches, etc., while asleep" (p. 120); "And as regards the so-called mental operations, we should maintain, with Descartes, that if anyone dreams that he believes, doubts, expects, desires, etc., then he really does" (p. 121); "People can really believe sentences to be true while they are dreaming" (*ibid.*); "A dreamer who is inspecting one dream-field could predict and expect certain later dream-fields; and when they occur he could recognize them to be or not to be the ones he predicted while inspecting earlier dream-fields" (p. 122). Apparently there is *a* sense of "dream" (dreaming when partly awake) in which it is possible for a dreamer to do the above things or at least some of them. But since there is another sense of "dream" (dreaming when sound asleep) in which none of them are possible, it follows that the general statements, "To say that one dreams is to say that one sees, hears, touches, etc., while asleep," and "If anyone dreams that he believes, doubts, expects, desires, etc., then he really does," are false.

he is awake. He who is half asleep *can* mistake the sights and sounds that he "dreams" for real sights and sounds; but the concept of half sleep does not *require* that he make this mistake.

A consequence of my argument is that there is no room left for the skeptical question (a) "How can I know whether I am awake or sound asleep?"—for the question is absurd, since if I raise it I am not sound asleep. It is still possible, however, for a philosopher to be troubled by the question (b) "How can I know whether I am fully awake or only partly awake?" This cannot be disposed of in the same way, and I do not try to deal with it in this paper. I will only remark that it is in essence the same as the question (c) "How can I know whether I am having an hallucination?" That questions (a) and (c) have a very different status is in itself a point of considerable interest.

XI

One result of the preceding treatment of the notions of sound sleep and dreaming is to show that Descartes' own solution of his problem of skepticism of the senses is untenable. In the *First Meditation* he observes that "there are no certain marks distinguishing waking from sleep." But after he has proved that God exists and is no deceiver, he goes on to declare, in the *Sixth Meditation*, that he ought

> to reject as hyperbolical and ridiculous all the doubts of these past days, more especially that regarding sleep, as being indistinguishable from the waking state. How marked, I now fiind, is the difference between them! Our memory can never connect our dreams with one another and with the whole course of our lives, in the manner in which we are wont to connect the things which happen to us while awake. If, while I am awake, someone should all of a sudden appear to me, and as suddenly disappear, as happens in dreams, and in such fashion that I could not know whence he came or whither he went, quite certainly it would not be unreasonable to esteem it a spectre, that is, a phantom formed in my brain, rather than a real man. When, on the other hand, in apprehending things, I know the place whence they have come, and that in which they are, and the time at which they present themselves to me, and while doing so can connect them uninterruptedly with the course of my life as a whole, I am completely certain that what I thus experience is taking place while I am awake, and not in dreams. And if after having summoned to my aid all my senses, my memory and my understanding, in scrutiny of these occurrences, I find that none of them presents me with what is at vari-

ance with any other, I ought no longer to entertain the least doubt as to their truth. God being no deceiver, it cannot be that I am here being misled [*DPW*, 264–265].

Descartes is undoubtedly intending to point out a criterion for distinguishing waking from sleep (although I do not believe that he is rejecting what he *meant* when he said in the *First Meditation* that there is no criterion): and undoubtedly this is intended to be a criterion that will enable me to tell whether *I* am awake or asleep, and not merely to tell whether some other person is awake or asleep. In the sentence "Our memory can never connect..." he is surely implying that if I cannot "connect" the things that I experience with one another and with the whole course of my life then I ought to *conclude* that I am asleep and that these things belong to a dream. To this there is the conclusive objection that in regard to a person who is sound asleep (and sound sleep has to come into the question here) there is no sense in speaking of his making a connection or drawing a conclusion. Similarly, in the sentence "When, on the other hand...," Descartes is implying that if I do not know where the things I apprehend come from and cannot connect them with the course of my life as a whole, then I am justified in *concluding* that I am asleep and dreaming. This involves the same absurdity. Descartes' criterion is identical with the principle of "coherence" or "consistency" that Leibniz,[17] Russell,[18] and others offer as a principle for distinguishing waking from sleeping. If my argument is correct, there cannot be such a principle.

[17] E.g., see Leibniz' paper "On the Method of Distinguishing Real from Imaginary Phenomena," *New Essays Concerning Human Understanding*, trans. by A. G. Langley (La Salle, Illinois, 1949), pp. 717–720, esp. pp. 718–719.
[18] E.g., see Russell's *Our Knowledge of the External World* (Chicago, 1914), p. 95.

Further Reading On
KNOWLEDGE, CERTAINTY, AND DOUBT

Abbott, W. R. "What Knowledge Is Not." *Analysis,* March 1971.

Aune, Bruce. "Two Theories of Scientific Knowledge." *Critica,* January 1971.

Bamborough, Renford. "The Disunity of Plato's Thought." *Philosophy,* October 1972.

Barker, John A. "Knowledge and Causation." *The Southern Journal of Philosophy,* Fall 1972.

Bearsley, Patrick J. "Another Look at the First Principles of Knowledge." *The Thomist,* October 1972.

Blizman, James. "Models, Analogies, and Degrees of Certainty in Decartes." *The Modern Schoolman,* November 1972.

Braine, David. "The Nature of Knowledge." *Proceedings of the Aristotelian Society,* 1972.

Cargile, James T. "On Near Knowledge." *Analysis,* April 1971.

Dilman, Ilham. "On Wittgenstein's Last Notes (1950–51) *On Certainty.*" *Philosophy,* April 1971.

Fain, Haskell, and A. Phillips Griffiths. "On Falsely Believing That One Doesn't Know." *American Philosophical Quarterly,* 1972.

Godwin, D. "The Structure of Knowledge." *Philosophy of Education: Proceedings,* 1970.

Johnson, Oliver A. "Is Knowledge Defensible?" *Southern Journal of Philosophy,* Fall 1971.

Kaiser, Nolan. "Plato on Knowledge." *Apeiron,* September 1972.

Levi, Issac. "Certainty, Probability, and the Correction of Evidence." *Nous,* September 1971.

McDermott, John. "I'm Free Because I Know That I Don't Yet Know What I'm Going to Do?" *British Journal for the Philosophy of Science,* November 1972.

Morris, William Edward. "Knowledge as Justified Presumption." *Journal of Philosophy,* March 1973.

Phillips, Hollibert E. "Evidence, Argument, and Certainty." *Philosophy of Education: Proceedings,* 1972.

Place, U. T. "The Infallibility of Our Knowledge of Our Own Beliefs." *Analysis,* June 1971.

Robinson, Richard. "The Concept of Knowledge." *Mind,* January 1971.

Schmidt, Paul F. "Knowledge Without Truth." *Southwestern Journal of Philosophy,* Winter 1971.

Thompson, Manley. "Who Knows?" *Journal of Philosophy,* November 1970.

White, Alan R. "Certainty." *The Aristotelian Society: Supplementary Volume,* 1972.

Zvara, Andrew A. "On Claiming to Know and Feeling Sure." *Philosophical Studies,* July 1973.

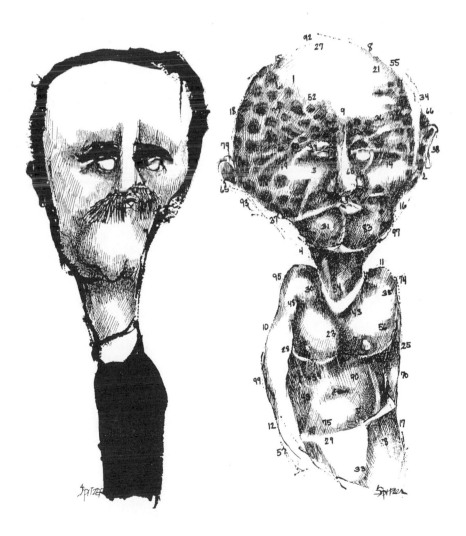

PART VI

SCIENTIFIC DISCOVERY

The Discovery of the Structure of DNA * †

J. D. Watson and F. H. C. Crick

* *DNA stands for deoxyribonucleic acid. Nucleic acids are large molecules, contained by every living cell of an organism, that control the production of proteins. Nucleic acids are made up of structural units called nucleotides, each with three parts: a five-carbon sugar, a phosphate group, and a nitrogen-containing compound. DNA molecules contain the genetic code by which the structural uniqueness of each protein molecule and of each new cell is retained during the production of new proteins and new cells. Discoveries concerning DNA, RNA (ribonucleic acid), and the genetic coding system have been said to be as important to biology and medicine as the discoveries of fission and fusion were to physics.*

† Watson and Crick, "The Structure of DNA," Cold Spring Harbor Symposia on Quantitative Biology, 1953, pp. 123–130. Permission to reprint granted by the authors and Cold Spring Harbor Laboratory, Copyright 1953.

. . . IN THIS PAPER WE SHALL DESCRIBE A STRUCTURE FOR DNA WHICH suggests a mechanism for its self-duplication and allows us to propose, for the first time, a detailed hypothesis on the atomic level for the self-reproduction of genetic material.

We first discuss the chemical and physical-chemical data which show that DNA is a long fibrous molecule. Next we explain why crystallographic evidence suggests that the structural unit of DNA consists not of one but of two polynucleotide chains. We then discuss a stereochemical model which we believe satisfactorily accounts for both the chemical and crystallographic data. In conclusion we suggest some obvious genetical implications of the proposed structure. . . .

I. EVIDENCE FOR THE FIBROUS NATURE OF DNA

The basic chemical formula of DNA is now well established. As shown in Figure 1 it consists of a very long chain, the backbone

D.N.A.

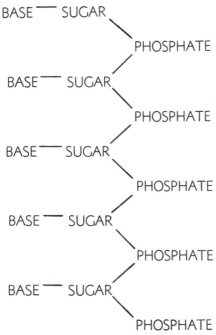

FIGURE 1. Chemical formula (diagrammatic) of a single chain of desoxyribo-nucleic acid.

of which is made up of alternate sugar and phosphate groups, joined together in regular 3′ 5′ phosphate di-ester linkages. To each sugar is attached a nitrogenous base, only four different kinds of which are commonly found in DNA. Two of these—adenine and guanine—are purines, and the other two—thymine and cytosine—are pyrimidines. . . .

It should be noted that the chain is unbranched, a consequence of the regular internucleotide linkage. On the other hand the sequence of the different nucleotides is, as far as can be ascertained, completely irregular. Thus, DNA has some features which are regular, and some which are irregular.

A similar conception of the DNA molecule as a long thin fiber is obtained from physico-chemical analysis involving sedimentation, diffusion, light scattering, and viscosity measurements. These techniques indicate that DNA is a very asymmetrical structure approximately 20 A wide and many thousands of angstroms long. . . . Surprisingly each of these measurements tends to suggest that the DNA is relatively rigid, a puzzling finding in view of the large number of single bonds (5 per nucleotide) in the phosphate-sugar backbone. Recently these indirect inferences have been confirmed by electron microscopy. . . .

II. EVIDENCE FOR THE EXISTENCE OF TWO
CHEMICAL CHAINS IN THE FIBER

This evidence comes mainly from X-ray studies. The material used is the sodium salt of DNA (usually from calf thymus) which has been extracted, purified, and drawn into fibers. These fibers are highly birefringent, show marked ultraviolet and infrared dichroism . . . and give good X-ray fiber diagrams. From a preliminary study of these, Wilkins, Franklin and their co-workers at King's College, London (Wilkins et al., 1953; Franklin and Gosling 1953a, b and c) have been able to draw certain general conclusions about the structure of DNA. Two important facts emerge from their work. They are:

1. *Two distinct forms of DNA exist.* Firstly a crystalline form, Structure A (Figure 2), which occurs at about 75 per cent relative humidity and contains approximately 30 per cent water. At higher humidities the fibers take up more water, increase in length by about 30 per cent and assume Structure B (Figure 3). This is a less ordered form than Structure A, and appears to be paracrystalline; that is, the individual molecules are all packed parallel to one another, but are not otherwise regularly arranged in space. In Table 1, we have tabulated some of the characteristic features which distinguish the two forms. The transition from A to B is reversible and therefore the two structures are likely to be related in a simple manner.

2. *The crystallographic unit contains two polynucleotide chains.* The argument is crystallographic and so will only be given in outline. Structure B has a very strong 3.4 A reflexion on the meridian. . . . this can only mean that the nucleotides in it occur in groups spaced 3.4 A apart in the fiber direction. On going from

Structure B to Structure A the fiber shortens by about 30 per cent. Thus in Structure A the groups must be about 2.5 per cent A apart axially. The measured density of Structure A (Franklin and Gosling, 1953c), together with the cell dimensions, shows that there must be *two* nucleotides in each such group. Thus it is very probable that the crystallographic unit consists of two distinct polynucleotide chains. Final proof of this can only come from a complete solution of the structure.

Structure A has a pseudo-hexagonal lattice, in which the lattice points are 22 A apart. This distance roughly corresponds with the diameter of fibers seen in the electron microscope, bearing in mind that the latter are quite dry. Thus it is probable that the crystallographic unit and the fiber are the one and the same.

FIGURE 2. X-ray fiber diagram of Structure A of desoxyribonucleic acid. (H. M. F. Wilkins and H. R. Wilson, unpub.)

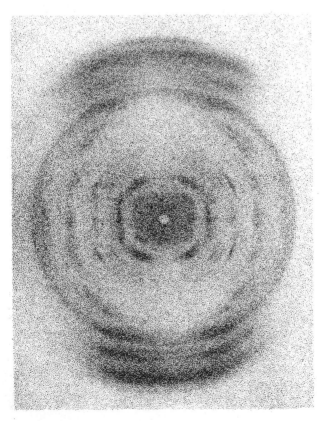

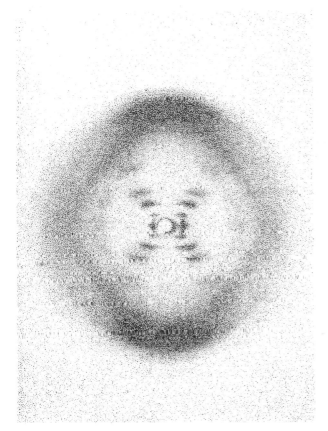

FIGURE 3. X-ray fiber diagram of Structure B of desoxyribonucleic acid. (R. E. Franklin and R. Gosling, 1953a.)

III. DESCRIPTION OF THE PROPOSED STRUCTURE

Two conclusions might profitably be drawn from the above data. Firstly, the structure of DNA is regular enough to form a three dimensional crystal. This is in spite of the fact that its component chains may have an irregular sequence of purine and pyrimidine nucleotides. Secondly, as the structure contains two chains, these chains must be regularly arranged in relation to each other.

To account for these findings, we have proposed . . . a structure in which the two chains are coiled round a common axis and joined together by hydrogen bonds between the nucleotide bases (see

Figure 4). Both chains follow right handed helices, but the sequences of the atoms in the phosphate-sugar backbones run in
opposite directions and so are related by a dyad perpendicular
to the helix axis. The phosphates and sugar groups are on the
outside of the helix whilst the bases are on the inside. . . . Our
structure is a well-defined one and all bond distances and angles
. . . are stereochemically acceptable.

The essential element of the structure is the manner in which
the two chains are held together by hydrogen bonds between the
bases. The bases are perpendicular to the fiber axis and joined
together in pairs. The pairing arrangement is very specific, and

FIGURE 4. This figure is diagrammatic. The two ribbons symbolize the two
phosphate-sugar chains and the horizontal rods. The paths of bases hold the
chain together. The vertical line marks the fiber axis.

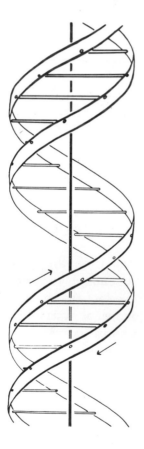

TABLE 1.
(From Franklin and Gosling, 1953a, b and c)

	Structure A	Structure B
Degree of orientation	Crystalline	Paracrystalline
Repeat distance along fiber axis	28 A	34 A
Location of first equatorial spacing	18 A	22–24 A
Water content	30%	> 30%
Number of nucleotides within unit	22–24	20 (?)

only certain pairs of bases will fit into the structure. The basic reason for this is that we have assumed that the backbone of each polynucleotide chain is in the form of a regular helix. Thus, irrespective of which bases are present, the glucosidic bonds (which join sugar and base) are arranged in a regular manner in space. In particular, any two glucosidic bonds (one from each chain) which are attached to a bonded pair of bases, must always occur at a fixed distance apart due to the regularity of the two backbones to which they are joined. The result is that one member of a pair of bases must always be a purine, and the other a pyrimidine, in order to bridge between the two chains. If a pair consisted of two purines, for example, there would not be room for it; if of two pyrimidines they would be too far apart to form hydrogen bonds.

In theory a base can exist in a number of . . . forms, differing in the exact positions at which its hydrogen atoms are attached. However, under physiological conditions one particular form of each base is much more probable than any of the others. If we make the assumption that the favored forms always occur, then the pairing requirements are even more restrictive. Adenine can only pair with thymine, and guanine only with cytosine. . . . This pairing is shown in detail in Figures 5 and 6. If adenine tried to pair with cytosine it could not form hydrogen bonds, since there would be two hydrogens near one of the bonding positions, and none at the other, instead of one in each.

A given pair can be either way round. Adenine, for example, can occur on either chain, but when it does its partner on the other chain must always be thymine. This is possible because the two glucoside bonds of a pair (see Figures 5 and 6) are symmetrically related to each other, and thus occur in the same positions if the pair is turned over.

It should be emphasized that since each base can form hydrogen bonds at a number of points one can pair up *isolated* nucleotides in a large variety of ways. *Specific* pairing of bases can only be obtained by imposing some restriction, and in our case it is in a direct consequence of the postulated regularity of the phosphate-sugar backbone.

It should further be emphasized that whatever pair of bases occurs at one particular point in the DNA structure, no restriction is imposed on the neighboring pairs, and any *sequence* of pairs can occur. This is because all the bases are flat, and since they are stacked roughly one above another like a pile of pennies, it makes no difference which pair is neighbor to which.

Though any sequence of bases can fit into our structure, the

FIGURE 5. Pairing of adenine and thymine. Hydrogen bonds are shown dotted. One carbon atom of each sugar is shown.

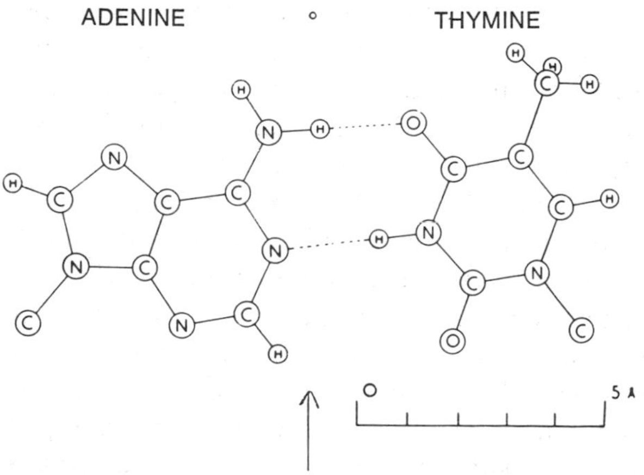

GUANINE   ○   CYTOSINE

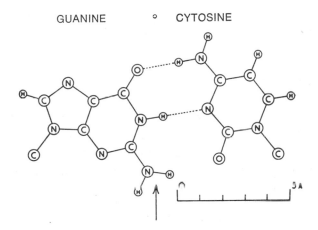

FIGURE 6. Pairing of guanine and cytosine. Hydrogen bonds are shown dotted. One carbon atom of each sugar is shown.

necessity for specific pairing demands a definite relationship between the sequences on the two chains. That is, if we knew the actual order of the bases on one chain, we could automatically write down the order on the other. *Our structure therefore consists of two chains, each of which is the complement of the other.*

IV. EVIDENCE IN FAVOR OF THE COMPLEMENTARY MODEL

The experimental evidence available to us now offers strong support to our model though we should emphasize that, as yet, it has not been proved correct. The evidence in its favor is of three types:

1. The general appearance of the X-ray picture strongly suggests that the basic structure is helical (Wilkins *et al.*, 1953; Franklin and Gosling, 1953a). If we postulate that a helix is present, we immediately are able to deduce from the X-ray pattern of Structure B (Figure 3), that its pitch is 34 A and its diameter approximately 20 A. Moreover, the pattern suggests a high concentration of atoms on the circumference of the helix, in accord

with our model which places the phosphate-sugar backbone on the outside. The photograph also indicates that the two polynucleotide chains are not spaced equally along the fiber axis, but are probably displaced from each other by about three-eighths of the fiber axis period, an inference again in qualitative agreement with our model.

The interpretation of the X-ray pattern of Structure A (the crystalline form) is less obvious. . . . It should be noted that the X-ray pattern of Structure A is much more detailed than that of Structure B and so if correctly interpreted, can yield more precise information about DNA. Any proposed model for DNA must be capable of forming either Structure A or Structure B and so it remains imperative for our very tentative interpretation of Structure A to be confirmed.

2. The anomolous titration curves of undegraded DNA with acids and bases strongly suggests that hydrogen bond formation is a characteristic aspect of DNA structure. . . . The fact that most of the ionizable groups are originally inaccessible to acids and bases is more easily explained if the hydrogen bonds are between bases within the same structural unit. This point would definitely be established if it were shown that the shape of the initial titration curve was the same at very low DNA concentrations, when the interaction between neighboring structural units is small.

3. The analytical data on the relative proportion of the various bases show that the amount of adenine is close to that of thymine, and the amount of guanine close to the amount of cytosine, . . . although the ratio of adenine to guanine can vary from one source to another (Chargaff, 1951; Wyatt, 1952). In fact as the techniques for estimation of the bases improve, the ratios of adenine to thymine, and guanine to cytosine . . . appear to grow very close to unity. This is a most striking result, especially as the sequence of bases on a given chain is likely to be irregular, and suggests a structure involving paired bases. In fact, we believe the analytical data offer the most important evidence so far available in support of our model, since they specifically support the biologically interesting feature, the presence of complementary chains.

We thus believe that the present experimental evidence justifies the working hypothesis that the essential features of our model are correct and allows us to consider its genetic possibilities.

V. GENETICAL IMPLICATIONS OF THE COMPLEMENTARY MODEL

As a preliminary we should state that the DNA fibers from which the X-ray diffraction patterns were obtained are not artifacts arising in the method of preparation. In the first place, Wilkins and his co-workers (see Wilkins *et al.*, 1953) have shown that X-ray patterns similar to those from the isolated fibers can be obtained from certain intact biological materials such as sperm head and bacteriophage particles. Secondly, our postulated model is so extremely specific that we find it impossible to believe that it could be formed during the isolation from living cells.

A genetic material must in some way fulfil two functions. It must duplicate itself, and it must exert a highly specific influence on the cell. Our model for DNA suggests a simple mechanism for the first process, but at the moment we cannot see how it carries out the second one. We believe, however, that its specificity is expressed by the precise sequence of the pairs of bases. The backbone of our model is highly regular, and the sequence is the only feature which can carry the genetical information. It should not be thought that because in our structure the bases are on the "inside," they would be unable to come into contact with other molecules. Owing to the open nature of our structure they are in fact fairly accessible.

A Mechanism for DNA Replication

The complementary nature of our structure suggests how it duplicates itself. It is difficult to imagine how like attracts like, and it has been suggested . . . that self duplication may involve the union of each part with an opposite or complementary part. In these discussions it has generally been suggested that protein and nucleic acid are complementary to each other and that self replication involves the alternate syntheses of these two components. We should like to propose instead that the specificity of DNA self replication is accomplished without recourse to specific protein synthesis and that each of our complementary DNA chains serves as a . . . mould for the formation onto itself of a new companion chain.

For this to occur the hydrogen bonds linking the complementary chains must break and the two chains unwind and separate. It seems likely that the single chain (or the relevant part of it) might itself assume the helical form and serve as a mould onto which free nucleotides (strictly polynucleotide precursors) can attach themselves by forming hydrogen bonds. We propose that polymerization of the precursors to form a new chain only occurs if the resulting chain forms the proposed structure. This is plausible because steric reasons would not allow monomers "crystallized" onto the first chain to approach one another in such a way that they could be joined together in a new chain, unless they were those monomers which could fit into our structure. It is not obvious to us whether a special enzyme would be required to carry out the polymerization or whether the existing single helical chain could act effectively as an enzyme.

. . .

A Possible Mechanism for Natural Mutation

In our duplication scheme, the specificity of replication is achieved by means of specific pairing between purine and pyrimidine bases; adenine with thymine, and guanine with one of the cytosines. This specificity results from our assumption that each of the bases possesses one tautomeric form which is very much more stable than any of the other possibilities. The fact that a compound is tautomeric, however, means that the hydrogen atoms can occasionally change their locations. It seems plausible to us that a spontaneous mutation, which as implied earlier we imagine to be a change in the sequence of bases, is due to a base occurring very occasionally in one of the less likely tautomeric forms, at the moment when the complementary chain is being formed. For example, while adenine will normally pair with thymine, if there is a tautomeric shift of one of its hydrogen atoms it can pair with cytosine (Figure 7). The next time pairing occurs, the adenine (having resumed its more usual tautomeric form) will pair with

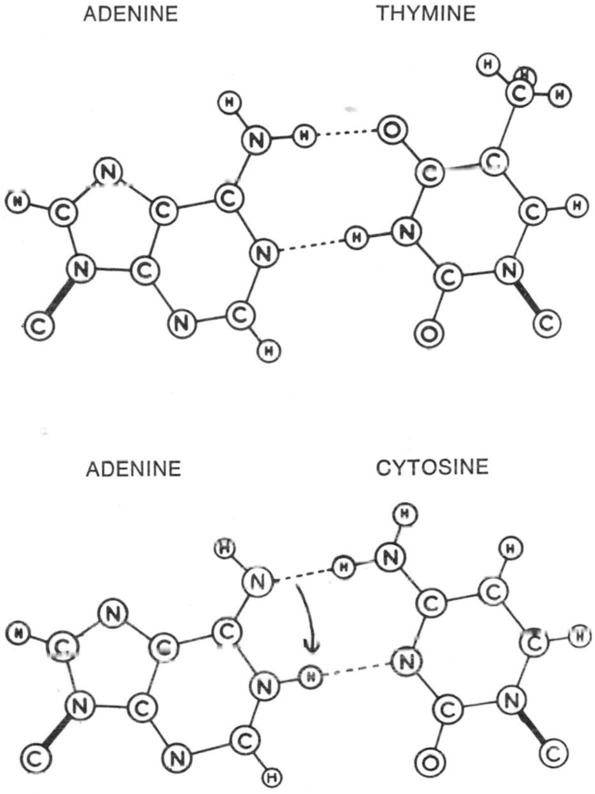

ADENINE   THYMINE

ADENINE   CYTOSINE

FIGURE 7. Pairing arrangements of adenine before (above) and after (below) it has undergone a tautomeric shift.

thymine, but the cytosine will pair with guanine, and so a change in the sequence of bases will have occurred. It would be of interest to know the precise difference in free energy between the various tautomeric forms under physiological conditions.

GENERAL CONCLUSION

The proof or disproof of our structure will have to come from further crystallographic analysis, a task we hope will be accomplished soon. It would be surprising to us, however, if the idea of complementary chains turns out to be wrong. This feature was initially postulated by us to account for the crystallographic regularity and it seems to us unlikely that its obvious connection with self replication is a matter of chance. On the other hand the plectonemic coiling is, superficially at least, biologically unattractive and so demands precise crystallographic proof. In any case the evidence for both the model and the suggested replication scheme will be strengthened if it can be shown unambiguously that the genetic specificity is carried by DNA alone, and, on the molecular side, how the structure could exert a specific influence on the cell.

REFERENCES

ASTBURY, W. T., 1947, X-Ray Studies of nucleic acids in tissues. Sym. Soc. Exp. Biol. 1:66–76.

CHARGAFF, E., 1951, Structure and function of nucleic acids as cell constituents. Fed. Proc. 10:654–659.

CRICK, F. H. C., and WATSON, J. D., 1953, Manuscript in preparation.

FRANKLIN, R. E., and GOSLING, R., 1953a, Molecular configuration in sodium thymonucleate. Nature, Lond. 171:740–741.

1953b, Fiber diagrams of sodium thymonucleate. I. The influence of water content. Acta Cryst., Camb. (in press).

1953c, The structure of sodium thymonucleate fibers. II. The cylindrically symmetrical Patterson Function. Acta Cryst., Camb. (in press).

FRASER, M. S., and FRASER, R. D. B., 1951, Evidence on the structure of desoxyribonucleic acid from measurements with polarized infra-red radiation. Nature, Lond. 167:760–761.

FRIEDRICH-FREKSA, H., 1940, Bei der Chromosomen Konjugation wirksame Krafte und ihre Bedeutung für die identische Verdoppling von Nucleoproteinen. Naturwissenshaften 28:376–379.

GULLAND, J. M., and JORDAN, D. O., 1946, The macromolecular behavior of nucleic acids. Sym. Soc. Exp. Biol. 1:56–65.

GULLAND, J. M., JORDAN, D. O., and TAYLOR, H. F. W., 1947, Electrometric titration of the acidic and basic groups of the desoxypentose nucleic acid of calf thymus. J. Chem. Soc. 1131–1141.

HUSKINS, C. L., 1941, The coiling of chromonemata. Cold Spr. Harb. Symp. Quant. Biol. 9:13–18.

JORDAN, D. O., 1951, Physiochemical properties of the nucleic acids. Prog. Biophys. 2:51–89.

KAHLER, H., and LLOYD, B. J., 1953, The electron microscopy of sodium desoxyribonucleate. Biochim. Biophys. Acta 10:355–359.

MANTON, I., 1950, The spiral structure of chromosomes. Biol. Rev. 25:486–508.

MULLER, H. J., 1947, The Gene. Proc. Roy. Soc. Lond. Ser. B. 134:1–37.

PAULING, L., and DEDBRÜCK, M., 1940. The nature of the intermolecular forces operative in biological processes. Science 92:77–79.

SIEGAL, A., and SINGER, S. J., 1953, The preparation and properties of desoxypentosenucleic acid. Biochim. Biophys. Acta 10:311–319.

VILBRANDT, C. F., and TENNENT, H. G., 1943, The effect of pH changes upon some properties of sodium thymonucleate solutions. J. Amer. Chem. Soc. 63: 1806–1809.

WATSON, J. D., and CRICK, F. H. C., 1953a, A structure for desoxyribose nucleic acids. Nature, Lond. 171:737–738.

1953b, Genetical implications of the structure of desoxyribose nucleic acid. Nature, Lond. (in press).

WILKINS, M. H. F., GOSLING, R. G., and SEEDS, W. E., 1951, Physical studies of nucleic acids—nucleic acid: an extensible molecule. Nature, Lond. 167:759–760.

WILKINS, M. H. F., and RANDALL, J. T., 1953, Crystallinity in sperm-heads: molecular structure of nucleoprotein in vivo. Biochim. Biophys. Acta 10:192 (1953).

WILKINS, M. H. F., STOKES, A. R., and WILSON, II. R., 1953, Molecular structure of desoxypentose nucleic acids. Nature, Lond. 171:738–740.

WILLIAMS, R. C., 1952, Electron microscopy of sodium desoxyribonucleate by use of a new freeze-drying method. Biochim. Biophys. Acta 9:237–239.

WYATT, G. R., 1952, Specificity in the composition of nucleic acids. In "The Chemistry and Physiology of the Nucleus," pp 201–213, N. Y. Academic Press.

WYATT, G. R., and COHEN, S. S., 1952, A new pyrimidine base from bacteriophage nucleic acid. Nature, Lond., 170:1072.

INQUIRY

Thus the world is divided into Scientists, who practice the art of infallibility, and non-scientists, sometimes contemptuously called "laymen," who are taken in by it.

ANTHONY STANDEN, *Science Is a Sacred Cow*

Surveyors are spiderlike contraptions with retrorockets to lower them gently on the moon's airless surface. They have "arms" for picking up rocks and TV "eyes" for analyzing specimens clenched in their claws.*

THIS description of a moon surveyor is almost humorous. It is typical of the writing in so-called scientific articles in magazines and newspapers that aim to "enlighten" the public on recent developments in various scientific fields, medicine to space technology. A kind of fictional aura has descended upon the whole framework of science in the eyes of the general public. The translator of science to the average man is the reporter, editor, or free-lance writer, publishing in the popular mass media; and unfortunately most of what we come to know as science reads like Jules Verne or H. G. Wells. The methodology of science and the concepts involved in theoretical reasoning, the presuppositions of science and scientific discovery, of prime interest to philosophers, seldom enter into the popular scientific report.

Astronomer Richard C. Hall of Flagstaff, Arizona, comments on the above description: "We may ask whether the quotes were left off 'claws' because the writer became convinced of the bestial quali-

---

* *U. S. News and World Report* (April 15, 1965).

ties of the Surveyor." * Hall maintains that the popular press has isolated many of us from the real workings of science by techniques of journalism designed to increase the gap between layman and scientist; those techniques make the scientist appear more like a wizard than a dedicated researcher into the relationship between facts of physical existence. (Similar ideas are expressed by C. P. Snow in his book *The Two Cultures*.)

Consider an example from *Time* magazine cited by Hall. *Time* gives us a verbal picture of a superhuman computer: "The scheduled maneuvers were perfectly calculated by one of the unsung heroes of the mission: an IBM 7094 Mode II computer. . . . (It has been taught all the incredible complications of orbital calculations." † Actually, the bases of all "orbital calculations" are Kepler's three simple laws of orbital motion; and the problem of a satellite in orbit around the earth, the two-body problem, is one of the most elemental in physics. The implication of the article, of course, is that science is far too difficult for the average man to comprehend. It alienates us from science instead of educating us. For most of us, science, though admittedly a major factor in our lives, is also a mysterious factor.

Our concern in this chapter is to examine philosophically the phenomenon of scientific discovery. Consider the account of their discovery of the structure of DNA by Watson and Crick. Can a well-defined method or procedure of science be determined from their report? Most of us have been told since elementary school that scientists proceed according to well-defined steps. It is often claimed that *the* scientific method is a series of concise procedures, memorized by the novice and used with the guarantee of reaching truth in the matter under consideration. Lionel Ruby, in his book *The Art of Making Sense*, organized the so-called scientific method into eight steps. He tells us that scientific inquiry begins when a situation generates interest, when the need to know why something happens or does not happen is felt. Second, the problem must be precisely formulated. The third step, Ruby tells us, is the observation of relevant facts based on the use of previous knowledge. (What makes a fact relevant? Is a theory or hypothesis needed before judgments of relevance can be made?) Then an explanatory hypothesis is to be formulated, and deductions from the hypothesis are to be made; that is, the implications of accepting a particular hypothesis are ex-

* Richard C. Hall, unpublished paper.
† *Time*, Vol. 86, No. 26, p. 33.

plored and tested by observation and/or experiment. The final step of the method, according to Ruby, is that the scientist must conclude that his hypothesis is confirmed or not confirmed on the basis of the evidence he has collected.*

Can we trace such a step-by-step procedure in Watson and Crick's work? If we could, would it be conclusive evidence of its success? Notice that, although the claim is to a precise formulation of a method of thinking, the actual plan is rather vague. We should wonder what generates the interest of a certain scientist in a problem while the majority of his colleagues are satisfied with current answers or do not even recognize the situation as problematic in the first place. Does nature change and thereby create new problems, or is the only change in the way people look at the same old events? How important is the crisis situation to discovery in science? Are experiments crucial in establishing hypotheses? What do we mean when we say that a particular hypothesis is established by the evidence? Are we only saying something about our language? Have we said anything about the physical world?

Francis Bacon, in his classic *Novum Organum,* maintains that the "true way" of "searching into and discovering truth" is to proceed gradually from the facts of nature to wider and wider generalizations, until the general axioms of nature are inductively derived. Theory, hypotheses, and conjectures play no role in Bacon's method of scientific discovery. He arrives at this idea of scientific method because he also holds a particular philosophy of nature. Nature, for Bacon, is an open book that the unprejudiced cannot misread. Bacon originally called his method *interpretatio naturae,* which means something like "reading out nature for those who cannot read themselves." Galileo may have had a similar idea when he wrote, "Philosophy [philosophy then meant all ways of knowing and especially what we now call science] is written in that vast book which stands open before our eyes, I mean the universe"; he adds, "but it cannot be read until we have learnt the language and become familiar with the characters in which it is written."†

Bacon's philosophy of science was aimed at establishing the best way of preparing oneself to read that book of nature. Of major importance in his method is ridding the mind of its biases and concepts. One must divest oneself of all preconceptions and allow

* Lionel Ruby, *The Art of Making Sense* (Philadelphia: Lippincott, 1954), pp. 220–221.
† Stuart Hampshire, ed., *The Age of Reason* (New York: New American Library, 1956), p. 33.

oneself to become familiar with the raw facts of nature. But is this possible? Are ideal scientists people with no preconceptions about nature? with no notions of what to expect?

What do we mean by "a fact"? We say such things as: "That's a fact!" "The facts of the case are . . ."; "I don't care what your opinion is, I just want the facts." When we use the word "fact," we seem to imply that what we are dealing with is separate from our theories, ideas, opinions. We suggest that *facts* are things that our opinions do not change, immutable objects, independent of our thinking about them. But what makes something a fact?

Benjamin Whorf's studies of the Hopi Indian language in "Science and Linguistics" provide us with a useful example. According to Whorf, Hopi language provides no dimensions for time, and time words cannot be pluralized, nor do they permit simultaneity (all major concepts in Western science). Action verbs apparently are not distinguishable in tenses. If a science were to be constructed in Hopi, Whorf claims that it would be based on ideas foreign to our sciences —intensity and variation—instead of our ideas of velocity and rate (among others). When called upon to report a chemical reaction, a Hopi would talk about its intensity, while a Western chemist would generally speak of its velocity. At first we might think both the Hopi and the Western chemist were reporting the same observations and simply using different words. But velocity has no place in a language without related time concepts. The Hopi does not see the velocity of a chemical reaction, and no analogies to moving objects, such as running horses, will serve to introduce the concept of velocity into a language with no place for it. All movement is satisfactorily described for the Hopi in terms of intensities. What then are the facts? Is the Hopi wrong, the Western chemist correct? Do the facts of velocity only apply to the situation when observed by someone who speaks the language of velocity? Whorf's conclusion is that "all observers are not led by the same physical evidence to the same picture of the universe unless their linguistic backgrounds are similar or can in some way be calibrated." *

The facts that we take to be immovable apparently depend to some degree upon the language we use to express them. Do we see facts? Or do we see objects, witness events? What would a fact look like? Could you take a picture of a fact? If facts are not picturable or observable, then they would seem to be in some sense linguistic. Reading the book of nature, as Bacon would have it, cannot be just

---

* See Selected Sources.

a matter of looking around. Learning the facts is not achieved by standing in the woods and letting your senses become stimulated. The facts of science do not arise miraculously from experience. Many are in direct opposition to common experience. Bacon, we are told, fought the acceptance of the Copernican (sun-centered solar system) point of view because it was not compatible with common sense. The Copernican theory, which called for placing the sun in a category exclusive of the planets and for putting the earth in a category with the bright moving objects in the sky, clearly was not consistent with Bacon's experience. After all, he could not even imagine standing on one of those bright moving objects, and the sun undoubtedly circled the earth every day. The facts, however, are Copernican.

If science is not just a matter of cataloguing experiences and drawing generalizations from them, what is its method of discovering truths of nature, and what is our criterion for saying some statement is a discovered truth of nature? William Whewell maintained that knowledge involves both subjective conjectures and empirical (physical) data: "Without Thought there could be no connexion; without Things there could be no reality." * For Whewell, a scientist begins with ideas that are clear and appropriate to the problem he confronts, not generalizations of data. The scientist invents a hypothesis by means of which he is able to order and structure his data. The mental ability of the scientist to conceive a new way of looking at things is a key to discovery. This involves a switch to a new point of view. Copernicus, Darwin, Einstein, and other leaders of scientific revolutions have been able to produce radical changes. Where do scientists get their new ideas? What is the source of new hypotheses? Is science only a natural outgrowth of its past? Is an act of creative genius involved in seeing everyday things in new and problematical ways?

Writing about Kepler, the great early astronomer, Albert Einstein says that "it seems that the human mind has first to construct forms independently before we can find them in things . . . knowledge cannot spring from experience alone but only from the comparison of the inventions of the intellect with observed fact." † Can this analysis be applied also to the discovery of the double helix structure of DNA? If scientific discovery is more than a matter of reporting, if it calls for subjective conjectures and concepts, how does it attain what we call truth? In what way is it objective?

---

* William Whewell, *History of Scientific Ideas* (London: John W. Parker and Son, 1858), Vol. I, p. 25.
† Albert Einstein, *Essays in Science* (New York: The Wisdom Library, 1934) p. 27.

The standard logics taught at the elementary college level usually include deduction and induction. Bacon championed induction as the logic of scientific discovery; but, as has been mentioned, there are many difficulties with such a view. Hence many philosophers have turned to the deductive model in their attempts to formulate the logic of science. In many ways the deductive model is attractive and does seem to fit the historical facts. In effect, hypotheses are plugged into a set of premises from which a statement describing some observable state of affairs is drawn. If, in fact, a situation exists that corresponds to the statement concluded, the hypothesis is taken to have been, at least to that extent, tested. The deductive model, however, provides a method only for the testing of hypotheses and really cannot be called a logic of discovery. The hypotheses must come from somewhere, but they cannot arise as the conclusions of the applications of the model.

In their description of the structure of DNA, Watson and Crick refer to their model as "a working hypothesis" that will either be proved or be disproved by further crystallographic analysis. The form such tests must take is a function of the hypothesis conjoined with a framework of premises to yield predictive statements. The double helix structure of DNA, however, is not revealed as a "working hypothesis" by a method of deduction. It is a discovery that if it has a logic at all does not seem to have the same logic as its test.

Simply put, the question of the source of such discoveries does not seem to be answered by explaining the logic of testing them. Many of those who have maintained that deduction is the primary logic of science have also argued that no logic of discovery *per se* is to be found. Instead, they tell us that discovery can be accounted for only in terms such as genius, accident, and/or psychological readiness to accept a certain hypothesis as probable, perhaps even on grounds as removed from logic as an aesthetic appreciation of one model over another. Indeed, Watson in his personalized history of the discovery writes of his exhilaration at having arrived at an aesthetically pleasing structural model of DNA.*

Norwood Russell Hanson has, however, argued persuasively that the proposal of a hypothesis has a logic conceptually different from the logic of accepting a hypothesis. In other words, as Hanson argues, a scientist's reasons for proposing hypothesis X (the double helix structure of DNA) are not necessarily and perhaps not at all the same as those he offers for its acceptance. Hanson calls the logic of discovery "retroduction." It is in basic form the searching for a

* James D. Watson, *The Double Helix* (New York: Atheneum, 1968).

cluster of premises from which an explanation of an anomalous event (unexplained data) can be unpacked. Scientific discovery begins, then, with a description of an event, an anomaly, that is incompatible with the standard scientific explanatory hypotheses and theories. It can be logically analyzed as the attempt to find premises, including a new hypothesis of a certain type, from which the description of the anomaly follows deductively.

DNA was assumed by Watson and Crick to be the carrier of the genetic specificity of virus and as such to possess "the capacity for exact self-duplication." But what structure of DNA would be consistent with that task? The basic chemical formula was well established, and it suggested that DNA is "a long thin fiber," asymmetrical in structure. Measurements tended to suggest that it is relatively rigid, an anomaly, "a puzzling finding in view of the large number of single bonds in the phosphate-sugar backbone." X-ray studies revealed at least two further important facts: (1) there are two distinct forms of DNA, one crystalline, the other paracrystalline; transitions from one form to the other are reversible; and (2) the crystallographic unit, the fiber, consists of two distinct chains. In order to account for these data, a number of hypotheses might have served. Watson and Crick, however, became convinced that the DNA structure must consist of two chains that complement each other coiled around a common axis and joined by hydrogen bonds between the nucleotide bases. Such a structure could account for the behavior of DNA and would be consistent with experimental data. The discovery of the structure of DNA as described by the two scientists seems to fit the logic of retroduction as expounded by Hanson.

The DNA experience suggests another issue of contemporary philosophy of science: the explanation of scientific revolutions. Thomas S. Kuhn, historian of science, has argued for a relativistic conception of science in which the business of science at any one time is dependent upon a nest of general assumptions, a way of looking at the world, which he calls a paradigm. Kuhn attempts to refute a long-standing view that the history of science is a history of the progressive building of one explanatory theory upon those that preceded it—that science is cumulative. Kuhn's analysis of science seems to undercut the claim that the established theories of science are objective. Instead they parade as objective when, in fact, they depend upon assumptions that are in no way open to scientific investigation.

Kuhn's notion of a paradigm is problematical, especially in so far as his descriptions of it are diverse. Sometimes paradigms are described as "networks of commitments," sometimes "theoretical and methodological beliefs," sometimes "patterns or models," and often "implicit metaphysical beliefs." What paradigm is central to the discovery of the structure of DNA, or is that discovery itself paradigmatic? When Watson and Crick predicted that the double helix model would generate new experimentation, explain the X-ray evidence, and provide the basis for a replication scheme (in time, they were proved correct), they seemed to intimate that their model was revolutionary, in that sense a Kuhnian paradigm. Scientists who accept the model view the world somewhat differently than before, and the problems as well as the acceptable scientific solutions to them are altered correspondingly.

1   FRANCIS BACON

(1561–1626)

Aphorisms Concerning the Interpretation of Nature and the Kingdom of Man*

Bacon attacks the rationalist tradition of the Middle Ages (the notion that the basic truths of the universe can be discovered simply by reflection). Knowledge, Bacon claims, must be based on unprejudiced empirical data. Before one can learn from nature, the mind must be freed from the traps of dogma and superstition. "Idols of the mind" are what Bacon calls the ways of thinking incorrectly about nature. Bacon argues that these idols must be torn down and replaced by an inductive method of deriving truths of nature. We must free ourselves from egocentric concerns and the theories of nature that men have constructed and allow nature to impart its secrets to us. Once having learned the secrets of nature, we are in a position to master it. Reliable knowledge is to be found by organizing the facts of nature in gradual inductive steps.

    Bacon's philosophy then has two distinct parts: a negative analysis of the "four idols of the mind" that distort truth, and a positive attempt to establish a new method of gaining knowledge by beginning with the particulars of experience and generalizing to more and more inclusive theories.

* Francis Bacon, *Novum Organum* (1620), Bk. 1, with omissions.

1. Man, being the servant and interpreter of nature, can do and understand so much and so much only as he has observed in fact or in thought of the course of nature: beyond this he neither knows anything nor can do anything.

3. Human knowledge and human power meet in one; for where the cause is not known the effect cannot be produced. Nature to be commanded must be obeyed; and that which in contemplation is as the cause is in operation as the rule.

12. The logic now in use serves rather to fix and give stability to the errors which have their foundation in commonly received notions, than to help the search after truth. So it does more harm than good.

15.   There is no soundness in our notions whether logical or physical. Substance, Quality, Action, Passion, Essence itself, are not sound notions: much less are Heavy, Light, Dense, Rare, Moist, Dry, Generation, Corruption, Attraction, Repulsion, Element, Matter, Form, and the like; but all are fantastical and ill defined.

16.   Our notions of less general species as Man, Dog, Dove, and of the immediate perceptions of the sense, as Hot, Cold, Black, White, do not materially mislead us; yet even these are sometimes confused by the flux and alteration of matter and the mixing of one thing with another. All the others which men have hitherto adopted are but wanderings, not being abstracted and formed from things by proper methods.

18.   The discoveries which have hitherto been made in the sciences are such as lie close to vulgar notions, scarcely beneath the surface. In order to penetrate into the inner and further recesses of nature, it is necessary that both notions and axioms be derived from things by a more sure and guarded way; and that a method of intellectual operation be introduced altogether better and more certain.

19.   There are and can be only two ways of searching into and discovering truth. The one flies from the senses and particulars to the most general axioms, and from these principles, the truth of which it takes for settled and immovable, proceeds to judgment and to the discovery of middle axioms. And this way is now in fashion. The other derives axioms from the senses and particulars, rising by a gradual and unbroken ascent, so that it arrives at the most general axioms last of all. This is the true way, but as yet untried.

20.   The understanding left to itself takes the same course (namely, the former) which it takes in accordance with logical order. For the mind longs to spring up to positions of higher generality, that it may find rest there; and so after a little while wearies of experiment. But this evil is increased by logic, because of the order and solemnity of its disputations.

21.   The understanding left to itself, in a sober, patient, and grave mind, especially if it be not hindered by received doctrines, tries a little that other way, which is the right one, but with little progress; since the understanding, unless directed and assisted, is a thing unequal, and quite unfit to contend with the obscurity of things.

22.   Both ways set out from the senses and particulars, and rest in the highest generalities; but the difference between them is infinite. For the one just glances at experiment and particulars in passing, the other dwells duly and orderly among them. The one, again, begins at once by establishing certain abstract and useless generalities, the other rises by gradual steps to that which is prior and better known in the order of nature.

23.   There is a great difference between the *Idols* of the human mind and the *Ideas* of the divine. That is to say, between certain empty dogmas, and the true signatures and marks set upon the works of creation as they are found in nature.

26.   The conclusions of human reason as ordinarily applied in matter of nature, I call for the sake of distinction *Anticipations of Nature* (as a thing rash or premature). That reason which is elicited from facts by a just and methodical process, I call *Interpretation of Nature*.

27.   Anticipations are a ground sufficiently firm for consent; for even if men went mad all after the same fashion, they might agree one with another well enough.

28.   ·For the winning of assent, indeed, anticipations are far more powerful than interpretations; because being collected from a few instances, and those for the most part of familiar occurrence, they straightway touch the understanding and fill the imagination; whereas interpretations on the other hand, being gathered here and there from very various and widely dispersed facts, cannot suddenly strike the understanding; and therefore they must needs, in respect of the opinions of the time, seem harsh and out of tune; much as the mysteries of faith do.

36.   One method of delivery alone remains to us; which is simply this: we must lead men to the particulars themselves, and their series and order; while men on their side must force themselves for awhile to lay their notions by and begin to familiarize themselves with facts.

37.   The doctrine of those who have denied that certainty could be attained at all, has some agreement with my way of proceeding at the first setting out; but they end in being infinitely separated and opposed. For the holders of that doctrine assert simply that nothing can

be known; I also assert that not much can be known in nature by the way which is now in use. But then they go on to destroy the authority of the senses and understanding; whereas I proceed to devise and supply helps for the same.

38. The idols and false notions which are now in possession of the human understanding, and have taken deep root therein, not only so beset men's minds that truth can hardly find entrance, but even after entrance obtained, they will again in the very instauration of the sciences meet and trouble us, unless men being forewarned of the danger fortify themselves as far as may be against their assaults.

39. There are four classes of idols which beset men's minds. To these for distinction's sake I have assigned names,—calling the first class *Idols of the Tribe;* the second, *Idols of the Cave;* the third, *Idols of the Market-place;* the fourth, *Idols of the Theater.*

40. The formation of ideas and axioms by true induction is no doubt the proper remedy to be applied for the keeping off and clearing away of idols. To point them out, however, is of great use, for the doctrine of idols is to the interpretation of nature what the doctrine of the refutation of sophisms is to common logic.

41. The Idols of the Tribe have their foundation in human nature itself, and in the tribe or race of men. For it is a false assertion that the sense of man is the measure of things. On the contrary, all perceptions, as well of the sense as of the mind, are according to the measure of the individual and not according to the measure of the universe. And the human understanding is like a false mirror, which, receiving rays irregularly, distorts and discolors the nature of things by mingling its own nature with it.

42. The Idols of the Cave are the idols of the individual man. For everyone (besides the errors common to human nature in general) has a cave or den of his own, which refracts and discolors the light of nature; owing either to his own proper and peculiar nature or to his education and conversation with others; or to the reading of books, and the authority of those whom he esteems and admires; or to the differences of impressions, accordingly as they take place in a mind preoccupied and predisposed or in a mind indifferent and settled; or the like. So that the spirit of man (according as it is meted out to dif-

ferent individuals) is in fact a thing variable and full of perturbation, and governed as it were by chance. Whence it was well observed by Heraclitus that men look for sciences in their own lesser worlds, and not in the greater or common world.

43. There are also idols formed by the intercourse and association of men with each other, which I call Idols of the Market-place, on account of the commerce and consort of men there. For it is by discourse that men associate; and words are imposed according to the apprehension of the vulgar. And therefore the ill and unfit choice of words wonderfully obstructs the understanding. Nor do the definitions or explanations wherewith in some things learned men are wont to guard and defend themselves, by any means set the matter right. But words plainly force and overrule the understanding, and throw all into confusion, and lead men away into numberless empty controversies and idle fancies.

44. Lastly, there are idols which have immigrated into men's minds from the various dogmas of philosophies, and also from wrong laws of demonstration. These I call Idols of the Theater; because in my judgment all the received systems are but so many stage-plays, representing worlds of their own creation after an unreal and scenic fashion. Nor is it only of the systems now in vogue, or only of the ancient sects and philosophies, that I speak: for many more plays of the same kind may yet be composed and in like artificial manner set forth; seeing that errors the most widely different have nevertheless causes for the most part alike. Neither again do I mean this only of entire systems, but also of many principles and axioms in science, which by tradition, credulity, and negligence have come to be received.

46. The human understanding when it has once adopted an opinion (either as being the received opinion or as being agreeable to itself) draws all things else to support and agree with it. And though there be a greater number and weight of instances to be found on the other side, yet these it either neglects and despises, or else by some distinction sets aside and rejects; in order that by this great and pernicious predetermination the authority of its former conclusions may remain inviolate. And therefore it was a good answer that was made by one who when they showed him hanging in a temple a picture of those who had paid their vows as having escaped shipwreck and would have him say whether he did not now acknowledge the power of the gods,—

"Aye," asked he again, "but where are they painted that were drowned after their vows?" And such is the way of all superstition, whether in astrology, dreams, omens, divine judgments, or the like; wherein men, having a delight in such vanities, mark the events where they are fulfilled, but where they fail, though this happen much oftener, neglect and pass them by. But with far more subtlety does this mischief insinuate itself into philosophy and the sciences; in which the first conclusion colors and brings into conformity with itself all that come after, though far sounder and better. Besides, independently of that delight and vanity which I have described, it is the peculiar and perpetual error of the human intellect to be more moved and excited by affirmatives than by negatives; whereas it ought properly to hold itself indifferently disposed towards both alike. Indeed in the establishment of any true axiom, the negative instance is the more forcible of the two.

48. The human understanding is unique; it cannot stop or rest, and still presses onward, but in vain. Therefore it is that we cannot conceive of any end or limit to the world; but always as of necessity it occurs to us that there is something beyond. Neither again can it be conceived how eternity has flowed down to the present day: for that distinction which is commonly received of infinity in time past and in time to come can by no means hold; for it would thence follow that one infinity is greater than another, and that infinity is wasting away and tending to become finite. The like subtlety arises touching the infinite divisibility of lines, from the same inability of thought to stop. But this inability interferes more mischievously in the discovery of causes: for although the most general principles in nature ought to be held merely positive, as they are discovered, and cannot with truth be referred to a cause; nevertheless the human understanding being unable to rest still seeks something prior in the order of nature. And then it is that in struggling towards that which is further off it falls back upon that which is more nigh at hand,—namely, on final causes; which have relation clearly to the nature of man rather than to the nature of the universe, and from this source have strangely defined philosophy. But he is no less an unskilled and shallow philosopher who seeks causes of that which is most general, than he who in things subordinate and subaltern omits to do so.

50. But by far the greatest hindrance and aberration of the human understanding proceeds from the dullness, incompetency, and decep-

tions of the senses; in that things which strike the sense outweigh things which do not immediately strike it, though they be more important. Hence it is that speculation commonly ceases where sight ceases, insomuch that of things invisible there is little or no observation. Hence all the working of the spirits inclosed in tangible bodies lies hid and unobserved of men. So also all the more subtle changes of form in the parts of coarser substances (which they commonly call alteration, though it is in truth local motion through exceedingly small spaces) is in like manner unobserved. And yet unless these two things just mentioned be searched out and brought to light, nothing great can be achieved in nature, as far as the production of works is concerned. So again the essential nature of our common air, and of all bodies less dense than air (which are very many), is almost unknown. For the sense by itself is a thing infirm and erring; neither can instruments for enlarging or sharpening the senses do much: but all the truer kind of interpretation of nature is effected by instances and experiments fit and apposite; wherein the sense decides touching the experiment only, and the experiment touching the point in nature and the thing itself.

59. The *Idols of the Market-place* are the most troublesome of all: idols which have crept into the understanding through the alliances of words and names. For men believe that their reason governs words; but it is also true that words react on the understanding; and this it is that has rendered philosophy and the sciences sophistical and inactive. Now words, being commonly framed and applied according to the capacity of the vulgar, follow those lines of division which are most obvious to the vulgar understanding. And whenever an understanding of greater acuteness or a more diligent observation would alter those lines to suit the true divisions of nature, words stand in the way and resist the change. Whence it comes to pass that the high and formal discussions of learned men end oftentimes in disputes about words and names; with which (according to the use and wisdom of the mathematicians) it would be more prudent to begin, and so by means of definitions reduce them to order. Yet even definitions cannot cure this evil in dealing with natural and material things; since the definitions themselves consist of words, and those words beget others: so that it is necessary to recur to individual instances, and those in due series and order; as I shall say presently when I come to the method and scheme for the formation of notions and axioms.

60. The idols imposed by words on the understanding are of two kinds. They are either names of things which do not exist (for as there

are things left unnamed through lack of observation, so likewise are there names which result from fantastic suppositions and to which nothing in reality corresponds), or they are names of things which exist, but yet confused and ill-defined, and hastily and irregularly derived from realities. Of the former kind are Fortune, the Prime Mover, Planetary Orbits, Elements of Fire, and like fictions which owe their origin to false and idle theories. And this class of idols is more easily expelled, because to get rid of them it is only necessary that all theories should be steadily rejected and dismissed as obsolete.

But the other class, which springs out of a faulty and unskillful abstraction, is intricate and deeply rooted. Let us take for example such a word as *humid,* and see how far the several things which the word is used to signify agree with each other; and we shall find the word *humid* to be nothing else than a mark loosely and confusedly applied to denote a variety of actions which will not bear to be reduced to any constant meaning. For it both signifies that which easily spreads itself round any other body; and that which in itself is indeterminate and cannot solidize; and that which readily yields in every direction; and that which easily divides and scatters itself; and that which easily unites and collects itself; and that which readily flows and is put in motion; and that which readily clings to another body and wets it; and that which is easily reduced to a liquid, or being solid easily melts. Accordingly when you come to apply the word,—if you take it in one sense, flame is humid; if in another, air is not humid; if in another, fine dust is humid; if in another, glass is humid. So that it is easy to see that the notion is taken by abstraction only from water and common and ordinary liquids, without any due verification.

There are however in words certain degrees of distortion and error. One of the least faulty kinds is that of names of substances, especially of lowest species and well-deduced (for the notion of *chalk* and of *mud* is good, of *earth* bad); a more faulty kind is that of actions, as *to generate, to corrupt, to alter;* the most faulty is of qualities (except such as are the immediate objects of the sense) as *heavy, light, rare, dense,* and the like. Yet in all these cases some notions are of necessity a little better than others, in proportion to the greater variety of subjects that fall within the range of the human sense.

2 NORWOOD RUSSELL HANSON

(1924–1966)

Retroductive Inference*

Hanson was a major contributor to a new outlook in contemporary philosophy of science. His book, Patterns of Discovery, has had a far-reaching effect upon reconsiderations of the process of discovery in science. This article is an attempt to distinguish two popular approaches to discovery in terms of their inferential and conceptual nature. The hypothetico-deductive method (called "HD" by Hanson) and the retroductive method ("RD") appear in completed form to be very much alike. The HD method is involved in conclusion-deducing, as is mathematics, but it is also a hypothesis-testing method. A hypothesis is linked to already confirmed premises; a conclusion is drawn and tested. If the observational consequences deduced from the premise cluster are confirmed, the hypothesis is said to be also confirmed to that extent. The RD scientific method centers on the attempted explanation of anomalies, events that appear unfamiliar or not explainable within the traditional framework. The RD scientist, as Hanson characterizes him, starts with the anomaly and seeks a set of premises that can account for it. It is an explanatory technique as opposed to the HD testing method. Formally these methods look alike, with premises and a conclusion, but Hanson argues that there is a major conceptual, not just psychological, difference that distinguishes these two ways of science. His examples from the history of astronomy provide interesting devices for testing his contention.

* Philosophy of Science, The Delaware Seminar, Bernard Baumrin, ed. (1961–1962), Vol. 1, pp. 21–37. Used by permission of the publishers, Interscience Publishers, Division of John Wiley & Sons, New York.

THE history of philosophy has in part been a history of attempts to describe scientific argument. In the *Posterior Analytics*, Aristotle writes of how naturalists argue from finite observations to general laws. Critics, like Sextus Empiricus, challenged Aristotle's account as unsound. A spectrum of views concerning scientific reasoning gradually proliferated. From Bacon through Reichenbach it was urged that all scientific argument reduces to induction by simple enumeration. From Mill through Braithwaite, scientists were seen to proceed by the hypothetico-deductive method (henceforth "HD"). Still others have espoused something called "retroduction" (RD) as the analysis of how scientists reason. Peirce, and Aristotle himself, opted for this view.

One objective of this paper will be to demonstrate that the differences between these philosophical accounts are not "merely psychological," but genuinely conceptual. Perhaps neither the HD nor the RD account has any application for the analysis of scientific argumentation. Or maybe both apply, but never at once. However this may be, it is not the case that the HD and the RD accounts constitute conceptually *equivalent* characterizations of any one scientific argument.

Our second objective is to distinguish yet again how people *do* argue from abstract questions about the form of argument. The delineation of the moves through which scientists reason while problem solving is as much the business of philosophy of science as is the *post factum* formal reconstruction of that argument for abstract logical purposes.

If these two objectives can be achieved, an historical point may then be made. The distinction drawn by 19th century astronomers between the Orthodox Problem of Perturbations and the Inverse Problem of Perturbations exemplifies the contrast we shall draw between the HD and RD accounts. Part of the conceptual excitement of the 19th century may be lost to logicians and historians who remain insensitive to this distinction.

The insight of the HD analysis consists in distinguishing the rational activity of the natural scientist from that of the mathematician, a distinction which Popper, Reichenbach, Braithwaite, Bergmann, and Carnap draw better and more finely than earlier inductive logicians like Hume, Mill, Jevons, Venn, and Johnson. The mathematician argues "typically" when he entertains certain premises solely to "unpack" them. His concern is neither with their contingent truth nor falsity, nor with that of the conclusions unpackable therefrom. It is the *unpacking relationship* which alone interests the formal scientist. The natural scientist, however, cares not only about consistency within a universe of discourse; he is concerned also with the contingent truth of claims about the universe in which we live. That a statement follows from *some* premise cluster may be a necessary condition for its descriptive utility. But it is not sufficient. False conclusions can follow validly from contingently false premises, or from logically false ones.

If each premise is contingently true, and if the deduction is valid, the conclusion will have "about" the same probability as has the premise cluster. There is thus a formal connection between a conclusion's probability and the joint probability of its premises. But problems seldom come to the scientist thus. Rarely is he given a list of claims and charged to draw up another list of their consequences. Usually he encounters some anomaly, and desires an explanation. It cannot follow from any *obvious* premise cluster else it would not be anomalous. So, one proceeds to cluster *some* established truths with hypotheses to see whether they may not jointly entail the anomaly. But now estimate the probability: the anomaly's description is assumed correct. The available premises obtain. From the joint probability of the anomaly plus these obvious premises one now estimates the probability of an hypothesis which, when conjoined with the premises, entails the anomaly.

The HD account is concerned not only with *conclusion deducing*, but with *hypothesis testing*. Hypotheses are tested by linking them with already confirmed statements to form a premise cluster. From this cluster, observational consequences are generated. If these are confirmed, the hypothesis is to that extent confirmed. But if further consequences turn out false, the probability of the hypothesis diminishes.

Much scientific reasoning and argumentation displays this HD pattern. Whenever the extension of a partially confirmed theory is in question, one generates further observational consequences of the theory and checks them against the facts. Indeed, detecting flaws in apparatus, and deviations in measuring instruments—as well as the theoretical discovery of "unexpected" phenomena—consists largely in deductively decomposing the premise clusters of theoretical science. This sets out the "logical expectations" of a given theory, and hence highlights any deviation from these expectations. The very identification of an event as "anomalous" depends on this HD elaboration of familiar premise clusters.*

The HD theorist attends thus to the scientist's inferences from contingent premise clusters to observationally vulnerable conclusions. The RD account focuses rather on the explanation of anomalies. RD enthusiasts think scientific argumentation to consist first in the recognition of anomalies, and then in the hunt for some premise cluster which, if confirmed, would explain the anomaly. This premise cluster will contain initial conditions and an hypothesis, the form of which "reveals itself" by its initial absence from the cluster. Thus, that the law of Universal Gravitation had an inverse square *form* seemed clear to the young Newton from the logical gap left in the cluster of known mechanical laws when he assumed that such laws were sufficient to explain *all* mechanical phenomena—the tides, hydrodynamics, ballistics, celestial motions, etc. A further hypothesis was needed. But although it was not

---

* There are other "less active" interpretations of the HD account. No matter. Even if every HD theorist were perfectly clear in setting out his views as *ex post facto* abstract logical analyses of scientific argumentation (which is not the case), this paper would still be making a distinction of import.

discovered until 1687, Newton perceived its form "lurking" in the very statement of his problem in 1665. So while the HD account pictures the scientist with a ready-made theory and a store of initial conditions in hand, generating from these testable observation statements, the RD account pictures him as possessing only the initial conditions and an upsetting anomaly, by reflections upon which he seeks an hypothesis to explain the anomaly and to found a new theory. Again, the HD account focuses on *hypothesis testing;* the RD account is concerned with *anomaly explaining.*

Some signal events in history have involved reasoning of this RD kind. The discovery of Neptune, and of the neutrino, are characterizable thus. Just as the discovery of Pluto, and of the antiproton, seem better described in HD terms. Here one runs out the consequences of an accepted theory and tests them. In the RD case, some facts surprisingly fail to confirm the consequences of an accepted theory; one then argues from these to some new hypothesis which may resolve the anomaly.

HD and RD enthusiasts both recognize that their formal criteria for success in argument are precisely the same. Thus, imagine that one scientist argues from premises A, B, C and hypothesis H, to conclusion D (which, although originally unexpected, ultimately is confirmed in fact). Another encounters the anomalous fact that D, and conjoins this with A, B, and C so as to "corner an hypothesis H which, when bracketed with A, B, and C, will "explain" D. Both scientists have been arguing; both have been using their heads. Differently. But the criterion for their having succeeded with their different tasks will be simply this: that D follows from A, B, C, and H. If either the first or the second scientist was mistaken in thinking D to be entailed by A, B, C, and H, then his reasoning fails.

But if the *logical* criteria for success or failure of reasoning in either case are the *same*, then whatever distinguishes these two scientific arguments must be nonlogical, and therefore (so the position develops) *merely psychological.* This is the strong form of the thesis that, though the aspects of scientific thinking distinguished by the HD and RD accounts may be interesting to psychologists, they contain nothing of importance for philosophers and logicians. My first objective is to attack that conclusion.

Consider a logic teacher presenting a problem to his class. One orthodox assignment might be this: "Here are three premises, A, B, and C. From these alone generate the theorem, D." The teacher is here charging his students to find what follows from premises written "at the top of the page." This is related to the traveler's puzzlement when he asks, "here I am, river to the left, mountains to the right, canyon ahead; *where do I go from here?*"

Contrast with this the different assignment a logic teacher might give: "Here is a theorem *D*. Find any three premises *A*, *B*, and *C* from which *D* is generable." Here, he gives his students *D* written, as it were, "at the bottom of a page." He asks them to work back from this to three premises which, if written at the top of the page, will be that from which D follows. Analogously, the traveler's question would be "*would I be able to return here from over there?* or there? or there?"

These two queries of the traveler will be answered, and appraised, by the same geographical criterion; "is there a geographical route connecting point *A* with point *B*?" Whether one is at *A* asking if he can get from there to *B*, or asking while at *B* whether he could return from some other point *A back* to *B*—the ultimate geographical issue is only whether some traversable route connects *A* and *B*.

Similarly, the criteria for assessing the logic students' answers are the same whether the teacher asks his question in terms of premise unpacking, or in terms of premise hunting. "Is there a logical route connecting *A*, *B*, *C* with *D*?" Whether one is at *D* and looking for some *A*, *B*, *C*, *H* from which he could get back to *D*, or whether one begins at *A*, *B*, *C*, *H* and asks whether he can make it to *D*—that these are different is not relevant in strict logic. The question of the existence of a route, logical or geographical, is independent of whether the route is traversed from one end to the other, or from the other end to the one: from *A*, *B*, *C*, *H*, to *D* or from *D* to *A*, *B*, *C*, *H*.

It is often supposed that when considering the *form* of an argument one should consider it as if it were *mathematical*. It is imagined that the ways logicians and mathematicians argue illuminates the issue of logical form. This is false. Mathematicians no less than other reasonable men argue sometimes from premises to conclusions, and sometimes from anomaly to its explanation independently of any *general* meta-mathematical question of whether some logical route connects the beginning point of the argument with its terminus. The actual arguments of mathematicians are just like ours. They have an arrow built into them; they progress from a starting point to a finish line.

The *logical form* of an argument, however, does not progress at all. It is static, time-independent, problem-neutral—above the battles of natural science and formal science alike. Hence, if deducing is what logicians and mathematicians *do* when arguing from premises to con-

clusions, then "deductive" cannot distinguish the formal characteristics
of one kind of argument as against others, i.e., probabilistic, analogical,
etc. If deduction is what someone does during the *de facto* business of
reasoning, the alternative ways of proceeding with one's reasoning
might be different and might have different names, e.g., "hypothetico-
deduction," "retroduction," etc. This may be so even though from a
strictly formal standpoint nothing may distinguish such procedures.

Just as arguing from premises at the top of a page down to a conclusion
differs from working from a conclusion "up" to premises at the top,
even when the logical form of each will be identical to that of the other
—so also, arguing from initial conditions plus hypothesis, A, B, C, H,
down to an observation statement D is different from working "up"
from an anomaly D to some H which, when conjoined with initial conditions A, B, C will entail, and hence explain, the anomaly. This, although the logical structure of each procedure is the same as that of
the other. The only question here is "does some logical route connect
A, B, C, and H with D?"

The HD account centers on hypothesis testing. It stresses the generating of observation statements D from premises A, B, C, and H. When
the D's square with the facts, H is, insofar, confirmed. The typical
description gives A, B, C, as known, H as conjectured, while D_1, D_2, D_3,
. . . have yet to be "unpacked" from this premise cluster. The analogy
between what the mathematician does during some of his problem
solving and what the scientist is taken to do by the HD philosopher, is
instructive. The natural scientist does not know in advance *what* observation statements D_1, D_2, D_3 may be generable from A, B, C, and H.
This is what makes this HD procedure an indirect test of H (*after* it
has been formulated and conjoined with A, B, *and* C). In both mathematics and natural science, arguments often exfoliate deductively; they
proceed from the "top of the page" down to the D-statements. This does
not identify the two procedures, however. The formal scientist is not
concerned with the empirical truth of A, B, C, or H or of the conclusions
drawn therefrom. That a conclusion D is validly generable from premises A, B, C, H, contingent truth or falsity aside, will be his one concern. A natural scientist proceeding in the HD manner, however, will
begin with initial conditions A, B, and C established as true. The status
of H remains unknown. After D is deduced from this set and discovered
to describe the facts, H may be said to have become "probabilified."
The natural scientist's concern is to determine whether a given H can
thus be raised to the same degree of acceptability as the initial condi-

tion A, B, and C. This he settles by enlarging and diversifying the set of observation statements D_1, D_2, D_3, . . . The regular confirmation of which will systematically raise H's probability. This distinguishes the epistemic context within which the mathematician and natural scientist work. Still, vis-à-vis the *direction* of argument, the mathematician and the natural scientist will both on occasion argue from the top of the page down, and this is traditionally described as "deducing."

When wearing his RD cap, the natural scientist begins his inquiry in puzzlement. After unpacking a well-established theory, replete with hypothesis H, into the expected observation statements D, he discovers that nature is not described by some of these latter. His normal expectations (and those of the theory) are thus thwarted. He has no reason to doubt initial conditions A, B, and C; their independent verification is what made them initial conditions. But he is astonished to note that the *orthodox* hypothesis H does not, when conjoined with A, B, C, generate descriptions of the facts. Thus the question: "Given the anomaly D, and the initial conditions A, B, C—from the hypothesis H' * does D follow when H' is bracketed with A, B, and C?"

Consider the two schemata on page 503.

Notice that the solid arrows represent the *actual* order of the scientist's argument. The "beginning" in the one case is H plus A, B, C, which set is then unpacked into the heretofore-unformulated D_1, D_2, D_3. In the other case, the occasion for the inquiry is the anomaly D: the rational moves from that point are towards a premise cluster A, B, C, H which can "explain" the anomaly. The dotted arrow, however, represents the *logical* order of the progressions. It points the same way in both cases—towards D_1, D_2, D_3; hence the logical criteria for appraising the validity of arguments of either form above are identical. Here then are two argument-schemata which, vis-à-vis logical structure, are the *same* argument, but, vis-à-vis their *de facto* development within the problem-solving context, are clearly different. The HD "starts from" initial conditions and an hypothesis and terminates in low-level observationally testable statements. The other "begins with" statements of actual observations—one unexpected on an HD basis—and terminates in a statement of initial conditions A, B, C, and some heretofore-unformulated hypothesis H.

Consider again the claim that this difference can be no more than psychological since both argument schemata are identical in logical

---

* *I.e.*, any hypothesis other than H.

HD characterization   RD characterization

$$\begin{bmatrix} A, B, C \text{ (initial conditions)} \\ \text{plus} \\ H \text{ (hypothesis)} \end{bmatrix}$$

D_1, D_2, D_3 ... (anomalies—
      ↑   descriptions
           of unex-
           pected ob-
           servations;
           these are in-
           compatible
           with the ex-
           pected HD
           unpacking
           of currently
           accepted hy-
           potheses)

D_1, D_2, D_3 ... (observation
    statements, as yet untested)

$$\begin{bmatrix} A, B, C \text{ (well-established} \\ \text{conditions of inquiry)} \\ \text{plus} \\ H_1, \text{ or } H_2, \text{ or } H_3 \text{ ...} \end{bmatrix}$$

form. This cannot be correct: the same conceptual probe leads to quite different reactions. That probe consists just in this: that from consistent premises, A, B, C, and H, any two resulting theorems, D_1 and D_2, must themselves be consistent. Whereas, it is not in general the ease that any two sets of premises, A, B, C and H, and A', B', C', and H'— either of which may resolve some anomaly D—will themselves be mutually consistent.

Thus consider the premise sets, A, B, C, *and* the claim "John is a bachelor." If these four premises are consistent, everything, D, which follows from them will also be mutually consistent, e.g., "John is unmarried," "John is male," "John is an adult," etc. But begin now from the low-level claim, D: "John is male." This *can* be shown to follow from A, B, C *and* "John is a bachelor." But it also follows from A, B, C, *and* "John is a married uncle." These two premise sets, however, are not consistent with each other. Since conceptually different answers result from this probe, the two characterizations must therefore be conceptually different and not merely psychologically so.

Here it might be objected, "Yes, 'John is a bachelor' and 'John is a married uncle' *are* inconsistent, and any premise sets in which they are imbedded will also be inconsistent. But these two premise sets are not inconsistent with respect to what is required in order to generate the single conclusion 'John is male.' Indeed, they could not be so, by the principle that if p entails q (and q is not necessary) then $\sim p$ cannot also entail q. The only analysis is this: that when $(r \cdot p)$ obtains and $p \to q$, then q will follow—and it will follow also from $(\sim r \cdot p)$ and $p \to q$. Hence a single anomaly D (i.e., q) can follow from two mutually incompatible premise sets only when the incompatibility plays no immediate role in the deduction."

This is an extremely potent objection. But it leaves the conceptual issue unscathed. It remains that A, B, C, H and R, if consistent, will entail only compatible conclusions D_1, D_2, D_3 . . . , etc. But an anomaly, D_3, might be explained not only by *different* premise sets—A B C H R and M N L O P—but also by *incompatible* premise sets—A B C H R and A B C H $\sim R$—where R and $\sim R$ are admittedly redundant to the derivation. Redundant or not, the conceptual distinction persists and rules out the "mere psychology" interpretation.

Moreover, in distinguishing premise sets *as embedded in scientific theories,* no premises are wholly redundant in the degenerate logical sense. For, although R and $\sim R$ may be redundant for this *one* accounting of D_3, they will not be redundant in general (as would a tautology) in the business of distinguishing the whole theories in which these arguments occur. Thus, in the wave theory of light, R may signify that a light ray *decelerates* on entering a denser medium, whereas in the particulate theory $\sim R$ will signify that the light *accelerates* on entering a denser medium. But neither R nor $\sim R$ will be needed immediately in the deduction of D—e.g., the proposition that the sines of the angles of incidence and refraction stand in ratio to each other. Nonetheless, *explaining* this latter phenomenon will involve reference ultimately not just to the premise set A, B, C, and H (which may be identical in both the wave theory and the particle theory): the explanations will sooner or later involve A, B, C, H, and R, on the one hand and A, B, C, H, and $\sim R$, on the other. So the conceptual difference remains, and is not trivialized by the redundancy move just noted.

Suppose someone urged that, so far as conceptual differences go, nothing distinguishes the "Classical Problem of Perturbations" and the "Inverse Problem of Perturbations." Such a person would not be taken seriously either by astronomers or by historians. I wish to describe these different approaches to perturbation theory, and to mark the analogies between them and the contrasts already drawn.

The Classical Problem of Perturbations may be characterized thus: Suppose we know the dynamical elements of some planet A (e.g., its mass, mean angular velocity, mean period of revolution, mean distance from the sun, orbital eccentricity, perihelial precession, etc.). And suppose also that we know the dynamical elements of some other planet B. Assuming the truth of the law of universal gravitation (H in this case), we can easily calculate the perturbation on B caused by A and vice versa. These calculations readily convert into predictions of the future positions of both planets. These are confirmed or disconfirmed by future observations. Should the observations confirm the predictions, they will indirectly reconfirm the law of gravitation, and reassure us also that the dynamical elements of both A and B have been properly described.

The Classical Problem of Perturbations thus reads remarkably like an HD reconstruction. So, knowing, as we do, the dynamical elements of the earth and Mars, we can predict the future positions of both by adding correction terms in the form of perturbation readjustments to the appropriate celestial theory. Indeed, by the systematic use of the HD method the discrepancies in unadjusted theories are regularly discovered, and the need for correction terms at the observational level clearly perceived. Nor is this HD technique *merely* a way of generating the detailed consequences of specific hypotheses. Nor is it merely ancillary to scientific theorizing; it is probably the only way of coming to perceive the need for further correction terms. The HD description is more accurate than any other in characterizing advances like the discovery of Halley's comet, of Pluto, of the antiproton and the antineutron. So, nothing in this paper is calculated to minimize the services rendered by cerebrations of the HD variety.

Other discoveries—of the planet Neptune, the neutrino, and the positive electron—are different from what has been discussed. The Inverse Problem of Perturbations is a case in point; it may be characterized thus: Suppose we know the dynamical elements of some planet B, and that we know from "unadjusted" celestial dynamics that the observed positions of B do not correspond to those predicted. B is perturbed from its expected path. The problem is now one of reasoning from this anomaly, these perturbations, to an hypothesis about some as-yet-undetected planet A whose specially designed dynamical elements would explain the observed perturbations. Explanation will have been achieved if B's observed perturbations logically follow from the hypothesis that A, with its tailor-made properties, exists. [This is precisely the argument which prepared us for the neutrino. Anomaly: Unlike α particles ejected from a spontaneously decaying radioactive source, the β particles display ranges, and hence energies covering a wide spectrum. But this conflicts with the accepted principle of the conservation of energy, since if the radioactive source is homogeneous, and all β particles have the same properties, then that some should have more energy than others suggests that in these "others" energy is not being conserved. Hypothesis: if β particles were always ejected *along with* some other as-yet-undetected particle (neutral charge, no rest mass, etc.) then each emitted particle-pair (β *and* neutrino) would have an aggregate energy equal to that of every other particle-pair. Emitted β particles do not leave a "star" of tracks, as do α particles, because these "neutrinos" are consuming different amounts of energy in each pair-emission: a fact which cannot show up in a Wilson chamber. *Therefore* neutrinos exist!] The existence of planet A will explain B's perturbations, if from this "existence hypothesis" B's perturbations can be shown to follow. And then we should be able to predict B's *future* perturbations on the basis of this same hypothesis. The HD procedure and the RD procedure are therefore indissolubly linked. They are even, indeed, conceptually linked. They are two stages of a three-stage rational process consisting in (*1*) unpacking the perhaps heretofore unformulated observational consequences of a given theory, or of a typical premise set within that theory, and (*2*) noting that one of these observational consequences, anomalously, does not square with the facts. The hunt is then on for some new hypothesis which, when conjoined with the orthodox premises *will* entail the anomaly, (*3*) unpacking in orthodox HD fashion this new premise set (containing the new hypothesis) into *other* as yet unformulated observational consequences: this is a further indirect test of the new anomaly explainer.

One of the great misunderstandings within the history of 19th century astronomy arose from this failure to distinguish arguing of the RD type from that of the HD type. My example is concerned with an exchange of letters between John Couch Adams and Professor George Airy, the distinguished Astronomer Royal.

Without engaging the vexed question of assigning ultimate priority, there can be little doubt that Adams' calculations in 1845 were sufficient for detecting the then-unknown planet which was perturbing Uranus. Adams' work was unknown to Leverrier when he took up this problem. But it is significant that both these astronomers, independently, concerned themselves with the Inverse Problem of Perturbations. Both of them recognized that they were departing from the usual perturbational problems of theoretical celestial mechanics.

As early as 1841 Adams formulated the problem of Uranus' orbit as follows: Given the anomalous motions of Uranus, from assuming the existence of what kind of planet, having what elements, could Uranus' observed positions be reconciled with orthodox Newtonian theory? *From* the anomaly, in other words, Adams envisages a rational process proceeding through the laws of celestial mechanics to some additional existence hypothesis which, if confirmed, would "explain" the Uranus' observed positions—rendering them thereby non-anomalous. Adams explicitly distinguishes this formulation of his problem from quite another one, namely the *arbitrary* assumption of some planets' existence —some planet having properties conjured up *de novo*. From this hypothesis of such a planet (plus associated initial conditions) to reason one's way in accordance with unadjusted Newtonian theory to observation statements—this is not Adams' idea of his own procedure. For even if this arbitrary hypothesis does explain the observed positions, it remains a different undertaking. Again, from the point of view of logical form, no distinction can be drawn between these two procedures: The inverse problem of perturbations and the orthodox problem of perturbations are thus indistinguishable in strict logic. But Adams sharply distinguishes the two as being different in *kind*. And no contemporary astronomer would be satisfied with being told by a philosopher that only a psychological difference demarcates the inverse from the orthodox problem of perturbations.

In one of his haughty letters to Adams, the Astronomer Royal thanks him for his detailed calculations and for having deduced the consequences of his *hypothesis* of a trans-Uranic premise. This convinced Adams that Airy had not really understood his work. For Adams did not arbitrarily select some hypothesis out of the air and unpack it into observation statements (some of which "accidentally" fit the facts). He began rather with incontrovertible observational facts (however "anomalous" in terms of the accepted theory) and slowly reasoned his way from these *back* to an hypothesis *H* which, almost as soon as it was formulated was seen *not* to be arbitrary in that it easily generated the anomaly.

Leverrier also sharply distinguishes the inverse from the orthodox problem of perturbations and definitely identifies his undertaking as being of the former variety. (Cf. Hanson, "Leverrier: The Zenith and Nadir of Newtonian Mechanics," in *Isis*, Vol. 53, Part 3, No. 173, Sept. 1962, pp. 359–378.)

Now this is a moment in the history of 19th century science which, I submit, could be misunderstood by one who minimized the *conceptual* differences between the HD description of scientific discoveries and the RD descriptions. These are not all-or-nothing exclusive accounts. You cannot recognize anomalies without the HD unpacking of accepted hypotheses. And you can't get new hypotheses for future HD unpacking without an RD type hunt for new hypotheses. Some HD theorists, by focusing only on logical form, which move has the consequence of conflating the HD and RD accounts, take all significant scientific *reasoning* in fact to be of the HD variety. A rationale of quite a different kind is often in evidence in the head work leading to discoveries such as that of the positive electron, the neutrino, and Neptune. To set out the conceptual structure of all of these examples as if they were instances of the same thing—and this the proponents of the HD analysis sometimes certainly do—would be to afford but a very incomplete understanding of the place of reason in the world of scientific discovery.

Long before this moment the following counter-claim will have been formulated: The HD philosopher had never purported to *describe* the process of scientific thinking. Since his interests are fundamentally *logical,* his concern is only to distinguish—in an *ex post facto* logical manner—arguments within formal science from arguments within natural science. Since the distinction between statements which are, within a given language, certifiably true or false, and hypotheses which are at most *probably* true or false, is a *logical* distinction—and since the HD theorist is concerned *only* with this distinction—his is not a descriptive undertaking, but a logical one.

This is unobjectionable. But many HD philosophers have gone further. They have characterized the HD account not simply in *ex post facto* terms, but as somehow relevant to the way in which scientists *actually proceed,* and the way in which science *actually develops.* Insofar as this is done it is an incomplete account; two stages of a irreducible trinity of processes. Moreover, *whether or not* HD theorists are concerned with the distinction we have drawn here, whether or not my exegesis of their views is correct, there *is* such a distinction to be drawn. And insofar as HD philosophers have denied that such a distinction can be drawn on anything but psychological grounds, it has been my objective here to deny precisely that.

3   BENJAMIN LEE WHORF

(1897–1941)

*Science and Linguistics**

*Whorf was a pioneer in the field of comparative linguistics. His thesis, derived
from a study of many different types of language, is that there is an essential
relationship between language and the way we think; that our language, in
fact, is the shaper of even our so-called most private thoughts. Whorf makes
two major points about science and linguistics. He claims, first, that all higher
levels of thinking are language-dependent and, second, that the structure of the
language used determines the way in which one understands his environment.
People who speak different languages see the universe differently and make
entirely different claims and evaluations of it. Whorf proposes what he calls a
new principle of relativity: "All observers are not led by the same physical
evidence to the same picture of the universe, unless their linguistic backgrounds
are similar, or can in some way be calibrated." Some languages cannot be
systematically standardized, and the sciences that necessarily would result
within these diverse patterns of thought would also be non-calibratable.*

* *Technology Review* (April, 1940), pp. 229–231, and 247–248. Used by
kind permission of the editor of *Technology Review*.

EVERY normal person in the world, past infancy in years, can and
does talk. By virtue of that fact, every person—civilized or uncivilized—carries through life certain naïve but deeply rooted ideas about
talking and its relation to thinking. Because of their firm connection
with speech habits that have become unconscious and automatic, these
notions tend to be rather intolerant of opposition. They are by no means
entirely personal and haphazard; their basis is definitely systematic,
so that we are justified in calling them a system of natural logic—a term
that seems to me preferable to the term common sense, often used for
the same thing.

According to natural logic, the fact that every person has talked
fluently since infancy makes every man his own authority on the process
by which he formulates and communicates. He has merely to consult a
common substratum of logic or reason which he and everyone else are
supposed to possess. Natural logic says that talking is merely an incidental process concerned strictly with communication, not with
formulation of ideas. Talking, or the use of language, is supposed only

to "express" what is essentially already formulated nonlinguistically. Formulation is an independent process, called thought or thinking, and is supposed to be largely indifferent to the nature of particular languages. Languages have grammars, which are assumed to be merely norms of conventional and social correctness, but the use of language is supposed to be guided not so much by them as by correct, rational, or intelligent THINKING.

Thought, in this view, does not depend on grammar but on laws of logic or reason which are supposed to be the same for all observers of the universe—to represent a rationale in the universe that can be "found" independently by all intelligent observers, whether they speak Chinese or Choctaw. In our own culture, the formulations of mathematics and of formal logic have acquired the reputation of dealing with this order of things: i.e., with the realm and laws of pure thought. Natural logic holds that different languages are essentially parallel methods for expressing this one-and-the-same rationale of thought and, hence, differ really in but minor ways which may seem important only because they are seen at close range. It holds that mathematics, symbolic logic, philosophy, and so on are systems contrasted with language which deal directly with this realm of thought, not that they are themselves specialized extensions of language. The attitude of natural logic is well shown in an old quip about a German grammarian who devoted his whole life to the study of the dative case. From the point of view of natural logic, the dative case and grammar in general are an extremely minor issue. A different attitude is said to have been held by the ancient Arabians: Two princes, so the story goes, quarreled over the honor of putting on the shoes of the most learned grammarian of the realm: whereupon their father, the caliph, is said to have remarked that it was the glory of his kingdom that great grammarians were honored even above kings.

The familiar saying that the exception proves the rule contains a good deal of wisdom, though from the standpoint of formal logic it became an absurdity as soon as "prove" no longer meant "put on trial." The old saw began to be profound psychology from the time it ceased to have standing in logic. What it might well suggest to us today is that, if a rule has absolutely no exceptions, it is not recognized as a rule or as anything else; it is then part of the background of experience of which we tend to remain unconscious. Never having experienced anything in contrast to it, we cannot isolate it and formulate it as a rule until we so enlarge our experience and expand our base of reference that we encounter an interruption of its regularity. The situation is somewhat analogous to that of not missing the water till the well runs dry, or not realizing that we need air till we are choking.

For instance, if a race of people had the physiological defect of being able to see only the color blue, they would hardly be able to formulate the rule that they saw only blue. The term blue would convey no meaning to them, their language would lack color terms, and their words denoting their various sensations of blue would answer to, and translate, our words "light, dark, white, black," and so on, not our word "blue." In order to formulate the rule of norm of seeing only blue, they would need exceptional moments in which they saw other colors. The phenomenon of gravitation forms a rule without exceptions; needless to say, the untutored person is utterly unaware of any law of gravitation, for it would never enter his head to conceive of a universe in which bodies behaved otherwise than they do at the earth's surface. Like the color blue with our hypothetical race, the law of gravitation is a part of the untutored individual's background, not something he isolates from that background. The law could not be formulated until bodies that always fell were seen in terms of a wider astronomical world in which bodies moved in orbits or went this way and that.

Similarly, whenever we turn our heads, the image of the scene passes across our retinas exactly as it would if the scene turned around us. But this effect is background, and we do not recognize it; we do not see a room turn around us but are conscious only of having turned our heads in a stationary room. If we observe critically while turning the head or eyes quickly, we shall see, no motion it is true, yet a blurring of the scene between two clear views. Normally we are quite unconscious of this continual blurring but seem to be looking about in an unblurred world. Whenever we walk past a tree or house, its image on the retina changes just as if the tree or house were turning on an axis; yet we do not see trees or houses turn as we travel about at ordinary speeds. Sometimes ill-fitting glasses will reveal queer movements in the scene as we look about, but normally we do not see the relative motion of the environment when we move; our psychic makeup is somehow adjusted to disregard whole realms of phenomena that are so all-pervasive as to be irrelevant to our daily lives and needs.

Natural logic contains two fallacies: First, it does not see that the phenomena of a language are to its own speakers largely of a background character and so are outside the critical consciousness and control of the speaker who is expounding natural logic. Hence, when anyone, as a natural logician, is talking about reason, logic, and the laws of correct thinking, he is apt to be simply marching in step with purely grammatical facts that have somewhat of a background character in his own language or family of languages but are by no means universal in all languages and in no sense a common substratum of reason. Second, natural logic confuses agreement about subject matter, attained through use of language, with knowledge of the linguistic process by which agreement is attained: i.e., with the province of the despised (and to its notion superfluous) grammarian. Two fluent speakers, of English let us say, quickly reach a point of assent about the subject matter of their speech; they agree about what their language refers to. One of them, A, can give directions that will be carried out by the other, B, to A's complete satisfaction. Because they thus understand each other so perfectly, A and B, as natural logicians, suppose they must of course know how it is all done. They think, e.g., that it is simply a matter of choosing words to express thoughts. If you ask A to explain how he got B's agreement so readily, he will simply repeat to you, with more or less elaboration or abbreviation, what he said to B. He has no notion of the process involved. The amazingly complex system of linguistic patterns and classifications, which A and B must have in common before they can adjust to each other at all, is all background to A and B.

These background phenomena are the province of the grammarian—or of the linguist, to give him his more modern name as a scientist. The word linguist in common, and especially newspaper, parlance means something entirely different, namely, a person who can quickly attain agreement about subject matter with different people speaking a number of different languages. Such a person is better termed a polyglot or a multilingual. Scientific linguists have long understood that ability to speak a language fluently does not necessarily confer a linguistic knowledge of it, i.e., understanding of its background phenomena and its systematic processes and structure, any more than ability to play a good game of billiards confers or requires any knowledge of the laws of mechanics that operate upon the billiard table.

The situation here is not unlike that in any other field of science. All real scientists have their eyes primarily on background phenomena that cut very little ice, as such, in our daily lives; and yet their studies have a way of bringing out a close relation between these unsuspected realms of fact and such decidedly foreground activities as transporting goods, preparing food, treating the sick, or growing potatoes, which in time may become very much modified, simply because of pure scientific investigation in no way concerned with these brute matters themselves. Linguistics presents a quite similar case; the background phenomena with which it deals are involved in all our foreground activities of talking and of reaching agreement, in all reasoning and arguing of cases, in all law, arbitration, conciliation, contracts, treaties, public opinion, weighing of scientific theories, formulation of scientific results.

Whenever agreement or assent is arrived at in human affairs, and whether or not mathematics or other specialized symbolisms are made part of the procedure, THIS AGREEMENT IS REACHED BY LINGUISTIC PROCESSES, OR ELSE IT IS NOT REACHED.

As we have seen, an overt knowledge of the linguistic processes by which agreement is attained is not necessary to reaching some sort of agreement, but it is certainly no bar thereto; the more complicated and difficult the matter, the more such knowledge is a distinct aid, till the point may be reached—I suspect the modern world has about arrived at it—when the knowledge becomes not only an aid but a necessity. The situation may be likened to that of navigation. Every boat that sails is in the lap of planetary forces; yet a boy can pilot his small craft around a harbor without benefit of geography, astronomy, mathematics, or international politics. To the captain of an ocean liner, however, some knowledge of all these subjects is essential.

When linguists became able to examine critically and scientifically a large number of languages of widely different patterns, their base of reference was expanded; they experienced an interruption of phenomena hitherto held universal, and a whole new order of significances came into their ken. It was found that the background linguistic system (in other words, the grammar) of each language is not merely a reproducing instrument for voicing ideas but rather is itself the shaper of ideas, the program and guide for the individual's mental activity, for his analysis of impressions, for his synthesis of his mental stock in trade. Formulation of ideas is not an independent process, strictly rational in the old sense, but is part of a particular grammar, and differs, from slightly to greatly, between different grammars. We dissect along lines laid down by our native languages. The categories and types that we isolate from the world of phenomena we do not find there because they stare every observer in the face; on the contrary, the world is presented in a kaleidoscopic flux of impressions which has to be organized by our minds—and this means largely by the linguistic systems in our minds. We cut nature up, organize it into concepts, and ascribe significances as we do, largely because we are parties to an agreement to organize it in this way—an agreement that holds throughout our speech community and is codified in the patterns of our language. The agreement is, of course, an implicit and unstated one, BUT ITS TERMS ARE ABSOLUTELY OBLIGATORY; we cannot talk at all except by subscribing to the organization and classification of data which the agreement decrees.

This fact is very significant for modern science, for it means that no individual is free to describe nature with absolute impartiality but is constrained to certain modes of interpretation even while he thinks himself most free. The person most nearly free in such respects would be a linguist familiar with very many widely different linguistic systems. As yet no linguist is in any such position. We are thus introduced to a new principle of relativity, which holds that all observers are not led by the same physical evidence to the same picture of the universe, unless their linguistic backgrounds are similar, or can in some way be calibrated.

This rather startling conclusion is not so apparent if we compare only our modern European languages, with perhaps Latin and Greek thrown in for good measure. Among these tongues there is a unanimity of major patterns which at first seems to bear out natural logic. But this unanimity exists only because these tongues are all Indo-European dialects cut to the same basic plan, being historically transmitted from what was long ago one speech community; because the modern dialects have long shared in building up a common culture; and because much of this culture, on the more intellectual side, is derived from the linguistic backgrounds of Latin and Greek. Thus this group of languages satisfies the special case of the clause beginning "unless" in the statement of the linguistic relativity principle at the end of the preceding paragraph. From this condition follows the unanimity of description of the world in the community of modern scientists. But it must be emphasized that "all modern Indo-European-speaking observers" is not the same thing as "all observers." That modern Chinese or Turkish scientists describe the world in the same terms as Western scientists means, of course, only that they have taken over bodily the entire Western system of rationalizations, not that they have corroborated that system from their native posts of observation.

When Semitic, Chinese, Tibetan, or African languages are contrasted with our own, the divergence in analysis of the world becomes more apparent; and, when we bring in the native languages of the Americas, where speech communities for many millenniums have gone their ways independently of each other and of the Old World, the fact that languages dissect nature in many different ways becomes patent. The relativity of all conceptual systems, ours included, and their dependence upon language stand revealed. That American Indians speaking only their native tongues are never called upon to act as scientific observers is in no wise to the point. To exclude the evidence which their languages offer as to what the human mind can do is like expecting botanists to study nothing but food plants and hothouse roses and then tell us what the plant world is like!

Let us consider a few examples. In English we divide most of our words into two classes, which have different grammatical and logical properties. Class 1 we call nouns, e.g., "house, man;" class 2, verbs, e.g., "hit, run." Many words of one class can act secondarily as of the other class, e.g., "a hit, a run," or "to man (the boat)," but, on the primary level, the division between the classes is absolute. Our language thus gives us a bipolar division of nature. But nature herself is not thus polarized. If it be said that "strike, turn, run," are verbs because they denote temporary or short-lasting events, i.e., actions, why then is "fist" a noun? It also is a temporary event. Why are "lightning, spark, wave, eddy, pulsation, flame, storm, phase, cycle, spasm, noise, emotion" nouns? They are temporary events. If "man" and "house" are nouns because they are long-lasting and stable events, i.e., things, what then are "keep, adhere, extend, project, continue, persist, grow, dwell," and so on doing among the verbs? If it be objected that "possess, adhere" are verbs because they are stable relationships rather than stable percepts, why then should "equilibrium, pressure, current, peace, group, nation, society, tribe, sister," or any kinship term be among the nouns? It will be found that an "event" to us means "what our language classes as a verb" or something analogized therefrom. And it will be found that it is not possible to define "event, thing, object, relationship," and so on, from nature, but that to define them always involves a circuitous return to the grammatical categories of the definer's language.

In the Hopi language, "lightning, wave, flame, meteor, puff of smoke, pulsation" are verbs—events of necessarily brief duration cannot be anything but verbs. "Cloud" and "storm" are at about the lower limit or duration for nouns. Hopi, you see, actually has a classification of events (or linguistic isolates) by duration type, something strange to our modes of thought. On the other hand, in Nootka, a language of Vancouver Island, all words seem to us to be verbs, but really there are no classes 1 and 2; we have, as it were, a monistic view of nature that gives us only one class of word for all kinds of events. "A house occurs" or "it houses" is the way of saying "house," exactly like "a flame occurs" or "it burns." These terms seem to us like verbs because they are inflected for durational and temporal nuances, so that the suffixes of the word for house event make it mean long-lasting house, temporary house, future house, house that used to be, what started out to be a house, and so on.

Hopi has one noun that covers every thing or being that flies, with the exception of birds, which class is denoted by another noun. The former noun may be said to denote the class $(FC-B)$—flying class minus bird. The Hopi actually call insect, airplane, and aviator all by the same word, and feel no difficulty about it. The situation, of course, decides any possible confusion among very disparate members of a broad linguistic class, such as this class (FC–B). This class seems to us too large and inclusive, but so would our class "snow" to an Eskimo. We have the same word for falling snow, snow on the ground, snow packed hard like ice, slushy snow, wind-driven flying snow—whatever the situation may be. To an Eskimo, this all-inclusive word would be almost unthinkable; he would say that falling snow, slushy snow, and so on, are sensuously and operationally different, different things to contend with; he uses different words for them and for other kinds of snow. The Aztecs go even farther than we in the opposite direction, with "cold," "ice," and "snow" all represented by the same basic word with different terminations; "ice" is the noun form; "cold," the adjectival form; and for "snow," "ice mist."

What surprises most is to find that various grand generalizations of the Western world, such as time, velocity, and matter, are not essential to the construction of a consistent picture of the universe. The psychic experiences that we class under these headings are, of course, not destroyed; rather, categories derived from other kinds of experiences take over the rulership of the cosmology and seem to function just as well. Hopi may be called a timeless language. It recognizes psychological time, which is much like Bergson's "duration," but this "time" is quite unlike the mathematical time, T, used by our physicists. Among the peculiar properties of Hopi time are that it varies with each observer, does not permit of simultaneity, and has zero dimensions; i.e., it cannot be given a number greater than one. The Hopi do not say, "I stayed five days," but "I left on the fifth day." A word referring to this kind of time, like the word day, can have no plural. The puzzle picture [shown here] will give mental exercise to anyone who would like to figure out how the Hopi verb gets along without tenses. Actually, the only practical use of our tenses, in one-verb sentences, is to distinguish among five typical situations, which are symbolized in the picture. The timeless Hopi verb does not distinguish between the present, past, and future of the event itself but must always indicate what type of validity the SPEAKER intends the statement to have: (a) report of an event (situations 1, 2, 3 in the picture); (b) expectation of an event (situation 4); (c) generalization or law about events (situation 5). Situation 1, where the speaker and listener are in contact with the same objective field, is divided by our language into the two conditions, 1a and 1b, which it calls present and past, respectively. This division is unnecessary for a language which assures one that the statement is a report.

Hopi grammar, by means of its forms called aspects and modes, also makes it easy to distinguish among momentary, continued, and repeated occurrences, and to indicate the actual sequence of reported events. Thus the universe can be described without recourse to a concept of dimensional time. How would a physics constructed along these

OBJECTIVE FIELD	SPEAKER (Sender)	HEARER (Receiver)	HANDLING OF TOPIC: A THIRD PERSON RUNNING
SITUATION 1a			ENGLISH: *He is running* HOPI: *Wari (Running, statement of fact)*
SITUATION 1b (Blank) (devoid of running)			ENGLISH: *He ran* HOPI: *Wari (Running, statement of fact)*
SITUATION 2			ENGLISH: *He is running* HOPI: *Wari (Running, statement of fact)*
SITUATION 3 (Blank)			ENGLISH: *He ran* HOPI: *Era wari (Running, statement of fact from memory)*
SITUATION 4 (Blank)			ENGLISH: *He will run* HOPI: *Warikni (Running, statement of expectation)*
SITUATION 5 (Blank)			ENGLISH: *He runs* (e.g. on the track team) HOPI: *Warikngwe (Running, statement of law)*

Contrast between a "temporal" language (English) and a "timeless" language (Hopi). What are to English differences of time are to Hopi differences in the kind of validity.

lines work, with no T (time) in its equations? Perfectly, as far as I can see, though of course it would require different ideology and perhaps different mathematics. Of course V (velocity) would have to go too. The Hopi language has no word really equivalent to our "speed" or "rapid." What translates these terms is usually a word meaning intense or very, accompanying any verb of motion. Here is a clue to the nature of our new physics. We may have to introduce a new term I, intensity. Every thing and event will have an I, whether we regard the thing or event as moving or as just enduring or being. Perhaps the I of an electric charge will turn out to be its voltage, or potential. We shall use clocks to measure some intensities, or, rather, some RELATIVE intensities, for the absolute intensity of anything will be meaningless. Our old friend acceleration will still be there but doubtless under a new name. We shall perhaps call it V, meaning not velocity but variation. Perhaps all growths and accumulations will be regarded as V's. We should not have the concept of rate in the temporal sense, since, like velocity, rate introduces a mathematical and linguistic time. Of course we know that all measurements are ratios, but the measurements of intensities made by comparison with the standard intensity of a clock or a planet we do not treat as ratios, any more than we so treat a distance made by comparison with a yardstick.

A scientist from another culture that used time and velocity would have great difficulty in getting us to understand these concepts. We should talk about the intensity of a chemical reaction; he would speak of its velocity or its rate, which words we should at first think were simply words for intensity in his language. Likewise, he at first would think that intensity was simply our own word for velocity. At first we should agree, later we should begin to disagree, and it might dawn upon both sides that different systems of rationalization were being used. He would find it very hard to make us understand what he really meant by velocity of a chemical reaction. We should have no words that would fit. He would try to explain it by likening it to a running horse, to the difference between a good horse and a lazy horse. We should try to show him, with a superior laugh, that his analogy also was a matter of different intensities, aside from which there was little similarity between a horse and a chemical reaction in a beaker. We should point out that a running horse is moving relative to the ground, whereas the material in the beaker is at rest.

One significant contribution to science from the linguistic point of view may be the greater development of our sense of perspective. We shall no longer be able to see a few recent dialects of the Indo-

European family, and the rationalizing techniques elaborated from their patterns, as the apex of the evolution of the human mind, nor their present wide spread as due to any survival from fitness or to anything but a few events of history—events that could be called fortunate only from the parochial point of view of the favored parties. They, and our own thought processes with them, can no longer be envisioned as spanning the gamut of reason and knowledge but only as one constellation in a galactic expanse. A fair realization of the incredible degree of diversity of linguistic system that ranges over the globe leaves one with an inescapable feeling that the human spirit is inconceivably old; that the few thousand years of history covered by our written records are no more than the thickness of a pencil mark on the scale that measures our past experience on this planet; that the events of these recent millenniums spell nothing in any evolutionary wise, that the race has taken no sudden spurt, achieved no commanding synthesis during recent millenniums, but has only played a little with a few of the linguistic formulations and views of nature bequeathed from an inexpressibly longer past. Yet neither this feeling nor the sense of precarious dependence of all we know upon linguistic tools which themselves are largely unknown need be discouraging to science but should, rather, foster that humility which accompanies the true scientific spirit, and thus forbid that arrogance of the mind which hinders real scientific curiosity and detachment.

4

THOMAS S. KUHN

(1922–   )

Historical Structure of Scientific Discovery *

*Thomas Kuhn's work in the field of history and philosophy of science has been
most influential since the publication of his book* The Structure of Scientific
Revolutions. *This paper contains some arguments for the major thesis of that book.
Kuhn, contrary to the majority of historians of science, offers documentation
designed to show that science is not cumulative, that each new theory is not built
upon all those that precede it. Instead, Kuhn argues, scientific discoveries demand
major adjustments in the way the world is viewed. Anomalous events do not
emerge in the course of doing normal science until some place for them has been
made conceptually, and the identification of the actual point in time of a scientific
discovery is usually quite arbitrary. A comparison of Kuhn's account of the role of
anomalies and Hanson's views on retroductive inference should be undertaken.
Note also that the case of the discovery of Uranus is common to both essays.*

* T. S. Kuhn, "Historical Structure of Scientific Discovery," *Science,* Vol. 136,
June 1, 1962, pp. 760–764. Reprinted by permission of the author and *Science.*
Copyright 1962 by the American Association for the Advancement of Science.

MY object in this article is to isolate and illuminate one small part
of what I take to be a continuing historiographic revolution in
the study of science.[1] The structure of scientific discovery is my
particular topic, and I can best approach it by pointing out that the
subject itself may well seem extraordinarily odd. Both scientists and,
until quite recently, historians have ordinarily viewed discovery as the
sort of event which, though it may have preconditions and surely has
consequences, is itself without internal structure. Rather than being
seen as a complex development extended both in space and time, discovering something has usually seemed to be a unitary event, one
which, like seeing something, happens to an individual at a specifiable
time and place.

This view of the nature of discovery has, I suspect, deep roots in the

[1] The larger revolution will be discussed in my forthcoming book, *The Structure of
Scientific Revolutions,* to be published in the fall by the University of Chicago
Press. The central ideas in this paper have been abstracted from that source,
particularly from its third chapter, "Anomaly and the emergence of scientific
discoveries."

nature of the scientific community. One of the few historical elements recurrent in the textbooks from which the prospective scientist learns his field is the attribution of particular natural phenomena to the historical personages who first discovered them. As a result of this and other aspects of their training, discovery becomes for many scientists an important goal. To make a discovery is to achieve one of the closest approximations to a property right that the scientific career affords. Professional prestige is often closely associated with these acquisitions.[2] Small wonder, then, that acrimonious disputes about priority and independence in discovery have often marred the normally placid tenor of scientific communication. Even less wonder that many historians of science have seen the individual discovery as an appropriate unit with which to measure scientific progress and have devoted much time and skill to determining what man made which discovery at what point in time. If the study of discovery has a surprise to offer, it is only that, despite the immense energy and ingenuity expended upon it, neither polemic nor painstaking scholarship has often succeeded in pinpointing the time and place at which a given discovery could properly be said to have "been made."

SOME DISCOVERIES PREDICTABLE, SOME NOT

That failure, both of argument and of research, suggests the thesis that I now wish to develop. Many scientific discoveries, particularly the most interesting and important, are not the sort of event about which the questions "Where?" and, more particularly, "When?" can appropriately be asked. Even if all conceivable data were at hand, those questions would not regularly possess answers. That we are persistently driven to ask them nonetheless is symptomatic of a fundamental inappropriateness in our image of discovery. That inappropriateness is here my main concern, but I approach it by considering first the historical problem presented by the attempt to date and to place a major class of fundamental discoveries.

The troublesome class consists of those discoveries—including oxygen, the electric current, x-rays, and the electron—which could not be predicted from accepted theory in advance and which therefore caught the assembled profession by surprise. That kind of discovery will

[2] For a brilliant discussion of these points see, R. K. Merton, "Priorities in scientific discovery: a chapter in the sociology of science," *Am. Sociol. Rev.* 22, 635 (1957). Also very relevant, though it did not appear until this article had been prepared, is F. Reif, "The competitive world of the pure scientist," *Science* 134, 1957 (1961).

shortly be my exclusive concern, but it will help first to note that there
is another sort and one which presents very few of the same problems.
Into this second class of discoveries fall the neutrino, radio waves, and
the elements which filled empty places in the periodic table. The existence of all these objects had been predicted from theory before they
were discovered, and the men who made the discoveries therefore
knew from the start what to look for. That foreknowledge did not
make their task less demanding or less interesting, but it did provide
criteria which told them when their goal had been reached.[3] As a
result, there have been few priority debates over discoveries of this
second sort, and only a paucity of data can prevent the historian from
ascribing them to a particular time and place. Those facts help to
isolate the difficulties we encounter as we return to the troublesome
discoveries of the first class. In the cases that most concern us here
there are no benchmarks to inform either the scientist or the historian
when the job of discovery has been done.

OXYGEN AS AN EXAMPLE

As an illustration of this fundamental problem and its consequences,
consider first the discovery of oxygen. Because it has repeatedly been
studied, often with exemplary care and skill, that discovery is unlikely
to offer any purely factual surprises. Therefore it is particularly well
suited to clarify points of principle.[4] At least three scientists—Carl
Scheele, Joseph Priestley, and Antoine Lavoisier—have a legitimate
claim to this discovery, and polemicists have occasionally entered the

---

[3] Not all discoveries fall so neatly as the preceding into one or the other of my two
classes. For example, Anderson's work on the positron was done in complete ignorance of Dirac's electron theory from which the new particle's existence had already
been very nearly predicted. On the other hand, the immediately succeeding work by
Blackett and Occhialini made full use of Dirac's theory and therefore exploited
experiment more fully and constructed a more forceful case for the positron's
existence than Anderson had been able to do. On this subject see N. R. Hanson,
"Discovering the positron," *Brit. J. Phil. Sci.* 12, 194 (1961): 12, 299 (1962).
Hanson suggests several of the points developed here. I am much indebted to
Professor Hanson for a preprint of this material.
[4] I have developed a less familiar example from the same viewpoint in "The caloric
theory of adiabatic compression," *Isis* 49, 132 (1958). A closely similar analysis
of the emergence of a new theory is included in the early pages of my essay "Conservation of energy as an example of simultaneous discovery," in *Critical Problems
in the History of Science,* M. Clagett, Ed. (Univ. of Wisconsin Press, Madison,
1959), pp. 321–356. Reference to these papers may add depth and detail to the
following discussion.

same claim for Pierre Bayen. [5] Scheele's work, though it was almost certainly completed before the relevant researches of Priestley and Lavoisier, was not made public until their work was well known.[6] Therefore it had no apparent causal role, and I shall simplify my story by omitting it.[7] Instead, I pick up the main route to the discovery of oxygen with the work of Bayen, who, sometime before March 1774, discovered that red precipitate of mercury (HgO) could, by heating, be made to yield a gas. That aeriform product Bayen identified as fixed air (CO_2), a substance made familiar to most pneumatic chemists by the earlier work of Joseph Black. [8] A variety of other substances were known to yield the same gas.

At the beginning of August 1774, a few months after Bayen's work had appeared, Joseph Priestley repeated the experiment, though probably independently. Priestley, however, observed that the gaseous product would support combustion and therefore changed the identification. For him the gas obtained on heating red precipitate was nitrous air (N_2O), a substance that he had himself discovered more than two years before.[9] Later in the same month Priestley made a trip to Paris and there informed Lavoisier of the new reaction. The latter re-

---

[5] The still classic discussion of the discovery of oxygen is A. N. Meldrum, *The Eighteenth Century Revolution in Science—The First Phase* (Calcutta, 1930), chap. 5. A more convenient and generally quite reliable discussion is included in J. B. Conant, *The Overthrow of the Phlogiston Theory: The Chemical Revolution of 1775–1789*, "Harvard Case Histories in Experimental Science, Case 2" (Harvard Univ. Press, Cambridge, 1950). A more recent and indispensable review, which includes an account of the development of the priority controversy, is M. Daumas, *Lavoisier, théoricien et expérimentateur* (Paris, 1955), chaps. 2 and 3. H. Guerlac has added much significant detail to our knowledge of the early relations between Priestley and Lavoisier in his "Joseph Priestley's first papers on gases and their reception in France," *J. Hist. Med.* 12, 1 (1957), and in his very recent monograph, *Lavoisier—The Crucial Year* (Cornell Univ. Press, Ithaca, 1961). For Scheele see J. R. Partington, *A Short History of Chemistry* (London, ed. 2, 1951), pp. 104–109.
[6] For the dating of Scheele's work, see A. E. Nordenskiöld, Carl Wilhelm Scheele, *Nachgelassene Briefe und Aufzeichnungen* (Stockholm, 1892).
[7] U. Bocklund ["A lost letter from Scheele to Lavoisier," *Lychnos* (1957–58), pp. 39–62] argues that Scheele communicated his discovery of oxygen to Lavoisier in a letter of 30 Sept. 1774. Certainly the letter is important, and it clearly demonstrates that Scheele was ahead of both Priestley and Lavoisier at the time it was written. But I think the letter is not quite so candid as Bocklund supposes, and I fail to see how Lavoisier could have drawn the discovery of oxygen from it. Scheele describes a procedure for reconstituting common air, not for producing a new gas, and that, as we shall see, is almost the same information that Lavoisier received from Priestley at about the same time. In any case, there is no evidence that Lavoisier performed the sort of experiment that Scheele suggested.
[8] P. Bayen, "Essai d'expériences chymiques, faites sur quelques précipités de mercure, dans la vue de découvrir leur nature, Seconde partie," *Observations sur la physique* (1774), vol. 3, pp. 280–295, particularly pp. 289–291.
[9] J. B. Conant (see 5, pp. 34–40).

peated the experiment once more, both in November 1774 and in February 1775. Only, because he used tests somewhat more elaborate than Priestley's, Lavoisier again changed the identification. For him, as of May 1775, the gas released by red precipitate was neither fixed air nor nitrous air. Instead, it was "[atmospheric] air itself entire without alteration ... even to the point that ... it comes out more pure." [10] Meanwhile, however, Priestley had also been at work, and, before the beginning of March 1775, he too had concluded that the gas must be "common air." To this point all of the men who had produced a gas from red precipitate of mercury had identified it with some previously known species. [11]

The remainder of this story of discovery is briefly told. During March 1775 Priestley discovered that his gas was in several respects very much "better" than common air, and he therefore re-identified the gas once more, this time calling it "dephlogisticated air," that is, atmospheric air deprived of its normal complement of phlogiston. This conclusion Priestley published in the *Philosophical Transactions,* and it was apparently that publication which led Lavoisier to reexamine his own results. [12] The reexamination began during February 1776 and within a year had led Lavoisier to the conclusion that the gas was actually a separable component of the atmospheric air which both he and Priestley had previously thought of as homogeneous. With this point reached, with the gas recognized as an irreducibly distinct species, we may conclude that the discovery of oxygen had been completed.

Only, to return to my initial question, when shall we say that oxygen was discovered and what criteria shall we use in answering that question? If discovering oxygen is simply holding an impure sample in one's hands, then the gas had been "discovered" in antiquity by the first man who ever bottled atmospheric air. Undoubtedly, for an experimental criterion, we must at least require a relatively pure sample like that obtained by Priestley in August 1774. But during 1774 Priestley was unaware that he had discovered anything except a new way to produce

---

[10] A useful translation of the full text is available in Conant (see 5). For this description of the gas see p. 23.

[11] For simplicity I use the term *red precipitate* throughout. Actually, Bayen used the precipitate; Priestley used both the precipitate and the oxide produced by direct calcination of mercury; and Lavoisier used only the latter. The difference is not without importance, for it was not unequivocally clear to chemists that the two substances were identical.

[12] There has been some doubt about Priestley's having influenced Lavoisier's thinking at this point, but, when the latter returned to experimenting with the gas in February 1776, he recorded in his notebooks that he had obtained "l'air dephlogistique de M. Priestley" [M. Daumas (see 5, p. 36)].

a relatively familiar species. Throughout that year his "discovery" is scarcely distinguishable from the one made earlier by Bayen, and neither case is quite distinct from that of the Reverend Stephen Hales who had obtained the same gas more than 40 years before.[13] Apparently to discover something one must also be aware of the discovery and know as well what it is that one has discovered.

But, that being the case, how much must one know? Had Priestley come close enough when he identified the gas as nitrous air? If not, was either he or Lavoisier significantly closer when he changed the identification to common air? And what are we to say about Priestley's next identification, the one made in March 1775? Dephlogisticated air is still not oxygen or even, for the phlogistic chemist, a quite unexpected sort of gas. Rather it is a particularly pure atmospheric air. Presumably, then, we wait for Lavoisier's work in 1776 and 1777, work which led him not merely to isolate the gas but to see what it was. Yet even that decision can be questioned, for in 1777 and to the end of his life Lavoisier insisted that oxygen was an atomic "principle of acidity" and that oxygen gas was formed only when that "principle" united with caloric, the matter of heat.[14] Shall we therefore say that oxygen had not yet been discovered in 1777? Some may be tempted to do so. But the principle of acidity was not banished from chemistry until after 1810 and caloric lingered on until the 1860's. Oxygen had, however, become a standard chemical substance long before either of those dates. Furthermore, what is perhaps the key point, it would probably have gained that status on the basis of Priestley's work alone without benefit of Lavoisier's still partial reinterpretation.

I conclude that we need a new vocabulary and new concepts for analyzing events like the discovery of oxygen. Though undoubtedly correct, the sentence "Oxygen was discovered" misleads by suggesting that discovering something is a single simple act unequivocally attributable, if only we knew enough, to an individual and an instant in time. When the discovery is unexpected, however, the latter attribution is always impossible and the former often is as well. Ignoring Scheele, we can, for example, safely say that oxygen had not been discovered before 1774; probably we would also insist that it had been discovered by 1777 or shortly thereafter. But within those limits any attempt to date the discovery or to attribute it to an individual must inevitably be arbitrary. Furthermore, it must be arbitrary just because discovering a

[13] J. R. Partington (see 5, p. 91).
[14] For the traditional elements in Lavoisier's interpretations of chemical reactions, see H. Metzger, *La philosophie de la matière chez Lavoisier* (Paris, 1935), and Daumas [see 5 (Chap. 7)].

new sort of phenomenon is necessarily a complex process which involves recognizing both *that* something is and *what* it is. Observation and conceptualization, fact and the assimilation of fact to theory, are inseparably linked in the discovery of scientific novelty. Inevitably, that process extends over time and may often involve a number of people. Only for discoveries in my second category—those whose nature is known in advance—can discovering *that* and discovering *what* occur together and in an instant.

URANUS AND X-RAYS

Two last, simpler, and far briefer examples will simultaneously show how typical the case of oxygen is and also prepare the way for a somewhat more precise conclusion. On the night of 13 March 1781, the astronomer William Herschel made the following entry in his journal: "In the quartile near Zeta Tauri . . . is a curious either nebulous star or perhaps a comet." [15] That entry is generally said to record the discovery of the planet Uranus, but it cannot quite have done that. Between 1690 and Herschel's observation in 1781 the same object had been seen and recorded at least 17 times by men who took it to be a star. Herschel differed from them only in supposing that, because in his telescope it appeared especially large, it might actually be a *comet!* Two additional observations on 17 and 19 March confirmed that suspicion by showing that the object he had observed moved among the stars. As a result, astronomers throughout Europe were informed of the discovery, and the mathematicians among them began to compute the new comet's orbit. Only several months later, after all those attempts had repeatedly failed to square with observation, did the astronomer Lexell suggest that the object observed by Herschel might be a planet. And only when additional computations, using a planet's rather than a comet's orbit, proved reconcilable with observation, was that suggestion generally accepted. At what point during 1781 do we want to say that the planet Uranus was discovered? And are we entirely and unequivocally clear that it was Herschel rather than Lexell who discovered it?

Or consider still more briefly the story of the discovery of x-rays, a story which opens on the day in 1895 when the physicist Roentgen

[15] P. Doig, *A Concise History of Astronomy* (Chapman, London, 1950), pp. 115–116.

interrupted a well-precedented investigation of cathode rays because he noticed that a barium platinocyanide screen far from his shielded apparatus glowed when the discharge was in process.[16] Additional investigations—they required seven hectic weeks during which Roentgen rarely left the laboratory—indicated that the cause of the glow traveled in straight lines from the cathode ray tube, that the radiation cast shadows, that it could not be deflected by a magnet, and much else besides. Before announcing his discovery Roentgen had convinced himself that his effect was not due to cathode rays themselves but to a new form of radiation with at least some similarity to light. Once again the question suggests itself: When shall we say that x-rays were actually discovered? Not, in any case, at the first instant, when all that had been noted was a glowing screen. At least one other investigator had seen that glow and, to his subsequent chagrin, discovered nothing at all. Nor, it is almost as clear, can the moment of discovery be pushed back to a point during the last week of investigation. By that time Roentgen was exploring the properties of the new radiation he had *already* discovered. We may have to settle for the remark that x-rays emerged in Würzburg between 8 November and 28 December 1895.

AWARENESS OF ANOMALY

The characteristics shared by these examples are, I think, common to all the episodes by which unanticipated novelties become subjects for scientific attention. I therefore conclude these brief remarks by discussing three such common characteristics, ones which may help to provide a framework for the further study of the extended episodes we customarily call "discoveries."

In the first place, notice that all three of our discoveries—oxygen, Uranus, and x-rays—began with the experimental or observational isolation of an anomaly, that is, with nature's failure to conform entirely to expectation. Notice, further, that the process by which that anomaly was educed displays simultaneously the apparently incompatible characteristics of the inevitable and the accidental. In the case of x-rays, the anomalous glow which provided Roentgen's first clue was clearly the result of an accidental disposition of his apparatus. But by 1895 cathode rays were a normal subject for research all over Europe; that

---

[16] L. W. Taylor, *Physics, the Pioneer Science* (Houghton, Mifflin, Boston, 1941), p. 790.

research quite regularly juxtaposed cathode-ray tubes with sensitive screens and films; as a result, Roentgen's accident was almost certain to occur elsewhere, as in fact it had. Those remarks, however, should make Roentgen's case look very much like those of Herschel and Priestley. Herschel first observed his oversized and thus anomalous star in the course of a prolonged survey of the northern heavens. That survey was, except for the magnification provided by Herschel's instruments, precisely of the sort that had repeatedly been carried through before and that had occasionally resulted in prior observations of Uranus. And Priestley, too—when he isolated the gas that behaved almost but not quite like nitrous air and then almost but not quite like common air—was seeing something unintended and wrong in the outcome of a sort of experiment for which there was much European precedent and which had more than once before led to the production of the new gas.

These features suggest the existence of two normal requisites for the beginning of an episode of discovery. The first, which throughout this paper I have largely taken for granted, is the individual skill, wit, or genius to recognize that something has gone wrong in ways that may prove consequential. Not any and every scientist would have noted that no unrecorded star should be so large, that the screen ought not have glowed, that nitrous air should not have supported life. But that requisite presupposes another which is less frequently taken for granted. Whatever the level of genius available to observe them, anomalies do not emerge from the normal course of scientific research until both instruments and concepts have developed sufficiently to make their emergence likely and to make the anomaly which results recognizable as a violation of expectation.[17] To say that an unexpected discovery begins only when something goes wrong is to say that it begins only when scientists know well both how their instruments and how nature should behave. What distinguished Priestley, who saw an anomaly, from Hales, who did not, is largely the considerable articulation of pneumatic techniques and expectations that had come into being during the four decades which separate their two isolations of oxygen.[18] The very number of claimants indicates that after 1770 the discovery could not have been postponed for long.

[17] Though the point cannot be argued here, the conditions which make the emergence of anomaly likely and those which make anomaly recognizable are to a very great extent the same. That fact may help us understand the extraordinarily large amount of simultaneous discovery in the sciences.
[18] A useful sketch of the development of pneumatic chemistry is included in Partington (*see* 5, chap. 6).

MAKING THE ANOMALY BEHAVE

The role of anomaly is the first of the characteristics shared by our three examples. A second can be considered more briefly, for it has provided the main theme for the body of my text. Though awareness of anomaly marks the beginning of a discovery, it marks only the beginning. What necessarily follows, if anything at all is to be discovered, is a more or less extended period during which the individual and often many members of his group struggle to make the anomaly law-like. Invariably that period demands additional observation or experimentation as well as repeated cogitation. While it continues scientists repeatedly revise their expectations, usually their instrumental standards, and sometimes their most fundamental theories as well. In this sense discoveries have a proper internal history as well as prehistory and a posthistory. Furthermore, within the rather vaguely delimited interval of internal history, there is no single moment or day which the historian, however complete his data, can identify as the point at which the discovery was made. Often, when several individuals are involved, it is even impossible unequivocally to identify any one of them as the discoverer.

ADJUSTMENT, ADAPTATION, AND ASSIMILATION

Finally, turning to the third of these selected common characteristics, note briefly what happens as the period of discovery draws to a close. A full discussion of that question would require additional evidence and a separate paper, for I have had little to say about the aftermath of discovery in the body of my text. Nevertheless, the topic must not be entirely neglected, for it is in part a corollary of what has already been said.

Discoveries are often described as mere additions or increments to the growing stockpile of scientific knowledge, and that description has helped make the unit-discovery seem a significant measure of progress. I suggest, however, that it is fully appropriate only to those discoveries which, like the elements that filled missing places in the periodic table, were anticipated and sought in advance and which therefore demanded no adjustment, adaptation, and assimilation from the profession. Though the sorts of discoveries we have here been examining are undoubtedly additions to scientific knowledge, they are also something more. In a sense that I can now develop only in part, they also react back upon what has previously been known, providing a new view of some previously familiar objects and simultaneously changing the way in which even some traditional parts of science are practiced. Those in whose area of special competence the new phenomenon falls often see both the world and their work differently as they emerge from the extended struggle with anomaly which constitutes that phenomenon's discovery.

William Herschel, for example, when he increased by one the time-honored number of planetary bodies, taught astronomers to see new things when they looked at the familiar heavens even with instruments more traditional than his own. That change in the vision of astronomers must be a principal reason why, in the half century after the discovery of Uranus, 20 additional circumsolar bodies were added to the traditional seven.[19] A similar transformation is even clearer in the aftermath of Roentgen's work. In the first place, established techniques for cathode ray research had to be changed, for scientists found they had failed to control a relevant variable. Those changes included both the redesign of old apparatus and revised ways of asking old questions. In addition, those scientists most concerned experienced the same transformation of vision that we have just noted in the aftermath of the discovery of Uranus. X-rays were the first new sort of radiation discovered since infrared and ultraviolet at the beginning of the century. But within less than a decade after Roentgen's work, four more were disclosed by the new scientific sensitivity (for example, to fogged photographic plates) and by some of the new instrumental techniques that had resulted from Roentgen's work and its assimilation.[20]

Very often these transformations in the established techniques of scientific practice prove even more important than the incremental knowledge provided by the discovery itself. That could at least be argued in the cases of Uranus and of x-rays; in the case of my third

[19] R. Wolf, *Geschichte der Astronomie* (Munich, 1877), pp. 513–515, 683–693. The pre-photographic discoveries of the asteroids is often seen as an effect of the invention of Bode's law. But that law cannot be the full explanation and may not even have played a large part. Piazzi's discovery of Ceres, in 1801, was made in ignorance of the current speculation about a missing planet in the "hole" between Mars and Jupiter. Instead, like Herschel, Piazzi was engaged on a star survey. More important, Bode's law was old by 1800 (R. Wolf, *ibid.*, p. 683), but only one man before that date seems to have thought it worth while to look for another planet. Finally, Bode's law, by itself, could only suggest the utility of looking for additional planets: it did not tell astronomers where to look. Clearly, however, the drive to look for additional planets dates from Herschel's work on Uranus.

[20] For α-, β-, and γ-radiation, discovery of which dates from 1896, see Taylor (*16*, pp. 800–804). For the fourth new form of radiation, N-rays, see D. J. S. Price, *Science Since Babylon* (Yale Univ. Press, New Haven, 1961), pp. 84–89. That N-rays were ultimately the source of a scientific scandal does not make them less revealing of the scientific community's state of mind.

example, oxygen, it is categorically clear. Like the work of Herschel and Roentgen, that of Priestley and Lavoisier taught scientists to view old situations in new ways. Therefore, as we might anticipate, oxygen was not the only new chemical species to be identified in the aftermath of their work. But, in the case of oxygen, the readjustments demanded by assimilation were so profound that they played an integral and essential role—though they were not by themselves the cause—in the gigantic upheaval of chemical theory and practice which has since been known as the "chemical revolution." I do not suggest that every unanticipated discovery has consequences for science so deep and so far-reaching as those which followed the discovery of oxygen. But I do suggest that every such discovery demands, from those most concerned, the sorts of readjustment that, when they are more obvious, we equate with scientific revolution. It is, I believe, just because they demand readjustments like these that the process of discovery is necessarily and inevitably one that shows structure and that therefore extends in time.

5   PETER CAWS

(1931–   )

The Structure of Discovery *

Peter Caws examines the claims of those who argue that scientific discovery is not
a logically analyzable enterprise, that it is purely the product of genius, intuition,
imagination, luck, etc. He maintains that such a view of discovery rests on a major
mistake: attributing to psychology what belongs to logic. Caws argues that
hypotheses arise naturally. He constructs a model designed to show that from
certain facts about human beings and human cultures it is quite natural that
certain hypotheses would emerge. One of the major difficulties that people have
had in trying to formulate a logic of scientific discovery is that they persist in drawing
sharp differences between deductive logic and discovery. Caws attempts to show
that such a difference actually does not exist. The logic of discovery is the everyday
logic of invention and is not mysterious, Caws argues. Particular heed should be
paid to Caws's accounts of genius and of structuralism. His position on these and
other topics should be compared with those of Kuhn, Hanson, and Whorf.

* P. Caws, "The Structure of Discovery," *Science*, Vol. 166, December 12, 1969,
pp. 1375–1380. Reprinted by permission of the author and *Science*. Copyright,
1969 by the American Association for the Advancement of Science.

IT has been widely held that, while logical analysis is appropriate to
the justification of claims to scientific knowledge, such knowledge
being expressed in hypotheses having empirical consequences, it is
not appropriate to an inquiry into the way in which such claims origi-
nate. Questions about origins are said to belong to the "context of
discovery" rather than to the "context of justification," and to require a
different kind of logic. The devising of hypotheses is ascribed to genius,
intuition, imagination, chance, or any number of other extralogical
processes; it comes to be regarded as a paradigm case of science in its
authentic natural state, inaccessible to logical reconstruction by philosophers who do not really know what it is like to be a scientist.

One of the tactics most often used by proponents of the mystique of
genius, who are always bandying about terms like *creativity, insight,
ripeness,* and so on, is the recounting of tales about moments of enlightenment in the lives of the great scientists. Everybody has heard
of Kekulé's dream about the snakes biting one another's tails, and of
Poincaré's long bout with the Fuchsian functions on his geological bus

trip through Normandy. Such stories no doubt give an accurate account of what "really happened"; they are suitably sensitive to the "actual development" of scientific theories. But to draw attention to them at all in connection with an analysis of the process of discovery seems to me a radical mistake. The mistake involved shows up clearly in a passage from Popper's *The Logic of Scientific Discovery,* where he says [1] (p. 31): "the initial stage, the act of conceiving or inventing a theory, seems to me neither to call for logical analysis nor to be susceptible of it. The question how it happens that a new idea occurs to a man—whether it is a musical theme, a dramatic conflict, or a scientific theory—may be of great interest to empirical psychology; but it is irrelevant to the logical analysis of scientific knowledge."

Popper thus dismisses the possibility of a logical analysis of the conception or invention of a theory because he thinks of these things in terms of "how it happens." But in the case of deductive argument nobody would think of asking how it happens; it would be the structure of the process, not its particular embodiment in a particular individual, that would be seen by everybody to be the crucial issue. In fact, in demonstrative argument just as in the process of discovery, there would be nothing strange in its not happening at all—the *actual movement* from the premises to a conclusion is just as intuitive, creative, and so on as the actual having of a new idea, and very stupid or very stubborn people, like the tortoise in Lewis Carroll's fable, may quite well decline, or be unable, to make it—but the fact that it failed to happen would not alter in any way the logical structure of the relationship between premises and conclusion. Even if one wished to maintain that, in the case of discovery, there are not any identifiable premises [or even any premises at all—a strategy I have explored elsewhere [2]] one could still choose to regard the process as in principle intelligible rather than unintelligible; what is disturbing about the passage from Popper is that he seems to opt for the latter. In fact he says explicitly: "My view may be expressed by saying that every discovery contains 'an irrational element,' or a 'creative intuition,' in Bergson's sense."

My point is that if this is to be said of the process of discovery it may just as well be said of the process of strict logical deduction, so we might add to the canon exciting tales about that activity too. I hope I may be forgiven an autobiographical example to try out this

[1] K. Popper, *The Logic of Scientific Discovery* [Harper, New York, new ed., 1965 (original German ed., 1934)].
[2] P. Caws, *Phil. Phenomenol, Res.* 25, 522 (1965).

parallel. I remember very clearly the moment when, as a schoolboy, I first understood the principle of linear simultaneous equations. The circumstances are engraved in my memory just as clearly as Poincaré's foot on the step of the bus became engraved in his; it was in the yard of my school, and I remember the red brick wall, the bicycle racks, and so on, in proper Proustian fashion. I saw, in a flash of intuition, why two equations were needed for two unknowns, and how the substitution from one equation into the other proceeded. Now, as I need hardly say, there was no question of originality here; I had had all the information for a number of weeks, during which my mathematics teacher had been trying to pound the principle into my head. As far as that goes, it wasn't that I *couldn't do* simultaneous equations —I could follow all the rules and get the right answer; it was just that I *hadn't seen* the underlying rationality of the process. When I finally saw it I got the "Eureka feeling," of which Koestler speaks,[3] just as surely as if I had invented simultaneous equations myself, but I didn't suppose that that had anything to do with the *logic* of the situation.

The trouble with "Eureka!" is that the temptation to shout it is a very poor index of success in the enterprise at hand. Such a feeling can *only* be a by-product of the process—a not unimportant one, perhaps, from some evolutionary point of view, but certainly a dispensable one. A discovery would still be a discovery if it were made in cold blood without any such affective concomitant, and if it turned out to be mistaken it would still be mistaken even though the heavens had opened upon the lucky discoverer at the moment he thought he was making it. It is perhaps conceivable that somebody might become addicted to the Eureka feeling and, in order to have it as often as possible, try very hard to make many discoveries, some of which might be valid. But scientists have to learn to be wary of emotional commitments to their hypotheses. Darwin says, "I have steadily endeavored to keep my mind free so as to give up any hypothesis, however much beloved (and I cannot resist forming one on every subject) as soon as facts are seen to be opposed to it. Indeed, I have had no choice but to act in this manner, for with the exception of the Coral Reefs, I cannot remember a single first-formed hypothesis which had not after a time to be given up or greatly modified." And he continues, "this has naturally led me to distrust greatly deductive reasoning in the mixed sciences." [4]

[3] A. Koestler, *The Act of Creation* (Hutchinson, London, 1964), pt. 2.
[4] C. Darwin, in *The Life and Letters of Charles Darwin*, F. Darwin, Ed. [Basic Books, New York, new ed., 1959 (original ed., 1888)], p. 83.

Another distinction frequently drawn between the logic of justification and the logic of discovery is that in the former case rules can
be given. This is only apparently true; on the one hand, although in
principle all deductions can be carried out by a rule-following technique, in practice good logicians and mathematicians are constantly
making wild leaps only later justified by rules, if at all, while on the
other hand certain workers—notably Polya [5]—have made significant
steps in the direction of formulating rules for "plausible inference."
Frege was among the first to try to carry out logical deductions strictly
according to rule, and he found it extraordinarily difficult, as he testifies in the preface to the *Begriffschrift*.[6] If there were *no* rules of
plausible inference, nobody could learn techniques of research, nor
could the agencies responsible for funding it have any confidence
whatever that the tasks undertaken by researchers would bear fruit.
Yet people do learn, and suitably financed campaigns of research (like
the Manhattan project) do regularly produce results. The task is then
to find out what is going on, not dismiss it all as ineffable or mysterious.

Scientists, as Norwood Russell Hanson points out, "do not start
hypotheses; they start from data." [7] The question, then, is what
happens between the data and the hypotheses, taken in that order—
not whether a deductive rule can be written to get from the former
to the latter, but whether some intelligible structure can be discerned
in the transition. I take "intelligible" in this context to be equivalent
to "logical"—a procedure which certainly has etymological sanction,
even if it means abandoning the narrower sense of "logical," which
requires the specification of rules. In fact it need not mean this, if we
remember that the use of "logic" in the expression "inductive logic"
is a perfectly orthodox one, and that it sanctions a use of "rule" in the
expression "inductive rule" which differs considerably in its connotations from the corresponding use in the deductive case. We have
come to think of deductive rules as *effective procedures*, leading with
certainty to the right result. In the inductive case, however, we have
to get accustomed to rules which lead, with finite probability, to the
wrong result. When people say "there could be no rule for making
discoveries," they generally have the first sense of the term in mind:
there could be no way of *being sure* of making discoveries. But there

---

[5] See, for example, G. Polya, *Patterns of Plausible Inference* (vol. 2 of *Mathematics
and Plausible Reasoning*) (Princeton Univ. Press, Princeton, N.J., 1954).
[6] G. Frege, in *From Frege to Gödel*, J. Van Heijenoorst, Ed. (Harvard Univ. Press,
Cambridge, Mass., 1950), p. 5.
[7] N. R. Hanson, *Patterns of Discovery* (Cambridge Univ. Press, Cambridge, England, 1958), p. 70.

might still be sets of rules, which, if faithfully followed, would increase the chances of making them. These, as inductive logicians have begun to realize, may include rules of acceptance as well as rules of inference. The manner of their implementation (their relation to rules of practice) needs further study, but it is not my purpose to pursue the question further here.

A MODEL FOR DISCOVERY

How do hypotheses arise? The answer I wish to suggest is that, strictly speaking, they arise *naturally;* hypotheses are to be accounted for in the same manner as the events they seek to explain—indeed the hypothesis that this is so has arisen in this way. The evidence for *this* hypothesis is of course far from conclusive; while I think it preferable to any alternative which calls upon nonnatural occurrences, it would admittedly be difficult to *show* that no such occurrences were involved in the process (just as it would be difficult to show this for deductive arguments). But if a model can be constructed within which the emergence of hypotheses follows obviously from other properties of the model, the nonnatural element will be shown to be dispensable, just as it might be shown to be dispensable in deductive arguments by remarking that anybody can follow the rules.

Such a model can, I think, be put together from a number of disparate sources. It shows that, given certain facts about human beings and human cultures, there is nothing odd about the emergence of science or about the rate of its development, or about the fact that some of the men who have contributed to this development have been geniuses. The model, it is true, gives the main part of its account in collective rather than in individual terms—but that has now become commonplace, since the analysis of individual discoveries has shown that, in practically every case, the individual acted as the catalyst for a complex process in which many other individuals played a role. This need not be taken to mean that no credit is due the individual for having advanced his science in a particular way at a particular time, but it does mean that (probably) no individual has been indispensable to the advance of science in general. "Very simple-minded people think that if Newton had died prematurely we would still be at our wits' end to account for the fall apples," says Medawar.[8] We must be able

---

[8] P. B. Medawar, *The Art of the Soluble* (Methuen, London, 1967).

to find a way of reconciling our admiration for Newton with the avoidance of this mistake.

I make no apology for beginning my exposition of this theory of discovery with Bacon, whose method has, I believe, been misunderstood in important respects. The feature of the method which has always struck me most forcibly occurs in book II of the *Novum Organum*,[9] where, after the construction of the inductive Tables, Bacon says (aphorism xx): "and yet since truth will sooner come from error than from confusion I think it expedient that the understanding should have permission, after the three Tables of First Presentation (such as I have exhibited) have been made and weighed, to make an essay of the Interpretation of Nature in the affirmative way; on the strength both of the instances given in the Tables, and of any others it may meet with elsewhere. Which kind of essay I call the *Indulgence of the Understanding* or the *Commencement of Interpretation* or the *First Vintage*." This is strikingly similar to Darwin's remark in the introduction to *The Origin of Species*, where he says:[10] "It occurred to me, in 1837, that something might perhaps be made out on this question by patiently accumulating and reflecting on all sorts of facts which could possibly have any bearing on it. After five years' work I allowed myself to speculate on the subject. . . ." He remarks elsewhere [11] that he worked on "true Baconian principles," a claim which is denied by a number of commentators who have not read Bacon as closely as Darwin himself evidently did. There is a hint of the same kind of thing in Frege's concern not to jump to conclusions in the course of his logical work.

The truth to which I think these and other citations point is that the practical problem is often one not so much of finding hypotheses as of holding them in check. Bacon's use of a word like "indulgence," Darwin's of the phrase "I allowed myself," suggest that, once the evidence is in, there is simply no need of a rule for getting the hypothesis—it has long since formed and is only waiting to be recognized. (Remember Darwin's comment: "I cannot resist forming one on every subject.") But two questions immediately present themselves: By what mechanism of thought did the hypothesis come into being? And, if it is a natural process, why isn't everybody a genius? (It was Bacon's

---

[9] F. Bacon, *The New Organon* [Liberal Arts Press, New York, new ed., 1960 (original ed., 1620)].

[10] C. Darwin, *The Origin of Species* [Modern Library, New York, new ed. (original ed., 1859)].

[11] Darwin, in *The Life and Letters of Charles Darwin*, p. 68.

failure to recognize that everybody is *not* a genius which constituted the chief weakness in his program for making the methods of science available to the population at large.)

As for everybody's not being a genius, the answer may be that everybody above a certain level of natural intelligence in principle *is*, until inhibiting factors supervene—which almost always happens. It may be worth making a more general point here about a habit of thought into which philosophers of science sometimes fall—a habit due largely, I suspect, to the influence of Hume's analysis of causality. We think of events as in general being *made* to happen (and ask what antecedent events *produced* them), rather than as just *happening* (in which case the relevant question would be what antecedent events, by failing to happen, failed to prevent them). It is noticeable however that, when scientists perform delicate experiments, they expend their energy not on making sure that the desired outcome occurs but on trying to make sure that some undesirable outcome does not occur; they take experimental precautions against Nature, rather than giving experimental encouragement to Nature. Similarly, a man engaged in logical argument doesn't really need a rule to tell him how to proceed; what he chiefly needs is a kind of single-minded concentration that keeps out irrelevant thoughts, and a facility for spotting wrong moves. The motive power of the enterprise doesn't come from the rules—they just keep it on the rails. Rules, it is true, can play a leading rather than a guiding part when the motive power is comparatively unintelligent, as in computers, but the critical thing seems to be to let the machinery run. The view is fully in keeping with the fact, frequently remarked upon, that the process of discovery may be unconscious: the scientist wakes up the next morning—or, in stubborn cases like Poincaré's, a week or so later—with the required solution. Whether or not all the steps are conscious is irrelevant to the question of whether or not they are logical.

If we are to admit biographical evidence, the point about inhibiting factors (and, on the other side of the coin, stimulating ones) may be illustrated by the fact that many men of genius have been characterized by a strong resistance to authority (that is, resistance to having their conclusions drawn for them) and, at the same time, by an openness to random suggestion amounting almost to credulity. Ernest Jones [12] observes this with respect to Freud, and Darwin [13] observes it with respect to himself. Ordinary social experience, and es-

[12] E. Jones, *Sci. Monthly* 8–4, 75 (1957).
[13] Darwin, in *The Life and Letters of Charles Darwin*, p. 82.

pecially education, work, of course, in precisely the opposite sense, imposing, even in the most well-meaning of democracies, an extraordinarily authoritarian view of the world and, at the same time, encouraging the belief that a man should be selective about what he takes in, and skeptical about all evidence from nonauthoritarian sources. These tendencies alone would be enough to account for the inhibition of discoveries in all but a handful of the population at any given time.

The hypothesis emerges naturally only when all the evidence is in—the conclusion follows only from a complete or almost complete set of premises. I add "almost complete" because there is a powerful *Gestalt* phenomenon to be observed here: closure is sometimes procured by the addition of a premise which is the obviously missing one, the only one which fits in with the rest of the pattern. Often, however, not even this much is required. *All* the premises for the hypothesis of the origin of species through natural selection were present both for Darwin and for Wallace, and, once they had them all (including the indispensable contribution from Malthus), they both got the point at once. Now there is of course no effective way of ever being sure that one has all the premises. But in this respect, also, the logic of discovery is in precisely the same boat as deductive logic: the rules there do not yield the premises either, they only yield the conclusion once the premises have been provided.

What are the premises which lead to a scientific discovery? Where do they come from? At this point, in the literature, the search for a logic of discovery frequently gets thrown off the scent by the insertion of a great deal of irrelevant talk about motivation, perplexity, or crisis; it is thought necessary to point out that discoveries do not happen if there is not some problem with the science we already have. This kind of thing is not only confusing but downright misleading. It suggests, again, a spurious difference between deductive logic and the logic of discovery. In fact, of course, nobody would carry out deductions either if there were not some reason to do so—and if that reason often amounts to nothing more than a passion for mathematics, having no direct relevance to the solution of any practical problem, a similar passion for investigation into nature has accounted for a great deal of inductive progress too.

The premises in question are of two principal kinds: on the one hand there are theories and observations made and confirmed by previous workers, and, on the other, observations not adequately covered by earlier theories, made by or communicated to the discoverer. The discovery consists, of course, in the provision of an adequate theory to cover these new observations. Premises of the former kind are part of the inheritance of the scientist, although he may have to search the literature for them. Those of the latter kind may come from plain observation or from experiment; they may come into the possession of the scientist quite by accident, in a disguised form, and so on. It is at this stage—in the provision of the premises, rather than in the structure of the argument—that the notorious uncertainty of the process of discovery arises, that serendipity plays a part, and so on.

By far the most important contribution, however, is made by what I have spoken of as the scientist's "inheritance," although it might be better to use the genetic term rather than the legal one and speak instead of "heredity." Newton's celebrated remark about "standing on the shoulders of giants" [14] reminds us that the development of science is a stepwise process; nobody starts from scratch, and nobody gets very far ahead of the rest. At any point in history there is a range of possible discovery; the trailing edge of the range is defined by everything known at the time (I overlook here the fact that people are constantly "discovering" what is already known, which blurs this edge somewhat), and the leading edge is a function of what is already known, together with variables representing available instrumentation, the capacity of human brains, and so on. But, within the range, all movement is not forward—quite the contrary. While the mind moves with a kind of subjective conviction and (as it persuades itself) unerringly to its inductive conclusion, that conclusion is not always the discovery it is thought to be. There may be several reasons for this: the "discovery," if it fits the facts, may have been made before; if it does not fit them, that may be because there are still, without the scientist's knowing it, some missing premises (some fact he does not know, some previously established theory he has not taken into account), or just because he has made a mistake. In order to get a clear picture of scientific discovery the account has to be broadened somewhat to take into consideration the population of scientific workers at the time, together with the nature of the development of science. The best analogy for this development is again a genetic one: Just as mutations arise naturally but are not all beneficial, so hypotheses emerge naturally but are not all correct. If progress is to occur, therefore, we require a superfluity of hypotheses and also a mechanism of selection. At any given epoch in the development of science—to deal with the first requirement first—hypotheses are in fact emerg-

14 Sir Isaac Newton, letter to Robert Houke (1676).

ing at a much higher rate than one might suspect from reading subsequent historical accounts. We all know about Darwin and Wallace, for example; but how many of the hundreds of other well-meaning naturalists of the middle 19th century, all tackling the problem of the persistance or mutability of species, are now remembered?

It may be useful in this connection to draw attention to a well known phenomenon which is more relevant to the development of science than most of us perceive it to be—namely, the phenomenon of the crackpot. We are accustomed to thinking of the advancement of science in terms of the half dozen great names in a given field; on reflection we may see that these half dozen are supplemented by a thousand or so working in more obscure laboratories. But we should also remember that there are myriads of people speculating, generally in a half-informed way, about the same topics from myriads of private vantage points; the occasional wild manifestos we all receive, showing how misguided Darwin and Einstein were represent a mere fraction of their output. In every epoch something like this has gone on, and the unrecorded history of unsuccessful speculation would swamp completely the history of science as we know it if it could ever be added to the literature. Unsuccessful hypotheses are weeded out, of course, by their failure to square with the facts, or if they can be made to do that, by their failure to be predictive. But in this connection certain social factors tend to interfere with the evolutionary pattern, just as they do in the biological case. Just as the children of rich families may, under a less than equitable social system, be comparatively better protected against the hostility of the environment than the children of poor ones, so some theories produced under powerful sponsorship may have a longer run than they deserve.

Despite the fact that parallels present themselves so readily, there are a couple of puzzling things about the development of science that make this evolutionary analogy suspect. First of all, there is the fantastic rate of its growth in the last three or four centuries, quite unlike the leisurely pace at which biological adaptation usually proceeds. Second, there is the remarkable fact, documented in the work of Robert Merton and others [15] that virtually all valid discoveries (let alone incorrect hypotheses) have been made by more than one worker, sometimes by many, while some great scientists appear to have made far more than their fair share of such discoveries. Clearly a random-mutation, Mendelian evolutionary model will not do.

[15] R. K. Merton, *New Sci.* 12, 306 (1961).

THE EVOLUTION OF SCIENCE

At this point it would be convenient to introduce some statistical analysis (already hinted at by the reference to Merton's work on multiple discoveries) to show how a given frequency of theoretical interest in a population, presumed to yield a rather smaller frequency of correct conjectures—these to be selected by the hostility of the experimental environment toward false theories—would account for the development of science. Unfortunately the necessary statistical apparatus has not been worked out, since statisticians have concentrated their attention on Mendelian genetics, whereas the form of genetic theory required for this purpose is clearly Lamarckian. The accumulated empirical and theoretical knowledge passed on from one generation of scientists to another counts as an acquired characteristic, the fruit of direct adaptation rather than of mutation. To make matters worse, the pattern of reproduction is quite evidently not sexual. I can offer one or two further genetic analogies—for example, it is easy to find parts of theory behaving like dominant characteristics, in that they exclude or subsume alternative views, and others behaving like recessive ones, in that they are passed on with the rest of the inherited material but do not become important until they are conjoined with some other factor—but I have not been able to work out the details of the appropriate model.

Still I think the general evolutionary point holds. Discoveries represent a kind of adaptation which is almost bound to occur in a number of individuals if they are subjected to roughly similar environmental pressures, the environment in this case being an intellectual one. Medawar, in an exchange with Arthur Koestler about the latter's book *The Act of Creation*, remarks: [16] "Scientists on the same road may be expected to arrive at the same destination, often not far apart. Romantics like Koestler don't like to admit this, because it seems to them to derogate from the authority of genius. Thus of Newton and Leibniz, equal first with the differential calculus, Koestler says 'the greatness of this accomplishment is hardly diminished by the fact that two among millions, instead of one among millions, had the exceptional genius to do it.' But millions weren't *trying* for the calculus. If they had been, hundreds would have got it." That is as close to backing on the statistical point as I am likely to come for the moment. It is notoriously difficult to confirm counterfactuals of this sort, but there does seem to be a practical sense in what Medawar says, borne out by the tendency of various agencies to bombard scientists with research grants in an expectation

[16] Medawar.

of results at least comparable to that of geneticists bombarding *Drosophila* with gamma rays.

I have now sketched the main outlines of a possible model for scientific discovery. But there are two important components still missing—namely, some explanation, on the one hand, of the tendency of the human mind to produce hypotheses at all and, on the other, of the tendency of some great minds to produce many correct ones. Given that hypotheses are in fact produced, in a sufficiently prodigal fashion to provide the grounds for natural selection and consequently for the origin of new theories, how are we to account for the phenomenon? It is not enlightening in this connection to talk about genius. To talk about imagination is a little better, although, as Peirce remarks in an essay on Kepler,[17] " 'imagination' is an ocean-broad term, almost meaningless, so many and so diverse are its species." I have already made reference to stresses from the intellectual environment, suggesting a theory of "necessity as the mother of invention," but that certainly can not be carried through for a large perhaps the greater—proportion of scientific discoveries.

Let me deal first with the special point about the disproportionate number of discoveries made by great scientists, and then go on to the more general, and concluding, point about the basic mechanism. Obviously no account which ignored "the distinctive role of scientific genius," as Merton calls it, can be considered satisfactory; but the term *genius,* meaning originally the spirit assigned a man at birth to guide his destiny, can now be admitted, if at all, only to describe the man who has already proved himself in the business of making discoveries, not to describe some potentiality he had before he started. There are clearly genetic determinants involved, having to do with brain capacity and other characteristics normally distributed in the population, with respect to which the genius will be found to lie under the right-hand shoulder of the bell-shaped curve, but none of them, nor any combination, can be equated with scientific genius, since a lot of similarly endowed people will be found living normal lives as stockbrokers, lawyers, and so on.

Once again, what makes a man a genius has nothing whatever to do with the logic he employs; and the point I wish to stress is that he need have no special logical endowment, no bag of creative tricks, in order to rise to the little eminence which, in the long historical view, he occupies for such a short time. I say "little eminence" not to mini-

17 C. S. Peirce, *Values in a Universe of Chance,* P. P. Wiener, Ed. (Doubleday, Garden City, N.Y., 1958), p. 255.

mize the respect we owe to genius—from close up, after all, we can properly refer to Einstein as a "towering genius"—but to reinforce the point made earlier about the comparatively narrow range within which at any time scientific discoveries can be made. The formation of a scientific genius, in fact, is comparable to the formation of an Olympic runner, or a tennis or chess champion. The chess analogy is a useful one; chess is, after all, a strictly deductive game, and all it takes to win every time is the ability to do a few billion calculations in the head within the period legally allowed for a move. Imagine a chess game in which there are some concealed pieces, moved by a third player, which influence the possible moves of the pieces on the board, and imagine that, instead of 16 pieces to a side, there are several million, some governed by rules of play not yet known to the players. In such a game a man who, after a long apprenticeship with the masters of his time, made three or four good moves during his career would have gained a place in history.

The kind of inference a great scientist employs in his creative moments is comparable to the kind of inference the master at chess employs; it involves an ability to keep a lot of variables in mind at once, to be sensitive to feedback from tentative calculations (or experiments), to assess strategies for the development of time and resources, to perceive the relevance of one fact to another, or of a hypothesis to facts. The difference between his logic and our logic is one of degree, not of kind; we employ precisely the same methods, but more clumsily and on more homely tasks. I wish to conclude by considering some crucial properties of the common logical mechanism with which we are all equipped, which explain, I think, the natural tendency for hypotheses to emerge, and in this connection to call on two diverse kinds of evidence, one from psychology and one from anthropology.

PSYCHOLOGY AND STRUCTURALISM

On the psychological side, Berlyne has recently drawn attention to a form of behavior among higher animals which he calls "exploration." Under this heading, he says, may be grouped activities describable as "curiosity" and "play," or, in a human setting, as "recreation," "entertainment," "art," or even "science." This kind of activity is not indulged in because of its utilitarian value, although it sometimes has useful by-products. "An animal looking and sniffing around may stumble upon a clue to the whereabouts of food. A scientist's discovery may contribute to public amenity and to his own enrichment or fame. Much of the time, however, organisms do nothing in particular about the stimulus patterns that they pursue with such avidity. They appear to seek them 'for their own sake.'" [18] Berlyne offers two lines of explanation for this exploratory activity. One of them is the conventional one of response to necessity, leading to "specific" exploration. The second, and more interesting, at least from the point of view of the problem of discovery, deals with what Berlyne calls "diversive" exploration. "It seems that the central nervous system of a higher animal is designed to cope with environments that produce a certain rate of influx of stimulation, information, and challenge to its capacities. It will naturally not perform at its best in an environment that overstresses or overloads it, but we also have evidence that prolonged subjection to an inordinately monotonous or unstimulating environment is detrimental to a variety of psychological functions. We can understand why organisms may seek out stimulation that taxes the nervous system to the right extent, when naturally occurring stimuli are either too easy or too difficult to assimilate." It looks, therefore, as if a certain kind of nondirected exploratory behavior is to be expected, both when the exterior world is too exciting (the intellectual withdraws into his ivory tower) and when it is not exciting enough (the explorer sets off to conquer new territories).

Now science is manifestly not the only possible kind of human exploration, even on the intellectual level, and this I think has to be recognized if scientific discovery is to be put in its proper context. The notion that true hypotheses emerge from the welter of speculation by a process of natural selection (the condition of survival being agreement with empirical evidence) can be extended by analogy to the emergence of science itself from a welter of natural mental activity. The final component of my model owes its inspiration to the work of the structuralists, notably Claude Lévi-Strauss, although it is an extension rather than a simple invocation of their views.

Lévi-Strauss observes, from the anthropologist's point of view, a phenomenon exactly analogous to that observed by Berlyne from the psychologist's. Primitive people, along with their totems and their myths, turn out to have an extraordinarily rich lore of a kind that can only be called scientific, since it represents a body of hypotheses about the natural world linked in some primitively acceptable way to a body of observations. This "science of the concrete," as Lévi-Strauss calls it, is not, in his words, "of much practical effect." But then "its main purpose is not a practical one. It meets intellectual requirements rather

18 D. E. Berlyne, *Science* 153, 25 (1966).

than or instead of satisfying needs. The real question is not whether the touch of a woodpecker's beak does in fact cure toothache. It is rather whether there is a point of view from which a woodpecker's beak and a man's tooth can be seen as 'going together'... and whether some initial order can be introduced into the universe by means of these groupings." [19]

This line of work is one which I think is at the moment of great interest and promise. What emerges from it is a view of mind as a structuring agent, which puts together a world of thought comparable in its complexity to the world of experience, thus satisfying the optimum conditions of mental activity described by Berlyne. The chief agency of structure is, of course, language. Of the various constructions made possible by language, science counts as only one, and initially enjoys no special advantage over myth. But sometimes what it says turns out to be true (the herb really does cure the disease), and although it is a long step from the truth of a report of practice to a genuinely theoretical truth, this realization is the starting point of the process of scientific development. A story told for no other initial purpose than to keep mind in a kind of dynamic balance with the world, to assert it over against the world, turns out to hold the clue to control of the world. Other people continue to tell stories for other purposes, and the accumulation of specialized linguistic habits, specialized techniques, and so on, may soon persuade the scientist that he is no longer like the others but is engaged on a different quest with its own creative character. It is true that scientists, on the whole, care more than other men do that the stories they tell should be true; but then truth itself is a comparative latecomer on the linguistic scene, and it is certainly a mistake to suppose that language was invented for the purpose of telling it.

Scientific theories are no longer created *ex nihilo;* the stories scientists tell are not free inventions. If the creative process starts from a very large set of premises already demonstrated to be true, its conclusion has a greater chance of being true than it would have if the process had started, like the conjecture of the primitive, from a random assortment of propositions indifferently true and false. When the conclusion is shown to be true by comparison with the evidence, we call the invention a discovery. ["Formulas are invented," as Bunge puts it, "but laws are discovered."] [20] The major point I have wished to make

[19] C. Lévi-Strauss, *The Savage Mind* [Univ. of Chicago Press, Chicago, new ed., 1966, p. 9 (original French ed., 1962)].
[20] M. Bunge, *The Search for System* (vol. 1 of *Scientific Research*) (Springer, New York, 1967), p. 345.

can be summed up in this way: In the creative process, as in the process of demonstration, science has no special logic but shares the structure of human thought in general, and thought proceeds, in creation as in demonstration, according to perfectly intelligible principles. Formal logic, whose history as a rigorous system started with Frege and ended with Gödel, represents a refinement and specialization of the principles of everyday argument; the logic of scientific discovery, whose rigorous formulation is yet to be achieved (not that it holds out the hope of completeness once entertained by deductive logic), will similarly prove to be a refinement and specialization of the logic of everyday invention. The important thing to realize is that invention is, in its strictest sense, as familiar a process as argument, no more and no less mysterious. Once we get this into our heads, scientific creativity will have been won back from the mystery-mongers.[21]

[21] This article, is dedicated to the memory of Norwood Russell Hanson, vice president of AAAS Section L in 1961–62 and for many years secretary of the section

Further Reading On
SCIENTIFIC DISCOVERY

Butterfield, Herbert. *The Origins of Modern Science.* New York: Free Press, 1957.

Feigl and Maxwell. *Current Issues in the Philosophy of Science.* New York: Holt, Rinehart and Winston, 1961.

George, Pulivelil M. "Problem of Value in Science and the Significance of History and Philosophy of Science." *Organon,* 1970.

Hanson, Norwood Russell. *Patterns of Discovery.* Cambridge: Cambridge University Press, 1958.

Hussain, Anwar. "Philosophy of Science." *The Pakistan Philosophical Journal,* July–December 1972.

Joy, Glenn C. "Can Science Give Us Truth?" *Journal of Thought,* April 1973.

King, M. D. "Reason, Tradition, and the Progressiveness of Science." *History and Theory,* 1971.

Kuhn, Thomas S. *The Structure of Scientific Revolutions.* Chicago: University of Chicago Press, 1962.

Mill, John Stuart. *Philosophy of Scientific Method.* New York: Hafner Publishing Company, 1950.

Nagel, Ernest. *The Structure of Science.* New York: Harcourt, Brace and World, 1961.

Popper, Karl. *Conjectures and Refutations.* New York: Basic Books, 1963.

Reichenbach, Hans. *The Rise of Scientific Philosophy.* Berkeley: University of California Press, 1951.

Smart, J. J. C. *Between Science and Philosophy.* New York: Random House, 1968.

Taylor, Alastair M. "For Philosophers and Scientists: A General Systems Paradigm." *International Philosophical Quarterly,* March 1973.

Tondl, Ladislav. "Problems of Empirical Basis of Science." *Organon,* 1971.

Vygotsky, Lev Semenovich. *Thought and Language.* Cambridge: M.I.T. Press, 1962.

Whorf, Benjamin Lee. *Language, Thought, and Reality.* Cambridge: M.I.T. Press, 1956.

Wisdom, J. O. "Science Versus the Scientific Revolution." *Philosophy of the Social Sciences,* May 1971.

PART VII

FAITH AND RELIGIOUS EXPERIENCE

Genesis 22: 1-14*

AND IT CAME TO PASS AFTER THESE THINGS, THAT GOD DID TEMPT Abraham, and said unto him, Abraham: and he said, Behold, *here I am.*

And he said, Take now thy son, thine only *son* Isaac, whom thou lovest, and get thee into the land of Moriah; and offer him there for a burnt offering upon one of the mountains which I will tell thee of.

And Abraham rose up early in the morning, and saddled his ass, and took two of his young men with him, and Isaac his son, and clave the wood for the burnt offering, and rose up, and went unto the place of which God had told him.

Then on the third day Abraham lifted up his eyes, and saw the place afar off.

And Abraham said unto his young men, Abide ye here with the ass; and I and the lad will go yonder and worship, and come again to you.

And Abraham took the wood of the burnt offering, and laid *it* upon Isaac his son; and he took the fire in his hand, and a knife; and they went both of them together.

And Isaac spake unto Abraham his father, and said, My father: and he said, Here *am* I, my son. And he said, Behold the fire and the wood: but where *is* the lamb for a burnt offering?

And Abraham said, My son, God will provide himself a lamb for a burnt offering: so they went both of them together.

And they came to the place which God had told him of; and Abraham built an altar there, and laid the wood in order, and bound Isaac his son, and laid him on the altar upon the wood.

And Abraham stretched forth his hand, and took the knife to slay his son.

* From *The Holy Bible*, King James Version.

And the Angel of the LORD called unto him out of heaven, and said, Abraham, Abraham: and he said, Here *am* I.

And he said, Lay not thine hand upon the lad, neither do thou any thing unto him: for now I know that thou fearest God, seeing thou hast not withheld thy son, thine only *son*, from me.

And Abraham lifted up his eyes, and looked, and behold behind him a ram caught in a thicket by his horns: and Abraham went and took the ram, and offered him up for a burnt offering in the stead of his son.

Sebastian in the Encantadas*

Tennessee Williams

MRS. VENABLE:

. . .

One long-ago summer—now, why am I thinking of this?—my son, Sebastian, said, "Mother?—Listen to this!"—He read me Herman Melville's description of the Encantadas, the Galápagos Islands. Quote—take five and twenty heaps of cinders dumped here and there in an outside city lot. Imagine some of them magnified into mountains, and the vacant lot, the sea. And you'll have a fit idea of the general aspect of the Encantadas, the Enchanted Isles—extinct volcanos, looking much as the world at large might look—after a last conflagration—end quote. He read me that description and said that we had to go there. And so we did go there that summer on a chartered boat, a four-masted schooner, as close as possible to the sort of boat that Melville must have sailed on. . . . We saw the Encantadas, but on the Encantadas we saw something Melville *hadn't* written about. We saw great sea-turtles crawl up out of the sea for their annual egg-laying. . . . Once a year the female of the sea-turtle crawls up out of the equatorial sea onto the blazing sand-beach of a volcanic island to dig a pit in the sand and deposit her eggs there. It's a long and dreadful thing, the depositing of the eggs in the sand-pits, and when it's finished the exhausted female turtle crawls back to the sea half-dead. She never sees her offspring, but we did. Sebastian knew exactly when the sea-turtle eggs would be hatched out and we returned in time for it. . . .

---

* Tennessee Williams, *Suddenly Last Summer* (New York: New Directions, 1958), pp. 18–21. Copyright © 1958 by Tennessee Williams. All rights reserved. Reprinted by permission of New Directions Publishing Corporation.

DOCTOR:
You went back to the—?

MRS. VENABLE:
Terrible Encantadas, those heaps of extinct volcanos, in time to witness the hatching of the sea-turtles and their desperate flight to the sea!
(*There is a sound of harsh bird-cries in the air. She looks up.*)
—The narrow beach, the color of caviar, was all in motion! But the sky was in motion, too. . . .

DOCTOR:
The sky was in motion, too?

MRS. VENABLE:
—Full of flesh-eating birds and the noise of the birds, the horrible savage cries of the—

DOCTOR:
Carnivorous birds?

MRS. VENABLE:
Over the narrow black beach of the Encantadas as the just hatched sea-turtles scrambled out of the sand-pits and started their race to the sea. . . .

DOCTOR:
Race to the sea?

MRS. VENABLE:
To escape the flesh-eating birds that made the sky almost as black as the beach!
(*She gazes up again: we hear the wild, ravenous, harsh cries of the birds. The sound comes in rhythmic waves like a savage chant.*)
And the sand all alive, all alive, as the hatched sea-turtles made their dash for the sea, while the birds hovered and swooped to attack and hovered and—swooped to attack! They were diving down on the hatched sea-turtles, turning them over to expose their soft undersides, tearing the undersides open and rending and eating their flesh. Sebastian guessed that possibly only a

hundredth of one per cent of their number would escape to the sea. . . .

DOCTOR:

What was it about this spectacle on the beach that fascinated your son?

MRS. VENABLE:

My son was looking for—
    (*Stops short: continues evasively—*)
Let's just say he was interested in sea-turtles.

DOCTOR:

You started to say that your son was looking for something.

MRS. VENABLE:

    (*defiantly*)
All right, I started to say that my son was looking for God and I stopped myself because I was afraid that if I said he was looking for God, you'd say to yourself, 'Oh, a pretentious young crack-pot!'—which Sebastian was not. All poets look for God, all good poets do, and they have to look harder for Him than priests do since they don't have the help of such famous guide-books and well-organized expeditions as priests have with their scriptures and churches. All right! Well, now I've said it, my son was looking for God. I mean for a clear image of Him. He spent that whole blazing equatorial day in the crow's nest of the schooner watching that thing on the beach of the Encantadas till it was too dark to see it, and when he came back down the rigging, he said, Well, now I've see Him!—and he meant God . . .

INQUIRY

Man has never been the same since God died,
He has taken it very hard.
Why, you'd think it was only yesterday
The way he takes it.

EDNA ST. VINCENT MILLAY, *Conversation at Midnight*

WHY was Abraham going to kill his son? No doubt you have heard of persons who, for whatever reasons, took their children from their homes and killed them; but such accounts usually are found in sensational tabloids, not in holy writ. Imagine your reaction if Abraham were your neighbor and you were reading of this event in the daily newspaper. He was willing to perform and all but completed an act that almost all societies would deem criminal and most moral codes would call evil. Would the fact that he claimed that God had directed him to do this thing sway your opinion of him? In a recent bizarre murder trial in Florida the fact that the accused claimed to talk with God was taken by friends and a psychiatrist as evidence for their conclusion that he was "psychotic, schizophrenic, a paranoid type." Even though your neighbor Abraham did not complete the act this time, would it not be wise to lock him up for society's protection? Assuredly you would no longer want him for a neighbor. How could you trust him?

The traditional interpretation of the story of Abraham aims to lead us into taking comfort in a God who rewards Abraham for obedience. Abraham was being tested by God; he had faith in God, and God is good, so everything turned out fine. We may go on and tell it to others without ever seeing the events from Abraham's point of view. Abraham had great faith in God; we may even add that all of us ought to follow his lead. But what do we mean by "great faith in God"? What is it that Abraham had or did that sets him apart and makes this a significant story?

In this chapter we shall examine the ideas of faith and religious experience and God. The statement "He had faith" is a key. Consider Abraham. Does he know something many of us do not know? Perhaps faith is a kind of knowledge, a certain sort of knowing, that is different from the kind of knowing we have in science and other human activities. Think of situations in which we normally use the word "faith." Mothers talk of having faith in baby aspirin. We might ask one of them on what evidence does she base this faith. She would most likely respond by recounting experiences: her own, her mother's, a neighbor's, or a report in *Parents' Magazine*. These experiences are offered as proof of the reliability of the object of her faith; and we might imagine that her "faith," used in this sense, could be strengthened or weakened by the addition of supporting or refuting evidence. Faith, used in this way, is either reasonable or unreasonable, given the evidence. If faith is not knowledge, at least it is not incompatible with our usual methods of obtaining knowledge. But is this what the religious man means when he talks of having faith? What would we think of our mother if she shook her head and said, "I have no evidence; I just give him the pills. I have faith they'll work." How much evidence is necessary to support a religious faith, and how much to destroy it?

We often talk as if faith were one of a number of ways of gaining truth; there is scientific truth, commonsense truth, religious truth, etc. We frequently distinguish between what we call religious knowledge and scientific knowledge and imply that both will lead in the long run to "truth." Consider Job's claim, "I know that my redeemer liveth." * Is the word "know" used here in the same way as in the statement "I know it's raining out" or "I know that water is composed of hydrogen and oxygen"? Theologians such as Paul Tillich call faith an act of ultimate concern that can only be expressed symbolically. It is not a matter of knowledge. It is a state of being something, not of knowing something.

Some major religions take the position that faith is the acceptance of certain statements as truths, statements revealed through prophecy, scripture, or ecclesiastical authority. The Bible, for instance, is accepted not only as inspiration from the divinity but as the written word of God. Thus faith amounts to believing certain propositions about the way things are upon scientifically insufficient evidence. The phrase *taking it on faith* comes to mean nearly the opposite of knowing for certain: believing without or despite evi-

---

* Job 19:25

dence. A good deal of criticism of religion arises because of this view of faith.

What evidence has Abraham to support his willingness to sacrifice his son? What could he expect to result from his actions? The man who knows something can predict certain things on the basis of his knowledge, but Abraham knows nothing of the events he is to perform except that he thinks he is called upon to perform them. How can he even know this is really the command of God? Abraham's position is not comparable to that of Agamemnon, who sacrificed his daughter with the assurance of the Greek gods that if he did so the winds would blow, carrying his ships to Troy and victory. If this is truly a test of Abraham's faith, then Abraham cannot expect anything. Or at least we might imagine that he expects the worst as he walks with his son to the mountain. Abraham cannot know this is only a test.

If we think of faith (Abraham's faith) as unrelated to knowledge, then we can understand why no amount of contradictory evidence affects the determination of the faithful. Consider how you might convince a man of faith that he is misguided, wasting his time, foolish. What kind of evidence can you bring to bear against his faith? Construct an argument that might convince Abraham to return home before this sacrifice thing goes too far. But Abraham tells you that all your arguments have occurred to him. He is not a fool. He knows what he is doing and what the circumstances are liable to be when he returns home. If he did not recognize the gravity of his deed, his act of faith would be of little significance. Why then does he proceed?

To have faith, according to Kierkegaard, is to have a particular point of view. You and the man of faith might agree on all the physical facts of a situation (an event in daily life or even the structure of the universe), but your interpretation of those facts might differ sharply from his. How would you then convince him that he is wrong? Bringing more facts to the argument in support of your position is not likely to help, for he does not disagree with you on the facts.

Here is an example suggested by Walt Kelly's *Pogo* cartoon strip. Albert, the alligator, announces to the other residents of the swamp that he has just discovered that they are living in the land of the Invisible Indians. Pogo asks what evidence Albert has to support his claim. Albert's answer is, "Look around," to which Pogo responds, "I don't see anything." And Albert retorts, "You see!" What is the difference between there being Invisible Indians and there being no Indians at all? What evidence for the existence of the Invisible Indians could be offered? Suppose you asked Albert if an Invisible Indian would leave a trail (broken twigs, bent brush, tracks), and he responded that these Indians are also intangible. You wonder why anyone would be interested in such Indians, to which Albert responds that of course we may not *know* whether the Indians are there, but certainly they might be there. And that, to him, is a very important "might."

Having faith is one thing, of course; the object of faith is quite another. Faith in a home remedy for chest colds and faith in the existence of a divine being are not on the same plane. Do we learn anything about the latter from examining the former?

One of the major philosophical problems related to religion is to determine a meaning for the statement "God exists" and how, if at all, it is to be used. Returning to your conversation with the man of faith, you discover that despite your argument on the facts, the man of faith finds it necessary to include the statement "God exists" as an explanation of those facts. You are not prepared to accept that without proof. Physical data as proof have been ruled out because you both agree on the physical facts. The man of faith could appeal to the powers of reflection and logic. Many "proofs" of the existence of God have been devised solely on the basis of definition and logic. St. Anselm's famous argument (used in a revised form by Descartes) rests on the kind of being we say that God is (called the "ontological argument" because "ontology" refers to the science of being). When Moses asked God at the burning bush to identify himself, God answered, "I am who I am." * If God is a perfect being, the ontological argument goes, and to be perfect is to lack nothing; then the perfect being must exist, for lacking existence would be an imperfection. Therefore, God exists. There are major problems with this type of thinking, as you may well imagine; not the least important of these is the claim of some philosophers that existence destroys perfection. A perfect circle, for example, cannot exist. All existing circles are less than perfect. It is suggested that the perfect God can only be perfect if he does not exist. David and Marjorie Haight also use the form of Anselm's proof to prove the existence of the Devil and in so doing maintain that it is only a matter of faith that one calls the entity whose existence has been proved by the name of the Divine.

The attributes of God are very important to some religious men.

* Exodus 3:14

We are told by religious people, as well as by Scripture, that God is (among other things) a loving being; we are also told that he is an all-powerful being, that no task is too difficult for his mastery. Yet as many philosophers (John Stuart Mill in particular) have pointed out, the world is filled with evil and suffering. If God were both loving and all-powerful, he ought to want to destroy the suffering and evil, and he ought to have the power to do so. Yet God doesn't seem to do anything to alter the evil state of affairs. Therefore we have no grounds for believing that God is loving; or, if he is loving, that he is powerful enough to overcome the evil of our situation.

How can a man of faith counter such an argument? Must he simply deny that there is evil or suffering in the world? He could claim that evil is an illusion, the result of our imperfect ability to understand the universe and God's plan; but, as in the Book of Job, such appeals to the imperfections of men do little to comfort the sufferer (and, in fact, reflect back upon God). If God is good and also the creator of the universe, he must be in some way responsible for the evil and suffering of his creatures.

The German existentialist philosopher Friedrich Nietzsche argued that there is no real human freedom (despite our illusion that we are free to act as we choose) if we accept the traditional notions of God as creator. Ultimately God must take the blame and punishment for our evil doings.

> How he raged at us, this wrath-snorter, because we understood him badly! But why did he not speak more clearly? And if the fault lay in our ears, why did he give us ears that heard him badly? If there was dirt in our ears, well! Who put it in them?

Nietzsche's prophet Zarathustra announces to man that God is dead. This concept has played a major role in contemporary theology. The statement is meant by Nietzsche to be taken as a historical pronouncement. Modern man no longer can have any relationship with God. Nietzsche did not mean that men no longer believe in God or that God is actually dead. His claim was that man had lost his own image as a responsible and dignified being in the centuries of feeling subservient to his image of God. Without an idea of meaningful human existence, the concept of God is valueless. Nietzsche was saying that the personality of man was incorporated in the idea of a personal god, and that because men have lost sight of themselves, they can find no way of identifying with God. Ugly man cannot stand the perfection and mercy of God. It demeans man, and so God must be killed for man to save face. Nietzsche wrote:

> Away with such a God! Better to have no God, better to set up des-
> tiny on one's own account, better to be a fool, better to be God
> oneself!

A nonpersonal God, a pantheistic God, a nature-God, or the identification of the Divine with the universe itself might be more appealing. Such concepts of God would both serve as explanations of nature and not be distinguishable from nature or the events in nature. But join Sebastian in the crow's nest watching that "thing" on the beach of the Encantadas. What you see is not a pleasant sight. Why call it God? What difference does it make to call a particular set of natural circumstances, no matter how awe-inspiring, God? Imagine what a religious relationship with such a God would involve. Is Sebastian having a religious experience?

In most Western religion the appropriate practice is worship, the adoration of the Divine-other by the believer. If, however, the Divine is identical with everything (as in the case of many Eastern religions), including the religious devotee, then worship would be, in a strange way, self-adoration. Meditation, the contemplation of the ultimate unity of all things, is then, within such a conception of the Divine, the true religious practice, and the attainment of that mystical experience is the goal of the devotee.

In many Oriental scriptures and mystical texts of both East and West, attaining oneness with all of nature, what Hindus call Brahman, the impersonal world soul, is the highest goal of man. Loss of self-identity in the Whole is the supreme aim of life. The salvation of man from his daily predicaments is said to consist in his identification with an insight into the essential singularity of the world soul and in freedom from the point of view of seeing things in nature as "particularizations." The ultimate experience is coming to see All without being confused by the diversity of parts.

There appears to be very little one can critically say about purported mystical experiences. The language used by mystics in their attempts to describe their experiences is, by their own testimony, inadequate, because it can only approximate the experience. In fact, it is one of the earmarks of having had such an experience that words are discovered to be useless in the attempt to express it. Hence mystics tend to write in poetic terms, in similes and metaphors. But metaphors for what?

William James cites four characteristics of mystical experiences. They are ineffable; they must be directly experienced, they cannot be transferred to others. When Sebastian claims to have seen God, he cannot transfer the experience to his listeners by that statement or by any further attempt at description. Mystical experiences impart a sense of insight, of knowledge, of what James calls a "curious state of authority" to the mystic. These experiences are transient, and, finally, the mystic himself is passive during the experience. It happens to him, not by him. Sebastian sits and watches. Compare him to Abraham, who *acts* on faith.

It is one thing to feel that one knows something of supreme importance, but it is quite another matter to be warranted in asserting any knowledge claims on the evidence of a mystical experience. What kind of authority is imparted by mystical experiences to those who undergo them? If they are not transferable, why should anyone who has not had a mystical experience uncritically accept the pronouncements of a mystic?

We are told that Sebastian was looking for God. The great Zen philosopher D. T. Suzuki, however, tells us that the ultimate Zen mystical experience of Satori is not to be pursued *per se*. The more one aims at the target, a novice Zen archer is told by his master, the less one succeeds in hitting it. Preparation for the experience is essential; then at the propitious moment: enlightenment. The following tale is characteristic.

> Tokusan was a great scholar of the *Diamond Sūtra*. Learning that there was such a thing as Zen, ignoring all the written scriptures, and directly laying hands on one's soul, he came to Ryutan to be instructed in the doctrine. One day Tokusan was sitting outside trying to see into the mystery of Zen. Ryutan said, "Why don't you come in?" Replied Tokusan, "It is pitch dark." A candle was lighted and handed over to Tokusan. When the latter was at the point of taking it, Ryutan suddenly blew the light out, whereupon the mind of Tokusan was opened.*

What is it for Sebastian to know that he has found God on that gory beach of the Encantadas?

* From D. T. Suzuki, *Essays in Buddhism* (New York: Grove Press, Inc., 1949), pp. 239–40.

1 SØREN KIERKEGAARD

(1813–1855)

*Faith and Abraham**

Kierkegaard is a dominant influence in theology today. His philosophy is existential, and his major concern is finding "authentic existence," salvation from the corruption of the social life of external convention. For Kierkegaard philosophy and truth are a subjective, individual matter. He attacks institutionalized Christianity as superficial and hypocritical and calls for understanding of the total commitment of a "knight of faith" in a subjectively oriented life. Kierkegaard's favorite example of a man called to act on faith is the Abraham-Isaac story in Genesis. Abraham acts without hope; he "leaps" to faith when his despair cannot be explained by reason or morality. Objectivity, Kierkegaard argues, is meaningless to faith. Abraham acts because he believes, and he does what cannot be rationally defended because he has restructured his life. He does nothing glorious. He does the absurd. We cannot understand his faith, Kierkegaard tells us; one must live it existentially. Seen from the point of view of faith, Abraham's actions have great significance in his life; his world can never be the same.

* Søren Kierkegaard, *Fear and Trembling and The Sickness unto Death,* transl. with Introduction and Notes by Walter Lowrie (Copyright 1941, 1954 by Princeton University Press; Princeton Paperback, 1968), "Problemata-Preliminary Expectoration." Reprinted by permission of Princeton University Press.

NO, not one shall be forgotten who was great in the world. But each was great in his own way, and each in proportion to the greatness of that which he *loved.* For he who loved himself became great by himself, and he who loved other men became great by his selfless devotion, but he who loved God became greater than all. Everyone shall be remembered, but each became great in proportion to his *expectation.* One became great by expecting the possible, another by expecting the eternal, but he who expected the impossible became greater than all. Everyone shall be remembered, but each was great in proportion to the greatness of that with which he *strove.* For he who strove with the world became great by overcoming the world, and he who strove with himself became great by overcoming himself, but he who strove with God became greater than all. So there was strife in the world, man against man, one against a thousand, but he who strove with God was greater than all. So there was strife upon earth: there was one who overcame all by his power, and there was one who overcame God by his impotence. There was one who relied upon himself and gained all, there was one who secure in his strength sacrificed all, but he who believed God was greater than all. There was one who was great by reason of his power, and one who was great by reason of his wisdom, and one who was great by reason of his hope, and one who was great by reason of his love; but Abraham was greater than all, great by reason of his power whose strength is impotence, great by reason of his wisdom whose secret is foolishness, great by reason of his hope whose form is madness, great by reason of the love which is hatred of oneself.

By faith Abraham went out from the land of his fathers and became a sojourner in the land of promise. He left one thing behind, took one thing with him: he left his earthly understanding behind and took faith with him—otherwise he would not have wandered forth but would have thought this unreasonable. By faith he was a stranger in the land of promise, and there was nothing to recall what was dear to him, but by its novelty everything tempted his soul to melancholy yearning—and yet he was God's elect, in whom the Lord was well pleased! Yea, if he had been disowned, cast off from God's grace, he could have comprehended it better; but now it was like a mockery of him and of his faith. There was in the world one too who lived in banishment from the fatherland he loved. He is not forgotten, nor his Lamentations when he sorrowfully sought and found what he had lost. There is no song of Lamentations by Abraham. It is human to lament, human to weep with them that weep, but it is greater to believe, more blessed to contemplate the believer.

By faith Abraham received the promise that in his seed all races of the world would be blessed. Time passed, the possibility was there, Abraham believed; time passed, it became unreasonable, Abraham believed. There was in the world one who had an expectation, time passed, the evening drew nigh, he was not paltry enough to have forgotten his expectation, therefore he too shall not be forgotten. Then he sorrowed, and sorrow did not deceive him as life had done, it did for him all it could, in the sweetness of sorrow he possessed his delusive expectation. It is human to sorrow, human to sorrow with them that sorrow, but it is greater to believe, more blessed to contemplate the believer. There is no song of Lamentations by Abraham. He did not mournfully count the days while time passed, he did not look at Sarah with a suspicious glance, wondering whether she were growing old, he did not arrest the course of the sun, that Sarah might not grow old, and his expectation with her. He did not sing lullingly before Sarah his mournful lay. Abraham became old, Sarah became a laughingstock in the land, and yet he was God's elect and inheritor of the promise that in his seed all the races of the world would be blessed. So were it not better if he had not been God's elect? What is it to be God's elect? It is to be denied in youth the wishes of youth, so as with great pains to get them fulfilled in old age. But Abraham believed and held fast the expectation. If Abraham had wavered, he would have given it up. If he had said to God, "Then perhaps it is not after all Thy will that it should come to pass, so I will give up the wish. It was my only wish, it was my bliss. My soul is sincere, I hide no secret malice because Thou didst deny it to me"—he would not have been forgotten, he would have saved many by his example, yet he would not be the father of faith. For it is great to give up one's wish, but it is greater to hold it fast after having given it up, it is great to grasp the eternal, but it is greater to hold fast to the temporal after having given it up.

Then came the fulness of time. If Abraham had not believed, Sarah surely would have been dead of sorrow, and Abraham, dulled by grief, would not have understood the fulfilment but would have smiled at it as at a dream of youth. But Abraham believed, therefore he was young; for he who always hopes for the best becomes old, and he who is always prepared for the worst grows old early, but he who believes preserves an eternal youth. Praise therefore to that story! For Sarah, though stricken in years, was young enough to desire the pleasure of motherhood, and Abraham, though gray-haired, was young enough to wish to be a father. In an outward respect the marvel consists in the fact that it came to pass according to their expectation, in a deeper sense the miracle of faith consists in the fact that Abraham and Sarah were young enough to wish, and that faith had preserved their wish and therewith their youth. He accepted the fulfilment of the promise, he accepted it by faith, and it came to pass according to the promise and according to his faith—for Moses smote the rock with his rod, but he did not believe.

Then there was joy in Abraham's house, when Sarah became a bride on the day of their golden wedding.

But it was not to remain thus. Still once more Abraham was to be tried. He had fought with that cunning power which invents everything, with that alert enemy which never slumbers, with that old man who outlives all things—he had fought with Time and preserved his faith. Now all the terror of the strife was concentrated in one instant. "And God tempted Abraham and said unto him, Take Isaac, thine only son, whom thou lovest, and get thee into the land of Moriah, and offer him there for a burnt offering upon the mountain which I will show thee."

So all was lost—more dreadfully than if it had never come to pass! So the Lord was only making sport of Abraham! He made miraculously the preposterous actual, and now in turn He would annihilate it. It was indeed foolishness, but Abraham did not laugh at it like Sarah when the promise was announced. All was lost! Seventy years of faithful expectation, the brief joy at the fulfilment of faith. Who then is he that plucks away the old man's staff, who is it that requires that he himself shall break it? Who is he that would make a man's gray hairs comfortless, who is it that requires that he himself shall do it? Is there no compassion for the venerable oldling, none for the innocent child? And yet Abraham was God's elect, and it was the Lord who imposed the trial. All would now be lost. The glorious memory to be preserved by the human race, the promise in Abraham's seed—this was only a whim, a fleeting thought which the Lord had had, which Abraham should now obliterate. That glorious treasure which was just as old as faith in Abraham's heart, many, many years older than Isaac, the fruit of Abraham's life, sanctified by prayers, matured in conflict—the blessing upon Abraham's lips, this fruit was now to be plucked prematurely and remain without significance. For what significance had it when Isaac was to be sacrificed? That sad and yet blissful hour when Abraham was to take leave of all that was dear to him, when yet once more he was to lift up his head, when his countenance would shine like that of the Lord, when he would concentrate his whole soul in a blessing which was potent to make Isaac blessed all his days—this time would not come! For he would indeed take leave of Isaac, but in such a way that he himself would remain behind; death would separate them, but in such a way that Isaac remained its prey. The old man would not be joyful in death as he laid his hands in blessing upon Isaac, but he would be weary of life as he laid violent hands upon Isaac. And it was God who tried him. Yea, woe, woe unto the messenger who had come before Abraham with such tidings! Who would have ventured to be the emissary of this sorrow? But it was God who tried Abraham.

Yet Abraham believed, and believed for this life. Yea, if his faith had been only for a future life, he surely would have cast everything away in order to hasten out of this world to which he did not belong. But Abraham's faith was not of this sort, if there be such a faith; for really this is not faith but the furthest possibility of faith which has a presentiment of its object at the extremest limit of the horizon, yet is separated from it by a yawning abyss within which despair carries on its game. But Abraham believed precisely for this life, that he was to grow old in the land, honored by the people, blessed in his generation, remembered forever in Isaac, his dearest thing in life, whom he embraced with a love for which it would be a poor expression to say that he loyally fulfilled the father's duty of loving the son, as indeed is evinced in the words of the summons, "the son whom thou lovest." Jacob had twelve sons, and one of them he loved; Abraham had only one, the son whom he loved.

Yet Abraham believed and did not doubt, he believed the preposterous. If Abraham had doubted—then he would have done something else, something glorious; for how could Abraham do anything but what is great and glorious! He would have marched up to Mount Moriah, he would have cleft the fire-wood, lit the pyre, drawn the knife —he would have cried out to God, "Despise not this sacrifice, it is not the best thing I possess, that I know well, for what is an old man in comparison with the child of promise; but it is the best I am able to give Thee. Let Isaac never come to know this, that he may console himself with his youth." He would have plunged the knife into his own breast. He would have been admired in the world, and his name would not have been forgotten; but it is one thing to be admired, and another to be the guiding star which saves the anguished.

But Abraham believed. He did not pray for himself, with the hope of moving the Lord—it was only when the righteous punishment was decreed upon Sodom and Gomorrha that Abraham came forward with his prayers.

We read in those holy books: "And God tempted Abraham, and said unto him, Abraham, Abraham, where art thou? And he said, Here am I." Thou to whom my speech is addressed, was such the case with thee? When afar off thou didst see the heavy dispensation of providence approaching thee, didst thou not say to the mountains, Fall on me, and to the hills, Cover me? Or if thou wast stronger, did not thy foot move slowly along the way, longing as it were for the old path? When a call was issued to thee, didst thou answer, or didst thou not answer perhaps in a low voice, whisperingly? Not so Abraham: joyfully, buoyantly, confidently, with a loud voice, he answered, "Here am I." We read further: "And Abraham rose early in the morning"—as though it were to a festival, so he hastened, and early in the morning he had come to the place spoken of, to Mount Moriah. He said nothing to Sarah, nothing to Eleazar. Indeed who could understand him? Had not the temptation by its very nature exacted of him an oath of silence? He cleft the wood, he bound Isaac, he lit the pyre, he drew the knife. My hearer, there was many a father who believed that with his son he lost everything that was dearest to him in the world, that he was deprived of every hope for the future, but yet there was none that was the child of promise in the sense that Isaac was for Abraham. There was many a father who lost his child; but then it was God, it was the unalterable, the unsearchable will of the Almighty, it was His hand took the child. Not so with Abraham. For him was reserved a harder trial, and Isaac's fate was laid along with the knife in Abraham's hand. And there he stood, the old man, with his only hope! But he did not doubt, he did not look anxiously to the right or to the left, he did not challenge heaven with his prayers. He knew that it was God the Almighty who was trying him, he knew that it was the hardest sacrifice that could be required of him; but he knew also that no sacrifice was too hard when God required it—and he drew the knife.

Who gave strength to Abraham's arm? Who held his right hand up so that it did not fall limp at his side? He who gazes at this becomes paralyzed. Who gave strength to Abraham's soul, so that his eyes did not grow dim, so that he saw neither Isaac nor the ram? He who gazes at this becomes blind.—And yet rare enough perhaps is the man who becomes paralyzed and blind, still more rare one who worthily recounts what happened. We all know it—it was only a trial.

If Abraham when he stood upon Mount Moriah had doubted, if he had gazed about him irresolutely, if before he drew the knife he had by chance discovered the ram, if God had permitted him to offer it instead of Isaac—then he would have betaken himself home, everything would have been the same, he has Sarah, he retained Isaac, and yet how changed! For his retreat would have been a flight, his salvation an accident, his reward dishonor, his future perhaps perdition. Then he would have borne witness neither to his faith nor to God's grace, but would have testified only how dreadful it is to march out to Mount Moriah. Then Abraham would not have been forgotten, nor would Mount Moriah, this mountain would then be mentioned, not like Ararat where the Ark landed, but would be spoken of as a consternation, because it was here that Abraham doubted.

Venerable Father Abraham! In marching home from Mount Moriah thou hadst no need of a panegyric which might console thee for thy loss; for thou didst gain all and didst retain Isaac. Was it not so? Never again did the Lord take him from thee, but thou didst sit at table joyfully with him in thy tent, as thou dost in the beyond to all eternity. Venerable Father Abraham! Thousands of years have run their course since those days, but thou hast need of no tardy lover to snatch the memorial of thee from the power of oblivion, for every language calls thee to remembrance—and yet thou dost reward thy lover more gloriously than does any other; hereafter thou dost make him blessed in thy bosom; here thou dost enthral his eyes and his heart by the marvel of thy deed. Venerable Father Abraham! Second Father of the human race! Thou who first wast sensible of and didst first bear witness to that prodigious passion which disdains the dreadful conflict with the rage of the elements and with the powers of creation in order to strive with God; thou who first didst know that highest passion, the holy, pure and humble expression of the divine madness which the pagans admired—forgive him who would speak in praise of thee, if he does not do it fittingly. He spoke humbly, as if it were the desire of his own heart, he spoke briefly, as it becomes him to do, but he will never forget that thou hadst need of a hundred years to obtain a son of old age against expectation, that thou didst have to draw the knife before retaining Isaac; he will never forget that in a hundred and thirty years thou didst not get further than to faith.

2

BRAND BLANSHARD

(1892–   )

Kierkegaard on Faith*

Blanshard attacks Kierkegaard's concept of faith as nonrational. Blanshard points out that Kierkegaard's faith is beyond reasonable understanding. Kierkegaard claims that we find what is absolutely true when we commit ourselves to the unintelligible and self-contradictory. Blanshard responds that such a definition of truth only creates meaningless assertions and a complete lack of common truths in religion. Blanshard's claim is that Kierkegaard can never succeed in establishing a basis for faith in the total subjectivity that is left after he has destroyed all uses of reason. Why must religion be reasonable? Does Kierkegaard have an insight that Blanshard ignores? Is Blanshard's concern with Kierkegaard's life relevant to his case against Kierkegaard's theory of faith and truth?

* *The Personalist*, Vol. XLIX, No. 1 (Winter, 1968). Used by kind permission of Professor Blanshard and *The Personalist*.

AT the center of Kierkegaard's thought is the idea of human life as lived on various plateaus, each with its special characteristics. The idea probably came from Hegel. Just as Hegel recognized three main stages on the way to the Absolute—being, essence, and the notion —so Kierkegaard distinguished three "stages on life's way," the aesthetic, the ethical, and the religious. The first two were preparatory stages, rungs on the ladder that led to the third, where the clearest and surest insights of which men are capable were to be reached. This highest stage was again divided into two, A and B, each with its special features. Of these it is 3B, the last stage of all, that is of most interest to the philosopher, since it carries us to the highest summit that man's knowledge can attain.

But Kierkegaard insists that this summit is not attained through any process of reflective thought. The final step is a passionate, nonrational "leap of faith," a commitment of feeling and will. What is the commitment *to?* Not to a way of life merely, as some readers have supposed, but also to Christian belief. And the central Christian belief, he holds, is the belief in the incarnation. "The object of faith is thus God's reality in existence as a particular individual, the fact that God has existed as an individual human being." This is the distinctive fact of Christianity, which marks it out from all other religions. And according to Kierkegaard it is a fact incapable of establishment by any process of objective thought. You can never *prove* the existence of any past fact. It might seem, then, that the proper attitude is one of doubt and suspended judgment, just as it would be if we were asked to accept the existence of King Arthur. The two facts, however, are not comparable. For the unique Christian fact, if a fact at all, is one of overwhelming moment, upon whose acceptance our eternal happiness depends, and if there is any chance of its reality, an attitude of reserve and detachment would be flippancy. So, "while objective knowledge rambles comfortably on by way of the long road of approximation without being impelled by the urge of passion, subjective knowledge counts every delay a deadly peril, and the decision so infinitely important and so instantly pressing that it is as if the opportunity had already passed." The decision is what James called a "forced option"; we cannot evade it, since with so high a prize at stake, to evade decision is in effect to reject the offer as illusory.

The man who attempts to make this decision on the ground of evidence is in an even worse position than we have suggested. For the incarnation is not a fact of more or less probability; to our reason it is an impossibility. Kierkegaard admits it to be a "contradiction that God has existed in human form." It is not knowable or even thinkable. "To speculate upon it is a misunderstanding, and the farther one goes in this direction the greater is the misunderstanding. When one finally reaches the stage of not only speculating about it, but of understanding it speculatively, one has reached the highest pitch of misunderstanding." The attempt to know religious truth by the intellect is thus fundamentally misguided because destined to defeat by the nature of its object. "For the absurd is the object of faith, and the only object that can be believed."

Fortunately this defeat of intelligence does not leave us without recourse. Faith remains. But there must be no looking back, no longing for the unprofitable old fleshpots of rational understanding and certainty. One must recognize the sophisticated intellect for the dangerous thing it is, and be content to become a child again. "When faith requires of a man to give up his reason, it becomes equally difficult for the cleverest and the most stupid person to believe, or it becomes in a sense more difficult for the clever." The difficulty must be overcome, not by thinking more critically, which is futile, but by a resolute act of will. The leap of faith is a daring, passionate non-rational commitment to the paradoxical and the unintelligible. "Faith begins where thought leaves off." "Without risk there is no faith." "The truth is precisely the venture which chooses an objective uncertainty with the passion of the infinite . . . the above definition of truth is an equivalent expression for faith. . . . Faith is precisely the contradiction between the infinite passion of the individual's inwardness and the objective uncertainty." "Faith is what the Greeks termed divine madness."

We shall say more in a moment about such faith as a means of insight in theology. But Kierkegaard's best known illustration of the meaning of faith is drawn not from theology, but from morals. The ultimate source of right and wrong is the will of God, and "the knight of faith," like the knights of the Round Table, will at every moment of life be in the service of his royal master. Not that he needs to renew the appeal to this will at every moment consciously; for the lower-level guidance of his own ethical faculties will normally suffice. The ethical level, says Kierkegaard, is the level of "the universal." By this cryptic pronouncement he seems to mean one or other of two things; either that the moral man will, in Kantian fashion, ask what conduct could in principle be consistently adopted by everybody, or, in Hegelian fashion, ask what the community would generally approve. Most modern moralists would regard either of these appeals as hopelessly inadequate, but Kierkegaard had little grasp of ethical theory. His chief contribution to it is to say that at times it breaks down, and that when it does, our resort must to be to a "teleological suspension of the ethical" at Divine behest. The nature of this behest can be ascertained only by faith.

How is he to show that our natural faculties do break down in morals? The most effective way would be to show that our clearest moral judgment may stand in radical conflict with the divine will. Can any case of such conflict be cited? Yes; we find it in scripture itself. The most revolting act of which a human being is capable·is to destroy his own flesh and blood. In the book of Genesis we find Abraham commanded by God to do just this, to take his only son, the son of his old age on whom the joy and hope of his life were concentrated, to the summit of Mount Moriah, to bind him, cut his throat, and use his body as a burnt offering. Anthropologists who have studied this legend have considered that it is probably a relic of the custom of human sacrifice which once held in many parts of the world, and apparently even in the prehistoric past of the Hebrew people. However that may be, Kierkegaard takes it in all historic and symbolic seriousness. Is it not the point of this story, which is clearly inspired, that it was Abraham's duty, and may at any moment be ours, to trample down the affections of the natural man and all his nicely calculated goods and evils? Kierkegaard's answer is an emphatic Yes.

In his essay *Fear and Trembling* he goes into the matter with gusto and in detail. After a "Preliminary Expectoration," as he calls it, in which he spews philosophy, ethics and even reflective theology out of his mouth as incompetent to deal with the case, he goes on to consider what is implied in the command to Abraham. There have been cases in history and literature in which a father's killing of a child may in some degree be reconciled with our moral sense. Brutus ordered the execution of his sons, but they were, after all, guilty of treason, and does not a general's duty to the state take precedence of his own affections? Jephthah made a grateful vow to Heaven to offer as a sacrifice the first person he met on his return from victory, and if this happened to be his daughter, he would nonetheless be breaking a sacred oath by sparing her. If Agamemnon kills Iphigenia, it is to appease the wrath of Artemis, who holds the power of destruction over his fleet and army. These are not, therefore, pure cases of "the teleological suspension of the ethical"; in all of them the killing of the child is dreadful, but it is not entirely pointless. The great thing about the act demanded of Abraham was that it was pointless absolutely. Isaac was wholly innocent; Abraham loved him beyond anyone else in the world; no conceivable good to anyone could be anticipated from killing him. It was an act in which every human consideration was lined up on one side and on the other nothing at all but the command from on high to kill. Abraham bowed to it and drew his knife. The fact that at the last moment he was relieved of the need to strike is irrelevant in appraising him. Whether he actually killed or not, he showed that he possessed the one thing needful, namely the readiness to kill.

For Kierkegaard this makes him the perfect knight of faith. "Venerable father Abraham! Second father of the human race! Thou who first didst know that highest passion, the holy, pure, and humble expression of the divine madness . . ." Abraham is "great by reason of his wisdom whose secret is foolishness, great by reason of his hope whose form is madness, great by reason of love which is hatred of oneself." He surrendered himself to the "paradox which is capable of transforming a murder into a holy act well pleasing to God." "Abraham believed and did not doubt, he believed the preposterous." "He believed by virtue of the absurd; for all human reckoning had long since ceased to function." He was called upon to renounce the moral for the religious, the finite for the infinite. "This is . . . clear to the knight of faith, so the only thing that can save him is the absurd, and this he grasps by faith." Here is the meaning of that most deceptive phrase, "the teleological suspension of the ethical." "Teleological" means "for an end," but what Kierkegaard is praising here is the abandonment of all thought of ends and the doing of something that in every human point of view is productive of nothing but evil. "As soon as the will begins to look right and left for results, the individual begins to become immoral."

What are we to say of a rhapsody (in forty thousand words) in praise of pure and holy murder, of a defense of the humanly immoral on the ground that it is religious duty? Kierkegaard, in choosing such ground, believes that he has cut off the possibility of rational criticism. And clearly if an appeal is taken to the unintelligible and the irrational, it is begging the question to protest against it on any grounds of sense or reason. Sense and reason have been deliberately left behind. But we can at least point out that the irrationalist defense is double-edged. If it undercuts its opponents, it also undercuts itself, in the sense that it has forgone all right to the rational criticism of others. If opponents claim a divine warrant for the opposite of what Kierkegaard proclaims, all he can do is denounce them as impostors.

Of course there have been countless claims of this sort. There were Jewish leaders who claimed a divine imperative to destroy the Amalekites, man, woman, and child. There were Christians—St. Louis described himself as one—who thought the proper Christian reply to an argumentative Jew was to bury one's sword in him to the hilt. John Woolman felt a divine interdict against his preparing papers as a magistrate for the sale of a slave. John Newton, the hymn-writer, reported that some of his sweetest hours of communion with the divine were spent while he was the captain of a slave-ship, separated by a few planks from a weltering mass of human misery. Joseph Smith claimed to know that the divine will approved of plural wives; Mohammed made a like claim, but limited the divine approval to four; the Christian fathers limited it still further to one; and St. Paul construed it as favoring those who did not marry at all. St. Basil, St. Gregory of Nyssa and St. Ambrose thought it a divine imperative that one should not accept interest on loans. St. Abraham the hermit appears to have thought it the divine will that, beginning with the day of his conversion and continuing for fifty years, he should wash neither his face nor his feet. There are few practices too trivial or too eccentric to have been included among actions enjoined or prohibited by divine will. If claims to such guidance are to be above rational criticism, what we have is a chaos of voices, each announcing itself as authoritative, each denouncing its opponents as deceivers, and none of them able to defend themselves against the others.

Abraham was enabled by faith to see what ordinary men were unable to see. What exactly was this? It was that an act which, so far as the human mind could judge, was productive only of evil was nevertheless right—a duty because the will of God. For the person who possesses the insight, the principles and consequences involved in the act are held to be irrelevant; its character as seen by faith is its true character, which takes precedence of any judgment of our merely human faculties. Faith thus revealed to Abraham in the most dramatic and decisive way that it may be duty to reduce rather than to increase, to destroy rather than to create, the values recognized by reason and conscience.

Now when "the knight of faith" claims that he has had this kind of insight, can we credit what he says? It is hard to take the claim seriously. A person may *say* that it is really better that the powers of youth should be frustrated than fulfilled, that excruciating pain is better than pleasure, that sorrow and anguish are better than happiness, but can we believe that he has in fact seen these things to be true? The question is not, of course, whether pain, misery, and the destruction of life may be *means* leading to later goods, this is true enough, but is irrelevant here; for we are expressly forbidden to try to justify the divine command by any such considerations. What was presented as Abraham's duty, what he was honored for accepting, was the production of these evils without any thought of compensating goods. When the question is thus clearly put, one must take leave to doubt not only whether such insight occurs in fact, but whether it could possibly occur. For what the insight amounts to is that there is no such thing as good or evil, right or wrong, better or worse. If the killing of innocent youth without regard to consequences may be right, then anything may be right, since our moral sense has proved delusive at the very point of its greatest confidence. If pleasure is intrinsically evil and pain intrinsically good, if misery is in truth more desirable than happiness, then the clearest and surest judgments about values are worthless, and it is no longer possible to hold that anything is really better than anything else. The entire realm of values, including moral values, becomes a mirage. Now one may talk as if it were, but one cannot live or think accordingly. Daily and hourly we make choices implying judgments that it is better to be happy or enlightened or at peace than it is to be the opposite; indeed the person who chooses to affirm that nothing is better than anything else presumably assumes that it is better so to affirm than not to do so. The Kierkegaardian "knight of faith," in electing the "absurd," is divesting himself of the shackles of all insights. But to do that is to be not a saint, but a moral nihilist.

Those who accept Kierkegaard's knight of faith as the true saint may well pause over this conclusion. The popularity of his religious ethics in our schools of theology is a genuine anomaly. The Christian saint, we must admit, has at times been a strange character whose asceticism and other-worldliness have set him apart from the run of men and caused him to be regarded with uncomprehending wonder. Still, in the main he has accepted and exemplified the values most prized by his fellows and has been honored by them accordingly; he has believed in the superiority of love to hate, in the relief of human misery, in refusing to count his own good as more important than that of others. These are virtues that we can see to be virtues with our unaided human faculties. But for Kierkegaard as for Luther, these faculties are corrupt; all the principles laid down by them are open to a "teleological suspension of the ethical" imposed from above; they are subject at any moment to cancellation by "the absurd"; and if, in the face of such a suspension we retain our old adherence to love or loyalty or even conscience in its natural sense, the charge of immorality is compounded with a charge of impiety. Furthermore, the saint or knight of faith, according to Kierkegaard, is a man whose leading concern is not the welfare of others, but his own "eternal happiness," a description, incidentally that applied to himself. "If ever a person was self-centered it was Kierkegaard; he hardly ever thinks of anyone but himself."[*] What we have in this strange version of Christianity is thus an insistence on the selfish character of the religious motive, combined with an insistence that the values of the Christian life, so far as these can be understood, are provisional only, and may at any time be overridden. Kierkegaard revelled in paradox; "if anyone has ever used the slogan *credo quia absurdum*," says Emil Brunner, "it was Kierkegaard."[†] Those who love daylight, even in religion, will greet the absurd with less acclaim. To them it will still seem odd that one should have to become immoral in order to be religious. They may recall Halevy's remark that "virtue is more dangerous than vice, because its excesses are not subject to the restraints of conscience."

---

[*] H. J. Paton, *The Modern Predicament*, 120.
[†] *Revelation and Reason*, 310.

We have been dealing with the absurdity apprehended by faith in the field of morals. But it will be remembered that the central dogmas of the creed are also apprehended by faith, and are regarded as equally absurd. Sometimes the absurd is presented as the merely improbable. "Faith has in fact two tasks: to take care in every moment to discover the improbable, the paradox; and then to hold it fast with the passion of inwardness." Sometimes, as we have seen, the paradox that must be held fast is more than improbable; it is impossible. The central fact of Christianity, Kierkegaard holds, is the incarnation. "The object of faith is . . . the fact that God has existed as an individual human being." But he admits that by rational standards, this fact is inconceivable and inconsistent with itself. A being who is eternal or out of time cannot have measured out his life in human years. A being who is omnipresent could not be confined in his movements to a small area in the eastern Mediterranean. A being who is omniscient cannot grow in knowledge, or a being who is perfect grow in grace. A son who is a separate person from his father cannot also be one with the father; still less can three persons be one. So speaks logic. But faith requires us to put logic aside and accept what Kierkegaard admits to be a "contradiction." "In my God-relationship I have to learn precisely to give up my finite understanding, and therewith the custom of discrimination which is natural to me . . ." A man must somehow learn "to relinquish his understanding and his thinking, and to keep his soul fixed upon the absurd . . ." He must achieve "a crucifixion of the understanding," and by a leap of faith embrace the improbable and even impossible as nevertheless certain.

The difficulty with this claim is to attach definite meaning to it. If we were told that though a certain belief were improbable, we should try to make ourselves believe it, that would be intelligible, whether ethical or not. If we were told that a belief, though beyond our present understanding was vouched for by others who did understand it, and that through provisionally accepting this assurance we might come to understand it ourselves, that too would make sense. But if we are told that although a belief is both unintelligible and self-contradictory, we shall see that it is absolutely true and certain if we commit ourselves to it passionately enough, we can only question whether the proposer knows what he is asking of us. The law of contradiction is not a principle that is valid in some cases and not in others; if it is invalid in any case, it is invalid *as such* and therefore in every case. But if it is thus universally invalid, then in no case does the assertion of something as true exclude the truth of its denial, and *nothing* is true rather than untrue. And that makes assertion meaningless, for *what* could one be asserting? Just as Kierkegaard's ethics implies the denial of a realm of value, so his trans-logical truth undermines truth as we know it. Not that he saw this implication or held to it. If he had, he would not have argued at all. He was in fact proud of his prowess as a dialectician, and took pleasure in pitting himself against Hegel. But his philosophy terminates in a rejection of those very principles of logic on which he proceeded as a philosopher. He can hardly have it both ways. If the logic he assumes in his philosophy is valid, then the faith which stands at the summit of "the stages on life's way" is meaningless. If that irrational faith is accepted, the principles on which reflection conducts itself are everywhere impugned. In that case, Kierkegaard should merely smile like Buddha and remain silent.

What would he reply to all this? Probably that he was not concerned with the truth of doctrines at all; "Christianity is not a doctrine but an existential communication expressing an existential contradiction." He would fall back on his notion of subjectivity; ". . . the passion of the infinite is the truth. But the passion of the infinite is precisely subjectivity, and thus subjectivity becomes the truth." (This is of course an illicit minor, if logic still has any importance.) He would renew his attack on the attempt to understand, insisting that "the objective acceptance of Christianity is paganism or thoughtlessness." He would remind us that religion is a commitment of the will, that "Christianity wishes to intensify passion to its highest pitch," not to induce in us belief or comprehension. But we have seen that this will not do. Christianity does include beliefs, and it insists rightly or wrongly that these beliefs are true in the common and ancient sense. To adopt Kierkegaard's new sense, peculiar to himself and inconsistently held, which reduces truth to a passionate commitment of feeling and will, would not save Christianity; on the contrary, it would largely destroy it. For it implies that there are no common truths for Christians to accept, no common principles by which their lives may be guided, indeed no common Deity for them to contemplate and worship. The Kierkegaardian subjectivity would dissolve these things away into a set of processes in individual minds where there would be as many Christianities as there were persons to exercise their "inwardness" and their passion.

In this review of Kierkegaard on faith and reason, we have been examining the thought, not the man. *Ad hominem* reasoning, besides being distasteful, is never conclusive and is often self-defeating. But I do not wish to conceal my own belief that psychological causes as distinct from logical reasons had much to do with his conclusions. I cannot think that a psychopathologist would have much trouble in connecting the irrationalism of his thought with the irrationality of his temper. He said himself that his thought must be understood through his personality, and his personality was profoundly abnormal —so abnormal as to have cut him off from his fellows, his friends, and his own family. His alternations of exaltation and depression, his temptations to suicide, the feverish activity of an over-pressed brain in darkened rooms, the hysterical-sounding claims to being "a genius in a market town" and his comparison of himself to Christ, the frantic excoriations of church and clergy in his later years, his own report that he had stood on the verge of insanity—it would be a mistake to pass over these things as if they were wholly irrelevant. They suggest, though with a force difficult to assess, that Kierkegaard's singularities of thought were less the product of judicial reflection than the by-product of a sick spirit.

I will take two examples that may serve to make clear what I mean. First, his overwhelming, persistent, and surely morbid sense of guilt. This was partly an infection from his father, who lived in terror of having committed the unpardonable sin, partly the reaction to youthful irregularities on the part of an excessively introspective mind brought up in a theological hothouse. Georg Brandes reminds us that "he lived his life through in an atmosphere saturated with theology and theological discussion; at least three fourths of his near acquaintances appear to have been theologians, chaplains, ministers, bishops, clerics of every rank." This atmosphere kept alive and flourishing in Kierkegaard's anxious mind a conviction which, if exposed to the air and light of free secular discussion, would probably have been dissipated, the inherited Lutheran conviction that we were born in sin, utterly corrupted by it, and doomed by it to condemnation unless faith could somehow be won. Kierkegaard, like his father, lived in fear. "The whole of existence frightens me; from the smallest fly to the mystery of the incarnation everything is unintelligible to me, most of all myself; the whole of existence is poisoned in my sight, particularly myself." The cure for this fear was faith, and Kierkegaard was terrified that, by losing his faith, he might also lose his "eternal happiness"; he must therefore keep it at all costs.

He saw clearly the tendency of "objective thinking" to undermine and disintegrate this faith. Is there any wonder that an imaginative mind, living in a "sickness unto death" of fear, despair, and dread, should come to conceive of philosophy as the enemy? If one wished to preserve one's faith, it was safer not to play the philosophical game at all. "The ungodly calmness with which the irresolute man would begin in the case of God (for he would begin with doubt), precisely this is insubordination; for thereby God is deposed from the throne, from being the Lord. And when one has done this, one really has chosen another master, wilfulness . . ." To argue the case with the philosopher is to risk defeat on an issue too important by far to be dealt with by a match of wits. It is better to ignore him, to insist that faith is one thing and reason another, and to settle the issue decisively by a leap of faith. That is the only escape from despair.

For the other example of how Kierkegaard's thought is rooted in his life, we may refer to his too celebrated love affair. Much in his philosophy seems to have been a rationalization, in the Freudian sense, of his conduct in this affair. He had long contemplated with growing passion a neighbor's daughter, a girl in her teens named Regina Olsen. He at last declared himself, led her on to a whole-hearted reciprocating passion, then threw her abruptly over and went off to Berlin where he wrote up his experience in *The Diary of a Seducer* and other edifying discourses. By merely secular standards, his behavior was that of a cad, and he seems to have realized this, for running through much of his work from this time on, there is a veiled attempt to justify himself. To his credit, he has occasional doubts. "If I had had faith, I would have remained with Regina," he once confided to his diary.

But the line he more commonly took was that he threw her over because he did have faith, or at least because renouncing her would give exaltation to his spiritual life. He prefers to write about it in parables, but the reference is unmistakeable. "Love for that princess became for him the expression for an eternal love, assumed a religious character, was transfigured into a love for the Eternal Being, which did to be sure deny him the fulfilment of his love, yet reconciled him again by the eternal consciousness of its validity in the form of eternity, which no reality can take from him." In this treatment of her, the simple Regina was unable to share "the eternal consciousness of its validity in the form of eternity," and was broken-hearted. Kierkegaard probably realized that, as mentally and sexually abnormal, he was no fit person to marry at all, and if he had rested his desertion on such ground, one could understand it, though wondering why the discovery came so late. But such an explanation was not satisfactory to a mind in which a messianic egotism was mixed in unwholesome fashion with eroticism and piety. He had done wrong; he knew it; and if he was to retain his picture of himself as genius and saint, he must explain his action by lofty motives. He chose the loftiest. As Buber suggested, God was Regina's successful rival. The desertion was in obedience to a secret imperative from on high, which, like the hero of *Fear and Trembling,* he was ready to obey, whatever the cost in renunciation.

CONCLUDING DISILLUSIONED POSTSCRIPT

This is a grim note on which to end a study of Kierkegaard. He is a figure who of late years has received almost lyrical praise for the profundity of his thought and the penetration of his psychological insight. We have been assured that he "belongs to all time and to all humanity, just as surely as do Plato and Aristotle, Spinoza and Hume and Kant and Hegel."* We have been assured over and over of how profound he is. "Kierkegaard's explanation of the dialectical relation of freedom and fate in sin is one of the profoundest in Christian thought," and again, "Kierkegaard's analysis of the relation of anxiety to sin is the profoundest in Christian thought."† "Harnack's once celebrated essay on *The Essence of Christianity* seems incredibly trivial when one has read S. K."‡ I recall that, stimulated by such fair words, I approached his books with high expectation. My experience was like that of John Laird, who wrote, after a determined attempt on *Either/ Or:* "By the time I had finished the first enormous volume I was sadly disconsolate. Even in a wide literary interpretation of 'philosophy'— and no other could be appropriate—I found very little that seemed to be worth stating in a formal way." One reads a few puzzling pages with the feeling that the writer must be catching his breath and getting slowly under way; some definite point will soon emerge. It does not. One reads on with gathering disillusionment, coming in the end to realize that Kierkegaard, if a philosopher at all, is a distinct species of philosopher, and that it is useless to look for clearly stated theses, still less for ordered arguments in support of them. He combined an undisciplined intellect with a remorseless, facile, unchecked, limitless, compulsive loquacity; he was, as Disraeli said of Gladstone, "inebriated with the exuberance of his own verbosity." He is alleged to have written twenty-two books by the time he was thirty-five; and since they have no firm construction, no obvious beginning or end, or any internal reason why they should ever end, one can read them only by allowing one's critical sense to be lulled into drowsiness and one's mind to be floated along on the tide of words.

* D. F. Swenson in E. Geismar, *Søren Kierkegaard,* xvii.
† R. Niebuhr, *The Nature and Destiny of Man,* I, 263; I, 182, note.
‡ W. Lowrie, *Kierkegaard,* 5.

Unfortunately, no sooner has one made one's peace with the in-discipline of thought and style than one must begin the battle over again with the man himself. The self-absorption, the strange blend of piety and contempt (his two dominant emotions, Georg Brandes said), the dogmatism, the proclamations of unappreciated genius, the im-precations on church and clergy, the gospel of universal guilt and despair, the homilies on love from a mind that was simmering with hatreds, the scorn for those who, in religion, try to understand—these things have an effect that the reader must manage to suppress if he is to go on. He must remind himself that though this is a sick and twisted mind, such minds have, on occasion, shown a sharp eye for truth.

What was the truth that Kierkegaard saw? The great insight claimed for him is that in religion objective thinking breaks down and that the insight it seeks is obtainable by faith. As for the inadequacy of thought, a case can certainly be made for it, and such a case was actually presented with a force of statement and argument far beyond Kierkegaard's range by an English contemporary, Dean Mansel. Kierkegaard's own case is unimpressive. His contention that thought cannot deal with existence is put so obscurely that there is difficulty in extracting from it a meaning clear enough to refute. Furthermore, he seems never to have worked out what was involved for the normal exercise of reason by its breakdown at crucial points—for ethics by the suspension of its clearest rules, and for logic by the admission of contradictions to the status of higher truths. As a philosopher he employed with scornful confidence the reason which, as a theologian, he dismissed with equal scorn. He was too impatient to get on with his writing to declare a moratorium on it while he achieved coherence in this theory of knowledge.

What of the second half of the great insight attributed to him—that where reason fails faith succeeds? Unfortunately this is more obscure than the first. Perhaps it is inevitably so. When one has bid good-bye to reason and made the prodigious non-rational leap into the rarefied air of paradox, one should presumably say nothing, since anything one did say would have to be said in the distorting accents of the reason one has left behind. The silence, nevertheless, is a pity. Men struggle onward and upward along the stages on life's way; a hardy few reach the summit; and when they descend, the many wait-ing below ask a report on the splendid vision from the top. Kierkegaard, so voluble elsewhere, here finds his tongue at last tied. The stage that was supposed to cast illumination downward on all the others turns out to be strangely dark and empty. Practically, indeed, it is rather worse than empty. Kierkegaard insists that the love felt by the knight of faith is not mere human love, and if one can make any inference from his own practice, he was right, since the love displayed in that practice permitted a selfishness and harshness toward others—toward Hans Andersen and Regina and his mother and his brother and Bishop Mynster and the unfortunate "Christians" about him—which the lower love would not have allowed. Nor is the insight of faith into truth comparable with a merely human knowledge. Just as it gave Luther the power to see through and around Aristotle, so it gave Kierkegaard the power to see how superficial were all the systems of philosophy, and to see of science, without the need to study it, that if it differed from faith at any point, it was wrong.

In the end Kierkegaard stands, in his thought as in his life, a defeated figure. He was like a business man who builds up a commercial empire by condemning and buying up the businesses of all his competitors on the strength of promissory notes which he cannot redeem. He indicts reason; he indicts rational ethics; he indicts love and justice of the merely human variety; he indicts with eloquent contempt the Christianity practiced around him. He invites them all to accept subordination to one directing head in return for grandiose, even infinite, promises. But when they present their claims, they find the bank empty. The large promises of a new directorate are never fulfilled. Just how reason is to be rectified or ethics reformed, just what the new golden affections are that are to replace the old leaden ones, just what we are to believe or do or feel—these all-important directions never transpire. Faith has leaped so high that it has shot up beyond the earth's atmosphere to where thought and conscience can no longer breathe. These may be poor things, but we know them, and know that they have served us not badly. We shall do well to keep them, even when notes are flourished before us that are stamped in infinite denominations, unless we can be sure that the issuing bank is solvent. That assurance Kierkegaard never supplies.

3 BERTRAND RUSSELL (1872–1970)

AND

FATHER F. C. COPLESTON (1907–)

The Existence of God—A Debate*

This debate between Russell and Copleston was originally broadcast on the BBC's Third Programme series. Russell is widely known as both a philosopher and a political activist. In matters of religion he has taken an agnostic point of view. Copleston, on the other hand, is a leading Catholic philosopher and historian of philosophy. The debate ranges over many of the issues related to the existence of God, particularly those arguments for God's existence based on moral issues and on religious experiences. Copleston argues that the existence of God is the only thing that will "make sense of man's moral experience and of religious experience." Russell, however, argues that there are many ways of accounting for the feeling of moral obligation and for so-called religious experiences that do not necessitate the existence of a God.

* This debate was broadcast in 1948. It is used by permission of the British Broadcasting Corporation and Earl Russell and Father Copleston.

COPLESTON: As we are going to discuss the existence of God, it might perhaps be as well to come to some provisional agreement as to what we understand by the term "God." I presume that we mean a supreme personal being—distinct from the world and creator of the world. Would you agree—provisionally at least—to accept this statement as the meaning of the term "God"?

RUSSELL: Yes, I accept this definition.

COPLESTON: Well, my position is the affirmative position that such a being actually exists, and that His existence can be proved philosophically. Perhaps you would tell me if your position is that of agnosticism or of atheism. I mean, would you say that the non-existence of God can be proved?

RUSSELL: No, I should not say that: my position is agnostic.

COPLESTON: Would you agree with me that the problem of God is a problem of great importance? For example, would you agree that if God does not exist, human beings and human history can have no other purpose than the purpose they choose to give themselves, which—in practice—is likely to mean the purpose which those impose who have the power to impose it?

RUSSELL: Roughly speaking, yes, though I should have to place some limitation on your last clause.

COPLESTON: Would you agree that if there is no God—no absolute Being—there can be no absolute values? I mean, would you agree that if there is no absolute good that the relativity of values results?

RUSSELL: No, I think these questions are logically distinct. Take, for instance, G. E. Moore's *Principia Ethica*, where he maintains that there is a distinction of good and evil, that both of these are definite concepts. But he does not bring in the idea of God to support that contention.

COPLESTON: Well, suppose we leave the question of good till later, till we come to the moral argument, and I give first a metaphysical argument. I'd like to put the main weight on the metaphysical argument based on Leibniz's argument from "Contingency" and then later we might discuss the moral argument. Suppose I give a brief statement on the metaphysical argument and that then we go on to discuss it?

RUSSELL: That seems to me to be a very good plan.

COPLESTON: Well, for clarity's sake, I'll divide the argument into distinct stages. First of all, I should say, we know that there are at least some beings in the world which do not contain in themselves the reason for their existence. For example, I depend on my parents, and now on the air, and on food, and so on. Now, secondly, the world is simply the real or imagined totality or aggregate of individual objects, none of which contain in themselves alone the reason for their existence. There isn't any world distinct from the objects which form it, any more than the human race is something apart from the members. Therefore, I should say, since objects or events exist, and since no object of experience contains within itself the reason of its existence, this reason, the totality of objects, must have a reason external to itself. That reason must be an existent being. Well, this being is either itself the reason for its own existence, or it is not. If it is, well and good. If it is not, then we must proceed farther. But if we proceed to infinity in that sense, then there's no explanation of existence at all. So, I should say, in order to explain existence, we must come to a being which contains within itself the reason for its own existence, that is to say, which cannot not exist.

RUSSELL: This raises a great many points and it is not altogether easy to know where to begin, but I think that, perhaps, in answering your argument, the best point at which to begin is the question of necessary being. The word "necessary," I should maintain, can only be applied significantly to propositions. And, in fact, only to such as are analytic—

that is to say—such as it is self-contradictory to deny. I could only admit a necessary being if there were a being whose existence it is self-contradictory to deny. I should like to know whether you would accept Leibniz's division of propositions into truths of reason and truths of fact. The former—the truths of reason—being necessary.

COPLESTON: Well, I certainly should not subscribe to what seems to be Leibniz's idea of truths of reason and truths of fact, since it would appear that, for him, there are in the long run only analytic propositions. It would seem that for Leibniz truths of fact are ultimately reducible to truths of reason. That is to say, to analytic propositions, at least for an omniscient mind. Well, I couldn't agree with that. For one thing, it would fail to meet the requirements of the experience of freedom. I don't want to uphold the whole philosophy of Leibniz. I have made use of his argument from contingent to necessary being, basing the argument on the principle of sufficient reason, simply because it seems to me a brief and clear formulation of what is, in my opinion, the fundamental metaphysical argument for God's existence.

RUSSELL: But, to my mind, "a necessary proposition" has got to be analytic. I don't see what else it can mean. And analytic propositions are always complex and logically somewhat late. "Irrational animals are animals" is an analytic proposition; but a proposition such as "This is an animal" can never be analytic. In fact, all the propositions that can be analytic are somewhat late in the build-up of propositions.

COPLESTON: Take the proposition "If there is a contingent being then there is a necessary being." I consider that that proposition hypothetically expressed is a necessary proposition. If you are going to call every necessary proposition an analytic proposition, then—in order to avoid a dispute in terminology—I would agree to call it analytic, though I don't consider it a tautological proposition. But the proposition is a necessary proposition only on the supposition that there is a contingent being. That there is a contingent being actually existing has to be discovered by experience, and the proposition that there is a contingent being is certainly not an analytic proposition, though once you know, I should maintain, that there is a contingent being, it follows of necessity that there is a necessary being.

RUSSELL: The difficulty of this argument is that I don't admit the idea of a necessary being and I don't admit that there is any particular meaning in calling other beings "contingent." These phrases don't for me have a significance except within a logic that I reject.

COPLESTON: Do you mean that you reject these terms because they won't fit in with what is called "modern logic"?

RUSSELL: Well, I can't find anything that they could mean. The word "necessary," it seems to me, is a useless word, except as applied to analytic propositions, not to things.

COPLESTON: In the first place, what do you mean by "modern logic"? As far as I know, there are somewhat differing systems. In the second place, not all modern logicians surely would admit the meaninglessness of metaphysics. We both know, at any rate, one very eminent modern thinker whose knowledge of modern logic was profound, but who certainly did not think that metaphysics are meaningless or, in particular, that the problem of God is meaningless. Again, even if all modern logicians held that metaphysical terms are meaningless, it would not follow that they were right. The proposition that metaphysical terms are meaningless seems to me to be a proposition based on an assumed philosophy. The dogmatic position behind it seems to be this: What will not go into my machine is non-existent, or it is meaningless; it is the expression of emotion. I am simply trying to point out that anybody who says that a particular system of modern logic is the sole criterion of meaning is saying something that is over-dogmatic; he is dogmatically insisting that a part of philosophy is the whole of philosophy. After all, a "contingent" being is a being which has not in itself the complete reason for its existence, that's what I mean by a contingent being. You know, as well as I do, that the existence of neither of us can be explained without reference to something or somebody outside us, our parents, for example. A "necessary" being, on the other hand, means a being that must and cannot not exist. You may say that there is no such being, but you will find it hard to convince me that you do not understand the terms I am using. If you do not understand them, then how can you be entitled to say that such a being does not exist, if that is what you do say?

RUSSELL: Well, there are points here that I don't propose to go into at length. I don't maintain the meaninglessness of metaphysics in general at all. I maintain the meaninglessness of certain particular terms—not on any general ground, but simply because I've not been able to see an interpretation of those particular terms. It's not a general dogma—it's a particular thing. But those points I will leave out for the moment. And I will say that what you have been saying brings us back, it seems to me, to the ontological argument that there is a being whose essence involves existence, so that his existence is analytic. That seems to me to be impossible, and it raises, of course, the question what one means by existence, and as to this, I think a subject named can never be significantly said to exist but only a subject described. And that existence, in fact, quite definitely is not a predicate.

COPLESTON: Well, you say, I believe, that it is bad grammar, or rather bad syntax to say for example "T. S. Eliot exists"; one ought to say, for example, "He, the author of *Murder in the Cathedral,* exists." Are you going to say that the proposition, "The cause of the world exists," is without meaning? You may say that the world has no cause; but I fail to see how you can say that the proposition that "the cause of the world exists" is meaningless. Put it in the form of a question: "Has the world a cause?" or "Does a cause of the world exist?" Most people surely would understand the question, even if they don't agree about the answer.

RUSSELL: Well, certainly the question "Does the cause of the world exist?" is a question that has meaning. But if you say "Yes, God is the cause of the world" you're using God as a proper name; then "God exists" will not be a statement that has meaning; that is the position that I'm maintaining. Because, therefore, it will follow that it cannot be an analytic proposition ever to say that this or that exists. For example, suppose you take as your subject "the existent round-square," it would look like an analytic proposition that "the existent round-square exists," but it doesn't exist.

COPLESTON: No, it doesn't, then surely you can't say it doesn't exist unless you have a conception of what existence is. As to the phrase "existent round-square," I should say that it has no meaning at all.

RUSSELL: I quite agree. Then I should say the same thing in another context in reference to a "necessary being."

COPLESTON: Well, we seem to have arrived at an impasse. To say that a necessary being is a being that must exist and cannot not exist has for me a definite meaning. For you it has no meaning.

RUSSELL: Well, we can press the point a little, I think. A being that must exist and cannot not exist, would surely, according to you, be a being whose essence involves existence.

COPLESTON: Yes, a being the essence of which is to exist. But I should not be willing to argue the existence of God simply from the idea of His essence because I don't think we have any clear intuition of God's essence as yet. I think we have to argue from the world of experience to God.

RUSSELL: Yes, I quite see the distinction. But, at the same time, for a being with sufficient knowledge it would be true to say "Here is this being whose essence involves existence!"

COPLESTON: Yes, certainly if anybody saw God, he would see that God must exist.

RUSSELL: So that I mean there is a being whose essence involves existence although we don't know that essence. We only know there is such a being.

COPLESTON: Yes, I should add we don't know the essence *a priori*. It is only *a posteriori* through our experience of the world that we come to a knowledge of the existence of that being. And then one argues, the essence and existence must be identical. Because if God's essence and God's existence was not identical, then some sufficient reason for this existence would have to be found beyond God.

RUSSELL: So it all turns on this question of sufficient reason, and I must say you haven't defined "sufficient reason" in a way that I can understand—what do you mean by sufficient reason? You don't mean cause?

COPLESTON: Not necessarily. Cause is a kind of sufficient reason. Only contingent being can have a cause. God is His own sufficient reason; and He is not cause of Himself. By sufficient reason in the full sense I mean an explanation adequate for the existence of some particular being.

RUSSELL: But when is an explanation adequate? Suppose I am about to make a flame with a match. You may say that the adequate explanation of that is that I rub it on the box.

COPLESTON: Well, for practical purposes—but theoretically, that is only a partial explanation. An adequate explanation must ultimately be a total explanation, to which nothing further can be added.

RUSSELL: Then I can only say that you're looking for something which can't be got, and which one ought not to expect to get.

COPLESTON: To say that one has not found it is one thing; to say that one should not look for it seems to me rather dogmatic.

RUSSELL: Well, I don't know. I mean, the explanation of one thing is another thing which makes the other thing dependent on yet another, and you have to grasp this sorry scheme of things entire to do what you want, and that we can't do.

COPLESTON: But are you going to say that we can't, or we shouldn't even raise the question of the existence of the whole of this sorry scheme of things—of the whole universe?

RUSSELL: Yes. I don't think there's any meaning in it at all. I think the word "universe" is a handy word in some connections, but I don't think it stands for anything that has a meaning.

COPLESTON: If the word is meaningless, it can't be so very handy. In any case, I don't say that the universe is something different from the objects which compose it (I indicated that in my brief summary of the proof), what I'm doing is to look for the reason, in this case the cause of the objects—the real or imagined totality of which constitute what we call the universe. You say, I think that the universe—or my existence if you prefer, or any other existence—is unintelligible?

RUSSELL: First may I take up the point that if a word is meaningless it can't be handy. That sounds well but isn't in fact correct. Take, say, such a word as "the" or "than." You can't point to any object that those words mean, but they are very useful words; I should say the same of "universe." But leaving that point, you ask whether I consider that the universe is unintelligible. I shouldn't say unintelligible—I think it is without explanation. Intelligible, to my mind, is a different thing. Intelligible has to do with the thing itself intrinsically and not with its relations.

COPLESTON: Well, my point is that what we call the world is intrinsically unintelligible, apart from the existence of God. You see, I don't believe that the infinity of the series of events—I mean a horizontal series, so to speak—if such an infinity could be proved, would be in the slightest degree relevant to the situation. If you add up chocolates you get chocolates after all and not a sheep. If you add up chocolates to infinity, you presumably get an infinite number of chocolates. So if you add up contingent beings to infinity, you still get contingent beings, not a necessary being. An infinite series of contingent beings will be, to my way of thinking, as unable to cause itself as one contingent being. However, you say, I think, that it is illegitimate to raise the question of what will explain the existence of any particular object?

RUSSELL: It's quite all right if you mean by explaining it, simply finding a cause for it.

COPLESTON: Well, why stop at one particular object? Why shouldn't one raise the question of the cause of the existence of all particular objects?

RUSSELL: Because I see no reason to think there is any. The whole concept of cause is one we derive from our observation of particular things; I see no reason whatsoever to suppose that the total has any cause whatsoever.

COPLESTON: Well, to say that there isn't any cause is not the same thing as saying that we shouldn't look for a cause. The statement that there isn't any cause should come, if it comes at all, at the end of the inquiry, not the beginning. In any case, if the total has no cause, then to my way of thinking it must be its own cause, which seems to me impossible. Moreover, the statement that the world is simply there if in answer to a question, presupposes that the question has meaning.

RUSSELL: No, it doesn't need to be its own cause, what I'm saying is that the concept of cause is not applicable to the total.

COPLESTON: Then you would agree with Sartre that the universe is what he calls "gratuitous"?

RUSSELL: Well, the word "gratuitous" suggests that it might be something else; I should say that the universe is just there, and that's all.

COPLESTON: Well, I can't see how you can rule out the legitimacy of asking the question how the total, or anything at all comes to be there. Why something rather than nothing, that is the question? The fact that we gain our knowledge of causality empirically, from particular causes, does not rule out the possibility of asking what the cause of the series is. If the word "cause" were meaningless or if it could be shown that Kant's view of the matter were correct, the question would be illegitimate I agree; but you don't seem to hold that the word "cause" is meaningless, and I do not suppose you are a Kantian.

RUSSELL: I can illustrate what seems to me your fallacy. Every man who exists has a mother, and it seems to me your argument is that therefore the human race must have a mother, but obviously the human race hasn't a mother—that's a different logical sphere.

COPLESTON: Well, I can't really see any parity. If I were saying "every object has a phenomenal cause, therefore, the whole series has a phenomenal cause," there would be a parity; but I'm not saying that; I'm saying, every object has a phenomenal cause if you insist on the infinity of the series—but the series of phenomenal causes is an insufficient explanation of the series. Therefore, the series has not a phenomenal cause but a transcendent cause.

RUSSELL: That's always assuming that not only every particular thing in the world, but the world as a whole must have a cause. For that assumption I see no ground whatever. If you'll give me a ground I'll listen to it.

COPLESTON: Well, the series of events is either caused or it's not caused. If it is caused, there must obviously be a cause outside the series. If it's not caused then it's sufficient to itself, and if it's sufficient to itself it is what I call necessary. But it can't be necessary since each member is contingent, and we've agreed that the total has no reality apart from its members, therefore, it can't be necessary. Therefore, it can't be (caused)—uncaused—therefore it must have a cause. And I should like to observe in passing that the statement "the world is simply there and is inexplicable" can't be got out of logical analysis.

RUSSELL: I don't want to seem arrogant, but it does seem to me that I can conceive things that you say the human mind can't conceive. As for things not having a cause, the physicists assure us that individual quantum transitions in atoms have no cause.

COPLESTON: Well, I wonder now whether that isn't simply a temporary inference.

RUSSELL: It may be, but it does show that physicists' minds can conceive it.

COPLESTON: Yes, I agree, some scientists—physicists—are willing to allow for indetermination within a restricted field. But very many scientists are not so willing. I think that Professor Dingle, of London University, maintains that the Heisenberg uncertainty principle tells us something about the success (or the lack of it) of the present atomic theory in correlating observations, but not about nature in itself, and many physicists would accept this view. In any case, I don't see how physicists can fail to accept the theory in practice, even if they don't do so in theory. I cannot see how science could be conducted on any other assumption than that of order and intelligibility in nature. The physicist presupposes, at least tacitly, that there is some sense in investigating nature and looking for the causes of events, just as the detective presupposes that there is some sense in looking for the cause of a murder. The metaphysician assumes that there is sense in looking for the reason or cause of phenomena, and, not being a Kantian, I consider that the metaphysician is as justified in his assumption as the physicist. When Sartre, for example, says that the world is gratuitous, I think that he has not sufficiently considered what is implied by "gratuitous."

RUSSELL: I think—there seems to me a certain unwarrantable extension here; a physicist looks for causes; that does not necessarily imply that there are causes everywhere. A man may look for gold without assuming that there is gold everywhere; if he finds gold, well and good, if he doesn't he's had bad luck. The same is true when the physicists look for causes. As for Sartre, I don't profess to know what he means, and I shouldn't like to be thought to interpret him, but for my part, I do think the notion of the world having an explanation is a mistake. I don't see why one should expect it to have, and I think what you say about what the scientist assumes is an over-statement.

COPLESTON: Well, it seems to me that the scientist does make some such assumption. When he experiments to find out some particular truth, behind that experiment lies the assumption that the universe is not simply discontinuous. There is the possibility of finding out a truth by experiment. The experiment may be a bad one, it may lead to no result, or not to the result that he wants, but that at any rate there is the possibility, through experiment, of finding out the truth that he assumes. And that seems to me to assume an ordered and intelligible universe.

RUSSELL: I think you're generalizing more than is necessary. Undoubtedly the scientist assumes that this sort of thing is likely to be found and will often be found. He does not assume that it will be found, and that's a very important matter in modern physics.

COPLESTON: Well, I think he does assume or is bound to assume it tacitly in practice. It may be that, to quote Professor Haldane, "when I light the gas under the kettle, some of the water molecules will fly off as vapor, and there is no way of finding out which will do so," but it doesn't follow necessarily that the idea of chance must be introduced except in relation to our knowledge.

RUSSELL: No it doesn't—at least if I may believe what he says. He's finding out quite a lot of things—the scientist is finding out quite a lot of things that are happening in the world, which are, at first, beginnings of causal chains—first causes which haven't in themselves got causes. He does not assume that everything has a cause.

COPLESTON: Surely that's a first cause within a certain selected field. It's a relatively first cause.

RUSSELL: I don't think he'd say so. If there's a world in which most events, but not all, have causes, he will then be able to depict the probabilities and uncertainties by assuming that this particular event you're interested in probably has a cause. And since in any case you won't get more than probability that's good enough.

COPLESTON: It may be that the scientist doesn't hope to obtain more than probability, but in raising the question he assumes that the question of explanation has a meaning. But your general point then, Lord Russell, is that it's illegitimate even to ask the question of the cause of the world?

RUSSELL: Yes, that's my position.

COPLESTON: If it's a question that for you has no meaning, it's of course very difficult to discuss it, isn't it?

RUSSELL: Yes, it is very difficult. What do you say—shall we pass on to some other issue?

COPLESTON: Let's. Well, perhaps I might say a word about religious experience, and then we can go on to moral experience. I don't regard religious experience as a strict proof of the existence of God, so the character of the discussion changes somewhat, but I think it's true to say that the best explanation of it is the existence of God. By religious experience I don't mean simply feeling good. I mean a loving, but unclear, awareness of some object which irresistibly seems to the experiencer as something transcending the self, something transcending all the normal objects of experience, something which cannot be pictured or conceptualized, but of the reality of which doubt is impossible —at least during the experience. I should claim that cannot be explained adequately and without residue, simply subjectively. The actual basic experience at any rate is most easily explained on the hypothesis that there is actually some objective cause of that experience.

RUSSELL: I should reply to that line of argument that the whole argument from our own mental states to something outside us, is a very tricky affair. Even where we all admit its validity, we only feel justified in doing so, I think, because of the consensus of mankind. If there's a crowd in a room and there's a clock in a room, they can all see the clock. The fact that they can all see it tends to make them think that it's not an hallucination: whereas these religious experiences do tend to be very private.

COPLESTON: Yes, they do. I'm speaking strictly of mystical experience proper, and I certainly don't include, by the way, what are called visions. I mean simply the experience, and I quite admit it's indefinable, of the transcendent object or of what seems to be a transcendent object. I remember Julian Huxley in some lecture saying that religious experience, or mystical experience, is as much a real experience as falling in love or appreciating poetry and art. Well, I believe that when we appreciate poetry and art we appreciate definite poems or a definite work of art. If we fall in love, well, we fall in love with somebody and not with nobody.

RUSSELL: May I interrupt for a moment here. That is by no means always the case. Japanese novelists never consider that they have achieved a success unless large numbers of real people commit suicide for love of the imaginary heroine.

COPLESTON: Well, I must take your word for these goings on in Japan. I haven't committed suicide, I'm glad to say, but I have been strongly influenced in the taking of two important steps in my life by two biographies. However, I must say I see little resemblance between the real influence of those books on me and the mystic experience proper, so far, that is, as an outsider can obtain an idea of that experience.

RUSSELL: Well, I mean we wouldn't regard God as being on the same level as the characters in a work of fiction. You'll admit there's a distinction here?

COPLESTON: I certainly should. But what I'd say is that the best explanation seems to be the not purely subjectivist explanation. Of course, a subjectivist explanation is possible in the case of certain people in whom there is little relation between the experience and life, in the case of deluded people and hallucinated people, and so on. But when you get what one might call the pure type, say St. Francis of Assisi, when you get an experience that results in an overflow of dynamic and creative love, the best explanation of that it seems to me is the actual existence of an objective cause of the experience.

RUSSELL: Well, I'm not contending in a dogmatic way that there is not a God. What I'm contending is that we don't know that there is. I can only take what is recorded as I should take other records and I do find that a very great many things are reported, and I am sure you would not accept things about demons and devils and what not—and they're reported in exactly the same tone of voice and with exactly the same conviction. And the mystic, if his vision is veridical, may be said to know that there are devils. But I don't know that there are.

COPLESTON: But surely in the case of the devils there have been people speaking mainly of visions, appearances, angels or demons and so on. I should rule out the visual appearances, because I think they can be explained apart from the existence of the object which is supposed to be seen.

RUSSELL: But don't you think there are abundant recorded cases of people who believe that they've heard Satan speaking to them in their hearts, in just the same way as the mystics assert God—and I'm not talking of an external vision, I'm talking of a purely mental experience. That seems to be an experience of the same sort as mystics' experience of God, and I don't see that from what mystics tell us you can get any argument for God which is not equally an argument for Satan.

COPLESTON: I quite agree, of course, that people have imagined or thought they have heard or seen Satan. And I have no wish in passing to deny the existence of Satan. But I do not think that people have claimed to have experienced Satan in the precise way in which mystics claim to have experienced God. Take the case of a non-Christian, Plotinus. He admits the experience is something inexpressible, the object is an object of love, and therefore, not an object that causes horror and disgust. And the effect of that experience is, I should say, borne out, or I mean the validity of the experience is borne out in the records of the life of Plotinus. At any rate it is more reasonable to suppose that he had that experience if we're willing to accept Porphyry's account of Plotinus's general kindness and benevolence.

RUSSELL: The fact that a belief has a good moral effect upon a man is no evidence whatsoever in favor of its truth.

COPLESTON: No, but if it could actually be proved that the belief was actually responsible for a good effect on a man's life, I should consider it a presumption in favor of some truth, at any rate of the positive part of the belief if not of its entire validity. But in any case I am using the character of the life as evidence in favor of the mystic's veracity and sanity rather than as a proof of the truth of his beliefs.

RUSSELL: But even that I don't think is any evidence. I've had experiences myself that have altered my character profoundly. And I thought at the time at any rate that it was altered for the good. Those experiences were important, but they did not involve the existence of something outside me, and I don't think that if I'd thought they did, the fact that they had a wholesome effect would have been any evidence that I was right.

COPLESTON: No, but I think that the good effect would attest your veracity in describing your experience. Please remember that I'm not saying that a mystic's mediation or interpretation of his experience should be immune from discussion or criticism.

RUSSELL: Obviously the character of a young man may be—and often is—immensely affected for good by reading about some great man in history, and it may happen that the great man is a myth and doesn't exist, but the boy is just as much affected for good as if he did. There have been such people. Plutarch's *Lives* take Lycurgus as an example, who certainly did not exist, but you might be very much influenced by reading Lycurgus under the impression that he had previously existed. You would then be influenced by an object that you'd loved, but it wouldn't be an existing object.

COPELSTON: I agree with you on that, of course, that a man may be influenced by a character in fiction. Without going into the question of what it is precisely that influences him (I should say a real value) I think that the situation of that man and of the mystic are different. After all the man who is influenced by Lycurgus hasn't got the irresistible impression that he's experienced in some way the ultimate reality.

RUSSELL: I don't think you've quite got my point about these historical characters—these unhistorical characters in history. I'm not assuming what you call an effect on the reason. I'm assuming that the young man reading about this person and believing him to be real loves him—which is quite easy to happen, and yet he's loving a phantom.

COPLESTON: In one sense he's loving a phantom, that's perfectly true, in the sense, I mean, that he's loving X or Y who doesn't exist. But at the same time, it is not, I think, the phantom as such that the young man loves; he perceives a real value, an idea which he recognizes as objectively valid, and that's what excites his love.

RUSSELL: Well, in the same sense we had before about the characters in fiction.

COPLESTON: Yes, in one sense the man's loving a phantom—perfectly true. But in another sense he's loving what he perceives to be a value.

RUSSELL: But aren't you now saying in effect, I mean by God whatever is good or the sum total of what is good—the system of what is good, and, therefore, when a young man loves anything that is good he is loving God. Is that what you're saying, because if so, it wants a bit of arguing.

COPLESTON: I don't say, of course, that God is the sum total or system of what is good in the pantheistic sense; I'm not a pantheist, but I do think that all goodness reflects God in some way and proceeds from Him, so that in a sense the man who loves what is truly good, loves God even if he doesn't advert to God. But still I agree that the validity of such an interpretation of a man's conduct depends on the recognition of God's existence, obviously.

RUSSELL: Yes, but that's a point to be proved.

COPLESTON: Quite so, but I regard the metaphysical argument as probative, but there we differ.

RUSSELL: You see, I feel that some things are good and that other things are bad. I love the things that are good, that I think are good, and I hate the things that I think are bad. I don't say that these things are good because they participate in the Divine goodness.

COPLESTON: Yes, but what's your justification for distinguishing between good and bad or how do you view the distinction between them?

RUSSELL: I don't have any justification any more than I have when I distinguish between blue and yellow. What is my justification for distinguishing between blue and yellow? I can see they are different.

COPLESTON: Well, that is an excellent justification, I agree, You distinguish blue and yellow by seeing them, so you distinguish good and bad by what faculty?

RUSSELL: By my feelings.

COPLESTON: By your feelings. Well, that's what I was asking. You think that good and evil have reference simply to feeling?

RUSSELL: Well, why does one type of object look yellow and another look blue? I can more or less give an answer to that thanks to the physicists, and as to why I think one sort of thing good and another evil, probably there is an answer of the same sort, but it hasn't been gone into in the same way and I couldn't give it you.

COPLESTON: Well, let's take the behavior of the Commandant of Belsen. That appears to you as undesirable and evil and to me too. To Adolf Hitler we suppose it appeared as something good and desirable. I suppose you'd have to admit that for Hitler it was good and for you it is evil.

RUSSELL: No, I shouldn't quite go so far as that. I mean, I think people can make mistakes in that as they can in other things. If you have jaundice you see things yellow that are not yellow. You're making a mistake.

COPLESTON: Yes, one can make mistakes, but can you make a mistake if it's simply a question of reference to a feeling or emotion? Surely Hitler would be the only possible judge of what appealed to his emotions.

RUSSELL: It would be quite right to say that it appealed to his emotions, but you can say various things about that; among others, that if that sort of thing makes that sort of appeal to Hitler's emotions, then Hitler makes quite a different appeal to my emotions.

COPLESTON: Granted. But there's no objective criterion outside feeling then for condemning the conduct of the Commandant of Belsen, in your view?

RUSSELL: No more than there is for the color-blind person who's in exactly the same state. Why do we intellectually condemn the color-blind man? Isn't it because he's in the minority?

COPLESTON: I would say because he is lacking in a thing which normally belongs to human nature.

RUSSELL: Yes, but if he were in the majority, we shouldn't say that.

COPLESTON: Then you'd say that there's no criterion outside feeling that will enable one to distinguish between the behavior of the Commandant of Belsen and the behavior, say, of Sir Stafford Cripps or the Archbishop of Canterbury.

RUSSELL: The feeling is a little too simplified. You've got to take account of the effects of actions and your feelings towards those effects. You see, you can have an argument about it if you say that certain sorts of occurrences are the sort you like and certain others the sort you don't like. Then you have to take account of the effects of actions. You can very well say that the effects of the actions of the Commandant of Belsen were painful and unpleasant.

COPLESTON: They certainly were, I agree, very painful and unpleasant to all the people in the camp.

RUSSELL: Yes, but not only to the people in the camp, but to outsiders contemplating them also.

COPLESTON: Yes, quite true in imagination. But that's my point. I don't approve of them, and I know you don't approve of them, but I don't see what grounds you have for not approving of them, because after all, to the Commandant of Belsen himself, they're pleasant, those actions.

RUSSELL: Yes, but you see I don't need any more ground in that case than I do in the case of color perception. There are some people who think everything is yellow, there are people suffering from jaundice, and I don't agree with these people. I can't prove that the things are not yellow, there isn't any proof, but most people agree with me that they're not yellow, and most people agree with me that the Commandant of Belsen was making mistakes.

COPLESTON: Well, do you accept any moral obligation?

RUSSELL: Well, I should have to answer at considerable length to answer that. Practically speaking—yes. Theoretically speaking I should have to define moral obligation rather carefully.

COPLESTON: Well, do you think that the word "ought" simply has an emotional connotation?

RUSSELL: No, I don't think that, because you see, as I was saying a moment ago, one has to take account of the effects, and I think right conduct is that which would probably produce the greatest possible balance in intrinsic value of all the acts possible in the circumstances, and you've got to take account of the probable effects of your action in considering what is right.

COPLESTON: Well, I brought in moral obligation because I think that one can approach the question of God's existence in that way. The vast majority of the human race will make, and always have made, some distinction between right and wrong. The vast majority I think has some consciousness of an obligation in the moral sphere. It's my opinion that the perception of values and the consciousness of moral law and obligation are best explained through the hypothesis of a transcendent ground of value and of an author of the moral law. I do mean by "author of the moral law" an arbitrary author of the moral law. I think, in fact, that those modern atheists who have argued in the converse way "there is no God; therefore, there are no absolute values and no absolute law," are quite logical.

RUSSELL: I don't like the word "absolute." I don't think there is anything absolute whatever. The moral law, for example, is always changing. At one period in the development of the human race, almost everybody thought cannibalism was a duty.

COPLESTON: Well, I don't see that differences in particular moral judgments are any conclusive argument against the universality of the moral law. Let's assume for the moment that there are absolute moral values, even on that hypothesis it's only to be expected that different individuals and different groups should enjoy varying degrees of insight into those values.

RUSSELL: I'm inclined to think that "ought," the feeling that one has about "ought," is an echo of what has been told one by one's parents or one's nurses.

COPLESTON: Well, I wonder if you can explain away the idea of the "ought" merely in terms of nurses and parents. I really don't see how it can be conveyed to anybody in other terms than itself. It seems to me that if there is a moral order bearing upon the human conscience, that that moral order is unintelligible apart from the existence of God.

RUSSELL: Then you have to say one or other of two things. Either God only speaks to a very small percentage of mankind—which happens to include yourself—or He deliberately says things that are not true in talking to the consciences of savages.

COPLESTON: Well, you see, I'm not suggesting that God actually dictates moral precepts to the conscience. The human being's idea of the content of the moral law depends certainly to a large extent on education and environment, and a man has to use his reason in assessing the validity of the actual moral ideas of his social group. But the possibility of criticizing the accepted moral code presupposes that there is an objective standard, that there is an ideal moral order, which imposes itself (I mean the obligatory character of which can be recognized). I think that the recognition of this ideal moral order is part of the recognition of contingency. It implies the existence of a real foundation of God.

RUSSELL: But the law-giver has always been, it seems to me, one's parents or someone like. There are plenty of terrestrial law-givers to account for it, and that would explain why people's consciences are so amazingly different in different times and places.

COPLESTON: It helps to explain differences in the perception of particular moral values, which otherwise are inexplicable. It will help to explain changes in the matter of the moral law in the content of the precepts as accepted by this or that nation, or this or that individual. But the form of it, what Kant calls the categorical imperative, the "ought," I really don't see how that can possibly be conveyed to anybody by nurse or parent because there aren't any possible terms, so far as I can see, with which it can be explained. It can't be defined in other terms than itself, because once you've defined it in other terms than itself you've explained it away. It's no longer a moral "ought." It's something else.

RUSSELL: Well, I think the sense of "ought" is the effect of somebody's imagined disapproval, it may be God's imagined disapproval, but it's somebody's imagined disapproval. And I think that is what is meant by "ought."

COPLESTON: It seems to me to be external customs and taboos and things of that sort which can most easily be explained simply through environment and education, but all that seems to me to belong to what I call the matter of the law, the content. The idea of the "ought" as such can never be conveyed to a man by the tribal chief or by anybody else, because there are no other terms in which it could be conveyed. It seems to me entirely——[Russell breaks in].

RUSSELL: But I don't see any reason to say that—I mean we all know about conditioned reflexes. We know that an animal, if punished habitually for a certain sort of act, after a time will refrain. I don't think the animal refrains from arguing within himself, "Master will be angry if I do this." He has a feeling that that's not the thing to do. That's what we can do with ourselves and nothing more.

COPLESTON: I see no reason to suppose that an animal has a consciousness of moral obligation; and we certainly don't regard an animal as morally responsible for his acts of disobedience. But a man has a consciousness of obligation and of moral values. I see no reason to suppose that one could condition all men as one can "condition" an animal, and I don't suppose you'd really want to do so even if one could. If "behaviorism" were true, there would be no objective moral distinction between the emperor Nero and St. Francis of Assisi. I can't help feeling, Lord Russell, you know, that you regard the conduct of the Commandant at Belsen as morally reprehensible, and that you yourself would never under any circumstances act in that way, even if you thought, or had reason to think, that possibly the balance of the happiness of the human race might be increased through some people being treated in that abominable manner.

RUSSELL: No. I wouldn't imitate the conduct of a mad dog. The fact that I wouldn't do it doesn't really bear on this question we're discussing.

COPLESTON: No, but if you were making a utilitarian explanation of right and wrong in terms of consequences, it might be held, and I suppose some of the Nazis of the better type would have held that although it's lamentable to have to act in this way, yet the balance in the long run leads to greater happiness. I don't think you'd say that, would you? I think you'd say that that sort of action is wrong—and in itself, quite apart from whether the general balance of happiness is increased or not. Then, if you're prepared to say that, then I think you must have some criterion of right and wrong, that is outside the criterion of feeling, at any rate. To me, that admission would ultimately result in the admission of an ultimate ground of value in God.

RUSSELL: I think we are perhaps getting into confusion. It is not direct feeling about the act by which I should judge, but rather a feeling as to the effects. And I can't admit any circumstances in which certain kinds of behavior, such as you have been discussing, would do good. I can't imagine circumstances in which they would have a beneficial effect. I think the persons who think they do are deceiving themselves. But if there were circumstances in which they would have a beneficial effect, then I might be obliged, however reluctantly, to say— "Well, I don't like these things, but I will acquiesce in them," just as I acquiesce in the Criminal Law, although I profoundly dislike punishment.

COPLESTON: Well, perhaps it's time I summed up my position. I've argued two things. First, that the existence of God can be philosophically proved by a metaphysical argument; secondly, that it is only the existence of God that will make sense of man's moral experience and of religious experience. Personally, I think that your way of accounting for man's moral judgments leads inevitably to a contradiction between what your theory demands and your own spontaneous judgments. Moreover, your theory explains moral obligation away, and explaining away is not explanation. As regards the metaphysical argument, we are apparently in agreement that what we call the world consists simply of contingent beings. That is, of beings no one of which can account for its own existence. You say that the series of events needs no explanation: I say that if there were no necessary being, no being which must exist and cannot not exist, nothing would exist. The infinity of the series of contingent beings, even if proved, would be irrelevant. Something does exist; therefore, there must be something which accounts for this fact, a being which is outside the series of contingent beings. If you had admitted this, we could then have discussed whether that being is personal, good, and so on. On the actual point discussed, whether there is or is not a necessary being, I find myself, I think, in agreement with the great majority of classical philosophers.

You maintain, I think, that existing beings are simply there, and that I have no justification for raising the question of the explanation of their existence. But I would like to point out that this position cannot be substantiated by logical analysis; it expresses a philosophy which itself stands in need of proof. I think we have reached an impasse because our ideas of philosophy are radically different; it seems to me that what I call a part of philosophy, that you call the whole, insofar at least as philosophy is rational. It seems to me, if you will pardon my saying so, that besides your own logical system—which you call "modern" in opposition to antiquated logic (a tendentious adjective)—you maintain a philosophy which cannot be substantiated by logical analysis. After all, the problem of God's existence is an existential problem whereas logical analysis does not deal directly with problems of existence. So it seems to me, to declare that the terms involved in one set of problems are meaningless because they are not required in dealing with another set of problems, is to settle from the beginning the nature and extent of philosophy, and that is itself a philosophical act which stands in need of justification.

RUSSELL: Well, I should like to say just a few words by way of summary on my side. First, as to the metaphysical argument: I don't admit the connotations of such a term as "contingent" or the possibility of explanation in Father Copleston's sense. I think the word "contingent" inevitably suggests the possibility of something that wouldn't have this what you might call accidental character of just being there, and I don't think this is true except in the purely causal sense. You can sometimes give a causal explanation of one thing as being the effect of something else, but that is merely referring one thing to another thing and there's no—to my mind—explanation in Father Copleston's sense of anything at all, nor is there any meaning in calling things "contingent" because there isn't anything else they could be. That's what I should say about that, but I should like to say a few words about Father Copleston's accusation that I regard logic as all philosophy—that is by no means the case. I don't by any means regard logic as all philosophy. I think logic is an essential part of philosophy and logic has to be used in philosophy, and in that I think he and I are at one. When the logic that he uses was new—namely, in the time of Aristotle, there had to be a great deal of fuss made about it; Aristotle made a lot of fuss about that logic. Nowadays it's become old and respectable, and you don't have to make so much fuss about it. The logic that I believe in is comparatively new, and therefore I have to imitate Aristotle in making a fuss about it; but it's not that I think it's all philosophy by any means—I don't think so. I think it's an important part of philosophy, and when I say that, I don't find a meaning for this or that word, that is a position of detail based upon what I've found out about that particular word, from thinking about it. It's not a general position that all words that are used in metaphysics are nonsense, or anything like that which I don't really hold.

As regards the moral argument, I do find that when one studies anthropology or history, there are people who think it their duty to perform acts which I think abominable, and I certainly can't, therefore, attribute Divine origin to the matter of moral obligation, which Father Copleston doesn't ask me to; but I think even the form of moral obligation, when it takes the form of enjoining you to eat your father or what not, doesn't seem to me to be such a very beautiful and noble thing; and, therefore, I cannot attribute a Divine origin to this sense of moral obligation, which I think is quite easily accounted for in quite other ways.

4 DAVID HAIGHT AND MARJORIE HAIGHT

(1941–   ) (1943–   )

An Ontological Argument for the Devil *

The Haights demonstrate that the famous ontological argument for the existence of God as originally conceived by St. Anselm can also be used to prove the existence of the devil. Many debates and discussions have centered upon the ontological argument since its inception. The Haights' paper is not so much a discussion of the argument's form as it is designed to show that the Anselm argument presupposes and cannot prove its major point, that God is the greatest possible being.

* Reprinted from *The Monist*, Volume 54, Number 2 (April, 1970), La Salle, Illinois with the permission of the publisher and the authors.

A FTER so many centuries of debate, much of it even quite recent, as to the credibility of Anselm's and others' ontological arguments for the existence of God, it seems only fair to the opposition that some such argument be proposed for Satan's existence. It must be noted, however, that in advocating the Devil's existence, we may be no more than playing the Devil's advocate.

We intend to argue that *if* Anselm's first ontological argument successfully proves that God indeed exists, then, by parity of reasoning, Satan, or the devil, exists as well. Or, to put it conversely, we shall claim that if Satan does not exist, then neither can God, at least in terms of what the Anselmian argument asserts. Finally, we shall claim that if Satan does not exist, it will *not* be because of the possible fact that the ontological argument establishes God's existence, but rather it will be because of something that the Anselmian argument *presupposes*, which may not be provable in any argument.

Anselm's first argument, roughly, is as follows:

1. I have a concept of something "than which nothing greater can be conceived."

2. If that "something" did not actually, or in fact, exist, it would not be "that than which nothing greater can be conceived," for something could always be conceived to be greater, viz., something that actually exists.

3. This "greatest something" is, by logical equivalence, or definition, "God."

∴. God exists.

An ontological argument for the devil, by analogue of reason, goes as follows:

1. I have a concept of something than which nothing *worse* can be conceived.

2. If that "something" did not actually, or in fact, exist, it would not be "that than which nothing worse could be conceived," because something could always be conceived to be much worse, viz., something that actually exists.

3. This "greatest something" we shall call the Devil.

∴. The Devil exists.

This second ontological argument, by parity of reasoning with the first, seems sound, if indeed, the first is. Is it not conceivable that not only do we have an idea of something that is the worst possible thing, but that it would *have* to exist if it truly *were* the worst possible thing? Hence, the very possibility of the Devil implies his actuality, just as the very possibility of God implies his existence. The logic is the same, in both cases. A devil would not be the Devil unless he existed and was therefore the most awful thing, just as a god would not be God unless he existed and was therefore the greatest thing.

This ontological argument for Satan seems shocking enough, at least at first reading, but something even more startling might be suggested: the two arguments are not only analogous—they are identical. Might it not be suggested that they both establish the existence of the *one* thing—call it God or Satan—namely, a supreme Being who is the "greatest" and the "worst" possible being. This suggestion, however, can be made good *only if* it can be plausibly argued that the word 'greater' in the first argument does *not* imply the word 'better'. For it is surely the case that if Anselm means "better" when he uses the word 'greater', there would be an overt contradiction between the two ontological arguments, viz., the conflict between a "best being" and a "worst being." But does Anselm, in fact, mean "better" by 'greater'? It has definitely been claimed, subsequent to Anselm, that his argument assumes "existence to be a perfection," or that it is *better* to be than not to be, and, with this supplementation, it certainly seems to be the case that Anselm equated the two terms or at least implied the one by the other.

But is this really explicit in Anselm's argument? Is he saying that existence is a perfection? If he is, then his argument seems question-begging, because the argument seems to assume what it purports to prove, viz., that it is better for God to exist than not to exist. Presumably, too, if existence is good, God must be good, but one may not be able to assume that existence is good without, first, proving that God exists and is good. Hence, one cannot, or must not, reverse the order of argument such as Anselm seems to do—one must not assume that existence is good or a perfection unless one has *already* proved God's existence. But, actually, the plausibility of Anselm's proof, at least as it has been here paraphrased, is partly contingent upon the word 'greater.' The "greatest" possible being must be God. Or, it might be the Devil, for it does not follow from Anselm's argument that God is good, only that he exists. And if the word 'greater' does not involve "perfection," then both ontological arguments establish the existence of one and only one being. It is then a matter of faith as to whether one calls it God or Satan, a benign *daemon* or a malicious demon. And this faith may, after all, be simply cause of itself.

5 WILLIAM JAMES

(1842–1910)

Mystical Religious Experiences *

James was famous as a psychologist and a philosopher. His brother was the distinguished novelist Henry James. The work of William James in philosophy was greatly influenced by C. S. Peirce, from whom he adopted pragmatism. James's scientific background fostered in his philosophy a concern for detail and description, which is reflected in this selection. His book The Varieties of Religious Experience, from which this material is taken, is considered a classic in the philosophy and psychology of religion. It is rich not only in James's own views but with a wealth of information including examples of mysticism from both Western and Eastern sources.

* From William James, *The Varieties of Religious Experience* (1902), Lects. XVI, XVII, with deletions.

OVER and over again in these lectures I have raised points and left them open and unfinished until we should have come to the subject of Mysticism. Some of you, I fear, may have smiled as you noted my reiterated postponements. But now the hour has come when mysticism must be faced in good earnest, and those broken threads wound up together. One may say truly, I think, that personal religious experience has its root and centre in mystical states of consciousness; so for us, who in these lectures are treating personal experience as the exclusive subject of our study, such states of consciousness ought to form the vital chapter from which the other chapters get their light. Whether my treatment of mystical states will shed more light or darkness, I do not know, for my own constitution shuts me out from their enjoyment almost entirely, and I can speak of them only at second hand. But though forced to look upon the subject so externally, I will be as objective and receptive as I can; and I think I shall at least succeed in convincing you of the reality of the states in question, and of the paramount importance of their function.

First of all, then, I ask, What does the expression 'mystical states of consciousness' mean? How do we part off mystical states from other states?

The words 'mysticism' and 'mystical' are often used as terms of mere reproach, to throw at any opinion which we regard as vague and vast and sentimental, and without a base in either facts or logic. For some writers a 'mystic' is any person who believes in thought-transference, or spirit-return. Employed in this way the word has little value: there are too many less ambiguous synonyms. So, to keep it useful by restricting it, I will do what I did in the case of the word 'religion,' and simply propose to you four marks which, when an experience has them, may justify us in calling it mystical for the purpose of the present lectures. In this way we shall save verbal disputation, and the recriminations that generally go therewith.

1. *Ineffability.*—The handiest of the marks by which I classify a state of mind as mystical is negative. The subject of it immediately says that it defies expression, that no adequate report of its contents can be given in words. It follows from this that its quality must be directly experienced; it canot be imparted or transferred to others. In this peculiarity mystical states are more like states of feeling than like states of intellect. No one can make clear to another who has never had a certain feeling, in what the quality or worth of it consists. One must have musical ears to know the value of a symphony; one must have been in love one's self to understand a lover's state of mind. Lacking the heart or ear, we cannot interpret the musician or the lover justly, and are even likely to consider him weak-minded or absurd. The mystic finds that most of us accord to his experiences an equally incompetent treatment.

2. *Noetic quality.*—Although so similar to states of feeling, mystical states seem to those who experience them to be also states of knowledge. They are states of insight into depths of truth unplumbed by the discursive intellect. They are illuminations, revelations, full of significance and importance, all inarticulate though they remain; and as a rule they carry with them a curious sense of authority for after-time.

These two characters will entitle any state to be called mystical, in the sense in which I use the word. Two other qualities are less sharply marked, but are usually found. These are:—

3. *Transiency.*—Mystical states cannot be sustained for long. Except in rare instances, half an hour, or at most an hour or two, seems to be the limit beyond which they fade into the light of common day. Often, when faded, their quality can but imperfectly be reproduced in memory; but when they recur it is recognized; and from one recurrence to another it is susceptible of continuous development in what is felt as inner richness and importance.

4. *Passivity.*—Although the oncoming of mystical states may be facili-

tated by preliminary voluntary operations, as by fixing the attention, or going through certain bodily performances, or in other ways which manuals of mysticism prescribe; yet when the characteristic sort of consciousness once has set in, the mystic feels as if his own will were in abeyance, and indeed sometimes as if he were grasped and held by a superior power. This latter peculiarity connects mystical states with certain definite phenomena of secondary or alternative personality, such as prophetic speech, automatic writing, or the mediumistic trance. When these latter conditions are well pronounced, however, there may be no recollection whatever of the phenomenon, and it may have no significance for the subject's usual inner life, to which, as it were, it makes a mere interruption. Mystical states, strictly so called, are never merely interruptive. Some memory of their content always remains, and a profound sense of their importance. They modify the inner life of the subject between the times of their recurrence. Sharp divisions in this region are, however, difficult to make, and we find all sorts of gradations and mixtures.

These four characteristics are sufficient to mark out a group of states of consciousness peculiar enough to deserve a special name and to call for careful study. Let it then be called the mystical group.

Our next step should be to gain acquaintance with some typical examples. Professional mystics at the height of their development have often elaborately organized experiences and a philosophy based thereupon. But you remember what I said in my first lecture: phenomena are best understood when placed within their series, studied in their germ and in their over-ripe decay, and compared with their exaggerated and degenerated kindred. The range of mystical experience is very wide, much too wide for us to cover in the time at our disposal. Yet the method of serial study is so essential for interpretation that if we really wish to reach conclusions we must use it. I will begin, therefore, with phenomena which claim no special religious significance, and end with those of which the religious pretensions are extreme.

The simplest rudiment of mystical experience would seem to be that deepened sense of the significance of a maxim or formula which occasionally sweeps over one. "I've heard that said all my life," we exclaim, "but I never realized its full meaning until now." "When a fellow-monk," said Luther, "one day repeated the words of the Creed: 'I believe in the forgiveness of sins,' I saw the Scripture in an entirely new light; and straightway I felt as if I were born anew. It was as if I had found the door of paradise thrown wide open." This sense of deeper significance is not confined to rational propositions. Single words, and conjunctions of words, effects of light on land and sea, odors and musical sounds, all bring it when the mind is tuned aright. Most of us can remember the strangely moving power of passages in certain poems read when we were young, irrational doorways as they were through which the mystery of fact, the wildness and the pang of life, stole into our hearts and thrilled them. The words have now perhaps become mere polished surfaces for us; but lyric poetry and music are alive and significant only in proportion as they fetch these vague vistas of a life continuous with our own, beckoning and inviting, yet ever eluding our pursuit. We are alive or dead to the eternal inner message of the arts according as we have kept or lost this mystical susceptibility.

A more pronounced step forward on the mystical ladder is found in an extremely frequent phenomenon, that sudden feeling, namely, which sometimes sweeps over us, of having 'been here before,' as if at some indefinite past time, in just this place, with just these people, we were already saying just these things. Sir James Crichton-Browne has given the technical name of 'dreamy states' to these sudden invasions of vaguely reminiscent consciousness. They bring a sense of mystery and of the metaphysical duality of things, and the feeling of an enlargement of perception which seems imminent but which never completes itself. In Dr. Crichton-Browne's opinion they connect themselves with the perplexed and scared disturbances of self-consciousness which occasionally precede epileptic attacks. I think that this learned alienist takes a rather absurdly alarmist view of an intrinsically insignificant phenomenon. He follows it along the downward ladder, to insanity; our path pursues the upward ladder chiefly. The divergence shows how important it is to neglect no part of a phenomenon's connections, for we make it appear admirable or dreadful according to the context by which we set it off.

. . .

A . . . more extreme state of mystical consciousness is described by J. A. Symonds; and probably more persons than we suspect could give parallels to it from their own experience.

> "Suddenly," writes Symonds, "at church, or in company, or when I was reading, and always, I think, when my muscles were at rest, I felt the approach of the mood. Irresistibly it took possession of my mind and will, lasted what seemed an eternity, and disappeared in a series of rapid sensations which resembled the awakening from anæsthetic influence. One reason why I disliked this kind of trance was that I could not describe it to myself. I cannot even now find words to render

it intelligible. It consisted in a gradual but swiftly progressive oblitera-
tion of space, time, sensation, and the multitudinous factors of experience which seem to qualify what we are pleased to call our Self. In
proportion as these conditions of ordinary consciousness were subtracted, the sense of an underlying or essential consciousness acquired
intensity. At last nothing remained but a pure, absolute, abstract Self.
The universe became without form and void of content. But Self per-
sisted, formidable in its vivid keenness, feeling the most poignant
doubt about reality, ready, as it seemed, to find existence break as
breaks a bubble round about it. And what then? The apprehension of
a coming dissolution, the grim conviction that this state was the last
state of the conscious Self, the sense that I had followed the last thread
of being to the verge of the abyss, and had arrived at demonstration
of eternal Maya or illusion, stirred or seemed to stir me up again. The
return to ordinary conditions of sentient existence began by my first
recovering the power of touch, and then by the gradual though rapid
influx of familiar impressions and diurnal interests. At last I felt myself
once more a human being; and though the riddle of what is meant by
life remained unsolved, I was thankful for this return from the abyss—
this deliverance from so awful an initiation into the mysteries of
skepticism.

"This trance recurred with diminishing frequency until I reached
the age of twenty-eight. It served to impress upon my growing nature
the phantasmal unreality of all the circumstances which contribute to
a merely phenomenal consciousness. Often have I asked myself with
anguish, on waking from that formless state of denuded, keenly sentient
being. Which is the unreality?—the trance of fiery, vacant, apprehen-
sive, skeptical Self from which I issue, or these surrounding phenomena and habits which veil that inner Self and build a self of flesh-and-
blood conventionality? Again, are men the factors of some dream, the
dream-like unsubstantiality of which they comprehend at such event-
ful moments? What would happen if the final stage of the trance were
reached?" [1]

In a recital like this there is certainly something suggestive of pa-
thology. The next step into mystical states carries us into a realm that
public opinion and ethical philosophy have long since branded as
pathological, though private practice and certain lyric strains of poetry
seem still to bear witness to its ideality. I refer to the consciousness
produced by intoxicants and anæsthetics, especially by alcohol. The
sway of alcohol over mankind is unquestionably due to its power to
stimulate the mystical faculties of human nature, usually crushed to
earth by the cold facts and dry criticisms of the sober hour. Sobriety

[1] H. F. Brown: J. A. Symonds, a Biography, London, 1895, pp. 29–31, abridged.

diminishes, discriminates, and says no; drunkenness expands, unites, and says yes. It is in fact the great exciter of the *Yes* function in man. It brings its votary from the chill periphery of things to the radiant core. It makes him for the moment one with truth. Not through mere perversity do men run after it. To the poor and the unlettered it stands in the place of symphony concerts and of literature; and it is part of the deeper mystery and tragedy of life that whiffs and gleams of something that we immediately recognize as excellent should be vouchsafed to so many of us only in the fleeting earlier phases of what in its totality is so degrading a poisoning. The drunken consciousness is one bit of the mystic consciousness, and our total opinion of it must find its place in our opinion of that larger whole.

Nitrous oxide and ether, especially nitrous oxide, when sufficiently diluted with air, stimulate the mystical consciousness in an extraordinary degree. Depth beyond depth of truth seems revealed to the inhaler. This truth fades out, however, or escapes, at the moment of coming to; and if any words remain over in which it seemed to clothe itself, they prove to be veriest nonsense. Nevertheless, the sense of a profound meaning having been there persists; and I know more than one person who is persuaded that in the nitrous oxide trance we have a genuine metaphysical revelation.

Some years ago I myself made some observations on this aspect of nitrous oxide intoxication, and reported them in print. One conclusion was forced upon my mind at that time, and my impression of its truth has ever since remained unshaken. It is that our normal waking consciousness, rational consciousness as we call it, is but one special type of consciousness, whilst all about it, parted from it by the filmiest of screens, there lie potential forms of consciousness entirely different. We may go through life without suspecting their existence; but apply the requisite stimulus, and at a touch they are there in all their completeness, definite types of mentality which probably somewhere have their field of application and adaptation. No account of the universe in its totality can be final which leaves these other forms of consciousness quite disregarded. How to regard them is the question,—for they are so discontinuous with ordinary consciousness. Yet they may determine attitudes though they cannot furnish formulas, and open a region though they fail to give a map. At any rate, they forbid a premature closing of our accounts with reality. Looking back on my own experiences, they all converge towards a kind of insight to which I cannot help ascribing some metaphysical significance. The keynote of it is invariably a reconciliation. It is as if the opposites of the world, whose contradictoriness and conflict make all our difficulties and troubles,

were melted into unity. Not only do they, as contrasted species, belong
to one and the same genus, but *one of the species,* the nobler and better
one, *is itself the genus, and so soaks up and absorbs its opposite into
itself.* This is a dark saying, I know, when thus expressed in terms of
common logic, but I cannot wholly escape from its authority. I feel as
if it must mean something, something like what the Hegelian philosophy means, if one could only lay hold of it more clearly. Those who
have ears to hear, let them hear; to me the living sense of its reality
only comes in the artificial mystic state of mind.

I just now spoke of friends who believe in the anæsthetic revelation.
For them too it is a monistic insight, in which the *other* in its various
forms appears absorbed into the One.

> "Into this pervading genius," writes one of them, "we pass, forgetting
> and forgotten, and thenceforth each is all, in God. There is no higher,
> no deeper, no other, than the life in which we are founded. 'The One
> remains, the many change and pass'; and each and every one of us
> is the One that remains. . . . This is the ultimatum. . . . As sure as
> being—whence is all our care—so sure is content, beyond duplexity,
> antithesis, or trouble, where I have triumphed in a solitude that God
> is not above."

This has the genuine religious mystic ring! I just now quoted J. A.
Symonds. He also records a mystical experience with chloroform, as
follows:—

> After the choking and stifling had passed away, I seemed at first in
> a state of utter blankness; then came flashes of intense light, alter-
> nating with blackness, and with a keen vision of what was going on
> in the room around me, but no sensation of touch. I thought that I
> was near death; when, suddenly, my soul became aware of God, who
> was manifestly dealing with me, handling me, so to speak, in an in-
> tense personal present reality. I felt him streaming in like light upon
> me. . . . I cannot describe the ecstasy I felt. Then, as I gradually awoke
> from the influence of the anaesthetics, the old sense of my relation
> to the world began to return, the new sense of my relation to God
> began to fade. I suddenly leapt to my feet on the chair where I was
> sitting, and shrieked out, 'It is too horrible, it is too horrible, it is too
> horrible,' meaning that I could not bear this disillusionment. Then I
> flung myself on the ground, and at last awoke covered with blood,
> calling to the two surgeons (who were frightened), 'Why did you
> not kill me? Why would you not let me die?' Only think of it. To
> have felt for that long dateless ecstasy of vision the very God, in
> all purity and tenderness and truth and absolute love, and then to
> find that I had after all had no revelation, but that I had been tricked
> by the abnormal excitement of my brain.

Yet, this question remains, Is it possible that the inner sense of reality which succeeded, when my flesh was dead to impressions from without, to the ordinary sense of physical relations, was not a delusion but an actual experience? Is it possible that I, in that moment, felt what some of the saints have said they always felt, the undemonstrable but irrefragable certainty of God? [2]

With this we make connection with religious mysticism pure and simple. Symonds's question takes us back to those examples which you will remember my quoting in the lecture on the Reality of the Unseen, of sudden realization of the immediate presence of God. The phenomenon in one shape or another is not uncommon.

. . .

Certain aspects of nature seem to have a peculiar power of awakening such mystical moods. Most of the striking cases which I have collected have occurred out of doors. Literature has commemorated this fact in many passages of great beauty—this extract, for example, from Amiel's Journal Intime:—

Shall I ever again have any of those prodigious reveries which sometimes came to me in former days? One day, in youth, at sunrise, sitting in the ruins of the castle of Faucigny; and again in the mountains, under the noonday sun, above Lavey, lying at the foot of a tree and visited by three butterflies; once more at night upon the shingly shore of the Northern Ocean, my back upon the sand and my vision ranging through the milky way; such grand and spacious immortal, cosmogonic reveries, when one reaches to the stars, when one owns the infinite! Moments divine, ecstatic hours; in which our thought flies from world to world, pierces the great enigma, breathes with a respiration broad, tranquil, and deep as the respiration of the ocean, serene and limitless as the blue firmament; . . . instants of irresistible intuition in which one feels one's self great as the universe, and calm as a god. . . . What hours, what memories! The vestiges they leave behind are enough to fill us with belief and enthusiasm, as if they were visits of the Holy Ghost.

The well-known passage from Walt Whitman is a classical expression of this sporadic type of mystical experience.

I believe in you, my Soul . . .
Loaf with me on the grass, loose the stop from your throat; . . .
Only the lull I like, the hum of your valved voice.

[2] Op. cit., pp. 78–80, abridged.

I mind how once we lay, such a transparent summer morning.
Swiftly arose and spread around me the peace and knowledge that
    pass all the argument of the earth,
And I know that the hand of God is the promise of my own,
And I know that the spirit of God is the brother of my own,
And that all the men ever born are also my brothers and the women
    my sisters and lovers,
And that a kelson of the creation is love.

I could easily give more instances, but one will suffice. I take it from
the Autobiography of J. Trevor.[3]

> One brilliant Sunday morning, my wife and boys went to the Unitarian
> Chapel in Macclesfield. I felt it impossible to accompany them—as
> though to leave the sunshine on the hills, and go down there to the
> chapel, would be for the time an act of spiritual suicide. And I felt
> such need for new inspiration and expansion in my life. So, very
> reluctantly and sadly, I left my wife and boys to go down into the
> town, while I went further up into the hills with my stick and my
> dog. In the loveliness of the morning, and the beauty of the hills and
> valleys, I soon lost my sense of sadness and regret. For nearly an
> hour I walked along the road to the 'Cat and Fiddle,' and then re-
> turned. On the way back, suddenly, without warning, I felt that I
> was in Heaven—an inward state of peace and joy and assurance in-
> describably intense, accompanied with a sense of being bathed in
> a warm glow of light, as though the external condition had brought
> about the internal effect—a feeling of having passed beyond the body,
> though the scene around me stood out more clearly and as if nearer
> to me than before, by reason of the illumination in the midst of which
> I seemed to be placed. This deep emotion lasted, though with de-
> creasing strength, until I reached home, and for some time after,
> only gradually passing away.

The writer adds that having had further experiences of a similar
sort, he now knows them well.

> "The spiritual life," he writes, "justifies itself to those who live it; but
> what can we say to those who do not understand? This, at least, we
> can say, that it is a life whose experiences are proved real to their
> possessor, because they remain with him when brought closest into
> contact with the objective realities of life. Dreams cannot stand this
> test. We wake from them to find that they are but dreams. Wander-
> ings of an overwrought brain do not stand this test. These highest
> experiences that I have had of God's presence have been rare and
> brief—flashes of consciousness which have compelled me to exclaim

[3] My Quest for God, London, 1897, pp. 268, 269, abridged.

with surprise—God is *here!*—or conditions of exaltation and insight, less intense, and only gradually passing away. I have severely questioned the worth of these moments. To no soul have I named them, lest I should be building my life and work on mere phantasies of the brain. But I find that, after every questioning and test, they stand out to-day as the most real experiences of my life, and experiences which have explained and justified and unified all past experiences and all past growth. Indeed, their reality and their far-reaching significance are ever becoming more clear and evident. When they came, I was living the fullest, strongest, sanest, deepest life. I was not seeking them. What I was seeking, with resolute determination, was to live more intensely my own life, as against what I knew would be the adverse judgment of the world. It was in the most real seasons that the Real Presence came, and I was aware that I was immersed in the infinite ocean of God." [4]

Even the least mystical of you must by this time be convinced of the existence of mystical moments as states of consciousness of an entirely specific quality, and of the deep impression which they make on those who have them. A Canadian psychiatrist, Dr. R. M. Bucke, gives to the more distinctly characterized of these phenomena the name of cosmic consciousness. "Cosmic consciousness in its more striking instances is not," Dr. Bucke says, "simply an expansion or extension of the self-conscious mind with which we are all familiar, but the super-addition of a function as distinct from any possessed by the average man as *self*-consciousness is distinct from any function possessed by one of the higher animals."

The prime characteristic of cosmic consciousness is a consciousness of the cosmos, that is, of the life and order of the universe. Along with the consciousness of the cosmos there occurs an intellectual enlightenment which alone would place the individual on a new plane of existence—would make him almost a member of a new species. To this is added a state of moral exaltation, an indescribable feeling of elevation, elation, and joyousness, and a quickening of the moral sense, which is fully as striking, and more important than is the enhanced intellectual power. With these come what may be called a sense of immortality, a consciousness of eternal life, not a conviction that he shall have this, but the consciousness that he has it already. [5]

It was Dr. Bucke's own experience of a typical onset of cosmic consciousness in his own person which led him to investigate it in others.

[4] Op. cit., pp. 256, 257, abridged.
[5] Cosmic Consciousness: a study in the evolution of the human Mind, Philadelphia, 1901, p. 2.

He has printed his conclusions in a highly interesting volume, from which I take the following account of what occurred to him:—

> I had spent the evening in a great city, with two friends, reading and discussing poetry and philosophy. We parted at midnight. I had a long drive in a hansom to my lodging. My mind, deeply under the influence of the ideas, images, and emotions called up by the reading and talk, was calm and peaceful. I was in a state of quiet, almost passive enjoyment, not actually thinking, but letting ideas, images, and emotions flow of themselves, as it were, through my mind. All at once, without warning of any kind, I found myself wrapped in a flame-colored cloud. For an instant I thought of fire, an immense conflagration somewhere close by in the great city; the next, I knew that the fire was within myself. Directly afterward there came upon me a sense of exultation, of immense joyousness accompanied or immediately followed by an intellectual illumination impossible to describe. Among other things, I did not merely come to believe, but I saw that the universe is not composed of dead matter, but is, on the contrary, a living Presence: I became conscious in myself of eternal life. It was not a conviction that I would have eternal life, but a consciousness that I possessed eternal life then; I saw that all men are immortal; that the cosmic order is such that without any peradventure all things work together for the good of each and all; that the foundation principle of the world, of all the worlds, is what we call love, and that the happiness of each and all is in the long run absolutely certain. The vision lasted a few seconds and was gone; but the memory of it and the sense of the reality of what it taught has remained during the quarter of a century which has since elapsed. I knew that what the vision showed was true. I had attained to a point of view from which I saw that it must be true. That view, that conviction, I may say that consciousness, has never, even during periods of the deepest depression, been lost.[6]

We have now seen enough of this cosmic or mystic consciousness, as it comes sporadically. We must next pass to its methodical cultivation as an element of the religious life. Hindus, Buddhists, Mohammedans, and Christians all have cultivated it methodically.

In India, training in mystical insight has been known from time immemorial under the name of yoga. Yoga means the experimental union of the individual with the divine. It is based on persevering exercise; and the diet, posture, breathing, intellectual concentration, and moral discipline vary slightly in the different systems which teach

---

[6] Loc. cit., pp. 7, 8. My quotation follows the privately printed pamphlet which preceded Dr. Bucke's larger work, and differs verbally a little from the text of the latter

it. The yogi, or disciple, who has by these means overcome the obscurations of his lower nature sufficiently, enters into the condition termed *samâdhi*, "comes face to face with facts which no instinct or reason can ever know." He learns—

> That the mind itself has a higher state of existence, beyond reason, a superconscious state, and that when the mind gets to that higher state, then this knowledge beyond reasoning comes. . . . All the different steps in yoga are intended to bring us scientifically to the superconscious state or samâdhi. . . . Just as unconscious work is beneath consciousness, so there is another work which is above consciousness, and which, also, is not accompanied with the feeling of egoism. . . . There is no feeling of *I*, and yet the mind works, desireless, free from restlessness, objectless, bodiless. Then the Truth shines in its full effulgence, and we know ourselves—for Samâdhi lies potential in us all—for what we truly are, free, immortal, omnipotent, loosed from the finite, and its contrasts of good and evil altogether, and identical with the Atman or Universal Soul.[7]

The Vedantists say that one may stumble into superconsciousness sporadically, without the previous discipline, but it is then impure. Their test of its purity, like our test of religion's value, is empirical: its fruits must be good for life. When a man comes out of Samâdhi, they assure us that he remains "enlightened, a sage, a prophet, a saint, his whole character changed, his life changed, illumined."

The Buddhists use the word 'samâdhi' as well as the Hindus; but 'dhyâna' is their special word for higher states of contemplation. There seem to be four stages recognized in dhyâna. The first stage comes through concentration of the mind upon one point. It excludes desire, but not discernment or judgment: it is still intellectual. In the second stage the intellectual functions drop off, and the satisfied sense of unity remains. In the third stage the satisfaction departs, and indifference begins, along with memory and self-consciousness. In the fourth stage the indifference, memory, and self-consciousness are perfected. [Just what 'memory' and 'self-consciousness' mean in this connection is doubtful. They cannot be the faculties familiar to us in the lower life.] Higher stages still of contemplation are mentioned—a region where there exists nothing, and where the meditator says: "There exists absolutely nothing," and stops. Then he reaches another region where he says: "There are neither ideas nor absence of ideas," and stops again.

---

[7] My quotations are from *Vivekananda*, Raja Yoga, London, 1896. The completest source of information on Yoga is the work translated by *Vihari Lala Mitra:* Yoga Vasishta Maha Ramayana, 4 vols., Calcutta, 1891–99.

Then another region where, "having reached the end of both idea and perception, he stops finally." This would seem to be, not yet Nirvâna, but as close an approach to it as this life affords.

. . .

Incommunicableness of the transport is the keynote of all mysticism. Mystical truth exists for the individual who has the transport, but for no one else. In this, as I have said, it resembles the knowledge given to us in sensations more than that given by conceptual thought. Thought, with its remoteness and abstractness, has often enough in the history of philosophy been contrasted unfavorably with sensation. It is a commonplace of metaphysics that God's knowledge cannot be discursive but must be intuitive, that is, must be constructed more after the pattern of what in ourselves is called immediate feeling, than after that of proposition and judgment. But *our* immediate feelings have no content but what the five senses supply; and we have seen and shall see again that mystics may emphatically deny that the senses play any part in the very highest type of knowledge which their transports yield.

In the Christian church there have always been mystics. Although many of them have been viewed with suspicion, some have gained favor in the eyes of the authorities. The experiences of these have been treated as precedents, and a codified system of mystical theology has been based upon them, in which everything legitimate finds its place. The basis of the system is 'orison' or meditation, the methodical elevation of the soul towards God. Through the practice of orison the higher levels of mystical experience may be attained. It is odd that Protestantism, especially evangelical Protestantism, should seemingly have abandoned everything methodical in this line. Apart from what prayer may lead to, Protestant mystical experience appears to have been almost exclusively sporadic. It has been left to our mind-curers to reintroduce methodical meditation into our religious life.

The first thing to be aimed at in orison is the mind's detachment from outer sensations, for these interfere with its concentration upon ideal things. Such manuals as Saint Ignatius's Spiritual Exercises recommend the disciple to expel sensation by a graduated series of efforts to imagine holy scenes. The acme of this kind of discipline would be a semi-hallucinatory mono-ideism—an imaginary figure of Christ, for example, coming fully to occupy the mind. Sensorial images of this sort, whether literal or symbolic, play an enormous part in mysticism. But in certain cases imagery may fall away entirely, and in the very highest raptures it tends to do so. The state of consciousness becomes then insusceptible of any verbal description. Mystical teachers are unanimous as to this. Saint John of the Cross, for instance, one of the best of them, thus describes the condition called the 'union of love,' which, he says, is reached by 'dark contemplation.' In this the Deity compenetrates the soul, but in such a hidden way that the soul—

> finds no terms, no means, no comparison whereby to render the sub-
> limity of the wisdom and the delicacy of the spiritual feeling with
> which she is filled. . . . We receive this mystical knowledge of God
> clothed in none of the kinds of images, in none of the sensible repre-
> sentations, which our mind makes use of in other circumstances.
> Accordingly in this knowledge, since the senses and the imagination
> are not employed, we get neither form nor impression, nor can we
> give any account or furnish any likeness, although the mysterious and
> sweet-tasting wisdom comes home so clearly to the inmost parts of our
> soul. Fancy a man seeing a certain kind of thing for the first time in
> his life. He can understand it, use and enjoy it, but he cannot apply
> a name to it, nor communicate any idea of it, even though all the
> while it be a mere thing of sense. How much greater will be his power-
> lessness when it goes beyond the senses! This is the peculiarity of the
> divine language. The more infused, intimate, spiritual, and super-
> sensible it is, the more does it exceed the senses, both inner and outer,
> and impose silence upon them. . . . The soul then feels as if placed in
> a vast and profound solitude, to which no created thing has access, in
> an immense and boundless desert, desert the more delicious the more
> solitary it is. There, in this abyss of wisdom, the soul grows by what it
> drinks in from the well-springs of the comprehension of love, . . . and
> recognizes, however sublime and learned may be the terms we employ,
> how utterly vile, insignificant, and improper they are, when we seek
> to discourse of divine things by their means.[8]

I cannot pretend to detail to you the sundry stages of the Christian mystical life.[9] Our time would not suffice, for one thing; and more-over, I confess that the subdivisions and names which we find in the

---

[8] Saint John of the Cross, The Dark Night of the Soul, book ii. of xvii., in Vie et Oeuvres, 3me édition, Paris, 1893, iii. 428–432. Chapter xi. of book ii. of Saint John's Ascent of Carmel is devoted to showing the harmfulness for the mystical life of the use of sensible imagery.

[9] In particular I omit mention of visual and auditory hallucinations, verbal and graphic automatisms, and such marvels as 'levitation,' stigmatization, and the healing of disease. These phenomena, which mystics have often presented (or are believed to have presented), have no essential mystical significance, for they occur with no consciousness of illumination whatever, when they occur, as they often do, in persons of non-mystical mind. Consciousness of illumination is for us the essential mark of 'mystical' states.

Catholic books seem to me to represent nothing objectively distinct. So many men, so many minds: I imagine that these experiences can be as infinitely varied as are the idiosyncrasies of individuals.

The cognitive aspects of them, their value in the way of revelation, is what we are directly concerned with, and it is easy to show by citation how strong an impression they leave of being revelations of new depths of truth. Saint Teresa is the expert of experts in describing such conditions, so I will turn immediately to what she says of one of the highest of them, the 'orison of union.'

> "In the orison of union," says Saint Teresa, "the soul is fully awake as regards God, but wholly asleep as regards things of this world and in respect of herself. During the short time the union lasts, she is as it were deprived of every feeling, and even if she would, she could not think of any single thing. Thus she needs to employ no artifice in order to arrest the use of her understanding: it remains so stricken with inactivity that she neither knows what she loves, nor in what manner she loves, nor what she wills. In short, she is utterly dead to the things of the world and lives solely in God. . . . I do not even know whether in this state she has enough life left to breathe. It seems to me she has not; or at least that if she does breathe, she is unaware of it. Her intellect would fain understand something of what is going on within her, but it has so little force now that it can act in no way whatsoever. So a person who falls into a deep faint appears as if dead. . . .
>
> "Thus does God, when he raises a soul to union with himself, suspend the natural action of all her faculties. She neither sees, hears, nor understands, so long as she is united with God. But this time is always short, and it seems even shorter than it is. God establishes himself in the interior of this soul in such a way, that when she returns to herself, it is wholly impossible for her to doubt that she has been in God, and God in her. This truth remains so strongly impressed on her that, even though many years should pass without the condition returning, she can neither forget the favor she received, nor doubt of its reality. If you, nevertheless, ask how it is possible that the soul can see and understand that she has been in God, since during the union she has neither sight nor understanding, I reply that she does not see it then, but that she sees it clearly later, after she has returned to herself, not by any vision, but by a certitude which abides with her and which God alone can give her. I knew a person who was ignorant of the truth that God's mode of being in everything must be either by presence, by power, or by essence, but who, after having received the grace of which I am speaking, believed this truth in the most unshakable manner. So much so that, having consulted a half-learned man who was as ignorant on this point as she had been before she was enlightened, when he replied that God is in us only by 'grace,' she disbelieved his

reply, so sure she was of the true answer; and when she came to ask wiser doctors, they confirmed her in her belief, which much consoled her. . . .

"But how, you will repeat, *can* one have such certainty in respect to what one does not see? This question, I am powerless to answer. These are secrets of God's omnipotence which it does not appertain to me to penetrate. All that I know is that I tell the truth; and I shall never believe that any soul who does not possess this certainty has ever been really united to God." [10]

The kinds of truth communicable in mystical ways, whether these be sensible or supersensible, are various. Some of them relate to this world,—visions of the future, the reading of hearts, the sudden understanding of texts, the knowledge of distant events, for example; but the most important revelations are theological or metaphysical.

> Saint Ignatius confessed one day to Father Laynez that a single hour of meditation at Manresa had taught him more truths about heavenly things than all the teachings of all the doctors put together could have taught him. . . . One day in orison, on the steps of the choir of the Dominican church, he saw in a distinct manner the plan of divine wisdom in the creation of the world. On another occasion, during a procession, his spirit was ravished in God, and it was given him to contemplate, in a form and images fitted to the weak understanding of a dweller on the earth, the deep mystery of the holy Trinity. This last vision flooded his heart with such sweetness, that the mere memory of it in after times made him shed abundant tears.[11]

Similarly with Saint Teresa. "One day, being in orison," she writes, "it was granted me to perceive in one instant how all things are seen and contained in God. I did not perceive them in their proper form, and nevertheless the view I had of them was of a sovereign clearness, and has remained vividly impressed upon my soul. It is one of the most signal of all the graces which the Lord has granted me. . . . The view was so subtile and delicate that the understanding cannot grasp it." [12]

She goes on to tell how it was as if the Deity were an enormous and sovereignly limpid diamond, in which all our actions were contained in such a way that their full sinfulness appeared evident as never before. On another day, she relates, while she was reciting the Athanasian Creed,—

---

[10] The Interior Castle, Fifth Abode, ch. i., in Oeuvres, translated by Bouix, iii. 421–424.
[11] Bartoli-Michel: Vie de Saint Ignace de Loyola, i. 34–36.
[12] Vie, pp. 581, 582.

Our Lord made me comprehend in what way it is that one God can be in three Persons. He made me see it so clearly that I remained as extremely surprised as I was comforted, . . . and now, when I think of the holy Trinity, or hear It spoken of, I understand how the three adorable Persons form only one God and I experience an unspeakable happiness.

On still another occasion, it was given to Saint Teresa to see and understand in what wise the Mother of God had been assumed into her place in Heaven.[13]

The deliciousness of some of these states seems to be beyond anything known in ordinary consciousness. It evidently involves organic sensibilities, for it is spoken of as something too extreme to be borne, and as verging on bodily pain.[14] But it is too subtle and piercing a delight for ordinary words to denote. God's touches, the wounds of his spear, references to ebriety and to nuptial union have to figure in the phraseology by which it is shadowed forth. Intellect and senses both swoon away in those highest states of ecstasy. "If our understanding comprehends," says Saint Teresa, "it is in a mode which remains unknown to it, and it can understand nothing of what it comprehends. For my own part, I do not believe that it does comprehend, because, as I said, it does not understand itself to do so. I confess that it is all a mystery in which I am lost." In the condition called *raptus* or ravishment by theologians, breathing and circulation are so depressed that it is a question among the doctors whether the soul be or be not temporarily dissevered from the body. One must read Saint Teresa's descriptions and the very exact distinctions which she makes, to persuade one's self that one is dealing, not with imaginary experiences, but with phenomena which, however rare, follow perfectly definite psychological types.

. . .

Mystical conditions may render the soul more energetic in the lines which their inspiration favors. But this could be reckoned an advantage only in case the inspiration were a true one. If the inspiration were erroneous, the energy would be all the more mistaken and misbegotten.

---

[13] Loc. cit., p. 574.

[14] Saint Teresa discriminates between pain in which the body has a part and pure spiritual pain (Interior Castle, 6th Abode, ch. xi.). As for the bodily part in these celestial joys, she speaks of it as "penetrating to the marrow of the bones, whilst earthly pleasures affect only the surface of the senses. I think," she adds, "that this is a just description, and I cannot make it better." Ibid., 5th Abode, ch. i.

So we stand once more before that problem of truth which confronted us at the end of the lectures on saintliness. You will remember that we turned to mysticism precisely to get some light on truth. Do mystical states establish the truth of those theological affections in which the saintly life has its root?

In spite of their repudiation of articulate self-description, mystical states in general assert a pretty distinct theoretic drift. It is possible to give the outcome of the majority of them in terms that point in definite philosophical directions. One of these directions is optimism, and the other is monism. We pass into mystical states from out of ordinary conciousness as from a less into a more, as from a smallness into a vastness, and at the same time as from an unrest to a rest. We feel them as reconciling, unifying states. They appeal to the yes-function more than to the no-function in us. In them the unlimited absorbs the limits and peacefully closes the account. Their very denial of every adjective you may propose as applicable to the ultimate truth,—He, the Self, the Atman, is to be described by 'No! no!' only, say the Upanishads,[15]—though it seems on the surface to be a no-function, is a denial made on behalf of a deeper yes. Whoso calls the Absolute anything in particular, or says that it is *this*, seems implicitly to shut it off from being *that*—it is as if he lessened it. So we deny the 'this,' negating the negation which it seems to us to imply, in the interests of the higher affirmative attitude by which we are possessed. The fountainhead of Christian mysticism is Dionysius the Areopagite. He describes the absolute truth by negatives exclusively.

> "The cause of all things is neither soul nor intellect; nor has it imagination, opinion, or reason, or intelligence; nor is it reason or intelligence; nor is it spoken or thought. It is neither number, nor order, nor magnitude, nor littleness, nor equality, nor inequality, nor similarity, nor dissimilarity. It neither stands, nor moves, nor rests. . . . It is neither essence, nor eternity, nor time. Even intellectual contact does not belong to it. It is neither science nor truth. It is not even royalty or wisdom; not one; not unity; not divinity or goodness; nor even spirit as we know it," etc., *ad libitum*. [16]

But these qualifications are denied by Dionysius, not because the truth falls short of them, but because it so infinitely excels them. It is above them. It is *super*-lucent, *super*-splendent, *super*-essential, *super*-sublime, *super* everything that can be named. Like Hegel in his logic,

---

15 MÜLLER's translation, part ii, p. 180.
16 T. DAVIDSON's translation, in Journal of Speculative Philosophy, 1893, vol. xxii. p. 399.

mystics journey towards the positive pole of truth only by the 'Methode der Absoluten Negativität.' [17]

Thus come the paradoxical expressions that so abound in mystical writings. As when Eckhart tells of the still desert of the Godhead, "where never was seen difference, neither Father, Son, nor Holy Ghost, where there is no one at home, yet where the spark of the soul is more at peace than in itself." [18] As when Boehme writes of the Primal Love, that "it may fitly be compared to Nothing, for it is deeper than any Thing, and is as nothing with respect to all things, forasmuch as it is not comprehensible by any of them. And because it is nothing respectively, it is therefore free from all things, and is that only good, which a man cannot express or utter what it is, there being nothing to which it may be compared, to express it by." [19]

. . .

Overcoming of all the usual barriers between the individual and the Absolute is the great mystic achievement. In mystic states we both become one with the Absolute and we become aware of our oneness. This is the everlasting and triumphant mystical tradition, hardly altered by differences of clime or creed. In Hinduism, in Neoplatonism, in Sufism, in Christian mysticism, in Whitmanism, we find the same recurring note, so that there is about mystical utterances an eternal unanimity which ought to make a critic stop and think, and which brings it about that the mystical classics have, as has been said, neither birthday nor native land. Perpetually telling of the unity of man with God, their speech antedates languages, and they do not grow old.

'That art Thou!' says the Upanishads, and the Vedantists add: 'Not a part, not a mode of That, but identically That, that absolute Spirit of the World.' "As pure water poured into pure water remains the same, thus, O Gautama, is the Self of a thinker who knows. Water in water, fire in fire, ether in ether, no one can distinguish them; likewise a man whose mind has entered into the Self." " 'Every man,' says the Sufi Gulshan-Râz, 'whose heart is no longer shaken by any doubt, knows with certainty that there is no being save only One. . . . In his divine majesty the *me*, the *we*, the *thou*, are not found, for in the One there can be no distinction. Every being who is annulled and entirely sepa-

---

[17] "Deus propter excellentiam non immerito Nihil vocatur." Scotus Erigena, quoted by ANDREW SETH: Two Lectures on Theism, New York, 1897, p. 55.
[18] J. ROYCE: Studies in Good and Evil, p. 282.
[19] JACOB BEHMEN's Dialogues on the Supersensual Life, translated by BERNARD HOLLAND, London, 1901, p. 48.

rated from himself, hears resound outside of him this voice and this echo: *I am God:* he has an eternal way of existing, and is no longer subject to death.'"

. . .

In mystical literature such self-contradictory phrases as 'dazzling obscurity,' 'whispering silence,' 'teeming desert,' are continually met with. They prove that not conceptual speech, but music rather, is the element through which we are best spoken to by mystical truth. Many mystical scriptures are indeed little more than musical compositions.

. . .

I have now sketched with extreme brevity and insufficiency, but as fairly as I am able in the time allowed, the general traits of the mystic range of consciousness. *It is on the whole pantheistic and optimistic, or at least the opposite of pessimistic. It is anti-naturalistic, and harmonizes best with twice-bornness and so-called otherworldly states of mind.*

My next task is to inquire whether we can invoke it as authoritative. Does it furnish any *warrant for the truth* of the twice-bornness and supernaturality and pantheism which it favors? I must give my answer to this question as concisely as I can.

In brief my answer is this,—and I will divide it into three parts.—

1. Mystical states, when well developed, usually are, and have the right to be, absolutely authoritative over the individuals to whom they come.

2. No authority emanates from them which should make it a duty for those who stand outside of them to accept their revelations uncritically.

3. They break down the authority of the non-mystical or rationalistic consciousness, based upon the understanding and the senses alone. They show it to be only one kind of consciousness. They open out the possibility of other orders of truth, in which, so far as anything in us vitally responds to them, we may freely continue to have faith.

I will take up these points one by one.

I

As a matter of psychological fact, mystical states of a well-pronounced and emphatic sort *are* usually authoritative over those who

have them. They have been 'there,' and know. It is vain for rationalism
to grumble about this. If the mystical truth that comes to a man proves
to be a force that he can live by, what mandate have we of the majority
to order him to live in another way? We can throw him into prison or
a madhouse, but we cannot change his mind—we commonly attach it
only the more stubbornly to its beliefs. It mocks our utmost efforts, as
a matter of fact, and in point of logic it absolutely escapes our jurisdiction. Our own more 'rational' beliefs are based on evidence exactly
similar in nature to that which mystics quote for theirs. Our senses,
namely, have assured us of certain states of fact; but mystical experiences are as direct perceptions of fact for those who have them as
any sensations ever were for us. The records show that even though
the five senses be in abeyance in them, they are absolutely sensational
in their epistemological quality, if I may be pardoned the barbarous
expression,—that is, they are face to face presentations of what seems
immediately to exist.

The mystic is, in short, *invulnerable*, and must be left, whether we
relish it or not, in undisturbed enjoyment of his creed. Faith, says
Tolstoy, is that by which men live. And faith-state and mystic state
are practically convertible terms.

II

But I now proceed to add that mystics have no right to claim that we
ought to accept the deliverance of their peculiar experiences, if we
are ourselves outsiders and feel no private call thereto. The utmost they
can ever ask of us in this life is to admit that they establish a presumption. They form a consensus and have an unequivocal outcome;
and it would be odd, mystics might say, if such a unanimous type of
experience should prove to be altogether wrong. At bottom, however,
this would only be an appeal to numbers, like the appeal of rationalism
the other way; and the appeal to numbers has no logical force. If we
acknowledge it, it is for 'suggestive,' not for logical reasons: we follow
the majority because to do so suits our life.

But even this presumption from the unanimity of mystics is far from
being strong. In characterizing mystic states as pantheistic, optimistic,
etc., I am afraid I over-simplified the truth. I did so for expository
reasons, and to keep the closer to the classic mystical tradition. The
classic religious mysticism, it now must be confessed, is only a 'privi-
leged case.' It is an *extract*, kept true to type by the selection of the
fittest specimens and their preservation in 'schools.' It is carved out
from a much larger mass; and if we take the larger mass as seriously

as religious mysticism has historically taken itself, we find that the supposed unanimity largely disappears. To begin with, even religious mysticism itself, the kind that accumulates traditions and makes schools, is much less unanimous than I have allowed. It has been both ascetic and anti-nomianly self-indulgent within the Christian church. It is dualistic in Sankhya, and monistic in Vedanta philosophy. I called it pantheistic; but the great Spanish mystics are anything but pantheists. They are with few exceptions non-metaphysical minds, for whom 'the category of personality' is absolute. The 'union' of man with God is for them much more like an occasional miracle than like an original identity. How different again, apart from the happiness common to all, is the mysticism of Walt Whitman, Edward Carpenter, Richard Jefferies, and other naturalistic pantheists, from the more distinctively Christian sort. The fact is that the mystical feeling of enlargement, union, and emancipation has no specific intellectual content whatever of its own. It is capable of forming matrimonial alliances with material furnished by the most diverse philosophies and theologies, provided only they can find a place in their framework for its peculiar emotional mood. We have no right, therefore, to invoke its prestige as distinctively in favor of any special belief, such as that in absolute idealism, or in the absolute monistic identity, or in the absolute goodness, of the world. It is only relatively in favor of all these things—it passes out of common human consciousness in the direction in which they lie.

So much for religious mysticism proper. But more remains to be told, for religious mysticism is only one half of mysticism. The other half has no accumulated traditions except those which the text-books on insanity supply. Open any one of these, and you will find abundant cases in which 'mystical ideas' are cited as characteristic symptoms of enfeebled or deluded states of mind. In delusional insanity, paranoia, as they sometimes call it, we may have a *diabolical* mysticism, a sort of religious mysticism turned upside down. The same sense of ineffable importance in the smallest events, the same texts and words coming with new meanings, the same voices and visions and leadings and missions, the same controlling by extraneous powers; only this time the emotion is pessimistic: instead of consolations we have desolations; the meanings are dreadful; and the powers are enemies to life. It is evident that from the point of view of their psychological mechanism, the classic mysticism and these lower mysticisms spring from the same mental level, from that great subliminal or transmarginal region of which science is beginning to admit the existence, but of which so little is really known. That region contains every kind of matter: 'seraph and snake' abide there side by side. To come from thence is no infallible credential. What comes must be sifted and tested, and run the gauntlet of confrontation with the total context of experience, just like what comes from the outer world of sense. Its value must be ascertained by empirical methods, so long as we are not mystics ourselves.

Once more then, I repeat that non-mystics are under no obligation to acknowledge in mystical states a superior authority conferred on them by their intrinsic nature.

III

Yet, I repeat once more, the existence of mystical states absolutely overthrows the pretension of non-mystical states to be the sole and ultimate dictators of what we may believe. As a rule, mystical states merely add a supersensuous meaning to the ordinary outward data of consciousness. They are excitements like the emotions of love or ambition, gifts to our spirit by means of which facts already objectively before us fall into a new expressiveness and make a new connection with our active life. They do not contradict these facts as such, or deny anything that our senses have immediately seized. It is the rationalistic critic rather who plays the part of denier in the controversy, and his denials have no strength, for there never can be a state of facts to which new meaning may not truthfully be added, provided the mind ascend to a more enveloping point of view. It must always remain an open question whether mystical states may not possibly be such superior points of view, windows through which the mind looks out upon a more extensive and inclusive world. The difference of the views seen from the different mystical windows need not prevent us from entertaining this supposition. The wider world would in that case prove to have a mixed constitution like that of this world, that is all. It would have its celestial and its infernal regions, its tempting and its saving moments, its valid experiences and its counterfeit ones, just as our world has them; but it would be a wider world all the same. We should have to use its experiences by selecting and subordinating and substituting just as is our custom in this ordinary naturalistic world; we should be liable to error just as we are now; yet the counting in of that wider world of meanings, and the serious dealing with it, might, in spite of all the perplexity, be indispensible stages in our approach to the final fullness of the truth.

In this shape, I think, we have to leave the subject. Mystical states indeed wield no authority due simply to their being mystical states. But the higher ones among them point in directions to which the religious sentiments even of non-mystical men incline. They tell of the supremacy of the ideal, of vastness, of union, of safety, and of rest. They offer us *hypotheses,* hypotheses which we may voluntarily ignore, but which as thinkers we cannot possibly upset. The supernaturalism and optimism to which they would persuade us may, interpreted in one way or another, be after all the truest of insights into the meaning of this life.

"Oh, the little more, and how much it is; and the little less, and what worlds away!" It may be that possibility and permission of this sort are all that the religious consciousness requires to live on.

6

D. T. SUZUKI

(1870–1966)

The Meaning of Satori *

Suzuki was a prolific writer on Buddhism and is probably the best known advocate of Zen to those of us in the Western world. This essay is an account of the culminating experience toward which all Zen devotees aim, satori. There is very little in the way of organized or systematized philosophy in the Zen sect of Mahayana Buddhism. Instead, disciples of Zen are instructed by Masters by studying poems (haiku) and koans (short, usually aphoristic accounts of conversations between a Master and a Monk). The experience of satori is, strictly speaking, not describable, but some things may be said about preparation for the experience and its meaning in the life of a disciple. Most importantly one must divest oneself of concern for self in daily life. Suzuki writes: "The satori intuition of reality consists of identifying oneself with becoming." It is important, however, as the story of the woodman emphasizes, that one cannot try to achieve satori. Satori comes only to those who are prepared in a state of consciousness to receive satori, after which all things will be understood.

* Reprinted from *The Middle Way,* The Journal of the Buddhist Society, 1969, London. Used by permission of the Society.

SATORI is a Japanese term, *wu* in Chinese. The Sanskrit *bodhi* and *buddha* come from the same root, *bud,* "to be aware of," "to wake". *Buddha* is thus "the awakened one", "the enlightened one", while *bodhi* is "enlightenment". "Buddhism" means the teaching of the enlightened one, that is to say, Buddhism is the doctrine of enlightenment. What Buddha teaches, therefore, is the realisation of bodhi, which is satori. Satori is the centre of all Buddhist teachings. Some may think satori is characteristic of Mahayana Buddhism, but it is not so. Earlier Buddhists also talk about this, the realization of *bodhi;* and as long as they talk about *bodhi* at all they must be said to base their doctrine on the experience of satori.

We have to distinguish between *prajna* and *vijnana.* We can divide knowledge into two categories: intuitive knowledge which is *prajna* whereas discursive knowledge is *vijnana.* To distinguish further: *prajna* grasps reality in its oneness, in its totality; *vijnana* analyses it into subject and object. Here is a flower; we can take this flower as representing the universe itself. We talk about the petals, pollen, stamen and stalk; that is physical analysis. Or we can analyse it chemically into so much hydrogen, oxygen, etc. Chemists analyse a flower, enumerate all its elements and say that the aggregate of all those elements makes up the flower. But they have not exhausted the flower; they have simply analysed it. That is the *vijnana* way of understanding a flower. The *prajna* way is to understand it just as it is without analysis or chopping it into pieces. It is to grasp it in its oneness, in its totality, in its suchness (*sono mame*) in Japanese.

We are generally attracted to analytical knowledge or discriminative understanding, and we divide reality into several pieces. We dissect it and by dissecting it we kill reality. When we have finished our analysis we have murdered reality, and this dead reality we think is our understanding of it. When we see reality dead, after analysing it, we say that we understand it, but what we understand is not reality itself but its corpse after it has been mutilated by our intellect and senses. We fail to see that this result of dissection is not reality itself, and when we take this analysis as a basis of our understanding it is inevitable that we go astray, far away from the truth. Because in this way we shall never reach the final solution of the problem of reality.

....*Prajna* grasps this reality in its oneness, in its totality, in its suchness. *Prajna* does not divide reality into any form of dichotomy; it does not dissect it either metaphysically or physically or chemically. The dividing of reality is the function of *vijnana* which is very useful in a practical way, but *prajna* is different.

Vijnana can never reach infinity. When we write the numbers 1, 2, 3, etc., we never come to an end, for the series goes on to infinity. By adding together all those individual numbers we try to reach the total of the numbers, but as numbers are endless this totality can never be reached. *Prajna*, on the other hand, intuits the whole totality instead of moving through 1, 2, 3 to infinity; it grasps things as a whole. It does not appeal to discrimination; it grasps reality from inside, as it were. Discursive *vijnana* tries to grasp reality objectively, that is, by addition objectively one after another. But this objective method can never reach its end because things are infinite, and we can never exhaust them objectively. Subjectively, however, we turn that position upside down and get to the inside. By looking at this flower objectively we can never reach its essence or life, but when we turn that position inside out, enter into the flower, and become the flower itself, we live through the process of growth: I am the shoot, I am the stem, I am the bud, and finally I am the flower and the flower is me. That is the *prajna* way of comprehending the flower.

In Japan there is a seventeen syllable poem called *haiku*, and one composed by a modern woman-poet reads in literal translation:

> Oh, Morning Glory!
> Bucket taken captive,
> I beg for water.

The following was the incident that led her to compose it. One early morning the poet came outdoors to draw water from the well, and saw the morning glory winding round the bamboo pole attached to the bucket. The morning glory in full bloom looks its best in the early morning after a dewy night. It is bright, refreshing, vivifying; it reflects heavenly glory not yet tarnished by things earthly. She was so struck with its untainted beauty that she remained silent for a little while; she was so absorbed in the flower that she lost the power of speech. It took a few seconds at least before she could exclaim: "Oh, Morning Glory!" Physically, the interval was a space of a second or two or perhaps more; but metaphysically, it was eternity as beauty itself is. Psychologically, the poet was the unconscious itself in which there was no dichotomization of any kind.

The poet was the morning glory and the morning glory was the poet. There was self identity of flower and poet. It was only when she became conscious of herself seeing the flower that she cried: "Oh, Morning Glory!" When she said that, consciousness revived in her. But she did not like to disturb the flower, because although it is not difficult to unwind the flower from the bamboo pole she feared that to touch the flower with human hands would be the desecration of the beauty. So she went to a neighbour and asked for water.

When you analyse that poem you can picture to yourself how she stood before the flower, losing herself. There was then no flower, no human poet; just a "something" which was neither flower nor poet. But when she recovered her consciousness, there was the flower, there was herself. There was an object which was designated as morning glory and there was one who spoke—a bifurcation of subject-object. Before the bifurcation there was nothing to which she could give expression, she herself was non-existent. When she uttered, "Oh, Morning Glory!" the flower was created and along with it herself, but before that bifurcation, that dualisation of subject and object, there was nothing. And yet there was a "something" which could divide itself into subject-object, and this "something" which had not yet divided itself, not become subject to bifurcation, to discriminative understanding (i.e. before *vijnana* asserted itself)—this is *prajna*. For *Prajna* is subject and at the same time object; it divides itself into subject-object and also stands by itself, but that standing by itself is not to be understood on the level of duality. Standing by itself, being absolute in its complete totality or oneness—that is the moment which the poet realised, and that is satori. Satori consists in not staying in that oneness, not remaining with itself, but in awakening from it and being just about to divide itself into subject and object. Satori is the staying in oneness and yet rising from it and dividing itself into subject-object. First, there is "something" which has not divided itself into subject-object, this is oneness as it is. Then this "something," becoming conscious of itself, divides itself into flower and poet. The becoming conscious is the dividing. Poet now sees flower and flower sees poet, there is mutual seeing. When this seeing each other, not just from one side alone but from the other side as well when this kind of seeing actually takes place, there is a state of satori.

When I talk like this it takes time. There is something which has not divided itself but which then becomes conscious of itself, and this leads to an utterance, and so on. But in actual satori there is no time interval, hence no consciousness of the bifurcation. The oneness dividing itself into subject-object and yet retaining its oneness at the very moment that there is the awakening of a consciousness—this is satori.

From the human point of view we talk of *prajna* and *vijnana* as the integral understanding and the discriminative understanding of reality respectively. We speak of these things in order to satisfy our human understanding. Animals and plants do not divide themselves; they just live and act, but humans have awakened this consciousness. By the awakening of consciousness we become conscious of this and that, and this universe of infinite diversity arises. Because of this awakening we discriminate, and because of discrimination we talk of *prajna* and *vijnana* and make these distinctions, which is characteristic of human beings. To satisfy this demand we talk about having satori, or the awakening of this self-identity consciousness.

When the poet saw the flower, that very moment before she spoke even a word there was an intuitive apprehension of something which eludes our ordinary intuition. This *sui generis* intuition is what I would call *prajna*-intuition. The moment grasped by *prajna*-intuition is satori. That is what made Buddha the Enlightened one. Thus, to attain satori, *prajna*-intuition is to be awakened.

That is more or less a metaphysical explanation of satori, but psychologically satori may be said to take place this way. Our consciousness contains all things; but there must be at least two things whereby consciousness is possible. Consciousness takes place when two things stand opposing one another. In our ordinary life, consciousness is kept too busy with all things going on in it and has not time to reflect within itself. Consciousness has thus no opportunity to become conscious of itself. It is so deeply involved in action, it is in fact action itself. Satori never takes place as long as consciousness is kept turning outwardly, as it were. Satori is born of self-consciousness. Consciousness must be made to look within itself before it is awakened to satori.

To get satori, all things which crowd into our daily-life conciousness must be wiped off clean. This is the function of *samadhi*, which Indian philosophers emphasize so much. "Entering into *samadhi*" is to attain uniformity of consciousness, i.e. to wipe consciousness clean, though practically speaking, this wiping clean is something almost impossible. But we must try to do it in order to attain this state of uniformity, which, according to early Buddhist thinkers, is a perfect state of mental equilibrium, for here there are no passions, no intellectual functions, but only a perfectly balanced state of indifference. When this takes place it is known as *samadhi*, or entering into the fourth stage of *dhyana* or *jhana*, as described in most early Buddhist sutras. This is not, however, a state of satori. *Samadhi* is not enough, which is no more than the unification of consciousness. There must be an awakening from this state of unification or uniformity. The awakening is becoming aware of consciousness in its own activities. When consciousness starts to move, begins to divide itself into subject-object and says: I am sorry, or glad, or I hear, and so on—this very moment as it moves on is caught up in satori. But as soon as you say "I have caught it" it is no more there. Therefore, satori is not something you can take hold of and show to others, saying, "See, it is here!"

Consciousness is something which never ceases to be active though we may be quite unconscious of it, and what we call perfect uniformity is not a state of sheer quietness, that is, of death. As consciousness thus goes on unceasingly, no one can stop it for inspection. Satori must take place while consciousness is going through stages or instant points of becoming. Satori is realized along with the becoming, which knows no stoppage. Satori is no particular experience like other experiences of our daily life. Particular experiences are experiences of particular events while the satori experience is the one that runs through all experiences. It is for this reason that satori cannot be singled out of other experiences and pronounced, "See, here is my satori!" It is always elusive and alluring. It can never be separated from our everyday life, it is forever there, inevitably there. Becoming, not only in its each particularisable moment but through its never-terminating totality is the body of satori.

The nature of human understanding and reasoning is to divide reality into the dichotomy of this and that, of "A" and "not-A" and then to take reality so divided as really reality. We do not seem to understand reality in any other way. This being so, as long as we are depending on "the understanding," there will be no grasping of reality, no intuitive taking hold of reality, and satori is no other than this intuitive taking hold of reality. There is no reality beside becoming, becoming is reality and reality is becoming. Therefore, the satori intuition of reality consists in identifying oneself with becoming, to take becoming as it goes on becoming. We are not to cut becoming into pieces, and, picking up each separate piece which drops from "becoming," to say to people, "Here is reality." While making this announcement we will find that becoming is no more there; reality is flown away into the realm of the irrevocable past.

This is illustrated by a Zen story. A woodman went to the mountains and saw a strange animal on the other side of the tree which he was cutting. He thought: "I might kill that animal." The animal then spoke to the woodman and said: "Are you going to kill me? Having his mind read, the woodman got angry and wondered what to do. The animal said: "Now you are thinking what to do with me." Whatever thought the woodman had, the animal intuited, and told him so. Finally, the woodman said: "I will stop thinking about the animal and go on cutting wood." While he was so engaged the top of the axe flew off and killed the animal.

This illustrates that when you are thinking of it there is satori. When you try to realise satori, the more you struggle the farther it is away. You cannot help pursuing satori, but so long as you make that special effort satori will never be gained. But you cannot forget about it altogether. If you expect satori to come to you of its own accord, you will not get it.

To realise satori is very difficult, as the Buddha found. When he wished to be liberated from the bondage of birth and death he began to study philosophy, but this did not avail him, so he turned to asceticism. This made him so weak that he could not move, so he took milk and decided to go on with his search for liberation. Reasoning did not do any good and pursuing moral perfection did not help him either. Yet the urge to solve this problem was still there. He could go no farther, yet he could not retreat, so he had to stay where he was, but even that would not do. This state of spiritual crisis means that you cannot go on, nor retreat, nor stay where you are. When this dilemma is genuine, there prevails a state of consciousness ready for satori. When we really come to this stage (but we frequently think that what is not real is real), when we find ourselves at this critical moment, something is sure to rise from the depths of reality, from the depths of our own being. When this comes up there is satori. Then you understand all things and are at peace with the world as well as with yourself.

7   WILLIAM ALSTON

(1921–　)

Ineffability *

There are many difficulties with a philosophical understanding of mystical experiences such as Zen satori and concepts of the supreme, the soul or the ultimate
union of all, found in both Western and Eastern forms of mysticism. One of the most
difficult problems concerns the meaning of the term ineffable, which is often used
by mystics to characterize their religious experiences. Alston, in this essay, has used
the dialogue form to examine the concept of ineffability. Philologos represents the
analytic philosopher who attempts to understand mystical pronouncements, while
Mysticus defends the mystical point of view and in particular the arguments of
W. T. Stace. The issue turns on the question, What does "God is ineffable" mean?
Is "ineffable" a predicate like "ill" or "tall"? Does the proposition "God is ineffable"
mean that nothing can be properly said of God?

* William Alston, "Ineffability," *The Philosophical Review*, 65, 1956, pp. 506–522.
Used by permission of the author and the Editor.

> It [the Godhead] is free of all names and void of all
> forms. It is one and simple, as God is one and
> simple, and no man can in any wise behold it.

MEISTER ECKHART

> Brahman has neither name or form, transcends
> merit and demerit, is beyond time, space, and the
> objects of sense-experience.... Supreme, beyond
> the power of speech to express ...

SHANKARA

> In them [mystical states] the mysterium is expe-
> renced in its essential, positive, and specific char-
> acter, as something that bestows upon man a
> beautitude beyond compare, but one whose real

nature he can neither proclaim in speech nor conceive in thought.

RUDOLPH OTTO

That Soul is not this, it is not that. It is unseizable, for it cannot be seized.

BRIHAD ARANYAKA UPANISHAD

No form belongs to Him, not even one for the Intellect. . . . What meaning can there be any longer in saying: "This and this property belongs to Him"

PLOTINUS

Philologus: How can anyone seriously make statements like this? They seem to be self-defeating. For in making such a statement as "Brahman has neither name nor form . . . [and is] beyond the power of speech to express," isn't one doing (or purporting to do) the very thing which the statement declares to be impossible, namely, attach a name or ascribe a form to Brahman or "express" it in speech? Of course we cannot press this charge until we know the authors' exact intentions. Perhaps they are indulging in rhetorical exaggeration, as I would in saying, "Oh, Jane is impossible." If I said this, you wouldn't charge me with self-contradiction on the ground that I was on the one hand implying that "Jane" names an actually existing person and on the other hand asserting that it is impossible (logically or causally) that this person exists. You would take me to be saying, hyperbolically, that Jane is very difficult to get along with, and/or expressing my irritation at her. (Cf. "That outcome is unthinkable," "I *always* say the line 'Scarf up the tender eye of pitiful day' wrong.") Similarly, Shankara may be hyperbolically saying that it is difficult to find the right words to talk about Brahman, and/or expressing the frustration he meets in such attempts. Or perhaps the authors are using terms like "name," "form," "express," and "property" with unstated restrictions and qualifications such that their statements do not involve naming, expressing, attributing forms or properties, and so on, in their use of these terms. On neither of these interpretations would their statements be logically objectionable. But the oracular style of these writings makes it very difficult to know what interpretation to give them.

Mysticus: It is true that most religious writers are rather obscure, on this point as on others. But there is at least one exception—Professor W. T. Stace. In his recent book, *Time and Eternity*,[1] Stace puts forward the proposition that God is ineffable and takes considerable pains to explain exactly what he means, thereby, so it seems to me, giving a precise expression to what the people such as you cited were getting at. He makes it quite clear that he is not speaking hyperbolically, and he makes it quite explicit that the assertions are to be taken unqualifiedly, without any sort of restriction. And yet I cannot see that they are self-defeating in the way you suggest. Here are some of his statements of the thesis:

> To say that God is ineffable is to say that no concepts apply to Him, and that He is without qualities. . . . And this implies that any statement of the form "God is *x*" is false.[2]

> Thus to the intellect He is blank, void, nothing. You cannot attach any predicate to Him . . . because every predicate stands for a concept, so that to affirm a predicate of Him is to pretend that He is apprehensible by the conceptual intellect.[3]

> It is not merely *our* minds which cannot understand God, nor is it merely *our* concepts which cannot reach Him. No mind could understand His Mystery—so long as we mean by a mind a conceptual intellect —and no concepts could apprehend Him. And this is the same as saying that He is, in His very nature, unconceptualizable, that His Mystery and incomprehensibility are absolute attributes of Him.[4]

Philologos: These utterances sound uncompromising enough. But there is something very queer about some of them, for example, "He is, in His very nature, unconceptualizable." Is this as if I should say, in speaking of a very bright but intractable student, "He is, by his very intelligence, incapable of learning"? Note that I *couldn't* be denying, in a literal sense, that he can learn. For my statement presupposes that he has intelligence, and we wouldn't say of anything that it has intelligence unless we suppose that it could learn something. Any evidence that it was in a strict sense incapable of learning would equally be evidence that it had no intelligence. In actually using this sentence I would be employing hyperbole to express vividly

[1] Princeton, N.J., 1952.
[2] *Op. cit.*, p. 33.
[3] *Op. cit.*, p. 42.
[4] *Op. cit.*, pp. 48–49.

the fact that the very intelligence which makes him capable of learning is so quick-triggered that it is *difficult* for him to submit to the
prolonged discipline which is essential for thoroughly learning anything. So in the same spirit I might say of an acquaintance, "He is, in
his very nature, unconceptualizable" (cf. "His nature is an absolute
enigma to me"), thereby exaggeratedly saying that he is hard to
understand and expressing my puzzlement at his dark and devious
ways. But again I could not mean "unconceptualizable" in a strict
sense here; [5] for in ascribing to him a nature. I have already admitted
that he is conceptualizable, that is, that concepts can be applied to
him. We speak of the nature of x only where we suppose ourselves
able to say various things about x. We wouldn't talk about human
nature unless we supposed we could apply certain concepts to men.
Hence I can suppose only that Stace in saying, "He is, in His very
nature, unconceptualizable" is hyperbolically expressing the *difficulty*
of forming concepts which apply strictly to God. And so we are back
to something like "Jane is impossible." [6]

Mysticus: No, I can't agree that Stace is just exaggerating. But I
must admit that the statements you cite are not happy ones. However,
I don't believe they are essential for the statement of his thesis. He
doesn't have to speak of God's *nature,* or of something being an absolute attribute of God. He used those locutions in order to emphasize
that God is unconceptualizable not just by the human mind but by
any mind whatsoever. But he could have made the point by saying
just that (as he also does) and thereby have avoided tripping himself
up in this way.

P.: Let's see what is left after the purge. "To say that God is ineffable is to say that no concepts apply to Him, . . . that any statement
of the form 'God is x' is false." "Thus you cannot attach any predicate

---

[5] A terminological note for the whole paper: I take Stace, and those who talk about
this matter in the same way, to be using "concept" within the philosophical tradition in which we can be said to apply a concept to x whenever we predicate anything of x (or attach a predicate to x); and in which to say that we can apply
concepts to x is equivalent to saying that x is conceptualizable, capable of being
apprehended by concepts or by the conceptual intellect, etc. These equivalences
are implicit in the second of the three above quotations from Stace and in the
quotation below, p. 510. Therefore, although I hold no brief for this double-barreled
lingo, I shall in the following use "apply a concept to x" as synonymous with
"attach a predicate to x" (or predicate something of x"). And, for stylistic purposes, I shall sometimes add as a further synonym "characterize x." I am under no
illusion that the boundaries of these three terms are precisely drawn in the tradition.
In fact a good part of this paper hinges, in part, on exhibiting their vagueness. But
I think that within the tradition they oscillate together for the most part.
[6] The same sort of considerations apply to "His Mystery and incomprehensibility
are absolute attributes of Him."

to Him." But if in saying, "God is ineffable" we are making a true statement, haven't we applied a concept to Him, viz., the concept of ineffability? Haven't we attached a predicate to Him, viz., "ineffable"? Haven't we made a true statement of the form "God is x"? Aren't we in the position of being able to make a true statement only by doing the very things which the statement declares impossible, thereby falsifying it? Is this like a man saying, "I can't speak English"? (Cf. the case of a town crier who cries that crying has been outlawed.)

M.: Surely you aren't serious. When I say, "God is ineffable," I am not attempting to apply a concept to Him or attach a predicate to Him, and so if the statement is true it would not be correct to say I have succeeded in doing these things. I am denying that any concepts or predicates can be applied to Him. Of course, the grammatical form of "God is ineffable" is misleading. It looks like a positive statement, such as "Jones is ill" or "Susie is pretty," but actually it doesn't involve attaching any predicate to anything. Its logical form would be more clearly exhibited if it were formulated: "It is not the case that any predicate can be attached to God." This shows that "God is ineffable" is not really of the *logical* form "God is *x*," although it looks as if it were. Similarly, saying "King Arthur is fictitious" does not constitute attaching a predicate to King Arthur, although it looks as if it did. Hence to say truly "God is ineffable" we are not required to do what we are declaring to be impossible.

P.: So the man who said, "I can't speak English," if charged with falsifying his own statement, might retort (in French) that he didn't mean that he couldn't say what he was saying. (And if the town crier were arrested, he might complain, "But surely the law doesn't forbid my crying *it*. It's the only way of publicizing it.") In both these cases the speaker trusts us to make the sort of qualification that would make his statement intelligible and proper. If we are tempted to interpret them in a paradoxical way, we draw back and say, "They couldn't have meant that" and look for some qualification that will remove the paradox. So Stace perhaps trusted to the circumstances to make it plain that he wouldn't count "ineffable" as a predicate because it is negative. But wouldn't it be better to make this explicit and restate the principle as: "No *positive* predicates can be applied to God"?

M.: This qualification is unnecessary. "Ineffability" is not a predicate, in the strict sense of the term. For to "predicate" ineffability of *x* is really to deny something of *x*.

P.: If a pupil who had been directed to give an example of a subject-predicate sentence were to present "Freedom is intangible" or even "God is ineffable," wouldn't he get credit for his answer? And isn't "the concept of impossibility" a proper phrase? So whatever the "strict" sense might be, the point is that Stace is deviating common usage and, in the interests of intelligibility, had best make his deviation explicit.

But now I want to bring out another feature of "God is ineffable" which puzzles me. Let me approach this by asking: "What is it of which ineffability is being predicated, or, if you prefer, of which 'ineffability' is being denied?"

M.: God, of course.

P.: Ah. But what do you mean by "God"?

M.: Stace identifies God with mystical experience. But that seems to me unduly restrictive. I would rather say that God is that toward which we direct religious activities of any sort: worship, prayer, and so forth.

P.: But when you and Stace explain in this way the meaning you attach to "God," aren't you thereby attaching predicates to Him, or at least putting yourself in a position to do so? In other words, in using "God," aren't you presupposing that you can predicate of God whatever phrase you would give to explain your meaning?

M.: There does seem to be something odd here. Perhaps we are overlooking some peculiarity in the way a proper name like "God" is used. Now that I recall, Stace says·

> As every logician knows, any name, any word in any language, except a proper name, stands for a concept or a universal.... Neither God nor Nirvana stand for concepts. Both are proper names. It is not a contradiction that Eckhart should use the name God and yet declare Him nameless. For though He has a proper name, there is for Him no name in the sense of a word standing for a concept.[7]

P.: This theory does not tally with the way you, and Stace, were just now explaining the meaning of "God." But never mind that. Let's look at this conception of proper names for a bit. And first I want to ask: "How do we determine whether a given person understands a given proper name?"[8] Let's start with something a little simpler than

[7] *Op. cit.,* p. 24.
[8] We do not ordinarily speak of "understanding a proper name." But we do speak of understanding sentences and using them meaningfully; and one of the conditions of understanding or using meaningfully a sentence in which a proper name occurs is knowing who the proper name is a name of (with certain qualifications which are noted below, p. 514). Hence, in the absence of any other compendious expression, I shall speak of "understanding a proper name, '*N*,'" as synonymous with "knowing who (or what) '*N*' is the name of" or "knowing who (or what) *N* is." This extension of the use of "understanding" will not cause confusion unless it is allowed to obscure the important differences involved.

"God." Suppose I say to you, "Jane is a spiteful wench." You nod, but for some reason I suspect you are bluffing. So I say, "I don't believe you know who I am talking about." What could you do to vindicate yourself?

M: I might point out a girl in the room and say, "That is Jane." Or I might go over and address her by name.

P.: Yes. But this obviously doesn't apply to our problem, since one can't in a literal sense, point out God, or go over and address Him. And so for our purpose we had better stipulate that I make my statement when Jane is not present and that for some reason we can't go to where she is. Or take the case of a historical figure, for example, "Richard II of England," where pointing out is *logically* impossible, How would you prove your understanding in these cases?

M.: In the case of Jane, I might reply to your charge by saying something like "She's Fred's sister-in-law" or "She's the girl with the auburn hair Bob introduced me to last night." In the case of Richard II, I might say, "He was the king deposed by Bolingbroke," or "He was ruler of England from 1377 to 1399."

P.: Good. But doesn't this show that a condition of your understanding me, when I use the proper name of something you cannot point out, is your capacity to provide some such identifying phrase? If you were unable to provide any such phrase, would we say you understand the name?

M.: I suppose not.

P.: And isn't the same true of "God"? Suppose I say to you, "God is a very present help in time of trouble." You nod piously, but for some reason I suspect a failure of communication; perhaps I have reason to think you use the word differently. And so I ask, "What do you mean by 'God'?" You might reply, "The first cause," or "The necessary being," or "The supreme mind holding moral relations with mankind," or "He Who revealed Himself to the prophets," or "The father of Jesus Christ," or "The judge of our sins." If you were unable to give *any* such answer, wouldn't I be justified in concluding that you didn't understand the word "God" in any way? This means that a condition of your understanding any statement containing "God" is your capacity to supply some such identifying phrase, and any such phrase would constitute a predicate which could be attached to God. Hence "God is ineffable" asserts that an essential condition of its meaningfulness does not hold.

M.: Hold on. I might agree with your premise that I couldn't be said to understand a sentence containing "God" unless I could supply an identifying phrase. But your conclusion doesn't follow. Suppose in order to identify Jane I use the phrase "the girl whose picture was on the back page of last night's paper," or in order to identify Richard II, I use the phrase "the protagonist of Shakespeare's play of that name." Would these responses be sufficient to convince you that I had understood your statements containing those proper names?

P.: I suppose so.

M.: But to say that a picture of Jane was on the back page of last night's paper is not to predicate anything of Jane or characterize her in any way. You might well complain that I had not told you what she is like and that you still can't form a concept of her. And still less have I predicated anything of Richard II when I have said that Shakespeare wrote a play about him.

P.: Maybe not. But you have said something about them.

M.: True. But to say that x is ineffable is obviously not to say that we can't say anything about x in any sense of "say something about." It is to say that we can't say anything which would involve attaching a predicate to x or characterizing it.

P.: You have overlooked one point, I fear. Even if you can't use those identifying phrases to characterize x, the information contained in these phrases gives you clues as to how to go about characterizing x. You can look at the back page of last night's paper, and on the basis of what you see, you can tell me all sorts of things about Jane. You can read Shakespeare's play and/or study his sources and thereby discover many characteristics of Richard II. Hence it isn't true that you could provide identifying phrases of this sort and yet *not be able* to characterize that which the phrase identifies.

M.: Perhaps. But what about "God"? That's the case we're really interested in. Couldn't I demonstrate my understanding of "God" by saying something like "the object of religious experience," or "the object of worship"? And surely saying that doesn't lead to any characterization lurking in the very *mode* of identification. For in identifying x as the protagonist of a drama, I am presupposing that x is a human being; and to identify x as that a picture of which . . . is to presuppose that x is a visible thing. But to identify x as the object of religious experience or worship is not to imply anything about what sort of entity it is. It does not involve any limitation on what can and cannot be said about it. It is like saying of something that it is an object of thought. That tells us nothing. *Anything* can be thought about.

P.: But doesn't your identifying phrase tell us where to look for more information, just as in the other cases? If you actually use "object of religious experience" as a criterion for identifying God (and aren't just mechanically repeating the phrase), you can find other things to say of God by reflecting on your own religious experience and/or reading what other people have said on the basis of theirs. Thus, depending on what you are willing to call "religious experience," you could discover that God is infinite bliss, a consuming fire, the ground of all being, the spirit of love, and so on. Or if your criterion is "object of worship," you could examine what you take to be cases of worship and discover what is said of God there, for example, that He is our father, King of Kings, creator of heaven and earth, judge of all men, and so forth.

M.: Ah, but the language we use to describe what we meet in religious experience or to address the object of our worship is metaphorical language. We don't mean that God is literally a fire, a father, a King, and so forth. Hence in saying these things we aren't really predicating anything of God.

P.: The standards for *real* predication seem to be steadily stiffening. Do you really wish to say that when the poet says:

> There is a garden in her face
> Where roses and white lilies grow,

he is not predicating anything of his lady fair?

M: Not in the strict sense.

P.: What would you take to be a case of predication in the strict sense?

M.: "This cup is blue."

P.: "God is a consuming fire" is certainly different from that. But until you have said just how it is different, that is, until you have given some criteria for recognizing *real* predication, your general thesis that no predicate can be applied to God doesn't come to much.

M.: Surely such criteria could be given. But there is something else we have overlooked. There are cases where we would say that someone understands a sentence even though he doesn't know who is named by a proper name occurring in the sentence. Suppose you are rambling on about your acquaintances and you say "John Krasnick is a queer duck." Perhaps we are interrupted them, and I don't have a chance to ask you who John Krasnick is. Or perhaps I am just not interested in following up this facet of the conversation. It would be strange, wouldn't it, to say that I didn't understand what you had said?

P.: Yes, it would. But note why. If I were called away just after uttering this sentence, and someone asked you, "Who is John Krasnick?" you would reply, "Oh, I don't know, one of P.'s acquaintances," or perhaps, "Someone P. was just talking about; that's all I know about him." You would have to supply at least this much of an identification if you are to be said to understand my remark.

M.: But if the ability to supply an identifying phrase like "the x named 'N,' " or "the x A calls 'N' " is sufficient for understanding a sentence containing a proper name, then I can certainly understand such a sentence without being able to characterize the nominatum. Surely not even you would hold that saying, "X is *named by* 'N' " constitutes a characterization of x.

P.: No, I wouldn't. But note what is going on here. Insofar as the only identifying phrase you gave for N is "the x called 'N," we are hesitant about saying that you understand, or fully understand, what is being said. If, when I said, "John Krasnick is a queer duck," you had nodded, assented, let it pass, or given other indications that you had understood me, and then it turned out later that the only identifying criterion you could give is "the man P. called 'John Krasnick,' " I could accuse you of practicing deception. I might say, "Why didn't you tell me you didn't know who I was talking about?" In other words, when we give the usual indications of having understood a sentence containing a proper name, we are purporting to be able to say more about the nominatum than this.

This is also brought out by the fact that if, after the interruption, someone were to ask you, "Who was P. talking about?" it would be misleading for you to reply, "John Krasnick." For in *using* the proper name, you would be representing yourself as knowing more about him than that I called him "John Krasnick." If that is all you know, the natural thing for you to say would be, "Oh, somebody named 'John Krasnick.' " Thus we put this case into a special category.

And this means that the philosopher who *says,* "God is ineffable" could not be interpreted as understanding "God" in this very weak sense. If I were to *say,* "John Krasnick is queer," and couldn't tell you anything about him (except for queerness), apart from the fact that his name is "John Krasnick," you could justifiably accuse me of shamming. You might retort, "You weren't really saying anything." And there is a good reason for this usage. There would be no point in my saying anything about John Krasnick or God or anyone else unless I had some way of identifying them in addition to their being so named. Why should I bother to say of God that He is ineffable rather than effable, why should I care whether He is omnipotent or limited, loving or cruel, conscious or unconscious, if I know Him only as what people call "God"? It is not only that in this case I would have no *basis* for saying one thing rather than the other. More fundamentally, I could have no interest in doing so. People are interested in saying things, and raising questions, about God because they identify Him as the source of their being, the promulgator of their moral laws, the judge of their sins, the architect of their salvation, the object of their worship, or (with Stace) mystical experience. It is because they identify God in such ways that they consider it important to ask and answer questions about Him.

M.: Perhaps you are right. But there is something else which has been worrying me. People differ enormously in verbal ability. Is it not possible for a man to understand a proper name and yet not be able to put this understanding, at least with any adequacy, in a formula?

P.: Perhaps. *Formulation* of an identifying phrase is not the only device for explaining one's understanding of a proper name, though it is the simplest. If the speaker lacks verbal facility, we might try to smoke out his criterion in some other way. We might, for example, present him with various passages from religious literature and note which ones he recognizes as describing God. Or we might describe (or present) various forms of worship and note which he considers appropriate. With sufficient pains we could, in this way, piece out a criterion which he would on reflection recognize as the one he actually uses. And if the most thorough attempts of this sort were persistently frustrated, wouldn't we again be justified in concluding that he wasn't using the word meaningfully?

Another thing. This point doesn't depend on any special features of *intersubjective* communication. I might be doubtful as to whether I really understood a certain name. If so, I would have to use the same devices to assure myself that I did (or didn't).

But let's forget all these difficulties for the moment and suppose that one can say, "God is ineffable" without thereby defeating one's purpose. We are still faced with the question why anyone should accept the statement. Isn't it amply refuted by the facts? Religious literature is crammed full of sentences attaching predicates to God, and there are many men who devote their lives to making such predications.

M.: Oh, no doubt there are many sentences which have a declarative grammatical form and contain "God" as subject. But if you examine them they will all turn out to be either negative or metaphorical. None of them express *conceptions* of God, and so none constitute predication in the strict sense of the term.

P.: Perhaps. But what positive reasons can be adduced for the position?

M.: Mystics, who are in the best position to know, have repeatedly declared God to be ineffable. Just consider, for example, the statements you cited at the beginning of our discussion.

P.: It is true that many mystics have said things which could be interpreted in this way. But if it is a question of authority, many deeply religious men who are not mystics have expressed themselves to the contrary. Of course you could rule out their testimony by defining "God" as what one encounters in mystical experience, or even (with Stace) simply as mystical experience.

M.: I would hesitate to do that. But if we approach God through mystical experience, without ruling out the possibility of other approaches, we can use a different line of argument. We can see that mystical experience has certain features which prevent it, or anything discovered in it, from being conceptualized. For example:

> It is of the very nature of the intellect to involve the subject-object opposition. But in the mystic experience this opposition is transcended. Therefore the intellect is incapable of understanding it. Therefore it is incomprehensible, ineffable.[9]

> But the oneness of God is indivisible and relationless. Now this relationless, indivisible unity is precisely the character of the mystic intuition as described by all mystics. . . . To say this is only to say that the mystic experience is beyond the capacity of the intellect to handle, since it is the very nature of the intellect to operate by means of separation, discrimination, and analysis.[10]

P.: Leaving aside questions as to the adequacy of the analysis of "intellect" employed here, there is something very strange about these arguments. The conclusion is "Mystical experience is unconceptualizable," and in order to prove it we adduce various characteristics of mystical experience. That is, we have made our success in conceptualizing mystical experience in a certain way a condition for proving that it can't be conceptualized. But how could a successful completion of a task ever enable us to prove that the task is impossible? Wouldn't it rather prove the opposite? Isn't this like giving an inductive argument for the invalidity of induction? Or presenting a documentary film to show that photography is impossible?

M: You keep making the same mistakes. To say that God is an indivisible unity is not to apply any concept to Him. It is simply to *deny* that there is any distinction of parts in Him.

P.: I begin now to see the situation more clearly. Several times I have pointed out that in saying or defending "God is ineffable," you were saying, or implying your ability to say, something about God. And each time you deny that what is being said involves attaching any predicate to God, applying any concepts to Him, or characterizing Him, either because it is negative, or because it is metaphorical, or

[9] *Op. cit.*, p. 40.
[10] *Op. cit.*, pp. 40–41.

because it is an extrinsic denomination, and so forth. It begins to appear that you are prepared to deny of anything you are committed to saying of God that it is a predicate and so on. But if this is your tack, then in uttering "God is ineffable," you are just exhibiting a certain feature of your use of "ineffable" (and "predicate," "concept," and so on), rather than saying anything about God. You are expressing your determination not to count as a predicate and so on anything which is said of God. You are like a man who says, "Only empirically testable sentences are meaningful" (cf. "Only scientific method gives us knowledge") and then, whenever presented with a sentence which can't be empirically tested, denies that it is meaningful, without giving any reason for all these denials except the lack of empirical testability. After a while we will begin to suspect that he is just showing us how he uses "meaningful," rather than ascribing some property to all the members of a class which has been defined in some independent way.

M.: But I am just using "predicate," "concept," and so on, in their ordinary senses. The only statements which you showed I was committed to making would not ordinarily be thought to involve applying concepts or predicates to God. Similarly if the positivist just accepts or rejects examples of meaningful statements according to our ordinary discriminations, he is saying something about the class of statements which would ordinarily be called meaningful.

P.: I'm not at all sure that you are using "predicate" and so on in just the way we ordinarily do, if, indeed, there is any one such way. At least you haven't made that out. Of course, it is only if you are taking "having 'God' as subject" as your sole and sufficient criterion for saying that a sentence doesn't involve predication and so on that you can be accused of uttering a tautology in the strict sense. Insofar as you have other criteria, you are not uttering a tautology. But if you don't state your criteria, and if, whenever you are forced to admit that certain statements containing "God" as subject can be made, you rule these out as examples of "predication" and so on, either without any justification or on the basis of a principle which looks tailor-made for the occasion, we can be excused for suspecting that your utterance approximates to a tautology. Of course alternatively I might suppose that you have no criterion. But then your utterance becomes so indefinite as to assert almost nothing.

If you want to prevent your thesis from oscillating in this limbo between tautology and maximum indefiniteness, you had better include a specification of the senses in which you wish to deny that concepts and predicates can be applied to God. With such a specification the thesis might well be significant and worthy of serious consideration.

For example, you might restate the position: "God cannot be positively characterized in literal terms." This assertion need not lead to such frustrations as we have been considering. For the speaker could use a nonliteral phrase to identify God; and although the statement itself is presumably literal, it is not positive. And, given a sufficiently precise explication of "literal," this is a thesis well worth consideration. Or you might wish to say, "We can speak only of extrinsic features of God, not of His intrinsic nature," or "God can never be characterized with the precision we can attain in science," or "We can speak of God only in a highly abstract way." None of these utterances need be self-defeating; for (1) in each case the sentence itself does not fall within the class of those declared impossible, and (2) a speaker or hearer can use a criterion for identifying God which does not involve attributing to Him a predicate of the sort which is ruled out. If you are interested in un-ambiguously communicating a definite thesis and avoiding tripping yourself up in the process, you would be well advised to make such specifications.

M.: Yes, I see that would be better. But how does it happen that so many philosophers make ineffability statements without qualification?

P.: Perhaps something like this is involved. There are many "un . . . able" words which can be applied with all sorts of qualifications, diminishing to an unqualified application. Thus I can say that our baseball team is unbeatable in our league; or unbeatable by any other amateur team; or well-nigh unbeatable (by any team); practically un-beatable; or, simply, unbeatable; or even, to make it still stronger, absolutely unbeatable. The final term in this series, "unbeatable" (or "absolutely unbeatable") is logically just as respectable as any of the others. Though it may be wildly improbable that our baseball team is unbeatable (without qualification), there is no logical self-stultification involved in saying so. (Cf. "unattainable," "unbreakable," "uncontrol-lable.") With such cases in mind it is easy to feel logically comfortable about saying of God without qualification that He is unconceptualiz-able or ineffable. But we still might feel more squeamish about this latter case were it not for the fact that there are contexts where we can employ even these terms (or terms very close to them) without qualification. For example: (a) "A fall in the stock market is incon-ceivable"; (b) "John is unspeakable." Of course as (a) is actually used, it doesn't imply that we can't apply a concept to the falling of the stock market. It simply means that we have every reason to sup-pose it won't happen. But the verbal similarity between this and "God is unconceptualizable" (where this is intended to imply that we cannot form a concept of God) helps us to suppose that the latter is as legitimate as the former. Similarly (b) is simply a way of saying that John is despicable. But the fact that it has a use helps us to suppose that the verbally similar utterance "God is ineffable" (taken to imply that God cannot be spoken of) also can be given a use. But fully to untangle the muddle in "God is ineffable," we should have to make explicit all the similarities and differences in the ways sentences of this sort function.

If we want to avoid such muddles, we must make explicit the sort of conception, predication, characterization, and so forth we are asserting to be impossible with respect to God in contrast to the sorts we are admitting as possible. To label something ineffable in an unqualified way is to shirk the job of making explicit the ways in which it *can* be talked about; just as to unqualifiedly label an expression (which is actually used) meaningless is to shirk the job of making explicit the sort of meaning it *does* have in these uses. There may be something in the world which can't be talked about in any way, but if so we can only signalize the fact by leaving it unrecorded.

Further Reading On
FAITH AND RELIGIOUS EXPERIENCE

Attfried, Robin. "Believing in God." *Sophia*, July 1973.

Baillie, John. *The Interpretation of Religion.* Nashville: Abingdon Press, 1928.

Baillie, John. *The Sense of the Presence of God.* New York: Scribner's, 1962.

Blackstone, Richard M. "Is Philosophy of Religion Possible?" *International Journal of Philosophy*, Fall 1972.

Buckley, M. J. *Motion and Motion's God.* Princeton: Princeton University Press, 1971.

Burrill, Donald (ed.). *The Cosmological Arguments.* New York: Doubleday, 1967.

Chryssides, George D. "Abraham's Faith." *Sophia*, April 1973.

Collins, J. *God in Modern Philosophy.* Chicago: Regnery, 1959.

De Nicolas, Antonio T. "Religious Experience and Religious Languages." *Main Currents*, November–December 1971.

Diamond, Malcolm L. "Miracles." *Religious Studies*, September 1973.

Dulles, Avery. "Faith, Reason, and the Logic of Discovery." *Thought*, Winter 1970.

Flew, Antony. *God and Philosophy.* New York: Harcourt, Brace and World, 1966.

Flew, Antony, and A. Macintyre. (eds.). *New Essays in Philosophical Theology.* New York: Macmillan, 1955.

Freud, Sigmund. *The Future of an Illusion.* New York: Liveright Publishing, 1955.

Garrigau-Lagrange, R. *God, His Existence and His Nature.* St. Louis: Herter, 1936.

Gastwirth, Paul. "Concepts of God." *Religious Studies*, June 1972.

Gini, A. R. "Facts and Faith." *Proceedings of the American Catholic Philosophical Association*, 1972.

Harrison, Frank R. "How to Go About Saying God Exists." *The New Scholasticism*, Fall 1970.

Hartshorne, Charles. *Man's Visions of God.* Chicago: Willett, Clark, 1941.

Hick, John. *Evil and the God of Love*. New York: Harper, 1966.

Hick, John. *Faith and Knowledge*. Ithaca: Cornell University Press, 1957.

Howe, LeRoy T. "A Preface to Theological Philosophy." *Heythrop Journal*, January 1972.

James, William. *The Varieties of Religious Experience*. New York: F. H. Revell, 1944.

Kaufmann, Walter. *Religion from Tolstoy to Camus*. New York: Harper Brothers, 1961.

Keene, J. Calvin. "Religion and Belief." *Philosophic Exchange*, Summer 1971.

Kenny, A. *The Five Ways*. London: Routledge, 1969.

Laird, John. *Mind and Deity*. New York: Philosophical Library, 1941.

Lewis, H. D. *Our Experience of God*. London: Allen & Unwin, 1959.

Macquarrie, J. *Studies in Christian Existentialism*. London: SCM Press, 1966.

Morrison, A. C. *Man Does Not Stand Alone*. New York: F. H. Revell, 1944.

Nietzsche, Friedrich. *Thus Spake Zarathustra*. Trans. by T. Common. London: Allen and Unwin, Ltd., 1909. (See esp. Sections 66 and 67.)

Phillips, R. P. *Modern Thomistic Philosophy*. Westminster, Maryland: The Newman Bookstore, 1935.

Pike, Nelson. *God and Evil*. Englewood Cliffs: Prentice-Hall, 1964.

Plantinga, Alvin. *God and Other Minds*. Ithaca: Cornell University Press, 1967.

Plantinga, Alvin. *The Ontological Argument*. Garden City: Doubleday, 1965.

Resnick, Lawrence. "Evidence, Utility, and God." *Analysis*, January 1973.

Ross, J. E. *Introduction to the Philosophy of Religion*. New York: Macmillan, 1969.

Russell, Bertrand. *Mysticism and Logic*. London: Allen & Unwin, 1917.

Swinburne, Richard. "Omnipotence." *American Philosophical Quarterly*, July 1973.

Taylor, Richard. *Metaphysics*. Englewood Cliffs: Prentice-Hall, 1963.

Tillich, Paul. *My Search for Absolutes*. New York: Simon and Schuster, 1967.

Watts, Alan. *The Spirit of Zen.* London: John Murray, 1936.

Young, Robert. "Miracles and Epistemology." *Religious Studies,* June 1972.

PART VIII

AESTHETIC JUDGMENT

The Rape of the Sabine Women by Poussin. The Metropolitan Museum of Art, Harris Brisbane Dick Fund, 1946.

Horizontal Tree by Mondrian. Munson-Williams-Proctor Institute, Utica, New York

Musical Forms by Braque. The Philadelphia Museum of Art: The Louise and Water Arensberg Collection

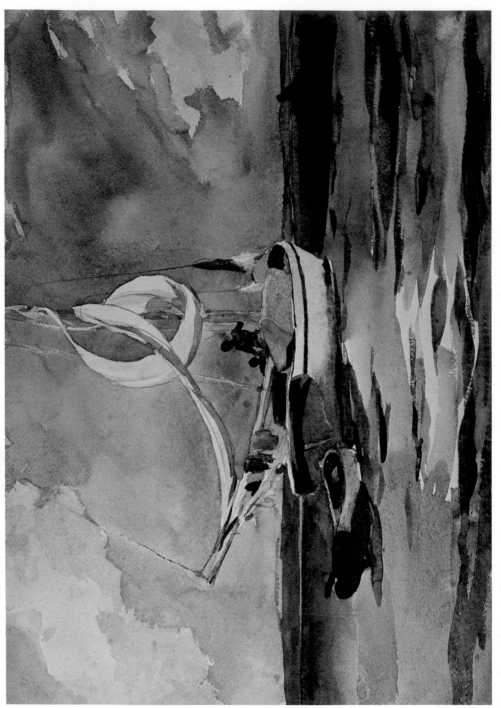

Sloop, Bermuda by Homer. The Metropolitan Museum of Art. Purchase, 1910, Amelia B. Lazarus Fund.

INQUIRY

The only unnatural thing in the world is a work of art.

ANDRE GIDE

CONTEMPORARY English philosopher Stuart Hampshire once said wryly, "It seems that there *ought* to be a subject called 'Aesthetics.' " * There is the philosophy of science and the philosophy of religion, why not the philosophy of art? The main thrust of those philosophies is the studying, clarifying, and analyzing of philosophical problems in the areas of science and religion. But what are the philosophical problems of art? In order to see some of these problems, we shall focus specifically upon the sorts of things people say and do when they evaluate fine art.

Imagine that a group of us are spending a rainy afternoon in an art gallery. Then construct a series of dialogues that concentrate on each of the four paintings: the Poussin, the Mondrian, the Braque, and the Homer. Such an exercise should produce a number of evaluative expressions, some in a class in which the paradigm might be "Mondrian's 'Horizontal Tree' is beautiful!" while others might be classified in a group with "The forms and colors of Homer's 'Sloop, Bermuda' are well-balanced." We shall call the first category I-type aesthetic judgments and the latter category A-type judgments, for reasons that will soon become clear.

What is someone saying when he makes a judgment of the I-type? Although in philosophical discussions the word *beautiful* has received an inordinate amount of attention, this class of judgments includes such expressions as "It's ugly," "It's nice," "It's pretty," "It's good," and "It's bad." The adjectives involved here do not function in ways similar to such descriptive adjectives as shape and color words. If you were to hear someone describe Poussin's "The Rape of the Sabine Women" to someone who had not seen the painting, as follows: "It has a dominant male figure in the upper

* "Logic and Appreciation," *The World Review*, October, 1952.

left who is dressed in a red toga, it is crowded with struggling human forms, and it is beautiful," the difference in adjectival functions would be easily recognizable. The word *beautiful* does not help the listener imagine the painting. If all that he heard were, "Poussin's 'The Rape of the Sabine Women' is beautiful," he would have no idea as to the style, forms, use of color, or composition of the painting. If *beautiful* is a descriptive adjective, what does it describe?

Suppose that instead of saying, "It's beautiful," someone just smiled and said, "Ah!" Is the same judgment of the painting being made? The word *Ah!* is in grammatical terms an interjection. It expresses in varying circumstances with different intonations and gestures, various emotions ranging from sorrow passing into regret to wonder and admiration. Wittgenstein says that words such as *beautiful* and *good* (also *ugly* and *bad*) are taught to children as interjections and are accompanied by exaggerated gestures and facial expressions. *Beautiful* is "an interjection of approval"; *ugly* is "an interjection of disapproval."

Do these interjections characterize their subjects, or do they say something only of those who utter them? Wittgenstein remarks that only people who cannot properly express themselves use these interjections frequently. Suppose that in the tour of the art gallery a dog accompanies the group and that while all are standing before the Poussin painting, the dog begins to wag its tail, as a dog does when getting a meal. The inclination might be to say, "The dog likes the Poussin painting." Here we would be treating the wagging tail as an expression of approval, just as we would treat a dog's howling while I'm singing as an expression of disapproval. What is the difference, however, between such an "expression of approval" by the dog and the utterance by a human being of any affirmative I-type judgment?

If one equates "Mondrian's 'Horizontal Tree' is beautiful" with "I (the speaker) like Mondrian's 'Horizontal Tree,' " then the I-type aesthetic judgment would be identical in meaning to a factual statement. Hence "Mondrian's 'Horizontal Tree' is beautiful" would be true if "I (the speaker) like Mondrian's 'Horizontal Tree' " were true; and otherwise, false. To follow out this type of analysis, if you say that the Mondrian is ugly, you are saying that you do not like the Mondrian. Thus "The Mondrian is ugly" is true in the case that "I (you, the speaker) dislike the Mondrian" is true. If this analysis holds, then the two statements, "The Mondrian is beautiful" and "The Mondrian is ugly," although they appear to, do not really contradict each other except when spoken by the same person. Real disagreement in aesthetics would be impossible if all aesthetic judgments were of the I-type; after all, can one interjection contradict any other? But does it really make sense to call an interjection a judgment?

Someone might say, "Braque's 'Musical Forms' is beautiful, but I don't like it." The fact that there does not seem to be a contradiction in that statement suggests that "X is beautiful" is not adequately interpreted simply as an interjection of approval. Suppose the discussion in the art gallery proceeds as follows :

A. The Mondrian is beautiful.
B: Does that mean that you like it?
A: It certainly does.
B: What makes it beautiful?
A: It is beautiful just because I like it.

A's last response seems to avoid rather than answer the question; doubtless B will press further:

B: Does your approval of the painting make it beautiful? Has the artist nothing to do with its beauty? Or the arrangement of the forms and colors that compose it?

If it is appropriate to ask Why questions when aesthetic judgments are made, a reiteration of an interjection, an expression of approval, or a report on one's likes and dislikes is not a totally acceptable answer. What kinds of reasons are valid reasons for aesthetic judgments?

Saying that Homer's "Sloop, Bermuda" is a good painting because it is a picture of a boat in the waters off Bermuda would not seem to be a reason why it is a good or beautiful painting. Person X might say, "The Homer is beautiful because it is well-balanced, the choice of color is very appropriate to the subject, and the paint is handled extremely well." In order to make judgments of this type with any degree of conviction, it is necessary to know certain things about painting, color, style, mediums, etc. Such A-type judgments are judgments of appreciation (after Wittgenstein). Included in this category we find such criticisms as, "It's too dark," "It's cluttered," "It exhibits a proper tension between space and solid forms," and "The perspective is poorly drawn." Wittgenstein maintains that to properly describe the role of these judgments one must understand their use in our culture and/or the culture of the time of the artist; and that, of course, entails knowing certain facts not only about the art but also about cultures. Art critic John Canaday makes the following remarks about Homer's watercolor "Sloop, Bermuda" that illustrate the use of A-type judgments and their dependence upon technical knowledge.

> The effect is very "wet"; the very feel of the flowing brush is still present. The texture of the paper, which is a part of this effect, is revealed in two ways. In some areas, as in the sky, the pigment has been allowed to settle into the grain of the paper. (Some heavy pigments never go into complete solution and when applied very wet they settle at the bottom of tiny puddles that form in the irregular surface of the paper.) In other places, as in the dark stroke indicating a wavelet in the extreme lower left corner, a relatively dry brushful of pigment has been dragged across the paper, leaving its grain showing as a speckling of white spots like flecks of foam or sparkles of light. Everywhere the paper tells; it is a part of the technique. It tells in brilliance beneath the transparency of the pigment itself. It tells in passages like the sails or the side of the sloop, where it may even remain entirely unpainted or tinted with only the barest suggestion of color.*

Paul Ziff maintains that the only reasons why a painting is beautiful or good are those reasons why it is worth contemplating. This seems to entail a definition of a work of art: a work of art is that which is worth contemplating. Surely there are, however, many phenomena in the world that are worth contemplating but that would not normally be called works of art: cascading waterfalls, idyllic country scenes, towering snow-capped mountains, etc. These are natural; works of art are human creations; hence at least one element in a proper characterization of a work of art would seem to be that it be the product of human hands, that it be an artifact. Yet herein arises another perplexing problem: should we consider paintings and other artistic creations as totally divorced from the artists who created them, or does the proper appreciation of a work of art necessarily entail an understanding of the artist's motives, what he was attempting to achieve?

People often say of a painting that it expresses the artist's feelings about the subject, or of a piece of music that it expresses the feelings of the composer. One may espouse the view that all art is an expression of human feelings (the artist's feelings) and that the only acceptable reasons for judging a painting good are those that explain how

---

* *Metropolitan Seminars in Art,* Portfolio 10, *Techniques* (New York: The Metropolitan Museum of Art, 1958), p. 6.

such expression is accomplished in the work. But the expression theory of art is a problematic one. Consider the following three sentences.

A. Homer's "Sloop, Bermuda" expresses serenity.

B. Homer expressed his feeling of serenity in painting "Sloop, Bermuda."

C. Homer's "Sloop, Bermuda" is serene.

Sentence A does not imply or entail B and, although it is not quite so obvious, B does not entail A. Suppose Homer while painting "Sloop, Bermuda" was feeling anything but serene. He was tense, perhaps angry at a friend, etc. Yet it still might be the case that A is true while B is false; Homer may not have been successful in the expression of his mood.

When A is spoken, how is it to be understood? Is it metaphoric? Paintings do not express feelings in the way people do. "The painting is sad" and "The painter is sad" do not seem to use "sad" in quite the same way. Perhaps A means that looking at Homer's "Sloop, Bermuda" will make one feel serene, but that is not guaranteed. One may look at the painting and feel nothing akin to serenity, yet admit that the painting is serene.

Do A and C mean the same thing? Some expression theorists would argue that they do mean the same thing, but that would seem to ignore some basic differences between being something and expressing something. Is the serenity in the painting? The sloop is in the painting, but serenity? The painting is predominately blue—but serene? Can serenity be a property of a painting? Why, to ask a question similar to the one upon which Bouwsma bases much of his analysis of the expression theory, do we use the word *serene* in regard to the painting at all? Is it only because the word is a part of our vocabulary of criticism, the language-game of aesthetics?

Philosophers dealing with problems of art criticism generally and with good reason focus upon what makes a work of art good or beautiful. The question, "What is good art?" however, is not the same as the question, "What is art?" Our consideration of the four famous paintings has perhaps obscured this important distinction. Consider then the drawing on page 670.

Is it a work of art? It is man-made. It is not functional. Hence it is an artifact, but not a particularly useful one or one designed for a useful purpose, as are most of the artifacts in a Sears Roebuck catalogue. It is achieved in a medium commonly identified with art. It even would appear to express a feeling. But is it art?

One might believe the determination of whether it is a work of art

"Me" (by Sean T. French [age 7]. Used by permission of the artist.)

is somehow a neutral or nonevaluative issue and after that decision has been reached the evaluative question of good or bad can be resolved. But is it not the case that "X is art" is itself an evaluative judgment dependent upon some not totally descriptive criteria: a theory of art? What is it about an amorphous five-foot-long mass of smooth plastic painted bright pink that qualifies it to be on display in an art gallery? A giant soup can label? Five strips of interwoven rusty metal? A giant canvas, bare save for one blue line? Is "X is art" an interjection-type (I-type) judgment, or is it an appreciation-type (A-type) judgment, or is it some other kind of judgment altogether?

1   LUDWIG   WITTGENSTEIN

(1889–1951)

*Lecture on Aesthetics**

Beyond any doubt, Wittgenstein has exerted great influence on the style and
form of most contemporary philosophy in the English-speaking world.
Wittgenstein's philosophical ideas cannot be easily summarized. His work
is more a method for investigating philosophical problems than a systematic
series of answers to those problems. He claims that he sets forth no theories in
philosophy. It is rather difficult, for that reason and because most of his work is
found in relatively short comments, to state Wittgenstein's position. Clearly he
is concerned with language and its many uses, and the contexts in which
language is the key to understanding philosophical difficulties. Philosophy, he
says, "leaves everything as it is." It does not add new information to the
perplexing problems of life; it attempts to clarify those problems by carefully
describing the language at work in them.

    This selection is taken from a lecture on aesthetics and is not written by
Wittgenstein, but is a compilation of his students' notes edited by Cyril Barrett.
One of the major ideas in Wittgenstein's later works, and a significant part of
this lecture, is his idea of forms of life. In his Philosophical Investigations he
tells us that "to imagine a language is to imagine a form of life." A form of
life is one of the things typical of a human being; it encompasses his
responses to his environment. Language plays a dominant role in expressing
and determining our form of life. Wittgenstein tells us that to use properly
aesthetic language (judgments of art), one must begin with a description of a
way of life. Aesthetic words play roles in the language in our culture and in
the culture of various periods of history. To understand their use it is necessary
to describe the circumstances in which they are appropriate expressions, to
know the culture, to have that form of life.

    Wittgenstein's way of doing philosophy is engaging. You cannot sit back and
read him. He demands your involvement. Consider the kinds of examples he
asks one to consider, i.e., "Why it is impossible to get a decent picture of your
friend even if you pay £1,000?" You must constantly stop and rethink the point
that at first seems so evident. Wittgenstein's analysis of aesthetic problems
revolves around the activities of judgment, not just aesthetic words such as
beautiful and moving. "We don't start from certain words, but from
certain occasions or activities," he believes.

* Cyril Barrett, *Wittgenstein Lectures and Conversations on Aesthetics,
Psychology and Religious Belief* (Berkeley, California: University of California
Press, 1967), pp. 1–11. Reprinted by permission of the Regents of the
University of California.

1.   The subject (Aesthetics) is very big and entirely misunderstood as far as I can see. The use of such a word as 'beautiful' is even more apt to be misunderstood if you look at the linguistic form of sentences in which it occurs than most other words. 'Beautiful' [and 'good'—R] is an adjective, so you are inclined to say: "This has a certain quality, that of being beautiful".

2.   We are going from one subject-matter of philosophy to another, from one group of words to another group of words.

3.   An intelligent way of dividing up a book on philosophy would be into parts of speech, kinds of words. Where in fact you would have to distinguish far more parts of speech than an ordinary grammar does. You would talk for hours and hours on the verbs 'seeing', 'feeling', etc., verbs describing personal experience. We get a peculiar kind of confusion or confusions which comes up with all these words. You would have another chapter on numerals—here there would be another kind of confusion: a chapter on 'all', 'any', 'some', etc.—another kind of confusion: a chapter on 'you', 'I', etc.—another kind: a chapter on 'beautiful', 'good'—another kind. We get into a new group of confusions; language plays us entirely new tricks.

4.   I have often compared language to a tool chest, containing a hammer, chisel, matches, nails, screws, glue. It is not a chance that all these things have been put together—but there are important differences between the different tools—they are used in a family of ways —though nothing could be more different than glue and a chisel. There is constant surprise at the new tricks language plays on us when we get into a new field.

5.   One thing we always do when discussing a word is to ask how we were taught it. Doing this on the one hand destroys a variety of misconceptions, on the other hand gives you a primitive language in which the word is used. Although this language is not what you talk when you are twenty, you get a rough approximation to what kind of language game is going to be played. Cf. How did we learn 'I dreamt so and so'? The interesting point is that we didn't learn it by being shown a dream. If you ask yourself how a child learns 'beautiful', 'fine', etc., you find it learns them roughly as interjections. ('Beautiful' is an odd word to talk about because it's hardly ever used.) A child generally applies a word like 'good' first to food. One thing that is immensely important in teaching is exaggerated gestures and facial expressions. The word is taught as a substitute for a facial expression or a gesture. The gestures, tones of voice, etc., in this case are expressions of approval. What *makes* the word an interjection of approval?* It is the

_____

* And not of disapproval or of surprise, for example?—R

game it appears in, not the form of words. (If I had to say what is the main mistake made by philosophers of the present generation, including Moore, I would say that it is that when language is looked at, what is looked at is a form of words and not the use made of the forms of words.) Language is a characteristic part of a large group of activities —talking, writing, travelling on a bus, meeting a man, etc. We are concentrating, not on the words 'good' or 'beautiful', which are entirely uncharacteristic, generally just subject and predicate ('This is beautiful'), but on the occasions on which they are said—on the enormously complicated situation in which the aesthetic expression has a place, in which the expression itself has almost a negligible place.

6.   If you came to a foreign tribe, whose language you didn't know at all and you wished to know what words corresponded to 'good', 'fine', etc., what would you look for? You would look for smiles, gestures, food, toys. ([Reply to objection:] If you went to Mars and men were spheres with sticks coming out, you wouldn't know what to look for. Or if you went to a tribe where noises made with the mouth were just breathing or making music, and language was made with the ears. Cf. "When you see trees swaying about they are talking to one another." ("Everything has a soul.") You compare the branches with arms. Certainly we must interpret the gestures of the tribe on the analogy of ours.) How far this takes us from normal aesthetics [and ethics—T]. We don't start from certain words, but from certain occasions or activities.

7.   A characteristic thing about our language is that a large number of words used under these circumstances are adjectives—'fine', 'lovely', etc. But you see that this is by no means necessary. You saw that they were first used as interjections. Would it matter if instead of saying "This is lovely", I just said "Ah!" and smiled, or just rubbed my stomach? As far as these primitive languages go, problems about what these words are about, what their real subject is, [which is called 'beautiful' or 'good'.—R.] don't come up at all.

8.   It is remarkable that in real life, when aesthetic judgments are made, aesthetic adjectives such as 'beautiful', 'fine', etc., play hardly any role at all. Are aesthetic adjectives used in a musical criticism? You say: "Look at this transition", or [Rhees] "The passage here is incoherent". Or you say, in a poetical criticism, [Taylor]: "His use of images is precise". The words you use are more akin to 'right' and 'correct' (as these words are used in ordinary speech) than to 'beautiful' and 'lovely'.

9.   Words such as 'lovely' are first used as interjections. Later they are used on very few occasions. We might say of a piece of music that it is lovely, by this not praising it but giving it a character. (A lot of

people, of course, who can't express themselves properly use the word very frequently. As they use it, it is used as an interjection.) I might ask: "For what melody would I most like to use the word 'lovely'?" I might choose between calling a melody 'lovely' and calling it 'youthful'. It is stupid to call a piece of music 'Spring Melody' or 'Spring Symphony'. But the word 'springy' wouldn't be absurd at all, any more than 'stately' or 'pompous'.

10. If I were a good draughtsman, I could convey an innumerable number of expressions by four strokes—

Such words as 'pompous' and 'stately' could be expressed by faces. Doing this, our descriptions would be much more flexible and various than they are as expressed by adjectives. If I say of a piece of Schubert's that it is melancholy, that is like giving it a face (I don't express approval or disapproval). I could instead use gestures or [Rhees] dancing. In fact, if we want to be exact, we do use a gesture or a facial expression.

11. [*Rhees*: What rule are we using or referring to when we say: "This is the correct way"? If a music teacher says a piece *should* be played this way and plays it, what is he appealing to?]

12. Take the question: "How should poetry be read? What is the correct way of reading it?" If you are talking about blank verse the right way of reading it might be stressing it correctly—you discuss how far you should stress the rhythm and how far you should hide it. A man says it ought to be read *this* way and reads it out to you. You say: "Oh yes. Now it makes sense." There are cases of poetry which should almost be scanned—where the metre is as clear as crystal—others where the metre is entirely in the background. I had an experience with the 18th century poet Klopstock. I found that the way to read him was to stress his metre abnormally. Klopstock put ˇ — ˇ (etc.) in front of his poems. When I read his poems in this new way, I said: "Ah-ha, now I know why he did this." What had happened? I had read this kind of stuff and had been moderately bored, but when I read it in this particular way, intensely, I smiled, said: "This is *grand*," etc. But I might not have said anything. The important fact was that I read it again and again. When I read these poems I made gestures and facial expressions which were what would be called gestures of approval. But the important thing was that I read the poems entirely differently, more intensely, and said to others: "Look! This is how they should be read." Aesthetic adjectives played hardly any rôle.

13. What does a person who knows a good suit say when trying on a suit at the tailor's? "That's the right length", "That's too short", "That's too narrow". Words of approval play no rôle, although he will look pleased when the coat suits him. Instead of "That's too short" I might say "Look!" or instead of "Right" I might say "Leave it as it is". A good cutter may not use any words at all, but just make a chalk mark and later alter it. How do I show my approval of a suit? Chiefly by wearing it often, liking it when it is seen, etc.

14. (If I give you the light and shadow on a body in a picture I can thereby give you the shape of it. But if I give you the highlights in a picture you don't know what the shape is.)

15. In the case of the word 'correct' you have a variety of related cases. There is first the case in which you learn the rules. The cutter learns how long a coat is to be, how wide the sleeve must be, etc. He learns rules—he is drilled—as in music you are drilled in harmony and counterpoint. Suppose I went in for tailoring and I first learned all the rules, I might have, on the whole, two sorts of attitude. (1) Lewy says: "This is too short." I say: "No. It is right. It is according to the rules." (2) I develop a feeling for the rules. I interpret the rules. I might say: "No. It isn't right. It isn't according to the rules." Here I would be making an aesthetic judgement about the thing which is according to the rules in sense (1). On the other hand, if I hadn't learnt the rules, I wouldn't be able to make the aesthetic judgement. In learning the rules you get a more and more refined judgement. Learning the rules actually changes your judgement. (Although, if you haven't learnt Harmony and haven't a good ear, you may nevertheless detect any disharmony in a sequence of chords.)

16. You could regard the rules laid down for the measurement of a coat as an expression of what certain people want. People separated on the point of what a coat should measure: there were some who didn't care if it was broad or narrow, etc.; there were others who cared an enormous lot. The rules of harmony, you can say, expressed the way people wanted chords to follow—their wishes crystallized in these rules (the word 'wishes' is much too vague). All the greatest composers wrote in accordance with them. ([Reply to objection:] You can say that every composer changed the rules, but the variation was very slight; not all the rules were changed. The music was still good by a great many of the old rules.—This though shouldn't come in here.)

17. In what we call the Arts a person who has judgement developes. (A person who has a judgement doesn't mean a person who says 'Marvellous!' at certain things.) If we talk of aesthetic judgements, we think, among a thousand things, of the Arts. When we make an aesthetic judgement about a thing, we do not just gape at it and say: "Oh! How

marvellous!" We distinguish between a person who knows what he is talking about and a person who doesn't. If a person is to admire English poetry, he must know English. Suppose that a Russian who doesn't know English is overwhelmed by a sonnet admitted to be good. We would say that he does not know what is in it at all. Similarly, of a person who doesn't know metres but who is overwhelmed, we would say that he doesn't know what's in it. In music this is more pronounced. Suppose there is a person who admires and enjoys what is admitted to be good but can't remember the simplest tunes, doesn't know when the bass comes in, etc. We say he hasn't seen what's in it. We use the phrase 'A man is musical' not so as to call a man musical if he says "Ah!" when a piece of music is played, any more than we call a dog musical if it wags its tail when music is played.

18.   The word we ought to talk about is 'appreciated'. What does appreciation consist in?

19.   If a man goes through an endless number of patterns in a tailor's, [and] says: "No. This is slightly too dark. This is slightly too loud", etc., he is what we call an appreciator of material. That he is an appreciator is not shown by the interjections he uses, but by the way he chooses, selects, etc. Similarly in music: "Does this harmonize? No. The bass is not quite loud enough. Here I just want something different. . . ." This is what we call an appreciation.

20.   It is not only difficult to describe what appreciation consists in, but impossible. To describe what it consists in we would have to describe the whole environment.

21.   I know exactly what happens when a person who knows a lot about suits goes to the tailor, also I know what happens when a person who knows nothing about suits goes—what he says, how he acts, etc. There is an extraordinary number of different cases of appreciation. And, of course, what I know is nothing compared to what one could know. I would have—to say what appreciation is—e.g. to explain such an enormous wart as arts and crafts, such a particular kind of disease. Also I would have to explain what our photographers do today—and why it is impossible to get a decent picture of your friend even if you pay £1,000.

22.   You can get a picture of what you may call a very high culture, e.g., German music in the last century and the century before, and what happens when this deteriorates. A picture of what happens in Architecture when you get imitations—or when thousands of people are interested in the minutest details. A picture of what happens when a dining-room table is chosen more or less at random, when no one knows where it came from.

23.   We talked of correctness. A good cutter won't use any words except words like 'Too long', 'All right'. When we talk of a Symphony of Beethoven we don't talk of correctness. Entirely different things enter. One wouldn't talk of appreciating the *tremendous* things in Art. In certain styles in Architecture a door is correct, and the thing is you appreciate it. But in the case of a Gothic Cathedral what we do is not at all to find it correct—it plays an entirely different rôle with us. The entire *game* is different. It is as different as to judge a human being and on the one hand to say 'He behaves well' and on the other hand 'He made a great impression on me'.

24.   'Correctly', 'charmingly', 'finely', etc. play an entirely different rôle. Cf. the famous address of Buffon—a terrific   man—on style in writing; making ever so many distinctions which I only understand vaguely but which he didn't mean vaguely—all kinds of nuances like 'grand', 'charming', 'nice'.

25.   The words we call expressions of aesthetic judgement play a very complicated rôle, but a very definite rôle, in what we call a culture of a period. To describe their use or to describe what you mean by a cultured taste, you have to describe a culture. What we now call a cultured taste perhaps didn't exist in the Middle Ages. An entirely different game is played in different ages.

26.   What belongs to a language game is a whole culture. In describing musical taste you have to describe whether children give concerts, whether women do or whether men only give them, etc., etc. In aristocratic circles in Vienna people had [such and such] a taste, then it came into bourgeois circles and women joined choirs, etc. This is an example of tradition in music.

27.   [*Rhees*: Is there tradition in Negro art? Could a European appreciate Negro art?]

28.   What would tradition in Negro Art be? That women wear cut-grass skirts? etc., etc. I don't know. I don't know how Frank Dobson's appreciation of Negro Art compares with an educated Negro's. If you say he appreciates it, I don't yet know what this means. He may fill his room with objects of Negro Art. Does he just say: "Ah!"? Or does he do what the best-Negro musicians do? Or does he agree or disagree with so and so about it? You may call this appreciation. Entirely different to an educated Negro's. Though an educated Negro may also have Negro objects of art in his room. The Negro's and Frank Dobson's are different appreciations altogether. You do something different with them. Suppose Negroes dress in their own way and I say I appreciate a good Negro tunic—does this mean I would have one made, or that I would say (as at the tailor's): "No . . . this is too long", or does it

mean I say: "How charming!"?

29. Suppose Lewy has what is called a cultured taste in painting. This is something entirely different to what was called a cultured taste in the fifteenth century. An entirely different game was played. He does something entirely different with it to what a man did then.

30. There are lots of people, well-offish, who have been to good schools, who can afford to travel about and see the Louvre, etc., and who know a lot about and can talk fluently about dozens of painters. There is another person who has seen very few paintings, but who looks intensely at one or two paintings which make a profound impression on him. Another person who is broad, neither deep nor wide. Another person who is very narrow, concentrated and circumscribed. Are these different kinds of appreciation? They may all be called 'appreciation'.

31. You talk in entirely different terms of the Coronation robe of Edward II and of a dress suit. What did *they* do and say about Coronation robes? Was the Coronation robe made by a tailor? Perhaps it was designed by Italian artists who had their own traditions; never seen by Edward II until he put it on. Questions like 'What standards were there?', etc. are all relevant to the question 'Could you criticize the robe as they criticized it?' You appreciate it in an entirely different way; your attitude to it is entirely different to that of a person living at the time it was designed. On the other hand 'This is a fine Coronation robe' might have been said by a man at the time in exactly the same way as a man says it now.

32. I draw your attention to differences and say: "Look how different these differences are!" "Look what is in common to the different cases", "Look what is common to Aesthetic judgements". An immensely complicated family of cases is left, with the highlight—the expression of admiration, a smile or a gesture, etc.

33. [Rhees asked Wittgenstein some question about his 'theory' of deterioration.]

Do you think I have a theory? Do you think I'm saying what deterioration is? What I do is describe different things called deterioration. I might approve deterioration—"All very well your fine musical culture; I'm very glad children don't learn harmony now." [*Rhees*: Doesn't what you say imply a preference for using 'deterioration' in certain ways?] All right, if you like, but this by the way—no, it is no matter. My example of deterioration is an example of something I know, perhaps something I dislike—I don't know. 'Deterioration' applies to a tiny bit I may know.

34.   Our dress is in a way simpler than dress in the 18th century and more a dress adapted to certain violent activities, such as bicycling, walking, etc. Suppose we notice a similar change in Architecture and in hairdressing, etc. Suppose I talked of the deterioration of the style of living. If someone asks: "What do you mean by deterioration?" I describe, give examples. You use 'deterioration' on the one hand to describe a particular kind of development, on the other hand to express disapproval. I may join it up with the things I like; you with the things you dislike. But the word may be used without any affective element; you use it to describe a particular kind of thing that happened. It was more like using a technical term—possibly, though not at all necessarily, with a derogatory element in it. You may say in protest, when I talk of deterioration: "But this was very good." I say: "All right. But this wasn't what I was talking about. I used it to describe a particular kind of development."

35.   In order to get clear about aesthetic words you have to describe ways of living. We think we have to talk about aesthetic judgements like 'This is beautiful', but we find that if we have to talk about aesthetic judgements we don't find these words at all, but a word used something like a gesture, accompanying a complicated activity.

36.   [*Lewy*: If my landlady says a picture is lovely and I say it is hideous, we don't contradict one another.]

In a sense [and in *certain examples*—R] you do contradict one another. She dusts it carefully, looks at it often, etc. You want to throw it in the fire. This is just the stupid kind of example which is given in philosophy, as if things like 'This is hideous', 'This is lovely' were the only kinds of things ever said. But it is only one thing amongst a vast realm of other things—one special case. Suppose the landlady says: "This is hideous", and you say: "This is lovely"—all right, that's that.

2   PAUL ZIFF

(1920–   )

Reasons in Art Criticism *

Ziff defends the view that the only reasons why a painting is good are reasons why the painting is worthy of contemplation. He examines the kinds of things critics might say of works of art and offers an analysis of what contemplating a work of art involves. Reasons for contemplation are distinguished from other kinds of statements made about the work of art. Hence to say that a painting is a seascape is not in itself to give a reason why it should be contemplated and therefore not a reason why it is good art. Note also the importance Ziff attaches to the education of the critic in judging a work of art.

* From *Philosophy and Education,* Israel Scheffler, ed., pp. 219–36. Copyright 1958 by Allyn and Bacon, Inc., Boston. Reprinted by permission of the publisher.

HSIEH Ho said one of the principles of painting is that "through organization, place and position should be determined." Le Brun praised Poussin's paintings to the French Academy, saying the figures were faithful copies of Roman and Greek statues.

If someone now says "P.'s painting is a faithful copy of a Roman statue," he is not apt to be offering a reason why the work is either good or bad. "The painting has a touch of blue," ". . . is a seascape," ". . . a picture of peasants," ". . . conforms to the artist's intentions," ". . . will improve men's morals": these too are not apt to be offered, and if offered cannot be accepted as reasons why the painting is good or bad.

But if someone says 'P.'s painting is disorganized," he is apt to be offering a reason why the work is bad (he need not be; this might be part of an answer to "Which one is P.'s?"). Even if it is right to say "P.'s painting is disorganized," it may be wrong to conclude "P.'s painting is bad," or even "P.'s painting is not good." Some good paintings are somewhat disorganized; they are good in spite of the fact that they are somewhat disorganized. But no painting is good because it is disorganized and many are bad primarily because they are disorganized.

To say "P.'s painting is disorganized" may be to offer a good reason why P.'s painting is bad. It is a consideration. It need not be conclusive. But it is a reason nonetheless. Much the same may be said of reference to the balance, composition, proportions, etc., of a painting; but much the same may not be said of certain references to the subject matter, of any reference to the size, shape, effect on morals, etc., of a painting. Why is this so? Is this so?

I

Someone might say this: "If a painting were disorganized and had no redeeming features, one would not call it 'a good painting.' To understand the relevant uses of the phrase 'a good painting' is to understand, among other things, that to say 'P.'s painting is disorganized' may be to offer a reason in support of an unfavorable opinion of P.'s painting."

This won't do at all even though it is plainly true that someone would not—I would not—call a painting "a good painting" if it were disorganized and had no redeeming features.

Maybe certain persons use the phrase "a good painting" in such a way that they would call a painting "a good painting" even if it were disorganized and had no redeeming features. Maybe some or even many or most in fact use the phrase "a good painting" in a way that no painting is good if it is not a seascape. Many people probably use the phrase "a good painting" in many different ways.

It is true that I and my friends would not call a painting "a good painting" if it were merely disorganized, unredeemed. That is no reason why anyone should accept the fact that a painting is disorganized as a reason in support of an unfavorable opinion of it. To say one would not call it "a good painting" if it were disorganized and had no redeeming features is primarily a way of indicating how strongly one is committed to the acceptance of such a fact as a reason, it is a way of making clear precisely what attitude one has here: it does not show the attitude is reasonable.

Why use the phrase in one way rather than another? Why bother with organization? Why not concentrate on seascapes? on pictures of peasants? Is it merely a linguistic accident that one is concerned with organization? This is not a matter of words. (And this is not to say that the words do not matter: "That is a good painting" can be queried with "According to what standards?"; "That is a magnificent painting" cannot be so queried and neither can "That is an exquisite painting," "... a splendid painting," etc.)

Only some of the remarks sometimes made while discussing a work of art are reasons in support of a critical evaluation of the work: to evaluate a work one must understand it, appreciate it; much of what is said about a work is directly relevant only to an appreciation of it.

Any fact is relevant to an appreciation of a work if a knowledge of it is likely to facilitate, to enhance, the appreciation of the work. A critic may direct attention to many different facts: the role of the supporting continuo is the central point in Tovey's discussion of Haydn's chamber music. Tovey points out that the supporting continuo was used to fill a crucial gap in the musical structure:

> The pioneers of instrumental music in the years 1600–20 showed an accurate instinct by promptly treating all groups of instruments as consisting of a firm bass and a florid treble, held together by an unobtrusive mass of harmony in the middle. Up to the death of Handel and beyond, throughout Haydn's boyhood, this harmonic welding was entrusted to the continuo player, and nobody ever supposed that the polyphony of the "real" orchestral parts could, except accidentally or by way of relief, sound well without this supplement.[1]

When Tovey then says: in the later chamber music Haydn abandoned the use of a supporting continuo, he is saying something of relevance to an appreciation of any one of Haydn's chamber works: who can then listen to an early Haydn quartet and not hear it in a new way? The supporting continuo acquires a new prominence in the structure of the whole work. But the end product of this process of re-examining the interrelations of the various parts, to which one has been impelled by the critic's information, is a keener feeling for the texture of the whole.

This is one instance of how historical information can be of value in directing and enlightening the appreciation of a work; there are others: the music of Bach has been compared with that of Schütz, Donne's poetry with that of Cavalcanti, Matisse's work with Egyptian wall paintings. Comparative studies are useful; they provide fresh means of directing and arousing interest in certain aspects of the works under consideration. When a critic shows that work A is intimately related or similar in some important respects to work B, this is of interest not only in that one is then aware of this particular relation between A and B, but more significantly, one may then see both A and B in a different way: A seen in the light of its relation to B can acquire a new lucidity.

Any fact may be relevant to an appreciation of a work, may thereby be indirectly relevant in evaluating it. Presumably every fact directly

[1] *Essays and Lectures on Music*, pp. 3–4.

relevant in evaluating the work is also relevant to an appreciation of it. But the converse is not true, e.g. that the work was executed while the artist was in Rome may be relevant to an appreciation of it but is likely to be relevant in no other way to an evaluation of it. What further requirements must a fact relevant to an appreciation of a work satisfy if it is also to be relevant in evaluating the work?

To say a painting is a good painting is here simply to say it is worth contemplating. (Strictly speaking, this is false but for the time being I am not concerned to speak strictly, but only for the time being. See II below.) Nothing can be a reason why the painting is good unless it is a reason why the painting is worth contemplating. (One can add: for its own sake, but that is redundant.)

Suppose we are in a gallery with a friend looking at P.'s painting; he somewhat admires the work, is inclined to claim that it is good; we wish to deny this, to claim it is a bad painting. We might attempt to support our counter claim by saying "The painting is clearly disorganized," offering this as a reason in support of our opinion of the work.

Saying this to him would be a way of drawing his attention to the organization of the painting, to the lack of it, a way of pointing to this aspect of the painting, saying "Notice this, see the disorder," not merely this, of course, but at least this.

> ("Here you see a single great curving diagonal holds together in its sweep nearly everything in the picture. And this diagonal is not built up by forms that are at the same distance from the eye. The forms are arranged so as to lead the eye gradually backwards until we pass out of the stable into the open air beyond. Here . . ." [2]

said Roger Fry, discussing a painting by Rubens, focusing the listening eye on the single great curving diagonal, drawing it back and forth across the picture plane, levelling the attention, directing it freely throughout the painting.)

This pointing is a fundamental reason why "The painting is clearly disorganized" is a reason, and the fact that it is indicates why "The work was executed while the artist was in Rome," ". . . conforms to the artist's intentions," ". . . is liked by Bernard," even though possibly relevant to an appreciation of the work, are not reasons why the painting is good or bad; for all this is not directly relevant. One cannot contemplate the fact that the work was done while the artist was in Rome in the painting; this is not an aspect of the painting, not a characteristic of it which one can either look at or look for. Suppose one

[2] *French, Flemish and British Art*, p. 125.

were told: "Notice that the work was done while the artist was in Rome," one could only reply: "But what am I supposed to look at?"

Of course one could do this: I say to you "Think of Rome; then look for things in the picture that will fit in with what you've just been thinking"; you might find a great deal in some pictures, little in others. If I want you to make out a lion in the picture which you seem not to have seen I could say this: "Remember the work was done in Africa," "The artist was much interested in animals," etc. So it won't do, in one sense, to say that remarks like "Notice that the work was done while the artist was in Rome" are not reasons because they do not direct or guide one in the contemplation of the work. But in another sense it is obvious that such remarks do not guide or direct one in the contemplation of a work; to suppose that they do is to suppose certain familiar locutions to be signifying in somewhat extraordinary ways.

What is important here is this: one looks at paintings; nothing can be a reason why a painting is good or bad unless it is concerned with what can be looked at in the painting, unless it is concerned with what can, in some sense, be seen.

If it be asked: "Why insist on this? How does this show that 'The work was done while the artist was in Rome' is not a reason why the painting is good?," a sufficient answer is: only in this way can the reason direct or guide one in the contemplation of the work; a "reason" that failed to do this would not be worth asking for, not worth giving; there would be no reason to be concerned with such a "reason."

But this is not to say that "The work was done while the artist was in Rome," ". . . is liked by Bernard," etc., are necessarily, apart from questions of appreciation, altogether irrelevant; these matters may in many ways be indirectly relevant to an evaluation of a work.

That the work was done while the artist was in Rome, is liked by Bernard, was done in the artist's old age, is detested by people of reputed good taste . . . may be indications, signs, that it is a poor work; these may be very good and important reasons to suppose the work is defective. It is for such reasons as these that one decides not to see a certain exhibition, not to read a certain book, not to hear a certain concert. But such facts as these do not in themselves constitute reasons why the painting is a poor work: indications or signs are never reasons why the painting is good or bad, but at best only reasons to suppose it is good or bad. The fact that C cannot remember D's name is often an indication or a sign of the fact that C dislikes D; it is a reason to suppose C dislikes D; in odd cases it may also be a reason why C dislikes D in that it is a contributing cause of the dislike; an indication or a sign is a reason why only when it is a cause. But one is not here concerned with causes: "What causes this to be a good painting?" has no literal meaning; "What makes this a good painting?" asks for the reason why it is a good painting, and this kind of question cannot be answered by citing indications or signs.

This pointing is not the only reason why certain facts are, and others are not, reasons why a painting is good or bad: "The painting is a seascape" points to a characteristic of the painting, directs one's attention to certain features of the work; for saying this to him could be a way of saying "Notice this, see that it is a seascape," yet this is not a reason why the painting is either good or bad.

To say to him "The painting is a seascape" could be a way of directing his attention to the subject matter of the painting, indicating that the painting was of a certain kind. While contemplating a painting one may consider what kind of work it is, who painted it, what kind of organization it has, what kind of subject matter (if any), what kind of pigmentation, etc. To learn that a painting is by a certain artist, has a certain kind of organization, subject matter, pigmentation, etc., may be relevant to an appreciation of the work; it may enable one to recognize, discern, make out, identify, label, name, classify things in the painting, aspects of the painting; such recognition, identification, classification, may be important in the appreciation of a painting; one who failed to recognize or discern or make out the man in Braque's *Man with a Guitar*, the printed letters in a cubist painting, a horse in *Guernica*, would be apt to misjudge the balance and organization of these works, would fail to appreciate or understand these works, would be in no position to evaluate them.

That a painting is of a certain kind may be an excellent reason to suppose it is good or bad. But is it ever a reason why the painting is good or bad? Is the fact that the painting is of a certain kind directly relevant to the contemplation of the painting? Does "The painting is a seascape" direct or guide one in the contemplation of the painting?

Being of a certain kind matters here primarily in connection with the recognition, identification, classification, etc., of various elements of the work. Shall we then say: "Contemplating the subject matter of a painting (or its organization, or its pigmentation, etc.) is not merely a matter of recognizing, identifying, the subject matter, not merely a matter of labelling, naming, classifying"?

That is not enough; it is not that contemplating a painting is not merely a matter of this or that, it is not a matter of recognizing or identifying or classifying or labelling at all.

Contemplating a painting is something one does, something one may be engaged in; one can and does say things like "I am contemplating this painting," "I have been contemplating this painting for some time." But in this sense, recognizing is not something one does; even though it may be true that while contemplating a painting (which has subject matter) I may recognize, or fail to recognize, or simply not recognize, the subject matter of the painting, it is never true that I am recognizing the subject matter; and this is a way of saying one cannot say "I am recognizing the subject matter of this painting," or "I am recognizing this painting," or "I have been recognizing it for some time," etc.

Recognition is like an event, whereas contemplation is like an activity (much the same may be said of identification, classification, etc., in certain relevant senses, though not in all senses, of these terms); certain events may occur during the course of an activity, recognition may or may not take place during the course of contemplation. While contemplating Braque's *Man with a Guitar* one may suddenly (or slowly and at great length) recognize, discern, make out, a figure in the painting; analytical cubistic works often offer such difficulties. If on Monday one recognizes a figure in the Braque painting, on Tuesday there is ordinarily no question of recognition; it has occurred, is over and done with, for the time being; "I recognize it every time I see it" would be sensible if each time it appeared in a fresh disguise, if I suffered from recurrent amnesia, if it appeared darkly out of a haze. (In the sense in which one can speak of "recognizing" the subject matter of an abstract or semi-abstract work, one often cannot speak of "recognizing" the subject matter of a characteristic Chardin still-life: one can see, look at, study, examine the apple in the Chardin painting, but there is not likely to be any "recognition.")

This is not to deny that if a work has recognizable elements, recognition may occur during the course of contemplation, nor that if it does occur then the contemplation of the work is, for some people at least, likely to be somewhat enhanced. If recognition is ever a source of delight, that is certainly true; this, too, would be true: the second time one contemplates the work the contemplation of it may be less worthwhile. But whether this is true or not does not really matter here. It appears to be of interest owing only to an ambiguity of "contemplating."

"Contemplating" may be employed to refer simply to contemplating, or to someone's contemplation of a work at a certain time and place and under certain conditions. "In contemplating the work one attends to the organization" is about contemplating, about what one is doing in contemplating the work; to speak of "contemplating a work," or of "the contemplation of a work," is a way of referring only to certain aspects of one's contemplation of a work at a certain time and place under certain conditions; it is a way of abstracting from considerations of person, place and time. "In contemplating the work one recognizes a figure in the foreground" is not about contemplating the work; it is not about what one is doing in contemplating the work; it is about something like an event that may occur while someone is contemplating the work for the first or second time under certain conditions. (Contrast "In walking one's leg muscles are continually being tensed and relaxed" with "In walking one finds an emerald.")

To say "Since the work has recognizable elements, recognition is likely to occur while contemplating the work and thus the contemplation of the work will be enhanced" would not be to refer to the contemplation of the work, it would not be to abstract from considerations of time; for it is not the contemplation of the work that would be enhanced, but only and merely the contemplation of the work on that particular occasion when recognition occurred. It is for this reason the fact that the work has recognizable elements—and thus admits of the possibility of recognition occurring during the course of contemplation, so enhancing the contemplation—is not a reason why the work is worth contemplating. To say "The work is worth contemplating," or "Contemplating the work is worthwhile," is here and ordinarily to speak of contemplating the work, it is here and ordinarily to abstract from considerations of person, place and time.

Were Guernica hung in Hell, contemplating it would hardly be worthwhile, would there be altogether tedious; yet it is not the work that would be at fault, rather the contemplation of the work in the galleries of Hell. But whether this would be the case has no bearing on whether Guernica is worth contemplating. It would ordinarily be at best foolish to reply to "Guernica is well worth contemplating" by asking "When?" or "Where?" or even "For whom?" That a certain person, at a certain time and place, finds Guernica not worth contemplating may be a slight reason to suppose Guernica is not worth contemplating, but it is not a reason why the work is not worth contemplating. If one knows that no one ever has found, or ever will find, Guernica worth contemplating, one has excellent reason to suppose Guernica is not worth contemplating; one can be absolutely sure it is not worth contemplating; yet this is not even the most trifling reason why Guernica is not worth contemplating. This does not ever entitle anyone to say "I know Guernica is not worth contemplating." All this is but an elaborate way of saying that in saying "The work is worth contemplating" one is abstracting from considerations of person, place and time.

What has been said of "recognition" could be said, in one way or another, of "identification," "classification," "labelling," "naming," etc.;

thus identification, as well as recognition, may occur during the course of contemplation, may enhance the contemplation, is over and done with after a time. But this is never a reason why the painting is good or bad. If recognition, identification, classification, etc. all fail, as they do in fact all fail, to be such a reason, and if nothing can be such a reason unless it is a fact about the work that directs or guides one in the contemplation of the work—thus comparisons, associations, etc., are out of order—it follows that the fact that a work is of a certain kind is also incapable of being a reason why the work is worth contemplating. "There can be no objective rule of taste by which what is beautiful may be defined by means of concepts," said Kant,[3] and he was right (but for the wrong reasons).

Let it be clear that nothing has been said to deny that one can be concerned only with recognition, or identification, or classification, or comparisons, etc., when contemplating paintings; one can treat a painting in the way an entomologist treats a specimen spider, or be concerned only with puzzle pictures, with conundrums. Nor has it been maintained that to say "The work is worth contemplating" is necessarily to abstract from considerations of person, place, and time; that this is what is here and ordinarily intended in speaking of "contemplating a painting" is primarily (though not exclusively) a verbal point and does not signify. There are other ways of speaking: a person may choose to say "The work is worth contemplating" and abstract only from considerations of person, or of place, or of time, or not at all. But if so, he cannot then say what one now wants to say and does say about paintings; for if a person fails or refuses to abstract from such considerations at all, it will be impossible either to agree or disagree with him about the worth of paintings; refusing to abstract from considerations of person, place, and time is tantamount to refusing ever to say, as one now says, "The work is worth contemplating," but insisting always on saying things like "The work is worth contemplating for me, here and now," or ". . . for him, yesterday, at two o'clock," etc. One can speak in this way if one chooses; one can do what one wills with paintings. But none of this has anything to do with art.

To state that a painting is a seascape, if it is simply to state that the work is of a certain kind, is not to state a reason why it is good or bad; for that the painting is of a certain kind cannot be such a reason. What can?

Contrast "The painting is a seascape" with "The painting is disorganized." To say the former to someone could be a way of directing his attention to the subject matter of the painting, indicating that it had a

[3] *Critique of Aesthetic Judgment,* Bk. I, sec. 17.

certain kind of subject matter; to say the latter not only could but would be a way of directing his attention to the organization of the painting, but it would not be indicating that it had a certain kind of organization.

The sense of "organization" with which one is here primarily concerned is that in which one can say of any painting "Notice the organization" without thereby being committed to the view that the painting is in fact organized; one can and does say things like "The main fault to be found with Pollock's paintings is in the organization: his work is completely disorganized." (Just so one can on occasion say "Notice the balance" of a certain painting, and yet not be committed to saying the painting is balanced.) Every work has an organization in the sense that no matter what arrangement there may be of shapes, shades, etc., there is necessarily a particular configuration to be found in the painting. In this sense, the organization is an aspect, a feature, of every painting; something that may be contemplated, studied, and observed, in every painting.

There are various kinds of organization, for the organization of a work is something which may be described, classified, analyzed:

> The chief difference between the classical design of Raphael and the Baroque lay in the fact that whilst the artists of the high Renaissance accepted the picture plane and tended to dispose their figures in planes parallel to that—Raphael's cartoons, for instance, almost invariably show this method—the Baroque designers disposed their figures along lines receding from the eye into the depths of the picture space.[4]

"Horizontally, crossing the picture plane," or "Primarily rectangular," or "Along a single curving diagonal," could be answers to the question "What kind of organization does it have?" in a way that "Organized" or "Disorganized" could not. "Organized" and "Disorganized" are more like states than like kinds of organization ("organized" is more like "happy" than like "healthy," and more like "healthy" than like "human").

Yet this is not to deny what cannot be denied, that a sensible answer to "What kind of painting is it?" might be "A fairly well organized seascape, somewhat reminiscent of the Maine coast." "What kind of painting is it?" is often a request not only to describe the painting, to identify it, name it, classify it, point out its similarities and dissimilarities to other paintings, but also to evaluate the painting, to say whether it is worth bothering with, etc.

[4] R. Fry, *op. cit.*, p. 22.

But seascapes are a kind of painting in a way disorganized or organized paintings are not; crocodiles are a kind of animal in a way healthy animals are not: unlike "seascape" and "crocodile," "organized" and "healthy" admit of questions of degree; one can say "He is quite healthy," "It is somewhat disorganized," "It would be less well organized if that were done," etc.; there are and can be no corresponding locutions employing the terms "seascape" and "crocodile." (One could introduce the terms "seascapish" and "crocodilish," but this is to say: one could invent a use for them.) One cannot discriminate between seascapes on the basis of their being seascapes, whereas one can and does discriminate between disorganized paintings on the basis of their being disorganized, for some are more and some are less.

That "organized," and "disorganized," unlike "seascape," admit of questions of degree is important (thus Tolstoi, who knew what art was, and knowing crucified it, spoke of ". . . those infinitely minute degrees of which a work of art consists"); [5] here it indicates that determining whether a painting is disorganized, unlike determining whether it is a seascape, is not a matter of recognition or identification, though it may, on occasion, presuppose such recognition or identification. In order to determine whether a painting is disorganized, it is necessary to contemplate the organization of the painting. To determine whether a painting is a seascape, it is sufficient to recognize or identify the subject matter of the work; it is not necessary to contemplate the subject matter. To say to someone "The painting is a seascape" could be a way of drawing his attention to the subject matter of the painting, but it would be a way of inviting recognition or identification of certain things in the painting, not a way of inviting contemplation of an aspect of the painting.

"Disorganized," unlike "seascape," reports on an aspect of the painting; one might also say: it refers to a point in a dimension, the particular dimension being that of organization; another point in this dimension is referred to by "clearly organized," another by "an incoherent organization," etc.; to say "The organization of the painting is defective," or "The painting has a defective organization," or "The painting is defectively organized," are ways—different ways—of attributing approximately the same location to the painting in the dimension of organization. To say "The painting is a seascape" is not to direct attention to a certain dimension, that of subject matter; it may direct attention to the subject matter, but not to the dimension of subject matter; such a dimension is found when one considers not the kind but the treatment or handling of subject matter (contrast "The painting is a

[5] *What Is Art?*, Oxford Univ. Press, p. 201.

seascape" with "The figures are too stiff, too impassive"); for it does not refer to a point in that dimension; it does not locate the painting in that dimension. (Just so to say "The painting has a diagonal organization" is not to direct attention to a certain dimension.)

But not any report on any aspect of the painting can be a reason why the painting is good or bad; "The painting is quite green, predominantly green" reports on an aspect of the painting, yet it is not a reason why the work is good or bad.

To say "The painting is quite green" could be somewhat like saying "Notice the organization of the painting" for it could serve to direct attention to an aspect of the painting; but it is not apt to be the relevant kind of report on this aspect. It is not such a report if it does not lead one either to or away from the work: if it were a reason, would it be a reason why the painting is a good painting or a reason why the painting is a bad painting?

But it would not be correct to say it is never a report, in a relevant sense; it is not apt to be, but it might; if someone were to claim that a painting were good and if, when asked why, replied, "Notice the organization!" it could be clear he was claiming that the painting was organized, perhaps superbly organized, that the organization of the work was delightful, etc.; just so if he were to claim "The painting is quite green, predominantly green," it could be quite clear he was claiming that the greenness of the painting was delightful, that the work was "sufficiently green," etc. "The painting is quite green" would here be a report on an aspect of the painting, a report leading in one direction. Even so, it is not a reason why the painting is good or bad.

This is not to deny that someone might offer such a statement as the statement of a reason why the painting is good. Nor is it to deny that "The painting is quite green" has all the marks of such a reason: it points to the painting: it directs one's attention to an aspect of the painting, an aspect that can be contemplated; it reports on this aspect of the painting and thus directs one to the contemplation of the painting. It could be a reason why the painting is good. But it is not. Is it because one simply does not care whether the painting is quite green? because it makes no difference?

One would not ordinarily say to someone "The painting is clearly disorganized" unless one supposed he had somehow not sufficiently attended to the organization of the work. But more than this: ordinarily one would not attempt to draw his attention to the organization of the painting, to the lack of it, unless one took for granted that if he did sufficiently attend to the organization and did in fact find the work to be disorganized, he would then realize that the painting was indeed defective.

One sometimes takes for granted that the absence of organization in a painting, once it is attended to, will in fact make much difference to a person; that he will be less inclined and perhaps even cease to find the work worth contemplating. And this is in fact sometimes the case; what one sometimes takes for granted is sometimes so.

This is one reason that a reference to the organization of the work may be a reason, and why a reference to the greenness of the painting is not; one ordinarily neither finds nor takes for granted one will find the fact that the painting is or is not quite green will make any such difference.

Being green or not green is not likely to make any difference to anyone in his contemplation of the painting; but the same is not true of being huge, or of having a sordid subject. Suppose a work were three miles high, two miles long: one simply could not contemplate it; suppose the subject matter of a work were revolting; certainly many could not contemplate it; or again, what if one knew that contemplating a work would have an insidious and evil influence: could one, nonetheless, contemplate it calmly?

There are many factors that may prevent and hinder one from contemplating a work; there are also certain factors that may facilitate the contemplation of a work; e.g., figure paintings, the Italian treatment of the figure, Raphael's, Signorelli's, Piero's handling, smoothes the path of contemplation.

> Therefore the nude, and best of all the nude erect and frontal, has through all the ages in our world—the world descended from Egypt and Hellas—been the chief concern of the art of visual representation.[6]

One is inclined to contemplate the nude (though not the naked—there is a difference).

That a painting has revolting subject matter, may seduce the beholder, is too large, too small, etc., does make much difference, but a difference of a different kind. That a painting is too large is in fact a reason why the painting is not good; yet it is a reason of a different kind, for it is also a reason why the painting is not bad: that the painting is too large is not a reason why the contemplation of the work is not worthwhile; rather it is a reason why one cannot contemplate the painting, a reason why one simply cannot evaluate the work.

That a painting is not too large, not too small, is not apt to seduce and is even apt to improve one, has splendid subject matter, etc., are not, in themselves, or in isolation, reasons why a work is a good work,

[6] B. Berenson, *Aesthetics and History*, pp. 81–82.

why the work is worth contemplating. Yet such factors as these, by rendering the work accessible to contemplation, can tend to enhance its value. (Memling's *Lady with a Pink* would be less lovely were it larger; *Guernica* would be less majestic were it smaller.) Such factors as these cannot stand alone; alone they are not reasons why the painting is a good painting. That the neighbouring woods are nearby does not prove them lovely, but if lovely, then by being nearby they are that much lovelier, and if ugly, that much uglier.

It is here, perhaps, that the locus of greatness, of sublimity, is to be found in art; a painting with a trivial subject, a shoe, a cabbage, may be a superb work, but its range is limited: even if it succeeds, it is not great, not sublime; and if it fails, its failure is of no consequence; it may be trivial, it may be delightful—nothing more. But a figure painting, Signorelli's Pan, was a great, a sublime painting; had it failed, its failure would have been more tragic than trivial.

Such factors as these often do make a difference, but unlike the fact that the work is well or poorly organized, they do not indicate that the work is or is not worth contemplating: they indicate only that if the work is worth contemplating, it will be well worth contemplating; and if it is not worth contemplating, then possibly it will be not merely not worth contemplating, but distressing.

One sometimes takes for granted that the presence or absence of organization will make a difference to the person. But what if it does not?

It is quite possible that it will not. It is possible that to some people it makes no difference at all whether a painting is disorganized. It may even be that some people prefer what are in fact disorganized paintings (though they might not call them "disorganized"). Perhaps some people greatly admire quite green paintings; the fact that a painting is or is not quite green will make much difference to them.

Someone might now want to say this: "even though you may happen to like a disorganized painting at a time, you won't like it after a time; disorganized paintings do not wear well." Or this: "Even though you may happen to like a disorganized painting, your liking of it will interfere with and narrow the range of your appreciation of many other paintings." Or even this: ". . . your liking of it is unlike that of someone who likes an organized painting; for such a person will not only like it longer, but will like it in a different and better way: 'not merely a difference in quantity, but a difference in quality.' Thus the satisfaction, the value, he finds in contemplating an organized painting is unlike and better than that you find in contemplating a disorganized painting."

It is sometimes true that disorganized paintings do not wear well, but it sometimes is not true; some people persist in liking unlikable paintings. Will perseverance do to transmute vice to virtue? It is sometimes true that a taste for disorganized paintings is apt to interfere with and narrow the range of one's appreciation of other paintings; but is it not likely that one who likes both organized and disorganized paintings will have the more catholic taste? Is it wise to be a connoisseur of wine and cut one's self off from the pleasures of the poor? There is a sense in which it is certainly true that the satisfaction one finds in contemplating an organized painting is unlike and superior to that one finds in contemplating a disorganized painting, but in the sense in which it is, it is here irrelevant: for of course it is certainly true that the satisfaction and value found in connection with a good painting is superior to that found in connection with a bad painting—this of course being a necessary statement. But apart from the fact that the satisfaction found in connection with a good painting is of course superior to that found in connection with a bad painting, what reason is there to suppose in fact—and not merely of course—this is the case? I find no satisfaction in connection with a bad painting, so how shall I compare to see which is superior?

One sometimes says: "Last year I found satisfaction in connection with what I now see to be a bad painting. Now I can see that my satisfaction then was inferior to my satisfaction now found in connection with a good painting." So you might predict to someone: "Just wait! Cultivate your taste and you will see that the satisfaction found in connection with good-A will be superior to the satisfaction, value, you now find in connection with bad-B."

And what if he does not? (Is it not clear that here aesthetics has nothing to do with consequences?) A man might say: "I find the very same kind of satisfaction in this 'disorganized' painting that you find in that 'organized' one: I too am greatly moved, greatly stirred. You may say of course that your satisfaction, the value you find, is superior to mine; in fact it is not." He might be lying, but could he be mistaken?

There is then an inclination to say this: "If being organized or being disorganized does make much difference to a person then for him it is a reason, whereas if it does not make any such difference, it is not." This would be to say that instead of speaking of "the reasons why the painting is good," one would have to speak of "his reasons why" and "my reasons why" and "your reasons why" if one wished to speak precisely. This will not do at all.

I or you or he can have a reason to suppose (think, believe, etc.) the work is worth contemplating; but neither I nor you nor he can have a reason why the work is worth contemplating; anyone may know such a reason, discover, search for, find, wonder about such a reason, but no one can ever have such a reason; even when one has found such a reason, one can only point to it, present it, never appropriate it for one's own; "What are your reasons?" makes sense in reply to "I believe it is worth contemplating," but it has no literal sense if asked of "I know it is worth contemplating." "My reasons why the work is worth contemplating . . . ," "The reason for me the work is worth contemplating . . . ," are also here without relevant literal meaning.

(It would be absurd to describe this fact by saying that what is a reason for me must be a reason for everyone else—as though what no one ever could own must therefore be owned by all alike. What one could say here is that a reason must be as abstract as the judgment it supports.)

If being organized or being disorganized does make much difference to a person then, not "for him" nor "in that case," nor "then and there," it is apt to be a reason, for in that case, then and there, one can forget about him then and there; whereas if it does not make any such difference then, for him, in that case, then and there, it is not apt to be a reason, for in that case, then and there, one cannot forget about him then and there.

To say "The work is worth contemplating" is here and ordinarily to abstract from considerations of person; but such abstraction is, as it were, a minor achievement, an accomplishment possible only when there either is or can be a community of interest. I can ignore the ground I walk on so long as it does not quake. This fact cannot be ignored: contemplating a painting is something that people do, different people.

Paradise gardens are not ever simply a place (one could not be there not knowing it, and it is in part because I know I am not there that I am not there); not being simply a place, paradise gardens are proportioned to everyman's need, even though these requirements may at times be incompatible. But these lesser perfections that paintings are are less adaptable, answer only to some men's need.

Reasoning about works of art is primarily a social affair, an attempt to build and map our common Eden; it can be carried on fruitfully only so long as there is either a common care or the possibility of one. But Kant was wrong in saying aesthetic judgments presuppose a common sense: one cannot sensibly presuppose what is often not the case.

A community of interest and taste is not something given, but something that can be striven for.

II

And now I can be more precise, and that is to say, more general, for we speak of "good poems," "good quartets," "good operas," etc., as well as "good painting." But the problem is always the same. A good anything is something that answers to interests associated with it. In art, this is always a matter of performing certain actions, looking, listening, reading, etc., in connection with certain spatio-temporal or temporal entities, with paintings, poems, musical compositions, etc.

Formulaically, there is only this: a person p_i, performs an action, a_i, in connection with an entity, e_i, under conditions, c_i; e.g. George contemplates Fouquet's *Madonna* in the gallery at Antwerp. e_i is good if and only if the performance of the relevant a_i by p_i under c_i is worthwhile for its own sake. To state a reason why e_i is good is simply to state a fact about e_i in virtue of which the performance of the relevant a_i by p_i under c_i is worthwhile for its own sake.

Someone says, pointing to a painting, "That is a good painting." There is (at least) a triple abstraction here, for neither the relevant persons, nor actions, nor conditions, have been specified. Is it any wonder we so often disagree about what is or is not a good painting.

Persons: George and Josef disagree about a Breughel. Say Josef is color-blind. Then here I discount Josef's opinion: I am not color-blind. But if they were concerned with a Chinese ink drawing, color-blindness would be irrelevant. George is not a peasant, neither does he look kindly on peasants, not even a Breughel painting of peasants. Well, neither do I, so I would not, for that reason, discount his opinion. Josef is a prude, that is, a moralist, and he looks uncomfortably at the belly of a Titian nude. I would discount his opinion, for I am not. (This is why it is horrible nonsense to talk about "a competent observer" in matters of art appreciation: no one is competent or not competent to look at the belly of a Titian nude.) But George has no stomach for George Grosz's pictures of butchers chopping up pigs, and neither do I, so I would not discount his opinion there. George has a horror of churches: his opinion of stained glass may be worthless. Not having an Oedipus complex, George's attitude towards Whistler's Mother is also eccentric. And so on.

If e_i is good then the performance of a_i by p_i under c_i is worthwhile for its own sake. But this obviously depends on the physical, psycho-

logical, and intellectual, characteristics of p_i. If p_i and p_j are considering a certain work then the relevant characteristics of p_i depend on
the particular p_j, e_i a_i, and c_i involved. It is worse than useless to stipulate that p_i be "normal"; what is that to me if I am not normal? and
who is? To be normal is not necessary in connection with some limited
works, and it is not enough to read *Finnegan's Wake*. Different works
make different demands on the person. The popularity of "popular art"
is simply due to the fact that it demands virtually nothing: one can be
as ignorant and brutish as a savage and still deal with it.

But there is no point in worrying about persons for practically nothing can be done about them. Actions are what matter. Art education
is a matter of altering the person's actions, and so, conceivably the
person.

Actions: here we have a want of words. Aestheticians are fond of
"contemplate," but one cannot contemplate an opera, a ballet, a cinema,
a poem. Neither is it sensible to contemplate just any painting, for not
every painting lends itself to contemplation. There is only one significant problem in aesthetics, and it is not one that an aesthetician can
answer: given a work e_i under conditions c_i what are the relevant a_i?
An aesthetician cannot answer the question because it depends on the
particular e_i and c_i: no general answer exists.

Roughly speaking, I survey a Tintoretto, while I scan an H. Bosch.
Thus I step back to look at the Tintoretto, up to look at the Bosch.
Different actions are involved. Do you drink brandy in the way you
drink beer? Do you drive a Jaguar XKSS in the way you drive a hearse?

A generic term will be useful here: "aspection," to aspect a painting
is to look at it in some way. Thus to contemplate a painting is to perform one act of aspection; to scan it is to perform another; to study,
observe, survey, inspect, examine, scrutinize, etc., are still other acts
of aspection. There are about three hundred words available here in
English, but that is not enough.

Generally speaking, a different act of aspection is performed in connection with works belonging to different schools of art, which is why
the classification of style is of the essence. Venetian paintings lend
themselves to an act of aspection involving attention to balanced
masses; contours are of no importance, for they are scarcely to be
found. The Florentine school demands attention to contours, the linear
style predominates. Look for light in a Claude, for color in a Bonnard,
for contoured volumes in a Signorelli.

George and Josef are looking at Van der Weyden's *Descent from the
Cross*. Josef complains, "The figures seem stiff, the Christ unnatural."
George replies, "Perhaps. But notice the volumes of the heads, the

articulation of the planes, the profound movement of the contours." They are not looking at the painting in the same way, they are performing different acts of aspection.

They are looking at the *Unicorn Tapestry*. Josef complains "But the organization is so loose!" So Spenser's great *Faerie Queene* is ignored because fools try to read it as though it were a sonnet of Donne, for the *Queene* is a medieval tapestry, and one wanders about in it. An epic is not an epigram.

George says "A good apple is sour" and Josef says "A good apple is sweet," but George means a cooking apple, Josef means a dessert apple. So one might speak of "a scanning-painting," "a surveying-painting," etc., and just so one speaks of "a Venetian painting," "a sonata," "a lyric poem," "an improvisation," etc.

If e_i is good then the performance of a_i by p_i under c_i is worthwhile for its own sake. If p_i performs a_i under c_i in connection with e_i, whereas p_j performs a_j under c_i in connection with e_i, p_i and p_j might just as well be looking at two different paintings (or poems, etc.). It is possible that the performance of a_i under c_i in connection with e_i is worthwhile for its own sake, while the performance of a_j under c_i in connection with e_i is not worthwhile for its own sake.

There is no easy formula for the relevant actions. Many are possible: only some will prove worthwhile. We find them by trial and error. The relevant actions are those that prove worthwhile in connection with the particular work, but we must discover what these are.

Imagine that *Guernica* had been painted in the time of Poussin. Or a Mondrian. What could the people of the time have done with these works? The question the public is never tired of asking is: 'What am I to look at? look for?" and that is to say: what act of aspection is to be performed in connection with e_i?

Before 1900, El Greco was accredited a second-rate hack whose paintings were distorted because he was blind in one eye. Who bothered with Catalonian frescoes? The Pompeian murals were buried.

Modern art recreates the art of the past, for it teaches the critics (who have the ear of museum and gallery directors who pick the paintings the public consents to see) what to look for and at in modern works. Having been taught to look at things in a new way, when they look to the past, they usually find much worth looking at, in this new way, that had been ignored. So one could almost say that Lehmbruck did the portal of Chartres, Daumier gave birth to Hogarth, and someone (unfortunately) did Raphael in.

Artists teach us to look at the world in new ways. Look at a Mondrian, then look at the world as though it were a Mondrian and you will see what I mean. To do this, you must know how to look at a Mondrian.

And now I can explain why a reason why a work is good or bad is worth listening to. One reason why a (good) Mondrian is good is that it is completely flat. If that sounds queer to you, it is because you do not know how to look at a Mondrian. And that is why the reason is worth considering.

A reason why e_i is good is a fact about e_i in virtue of which the performance of a_i by p_i under c_i is worthwhile for its own sake. So I am saying that the fact that the Mondrian is completely flat indicates that the performance of a_i by p_i under c_i is worthwhile in connection with the Mondrian painting. In telling you this, I am telling you something about the act of aspection to be performed in connection with the work, for now you know at least this: you are to look at the work spatially, three-dimensionally. (Without the painting to point to, I can only give hints: look at it upside down! Right side up, each backward movement into space is counterbalanced by an advancing movement. The result is a tense, dynamic, and dramatic picture plane held intact by the interplay of forces. Turn the painting upside down and the spatial balance is destroyed: the thing is hideous.)

Reasons in criticism are worthwhile because they tell us what to do with the work, and that is worth knowing. Yao Tsui said:

> It may seem easy for a man to follow the footsteps of his predecessors, but he does not know how difficult it is to follow the movements of curved lines. Although one may chance to measure the speed of the wind which blows through the Hsiang Valley, he may have difficulty in fathoming the water-courses of the Lü-liang mountain. Although one may make a good beginning by the skilful use of instruments, yet the ultimate meaning of an object may remain obscure to him until the end. Without knowing the song completely, it is useless to crave for the response of the falling dust.

3

O. K. BOUWSMA

(1898–   )

The Expression Theory of Art *

Bouwsma's style of doing philosophy is unusual. His works seem whimsical, even
farcical, when compared with the writings of the great philosophers of the past.
But Bouwsma is no less serious in his pursuit of clarifications of major philosophical
perplexities. In this essay he tackles the expression theory of art. His concern is to try
to understand what might be meant when an emotion term is predicated of a work
of art. His prime example is "The music is sad," but what he says of music can be
applied to painting and other types of art. When someone says that the music is
sad, does that say of the music something similar to what is said when sadness is
predicated of a person? What is the meaning of emotion terms when they are
applied, as they often are, to works of art?

* From *Philosophical Analysis*, edited by Max Black. Reprinted by permission of
the Editor and the Author.

THE expression theory of art is, I suppose, the most commonly
held of all theories of art. Yet no statement of it seems to satisfy
many of those who expound it. And some of us find all statements
of it baffling. I propose in what follows to examine it carefully. In
order to do this, I want first of all to state the question which gives
rise to the theory and then to follow the lead of that question in providing an answer. I am eager to do this without using the language
of the expression theory. I intend then to examine the language of that
theory in order to discover whether it may reasonably be interpreted
to mean what is stated in my answer. In this way I expect to indicate
an important ambiguity in the use of the word "expression," but more
emphatically to expose confusions in the use of the word "emotion."
This then may explain the bafflement.

I

And now I should like to describe the sort of situation out of which
by devious turnings the phrase "expression of emotion" may be conceived to arise.

700

Imagine then two friends who attend a concert together. They go together untroubled. On the way they talk about two girls, about communism and pie on earth, and about a silly joke they once laughed at and now confess to each other that they never understood. They were indeed untroubled and so they entered the hall. The music begins, the piece ends, the applause intervenes, and the music begins again. Then comes the intermission and time for small talk. Octave, a naïve fellow, who loves music, spoke first. "It was lovely, wasn't it? Very sad music, though." Verbo, for that was the other's name, replied: "Yes, it was very sad." But the moment he said this he became uncomfortable. He fidgeted in his seat, looked askance at his friend, but said no more aloud. He blinked, he knitted his brows, and he muttered to himself. "Sad music, indeed! Sad? Sad music?" Then he looked gloomy and shook his head. Just before the conductor returned, he was muttering to himself, "Sad music, crybaby, weeping willows, tear urns, sad grandma, sad, your grandmother!" He was quite upset and horribly confused. Fortunately, about this time the conductor returned and the music began. Verbo was upset but he was a good listener, and he was soon reconciled. Several times he perked up with "There it is again," but music calms, and he listened to the end. The two friends walked home together but their conversation was slow now and troubled. Verbo found no delight in two girls, in pie on earth, or in old jokes. There was a sliver in his happiness. At the corner as he parted with Octave, he looked into the sky, "Twinkling stars, my eye! Sad music, my ear!" and he smiled uncomfortably. He was miserable. And Octave went home, worried about his friend.

So Verbo went home and went to bed. To sleep? No, he couldn't sleep. After four turns on his pillow, he got up, put a record on the phonograph, and hoped. It didn't help. The sentence "Sad, isn't it?" like an imp, sat smiling in the loud-speaker. He shut off the phonograph and paced the floor. He fell asleep, finally, scribbling away at his table like any other philosopher.

This then is how I should like to consider the use of the phrase "expression of emotion." It may be thought of as arising out of such situations as that I have just described. The use of emotional terms—sad, gay, joyous, calm, restless, hopeful, playful, etc.—in describing music, poems, pictures, etc., is indeed common. So long as such descriptions are accepted and understood in innocence, there will be, of course, no puzzle. But nearly everyone can understand the motives of Verbo's question "How can music be sad?" and of his impulsive "It can't, of course."

Let us now consider two ways in which one may safely escape the expression theory.

Imagine Verbo at his desk, writing. This is what he now writes and this gives him temporary relief. "Every time I hear that music I hear that it's sad. Yet I persist in denying it. I say that it cannot be sad. And now what if I were wrong? If every day I met a frog, and the frog said to me that he was a prince, and that there were crown jewels in his head ('wears yet a precious jewel in his head'), no doubt I should begin by calling him a liar. But the more I'd consider this the more troubled I should be. If I could only believe him, and then treat him like a prince, I'd feel so much better. But perhaps *this* would be more like the case of this music: Suppose I met the frog and every day he said to me, 'I can talk,' and then went on talking and asked me, 'Can I talk?' then what would I do? And that's very much how it is with the music. I hear the music, and there it is again, sad, weeping. It's silly to deny this. See, now, how it is? There's a little prince, the soul of a prince, in the frog, and so there's the soul in this music, a princess, perhaps. See then how rude I was denying this princess her weeping. Why shouldn't music have a soul too? Why this prejudice in favour of lungs and livers? And it occurs to me that this is precisely how people have talked about music and poems. Art lives, doesn't it? And how did Milton describe a good book? Didn't Shelley pour out his soul? And isn't there soul and spirit in the music? I remember now that the poet Yeats recommended some such thing. There are spirits; the air is full of them. They haunt music, cry in it. They dance in poems, and laugh. Pan-psychism for the habitation of all delicacies! So this is how it is, and there is neither joke nor puzzle in this sad music. There's a sad soul in it."

And then it was that Verbo fell asleep. His resistance to the music had melted away as soon as he gave up his curious prejudice in favor of animal bodies, as soon as he saw that chords and tones, like rhymes and rhythms, may sigh and shed invisible tears. Tears without tear glands—oh, I know the vulgar habit! But surely tones may weep. Consider now how reasonable all this is. Verbo is suddenly surprised to discover something which he has always known, namely that music is sad. And the discovery startles him. Why? Because in connection with this, he thinks of his sister Sandra (Cassie to all who saw her cry). And he knows what her being sad is like. She sobs, she wipes her eyes, and she tells her troubles. Cassie has a soul, of course. So Cassie is sad and the music is sad. So the question for Verbo is "How can the music be like Cassie?" and he gives the answer "Why shouldn't there be a soul of the music, that flits in and flits out (People die too!) and inhabits a sonata for a half-hour? Or why shouldn't there be a whole troupe of them? 'The music is sad' is just like 'Cassie is sad,' after all. And Octave who was not disturbed was quite right for he must have a kind of untroubled belief in spirits. He believes in the frog-prince, in the nymphs in the wood, and in the psyche of the sonnet."

This then is one way of going to sleep. But there is another one, and it is based upon much the same sort of method. Both accept as the standard meaning for "The music is sad," the meaning of "Cassie is sad." We saw how Verbo came to see that the meaning is the same, and how then it was true in the case of the music. He might however have decided that the meaning was certainly the same, but that as applied to the music it simply made no sense at all, or was plainly false. Souls in sonnets! Don't be silly. There is the story about Parmenides, well-known to all readers of Dionoges,[1] which will illustrate the sort of thing I have in mind. According to the story, Parmenides and his finicky friend Zeno once went to a chariot race. The horses and chariots had been whizzing past and the race had been quite exciting. During the third round, at one turn a chariot broke an axle and horse and chariot and rider went through the fence. It was a marvelous exhibition of motion done to a turn at a turn. Parmenides was enjoying himself thoroughly. He clutched at the railing and shouted at the top of his voice, "Go, Buceph! Run!" The race is close. But at about the seventh round, with Buceph now some part of a parasang behind, Parmenides began to consider: "Half the distance in half the time; a quarter of the length of a horse in a quarter of the pace it takes. . . ." Suddenly, before the race was half over, Parmenides turned to Zeno. "Zeno," he said, "this is impossible." Zeno, who was ready for his master, retorted, "I quit looking a long time ago." So they left the chariot race, a little embarrassed at their non-existence showing as they walked, but they did not once look back to see how Buceph was doing.

This then is the story about Parmenides. It may be, of course, that this story is not true; it may be one of Dionoges' little jokes. But our concern is not with Parmenides. The point is that it illustrates a certain way of disposing of puzzles. Parmenides has been disciplined to a certain use of such words as "run," "go," "turn," "walk," etc., so that when he is thoughtful and has all his careful wits about him, he never uses those words. He is then fully aware that all forms of motion are impossible. Nevertheless the eyes are cunning tempters. In any case as soon as Parmenides reflects, he buries himself in his tight-fitting vocabulary, and shuts out chariots and horses, and Buceph, as well. "Motion is impossible, so what am I doing here? Less than nothing. N'est pas is not." This disposition of the puzzle is, of course, open only to very strong men. Not many of those people who believe in the impossibility of

[1] An author of no repute at all, not to be confused with Diogenes.

motion are capable of leaving a horse race, especially when some fleet favorite is only a few heads behind.

Now something like this was a possibility also for Verbo. When, puzzled as he was, asking, "How can that be?" he hit upon the happy solution "Why not?" But he might surely have said, stamping his foot, "It can't be." And in order then to avoid the pain of what can't be, he might have sworn off music altogether. No more concerts, no more records! The more radical decision is in such cases more effective. One can imagine Parmenides, for instance, sitting out the race, with his eyes closed, and every minute blinking and squinting, hoping he'd see nothing. So too Verbo might have continued to listen to music, but before every hearing invigorating his resolution never to say that the music was sad. Success in this latter enterprise is not likely to be successful, and for anyone who has already been puzzled it is almost certainly futile.

We have now noticed two ways in which one may attempt to rid oneself of the puzzle concerning "The music is sad," but incidentally we have also noticed the puzzle. The puzzle is identified with the question "How can music be sad?" We have also noticed how easy it is, once having asked the question, to follow it with "Well, it can't." I want now to go on to consider the expression theory in the light of the question "How can it be?" In effect, the expression theory is intended to relieve people who are puzzled by music, etc. They listen and they say that the music is sad. They ask, troubled and shaking their heads, "How can it be?" Then along comes the expression theory. It calms them, saying, "Don't you see that the music expresses sadness and that this is what you mean by its being sad?" The puzzled one may be calmed too, if he isn't careful. In any case, I propose to consider the question "How can it be?" before going on further.

This question "How can it be?" is apparently then not a question primarily about the music. One listens to the music and hears all that there is to hear. And he is sure that it is sad. Nevertheless when he notices this and then returns to the music to identify just what is sad in it, he is baffled. If someone, for instance, had said that there is a certain succession of four notes on the flute, in this music, and he now sought to identify them, he could play the music, and when they came along, he would exclaim, "There they are," and that would be just what he aimed at. Or again if someone had said that a certain passage was very painful, and he explained that he meant by this that when it is heard one feels a stinging at one's finger tips, then again one could play the music and wait for the stinging. Neither is it like the question which leaped out of the surprise of the farmer at the birth of his first two-headed calf. He looked, amazed, and exclaimed, "Well, I'll be switched! How can that be?" He bedded the old cow, Janus, tucked in the calf, and went to consult his book. He did not stand muttering, looking at the calf, as Verbo did listening to the record on the phonograph. He took out his great book, *The Cow*, and read the chapter entitled "Two Heads Are Better than One?" He read statistics and something about the incidence of prenatal collusion and decided to keep an eye on collaborators among his herd. And that was all. When now it comes to "The music is sad," there's no such easy relief. What is there to listen for? What statistics are there?

We have noticed before how Verbo settled his difficulty. He did this, but not by examining the music further. He simply knew that the music was sad, and supplied the invisible tears, the unheard sobs, the soul of the music. If you had asked him to identify the tears, the unheard sobs, the soul of the music, he could not have done this. He might have tried, of course, and then he would have been baffled too. But the point is that he tries to think of the sadness of the music in the way in which he thinks of Cassie's sadness. Now we may be ready to explain the predicament, the bafflement. It arises from our trying to understand our use of the sentence "The music is sad" in terms of our uses of other sentences very much like this. So Verbo understands in terms of the sentence "Cassie is sad." One can imagine him saying to himself, "I know what sadness is, of course, having Cassie in the house, so that must be how it is with the music." Happily, as in the case of Parmenides, he thought of only one use, and as with a sharp knife he cut the facts to suit the knife. But suppose now that there are several uses of sentences much like "The music is sad"; what then? Is it like this use or this use or this use? And supposing sometimes it's like this and at other times like this, and sometimes like both. Suppose further that one is only vaguely aware that this is so, and that one's question "How can that be?" is not stated in such a way as to make this possibility explicit, would it then be any wonder that there is bafflement?

Let us admit then that the use of "The music is sad" is baffling, and that without some exploration, the question "How can that be?" cannot be dealt with. Merely listening to the music will not suffice. We must then explore the uses of other sentences which are or may not be similar to this, and we may hope that in this process we may see the expression theory emerge. At any rate, we'll understand what we are about.

II

What now are some of these other types of sentences which might be helpful? Well, here are a few that might serve: "Cassie is sad," "Cassie's dog is sad," "Cassie's book is sad," "Cassie's face is sad." Perhaps, one or other of these will do.

Though we have already noticed how Verbo came to use "Cassie is sad," I should like to consider that sentence further. Verbo understood this. When, as he remembered so well, the telephone call came and little Cassie answered—she had been waiting for that call—she was hurt. Her voice had broken as she talked, and he knew that the news had been bad. But he did not think she would take it so hard. And when she turned to him and he asked her what the man had said, at first her chin quivered and she didn't speak. Then she moved towards him and fell into his arms, sobbing: "Poor Felicia, poor Felicia!" He stroked her hair and finally when she was calm, she began to pour out her confidences to him. She loved her cat so; they had been brought up together, had had their milk from the same bottle, and had kept no secrets from each other. And now the veterinary had called to say that she had had another fit. And she burst into tears again. This was some years ago. Cassie is older now.

But this is not the only way in which "Cassie is sad" is used. Verbo had often heard his father and mother remark that it was good that Cassie could cry. They used to quote some grandmother who made a proverb in the family. It went: "Wet pillows are best." She had made this up many years ago when some cousin came to sudden grief. This cousin was just on the verge of planned happiness, when the terrible news came. (Her picture is the third in the album.) She received the news in silence and never spoke of it or referred to it as long as she washed the dishes in her father's house, for, as you may have guessed, she never married. She never cried either. No one ever heard her sniffling in the middle of the night. She expressed no regrets. And she never told cat or mirror anything. Once she asked for a handkerchief, but she said she had a cold. All the family knew what had happened, of course, and everyone was concerned, but there was nothing to do. And so she was in many ways changed. She was drooping, she had no future, and she tried to forget her past. She was not interested. They all referred to her as their sad cousin, and they hoped that she would melt. But she didn't. Yet how can Cassie's cousin be sad if she never cries?

Well, there is a third use of "Cassie is sad." Tonight Cassie, who is eighteen now, quite a young lady, as the neighbours say, goes up to her room with her cat, her big book, and a great bowl of popcorn. She settles into her chair, tells kitty to get down, munches buttery corn, and reads her book. Before very long she is quite absorbed in what she reads and feels pretty bad. Her eyes fill with tears and the words on the page swim in the pool. It's so warm and so sweet and so sad! She would like to read this aloud, it's so wonderful, but she knows how the sadness in her throat would break her words in two. She's so sorry; she's so sad. She raises her eyes, closes them, and revels in a deep-drawn sigh. She takes up a full hand of popcorn and returns to her sadness. She reads on and eats no more corn. If she should sob in corn, she might choke. She does sob once, and quite loud, so that she is startled by it. She doesn't want to be heard sobbing over her book. Five minutes later she lays her book aside, and in a playful mood, twits her cat, pretending she's a little bird. Then, walking like old Mother Hubbard, she goes to the cupboard to get her poor cat a milk.

Cassie is sad, isn't she? Is she? Now that you consider it, she isn't really sad, is she? That cozy chair, that deliberate popcorn, that playing sparrow with her cat, that old Mother Hubbard walk—these are not the manners of a sad girl. She hasn't lost her appetite. Still one can see at once how we come to describe her in this way. Those are not phony tears, and she's as helpless in her sobs and in keeping her voice steady and clear as she was years ago when her dear cat had that fit. And she can, if you are so curious, show you in the book just what made her feel so sad. So you see it is very much like the case in which Cassie was sad. There's an obvious difference, and a similarity too. And now if you balk at this and don't want to say that Cassie in this situation is sad, your objection is intelligible. On the other hand if Cassie herself laughingly protests, "Oh, yes, I was sad," that will be intelligible too. This then may serve as an illustration of the way in which a puzzle which might become quite serious is fairly easily dealt with. How can Cassie be sad, eating popcorn and playing she's a sparrow?

In order to make this clear, consider Cassie now a grown woman, and an accomplished actress. She now reads that same passage which years ago left her limp as a willow, but her voice is steady and clear, and there are no tears. She understands what she reads and everyone says that she reads it with such feeling—it's so sad!—but there isn't a sign of emotion except for the reading itself, which as I said, goes along smoothly and controlled even to each breath and syllable. So there are no wet eyes, no drunken voice, and not a sob that isn't in the script. So there. Is she sad? I take it not. The spoken words are not enough. Tears, real tears, a voice that breaks against a word, sighs that happen to one, suffered sobs— when the reading occasions these, then you might say that Cassie was sad. Shall we say however, that the reading is sad? How can that be? Well, you see, don't you?

Let us now attend to a sentence of a different type: "Cassie's dog is sad." Can a dog be sad? Can a dog hope? Can a dog be disappointed? We know, of course, how a Cartesian would answer. He might very well reply with this question, "Can a locomotive be sad?" Generous, he might allow that a locomotive might look sad, and so give you the benefit of a sad look for your dog. But can a dog be sad? Well, our dog can. Once during the summer when Cassie left her for three weeks, you should have seen her. She wouldn't look at the meatiest bone. She'd hang her head and look up at you as woebegone as a cow. And she'd walk as though her four hearts would break. She didn't cry, of course, and there were no confidences except those touching ones that come by way of petting and snuggling and looking into those wailing eyes. In any case our dog acted very much like that sad cousin who couldn't cry. She had plenty of reason, much too much, but she kept her wellings-up down. It's clear in any case what I mean when I say that our dog was sad. You mustn't expect everything from a sad dog.

So we pass to another type of sentence: "Cassie's book is sad." Well, obviously books don't cry. Books do not remember happier days nor look upon hopes snuffed out. Still, books that are sad, must have something to do with sadness, so there must be sadness. We know, of course. Books make people sad. Cassie reads her book and in a few minutes if she's doing well, she's sad. Not really sad, of course, but there are real tears, and one big sob that almost shook the house. It certainly would be misleading to say that it was imaginary sadness, for the sadness of Cassie isn't imagined by anyone, not even by herself. What she reads on the other hand is imaginary. What she reads about never happened. In this respect it's quite different from the case in which she is overwhelmed by the sad news over the telephone. That was not imaginary, and with the tears and sobs there was worry, there was distress. She didn't go twittering about, pretending she was a little bird five minutes after that happened. So a sad book is a book that makes Cassie, for instance, sad. You ask, "Well, what are you crying about?" And she says, "Booh, you just read this." It's true that that is how you will find out, but you may certainly anticipate too that it will be a story about a little boy who died, a brave little boy who had stood up bravely for his father, about a new love and reconciliation come almost too late, about a parting of friends and tender feelings that will die, and so on. At any rate, if this is what it is like, you won't be surprised. It's a sad book.

There is one further sentence to consider: "Cassie's face is sad." The same sort of thing might be said about her speaking, about her walk, about her eyes, etc. There is once again an obvious way of dealing with this. What makes you say her face is sad? Anyone can tell. See those tear stains and those swollen eyes. And those curved lines, they all turn down. Her face is like all those sad faces in simple drawings where with six strokes of my neighbor's pencil I give you "Sad-Eye, the Sorry Man." The sad face is easily marked by these few unmistakable signs. Pull a sad face, or droop one, and then study it. What have you done? In any case, I am supposing that there is another use of "Cassie's face is sad," where this simplicity is absent. Oh, yes, there may be certain lines, but if you now ask, "And is this all you mean by Cassie's face being sad," the answer may very well be "No." Where then is the sadness? Take a long look and tell me. Cassie, hold still. The sadness is written all over her face, and I can't tell you it's here and not there. The more I look, the more I see it. The sadness in this case is not identified with some gross and simple signs. And you are not likely to find it there in some quick glance. Gaze into that face, leisurely, quietly, gently. It's as though it were composed not of what is sad in all sad faces, but rather of what is sad only in each sad face you've ever known. This sad face is sad but when you try now to tell someone what is sad in it, as you might with the drawing I made, you will have nothing to say. But you may say, "Look, and you will see." It is clear, of course, that when Cassie's face is sad, she need not be sad at all. And certainly when you look as you do, you need not be sad.

We have noticed briefly several types of sentences similar to "The music is sad," and we have seen how in respect to several of these the same sort of puzzling might arise that arose in respect to "The music is sad." We have also seen how in respect to these more obvious cases this puzzling is relieved. The puzzling is relieved by discerning the similarity between the offending use and some other use or uses. And now I should like to ask whether the puzzle concerning "The music is sad" might not also be relieved in some similar fashion. Is there not a use of some type of sentence, familiar and relatively untroubled, which is like the use of "The music is sad"?

We have these types of sentences now ready at our disposal: There are two uses of "Cassie is sad," in the first of which she is concerned about her cat, and in the second of which she is cozy and tearful, reading her book. We have "Cassie's cousin is sad," in which Cassie's cousin has real cause but no tears, and "Cassie's dog is sad," in which her dog is tearless as her cousin, but with a difference of course. You could scarcely say that Fido restrained his tears. Then there were the uses of "Cassie's face is sad" and "Cassie's reading is sad." And, of course, there is the use of "Cassie's book is sad." I am going to take for granted that these uses are also intelligible. Now then is the use of "The music is sad" similar to any of these?

I suppose that if the question is stated in this way, one might go on by pointing out a similarity between it and each one of these other types of sentences. But what we must discover is enough similarity, enough to relieve the puzzle. So the question is: To which use is the use of "The music is sad" most similar? Certainly not to "Cassie is sad (about her cat)," nor to "Cassie's cousin is sad," nor to "Cassie's dog is sad."

There are two analogies that one may hopefully seize upon. The first is this: "Cassie is sad, reading a book," is very much like "Verbo is sad, listening to music." And this first is also very much like "Cassie is sad, hearing the news over the telephone." And just as the first involves "The book is sad," so the second involves "The music is sad," and the third involves "The news is sad." Now let us consider the first. Reading the book is one thing, and feeling sad is quite another, and when you say that the book is sad, you mean by this something like this: When Cassie reads, she feels sad about what she reads. Her feeling sad refers to her tears, her sobs, etc. So too listening to the music and hearing it is one thing, and feeling sad is another, and when you say that the music is sad, you mean that while Verbo listens to the music, he feels sad. And shall we add that he feels sad about it? This might, if you like, refer to something like his half-tears, sub-sobs, etc.

Suppose now we try to relieve Verbo in this way. We say, "Don't you see? 'This music is sad' is like 'The book is sad.' You understand that. That's very much like 'The news is sad.'" Will that satisfy him? I think that if he is very sharp, it won't. He may say, "I can see how 'The book is sad' is like 'The news is sad.' But when it comes to these you can easily point out the disturbance, the weeping, but the music—that's different. Still there might be something." What now bothers him?

I think what bothers him may be explained in this way. When you say that a book is sad, or a certain passage in a book is sad, you may mean one or other or both of two things. You may mean what has already been defined by the analogy above. But you may also mean something else. The following illustration may exhibit this. Imagine Cassie, then, in her big chair, reading, and this is the passage she reads:

> "I say this in case we become bad," Alyosha went on, "but there's no reason why we should become bad, is there, boys? Let us be, first and above all, kind, then honest, and let us never forget each other! I say that again. I give you my word, for my part, that I'll never forget one of you. Every face looking at me now I shall remember even for thirty years. Just now Kolya said to Kartashov that he did not care to know whether he exists or not. But I cannot forget that Kartashov exists and that he is blushing now as he did when he discovered the founders of Troy, but is looking at me with his jolly, kind, dear little eyes. Boys,

my dear boys, let us all be generous and brave like Ilusha, clever, brave and generous like Kolya (though he will be ever so much cleverer when he grows up), and let us all be as modest, as clever and sweet as Kartashov. But why am I talking about those two! You are all dear to me, boys, from this day forth I have a place in my heart for you all, and I beg you to keep a place in your hearts for me! Well, and who has united us in this kind, good feeling which we shall remember, and intend to remember all our lives? Who, if not Ilusha, the good boy, the dear boy, precious to us forever! Let us never forget him. May his memory live forever in our hearts from this time forth."

Cassie reads this and Cassie cries. Let us call this Cassie's sadness. But is there now any other emotion, any other sadness, present? Well, there may very well be. There may be the Alyosha emotion. Whether that is present however depends upon how the passage in question is read. It may be read in such a way, that though Cassie understands all she reads, and so knows about the Alyosha emotion, yet she will miss it. This will be the case if she cries through the reading of it. If she reads the passage well, controlled, clear, unfalteringly, with feeling, as we say, which does not mean with crying, then the Alyosha emotion will be present. Otherwise only signs of it will be present. Anyone who has tried to read such a passage well, and who has sometimes failed and sometimes succeeded, will understand what I have in mind. Now then we have distinguished the Cassie emotion and the Alyosha emotion. They may be present together, but only, I think, when the Cassie emotion is relatively weak. And so when someone says that the passage in question is sad, then in order to understand we must ask, "Is it sad in the Cassie emotion or is it sad in the Alyosha emotion?"

And now we are prepared again to examine the analogy: "The music is sad" is like "The book is sad," where it is sad with the Alyosha emotion. This now eliminates the messiness of tears. What we mean by Alyosha's emotion involves no tears, just as the sadness of the music involves no tears. And this now may remind us of Cassie reading the passage, cool, collected, reading with feeling. But more to the point it suggests the sentence "Cassie's face is sad." For see, when the music is sad, there are no tears, and when the passage is read, well read, there are no tears. And so when I look into this face and find it sad, there are no tears. The sadness in all these cases may be unmistakable, and yet in none of these is there anything to which I might now draw your attention, and say, "That's how I recognize it as sad." Even in the case of the reading, it isn't the sentences, it isn't the subject, that make it sad. The sadness is in the reading. Like a musical score, it too may be played without feeling. And it isn't now as though you both read and have these feelings. There is nothing but the reading, and the feeling is nothing apart from this. Read the passage with and without feeling, and see that the difference consists in a difference in the reading. What baffles in these cases is that when you use the word "sadness" and the phrase "with feeling," you are certain to anticipate sadness and feeling in the ordinary sense. But if the sadness is in the sounds you make, reading or playing, and in the face, once you are forewarned you need no longer anticipate anything else. There is sadness which is heard and sadness which is seen.

This then is my result. "The music is sad" is like "the book is sad," where "The book is sad" is like "The face is sad." But "The music is sad" is sometimes also like "The book is sad," where "The book is sad" is like "The news is sad." If exhibiting these analogies is to be helpful, then, of course, this depends on the intelligibility of such sentences as "The book is sad," "The face is sad," "The news is sad," etc.

III

So far I have tried to do two things. I have tried to state the problem to which the expression theory is addressed, and then I have gone on to work at the solution of that problem in the way in which this statement of the problem itself suggests that it be worked out. In doing this I have sought deliberately to avoid the language of the expression theory.

Here then is the phrase to be studied. The expression theory maintains: The music is sad means: The music is the expression of sadness or of a certain sadness. The crucial word is the word "expression." There are now at least two contexts which determine the use of that word, one is the language of emotion, and the other is the language of or about language.

Let us consider first the use of the word "expression" in the language of emotion. In the discussion of the types of sentences above, it will be remembered that Cassie's cousin is sad, but doesn't cry. She does not "express" her emotion. Cassie on the other hand carries on, crying, sobbing, and confiding in everyone. She "expresses" her emotion, and the expression of her emotion is tears, noises, talk. That talk is all about her cat, remember. When she reads her book, she carries on in much the same way. In this latter case, there was some question as to whether there was really any emotion. She was so sad, remember, and ate popcorn. But in terms of what we just now said, whether there is emotion or not, there certainly is "expression" of emotion. These tears are just as wet as other tears, and her sobs are just as wet too. So in both cases there is expression of emotion, and in the first case there is emotion, thick as you please, but in the second case, it's not that thick. It appears then that you might find it quite natural to say that there is expression of emotion but no emotion, much as you might say that there was the though of an elephant, but no elephant. This may not seem so strange, however, if we reflect that as in the case of Cassie's cousin, there may be emotion, but no or very little expression of emotion.

In order to probe the further roots of the uses of this phrase, it may be useful to notice that the language of emotion is dominantly the language of water. So many of our associations with the word "emotion" are liquid. See then: Emotions well up. Children and young girls bubble over. There are springs of emotion. A sad person is a deep well. Emotions come in waves; they are like the tides; they ebb and flow. There are floods and "seas of passion." Some people gush; some are turbulent. Anger boils. A man blows up like a boiler. Sorrow overwhelms. The dear girl froze. We all know the theory of humors. In any case, it is easy enough, in this way, to think of a human being as like a reservoir and an ever flowing pool and stream of emotions. All flow on toward a dam, which may be raised or lowered, and over and through which there is a constant trickle. Behind the dam are many currents, hot, cold, lukewarm, swift, slow, steady, rippling, smooth. And there are many colors. Perhaps we should say that currents are never exhausted and do not altogether trickle away. Emotions, like our thoughts, are funded, ready to be tapped, to be rippled, to be disturbed.

Let us see how the term "expression" fits into this figure. How was it with Cassie's cousin? Well, once there was a clear, smoothflowing current of affection, and it flowed, trickle, trickle, over the dam in happy anticipation and a chestful of hope's kitchen and linen showers. And suddenly a planet falls, in the form of a letter, into that deep and flowing pool. Commotion follows, waves leap, eddies swirl. The current rushes on to the dam. And what happens? The dam rises. Cassie's cousin resists, bites her lip, intensifies her fist. She keeps the current back. Her grief is impounded. She does not "express" her emotion. And what happens to Cassie, when she felt so bad about the cat? That's easy. Then too there was a disturbance. The current came down, splashed over the dam which did not rise at all, and it flowed away in a hurly-burly of "Oh! It's awful! My poor kitty!" Cassie let herself go. She "expressed" her emotion.

The use of the word "expression" in the light of this figure is, I take it, clear enough. And the use of the word in this way describes a familiar difference in the way in which good news and bad news may affect us. And now we may ask, "And is it something like this that people have

in mind when they say that art is the expression of emotion?" Certainly
something like this, at least part of the time. Consider how Wordsworth
wrote about poetry: "Poetry is the spontaneous overflow of powerful
emotions." Overflow! This suggests the pool and the dam and the
"powerful" current. An emotion, lying quiet, suddenly gets going and
goes over. There is spontaneity, of course. No planet falls and no cat is
sick. The emotion is unprovoked. There is also the common view that
artists are people who are more emotional than other people. They are
temperamental. This once again suggests the idea that they have particular need of some overflow. Poetry is a little like blowing off steam.
Write poetry or explode!

This isn't all that Wordsworth said about poetry. In the same context
he said: "Poetry is emotion recollected in tranquility." Again this suggests a hiding place of emotion, a place where past heartaches are
stored, and may be taken up again, "recollected." We store ideas. We
also put away emotions. So we have the pool as we had the pool before
in describing Cassie's cousin and Cassie. But now we have something
else, "the spontaneous overflow" and the "recollection in tranquility."

Let us consider this for a moment, again in order to notice the use
of the word "expression." Cassie hears bad news and cries. She "expresses" her emotion. The emotion is aroused and out it flows. What
now happens in the case of the poet? Ostensibly in his case too emotions
are aroused, but they do not flow out. Poets do not cry enough. Emotions
are stored up, blocked. Emotions accumulate. And what happens now?
Well, one of two things may happen. Emotions may quite suddenly
leap up like spray, and find a way out, or again a poet may dip into
the pool with his word dipper, and then dip them out. It's as though
the emotions come over the dam in little boats (the poems) and the
little boats may be used over and over again to carry over new surges.
And this too may be described in this way: The poet "expresses" his
emotion. Cassie cries. The real incident is sufficient. The poet does not
cry. The real incident is not sufficient. He's got to make poems in order
to cry. All men must cry. This may seem a bit fantastic, but this sort of
phantasy is common in explaining something as old, for instance, as
Aristotle's use of the word "catharsis."

The analogy which we have tried to exhibit now is this one: As Cassie
"expresses" her emotion at hearing the news, so the poet or reader "expresses" his emotion at reading the poem. The news and the poem
arouse or evoke the respective emotions. Now most people who expound the expression theory are not content with this analogy. They say
that Cassie merely vents or discharges her emotion. This is not "expression" of emotion. Cassie merely gets rid of her emotion. And what does

the poem do? Perhaps in terms of our figure we may say: It ripples it, blows a gentle wind over it, like a bird skimming the water. At any rate the emotion stays. And so the theory seeks a more suitable analogy and finds it conveniently in the language about language.

I should like first to notice certain distinctions which lead to this shift from the first to the second analogy. In the first place poems and music are quite different from the occasions that make Cassie and Cassie's cousin so sad. Tones on a piano and a faithless lover or dying cat are not much alike, and this is enough to disturb the analogy. But there is also an unmistakable difference in the use of the word "emotion" in the two cases. An "emotion recollected in tranquility" is, after all, as I suggested before, more like a ripple than like a tempest. It is, accordingly, these distinctions that determine the shift. It may be useful to notice that the general form of the first analogy is retained in the second. For the poem and the music are still conceived as "arousing," as "evoking," the emotion.

The new analogy accordingly is this one: Music "expresses" sadness (art expresses emotion) as sentences "express" ideas. And now, I think, it is easy to see why this analogy should have been seized upon. In the first place so much of art involves symbols, sentences themselves, and representations. There are horses in pictures. It is quite easy then to fall into regarding art as symbolic, that is, as like sentences. And now just as sentences symbolize ideas and serve to evoke them as distinguished from real things, of which ideas are more like shadows, so too music and poems serve to evoke emotions of a peculiar sort, emotions which are like the shadows of real emotions. So this analogy is certainly an improvement. Art is after all an artifice, like sentences, and the emotions involved are related to the real things in much the way that ideas are to real things, faint copies. All this fits in very well with the idea that art is like a dream, a substitute of real life, a vicarious more of what you cannot have, a shadowland.

And now how does this analogy succeed?

Before answering this question, I should like to notice the use of the words "evoking" and "arousing." Sentences "evoke" ideas. As one spieler I know, says: "When I read a sentence, an idea pops into my head." Pops! This is something like what, according to the analogy, is meant by sentences "expressing" ideas. I am not interested in criticizing this at this point. I wish only to clarify ideas. Pop! Consider the sentence "The elephant ate a jumbo peanut." If at the moment that you read this sentence you see in your mind's eye a big elephant nuzzling around a huge peanut, this will illustrate what "evoking" is like. The sentence evokes; the idea pops. There is the sentence and there is this unmistakable seeing in your mind's eye. And if this happened, surely you would have got the idea. What I wish to point out is that it is this view or some similar view of how sentences work, that underlies this present analogy. They "evoke." But the word "evoke" has other contexts. It suggests spirits, witchcraft. The spirit of Samuel appearing at the behest of the witch of Endor is an "evocation." Spiritualistic mediums "evoke" the living spirits of the dead. And the point of this association is that the spirits are waiting, in the second or third canto of Dante's *Comedy,* perhaps, to be called. They are in storage like our ideas, like our emotions. And the word "arouse" is like the word "evoke." Whom do you arouse? The sleeper. And so, sleeping ideas and sleeping emotions lie bedded in that spacious dormitory—hush!—we call the mind. Waiting to be called! And why now have I made a point of this? Because this helps to fill out this analogy by which in particular we are led to use the word "feeling" or "emotion" in the language of the expression theory. The music "evokes," "arouses" feelings.

The difficulty then does not arise concerning experiences of this sort. The puzzle arises and remains most stubbornly where the sadness is dry-eyed. And here the analogy with language seems, at least, to be of no use. Cassie may read the passage with feeling, but without the flicker of an eyelash. And she may listen to sad music as cool and intent as she is gazing at a butterfly. She might say that it was more like watching, fascinated, the pain in a suffering face, herself quite undistressed. Santayana identifies the experience in this way: "Not until I confound the impression (the music; the sentences) and suffuse the symbols with the emotions they arouse, and find joy and sweetness in the very words I hear, will the expressiveness constitute a beauty. . . ." [2] I propose now to study this sentence.

Now notice how curious this is. Once more we have the sentences or the music. And these arouse emotions. This describes Cassie reading her book. So we might expect that Cassie would cry and would sob and so on. But this isn't all. Cassie is confused. Actually she is crying but she thinks the words are crying. She wipes her tears off those words. She sighs but the words heave. The sentence of Santayana suggests that she sees the sentences she reads through her tears and now her tears misserve her much as blue moods or dark glasses do. So Cassie looks through sadness and the sentence is tearful. What a pathetic fallacy! From confusion to suffusion! Are there misplaced emotions? Imagine what this would be like where sentences aroused not emotions but a toothache.

[2] *The Sense of Beauty* (1896), p. 149.

And now you confused the toothache with the sentence, and before someone prevented you, you sent the sentence to the dentist.

Nevertheless, Santayana has almost certainly identified an experience that is different from that in which Cassie is sad over her book. We find "joy and sweetness in the very words" we hear. Certainly, too, Santayana has been misled by these words "joy and sweetness." For if there is joy and sweetness, where should these be but where they usually are? Where is joy then and where is sweetness? In the human breast, in the heart ("my heart leaps up when I behold"), in the eye. And if you say this, then indeed there must be some illusion. The sentence is like a mirror that catches and holds what is in the heart. And so artful are poets' sentences that the best readers are the best confused. I want now, however, to suggest that indeed joy and sweetness, and sadness too, are in the very words you hear. But in that case, joy and sweetness must be of the sort that can be in sentences. We must, accordingly, try to figure out what this "joy and sweetness in the very words" is like. For even though, making a mistake, one imagined they were in the words, their being there must make some sense. And Santayana too does not imagine that sentences cry.

Let me return now to the analogy: The music is sad is like: The sentence expresses an idea. We saw before how the sentence "The elephant ate a jumbo peanut" might be accompanied by an image and how this was like sentences or music arousing emotions. We want now to see how we might use the phrase "joy and sweetness in the very words." Do we have a meaning for "The idea in the very words you hear." Where is the idea of the elephant eating a jumbo peanut? Suppose we say, "It's in the very words you hear." Have you ever seen, in your mind's eye, that is, an elephant eating a peanut in the very words you hear? A sentence is like a circus tent? I do not suppose that anyone who said that joy and sweetness are in the very words you hear would be likely to say that this was like the way in which you might also see an image in the very sentence which you hear—a bald head in the word "but." I should like in any case to try something different.

I do not intend to abandon the analogy with language yet. Music is expression of emotion as sentences are expression of ideas. But now how do sentences express ideas? We have noticed one way in which sentences do sometimes have meaning. Sentences, however, have been described in many ways. Sentences are like buzzers, like doorbells, like electric switches. Sentences are like mirrors, like maps, like pictures; sentences are like road signs, with arrows pointing the way. And so we might go on to ask, "Is music like buzzers, like pictures, like road sign arrows?" I do not however intend to do this. It will be noticed that the same analogy by which we have been trying to understand music, art, etc., may serve us also to understand what language is like. The analogy pre-supposes that we do know something about music, and so turning the analogy to this use may be fruitful. It might show us just how enlightening and how unenlightening the analogy is.

In order to study the analogy between music and the sentence and to try in this way to find out what the sentence is like, I now intend to offer a foolish theory. This may throw into clearer relief what Santayana says. What is understanding a sentence like? Understanding a sentence is speaking the sentence in a certain way. You can tell, listening to yourself talk, that you are understanding the sentence, and so can anyone else who hears you speak. Understanding has its rhythm. So the meaning of the sentence consists in a certain reading of the sentence. If, in this case, a sentence is spoken and not understood by someone, there would be only one thing to do, namely, speak the sentence again. Obviously this account will not do for there are other ways of clarifying what we mean. Nevertheless in some cases it may be all that is necessary.

Now notice. If this were what the meaning of a sentence is like, we should see at once what was meant if someone said that the meaning or the idea is in the sentence. For if there is meaning, where could it be but in the sentence, since the sentence is all there is. Of course, it is true that the sentence would have to be spoken and, of course, spoken in some way or other. And with every variation in reading it might then be said to have a different meaning. If anyone asked, "And what does the sentence mean?" expecting you to point to something or to elaborate the matter in gestures or to translate, it would be clear that he quite misunderstood what meaning is like. One might even correct him, saying it is even misleading to say that the meaning is in the sentence, as though it were only a part of the sentence, or tucked away somehow under overlapping syllables. A sentence having meaning in a case like this would be something like a living thing. Here too one might ask, "Where is the life in a squirrel and in a geranium?" Truly the life is the squirrel and is the geranium and is no part of either nor tucked away in some hidden fold or tiny vein. And so it is with the sentence, according to our imaginary theory. We might speak of the sentence as like a living thing.

And now let us see whether we have some corresponding use for "The joy and sweetness are in the very words you hear." People do ask about the meaning of poems and even about the meaning of music. Let us first of all say that the meaning is "the joy and sweetness," and the sadness. And where are these? In the very words you hear, and in the music. And now notice that what was admittedly a foolish theory in respect to sentences is not a foolish theory in respect to poems or music. Do you get the poem? Do you get the music? If you do not, pointing, gestures, translations will not help. (Understanding the words is presupposed.) There will be only one thing to do, namely, read the verses again, play the music once more. And what will the joy and sweetness and the sadness be like? They will be like the life in the living thing, not to be distinguished as some one part of the poem or music and not another part, or as some shadow that follows the sounded words or tones. "In the very words you hear," like the squirrel in fur!

I infer now that the analogy between the "joy and sweetness" in words and the meaning in sentences is misleading and is not likely to be helpful. The meaning of sentences is translatable, but the "meaning" of poems, of music is not. We have seen how this is so. There may, of course, be something in the sounding of all sentences which is analogous to the "joy and sweetness in the very words," but it is not the meaning of those sentences. And now this is an interesting consequence. It makes sense to ask, "What does the sentence express?" It expresses a meaning, of course, and you may have some way of showing what this is, without using the sentence to do so. But it now makes no sense to ask, "What does the poem express?" or "What does the music express?" We may say, if we like, that both are expressive, but we must beware of the analogy with language. And we may prevent the helpless searching in this case, by insisting that they "express" nothing, nothing at all.

And now let us review. My assumption has been that the expression theory is plagued with certain analogies that are not clearly distinguished, and none of which finally is helpful without being misleading. The first analogy is that in terms of which we commonly think of emotions. The second is that in terms of which we think of language, the doorbell view. Besides this there are two different types of experience that arise in connection with art. One of these types may be fairly well described by the analogy with doorbell language. The similarity of our language, however, in respect to both these types of experience, conceals the difference between those two types. Santayana's sentence reveals the agony that follows the recognition of this difference in these types of experience and the attempt to employ the language which describes the one to describe the other. The language requires very interesting translation. My conclusion, accordingly is this: The analogy drawn from language may be useful in describing one type of experience. It is practically useless in describing the other. Since, then, these two analogies dominate the use of the word "expression," I suggest that, for the sake of clarity and charity, they be abandoned in seeking to describe that "expressiveness" which Santayana says constitutes "a beauty."

If we now abandon these analogies, are we also to abandon the use of the word "expression"? Not unless we please to do so. But we do so at our risk, for these analogies are not easily abandoned. We may, however, fortify our use of this word by considerations such as these. We use the word "expressive" to describe faces. And we use "expressive" in much the same way that we use the phrase "has character." A face that is expressive "has character." But when we now say that a face has character, this may remind us that the letters of the alphabet are characters. Let us suppose for a moment that this is related to "He's a character!" I suppose that he's a character and he has a character do not mean quite the same thing. There are antics in he's a character. Try again: The zigzag line has character and the wavy line has character. Each letter of the alphabet is a character, but also has character. The number tokens, 1 2 3 4 5 6 7 8 9—each has its character. In the same way sounds have character. Let me see whether we can explain this further. You might say that if some dancing master were to arrange a dance for each of the numbers, you might see how a dance for the number one would not do at all for number five. Or again if the numbers were to be dressed in scarfs, again a certain color and a certain flimsy material would do for six but would not suit five at all. Now something of the same sort is true of words, and particularly of some. Words have character. I am tempted to say that all these things have their peculiar feel, but this then must be understood on the analogy with touch. If we, for instance, said that all these things have their peculiar feeling, then once again it might be supposed that in connection with them there is a feeling which is aroused by them.

Let your ears and your eyes, perhaps, too, feel these familiar bits of nonsense:

> Hi diddle diddle!
> Fee! fi, fo, fum!
> Intery, mintery.
> Abra ca da bra.

Each has its character. Each is, in this sense, expressive. But to ask now "What is its character or what does it express?" is to fall into the pit. You may, of course, experiment to exhibit more clearly just what the character, in each case, is. You may, for instance, contrast the leaping, the stomping, the mincing, the shuffle, with what you get if you change the vowels. Try the following:

> Ho! doodle doodle!
> Fa, fo, fu, fim!
> Untery, muntery.
> Ay bray cay day bray.

One also might go on to change consonants in order again to exhibit character by giving the words new edges and making their sides steeper or smoothing them down.

I do not intend, in proposing illustrations of this sort, to suggest that art is nonsense and that its character is simple as these syllables are. A face, no doubt may bear the impress, the character, of a life's torment and of its hope and victory. So too words and phrases may come blazing out of the burning past. In art the world is born afresh, but the travail of the artist may have had its beginnings in children's play. My only point is that once the poem is born it has its character as surely as a cry in the night or intery, mintery. And this character is not something that follows it around like a clatter in a man's insides when he reads it. The light of the sun is in the sun, where you see it. So with the character of the poem. Hear the words and do not imagine that in hearing them you gulp a jigger to make yourself foam. Rather suppose that the poem is as hard as marble, ingrained, it may be, with indelible sorrow

If, accordingly, we now use the sentence "Art is expression," or "Art is expressive," and the use of this sentence is determined by elucidations such as I have just now set out, then, I think, that our language may save us from some torture. And this means that we are now prepared to use freely those sentences that the expression theory is commonly inclined to correct. For now, unabashed, we shall say that the music is sad, and we shall not go on to say that this means that the music expresses sadness. For the sadness is to the music rather like the redness to the apple, than it is like the burp to the cider. And above all we shall not, having heard the music or read the poem, ask, "What does it express?"

IV

And now it's many words ago since we left Verbo and his friend at the corner. Verbo was trying to figure out, you remember, how the music was related to his grandmother. How can music be sad? I suggested then that he was having word trouble, and that it would be necessary to probe his sentences. And so we probed. And now what shall we tell Verbo?

Verbo, we will say, the music is sad. And then we will remind him that the geranium is living, and that the sun is light. We will say these things so that he will not look away from the music to discover the sadness of it. Are you looking for the life in the geranium? Are you looking for the light in the sun? As then the life and the light describe the geranium and the sun, so too does sadness describe the music. And then we shall have to go on to tell him about these fearful analogies, and about Santayana's wrestle on the precipice. And about how we cut the ropes! And you may be sure that just as things are going along so well, Verbo will ask, flicking the ashes from his cigarette, "And what about the sadness?"

And now it's time to take the cat out of the bag, for so far all that has been exposed is the bag. The sadness is a quality of what we have already described as the character, the expressive. One piece of music is like and unlike some other pieces of music. These similarities and these differences may be perceived. Now then, we have a class of sad music. But why sad, that is, why use this word? It must be remembered, of course, that the use of this word is not precise. So there may be some pieces of music which are unmistakably sad, and others which shade off in gradations to the point where the question "Is it sad?" is not even asked. Suppose we ask our question "Why sad?" in respect to the unmistakable cases. Then, perhaps, some such answer as this will do. Sad music has some of the characteristics of people who are sad. It will be slow, not tripping: it will be low, not tinkling. People who are sad move more slowly, and when they speak, they speak softly and low. Associations of this sort may, of course, be multiplied indefinitely. And this now is the kitten in whose interest we made so much fuss about the bag. The kitten has, I think, turned out to be a scrawny little creature, not worth much. But the bag was worth it.

The bag was worth it? What I have in mind is that the identification of music as the expressive, as character, is crucial. That the expressive is sad serves now only to tag the music. It is introspective or, in relation to the music, an aside. It's a judgment that intervenes. Music need not be sad, nor joyous, nor anything else. Aestheticians usually account for this by inventing all sorts of emotions without names, an emotion for every piece of music. Besides, bad music, characterless music, the unexpressive, may be sad in quite the same way that good music may be. This is no objection, of course, to such classifications. I am interested only in clarifying the distinction between our uses of these several sentences.

And now that I have come to see what a thicket of tangle-words I've tried to find my way through, it seems to me that I am echoing such words as years ago I read in Croce, but certainly did not then understand. Perhaps if I read Croce again now I shouldn't understand them either. "Beauty is expression."

Further Reading On
AESTHETIC JUDGMENT

Amos, Van Meter. "Is It Art?" *Journal of Aesthetics and Art Criticism,* Fall 1971.

Beardsley, Monroe. *Aesthetics.* New York: Harcourt, Brace and World, 1958.

Carritt, E. F. *What Is Beauty?* Oxford, 1962.

Daubner, Edith. "Defining Art: A Classroom Discussion." *Journal of Aesthetic Education,* October 1972.

Dewey, John. *Art as Experience.* New York: Capricorn Books, 1934.

Feibleman, James K. "Bad Art." *Tulane Studies in Philosophy,* 1971.

Harrison, John L. "Cognitive Aspects of Aesthetic Response." *Philosophy of Education: Proceedings,* 1971.

Iseminger, Gary. "Aesthetic Judgements and Non-Aesthetic Conditions." *Analysis,* March 1973.

Hofstradter and Kuhns. *Philosophies of Art and Beauty.* New York: Modern Living, 1964.

Kant, Immanuel. *Observations on the Feeling of the Beautiful and Sublime.* Trans. by J. T. Goldwaitt. Berkeley: University of California Press, 1960.

Levich, Marvin. *Aesthetics and the Philosophy of Criticism.* New York: Random House, 1963.

Mace, C. A. "The Aesthetic Attitude." *British Journal of Aesthetics,* Summer 1972.

Margolis, Joseph. "Critics and Literature." *British Journal of Aesthetics,* Autumn 1971.

Meager, R. "Aesthetic Concepts." *British Journal of Aesthetics,* October 1970.

Morawski, Stefan. "Artistic Value." *Journal of Aesthetic Education,* January 1971.

Osborne, H. "Definition and Evaluation in Aesthetics." *Philosophical Quarterly,* January 1973.

Peltz, Richard. "Classification and Evaluations in Aesthetics: Weitz and Aristotle." *Journal of Aesthetics and Art Criticism,* Fall 1971.

Puravs, Olgerts. "Criticism and Experience." *Journal of Aesthetic Education,* January 1973.

Tatarkiewicz, Wladyslaw. "The Great Theory of Beauty and Its Decline." *Journal of Aesthetics and Art Criticism,* Winter 1972.

EPILOGUE

METAPHILOSOPHY

INQUIRY

AFTER having explored the irregular topography of the territory of philosophy by focusing upon specific landmark problems and after having discerned and hopefully applied the differing techniques of a number of philosophers, one might have the feeling: "It does not all belong; it is too diverse. Can it all be philosophy?"

Philosophy: a discipline lacking in unity, at first a desert; then a pine forest, then red rocks, cliffs dropping off into the green-blue waters of yet another uncharted sea; a fog. The explorer is frustrated, bewildered, his maps incomplete, his trail markings scattered by the fury of a shifting gale. Ludwig Wittgenstein wrote, "A philosophical problem has the form 'I don't know my way about' "[1]

If only one could observe the terrain of philosophy from above, play the philosophical astronaut. It is said that on a certain plain in Peru odd markings have been discovered when seen from an airplane which on earth hardly resemble the beetle-like creature which they outline. Some things, such as the Peruvian beetle, are "meant" to be seen from above. But to get "above" philosophy is to leave philosophy. As one recedes from the activity, its stark cliffs and majestic mountains, its hazards, pitfalls, and triumphs flatten. The burning browns of the deserts, the icy whites of the peaks, the somber greens of the forests, and the salty blues of the sea as one ascends blend into a dull gray. No philosophical exploration has ever been conducted from 40,000 feet above the activity of philosophy, and none ever will.

There is, nevertheless, a good deal of literature on the question "What is philosophy?" not unlike an over-large collection of photographs of the Grand Canyon, all of which, although taken from different positions and angles, look remarkably similar; none quite "captures" the vista. The following selections by R. M. Hare on the style of doing philosophy at Oxford University and by Gilbert Ryle on the nature of philosophical activity are included for those who feel that it is necessary to say something in a general sort of way about the aims and methods of the philosophical enterprise in an introductory textbook on philosophy. They are also offered for their inspirational value.

[1] *Philosophical Investigations* (New York: Macmillan Co., 1953), #123.

R. M. HARE

(1919–   )

Philosophy at Oxford*

*From "A School for Philosophers," *Ratio*, II, No. 2, 1960 (also printed in *Essays on Philosophical Method*, London Macmillan, 1971) © by R. M. Hare 1960, used by permission of R. M. Hare.

. . .

We have at Oxford about sixty professional philosophers; the bulk of these, apart from the three professors at the top, and a very few university readers, lecturers, etc., are, like myself, fellows and tutors in one or other of the many colleges which make up the university. Each of us has committed to his charge some twenty or so students from his own college; these are normally studying some other subject in addition to philosophy—for we do not think it healthy to study philosophy in complete isolation; we put it with some other, less abstract subject such as history or economics or psychology. It should, perhaps, be mentioned also that philosophy is studied at Oxford by very large numbers of students. It is not, as at most other places, a small specialist course. Most of my pupils are going to be, not professional philosophers, but businessmen, politicians, schoolmasters, clergymen, lawyers, journalists, civil servants, and, indeed, almost anything but philosophers; and a substantial number of these may be expected to reach the highest ranks of their professions. So the Oxford tutor, if he can teach his pupils how to think more clearly and to the point, can have much more influence on the life of the country in this way than he is likely to achieve by writing books, unless the books are outstandingly successful.

Each of these students goes to his philosophy tutor once a week, either by himself or in the company of one other student, for what is known as a *tutorial*. He will have been told the week before to read certain books or articles and to write an essay on some subject chosen by the tutor to bring out the most important questions raised in the book. At the beginning of the tutorial he will read this essay aloud; this will take about fifteen minutes. If he gets to the end of it without interruption, the rest of the hour will be spent in discussing the subject of the essay. The average tutor's working week during the term will consist of from ten to twenty hours spent seeing pupils in this way, and about two hours' public lectures or seminars. The rest of his time, after some part of it has been devoted to practical business in connection with the administration of the college, is his own.

. . .

What, then, is the effect of this system on the student and on his tutor? It is profound. The student is very soon made to realise that everything that he says in an essay has to be justified before a highly skilled and usually merciless critic, not only in respect of its truth, but also in respect of relevance, accuracy, significance and clarity. Anything that is put in to fill in space, or which is ambiguous or vague or pretentious, or which contains more sound than significance, or whose object is anything else but to express genuine thought, is ruthlessly exposed for what it is. The tutor knows that he cannot be sure of getting his pupil to see the truth; for, even if it were not possible in philosophy for there to be sincere differences of opinions about the truth, nobody can see the truth about a philosophical question until he has by his own efforts reached the point from which it is visible. What the tutor can do is to teach his pupil to think effectively; to express his thought clearly to himself and to others; to make distinctions where there are distinctions to be made, and thus avoid unnecessary confusion—and not to use long words (or short ones) without being able to explain what they mean. Enormous stress is laid on style, not in the sense of literary elegance—for this is esteemed of small value—but in the sense of an effective, unambiguous, clear and ordered expression of one's thought, which cannot be achieved unless the thought itself has the same qualities.

The effect of this treatment on the student is what might be expected. But its effect on the tutor himself should not escape notice. He has continually to set an example of the virtues which he is seeking to inculcate. Though he may have been studying a question for twenty years or more, he has hour after hour—sometimes for five hours or even seven in a day—to explain it afresh to a succession of people who are considering it for the first time. For a historian or a language-scholar such a routine might well be called deadening—though for a man whose vocation it is to teach, the task has a continuing and absorbing interest. But for a philosopher this life is just what is required to perfect his understanding of the subject. I can honestly say that I have learnt more from my pupils than I have from books. For is it not true that the really fundamental steps in any philosophical theory are those taken at the outset? It is the *ways in* to philosophy that are the most interesting part of the subject; for it is the course taken at the outset—in the first steps from ordinary ways of speaking to the extraordinary things which philosophers habitually say— that determines the whole of a thinker's theories. For example, how do we find ourselves saying 'Free will is an illusion' or 'Time is unreal' or any other of the things that philosophers say in their books? Under the Oxford system, the professional philosopher is compelled continually to explore these foundations of the subject, to see if they are sound. Not for him the delights of erecting, in solitary thought, imposing edifices—of writing huge volumes which only a handful of people will ever understand. He has to spend his time asking the question 'How can philosophy begin?'; for he has to spend it getting people to philosophise who have probably never done it before.

. . .

When I have read a paper or given a lecture to a German audience, what has frequently happened after the paper has been something like this: each of the audience who wants to say something has made a little speech, lasting some minutes, setting out his point of view on the subject of the paper, or about philosophy in general. After everyone who wants to has had his say, the proceedings have closed with a formal reply by the speaker. There has seldom, in my experience, been any dialogue or argument—just a succession of different views, none of which, not even the principal speaker's, is subjected to any elenchus. In Oxford it is very different. After a paper has been read, somebody may reply briefly to the paper, or the meeting may be immediately thrown open to discussion. What happens thereafter is rather like what happens in the Socratic dialogues of Plato—or perhaps, since Plato has organised his dialogues in a rather literary way, like the original Socratic discussions on which the dialogues are modelled. Speeches of more than a few sentences are rare; if anybody says more than about five sentences in succession, people begin to look embarrassed. We have instead a series of dialogues of the question-and-answer type, usually between two people, but sometimes with more intervening, and when one of the participants has nothing further to say, or begins to flag, or cannot answer his opponent, the cudgels are taken up by somebody else. When the thing is done properly, which it is not always, there is a great feeling for relevance. To introduce a new topic which does not grow naturally out of the one being discussed (unless that is obviously exhausted) is to risk being politely ignored. And one is not supposed to butt into a dialogue which is already, so to speak, fully manned. The rules of this game are so well understood, among the professionals at any rate, that the office of chairman is purely titular; the chairman joins in the discussion on the same terms as everyone else if he feels like it; otherwise he has nothing to do. The size of the meeting, which may be up to fifty people, does not make much difference to this, since at any one time only a handful of people are actively concerned in the discussion; the rest listen.

Here again, as in all our philosophy, the virtues which we seek are clarity, relevance and brevity—and, of course, at this level, some degree of originality; for these discussions take up so large a part of our time that the obvious moves in the various philosophical chess games that are in fashion are well known, and can be taken for granted. I say 'games,' not because I think philosophy is not a serious matter, but because philosophical arguments, conducted in the way that I have described, have the same sort of objectivity that chess games have. If you are beaten at chess you are beaten, and it is not to be concealed by any show of words; and in a philosophical discussion of this sort, provided that an unambiguously stated thesis is put forward, objective refutation is possible. Indeed, the whole object of our philosophical training is to teach us to put our theses in a form in which they can be submitted to this test. Ambiguities and evasions and rhetoric, however uplifting, are regarded as the mark of a philosopher who has not learnt his craft; we prefer professional competence to a superficial brilliance.

The conditions I have described are those obtaining in Oxford. At other universities you will find differences, some of them considerable. But the tone of British philosophy is at present set by Oxford (thirty years ago it was Cambridge); and the sort of philosophy that is done in England now is the result, more than anything else, of the kind of philosophical training which I have been picturing. British philosophers, by and large, will not be bothered with a philosophical thesis which is not stated briefly and in clear terms, such as make it possible to discuss it in the manner I have described; and it is much more highly esteemed if it is the sort of thesis which can be explained without technicalities, if possible in everyday language. We have not taken to mathematical logic with any enthusiasm, though a number of us can do it. The reason for this bias towards everyday language is that our dealings with our pupils have shown us that it is in the passage from everyday language to technical language that all the most vexatious problems of philosophy have their origin. Thus, when we examine a work of mathematical logic, we shall normally take it for granted that the writer has made no errors in the calculations; what we shall observe closely is the process by which he sets up his calculus, often using terms of common speech to do so. And the same may be said of our attitude to any other kind of technical vocabulary.

. . .

One of my purposes in saying all this is to give my own explanation of what usually happens on those occasions (unfortunately rare) when a typical Oxford philosopher meets a typical German philosopher in a philosophical discussion. The German philosopher will say something relating to his own philosophical views; the British philosopher will then say that he cannot understand what has been said, and will ask for an elucidation. The German will take this, the first time that it happens to him, for an encouragement, and will go on expounding his views; but he will be disappointed by the reaction. What was desired, it turns out, was not more of the same sort of thing; what the British philosopher wanted was to take just one sentence that the German had uttered—say the first sentence—or perhaps, for a start, just one word in this sentence; and he wanted an explanation given of the way in which this word was being used. One of the sources of this procedure is to be found in a piece of advice given by Wittgenstein:

> The right method of philosophy would be this. To say nothing except what can be said . . . i.e. something that has nothing to do with philosophy: and then always, when someone else wished to say something metaphysical, to demonstrate to him that he had given no meaning to certain signs in his propositions. (*Tractatus*, 6.53)

Present-day Oxford philosophers do not now take such a destructive view as this; they are perfectly prepared to have metaphysical things said; in fact, as I shall argue, what we spend most of our time in Oxford doing is metaphysics. But we have absorbed Wittgenstein's advice to this extent, that we have the greatest aversion to cutting ourselves off from our base in ordinary speech; we have seen what monstrous philosophical edifices have been erected by slipping, surreptitiously, from the ordinary uses of words to extraordinary uses which are never explained; we spend most of our working time explaining our *own* uses of words to our pupils; and when we find ourselves in the position of pupil, nothing pleases us so much as to sit back and have a German metaphysician explain to us, if he can, how he is going to get his metaphysical system started. And as he is usually unable to do this, the discussion never gets on to what he thinks of as the meat of the theory. This is a great disappointment to him, and leads easily to the accusation that we in Oxford are antagonistic to metaphysics. But actually we do a lot of metaphysics ourselves, only we have an obsession that it must be done rigorously as we understand the word; this means, among other things, that nothing should be said whose meaning cannot be explained. I wish to emphasise that, although we do as a matter of fact in Oxford do metaphysics in plainer language than is fashionable in other places, we by no means insist on people saying nothing that cannot be said in plain language; there is no ban on using words in any way one pleases, provided that a sense, and a precise one, is given to them. We insist only on distinguishing between serious metaphysical inquiry and verbiage disguised as such.

I have used the word 'metaphysics'; and I know that the suggestion that metaphysics is done at Oxford will meet with some incredulity. But this is largely due to a terminological muddle. We *do* metaphysics at Oxford; but we *call* it something else—usually 'logic' in an eccentrically wide sense of the word. In philosophy examinations at Oxford, the paper to which perhaps more attention is paid than to any other in assessing the merits of candidates is called 'Logic'; but it includes many questions which would be called in other places metaphysical. There are, for example, questions about time and space and their nature; about substance; about the nature of universals, and so on; as well as more narrowly logical questions. The title of the paper is traditional, and dates from long before the rise of the analytical movement; but although this nomenclature may be due to fortuitous historical causes, it serves to draw attention to an age-old difficulty in making a distinction between logic and metaphysics.

Metaphysics began when Socrates refused to answer first-order questions about, for example, what things are right, before he had had a satisfactory answer to second-order questions such as 'What is rightness?' This refusal was called by Plato 'demanding, in the case of everything, a definition (or account) of what-it-is-to-be that thing, or of its essential being (λόγον ἑκάστου λαμβάνειν τῆς οὐσίας),' and was said by him to be the mark of the true dialectical philosopher. Aristotle's *Metaphysics* is centred round a study of this Socratic question, and may be regarded as a third-order inquiry—an inquiry, not into what-it-is-to-be any *particular* kind of thing, but into the very concept *what-it-is-to-be* something (τὸ τί ἦν εἶναί τινι, οὐσία). That is why it is called a study of being *qua* being (τὸ ὄν ἦ ὄν). In more modern terms, Socrates would not have words used before an account was given of their meaning; Plato said that this attitude was characteristic of the philosopher, and Aristotle tried to give a general account of what it was philosophers were after. At that time, and ever since, the ordinary man has found something trifling about such second- and third-order enquiries: 'Trivial disputes about words!' say the enemies of modern philosophy; 'Abstract and metaphysical questions divorced from reality!' has always been the cry of those who do not like philosophers. Even at the very beginning, Aristophanes attacked Socrates for occupying himself with trivial verbal questions, and no doubt Plato's *Cratylus*, in the eyes of the ordinary man, lent colour to the accusation. We at Oxford, who in England are the chief butt of such attacks, are content to be the successors of Socrates, Plato and Aristotle, the study of whose philosophies remains a large part of our syllabus; we do not think it a trivial matter that people should understand what they are saying.

. . .

It would be incorrect, even, to tie to us, without qualification, the label 'Empiricists'—a label which gets almost automatically affixed to the English by Continental philosophers. For we practise a radical methodological scepticism with regard to the meaningfulness or usefulness of *all* these old philosophical labels. An empiricist is a person, presumably, who believes that all knowledge springs from experience. But what is 'knowledge'? What is 'experience'? What is it for knowledge to 'spring from' experience? As soon as we ask ourselves these questions, we are afflicted by doubts, which we seek to resolve by asking ourselves, 'How did we find ourselves using these terms?' So we go back over the ground that philosophy has covered, trying to pick up the trail of significance. The trail undoubtedly started from common language. Plato, for example, had no technical vocabulary to start with; and we cannot understand what he may have meant by a word like *eidos* without studying how, in the dialogues, he introduces the term and gives it a use.[1] But his explanations are always, and have to be, made in terms of ordinary words of Greek common speech; and if we are to understand the philosophy of Plato, or of anybody who takes over Plato's philosophical apparatus, it is absolutely necessary to make sure that, in passing from ordinary uses of words to their technical uses, they have not parted company with sense. In general our reaction, when confronted with a piece of philosophical diction, is to demand that the words in it be given a definite and unambiguous use.

This is not to say that for us the terms of common speech (in Greek, English, or any other language) are themselves above suspicion. We are not, as has been often suggested, uncritical worshippers of common speech; nor do we insist that all philos-

---

[1] Oxford is one of the few places where ancient philosophy is studied, in Greek, as part of the philosophical curriculum, under tutors who have both an up-to-date philosophical training and a thorough classical education. In most other universities one may study Plato either in Greek but not as a philosopher, or as a philosopher but in translation.

ophy must be expressed in common speech—though obviously
it would be an advantage if it could be. Apart from the fact that
many common words have a philosophical origin (for example,
'cause,' 'accident' and 'quality'), the most that we can know from
the fact that the word has a use in common speech is that it has
a use; *what* precisely its use may be, or whether it has more than
one use, easily confused with one another, or whether its use is
quite different in kind from expressions of apparently similar
grammatical form—these are questions which require a very
careful investigation of the actual use of expressions. There is no
sure way of avoiding being deceived by words, except to pay
very careful attention to words—that is one reason why the accusation that 'linguistic philosophers' are likely to take the linguistic form for the philosophical reality is the very reverse of the
truth. A few Oxford philosophers are so impressed by these difficulties that they concentrate on a systematic mapping of the
categories and conceptual apparatus of common language,
whether or not philosophical problems have yet arisen concerning
them. These philosophers are far from denying the value of other
sorts of philosophical enquiry, but are convinced of the usefulness
of such a basic study as a foundation for philosophy. The majority,
however, are content to go on investigating those problems which
are by common consent called philosophical—but investigating
them with at least one eye fixed on the need for knowing, all the
time, precisely what one is saying. These two kinds of study are
of great assistance to each other; the relation between them is
similar to that between geologists who prospect for minerals and
those who seek to advance our systematic knowledge of the subject.

It is frequently said of the so-called 'linguistic philosophers'
that, through concentrating their attention on words and their
meanings, they have abandoned the study of 'the world' or of
'reality.' This accusation reveals a curious misconception about
what a *word* is. There is, I suppose, a sense of the word 'word'
in which, if I were to cut out of the page of a book a piece of
paper carefully chosen as to position, what I should have would
be a word. *This* could be studied without studying any more of
reality than the piece of inky paper. Perhaps, even, there are
certain aspects of linguistic studies which do not involve any

consideration of meanings. If so, they have little to do with philosophy—even 'linguistic philosophy.' But philosophers are concerned with words as having meanings or uses; and these at any rate cannot be studied without seeing how words are used, in concrete situations, to say various things; and, of course, this involves (as is evident from our practice) a careful study of the situations, in order to find out what is being said. Thus, the philosopher who asks what is meant by saying 'I intend to kill him' has to ask himself how this expression would, concretely, be used; and this involves a study of more than pieces of inky paper. A full philosophical examination of language would involve a full examination of everything that can be talked about—and if there are things that cannot be talked about, they cannot in any case become the subject of a philosophical enquiry.

It is sometimes said that if the philosopher studies words, he will get caught in the meshes of his own language—English or whatever it may be. Now, the fact that a thing can be said in any particular language is sufficient proof that it can be said—and this may be of philosophical interest. In so far as the same thing can be exactly translated into some other language, the philosophical results established in terms of the first language will be statable in the second language. How far various sentences in the two languages are equivalent to one another is a philological, not a philosophical question (though it is an interesting philosophical question, what we mean by saying that they are equivalent). It is of interest to the philosopher, however, if some foreign language can be used to say things that cannot be said in his own. For example, the fact that to the English expression 'I could have' there correspond in Latin two expressions, *potui* and *potuissem,* which have different meanings, has been used by Professor Austin to bring out an important and unsuspected ambiguity in the English expression, which has far-reaching implications for the study of the problem of moral responsibility.[2] One can also *coin* expressions if they do not exist in one's own language (though one must be careful to give them a meaning); and this to some extent exempts the philosopher from an exhaustive search for

[2] 'Ifs and Cans,' *Proceedings of the British Academy,* XLII (1956) 109. Reprinted in J. L. Austin, *Philosophical Papers,* p. 164.

logical specimens in foreign languages. One can *experiment* with language. If one is successful in giving sense to a newly coined form of expression, that, too, proves something. So the philosopher who uses and studies no language but his own is not necessarily the prisoner of that language's conceptual structure. But knowledge of other languages can provide important stimuli to enquiry —stimuli which are certainly not lacking in Oxford.

And so the subject-matter of 'linguistic philosophy' is not, after all, clearly divided from the subject-matters of other sorts of philosophy. 'Linguistic philosophy' is simply philosophy, but done with a proper awareness of the pitfalls of language, which others ignore, and a determination to avoid these pitfalls, both by carefully charting those which have been discovered, and by keeping a good look-out for any uncharted ones that there may be. Nor have philosophers at Oxford any obvious common tenets. If one took any of the well-known controversies in philosophy, such as that between the realists and nominalists, or that between objectivism and subjectivism in ethics, and asked a lot of Oxford professors what they thought, they would probably agree in rejecting as inadequate or unclear all of the best-known formulations of either side in these controversies. But this would be likely to be the full extent of their agreement; they would be sure to dispute hotly with one another about the correct way of resolving the problems. The most obvious common characteristic of Oxford philosophers is, indeed, their propensity for arguing with one another—here is one place in the world, at any rate, where people holding opposing views on philosophical problems can meet and understand one another's arguments—and this presupposes, first that Oxford philosophers seldom agree, but secondly that they have sufficient confidence in the rigour and honesty and clarity of each other's thought to hope that argument will not be a waste of time. In fact, what we share are not tenets but standards (which we may or may not live up to, but go on trying); Oxford, that is to say, is not so much a school of philosophy as a school for philosophers.

GILBERT RYLE

(1900–   )

*Proofs in Philosophy**

*From "Proofs in Philosophy," *Revue Internationale de Philosophie*, No. 27–28, 1954, pp. 150–157. Used by permission of Max Servais, administrative deputy of the *Revue,* and Gilbert Ryle.

Philosophers do not provide proofs any more than tennis-players score goals. Tennis-players do not try in vain to score goals. Nor do philosophers try in vain to provide proofs; they are not inefficient or tentative provers. Goals do not belong to tennis, nor proofs to philosophy.

Certainly some philosophers are also mathematicians, like Descartes, Leibniz and Frege. Some philosophers are also Formal Logicians, like Aristotle, Frege and Russell. Philosophers may prove theorems in mathematics and Formal Logic, just as tennis-players may score goals in the winter. But the strengths and weaknesses of Aristotle or Frege in discussing philosophical points are distinct from their strengths and weaknesses in proving theorems in Formal Logic or in mathematics. There could be persons, who were superior to Aristotle in proving theorems in Formal Logic, whom we should still rank below Aristotle as philosophers.

But to say that philosophers do not prove or even try to prove things sounds over-violent in two ways. (1) First, some philosophers, like Spinoza, have deliberately tried to do for certain philosophical matters what Euclid did for geometrical matters. Attempted proofs of the existence of God and the immortality of the soul bespatter the chronicles of philosophy from Plato to 1953. I do not want to waste your time in debating whether such attempts should be listed as a peculiar variety of philosophising or as bad philosophising or as non-philosophical enterprises undertaken by men who, in other parts of their work, were genuine philosophers. So let me say, more guardedly, that anyhow some of the characteristically philosophical products of anyhow some of the best philosophers have not been proofs, quasi-proofs, pseudo-proofs or even would-be proofs.

(2) But for another reason also it sounds over-violent to say that anyhow some characteristic and excellent specimens of philosophising are not either good or bad attempts at proving. For it sounds like saying that some good philosophising is like most poetry or like much preaching, namely that it is not argumentative or not ratiocinatory. I maintain, on the contrary, that the best products of the best philosophers are argumentative, indeed that they are not merely argued, but are themselves arguments. It is for the powerfulness and originality of his arguments that a philosopher merits the respect of his colleagues.

Yet these powerful arguments of his are not rigorous proofs, and they are not unrigorous proofs either. Frege, for example, uses some powerful arguments in his philosophical discussions of the concept of number, yet these arguments are neither inferior nor superior to his proofs of his theorems in the body of his *Grundgesetze*. They are not exercises in the same genre; they are not candidates for the same honours.

When I say that a philosophical argument employed by Frege, say, or Plato is powerful, I do not mean that it is rhetorically persuasive. On the whole, Plato is rhetorically more efficient than Aristotle, but we can distinguish the question whether a certain argument of Aristotle is more or less powerful than a corresponding argument of Plato from the question whether the presentation of the one is more or less persuasive than the other. Philosophical arguments can be or fail to be logically powerful in a sense of 'logically' closely related to the sense in which a proof may be or fail to be logically rigorous. Why do I say that anyhow some characteristically philosophical arguments are not proofs?

Theorems can be learned, understood and used in abstraction from their proofs. Sometimes a proposition of which there does not yet exist a proof may be intuitively obvious, so that the discovery of its proof is posterior to the discovery of the truth of that proposition. The corresponding things do not hold of philosophical arguments. It would be absurd to try to tell a student the results of Plato's ratiocinations about the concepts of knowledge and false belief, without introducing him to those ratiocinations themselves; or to make him learn by heart and use Frege's elucidation of the concept of number while exempting him from appreciating the argumentation which gave that elucidation. There could not be a list of Aristotle's or Kant's findings. There are no philosophical theorems, not even slippery or foggy theorems.

Sometimes, I think, this absence of a list of philosophical theorems is mis-diagnosed. It is supposed that while ideally there would exist such listable theorems, in fact they do not exist because the philosopher, unfortunately, has to operate with the soft and vaporous concepts of everyday untechnical discourse, where the mathematician operates with hard and chiselled, technical concepts. But this sort of apology is mistaken. The concept of number for which Frege gave his philosophical elucidation was that hard and chiselled concept which is used in counting and calculating—yet still his philosophical arguings were totally unlike his establishings of logistical theorems. The concepts of *infinitesimal* and *point* which exercised philosophers like Zeno, Aristotle, Berkeley and Whitehead were the non-vernacular concepts which were actually and efficiently employed by mathematicians in the course of their far from vaporous work.

Next, where proofs exist, premisses exist. A proof is unsatisfactory if, among other things, it is left unclear just what premisses have been used and if it is doubtful whether they are true. Philosophers' arguments are not laid out in this way—or when, in pious imitation of Euclid's Elements or *Principia Mathematica*, philosophers do pretend to display sets of necessary and sufficient premisses, the debate instantly moves back a step. The philosophical point at issue is seen to be lodged not in the use to which these premisses were put by their employer, but in those pretended premisses themselves. Cartesians like to trumpet 'cogito, ergo sum' as a premiss to some promised philosophical theorems. Moore, I think, has sometimes thought of Common Sense as a budget of premisses for philosophers. The reaction of philosophers has always been the critical one, 'We don't want to build anything on these premisses.' Their reaction, I suggest, ought to be 'we don't want premisses at all, because we don't want theorems.' Only we have been shy of saying anything of the sort, because we have inadvertently assumed that any argument, with any degree of logical powerfulness must have the shape of a premiss-theorem proof.

Well then what can be positively said about the arguments which we expect to find in the debates of good philosophers and to produce in our own debates? I am not going to lay down any wide generalisation or suggest any piece of legislation. I want to consider just one thing which we sometimes have to do by argument in the course of some philosophical discussions. Whether it is typical or not, I do not want to debate.

Let me begin by reminding you of the familiar distinction between techniques and technologies, or methods and methodologies, between, say, music and musicology. It is one thing to have learned to do a thing correctly or well; it is quite another thing to be able to tell how to do it correctly or well. A surgeon who has learned or invented a trick can perform it, but he may lack the quite different skill of formulating verbal instructions telling other surgeons what to do and what to avoid when essaying the trick.

Between the naive performance of his trick and the sophisticated business of giving verbal instructions about its performance, there is an intermediate activity, less naive than the first and less sophisticated than the second, namely that of demonstrating or showing the trick—rehearsing its operations one by one, in a conspicuous manner, and at a deliberately reduced speed.

Now suppose that the surgeon himself tries to formulate the verbal instructions or recipe for the performance of this trick. How does the surgeon test these proposed instructions—how does he satisfy himself that the suggested recipe does or does not answer to the operations that he knows how to perform? He must go through his trick, as he has learned to do it, yet rehearse it with one eye on the corresponding items of the suggested recipe. He must show off the ingredient operations of his trick in order to match them against the ingredient prescriptions of the recipe; and this is not easy—especially since the first verbal recipe or instruction-formula to be suggested will certainly be only a very schematic, outline affair.

Now to apply this to our concern.

It is one thing to be able to count, add, subtract and multiply, i.e. to operate with numbers. Schoolboys can do these things. It is quite another thing to formulate verbal recipes or instructions for correct operations with numbers. Schoolboys do not have to try to do this new, sophisticated thing, but, for certain purposes, certain adults do have to try to do this. They have, so to speak, to try to codify the operation-rules for numerical expressions, as primitive tribal legislators have to try to codify the conduct-rules which the tribe observes but does not propound. What is true of numerical expressions is true of nearly all expressions, whether non-technical, technical or semi-technical. We learn how to operate with them consistently and systematically before we can consider verbal instructions for operating with them. We first have to learn how to operate with them properly, e.g. in asking answerable questions, in giving obeyable orders, in making checkable statements, and so on. Later on we may have also to consider codifications of these previously uncodified, yet still rule-governed practices of ours. As it is sometimes not very happily put, we have to make explicit the previously implicit 'logic' of their employment. This means that we have a matching-problem just like that of my surgeon, namely the problem of matching already well-mastered operations with these expressions, against suggested and more or less schematic, instructions for those operations. In particular, we have to rehearse arguments pivoting on these expressions in order to match these arguments against the more or less roughly outlined argument-patterns which the suggested instructions codify. Notice that here, unlike the case of the surgeon, the procedure under examination is itself a batch of operations with expressions. We are trying to codify in words of one level the rules observed in the employment of words of another level. I shall give two examples. Plato needed to discuss the place in human life of *pleasure;* he needed, therefore, to put it crudely, to be able to say what sort of a thing pleasure is. He noticed that among things that we enjoy are such things as eating when we are hungry and drinking when we are thirsty. Eating and drinking are processes, namely transitions from emptiness to repletion. They are processes of replenishment. He then suggested that the pleasures of eating and drinking, the enjoyment we get from them, are in the same manner processes, or more specifically, transitions from one state to another. Against this, Aristotle argued in effect as follows. If enjoying something were a process from state to state, it would follow that a person could have begun to enjoy something but been prevented from finishing, as a person can begin his dinner but be prevented from completing it. But, though a person may enjoy something for a short time or for a long time, he cannot have half an enjoyment. Enjoyments can be great or small, but not fractional. This demolishes Plato's assimilation of the concept of pleasure to the general type of concepts of process or transition. Aristotle has shown that a batch of elementary argumentative operations which are legitimately made with process-expressions, like 'dine,' cannot be made with expressions like 'enjoy.' But in doing this he has not merely done something destructive; he has done something constructive. He has added a new item to the formulation of the needed recipe. He has found a specific fault in a suggested codification; he has thereby fixed a specific positive element in the required codification. To correct is to rectify.

Next, consider one of the things that Frege had to do and did. Certain thinkers who were as competent at simple arithmetic as Frege, suggested that adjectives such as 'one,' 'two' and 'three' stood, like the adjectives 'green,' 'square' and 'honest' for qualities of things—somewhat mysterious qualities, perhaps, but still qualities.

Frege demolished this matching-suggestion by, so far as I recall, such arguments as this. If the men in this room are honest then I, who am in this room, am honest. But if the men in this room number thirty five, it does not follow that I number thirty five. Moreover not merely do I not number 35, but I do not even number 1, or any other number. The Oxford Professors in this room number 1, and I am an Oxford Professor in this room and no one else is. But 'numbering 1' is not, as 'honest' is, the sort of predicate which can characterise me. It can characterise only such subjects as 'the Oxford Professors in this room.' Numerical expressions will not go through all the same inference-hoops as quality-expressions. The suggested matching of those with these collapses. But with this collapse, something positive arises; we can now say one positive thing about the logical behaviour of numerical expressions—a positive thing which is akin to an important feature of existence-expressions.

Notice that in these two examples, the suggested verbal recipes were worded with the aid of logicians' classificatory words such as 'process' and 'quality.' But there are lots of other ways in which one may formulate our codifications of the inference-métiers of concepts.

I suggest now that we can see the reason why anyhow some characteristically philosophical arguments are not of the premiss-theorem pattern. For they are operations not *with* premisses and conclusions, but operations *upon* operations with premisses and conclusions. In proving something, we are putting propositions through inference-hoops. In some philosophical arguments we are matching the hoops through which certain batches of propositions will go against a worded recipe declaring what hoops they should go through. Proving is a one-level business; philosophical arguing is, anyhow sometimes, an inter-level business.

Moreover to prove something, we must have true premisses. For the philosopher's business what matters is not whether a concrete proposition incorporating (non-vacuously) the concept, say, of *pleasure* is true, but only what *would* confirm it, what *would* refute it etc. He is, so to speak, not making real inferences, but rehearsing them for his own matching-purposes. Similarly the surgeon who is trying to teach his tricks to others by showing them off, step by step, in a conspicuous manner and at a reduced speed is not then and there trying to extract an invalid's appendix. Still less is he trying to do this when he is matching his procedure against some suggested verbal instructions in this procedure. He is only *rehearsing* his trick for his new non-clinical purpose.

One last word. Philosophers' problems do not in general, if ever, arise out of troubles about single concepts, like that say of *pleasure* or that of *number*. They arise, rather, as the traffic-policeman's problems arise, when crowds of conceptual vehicles, of different sorts and moving in different directions meet at some conceptual cross-roads. All or a lot of them have to be got under control conjointly. This is why, in its early stages, a philosophical dispute strikes scientists and mathematicians as so messy an affair. It *is* messy, for it is a traffic-block—a traffic-block which cannot be tidied up by the individual drivers driving their individual cars efficiently.

GLOSSARY

This list certainly is not exhaustive of those words which might be trouble-some in the text. It is recommended that students consult a good dictionary, such as the *Oxford English Dictionary*, when difficulties arise. For further elaboration on these and other philosophical terms, consult the *Encyclopedia of Philosophy*, edited by Paul Edwards (New York: Macmillan, 1967).

abduction (retroduction)

An argument form in which one of the premises is known to be true and the other premise is a hypothesis, from which a conclusion is deduced, which if then proved to be true, establishes the hypothesis.

ad hominem

Attacking one's opponent rather than the subject under discussion, as an ad hominem argument.

aesthetics

The philosophical study and/or analysis of problems regarding the evaluation of artifacts and works of art.

agnosticism

In the philosophy of religion, the view that knowledge of God is impossible and hence that one cannot answer the question regarding the existence of God.

apodictic

For Kant, referring to that which is necessarily true, in itself, without reference to any outside purpose (e.g. the Categorical Imperative).

a posteriori

Based on experience.

a priori

Independent of experience.

atman (Atman)

In Hinduism, used interchangeably for both the individual soul (not capitalized) and the universal soul (capitalized).

atheism

The theological position that no god exists.

behaviorism
The psychological and philosophical position that proper explanations of human behavior are to be made solely in terms of observable human actions, to the exclusion of reference to the concept of mind and the use of mental terminology.

Brahman
In Hinduism, the absolute, One, with which all in the universe is ultimately identified.

categorical imperative
For Kant, the unconditional moral law which applies to all rational beings, given three formulations in *Fundamental Principles of the Metaphysics of Morals.*

causation
The relationship between a cause and its effect.

concomitant variation
A test for causal relatedness by which one variable is altered to see if it modifies the result and hence indicates a causal relationship between the variable and the result.

contingent
Referring to that which is not necessary, hence that which may or may not occur.

cosmology
The formulation and analysis of philosophical theories regarding the origin and nature of the universe.

deduction
An argument form in which the conclusion follows necessarily from one or more premises.

dualism
Any philosophical theory which maintains the independent and irreducible existence of two substances (e.g. natural and supernatural, mind and body, good and evil).

egalitarianism
The philosophical position that all human beings ought to possess equal rights in all matters.

empirical
Referring to experience, actual facts.

empiricism
The theory that sense experience is the only legitimate source of human knowledge.

epistemology
The investigation of the possibility and nature of human knowledge.

essence
The nature of anything independent of its existence.

ethics
The philosophical study and/or analysis of those issues directly related to standards of human conduct.

etymology
The study in linguistics of the origin and development of words.

existentialism
The philosophical position that the existence of every person precedes his/her essence, and hence that each person through free action creates what he/she is.

hypothetical
Conditional, qualified, not absolute. In Kant, contrasted with categorical.

hedonism
The theory that ultimate value is to be found in pleasure alone.

induction
An argument form in which a generalization is derived from a collection of particular facts.

interactionism
The theory that there is direct causal influence between mind and body.

intuition
The immediate knowing of something without the use of reason.

libertarianism
The theory that every human being possesses a will that is free. Opposed to deterministic theories.

materialism
Any philosophical theory that maintains that reality is ultimately to be explained only in terms of matter. The view that only matter exists, that matter is the fundamental constituent of the universe.

metaphysics
The investigation of the nature of reality or being.

monism
Any philosophical theory which maintains that there is only one basic reality.

mysticism
The theological position that direct and immediate awareness of the divine is attainable.

necessary being
An entity whose existence is not contingent upon the occurrence of any state of affairs.

objective
Referring to that which is independent of the mind of the knowing subject, contrasted with subjective.

ontological proof
The proof of the existence of God based on the idea that a perfect being cannot lack existence.

ontology
An investigation of the nature of being.

paradox
Something that appears to be self-contradictory.

parallelism
The view that mind and body are independent and do not interact but that their functions are parallel.

phenomenalism
The view that we can have knowledge of things only as they appear to us.

pluralism
The theory that not one (monism), not two (dualism), but many ultimate substances exist.

pragmatism
The philosophical position that defines the truth of concepts in terms of their practical results (their "cash value" in experience).

presupposition
That which is antecedently assumed in an argument.

psychical (restricted sense)

Concerning mental phenomena, such as telepathy, clairvoyance, mediumship, etc.

rationalism

Any philosophical theory which maintains that reality can be known by human reason alone; that is, that human reasoning without dependency upon sensory experience can deduce knowledge that is certain.

reductio ad absurdum

The logical method of showing the truth of a proposition by deducing a contradiction from premises which include other previously proved propositions and the negation of the proposition being tested. Also the method of proving the negation of a proposition by deducing a contradiction from premises which include the proposition and other previously proved propositions.

relativism

The view that there are no objective standards that apply universally.

Satyagraha

Literally, truth seeking. Term used by Gandhi to characterize his doctrine of passive resistance and noncooperation in order to bring about political ends.

skepticism

The view that human beings can obtain no certain knowledge.

subjective

Limited to the operations of the mind, contrasted with objective.

substance

The essential part of something or that which has independent existence. Monists argue that there is only one substance, dualists that there are two substances, pluralists that there are many.

survival hypothesis

The view that a person or some essential element of a person (e.g. the mind) exists in some form after physical death.

tautology

A propositional form that maintains a truth value of true no matter what truth value is assigned to its variable components.

teleological

In reference to ends, hence a teleological explanation of an event is one given in terms of consequences rather than antecedent causes.

theism

The theological position that a god exists. .

transcendental

In Kantian philosophy, that which is not derived from experience but is based on certain a priori elements of experience. Descriptive of the necessary conditions of knowledge.

utilitarianism

The ethical theory that an act is right if of all those acts open to an agent, it is the one which actually or with a high probability will produce the greatest amount of happiness for the greatest number of people. There are various forms of utilitarianism, in particular, act utilitarianism and rule utilitarianism, which are based upon modifications of the above description.

INDEX

M

T

Taft, Robert, 242
Tannery, P., 441n
Taylor, L. W., 527n
Taylor, Richard, *see* Diodorus
  Cronus
Technology Review, 509
Teilhard de Chardin, Pierre, 219
Telepathy (Carington), 351
Tempest, The (Shakespeare), 352
Teresa, Saint, 623–625
  on God, 623–625
Theaetetus (Plato), 391–409
Third Man, The (movie), 370
Thoreau, Henry David, 221, 222
"Three Ways of Spilling Ink"
  (Austin), 18
Thymine, 471, 472, 476, 477
Tilley, Charles, 261n
Time, 481
Time and Eternity (Stace), 642
Tintoretto, 697
Toch, Han, 257n
Tolstoy, Leo, 221, 690
Tovey, Sir Donald Francis, 682
*Toward a Theory of War
  Prevention* (eds. Falk and
  Mendelovitz), 247n
Tractatus (Wittgenstein), 735
Treatise of Human Nature, A
  (Hume), 301–310
Trevor, J., 617–618
Truth
  Bacon on, 488
  Gandhi on, 221–229
Tucker, Lord, 190, 191
Tulsidas, 226
Turnbull, Colin, 205–206
Two Cultures, The (Snow), 481
Two Lectures on Theism (Seth),
  627n
Two Treatises of Government
  (Locke), 141–150, 232

U

Uganda, 205–206
Union of Soviet Socialist Republics,
  U.S. and, 7, 8
United Nations, violence, 209
United States of America
  Commission on Obscenity and
    Pornography, 109–123, 127
  Europe and, 7–8
  Middle East and, 8
  Southeast Asia and, 8
  U.S.S.R. and, 7, 8
  Vietnam War, 8, 205, 215, 217
  violence, 209, 212, 215, 218,
    237–239, 243–244
  Watergate affair, 3–12, 13, 16
  West Germany and, 7
U.S. News and World Report, 480
U.S. Supreme Court, on obscenity,
  120
Universal law, 62–64, 67–68, 71,
  73–75
*University of Pennsylvania Law
  Review*, 180
Unsafe at Any Speed (Nader), 254n
Upanishads, 325–327, 627, 641
"Uses of Violence, The" (Nieburg),
  247n
Utilitarianism
  duty and, 16
  responsibility and, 16

V

Values in a Universe of Chance
  (ed. Wiener), 543n
Van der Weyden, Rogier, 697
Van Heijenoorst, J., 535n
*Varieties of Religious Experience,
  The* (James), 609–632
Vedantists, 620, 627
Venn, John, 497
Vergil, 359–360
Verne, Jules, 480